THE DEFENCE OF INDIA

THE

DEFENCE OF INDIA:

A STRATEGICAL STUDY

C. M. MACGREGOR

GYAN

Published by

Gyan Publishing House
5, Ansari Road
Daryaganj, New Delhi-110002
Phone: 011-47034999, 9811692060
E-mail: books@gyanbooks.com

Distribution Network
gyanbooks.com
India, USA, Canada, UK, Australia

ISBN: 978-93-6433-039-8 (PB)
First Published, 1884

2nd Impression 2024

Printed at: Gyan Press, Delhi.

THE DEFENCE OF INDIA: A STRATEGICAL STUDY
Author: C. M. MACGREGOR

THE

DEFENCE OF INDIA:

A STRATEGICAL STUDY.

BY

MAJOR-GENERAL SIR C. M. MACGREGOR, K.C.B., C.S.I., C.I.E.,
QUARTER MASTER GENERAL IN INDIA.

SIMLA:
GOVERNMENT CENTRAL BRANCH PRESS.

1884.

PREFACE.

THE following pages have been written under the strong belief that a great danger is impending over our Indian Empire, and therefore that it behoves all Englishmen to try to realize exactly what that danger is, and what measures should be undertaken to meet it. It may be taken for certain that the ranks of those who believe that there is no danger to India from Russian encroachments in Asia have been very much diminished by the late uncalled for and deceitful advance of that Power to Merv, and that therefore any warning is now but little required. However this may be, I hope what I have to say will at last open the eyes of *all* Englishmen, and decide those who may yet be wavering that the danger is now real.

I have proposed certain measures (drastic I allow) to meet the Russian menace. I believe all are sound and all are feasible; but as long as my readers agree with me that the danger is real and must be met adequately, I have no wish to split hairs as to what is best to be done. Once those in power in England and India are roused to a just appreciation of the situation, I shall have no fear of the result.

Therefore, I earnestly appeal to each one who reads my paper to do all that lies in his power to aid in the great work which it recommends; for that work is no less than the preservation of our Indian Empire.

It may be asked why I have not addressed myself to the general public of England and India by means of the Press. My answer is,—Because, I believe, doing so would do more harm than good, inasmuch as though I believe if I did so it would raise a strong popular feeling on the subject, still there is much of what I have said that should not be known to the Russian Government, who, with all their *finesse*, are not so well informed on many points as they would wish to be and are trying to be.

I therefore, instead of addressing myself to the general public of England, appeal to those whom I believe to have the power to aid; and I ask each one who reads this paper, while keeping it strictly confidential, to do what he can to assist in getting done what is necessary and advisable.

C. M. MACGREGOR, *Major-Genl.*,
Quarter Master General in India

NOTE.

I SHALL be very pleased to receive from any gentleman who may read this 'Study' any remarks he may have to offer in favour of or against the views I have set forth. In fact, as my only object is to get the right thing done, whatever that may be I earnestly invite such remarks, and promise to give them every consideration in a second edition of this work.

Communications addressed as under will reach me :—

MAJOR-GENL. SIR C. MACGREGOR, K.C.B., C.S.I., C.I.E.,
Quarter Master General in India,
Army Head Quarters,
India.

C. M. MACGREGOR, *Major-General,*
Quarter Master General in India.

THE

DEFENCE OF INDIA:

A STRATEGICAL STUDY.

CHAPTER I.

CAN RUSSIA INVADE INDIA.

MUCH has been written and said to prove and disprove the possibility of Russia invading India, and the probability of her having any such design. Many of these papers, and much of this talk, have been based on inaccurate information and issued to fall in with a preconceived view, or framed to meet purely personal or party interests; and although there have been many very able opinions delivered on this subject, the value of which has not been lessened by any of the above causes, I have never yet seen any paper which has clearly worked out, stage by stage, an answer to the important question—" Is an invasion of India by Russia possible ? "

I hold it to be of no sort of use to meet such a question by any such answer as—" Yes, of course. Did not Changez and Timur, Nadir and Ahmed Shah, &c., &c., invade India ? Then why should not the Russians, who are more powerful and better organized " ; or—" No, of course not. Between us and the Russians is there not the broad impassable Oxus ; the frightful wastes of the Turkoman desert, where no living thing can exist ; the terrible defiles and snow-clad passes of the Hindu Kush ; the unconquerable Afghans ; the gloomy gorges of Jagdalak, the Bolan, and the Khaibar ; and, lastly, our own numerous, well disciplined, and thoroughly faithful army, backed by a completely loyal population ? "

I propose to adopt neither of these styles, but to review the whole question as far as possible, calmly and dispassionately, with as little bias for one view as the other. I propose to imagine myself for the nonce a Russian officer ordered to draw up a project for the invasion of India, and show my readers how such an idea would be worked out; take them step by step over the ground intervening between Russia and India; and give them such data and facts as they can judge for themselves, whether an invasion of India is feasible, as some say, or only the nightmare of a few madmen, according to others.

The problem then is—"Can Russia from her present position in Asia invade India now, or at any future time?"

First, then, what is her present position in Asia? Commencing from the west, it is as follows: *1st,* the whole of the Caucasus has been conquered and subdued so far as to make it improbable Russia need fear any insurrection in this quarter; *2nd,* Turkey has at least been made to see the hopelessness of a struggle with Russia single-handed; *3rd,* the ruling dynasty of Persia and the whole of its northern provinces are completely under Russian domination; *4th,* the Turkomans have felt the weight of Russia's hand, and fear her; *5th,* Khiva and Bokhara are completely under her thumb; *6th,* Khokand has been annexed; *7th,* Kashgar is hostile but afraid; *8th,* China is hostile and more than half-afraid; and, lastly, *9th,* her advanced posts are now at Merv, Petro-Alexandrovsk, Jam and Ush, and her communications with the rear are quite safe from attack.

Taking it then for granted that no exception can be advanced to this statement of the present position of Russia in Asia, I also ask to be allowed to assume, for the sake of argument, that all that has been written for and against the possibility of an invasion of India has left the question in such a state, that it is worth while to go into it more thoroughly than has ever yet been done, and satisfy ourselves, not by calculating probabilities, or allowing a free rein to our imaginations, but by examining into the incontestable facts of the case, and determining whether it is feasible or not.

The first point then which I shall consider is—Has Russia the necessary force for such an undertaking? I propose to show what is the total fighting strength of Russia; then to endeavour to estimate what proportion of this strength it would be necessary for her to retain—*1st,* for the defence of her German and Austrian frontiers; *2nd,* for the frontier of Turkey in Europe; *3rd,* for the frontier of Turkey in Asia; *4th,* for the internal defence of her European dominions; *5th,* for her secure hold of the Caucasus; *6th,* for the keeping in subjection her recent conquests in Central Asia; and, *7th,* for her Chinese frontier.

I find that the total strength of Russia, inclusive of all reserves, to be as follows*:—

	Infantry and engineers.	Cavalry.	Guns.
On a peace footing	460,897	89,884	1,538
„ war „	1,286,122	176,268	3,630

* *N.B.*—In the above figures all the troops destined for service in the field are included, but not depôt battalions, local troops, nor garrison artillery. Cavalry, engineers, and infantry are taken at their full strength of combatants and non-combatants; but artillerymen, artillery and engineer parks, and the staff of army corps and divisions are not included.

Peace Footing.

This enormous force is distributed in peace as follows :—

		Infantry and engineers.	Cavalry.	Guns.
Guard Corps, St. Petersburg	...	26,581	9,183	102
Grenadier Corps, Moscow	...	23,664	......	72
1st Army Corps, St. Petersburg	...	23,619	3,484	84
2nd „ Vilna	...	23,619	3,484	84
3rd „ Riga	...	15,746	3,484	60
4th „ Minsk	...	15,746	3,484	60
5th „ Warsaw	...	15,746	3,484	60
6th „ ditto	...	23,619	3,484	84
7th „ Sevastopol	...	15,746	3,484	60
8th „ Odessa	...	15,746	3,484	60
9th „ Orel	...	15,746	3,484	60
10th „ Kharhov	...	15,746	3,484	60
11th „ Titomir	...	15,746	3,484	60
12th „ Kiev	...	15,746	3,484	60
13th „ Moscow	...	23,619	3,484	84
14th „ Lublin	...	15,746	3,484	60
15th „ Kazan	...	15,746	......	48
23rd Division, Helsingfors	...	7,873	......	24
Don Cossack Division, Zamost	...	......	3,976	12
5 Rifle Brigades (various)	...	9,940	......	...
8 Finnish Battalions, Helsingfors	...	4,400	......	...
Cossacks (various)	...	247	637	4
Engineer Brigades (various)	...	16,391	......	...
Army of the Caucasus (various)	...	61,224	17,107	196
„ „ Turkistan (various)	...	26,743	7,618	76
Siberian Troops, Omsk	...	4,212	987	32
„ „ Eastern	...	11,940	1,600	36
Grand Total	...	460,897	89,884	*1,538

* *Note.*—These figures include regimental non-combatants, but not brigade nor divisional staff, &c.

On mobilization the foregoing becomes as follows :—

		Infantry and engineers.	Cavalry.*	Guns.
Guard Corps, St. Petersburg	...	53,919	10,976	180
Grenadier Corps, Moscow	...	48,816	......	144
1st Army Corps, St. Petersburg	...	47,295	3,477	156
2nd " Vilna	...	47,295	3,477	156
3rd " Riga	...	31,530	3,477	108
4th " Minsk	...	31,530	3,477	108
5th " Warsaw	...	31,530	3,477	108
6th " ditto	...	47,295	3,477	156
7th " Sevastopol	...	31,530	3,477	108
8th " Odessa	...	31,530	3,477	108
9th " Orel	...	31,530	3,477	108
10th " Kharhov	...	31,530	3,477	108
11th " Titomir	...	31,530	3,477	108
12th " Kiev	...	31,530	3,477	108
13th " Moscow	...	47,295	3,477	156
14th " Lublin	...	31,530	3,477	108
15th " Kazan	...	31,530	......	96
23rd Division, Helsingfors	...	15,765	......	48
Don Cossack Division, Zamost	...	......	3,800	12
5 Rifle Brigades (various)	...	20,500	......	...
8 Finnish Battalions (various)	...	9,208	......	...
Cossacks, 30 Don† Regiments, 2nd and 3rd (categories)	...	......	29,250	...
14 Don Batteries	...	......	......	84
3 Astrakhan Regiments	...	......	2,019	...
Crimean Battalion	...	1,825	......	...
4 Engineer Brigades	...	18,271	......	...
24 Reserve Infantry Divisions and Artillery Brigades	...	385,152	......	768
Army of the Caucasus	...	138,288	42,538	388
Ural Cossacks (2nd and 3rd) (categories)	...	......	6,972	...
Orenburg Cossacks (ditto)	...	......	11,952	24
Turkistan Army	...	26,743	7,618	76
8 Reserve Turkistan Battalions (as formed 1878)	...	8,424	......	32
Omsk District	...	7,381	987	32
East Siberian District	...	11,940	1,600	36
Semirietchie, trans-Baikal, Siberian and Amur Cossacks (2nd and 3rd categories)		4,680	9,778	6
Total	...	1,286,122	176,268	3,630

* By a recent order all cavalry regiments have been raised to six squadrons; but as no figures of strengths, &c., have been published, the old establishments are here reckoned.

† Recently reduced to 15 regiments of each category.

To the above must be added the forces of Servia, Bulgaria, Roumania, and Eastern Roumelia, which may safely be considered available for Russian purposes.

Those of Servia on mobilization consist of—

1st category.	15 regiments of infantry @ 4 active and 1 reserve battalions	107,436 men.
	5 regiments of cavalry	
	5 reserve squadrons	
	40 field batteries (240 guns)	
	6 mountain batteries (24 guns)	
	6 reserve batteries	
	5 pioneer companies with bridge train, &c., &c. ...	
2nd category.	15 regiments of infantry @ 4 battalions ...	56,044 "
	10 squadrons of cavalry	
	20 field batteries (120 guns)	
	5 pioneer companies	
3rd category.	60 battalions (of little worth)	53,640 "
	Total ...	217,120 "
		384 field guns.

Bulgaria could put in the field—

24 battalions @ 1,000 men	36,000 men.
8 squadrons @ 150 men	88 guns.
11 batteries @ 8 guns	
4 engineer companies	
2 garrison artillery companies	
7 reserve battalions	

Roumania can mobilize—

4 army corps with each 30 battalions, 15 squadrons, 12 guns and 5 engineer companies, 1 cavalry division of 16 squadrons.

Total.	120 battalions	150,000 men.
	70 squadrons	288 guns.
	48 batteries	
	20 engineer companies	

The Roumanian militia could form four other army corps of the above strength, but slightly weaker in cavalry and artillery.

East Roumelia could place on a war footing—

12 battalions @ 1,000 men	13,000 men,
2 squadrons @ 150 men	4 guns;
1 battery of 4 guns @ 200 men	
2 engineer companies @ 100 men	

besides a partially trained militia of about 40,000.

Montenegro's forces (about 10,000 men) should also be reckoned, as they are trained by Russians.

The total forces then which Russia has available therefore are—

Russia ...	1,462,390	cavalry, infantry and engineers, and	3,630 guns.
Servia ...	217,120	" " "	384 "
Bulgaria ...	36,000	" " "	88 "
Roumania ...	150,000	" " "	288 "
East Roumelia ...	53,000	" " "	4 "
Montenegro ...	10,000	" " "	...
	1,928,510		4,394

The number of troops which Russia would have to keep on her German and Austrian frontiers would of course depend on whether she had secured the neutrality of those Powers during any other operations she was about to engage in ; and it is evident unless such neutrality had been made very secure, she must keep up considerable forces on those frontiers.

During the Russo-Turkish war of 1877-78, the following preparations were made by Russia on her German and Austrian frontiers. The garrison troops of the following fortresses were mobilized and the fortresses armed at the following periods :—

In November 1876 ...	Kertch. Bender. Dunaburg. Bobruisk.
In January 1878 ...	Novo Georgievsk. Kronstadt. Sveaborg. Wiborg.
During the Berlin Congress.	Ivangorod. The coast defences on the Baltic were organized and the batteries armed, Kronstadt and Sveaborg being the centres chosen.

In 1877-78 there were no such cadres for reserve troops as now exist in Russia, and local and fortress battalions had to be used as a basis for these formations. The orders for the formation of the battalions were given on the following dates :—

18th April 1877	...	...	...	10 battalions.
12th August 1877	...	...	...	36 ,,
16th August 1877	...	...	...	6 ,,
31st January 1878	...	...	...	44 ,,
17th April 1878	...	...	...	36 ,,
		Total	...	132 battalions = 118,800 men.

Those were formed by drafts from the local and fortress battalions and by men of the first category of the militia. They were formed into 11 divisions of 12 battalions, of which the 1st and 2nd served in Roumania and the 3rd in the Caucasus as *étappen* troops, the 4th to 8th were employed in Poland and the South-West Provinces, and the 9th to 11th on the Baltic coast. Eighteen reserve brigades of artillery (72 batteries) were formed in European Russia.

In *Turkistan*, in May and June 1878, eight reserve battalions (7,200 men) and a reserve brigade of artillery were formed.

The Cossack troops were mobilized as follows* :—

Cossacks Don—
- 60 regiments = 360 sotni
- 20 batteries = 120 guns

Kuban—
- 20 regiments = 120 sotni
- 12 battalions
- 5 batteries = 40 guns

Terek—
- 10 regiments = 40 sotni
- 2 batteries = 8 guns

Orenburg—
- 14 regiments = 84 sotni
- 4 batteries = 24 guns

Astrakhan—
- 2 regiments = 8 sotni

Total—
- 612 sotni = 91,800
- 12 battalions = 10,800
- 31 batteries = 192 guns

were in all mobilized by the Cossack armies of European Russia, though all were not employed on active service.

---

* *Note.*—The above details from Thilo von Trotha's "Mobilizirung der Russischen Armée 1877-78."

According to Blume, the active army of the Germans in France on the 1st March 1871, when the battalions, &c., had been filled up after their heavy losses, numbered (including three mobilized reserve divisions) 455,782 infantry, 57,779 cavalry, and 1,674 guns. It may therefore be assumed that a force of 450,000 infantry, 50,000 cavalry, and 1,500 guns, aided by the militia and supported by the fortresses of the Polish quadrilateral would be a sufficient army of observation against Germany, with perhaps 300,000 infantry, 30,000 cavalry, and 900 guns against Austria.

The number of troops which Russia would have to mobilize on the Turkish frontier in Europe would depend altogether on whether an alliance had been made with Turkey by England, and whether that alliance was offensive as well as defensive.

I find that the troops mobilized in Russia for employment in European Turkey in 1877-78 were as follows :—

		Battalions.	Squadrons.	Guns.
Original "Army of the South."	8th Army Corps	24	18	108
	9th " "	24	18	108
	11th " "	24	18	108
	12th " "	24	18	108
	3rd Rifle Brigade	4	...	...
	4th " "	4	...	...
	Cossack combined division ...	...	20	6
	Don Cossack Regiments (attached to infantry divisions) ...	...	54	46
	3rd Engineer Brigade, 3rd and 4th Pontoon, and 7 Sapper Battalions	...	...	...
	Total ...	104	146	484
Added 6th May ...	4th Army Corps	24	18	108
	13th " "	24	18	108
	14th " "	24	24	108
	Bulgarian Militia	6	...	...
	Total ...	78	60	324
Added 3rd August	Guard Corps	53	24	160
	2nd and 3rd Grenadier Divisions	24	...	96
	2nd, 3rd, 24th, and 26th Infantry Divisions	48	...	192
	1 Cavalry Division ...	...	18	12
	Total ...	125	42	460

GRAND TOTAL.

	Battalions.	Squadrons.	Guns.
1st mobilization	104	146	484
1st reinforcement	78	60	324
2nd "	125	42	460
Total ...	307	248	1,268 *or*

307 battalions @ 900 rifles = 276,300
248 squadrons @ 150 sabres = 37,000

313,300 men.
1,268 guns. *

* *Note.*—In Russia, the 7th and 10th Corps (48 battalions, 36 squadrons, 216 guns) were mobilized and placed to watch the Black Sea coast, but only a few squadrons of the 7th Corps crossed the Turkish Frontier.

I think that a consideration of the above will show clearly—"*1st*, even if Turkey did not enter openly into an alliance with England, Russia would still have to maintain in a state of readiness a force at least equal to the original Army of the South, namely (in round numbers), 93,600 infantry, 21,900 cavalry, 484 guns; and if Turkey formed an offensive-defensive alliance with England, she could not well keep a much smaller force in hand than she employed in European Turkey in the war of 1877-78, namely (in round numbers), 276,300 infantry, 37,000 cavalry, and 1,268 guns.

The troops mobilized on the Asiatic theatre of operations in 1877-78 were—

		Battalions.	Squadrons.	Guns.
Caucasus Army ...	Caucasus Grenadier Division ...	16	...	48
	19th, 38th, 39th, and 41st Divisions	64	...	192
	Of 20th Division ...	...	...	8
	Of 21st " ...	...	...	8
	Caucasus Rifle Brigade ...	4	...	...
	Caucasus Dragoon Division (two Don Cossack H. A. Batteries attached)	...	16	12
	Kuban Cossack Infantry ...	1	...	...
	" Cossacks, 1st category ...	...	60	12
	" " 2nd " ...	...	48	...
	Terek " 1st " ...	...	16	18
	" " 2nd " ...	...	20	...
Reinforcements from Europeans, Russia.	1st Grenadier Division ...	12	...	48
	40th Infantry " ...	12	...	48
	2nd Astrakhan Cossacks ...	...	6	...
	6th and 7th Orenburg Cossacks ...	...	8	...
	Total ...	109	174	394

besides sappers and a large number of militia cavalry.

Total ...	109 battalions @ 900 =	98,100
	174 squadrons @ 150 =	25,500
	Total =	123,600 men.
		394 guns.

Thus it is clear that if Turkey entered into an offensive-defensive alliance with England, Russia could not dare to maintain on her Armenian frontier a much less force than the above, namely,—

98,100 infantry. 25,500 cavalry. 394 guns.

The total war strength of the army of the Caucasus is, we have seen,—

138,288 infantry, 42,538 cavalry, 388 guns;

from this we must deduct the army which would have to be kept ready on the Armenian frontier, with the result that there would be available in the Caucasus for exterior operations about—

40,188 infantry. 17,038 cavalry. 6 guns.

The army of Turkistan numbers—

26,743 infantry. 7,618 cavalry. 76 guns.

It is evident that none of these can be spared for exterior operations; and the same remark may be applied to the troops in East and West Siberia: indeed, these provinces are clearly already dangerously weak.

We can now arrive at some idea of the smallest force which Russia would have to maintain on her frontiers and for internal purposes :—

		Infantry.	Cavalry.	Guns.
On the German frontier	...	450,000	50,000	1,500
" Austrian "	...	300,000	30,000	900
" European Turkey frontier	...	200,000	25,000	600*
" Asiatic " "	...	75,000	16,000	200
Caucasus ...	For internal defence	30,000	5,000	100
Turkistan ...	For internal defence	26,000	7,500	75
Siberia, East and West	For internal defence	20,000	2,500	64
Total	...	1,101,000	136,000	5,439

Interior Russia. The local and depôt troops are specially designed for internal police purposes during war.

Deducting then these numbers from the total armed strength of Russia (*vide* page 5), I find there would be a balance of about 185,000 infantry, 40,000 cavalry, and 191 guns available for operations in the direction of India, and this without counting on any aid at all from the tributary States of Servia, Bulgaria, &c. But if the troops of these States were added, Russia would then have an available field army of no less than 691,000 men and 955 guns. I think then it may be allowed that Russia has at her disposal sufficient men for the invasion of India.

The next necessity in making war is money ; and the finances of Russia are known to be in a bad way. But as she makes no sign of reducing her forces in peace time,—and I am informed that the loan of 15 millions she lately put into the Berlin market was taken up thirty times over,—I think we may safely assume that for such a popular operation as the invasion or threatening of India, money in abundance would be forthcoming. Still I regret I have not the data to prove this, nor do I know where to find data to do so ; therefore I must confine myself to saying that tightness of the money market never yet prevented a nation from going to war.

I have now proved that Russia has the necessary men ; I have assumed she will find the money should it be required ; and now I proceed to consider what steps would be taken towards ascertaining the feasibility of the operation we are considering.

I have said that the Russians now have their outposts at Merv, Petro-Alexandrovsk, Jam and Ush ; they have crept up to these places very unobtrusively. This may be owing to a very natural modesty in supposing that the world in general cannot be interested in movements directed towards such legitimate, even praiseworthy, ends as improving their commercial relations and consolidating the large extent of territory which the chances and changes of events have placed under their control.

But there can be no doubt that, supposing the Russian Government to have ulterior aims against India, this unobtrusive method of advancing their frontier is excellently well calculated to gain their ends ; and undoubtedly one of the first things which would suggest itself to a General ordered to arrange for an invasion of India would be that this silent advance should continue as long as possible. He would point out that the invasion of India was much

* I have here put the force which would have to be maintained by Russia on the European and Asiatic Turkish frontier at the lowest which would have to be kept up. If England and Turkey had entered into an offensive-defensive alliance, these numbers would have to be increased, and could not be less than about 340,000 men and 1,660 guns.

like the attack on a fortress; and it would consequently be advisable to ascertain whether there were any vantage points which, once seized, would give an advantage to his operations. "Oddly enough, he might remark, the points to which the Russians have already advanced are admirably suited to the end in view, and it will only be necessary to continue to conduct matters in the same way to secure like results."

The archives of the Intelligence Department of St. Petersburg and Tashkand would show him that such vantage points clearly existed; and I think it is not too much to say that he would select the points Herat, Kabul, and Chitral. The first because, *inter alia*, it is a strong fortress in a fertile valley capable of feeding a large number of men, and it is situated on the most practicable road to India from the west, while it can be, with equal ease, supported either from the north or the west by roads which are beyond any possibility of counter-attack. The second because, though a position of less importance, it is also situated in a fertile valley, with large food resources, within a very short distance of Peshawar, and in the midst of a population every man of whom is bitterly hostile to the English. The third because, though not of so great value as the others, it would place the General in command of a force at it in direct communication with a more than doubtful ally of the English, and with several tribes bitterly hostile to them.

I suppose then these three are the points selected. I don't say these would be, or need be, the exact points which would be selected; but as it would be very advisable to endeavour to seize some points in advance of those the Russians are now in possession of, these three seem on the whole to be the best.

And, further, it would clearly be an additional advantage that these points should be seized, either with the acquiescence of the English Government, or before that Government could take measures to prevent their falling into the hands of Russian Generals. It is also evident that every possible step should be taken to lull the suspicions of the English until such time as the Russians were in a position to seize them with tolerable certainty.

These points gained, it is evident it would only be necessary to hold them in sufficient strength to prevent their being retaken by the English, or by protestations of friendliness to induce that people to acquiesce in their loss as a *fait accompli*. In either case, it may be granted that a lull might then take place in the operations exactly as, to continue the analogy, would happen in the siege of a fortress. During this lull, the vantage points would be strengthened; the roads to the rear would be improved to admit of the storing of ammunition for the batteries; reconnaissances, up even to the walls of the fortress, would be undertaken; and communications would be opened with any of the garrison whose fidelity was doubtful.

This then shows us that an invasion of India like the operations of a siege naturally divides itself into two operations, separated from each other by a greater or less interval of time, according to the exigencies of the moment, but always also according to the convenience of the assailants.

I will therefore consider the question under these two headings—*1st*, measures advisable to place the Russians in possession of these vantage points; *2nd*, final measures for the invasion of India. It is necessary to give the Russians credit for a certain amount of forethought, and, in all operations of war, to allow for a certain amount of preliminary manœuvring before the opposing forces are ranged for the final struggle.

It having been settled thus which are the most important outworks of India, it is now necessary to consider what steps would be taken by the

Russians to prevent attention of the English being directed to these points; and at this stage, the question which a General entrusted with the preparations of this plan would ask would be—By what means can the suspicion of the English be lulled; and what steps should be taken to place the Russian forces within *coup de main* distance of these points?

To answer the last first, I think it must be allowed that the completion of the railway from the Caspian to the furthest limit of Russian territory on the Atak; the completion of a railway across the Ust Urt, from the Airakti Bay to the Oxus; the improvement of the marine on the Caspian, of the navigation of the Oxus, of the roads from Jam to the Oxus (through Bokhara) and towards Alai from Ush; and, finally, gradually to reinforce all points of the line in as quiet and unobtrusive a manner as possible,—would be the probable answer.

And as regards the pretexts for these steps and movements which would appear to be most likely to silence English suspicions, what seems the best to offer would be—*1st*, the vital necessity of so improving the communications to her possessions in Central Asia as would enable Russia to get such a firm grip of them as would at last enable her to consolidate and improve her commercial relations with her new subjects; *2nd*, to do all this it would also seem to be necessary to be very strong, so as to make any attempt on the part of the only half-subdued Khanates and tribes to disturb the peace impossible. Unfortunately, it might be pointed out, the elements of disorder within the Russian frontier were still numerous; the warlike Merv Tekkes only recently defied the Russians; and no reliance can even now be placed on their very qualified show of submission. Then in Khiva, Bokhara, and Khokand a seditious spirit has long been apparent which renders the greatest caution necessary, especially as Kashgar held by the Chinese is known to be bitterly hostile, and is the refuge of all the discontented spirits of the three Khanates. Then as the time drew near for throwing off the mask, it would be advisable to circulate rumours of an impending outbreak in Merv, and of the proposed further annexation of all Bokhara and Khiva.

The objects which would now have to be attained would be the possession of Herat, Kabul, and Chitral; or, if at the moment of the attempt it was not found advisable to push the advance through, of some points as near as possible to those places which could, without any cavil on the part of the English, be seized. These points would appear to be Sarakhs, Charjui, Kilif, and Samti Bala.

For this purpose it would be necessary to prepare five columns, and to undertake the measures described below under the name of each column, which will be called—1st, The Atak column; 2nd, The Oxus column; 3rd, The Jam column; 4th, The Margilan column; 5th, The Pamir column.

First, then, the Atak column. The objective of this force would be the seizing of Herat; but the probable ostensible reason of its assembly would be the punishment of the Merv Tekkes. To enable it to accomplish this object in a thoroughly effective manner, it will be necessary to provide (*a*) a force for the seizure of Herat, (*b*) a force for the protection of the communications from the Caspian in the Akhal country, (*c*) a force at Sarakhs and Merv to overawe the Merv Tekkes and protect the left flank of the advance, (*d*) a force at Charjui to overawe the Merv Tekkes from the north, (*e*) a force to reinforce Herat when taken.

For the first object (*a*), I consider that a force of the following strength would be ample: 16,200 infantry, 900 engineers, 3,850 cavalry, 1,600 artillery, and 64 guns.

For the second (*b*), a force of 8,000 infantry, 1,800 cavalry, 200 engineers, and 40 guns (which is the number Skobeleff took Geok-Tepe with) would be quite ample. For the third (*c*), I should say a force of 4,000 infantry, 1,000 cavalry, 200 engineers, and 16 guns would suffice; while the force for the fourth (*d*) will be found described under the heading—"The Oxus Column" (*e*).* In addition to the above, a force (*e*) of about the same strength as the advance would be held in readiness as a reserve to reinforce Herat when taken.

That is to say, omitting the Oxus column, a total of 44,400 infantry, 2,200 engineers, 10,500 cavalry, 4,000 artillery, and 184 guns would be required.

The force at present in the Akhal country consists of—

6 rifle battalions of the trans-Caspian Rifle Brigade at 900 = 5,400.
1 railway battalion ... ... 900.
1½ regiments of Cossack cavalry (1 Taman, ½ Laba), 9 sotnias at 150 = 1,350.
4 batteries artillery at 200 men and 8 guns = 32 guns and 800 men.

Consequently this force would have to be reinforced by 39,000 infantry, 2,200 engineers,† 8,150 cavalry, 3,800 artillery, and 152 guns to bring it to the strength required for the occupation of Herat.

In considering where this force is to come from, I cannot of course do more than take for granted that it will be drawn from the most convenient and readily accessible sources, namely, the Caucasus, any deficiency in the garrison of that province being made up from other parts of Russia.

Therefore, I suppose that the following troops have been selected for the advance force by reason of their being nearest to the three ports on the Caspian, *viz.*, Baku, Derband, and Petrovski, and having regard to the routes connecting their peace stations therewith :—

18 battalions infantry at 900	=	16,200
2 regiments Dragoons at 750; 2 Terek Cossack regiments at 600; 1 Kuban Cossack regiment at 900	=	3,850
8 batteries at 200	=	1,600, 64 guns
1 sapper battalion	=	900
		22,550, 64 guns

or with staff and departments, 23,000 men.

These troops might be composed of—

20th Division ...	2 battalions 78th Regiment, Vozdvijenskoe. 2 battalions 79th Regiment, Groznaya. 2 battalions 80th Regiment, Hasar Yurt. 2 batteries 20th Artillery Brigade, Vladikavkaz.
21st Division ...	2 battalions 82nd Regiment, Tchir Yurt. 2 battalions 83rd Regiment, Deshlagar. 2 battalions 84th Regiment, Kusari. 2 batteries 21st Artillery Brigade, Temir Khan Shura.
Caucasus Grenadiers Division.	2 battalions 13th Grenadiers, Manglis. 2 battalions 15th Tiflis, Manglis. 2 battalions 16th Tiflis, Manglis. 2 batteries Caucasus Grenadier Artillery Brigade, Tiflis.

* *Vide* page 30.

† The Railway battalion being required for the line from Mikhaelovsk to Kizil-Arvat is left out of the calculation.

44th Dragoons, Piatigorsk.
45th Dragoons, Mozdok.
Kisliar Greben (Terek) Cossacks, Mozdok.
Sundja (Terek) Cossacks, Groznaya.
Poltava (Kuban) Cossacks, Elisavetpol.
2nd Kuban H. A. Battery, Shusha.
5th Kuban H. A. Battery, Bieli Kliutch.
1st Sapper Battalion, Tiflis.
Telegraph Park, Tiflis.
½ 42nd Ammunition Park, Tiflis.
45th Ammunition Park, Petrovsk.

The corps chosen are all taken from the Caucasus Army, as the country east of the Caspian is under the same Government, and all operations in that country have hitherto been undertaken by troops of that army.

The troops in the Caucasus are on the peace footing, roughly speaking, at half war strength, with the notable exception of the cavalry, who are kept at somewhat over war strength both in men and horses. The war strengths, in round numbers, of the various units are as follows :—

Infantry battalions	... ...	900 men		
Dragoon regiments	... ...	750 „		
Cossack 6-sotnia regiments	... ...	900 „		
„ 4 „ „	... ...	600 „		
Heavy Battery (2 per brigade)	... ...	200 „	8	guns.
Light „ („)	... ...	200 „	8	„
Mountain „ („)	... ...	200 „	8	„
Cossack H. A. „ („)	... ...	200 „	6	„

Each infantry battalion would require therefore 450 reservists, each battery 40 to 100 men. The sapper battalions would require 300 men to complete; the ½ engineer and telegraph parks could be completed from the ½ remaining. It is not known how the ammunition columns would be completed. Details as to the mobilization of regimental and army corps and trains, &c., are not available. The wagons are stated to be in store; but how men and horses are obtained is unknown : the latter probably by requisition. If each battalion called up 650 instead of 450 reservists, all needs of artillery, sappers, and train would probably be filled. This number has therefore been taken as the basis of calculation, and the experience of 1877 would seem to justify it.

The depôt battalions of the Caucasus troops are stationed in the interior of Russia in the Eastern Provinces, with the exception of those of the 21st division who are on the Moskov Railway line, and would come *viâ* Nikolaievsk and Poti. There does not appear to be any strict rule as to the mobilization of regiments from their own territorial districts ; therefore to relieve the strain on the Poti-Tiflis-Baku Railway, the reserves of the 38th (Caucasus) Division in the Government of Voronej have been affiliated to this division. The 20th Division utilizes its own reserves from the Volga districts. The Caucasus Grenadiers have no territorial districts nor depôt battalions ; the reserves of the 41st (Caucasus) Division from the Volga districts have been supposed to complete it.

Although in 1870 the French system of sending regiments to the front without their reservists, and sending the latter after them, worked most disastrously for France, it has been adopted in this case—

(1) on account of the great distances the reservists would otherwise have to travel ;

(2) because there would be no fear of the troops being attacked before their reserves arrived as in 1870 ;

(3) on account of the small number of troops mobilized.

The reservists have therefore been supposed sent to the ports on the eastern side of the Caspian, to which their corps have been directed. Regiments, &c., have their augmentation stores of clothing, arms, equipment, wagons, &c., in their own possession, and the reservists could therefore be equipped on arriving at their corps.

Routes in the Caucasus to the ports on the Caspian, and Russian Railways in the interior.

The principal roads in the Caucasus which would be utilized for the concentration of troops at the ports are :—

Mozdok Vladikavkaz	} *viâ* Tcherevlennaya to Petrovsk	
Temir Khan Shura	,,	,,
Deshlagar	,,	Darband
Kusari	,,	,,

which are all excellent macadamized roads. Of the Tiflis-Baku Railway, the following details only are known :—

Length of line	345	miles.
Longest distance between stations	19½	,,
Time interval	3	hours.
Speed	15	miles.
Time of transit	23	hours.
Number of trains per diem (maximum) ...	8	

No details of the amount of rolling stock are available ; but there can be little doubt that sufficient exists to furnish 4 trains per diem of the maximum of 120 axles, which would require 8 to 10 engines and 480 vans and trucks. The data upon which calculations for military transport by rail are made in Germany are here assumed, and according to these a train can convey either a battalion of 1,000 men, a squadron (150 horses), or a battery. Two of the weak peace battalions may therefore be carried in one train.

The railway sections in the interior of Russia utilized are—

Buzuluk to Samara ...	162	versts =	6	hours	20	minutes.
Atkarsk to Sarato ...	54	,, =	1	,,	58	,,
Liski to Griazi ...	198	,, =	6	,,	15	,,
Griazi to Tsaritsin ...	564	,, =	21	,,	10	,,

On these railways rolling stock may be supposed unlimited, as they are connected with the Russian Railway system, and 6 trains per diem may (if required) be counted upon.

Concentration of the troops at the ports of embarkation.
A. Cadres, &c. (exclusive of reserves).

The Caucasus could easily furnish the number of horses required to complete the trains, batteries, &c., and from statistics it appears that the requisitioned horses would be all available in an average of about *seven* days. This then may be taken as the time in which, from date of receipt of the telegraphic order for mobilization, the battalions and batteries (minus their reserve men) are ready to march. Cavalry may be considered ready on the third day, as the small number of horses required for their trains would probably in that time be available. The following tables shew the dates of arrival at Petrovsk and Darband of the troops destined to embark there :—

At Petrovsk.

Division.	Regiment, Brigade, &c.	Place of mobilization.	Day of departure.	Distance (versts).	Number of days' march.	Day of arrival at Petrovsk.	Remarks.
20th	78th Regiment (2 battalions) ...	Vozdvijensk ...	8th	190	8	16th	Route march.
20th	79th „ („) ...	Groznaya ...	8th	160	7	14th	Route march.
20th	80th „ („) ...	Hasav Vurt ...	8th	80	3	10th	Route march.
20th	20th Artillery Brigade (2 batteries).	Vladikavkaz ...	8th	260	10	17th	Route march.
21st	82nd Regiment (2 battalions)...	Tchir Yurt ...	8th	40	2	9th	Route march.
21st	21st Artillery Brigade (2 batteries).	Shura ...	8th	50	2	9th	Route march.
	44th Dragoons	Piatigorsk ...	4th	260	7	11th	By rail (12 hours) on 4th day to Vladikavkaz; thence route march.
	45th Dragoons	Mozdok ...	4th	230	7	10th	Route march.
	Kisliar Greben Cossacks ...	Ditto ...	4th	230	7	10th	Route march.
	Sundja Cossacks	Groznaya ...	4th	160	5	8th	Route march.
	45th Field Park	Petrovsk ...	8th	...	...	8th	Route march.

At Darband.

Division.	Regiment, Brigade, &c.	Place of mobilization.	Day of departure.	Distance (versts).	Number of days' march.	Day of arrival at Darband.	Remarks.
21st	83rd Regiment (2 battalions) ...	Deshlagar ...	8th	75	3	10th	
21st	84th „ („) ...	Kusari ...	8th	75	3	10th	

At Baku.

It may be assumed that the necessary extra platform accommodation required and other preparations necessary for a large movement of troops would be made during the mobilization period, and that on the conclusion of this the railway would be ready to begin the transport of troops to Baku. The table overleaf shews the dates of arrival at that port.*

Note.—If considered necessary, the garrisons of the troops moved might be taken over by troops of the 7th (Sebastopol) and 8th (Kharkov) Corps brought by sea and rail.

N.B.—25 versts = 15½ miles is taken as a day's march for infantry and artillery ; 35 versts = 20½ miles for cavalry marching independently, which Russian troops could easily do.

* At Baku large preparations for the embarkation of large bodies of troops have already been made.

Corps.	Place of mobilization.	Day of completion.	Route March.					Railway.		
			Day of start.	Distance (versts).	Number of marches.	*Arrival.* At	*Arrival.* Day.	Entrained at	Date.	Arrive at Baku.
13th Grenadier (2 battalions)	Manglis ...	7th	8th	50	2	Tiflis ...	9th	Tiflis ...	10th	11th
15th " (")	Tiflis ...	7th	...	...	...	...	...	" ...	8th	9th
16th " (")	" ...	7th	...	...	...	...	...	" ...	8th	9th
Caucasus Grenadier Artillery (2 batteries)	" ...	7th	...	...	...	...	...	" ...	8th	9th
Poltava Cossacks	Elisavetpol ...	3rd	...	...	...	...	...	Elisavetpol ...	4th 5th	5th 6th
2nd Kuban Horse Artillery Battery	Shusha ...	7th	8th	140	4	Elisavetpol ...	12th	Tiflis ...	13th	14th
5th " "	Bieli Klintch	7th	8th	40	2	Tiflis ...	9th	" ...	10th	11th
1st Sapper Battalion	Tiflis ...	7th	...	...	...	...	...	" ...	9th	10th
Telegraph Park	" ...	7th	...	...	...	...	...	" ...	9th	10th
½ 42nd Ammunition Park	" ...	7th	...	...	...	...	...	" ...	9th	10th

B. Concentration of the Reserves.

The experience of 1877 has shown that in the populous districts of Russia the reservists may be expected to be assembled at their district head-quarters in (on an average) five days; in the less densely peopled districts in eight days. The former figure has been adopted for the reserves of the 21st Division; the latter for those of the Grenadiers and 20th.

Marvin in his "Russian Campaign against the Turkomans" says that on the Volga there are "650 steamers and 15,000 flat-bottomed barges (many of 750 to 1,000 tons burden)." The river transport of the reservists from Tsaritsin, Saratov, Syzran, Samara, and Stavropol to Astrakhan (where they must be shipped in deep-sea steamers) may therefore be considered assured. The distances are approximately (no exact figures are available) :—

Tsaritsin to Astrakhan	...	...	400 versts	=	33 hours.
Saratov "	...	...	720 "	=	60 "
Syzran "	...	...	960 "	=	80 "
Samara "	...	...	1,060 "	=	88 "
Stavropol "	...	...	1,140 "	=	95 "

Allowing 8 miles = 12 versts (nearly) as the average rate of a steamer down-stream, the table overleaf shows the date of concentration of reserves at Astrakhan.

Number of regimental district.	Head-quarters.	Regiment of infantry to which infantry reserves will be attached.	Day of completion of assembly.	By Route March.				By Rail.				By Steamer.				Remarks.
				Distance (versts).	Day's march.	Arrive at	Day of arrival.	Entraining stations.	Day of entraining.	Detraining stations.	Date.	Embarking station.	Date.	Arrival at	Date.	
78	Stavropol ...	78th ...	8th	...	...	......	...	......	...	......	...	Stavropol	9th	Astrakhan	13th	
79	Buzuluk ...	79th ...	8th	...	...	......	...	Buzuluk ...	...	Samara ...	9th	Samara ...	10th	"	14th	
80	Syzran ...	80th ...	8th	...	...	......	...	......	...	......	...	Syzran ...	9th	"	12th	
149	Babrov ...	84th ...	5th	50	2	Lirki ...	7th	Lirki ...	8th	Tsaritsin ...	9th	Tsaritsin ...	10th	"	13th	
150	Ostrogojsk ...	82nd ...	5th	25	1	" ...	6th	" ...	7th	" ...	8th	" ...	9th	"	11th	
151	Birioutch ...	83rd ...	5th	100	4	" ...	9th	" ...	10th	" ...	11th	" ...	12th	"	14th	
161	Saratov ...	13th Grenadier ...	5th	...	...	......	...	......	...	......	...	Saratov ...	9th	"	12th	
162	Atkarsk ...	15th " ...	8th	...	...	......	...	Atkarsk ...	9th	Saratov ...	9th	" ...	10th	"	13th	
164	Tsaritsin ...	16th " ...	8th	...	...	......	...	......	...	......	...	Tsaritsin ...	9th	"	11th	

V. Means of transport on the Caspian Sea, rates of passage, and ports of landing on the east coast.

From Mr. Marvin's "The Russians at Merv and Herat," I extract the following notes on the marine of the Caspian :—

The *Caucasus and Mercury Company* possess a fleet of 19 steamers with a collective tonnage of 20,000 tons, which, by the conditions of the Government subsidy, are always available for troop-transport.

Nobel Brothers have 12 large steel steamers 245 feet long and 27¾ feet broad, steaming 10 knots an hour. These would afford transport for 6,000 troops at a trip, and in fine weather this might be doubled.

There are besides numerous large steamers owned by private individuals.

The entire marine now exceeds 1,500 vessels of all classes, of which the larger number belong to the port of Baku.

I may therefore consider the transport of the troops across the Caspian as completely assured, more especially as all are not to be conveyed at once.

The lengths of passage by steamer on the various routes are as follows :—

Astrakhan	to Krasnovodsk	...	...	...	48-60 hours.
"	to Tchikishlar	...	...	...	72-84 "
Darband	to Krasnovodsk	...	...	...	27 "
Petrovsk	to "	...	...	...	30 "
"	to Tchikishlar	...	...	...	60 "
Baku	to Krasnovodsk	...	...	...	24 "
"	to Tchikishlar	...	...	...	48 "

The capabilities of the ports of Krasnovodsk and Tchikishlar will be seen from the three following papers in Appendix A, B, C, from which it appears that there would be little difficulty in landing the amount of troops laid down to arrive daily. The most serious difficulty is the scarcity of water at Krasnovodsk, and extensive preparations would be required in the way of setting up condensers; but a camp at Mikhailovsk (to which troops can only be conveyed in barges from Krasnovodsk after debarkation) would relieve the strain.

However, as the preparation of proper watering arrangements would take time, it would clearly be necessary to be most careful to make them secretly, so that this dangerous and unmistakeable hint of the preparation for a large force should not become known to the English prematurely.*

* Considering that the English have no means of getting information from the Caspian, the danger is not very great.

The transport of the troops across the Caspian would be effected by the following dates :—

Division.	Regiment, &c.	Embarked at	Date.	Arrive at	Date.	Ready to march on	Remarks.
	78th Regiment, 2 battalions ...	Petrovsk ...	17th	Krasnovodsk	18th	} 20th	
	78th ,, reserves ...	Astrakhan ...	15th	,,	18th		
	79th ,, 2 battalions ...	Petrovsk ...	15th	,,	16th	} 20th	
	79th ,, reserves ...	Astrakhan ...	15th	,,	18th		
	80th ,, 2 battalions ...	Petrovsk ...	11th	,,	12th	18th	
	80th ,, reserves ...	Astrakhan ...	13th	,,	16th	} 20th	
	20th Artillery Brgade, 2 batteries ...	Petrovsk ...	18th	,,	19th		
	82nd Regiment, 2 battalions ...	,, ...	10th	,,	11th	} 17th	
	82nd ,, reserves ...	Astrakhan ...	12th	,,	15th		
	83rd ,, 2 battalions ...	Darband ...	11th	,,	12th	} 20th	
	83rd ,, reserves ...	Astrakhan ...	15th	,,	18th		
	84th ,, 2 battalions ...	Darband ...	11th	,,	12th	} 18th	
	84th ,, reserves ...	Astrakhan ...	13th	,,	16th		
	21st Artillery Brigade, 2 batteries ...	Petrovsk ...	10th	,,	11th	} 17th	
	13th Grenadiers, 2 battalions ...	Baku ...	12th	,,	13th		
	13th ,, reserves ...	Astrakhan ...	13th	,,	16th	18th	
	15th ,, 2 battalions ...	Baku ...	10th	,,	11th	} 19th	
	15th ,, reserves ...	Astrakhan ...	14th	,,	17th		
	16th ,, 2 battalions ...	Baku ...	10th	,,	11th	} 17th	
	16th ,, reserves ...	Astrakhan ...	12th	,,	15th		
	Grenadiers Artillery Brigade, 2 batteries	Baku ...	10th	,,	11th	17th	
	44th Dragoons	Petrovsk ...	12th	Tchikishlar ...	15th	17th	
	45th ,, ...	,, ...	11th	,,	14th	16th	
	Kislar Greben Cos.	,, ...	12th	,,	15th	17th	
	Sundja Cos.	,, ...	9th	,,	12th	14th	
	Poltava ,, ...	Baku ...	8th	,,	11th	13th	
	2nd Kuban H. A. Battery ...	,, ...	15th	,,	17th	19th	
	5th ,, ,, ,, ...	,, ...	12th	,,	14th	16th	
	1st Sapper battalion	,, ...	12th	Krasnovodsk	13th	17th	
	Telegraph Park ...	,, ...	12th	,,	13th	15th	
	½ 42nd Ammunition Park ...	,, ...	12th	,,	13th	17th	
	45th ,, ,, ...	Petrovsk ...	8th	,,	9th	17th	

That is to say, by the 20th day after the order for the move was given the last regiment would have landed on the east coast of the Caspian.

It would be necessary now to provide this force with transport, and therefore we must first see what it would be necessary for it to carry with it. Of course large depôts of such provisions as the country would afford would have been formed at Kizil-Arvat, Ashkabad, and Sarakhs, or near it, so that it would only be necessary for a supply sufficient for about one month to be taken.

In order to enable us to make these calculations, we cannot have a better guide than the scale of transport laid down by Skobeleff for the Akhal Tekke Expedition of 1880-81. This is as follows :—

(A) Wheeled transport—

Infantry.—Two 4-wheeled wagons per battalion.

(B) Pack transport (horse)—

Cavalry.—1 pack-horse for every 10 horses.

(C) Camel transport—

Infantry.—Per battalion—

	Camels.
Men's kits	100
Officers' kits	21
Forage for officers' horses	6
Water	60
Ammunition	18
Eight days' rations of biscuit	89
One month's tinned provisions	147
Tents	15
Felts	79
Field ovens	25
Total ...	549

Artillery—

(*a*)—*Field Battery* @ 200 non-commissioned officers and men and 107 artillery and spare horses—

	Camels.
Men's kits	22
Officers' kits	6
Water	6
Eight days' rations of biscuit	28
One month's tinned provisions	30
Tents	3
Felts	16
Field ovens	5
Forage for five days	53
Total ...	163

(*b*) *Mountain Battery* @ 250 non-commissioned officers and men and 5 officers' horses—

	Camels.
Men's kits	30
Officers' kits	6
Water	9
Eight days' rations of biscuit	30
One month's tinned provisions	43
Tents	4
Felts	25
Field ovens	6
Five days' forage	66
Total ...	219

Cavalry.—Per squadron or sotnia—

	Camels.
Men's kits	10
Officers' kits	4
Five days' forage	37
Eight days' rations of biscuit	10
One month's tinned provisions	15
Tents	1
Felts	8
Field ovens	3
Total ...	86

These figures are taken from Grodekoff's account of Skobeleff's campaign in the Akhal; and if that General considered the stores herein laid down sufficient for the above campaign, where the Russians had no secure hold of the country beyond Chat, it must be allowed that they would be sufficient for our purpose; for it is evident that any amount of stores can be collected at Ashkabad without the attention of the English being called to the fact, and of course that such a collection of stores shall have been made beforehand must be taken as a *sine quâ non* in carrying out the operation I am now considering.

The force which is to form the advance of Herat is to consist of—

18 battalions of infantry.
20 squadrons of cavalry.
1 battalion of sappers.
8 batteries of artillery.

Therefore the transport required to move it with one month's tinned provisions will be in round numbers—

Infantry battalions	18 × 550 camels	=	10,000	camels,	36 four-wheeled wagons.
Cavalry squadrons	20 × 90 „	=	1,800	„	350 pack-horses.
Sapper battalion	1 × 550 „	=	550	„	
Batteries	8 × 190 „	=	1,520	„	
	Total ...		13,870		

In addition to the above it would be necessary to provide an ammunition column and an engineer park.

The calculations for these are made out as follows :—

An artillery and infantry ammunition column has 130 ammunition wagons, the *load* of each of which is 1 ton 4 cwt. 1 lb. = 1⅕ tons.

Therefore 1½ columns have 195 wagons loaded with in all 524,160 lbs. = say 1,100 camel-loads. If the ammunition is not to be carried on camels but drawn by horses in the usual wagons, then an ammunition column may be calculated for transport as the equivalent of 6 batteries.

If all the engineer field park stores (58 carriages at 30 cwt. each) are to be carried on camels, for the 194,880 lbs. 389 (say 400) camels will be required. If the usual horse wagons are to be taken, the park may be considered as the equivalent of 2 batteries.

The total transport required would therefore be—

	Camels.
As above	13,870
Ammunition	1,100
Engineer park	400
Total ...	15,370, or allowing about 10 per cent. spare, say 17,000 camels.

In addition there would be required some 36 of the 4-wheeled wagons used by the Russians and 350 pack-horses for the cavalry.

This transport of course need not all be camels; but as a considerable portion of it must be camels, and the rate of a march is regulated by the pace of the slowest member of a column, the distances traversed each day will not be practically effected :—

A camel equals about 2 mules.
„ „ „ ¼ of a 1-horse cart.
„ „ „ ⅐ of a 2-horse cart.

The question now is where all this transport is to come from, and how soon could it be collected.

In the first place it must, I hold, be assumed that any number of horses and wagons that might be necessary could be gradually sent over the Caspian so as to be ready for the troops. What the resources of Russia are in this respect may be gathered from the following extract from the *St. James's Gazette*.*

* The Russian Government have recently published a summary of a horse census, carried out systematically, last autumn, in all the fifty-eight provinces of European Russia. The results of this census show that the military district of St. Petersburg has nearly eight hundred thousand horses, of which rather more than six hundred thousand are fit for military service in the event of a general mobilization. Vilna has about two millions, of which one million seven hundred thousand are reported as effectives. Warsaw has seven hundred thousand effectives out of a total of nearly a million. Kiev, Odessa, and Charkov are returned as possessing 1,210,132, 1,094,616, and 2,157,623 effective animals, respectively. Moscow has three and Kazan four million horses fit for transport service, &c. The grand result, according to the *Invalide Russe*, is that, out of nearly twenty million horses, Russia has some fifteen millions available for war in the eight military districts west of the Caucasus. Charkov and Kazan are the great recruiting grounds for horses of the line; and the Russian authorities are said to be agreeably surprised at the number of horses returned as available for transport duties.

But in addition to these the resources in transport of Turkomania could undoubtedly be tapped. Major Napier, the best available authority I have to refer to, calculates that within a fortnight of receipt of orders by telegraph there might be collected—

	Camels.
At Bami	7,000
From Krasnovodsk	1,000
From the Yamud	3,000
From the Akhal on the Persian border	3,000
From the Goklan near Astrabad, from Shahrood and Mazanderan	2,000
Total ...	16,000

A fortnight later there might be collected at Bami—

	Camels.
From Mangishlak and the Kirghiz	3,000
From the Yamud	2,000
From the Akhal	2,000
From Merv	3,000 to 4,000
Total ...	10,000

Thus the transport requirements of the force could be completely met in less than a month, and a considerable margin left, and moreover no intimation of their collection need reach the English.

I have said above that on the 20th day the last regiment would have landed at Krasnovodsk; and as of course the transport could have been collected before their arrival, it may be said that the advance could commence on the 21st day.

The various data of the onward routes, &c., are as follows :—

Krasnovodsk to Tash Arvat Kala (near the railway), 95 miles = 6 marches.

The railway from Mikhailovsk to Kizil Arvat, 144 miles.

Six trains per diem available.

Time of transit,—14 hours.

There are two tugs which work between Krasnovodsk and Mikhailovsk, each of which can in 24 hours tow barges with ½ battalion or 2 sotni from one place to another and return; but these had perhaps better be left for the conveyance of stores and troops sent by road :—

Kizil Arvat to Sarakhs is 323⅛ miles (see detailed route in Appendix E).

Chikishlar to Bami as 215¾ miles (see detailed route in Appendix D).

The following tables show the concentration of the troops from Krasnovodsk and Chikishlar at Kizil Arvat and Bami. The average marches are about 15 miles, and this is nearly the rate maintained by the troops under Sir Frederick Roberts on the march from Kabul to Kandahar; and it is evident that it would with difficulty be exceeded by troops of any other army, especially if equipped to any extent, as I take it this force must be with camels. I have allowed two halts on the march of the cavalry between Chikishlar and Bami.

Advance from Krasnovodsk to Kizil Arvat.

Regiment, &c.	Route.	March.	Railway.		Remarks.
	Leave Krasnovodsk	Arrive Tash Arvat Kala	Leave Tash Arvat Kala	Arrive Kizil Arvat	
2 battalions, 78th Regiment ...	21st	26th	31st	32nd	Two trains per diem being reserved for stores, only four will be available for troops. No *time* would be gained by moving troops by road to Kizil Arvat, and the character of the country would appear to render it advisable to send all troops by rail. Supplies at Kizil Arvat would have been collected by the trans-Caspian troops, or pushed up in the first three weeks of the movement.
2 ,, 79th ,, ...	21st	26th	30th	31st	
2 ,, 80th ,, ...	19th	24th	29th	30th	
2 batteries, 20th F. A. ...	21st	26th	30th	31st	
2 battalions, 82nd Regiment ...	18th	23rd	26th	27th	
2 ,, 83th ,, ...	21st	26th	31st	32nd	
2 ,, 84th ,, ...	19th	24th	29th	30th	
2 batteries, 21st F. A. ...	18th	23rd	26th	27th	
2 battalions, 13th Grenadiers ...	19th	24th	27th	28th	
2 ,, 15th ,, ...	20th	25th	27th	28th	
2 ,, 16th ,, ...	18th	23rd	24th	25th	
2 batteries, Grenadier A. ...	18th	23rd	24th	25th	
1 sapper battalion ...	18th	23rd	25th	26th	
Telegraph park ...	16th	21st	22nd	23rd	
½ 42nd Ammunition Park ...	18th	23rd	25th	26th	
45th ,, ,, ...	18th	23rd	28th	29th	

The troops from Chikishlar would arrive as follows at Bami :—

44th Dragoons	leave Chikishlar	18th ;	arrive	34th	day.
45th ,,	,, ,,	16th ;	,,	33rd	,,
Kisliar Greben Cossacks	,, ,,	18th ;	,,	34th	,,
Sundja Cossacks	,, ,,	15th ;	,,	32nd	,,
Poltava ,,	,, ,,	15th ;	,,	32nd	,,
2nd Kuban H. A. Bty.	,, ,,	20th ;	,,	36th	,,
5th ,, H. A. Bty.	,, ,,	18th ;	,,	34th	,,

The transport required for this force having been collected at Kizil Arvat would be served out to each detachment on arrival, and these would consequently be in a position to move from these places on the day after their arrival is necessary. The cavalry and horse artillery would have to be equipped at Chikishlar.

The troops would advance from Kizil Arvat in echelons organized with a due proportion of all arms of the services, as—

(1) troops would probably be more easily fed at Kizil Arvat than at Ashkabad while waiting to advance;

(2) it might be advisable for the advanced troops to push on at once from Ashkabad to take advantage of any partial surprise, and this necessitates their being organized properly.

Echelons composed as under would therefore advance from Kizil Arvat as follows :—

45th Dragoons, Sundja Cossacks ...	= 8 sq.	Leave 35th day; arrive 58th day at Sarakhs.
15th, 16th, and 13th Grenadiers ...	= 6 bns.	
2 Battr. Gren. Artillery Brig. ...	= 16 guns.	
1 Sapper Bn. and Park		
Telegraph Park		
½ Ammunition column		

44th Dragoons, Poltava Cossacks ...	= 10 sq.	Leave 36th day; arrive 59th day.
82nd, 83rd, and 84th Regiments ...	= 6 bns.	
2 Battr. 21st Artillery Brig. ...	= 22 guns.	
5th Kuban H. A. Battery ...		
½ Ammunition column		

Kisliar Greben Cossacks ...	= 4 sq.	Leave 37th day; arrive 60th day.
78th, 79th, and 80th Regiments ...	= 6 bns.	
2 Battr. 20th Artillery Brig. ...	= 22 guns.	
2nd Kuban H. A. Battery ...		
⅓ Ammunition column		

The cavalry and horse artillery would join the columns at Bami.

The force which the Russians would thus have available at Sarakhs, where it would arrive on the 60th day for a further advance on Herat, would consist of about 23,000 men of all arms and 64 guns.

The ostensible object of this force would be the coercion of the Merv Tekkes, and it certainly could not seem to the English that this force was, to any great extent, more than sufficient for the purpose, and Her Britannic Majesty's Government could therefore hardly remonstrate with Russia on this plea.

But this force, which does not seem more than sufficient to subdue the Mervlis, *is quite sufficient to take Herat by a coup de main*, and it would on the 60th day be within 16 days of that place, and it may be expected that the English, with their imperfect intelligence arrangements, would probably be at least in great doubt as to its destination.

Lessar's route from Sarakhs to Herat through Afghan territory* is the best road to Herat, as it avoids the high mountains met with on the route by Meshed, and is most suitable for wheeled traffic. It runs as follows:—

	Miles.
Sarakhs to Din Kala ...	9⅓
Naurozabad ...	15
Adam Yolan ...	27
Agar Chashma ...	8⅓
Kungrueli Rabat ...	5⅔
Kizil Bulak ...	26
Kambou ...	24
Kazan ...	30
Herat ...	64
Total ...	209⅓

At the above average of 15 miles per diem, this distance could be accomplished in 13 marches or 16 days, allowing three halts. That is to say, in 60 days from commencing, the Russians could put 23,000 men and 64 guns at Sarakhs, and this without giving the English an excuse for a declaration of war; and 16 days after reaching Sarakhs, or after throwing off the mask, they could be at Herat. If the Russians got to Herat before the English, it must be clear that they could not be turned out without enormous efforts on the part of the latter, because the mask once thrown off by the Russians, their army in Herat could then be reinforced to any extent desirable by marching troops through Persia as well as by the Kizil Arvat Railway line.

The force required for the (*b*) Akhal communications and (*c*) Sarakhs I have put at—

	infantry.	engineers.	cavalry.	artillery.	guns.
(*b*)	8,000	200	1,800	1,000	40
(*c*)	4,000	200	1,000	400	16
Total	12,000	400	2,800	1,400	56

* *Vide* Appendix F.

Of this force, the following are already on the spot (their reserves having been sent with those for the advanced force) :—

5,400, infantry, 1.350 cavalry, and 32 guns.

Therefore only the balance would have to be provided, and these could move from the western ports of the Caspian, and push on to the respective destinations immediately after the above advance force had passed on. There would in all probability be but little risk in doing this, as the Akhal and Merv Turkomans would certainly remain quiet until the advance force had passed on. The following troops would probably be selected :—

2 battalions, 77th Regiment, Vladikavkaz 2 „ 81st „ Iskharti 2 „ 14th Grenadiers, Bieli Klintch	7 battalions.
3rd Rifle Battalion, Vladikavkaz	
½ Laba Cossack Regiment, Geok Tapa (near Lenkoran)	= 3 squadrons.
Volga „ „ Tiflis	= 4 „
Kutais Irregular Cossack Regiment, Kutais ...	= 4 „
1 battery, 20th Artillery Brigade, Vladikavkaz 1 „ 21st „ „ Khan Shura 1 „ Caucasus Grenadier Artillery Brigade, Tiflis	= 3 batteries = 24 guns.
2 companies 2nd Sapper Battalion, Vladikavkaz.	

These troops could be at the ports on the western shore of the Caspian as follows :—

2 battalions, 77th Regiment,	at Petrovsk	on the	17th day.
2 „ 81st	„ „	„	10th „
2 „ 14th Grenadiers	„ Baku	„	11th „
3rd Rifle Battalion	„ Petrovsk	„	17th „
½ Laba Cossacks	„ Lenkoran	„	5th „
Volga „	„ Baku	„	6th and 7th day.
Kutais „	„ „	„	12th and 13th „
1 battery, 20th Brigade	„ Petrovsk	„	17th day.
1 „ 21st „	„ „	„	9th „
1 „ Grenadier Brigade	„ Baku	„	11th „
2nd Sapper Battalion (2 cos.)	„ „	„	17th „

It may therefore be assumed that there would be no difficulty in providing for the *étappen* line posts as the main body advanced, and that by the time (60th day) that the latter arrived at Sarakhs all these posts will be occupied by their garrisons. The trans-Caspian battalions, &c., from Ashkabad might even be pushed on to Sarakhs as an advanced guard if required. The 13 battalions, 20 squadrons, 7 batteries, and 2 sapper companies might be distributed as under :—

	Battalions.	Squadrons.	Sap. cos.	Guns.
Sarakhs	4½	7	1	16
Chacha	½	1	...	4
Mehna	½	1	...	...
Dushak	1	1	...	...
Kahka and Abiverd ...	1	2	...	4
Baba Durmaz	½	1	...	4
Ashkabad	3	4	1	12
Geok Tapa	½	½	...	4
Archman	½	1	...	4
Bami	1	½	...	4
Kizil Arvat	½	1	...	4
Total ...	13	20	2	56

The reserve force for Herat has now to be arranged for. This would be of the same strength as the advance force, and would be formed into two equal divisions.

I have shown that it would not be necessary for the Russians to throw off the mask which had veiled their intention of striking at Herat until the arrival of the advance force at Sarakhs on the 6(th day after the order for mobilization had been given; but it is evident it would be perfectly eligible for them to concentrate any number of troops they pleased at the Caspian ports of Baku, Darband, and Petrovski on the plea of their being a reserve for the force which had been despatched against Merv.

The Russian Government would then be informed by telegraph by the General Officer in command of the Atak column of the day on which he would be in a position to continue his march from Sarakhs to Herat. On that day the mask would have to be abandoned, and therefore on that day the embarkation of the reserve force might commence.

For this force, most of the remaining troops of the 20th and 21st and Caucasus Grenadier Divisions, and Caucasus Rifle Brigade, would probably be utilized, and would be distributed into two divisions, each consisting of—

8 battalions infantry 1 battalion rifles	= 9 battalions @ 900	...	= 8,100
1 regiment Dragoons	@ 750 ...	... ...	= 750
1 " Cossacks	@ 900 ...	... ...	= 900
1 " "	@ 600 ...	... ...	= 600
4 batteries artillery	@ 200 and 8 guns	... ...	= 800 and 32 guns.
½ sapper battalion	...	... ...	= 450
	Total	...	10,600 men,* 32 guns.

One of those would be concentrated at Petrovski, the other at Baku; the voyage from Baku to Bandar Gaz would take two days, and from Petrovski to the same place three days; and as there is ample sea transport available, it may be safely presumed that both divisions would be disembarked at Bandar Gaz by the 4th day, after receiving the order and after the advance force had left Sarakhs for Herat.

These divisions would concentrate at Astrabad, 23 miles distant, on the 6th day. At this place they would receive their equipment of transport, their requirements being calculated on the same scale as for the advance force, *viz.*, 17,000 camels, or an equivalent. This transport, it is stated by Major Napier, would be procurable as follows :—

Within a fortnight of receipt of orders, the following could be collected :—

From the Goklan, near Astrabad. from Shahrud and Mazanderan	9,000 camels.
From Astrabad, Mazanderan, and Shahrud	500 mules.

In another fortnight—

From Damghhan and the hills about Hazar Jarib	19,000 camels.
Semnan, Jagatai, Mazinan, &c.	1,500 mules.

Besides, as shown above, any number of horses and carts could be sent over from the Caucasus.

It is scarcely to be hoped that such a collection of animals could be made without being known to the English, and it would therefore be necessary to state that they were being collected to be sent on to Bami and Kizil Arvat for the force advancing on Merv; and if they were driven past Astrabad to the Gurgan, and arrangements made that no news of them should become

* Besides half an ammunition park.

known, it would be quite possible to recall them to Astrabad in the time the reserve divisions would take to concentrate at this place. It may therefore be taken for granted that there would be no difficulties about transport that money, energy, and hard lying would not get over.

Of course very extensive arrangements would have to be made by the Russians for supplies in Persia. This would be done by sending officers disguised as merchants to buy up all the necessary supplies procurable and arrange for their being forthcoming when wanted.* Secrecy would in this matter certainly be very difficult to maintain; but looking to the very ineffective arrangements of the English for getting intelligence from Persia, very much would probably be done before their suspicions were thoroughly aroused. These two divisions would advance from Astrabad in separate bodies,—the 1st taking the route by the Gurgan Pass, the Armutli plain, and Nishapur to Sharifabad; and the 2nd would move by Shahrud, Subzawar, Turshiz, and Turbat Haidari on Herat.

The first division would land at Bandar Gaz, and would march by the following route, the stages named being provided with supplies from the neighbouring country under the arrangements of the Persian Government:—

Stage.	Distance.	Source of supply.
1. Kurd Mohala	7	Village of adjacent belooks of Mazanderan, Hazarja rib and the Anazan belook.
2. Astrabad	16	Town and surrounding villages.
3. Camp	16	Sadan Rustak and Finderisk belooks and Turkoman camps.
4. Finderisk	16	Finderisk belook and Turkoman camps.
5. Camp	16	Finderisk, Kohsar, and Turkoman camps.
6. Pisarak	16	Kohsar, Sangor, and Turkoman camps.
7. Camp	15	Goklan camps.
8. Camp	15	"
9. Obah Chakir	16	"
10. Nowsherwan Rabat ...	25	"
11. Karoguez	20	Nardin (1 day caravan), Jahjarm (2 days), Shahrud (6 days).
12. Rabat-i-Ask	21	Shahrud and Jahjarm.
13. Showgan	27	Bujnurd and Mana.
14. Hajugan	26	Local and Sungkhas and Chardeh hamlets.
15. Dowlutabad	21	Isperayin and Safiabad.
16. Camp	22	Jogatai, Juven (2 days' caravan), Mazinan (5 days), Subzawar (5 days).
17. Rabat-i-Gaz	22	Jogatia, Juven, and Subzawar.
18. Pahnay	14	" "
19. Madan	12	Nishapur and Subzawar.
20. Hissar	16	" "
21. Nishapur	12	" "
22. Kadamgah	15	" "
23. Camp	13	" "
24. Sharifabad	12	" "
Total	411 miles.	

This distance I calculate would be traversed by the division in 32 days, allowing a fair time for halts en route, that is to say, it would arrive at Sharifabad on the 36th day after leaving the port of embarkation, or the 96th day from the commencement of operations; and on that day it would be in a position either to overawe (if this should be necessary) the authorities in Mashad, or to advance to the reinforcement of the corps in Herat.

* Appendix G.

If the latter alternative should be necessary, the division would arrive at Herat in 18 days by the following route from Sharifabad* :—

		Miles.			Miles.
1.	Turukh	19	10.	Camp	17
2.	Sangbast	17½	11.	Karez	13
3.	Farimun	19	12.	Kohsan	21
4.	Halt	...	13.	Halt	...
5.	Camp	12	14.	Camp	13½
6.	Burdu	12	15.	Ghorian	11½
7.	Mahmudabad	19	16.	Zindehjan	13
8.	Turbat-i-Shaikh-Jam	16	17.	Ab-i-Salil	15
9.	Halt	...	18.	Herat	11
				Total	229½

The 2nd Division would in the same manner land at Bandar Gaz, and march by the following route,† full details of which will be found in the Appendix. The stages would be provided with supplies from the neighbouring country under arrangements with the Persian Government :—

		Miles.			Miles.
1.	Kurd Mahala	7	23.	Badraskand	14
2.	Astrabad	16	24.	Naobulhakim	21
3.	Camp	14	25.	Saadadi	21
4.	Galugah	15	26.	Camp	14
5.	Radkan	12	27.	Turshiz	14
6.	Halt	...	28.	Halt	...
7.	Asp-o-Neza	8	29.	Camp	12
8.	Shahkob Pain	13½	30.	Zurmir	13
9.	Tush Rubat	15½	31.	Camp near Turbat-i-Haidari	15
10.	Shahrud	19½	32.	Camp	20
11.	Halt	...	33.	,,	20
12.	Khairabad	8	34.	Himatabad	20
13.	Camp	14	35.	Shahr-i-Nao	14
14.	Maiomai	18	36.	Mushadi Reza	17
15.	Miandasht	22	37.	Karez	14
16.	Abbasabad	19	38.	Halt	...
17.	Muzinan	21	39.	Kohsan	21
18.	Mehr	18	40.	Camp	13½
19.	Camp	15	41.	Ghorian	11½
20.	Subzawar	15	42.	Zindehjan	13
21.	Halt	...	43.	Ab-i-Julil	15
22.	Bizwat	14	44.	Herat	11
				Total	598½

From the foregoing it is evident that the forces I have named above would each arrive at their destinations on the following days after the order was given :—

Atak column—advanced force for Herat...	At Herat on the 77th day.
Sarakhs Brigade	At Sarakhs by the 60th day.
Akhal communications force ...	At various places, *viz.*, Kizil Arvat, Bami, Ashkabad, Abivurd, and Chacha ; at the last on the 60th day.
Reserve force for Herat	1st Division at Sharifabad on the 96th day. 2nd Division at Turbat-i-Haidari on the 96th day. The whole force at Herat on the 112th day.

It is thus evident that from the 77th day on which the advance force arrives at Herat until the 112th day, on which its reserve could join it, the former must depend on its own exertions to maintain its position.

* All such supplies would be brought ostensibly for the Russian troops in the Atak.
† Appendix H.

It would be useless to attempt to say on what day after arrival the Russians would be in possession of Herat. This would entirely depend on what resistance they met with. But of course intrigues would have been set on foot to prepare the way for a peaceable occupation of this city, and there does seem fair ground for supposing that the Russians would not have much difficulty in gaining over a party in Herat, and by its means being admitted without any very great delay; and as the plans of this fortress would have been in the hands of Russian engineers for a considerable time, it is fair to assume that the improvement of its defences could be begun the day after they gained possession of it; and that in a very short time afterwards the place would be rendered beyond the power of any force unprepared with a large siege train to retake.

So much for what can be done from the Caspian. I will now consider what can be done from other directions, and first from Petro-Alexandrovsk or Shurakhana, the cantonment in Khiva. At this place the Russians have, according to our latest information, a garrison consisting of the 5th and 13th Battalions of the Turkistan Infantry, 4th Orenburg Cossack Regiment, numbering in all 2,106 infantry and 994 cavalry. This force is clearly not more than sufficient to hold its own against Khiva: indeed it is certain that it must be reinforced in order to be able effectually to keep that State in check in the event of hostile operations going on in its vicinity; and I am disposed to think that it would have to be increased by at least six more battalions of infantry, one regiment of cavalry, and four batteries of artillery. Besides this a force, (*d*) the Oxus column, is required to advance to Charjui to threaten Merv from the north, and, if necessary, afterwards to advance to that place; and this would not consist of less than four battalions infantry, one regiment cavalry, two batteries artillery. That is to say, the Petro-Alexandrovsk garrison would have to be reinforced by ten battalions of infantry, three regiments cavalry, and six batteries of artillery.

The troops most convenient for this purpose are those of the 40th Division stationed on the Volga at Saratov and Samara, to which the Astrakhan Cossack Regiment at Astrakhan and the two Orenburg Cossack Regiments at Nijni Novgorod might be added. The troops selected would be mobilized and ready to move on the following dates:—

Regiment, &c.	Place of mobilization of regiment, &c.	Head-quarters of regimental district.	Movements of reserve men.	The reserves arrive	The regiment is ready to march
157th Regiment ...	Saratov ...	Khvalinsk ...	Reserves 234 versts = 18 hours by steamer.	9th	11th
158th " ...	" ...	Kuznetsk ...	Reserves 6½ hours rail to Syzran; 27 hours steamers.	10th	12th
159th " (2 bns.)...	Samara ...	Penza ...	Reserves 14 hours rail.	9th	11th
40th Artillery Brigade...	Saratov ...	......	......	...	12th
Astrakhan Cossacks ...	Astrakhan ...	......	A few reserves required ...	7th	8th
2 Orenburg Regiments...	Nijni Novgorod	......	......	...	3rd

The same data as previously assumed for the Caucasus troops are here used as a basis of calculation. The troops would be brought down the Volga to Astrakhan in barges towed by steamers, the lengths of voyage being as follows:—

Nijni Novgorod to Astrakhan	...	...	180 hours;
Saratov to "	...	...	60 "
Samara to "	...	...	88 "

and they would, therefore, arrive there—

157th Regiment on the	...	...	14th day.
158th " "	...	...	15th "
159th " (2 battalions) on the	...	...	15th "
40th Artillery Brigade on the	...	...	15th "
2 Orenburg Cossack Regiments	...	...	10th "

From Astrakhan to Kinderli Bay would take less than 48 hours.

Having landed at Kinderli Bay, it would be marched by the route across the Ust Urt taken by Lamakin's column in 1873. The force consists of ten battalions of infantry, three regiments of cavalry, six batteries of artillery, and it would probably be divided into three columns, the first consisting of four battalions infantry, one regiment cavalry, two battalions artillery (required for Charjui), the second of three battalions infantry, two batteries artillery, one regiment of cavalry, and the third of three battalions infantry, two batteries artillery, one regiment of cavalry.

According to the calculations made on a preceding page, this force would require transport as follows:—

10 battalions	infantry	at 550 =	5,500
10 squadrons	cavalry	at 90 =	900
6 batteries	artillery	at 170 =	1,020
	Total	...	7,420

add 10 per cent. spare, and about 8,200 camels would be required.

This would only provide 30 days' rations for men, whereas Lamakin took 45 days'; but as supplies would probably be sent out from Khiva to meet them, I suppose 30 days' sufficient to carry with them. This transport could without doubt be supplied by Khiva and the neighbouring Turkomans, and could be ready at Kinderli Bay in 30 days after the order was given or before they were wanted.

Allowing one day for transhipment at Astrakhan and two for the voyage to Kinderli Bay, the force would disembark complete at Kinderli Bay by the 18th day. Then allowing two days' halt here to get everything shipshape, the first echelon could start on the 20th day. Lamakin in 1873 reached Kungrad, 150 miles from Khiva, in 28 days. This was with no sort of extra assistance and going over a road that was then unknown. Therefore knowing what Russian troops are capable of, and taking into consideration that this force would be helped on its way with camels and water sent out from Khiva, I think it is only fair to suppose that on the 48th day or thereabouts after leaving Astrakhan it would reach Kungrad, and ten days more would take it to Petro-Alexandrovsk. Here I suppose them to require a week to recruit after their trying march; therefore on the 8th day after arriving at Petro-Alexandrovsk they would march by the bank of the Oxus to Charjui. The distance is about 250 miles, and this they would accomplish in 20 days at the latest. Therefore on the 85th day after receiving orders they would be in position at Charjui; but as this detachment might be sent on ahead, irrespective of the Atak column, it is evident it could arrive at Charjui on the same day as the Atak column arrived at Sarakhs.

Having reached Charjui, it would depend on the disposition and intentions of the Russian Commander-in-Chief on the Atak line what became of them afterwards. They might be directed to remain at Charjui so as to threaten the Merv Tekkes; or if these tribes had been reduced to a proper spirit of subserviency, they might advance and take possession of a position in the Merv oasis for the purpose of protecting the left flank of the Atak army. But whatever was its ultimate duty, it is not necessary to follow the fortunes of this column further, as it would not be directly employed in the operations I am considering.

By the new road, which was discovered and tried by Vaniushin, the above operation would be carried out as follows.

From Astrakhan the troops would cross the Caspian to the Yaman Airakti Creek of the Mertvi Kultak Bay. This creek is sheltered on three sides by hills, within 70 fathoms of the beach; the depth of water is 15 to 18 feet; and a pier of 630 feet would suit all vessels. Sailing vessels freely navigate Mertvi Kultak Bay, and Russian steamers occasionally, and the entrance is quite practicable. From Yaman Airakti to Kungrad the distance is 298 miles. Commencing from the latter, the direction of the road is west-south-west, and at 12 miles it ascends the Chink at a point called Adchul. It then follows the same direction for 25 miles to the junction of a road leading to Kohna Urganj; it then turns north-west and continues in that direction to the Caspian. The surface of the ground is of a sandstone formation. In the spring and autumn, after the accumulation of the waters, the road across the Dibugir is sometimes flooded; but the flooded parts can be avoided.

As far as the Amandjul well, which occurs midway, the road ascends a series of terraces, and from Turlugal well to the Caspian it descends in the same way; but the ascents and descents are easy, and present no difficulties whatever. The Adchul ascent is very easy, as is also the descent to the Caspian through a defile in the Djagylgan hills. A large quantity of saxaul, covering areas of 200 square versts, grows in the vicinity of the Sumbe and of the Issen Kazak wells, which divide the road into three equal lengths of about 150 versts each. Saxaul and prickly shrubs are found in other parts along the road, and the reeds on the shores of the Caspian are equally fit for fuel. Fodder is procurable all the way, the grass (djuzam) which grows between Amandjul well and the Caspian being particularly good. From Atabai and Yassabai wells (112 versts = 74¾ miles from Kungrad) other wells are of frequent occurrence along this road, about 10 to 15 versts (7 to 10 miles) apart. Sometimes there are groups of four or five wells on one spot. They are all faced with stone and some have stone troughs, which would indicate a traffic along this line at some past period. In most of the wells the water is perfectly good, but in some it is brackish, containing sulphuric hydrogen gas; yet horses and camels drink it freely. Three hundred camels may be watered at any of the wells. Generally speaking, this road is perfectly suited for wheel traffic, and the only one drawback to it is the waterless track of 94 versts (62¾ miles) between the Adchul ascent and the Atabai well. However, even this portion of the road can be avoided by taking the Chibin ascent of the Chink, a little farther north, and making for the Irbasan well, and proceeding thence due west to Amandjul. This way the waterless tract is reduced to 50 versts (33 miles); but the road in this direction would require some small improvement. By this route I should imagine this column would reach Kohnah Urganj in 25 days from leaving Yaman Airakti. From this to Petro-Alexandrovsk is about 100 miles, or say 8 days' march; so that on the 33rd day they could reach the latter place, allowing a halt of 7 days, as on the above route they would march for Petro-Alexandrovsk on the 40th, and reach Charjui in 60 days after leaving the Caspian, or in 80 days after the order was given.

I now turn to the Turkistan Army, and will consider what part it would take in the above operations.

The strength of the Turkistan Army, according to our latest accounts, is said to be as follows :—

26,213 infantry, 7,618 cavalry, 76 guns ;

from this we must deduct the present garrison of Petro-Alexandrovsk, *viz.*,—

2,106 infantry, 994 cavalry, thus leaving
24,107 „ 6,624 „ 76 guns ;

and I think it may be allowed that it will be necessary to leave at least that strength as garrison for Turkistan. I am aware this seems but a small garrison for such an extent of country ; but when the Russians proposed to advance on Afghanistan in 1878, they must have left even a smaller force than this.

The part which under present conditions the Russian troops in Turkistan are likely to be called on to play in an invasion or threatening of India would, no doubt, be a comparatively subordinate one ; but still it might be one that should not fail to cause the English great anxiety and uncertainty. The forces sent from Turkistan would probably be divided into three columns—*1st*, assembling at Jam would operate by the line Shahr-i-Sabz, Hazar, Shirabad, Khilif, and Balkh on Kabul ; *2nd*, assembling at Marghilan would operate by Karategin, Kolab, Faizabad, to Chitral, whence it would threaten the lines Kunar-Jalalabad-Peshawar or Dir-Swat-Peshawar ; *3rd*, assembling at Marghilan would operate by Alai, the Pamir, and Kanjut and threaten or open communications with Kashmir.

These three columns would of course be properly organized and of sufficient strength, and I think the following numbers would be found quite sufficient :—

		Infantry		Cavalry		Guns	
1st (Jam) column—							
Advance force for Kabul		10,000	infantry,	3,000	cavalry,	40	guns.
Reserve „ „		10,000	„	...		40	„
Communications, *viz.*,—							
At Chuskhaguzar	...	1,000	„	500	„	8	„
At Balkh	...	3,000	„	1,000	„	16	„
At Chehl Burj	...	1,500	„	...	„	8	„
At Gardan Diwar	...	3,000	„	500	„	16	„
Total	...	28,500	„	5,000	„	128	„
2nd (Marghilan) column—							
Advance force	...	6,000	„	1,500	„	24	„
Communications—							
At Alai	...	1,000	„	500	„	8	„
At Kolab	...	2,000	„	750	„	16	„
Total	...	9,000	„	2,750	„	48	„
3rd (Pamir) column—							
Advance force	...	3,000	„	600	„	16	„
Communications	...	...	„	...	„	...	„
GRAND TOTAL	...	40,500	„	8,350	„	192	„

But it will be seen that, after providing the necessary garrison for Turkistan, practically no troops could be spared for the field army; therefore the whole force required must be a reinforcement from Russia.

The arrangements which would appear to be necessary to reinforce the Turkistan army to the above extent therefore would seem to be as follows :—

The troops most likely to be selected would be—

2nd Division	from	Kazan ...	16	battalions,	48	guns.
3rd „	„	Nijni Novgorod	16	„	48	„
1st Brigade, 35th Division	„	Yaroslavl ...	8	„	...	
35th Field Artillery Brigade	„	Rostov ...	...	„	48	„
		Total ...	40	„	144	field guns.

13th Cavalry Division, Moscow.				
37th, 38th, and 39th Dragoons	12	squadrons.		
20th and 22nd Horse Artillery Batteries ...	...		12	field guns.
4th Ural Cossacks (2nd category), Uralsk ...	6	„	...	
7th, 8th, 9th, 10th, 11th, and 12th Orenburg Cossack Regiments (all of 2nd category) ...	36	„	...	
2nd, 6th, 7th, and 8th Orenburg Horse Artillery Batteries	...		24	„
4th and 5th Siberian Cossack Regiments (2nd category)	12	„	...	
Total ...	66	„	36	Horse Arty. guns.

34th and 35th Ammunition Parks.
18th Cavalry „ „
Grenadier and 1st Sapper Battalions.
1st and 2nd Pontoon Battalions.
1st Engineer Field Park.
1st and 2nd Field Telegraph Parks.

Of those troops, the 2nd Division, the 1st Brigade of the 35th Division, and the 2nd and 35th Artillery Brigades are all at stations on the Volga; and of the 3rd Division, two regiments are at Nijni Novgorod, the other two at Schuia and Vladimir, and the 3rd Artillery Brigade at Pavlovskaya, all of which are connected by rail with Nijni Novgorod. The reserves of all these troops are those of the districts in which they are stationed, and would probably be all collected by the 8th day. The three dragoon regiments are at Gjatsk, Kolomna, and Murom, and are in railway communication with Samara. The Ural, Orenburg, and Siberian Cossacks of the 2nd category would take at least 14 days to complete their mobilization, and they are all stationed in their homes in the districts of Orenburg, Ural, Omsk, and Semipalatinsk. The three ammunition parks are at Bronnitzi near Moscow and in railway communication with Samara, and the various engineer troops are quartered in and about St. Petersburg. As will be seen by the description of the routes, there is no necessity for hurrying those troops to the initial points of the roads to Tashkand, as over the latter troops can only pass in small echelons, and I therefore consider it unnecessary to enter minutely into details of mobilization, &c., but proceed at once to the description of the routes. From Moscow, two great routes lead to Tashkand,—the first by Orenburg, Turgui, Fort Perovski, and Chemkend ; the second by Nijni Novgorod, Kazan, Perm, Ekaterinburg, Omsk, Semipalatinsk, and Viernoe.

On the first route from Moscow there is railway communication by Riajsk, Penza, and Samara to Orenburg. This line is double as far as Riajsk, and thence single. The single line must therefore be taken as a basis of calculation.

The greatest distance between stations is 25 versts; and allowing for a speed of 20 versts ($13\frac{1}{3}$ miles) an hour only, to include the necessary halts on those long journeys, the trains could not run at less time-intervals than $2\frac{1}{2}$ hours. Leaving therefore, as is usual in Germany, 6 out of the 24 hours free at every station, eight trains each way per diem is about the maximum which could be got out of the line. From Orenburg to Tashkand the following route is given by Kostenko*:—

Orenburg to Orsk	265 versts	=	12 days' march.
Orsk by Turgai to Turkistan ...	1,174 „	=	34 „ „
Turkistan to Tashkand	266 „	=	12 „ „
Total ...	1,705 „	=	58 „ „

As it is usual for the yearly reinforcements to march three days and halt on the fourth, and as some of the stages are very long, it is advisable to add one-third to the above, giving a total of about 80 days' march. The country through which the first and last thirds of this road pass is fairly populous, and it is believed that there would be no difficulty in feeding echelons of about 2,000 men moving at three days' interval apart, if preliminary orders as to the collection of supplies were given. To assist in the conveyance of rations and forage, it would be advisable to send all the ammunition and stores of the artillery and engineer parks by camels from Orsk to Kazala, and thence up the Syr Darya to Chinaz by boat. The distance to Kazala is 747 versts, 39 marches, and the time taken by steamers up the Syr is at the outside 32 days. The total carrying power of the fleet of barges is 900 tons, which would amply suffice to carry all those stores and have a large margin over. The park wagons would then be available for the carriage of rations and forage, to be supplemented by camels. Five days' rations are carried in regimental trains. Forage would be the great difficulty, and recourse would probably have to be had to compressed food, horse biscuit, Turkoman cakes, &c.

The route from Moscow by Semipalatinsk begins with the railway to Nijni Novgorod, whence to Kazan is one day by steamer on the Volga; the latter town may be considered as the starting point of this route, the time required to reach Tashkand being—

Kazan to Perm by steamer and barges	2 days.
Transfer steamer to rail	1 day.
Rail to Ekaterinburg (20 hours)	1 „
March to Tiumen (220 miles)	17 days.
Transfer to steamer and barges	1 day.
Tiumen to Semipalatinsk by Omsk by steamers towing barges (287 hours)	12 days.
March to Tashkand (1,803 versts)	93 „
Total ...	127 days.

Although this route† is so much longer than the other, it is less trying for foot-soldiers, as the march across the Turgai steppe is thus avoided, and it

* Appendix N. | † Appendices P. and Q.

is valuable as affording a second route to Tashkand. The troops would march by echelons at three days' distance apart of the same strength as above, camels being provided between Semipalatinsk and Tashkand for the conveyance of rations. The same steamers can run from Kazan to Perm and from Tiumen to Semipalatinsk; but it must be noted that steamers of the size necessary to tow barges can only navigate the Tobol from spring to August.

By the first route there would advance—

13th Cavalry Division and 4th Ural Cossacks ...	in 4 echelons.
6th Orenburg Cossack Regiment 4th „ „ Battery ...	„ 6 „
2 Sapper battalions and parks ...	„ 1 „
1st Brigade, 35th Division 4 Batteries, 35th Artillery Brigade ...	„ 4 „

The ammunition parks would march to Orsk with an echelon of the 13th Cavalry Division, and there be broken up among the succeeding ones.

By the second routs there would advance—

2nd Division in 8 echelons.

3rd „ in 8 „ with 2 batteries 35th Artillery Brigade.

4th and 5th Siberian Cossack Regiments.

On the 1st route, the 37th Dragoons could leave Gjutsk on the 4th day, reaching Orenburg on the 7th, and marching on the 8th, followed at three days' interval by the rest of the troops using this road, who would arrive at Tashkand as follows:—

	Leave Orenburg.	Arrive Tashkand.
37th Dragoons ... 2nd Orenburg Cossack, H. A. Battery ...	8th	88th
38th Dragoons ... 20th H. A. Battery, 18th Cavalry Park ...	11th	91st
39th Dragoons ... 34th and 35th Ammunition cols. ...	17th	97th
4th Ural Cossacks ... ... 22nd H. A. Battery	17th	97th
Grenadier and 1st Sapper Battalions ... Sapper Parks	20th	100th
2 battalions, 137th Regiment ... ... 1 battery, 35th F. A. Brigade	23rd	103rd
2 battalions, 138th Regiment ... ... 1 battery, 35th F. A. Brigade	26th	106th
2 battalions, 139th Regiment ... ... 1 battery, 35th F. A. Brigade	29th	109th
2 battations, 140th Regiment ... ... 1 battery, 35th F. A. Brigade	32nd	112th
7th Orenburg Cossacks	35th	115th
8th „ „	35th	115th
9th „ „ ... ... 6th „ H. A. Battery	41st	121st
10th „ Cossacks	44th	124th
11th „ „ ... ... 7th „ H. A. Battery	47th	127th
12th „ Cossacks ... ... 8th „ H. A. Battery	50th	130th

Of the troops moving by the second route, the first would be the 5th Regiment, whose station and reserve district is Simbrik. It could move on the 8th day, and the troops by this route would arrive as follows :—

	Leave Kazan.	Arrive Tashkand.
2 battalions, 5th Regiment (leave Simbrik)...	8th	135th
2 battalions, 5th „	11th	135th
2 battalions, 6th „ ... ... 1 battery, 2nd F. A. Brigade	14th	136th
2 battalions, 6th Regiment ... ... 1 battery, 2nd F. A. Brigade	17th	139th
2 battalions, 7th Regiment ... ... 1 battery, 2nd F. A. Brigade	20th	142nd
2 battalions, 7th Regiment ... ... 1 battery, 2nd F. A. Brigade	23rd	145th
2 battalions, 8th Regiment ... ... 1 battery, 2nd F. A. Brigade	26th	148th
2 battalions, 8th Regiment ... ... 1 battery, 2nd F. A. Brigade	29th	151st
2 battalions, 9th Regiment ... ... 1 battery, 3rd F. A. Brigade	32nd	154th
2 battalions, 9th Regiment ... ... 1 battery, 3rd F. A. Brigade	35th	157th
2 battalions, 10th Regiment ... ... 1 battery, 3rd F. A. Brigade	38th	160th
2 battalions, 10th Regiment ... ... 1 battery, 3rd F. A. Brigade	41st	166th
2 battalions, 11th Regiment ... ... 1 battery, 3rd F. A. Brigade	44th	166th
2 battalions, 11th Regiment ... ... 1 battery, 5th F. A. Brigade	47th	169th
2 battalions, 12th Regiment ... ... 1 battery, 35th F. A. Brigade	50th	172nd
2 battalions, 12th Regiment ... ... 1 battery, 35th F. A. Brigade	53rd	175th

The 4th and 5th Siberian Cossacks could probably leave Semipalatinsk on the 20th day, arriving at Tashkand on the 110th day.

Some troops of those moving by this route could be sent by the Orenburg route, if required ; but extra fatigue would be entailed on them.

There can be no doubt but that to the Turkistan troops, who have borne the heat and burden of the day in Central Asia, would be delegated the honor of leading the way to India. By this means also the first line, who would have most difficulties to overcome, could be composed of troops thoroughly seasoned and accustomed to the climate. The following are the various distances in Turkistan :—

	Miles.		Stages.		Days.
Tashkand to Jam	193	=	12	=	15
Samarkand to Jam	$46\frac{1}{2}$	=	3	=	3
Tashkand to Marghilan	$181\frac{1}{3}$	=	12	=	15
Khokand to Marghilan	$56\frac{1}{4}$	=	3	=	3
Kata Kurgan to Jam	40	=	3	=	3
Lepsinsk to Vierni	$347\frac{5}{8}$	=	21	=	25
Jarkand to Vierni	$209\frac{7}{8}$	=	12	=	15
Vierni to Tashkand	$537\frac{5}{8}$	=	38	=	45
Ush to Marghilan	$59\frac{1}{8}$	=	4	=	4
Andijan to Marghilan	$47\frac{1}{3}$	=	3	=	3
Namangham to Marghilan	45	=	4	=	4
Khodjent to Marghilan	$139\frac{1}{3}$	=	9	=	10

The following would be a probable distribution of the troops and the dates of their arrival in position at the points of concentration, seven days being in the case of the infantry and artillery, and three in that of the cavalry, allowed for mobilization :—

1st column to assemble at Jam—

12 battalions	3rd, 6th, 9th, 11th, and 19th Turkistan Line Battalions	from	Samarkand ;	arrive	10th	day.
	8th Turkistan Line Battalion	... "	Kata Kurgan	"	10th	"
	1st " "	... "	Vierni	"	67th	"
	1st, 2nd, 3rd, and 4th Turkistan Rifle Battalions 18th Turkistan Line Battalions	... "	Tashkand	"	22nd	"
30 guns	2 light and 1 mountain batteries, Turkistan Artillery. 5th Orenburg Cossack, H. A. Battery	... "	Tashkand	"	22nd 22nd	" "
1 Sapper Company	1 Company Turkistan Sappers	... "	Tashkand	"	22nd	"
18 squadrons	2nd Ural Cossack Regiment	... "	Samarkand	"	6th	"
	1st Siberian Cossack Regiment	... "	Jarkand	"	78th	"
	2nd Siberian Cossack Regiment	... "	Lepsinsk	"	88th	"

2nd column to assemble at Marghilan—

7 battalions	2nd Turkistan Line Battalion ...	... from	Khokand ;	arrive	10th	day.
	4th " " " ...	... "	Ush	"	11th	"
	7th " " " ...	... "	Namanghan	"	11th	"
	10th, 12th, 17th Turkistan Line Battalions	... "	Tashkand	"	22nd	"
	16th Turkistan Line Battalion ...	... "	Andijan	"	10th	"
24 guns	1 light, 1 mountain and 1 heavy battery, Turkistan Artillery ...	... "	Tashkand	"	22nd	"
12 squadrons	5th Orenburg Cossack Regiment ...	... "	Khodjent	"	13th	"
	3rd Orenburg " " ...	... "	Marghilan ;	ready	3rd	"
1 Sapper Company	1 Sapper Company, Turkistan, ½ battalion	... "	Tashkand ;	arrive	22nd	"

3rd column to assemble at Marghilan—

3 battalions	14th, 15th, and 20th Turkistan Line Battalions	...	at Marghilan ; ready 7th day.
14 guns	Mountain, H. A. Battery 1st Orenburg Cossack, H. A. Battery		
4 squadrons	1st Semirietchie Cossack Regiment		from Jarkand ; arrive 78th "

From the above it will be seen that, with the exception of 1 battalion and 16 squadrons, the whole force could be in position on the 22nd day after leaving their stations in Russian Turkistan.* But† before the Khiva expedition in 1873, the 4th Rifle Battalion traversed the 670 miles between Orenburg and Kazalinsk in less than four weeks, the men being carried in sledges ; and therefore there is no reason why the battalion from Viernoi, travelling by cart on a good road, should not arrive at Jam in 30 days. In the same manner, the cavalry regiments from Jarkand might make double marches, arriving at Jam Marghilan in about 40 days, while the regiment from Lepsinsk would arrive on the 45th day. Leaving the latter regiment to follow the main column to Kilif, to which it proceeds by easy marches and where it could doubtless overtake the column, there can be little doubt that the 1st and 3rd columns would be ready to start by the 40th day, the 2nd on the 24th day. Besides all movements north of the Oxus would be made in countries over which Russian influence is supreme, and with which we have no concern. But let us assume 40 days as necessary for all.

---

* The concentration of troops in Turkistan would of course be carried out before the commencement of the movement of the Atak column, and it could be timed to fit in with that movement. It is certain the English would have no certain news of this movement ; and even if they had, it could easily be explained sufficiently to satisfy them.

† Rumours of large assemblages of Russian troops have already reached us from several independent sources, so that it may be a fact that this preliminary concentration *has already been carried out*.

As I have shown above, the reinforcements from Russia, always supposing that orders to all the troops considered in this paper were issued simultaneously by telegraph, begin to arrive on the 88th day at Tashkand, the first infantry battalions arriving on the 105th day. These troops would constitute the reserves of the 1st and 2nd columns and their *étappen* troops, and also the garrisons of the country. But pending their arrival, there would be in the Turkistan military district (besides the troops at Petro-Alexandrovsk)—

6th Orenburg Cossacks at Tashkand.
4 batteries, West Siberian Artillery at Viernoi } Those could move on Tash-
6th Orenburg H. A. Battery at Troitsk } kand, &c.
8th Turkistan Reserve Battalions (as mobilized in 1878).
3rd W. Siberian Battalion.
2nd and 3rd category regiments of the 1st and 2nd Siberian Cossacks.
2nd and 3rd Semirietchie Cossacks (of 2nd and 3rd categories, who could be mobilized within a month).

Besides which some troops could probably be required from Semipalatinsk to garrison Lespinsk and Jarkand on the Kuldja frontier. Bearing in mind that on the 70th day the leading troops from Russia would reach the town of Turkistan, and that on the 32nd day the leading troops on the other road would reach Semipalatinsk and Viernoi on the 77th, I think it may be assumed that the above force would be sufficient to hold the principal places in Turkistan.

Thus the 1st or Jam column could be at Kilif on the 60th day, or just at the time the force from Sarakhs would be starting for its advance on Herat, and Kilif would be on the frontier of Afghanistan.

The 1st (Jam) column would, according to the calculations made for the other columns, require about 23,000 camels, the 2nd (Marghilan) 9,000, and the 3rd (Marghilan) 2,000; and there can be no doubt that those numbers could easily be collected in time. The Jam column would operate by Shahr-i-Sabz, Huzar, Shirabad, Kilif, and Balkh on Kabul. The following is the route* it would in all probability adopt :—

* Full details of this route, as also of a route from Samarkand and to Kabul, will be found in Appendices I and J.

Route from Jam to Kabul viâ Chihal Burj.

Days.	Halting places.	Miles. Intermediate.	Miles. Total.	Remarks.
1	Kara Kiya	13	13	The road as far as Balkh, according to Mayeff, Minayeff, Kostenko, and others, appears to present obstacles to wheeled transport here and there, especially on the seven marches from Chashma-i-Hafiz-gan to Gaz Keshlak, the worst bit being from Lailakam to Shirabad; but it may be presumed that no natural obstacles exist which would not succumb to military engineering in a very short space of time. The authorities are not very precise in their descriptions, occasionally stating specifically that the road is fit for wheeled traffic, but more frequently merely mentioning it as good or bad for travelling in general. As to the state of the road for the last 26 marches, we know for certain that it has several times been traversed by Afghan wheeled artillery during the last ten years under Muhammad Sharif Khan and the ex-Amir Yakub Khan. The mountain roads on this section are said to run chiefly through clay soil, and to require nothing but spade and pick labour (no blasting) to improve them. Water is everywhere abundant, and grain and forage are generally plentiful.
2	Kok Tash Wells	13	26	
3	Chirakchi	12	38	
4	Kara Bagh	16	54	
5	Huzar	23	77	
6	Halt	...	...	
7	Kush Sush	11	88	
8	Tanga	13	101	
9	Chashma-i-Hafiz Jan	15	116	
10	Tash Kalama	7	123	
11	Shorab	10	133	
12	Sar-i-Ab	17	150	
13	Igerchi	10	160	
14	Halt	...	...	
15	Lailakan	8	168	
16	Shirabad	11	179	
17	Gaz Kishlak	17	196	
18	Kempir Balak	12	208	
19	Kempir Dagan	10	218	
20	Kalif	13	231	
21 22	Passage of Oxus	...	...	
23	Sardaba	18	249	
24	Khan-i-Naobat	12	261	
25	Chárbagh	11	272	
26	Paimast	5	280	
27	Balkh	10	290	
28	Halt	...	...	
29	Halt	...	...	
30	Mazar-i-Sharif	12	302	
31	Bakaolang	16	318	
32	Kishindeh Pain	15	333	
33	Kishindeh Bala	8	341	
34	Darai-i-Yusuf	12	353	
35	Garmab	12	365	
36	Walishan	8	373	
37	Halt	...	...	
38	Chashma-i-Duzdan	9	382	
39	Zardgia	11	393	
40	Band-i-Char-Asman	12	405	
41	Camp	...	...	
42	Chihal Burj (or Shahar-i-Kolona) ...	21	426	
43	Yak Aolang	11	437	
44	Camp	...	...	
45	Tagas-i-Bark	24	461	
46	Halt	...	...	
47	Siah Darra	11	472	
48	Daraz Kol	11	483	
49	Kotal-i-Mushak	12	495	
50	Badasia	10	505	
51	Camp	...	...	
52	Farogh Olem	18	523	
53	Camp	...	...	
54	Gurdan Diwar	18	541	
55	Halt	...	...	
56	Yunt	7	548	
57	Unai Pass	5	553	
58	Sar-i-Chashma	9	562	
59	Gabrez	10	572	
60	Rustam Khel	10	582	
61	Argandeh	8	590	
62	Kabul	14	604	

From the above it is clear that it would appear quite a feasible operation for the Russians to put such a force as I have given above, *viz.*, 10,000 infantry,

3,000 cavalry, and 32 guns into Kabul in any time from 70 to 103 days after leaving Jam. The intervening country is, I submit, quite practicable, and the force is quite sufficient to take Kabul* and hold it against all comers. I doubt if such a force would have to fight at all on its way; but if so, one battle in the plains of Balkh would certainly clear the way for them. Once in Kabul there could be little difficulty in raising 20,000 splendid and well-armed fighting men, and it is very doubtful if the English would have the power to turn them out when once established. But of course it must not be supposed that the Russians would be foolhardy enough to attempt to seize Kabul and remain there unless they were properly supported from the rear. This could be done either by reinforcing them from the direction of the Caspian; from Herat by way of Obeh, Daolatyar, Chehl Burj, and Gardan Diwar; from Sarakhs by way Panjdeh, Maimana, Sar-i-pul, and thence by the same route as from Balkh. But as I suppose the troops at Herat will have enough to do, and there would be every advantage in their keeping to as many lines of operations as they could, I therefore suppose that all reinforcements for Kabul would be sent by the same line by which the force advanced and that line is held in strength.†

The second column would operate by Karategin, Kolab, Faizabad to Chitral, and thence threaten either the route Kunar-Jalalabad-Peshawar or Dir-Swat-Peshawar.

It would be assembled with the third column at Marghilan and proceed by the following route‡:—

From Marghilan to Chitral.

Days.			
1.		...	By Ming Japa and Airavan on the postal road practicable for carts.
2.		...	
3.		...	
4. Ush,	60 miles	...	
5. „ Halt.			
6. Langar,	20 „	...	By cart road.
7.			
8. Gulcha,	30 „	...	Ditto.
9. Kizil Kurghan,	12 „	...	
10. Halt.			
11. Yangi Arik,	5⅓ „		All thesches bye mar a cartroad.
12. Sufi Kurghan,	8⅔ „		
13. Kizil Jar,	14⅔ „		
14. Koijol Diwan Pass,	10⅔ „		
15. Kulin Ort Pass,	5⅓ „		
16. Alai Valley,	4 „		
17. Halt.			
18.			
19.	55 „	...	Cart road ceases, but road is good for pack-animals; some difficult places.
20.			
21. Darawat Kurghan,			
22. Darawat Kurghan,		...	Halt.
23.			
24. Kata Karamukh,	19 „		
25.			
26.			

* Provided the way had been prepared beforehand, as it undoubtedly should have been.

† At Khushkaguzar ... 1,000 infantry, 500 cavalry, 8 guns.
„ Balkh ... 3,000 „ 1,000 „ 16 „
„ Chehl Burj ... 1,500 „
„ Gardan Diwar ... 3,000 „ 500 „ 16 „

‡ Appendices K, L, M.

Days.				
27.				
28.	Zinkhab,	60	miles.	
29.	Halt.			
30.				
31.				
32.	Gharam,	40	,,	
33.	Kamchurik,	10⅔	,,	
34.	Chehl Dara,	9⅓	,,	
35.	Halt.			
36.	Tabidara,	16	,,	
37.	Saghri Dasht,	10⅔	,,	
38.	Talbur,	17	,,	
39.	Saripul,	16	,,	
40.	Khowalim,	7½	,,	
41.	Mominabad,	16	,,	
42.	Kolab,	13½	,,	
43. } 44. }	Halt.			
45.	Sar-Chashma.			
46.	Samti Bala ...		...	Cross Oxus.
47.	Camp.			
48.	Chaiab,	46	miles.	
49.	Rustak,	17	,,	
50.	Ilkashan,	12	,,	
51.	Sarai Dara,	18	,,	
52.	Faizabad,	16½	,,	
53. } 54. }	Halt.			
55.				
56.	Chapchi,	23	,,	
57.				
58.				
59.	Tirgaran,	35	,,	
60. } 61. }	Halt.			
62.				
63.	Zebak,	30	,,	
64.	Halt.			
72.	Chitral ...		...	From Zebah there are several roads to Chitral, *viz.*, by the Dura, Nukshan, Agram, and Khartega Pass. The distance from the S, *i.e.*, from Chitral to the head of the Dura pass (which is the easiest, and is 14,800 feet in elevation), is 42 miles, or four marches. The distance from the head of the Dura Pass to Zebah is much less; but I have allowed 8 days for the whole journey.
	Total about	740	miles.	

The total distance is about 740 miles, and I have allowed for 12 halts, supposing this column would arrive on the 72nd day at Chitral; but I think it would be advisable to allow more time and bring the force to Chitral in 90 days after leaving Samti Bala.

It cannot be denied that it would be very unlikely that the English would hear anything of this move, until the column was well past Faizabad, and within a little over 100 miles of Chitral.

It is pretty certain the column would meet with no opposition until they crossed the Oxus; and as there is nothing in Badakhshan to withstand half its numbers, the opposition in that district could not be of a very serious nature.

I think it probable that the Kafirs would contest the passage of the Hindu Kush; but when we consider how badly armed they are, it would not be fair to suppose they could do so successfully without proper leading or organization.

Were the orders for the Turkistan troops issued at the same time as those for the Caucasus troops, the 2nd column would reach Samti Bala on the Oxus on the 23rd + 46th = 69th day; but by giving orders sooner, it could, as in the case of the Kabul column, arrive on the Oxus at about the time the Atak column was ready to leave Sarakhs for Herat, *viz.*, the 60th day.

The 3rd column being a very weak one, composed of 3,000 infantry, 600 cavalry, and two light batteries of artillery, would march by the same route as the 2nd column for the first 11 or 12 marches; it would then turn south by the Karakul Lake and the Khargosh Pamir, Sares Pamir, Alechur Pamir, and threaten the Baroghil pass and the road which Mr. Dalgleish states leads through Kanjut to Gilgit and Skardoh.*

This column would not be intended to do more than create alarm all along the northern frontier of Kashmir, and the commander would be instructed, if possible, to open communication with the Kashmir authorities in Gilgit and Skardoh. As soon as its object had been obtained, and the weather became unfavourable, it would be withdrawn, probably crossing the Little Pamir and wintering at Ishkashm. It would form a support to the 2nd column at Chitral. The time of its advance might or might not correspond with that of the other columns. It could not leave Marghilan before the end of May, and could not stay on the inhospitable Pamirs longer than the end of August.

I am now in a position to show at a glance what would be the position of the Russian columns whose operations have been sketched in the foregoing pages on any given date. I have said that until the arrival of the Russian General on command of the Atak force at Sarakhs, every effort would be made to throw dust in our eyes, and induce the English to take no steps to counteract these very formidable combinations. On that day, *viz.*, the 60th day after a Russian force has been ordered to start on the ostensible errand of coercing the Merv Tekkes, there can be little doubt that the Russian columns would be in the following positions :—

1° Atak column at Sarakhs.
2° Reinforcements for ditto ready to embark at Baku, Petrovski, and Darband.
3° Jam column at Kilif.
4° Marghilan column at Samti Bala.
5° Pamir column at Terek Diwan Pass.

And the following table will show where they would probably be on each succeeding day :—

Table showing where each body of troops would be on any named day.

Troops.	61st.	62nd.	63rd.	64th.	65th.	66th.	67th.
Atak column ...	Sarakhs ...	Din Kala...	Naorozabad	Camp ...	Adam Yolan sh	Agar Chama.	Halt.
1st division of reinforcement.	Baku ...	Crossing	Caspian†	Khurd Mohala.	Astrabad ...	Camp ...	Finderisk.
	Petrovski						
2nd division of reinforcement.	Darband...			Khurd Mohala.	Astrabad ...	" ...	Galuzah.
Jam column ...	Kilif ...	Crossing	of Oxus ...	Surdoba ...	Khan-i-Nsbat	Charbagh ..	Palmast.
Marghilan column...	Samti Bala	Chaiab ...	Chaiab ...	Rustak ...	Il Kashan ...	Sarai Dara	Faizabad.

* Appendix L.

† This presupposes that extensive arrangements had been made for landing troops at Bandar Gaz in the preceding 53 days.

The divisions would probably march in echelons. The dates show where the leading echelon each would be, and the whole shows the *minimum* time possible.

Troops.	68th.	69th.	70th.	71st.	72nd.	73rd.	74th.
Atak column ...	Camp ...	Kizil Buluk	Kombov ...	Halt ...	Camp ...	Kusan ...	Ghorian.
1st division of reinforcement.	Pisarak ...	Camp ...	Halt ...	Camp ...	Obah Chakir	Camp ...	Nowsherwan.
2nd division of reinforcement.	Rudkan ...	Halt ...	Asp-o-Neza	Shulikoh ...	Tash Rubut	Shahrud ...	Halt.
Jam column ...	Balkh ...	" ...	Halt ...	Mazar-i-Shahrif ...	Bakaolang ...	Kishindeh Pain.	Kishindeh Bala
Marghilan ...	Halt ...	" ...	Camp ...	Chapchi ...	Camp ...	Camp ...	Tirgaran.

Troops.	75th.	76th.	77th.	78th.	79th.	80th.	81st.
Atak column ...	Zindehjan	Ab-i-Jalil ..	Herat ...	...	...	...	...
1st division of reinforcement.	Camp ...	Karoguez...	Halt ...	Rabut-i-Ask	Camp ...	Showgan...	Camp.
2nd division of reinforcement.	Khairabad	Camp ...	Maiomai ...	Miandasht ...	Abbasabad ...	Mazinan ...	Halt.
Jam column ...	Dara-i-Yusuf.	Garmab ...	Walishan ..	Halt ...	Duzdan ...	Zardgia ...	Band-i-Char-Asman.
Marghilan column ...	Halt ...	Camp ...	Camp ...	Zebah ...	Halt ...	Camp ...	Camp.

Troops.	82nd.	83rd.	84th.	85th.	86th.	87th.	88th.
Atak column ...	...	...	...	...	...	...	...
1st division of reinforcement ...	Hajugan ...	Dowlatabad	Halt ...	Camp ...	Camp ...	Rabat-i-Guz	Pahnay.
2nd division of reinforcement ...	Nuhr ...	Camp ...	Sabzawar...	Halt ...	Bigwat ...	Budraskund	Naobulnakim.
Jam column ...	Camp ...	Chehl Burj	Yak Aolang	Camp ...	Tagao-i-Bark	Halt ...	Sia Dara.
Marghilan column	" ...	Camp ...	Camp ...	" ...	Camp ...	Chitral ...	...

Troops.	89th.	90th.	91st.	92nd.	93rd.	94th.	95th.
Atak column ...	...	...	...	...	...	...	...
1st division of reinforcement.	Halt ...	Madan ...	Hissar ...	Nishapur ...	Kadamgah ...	Camp ...	Sharifabad.
2nd division of reinforcement.	Sundadi ...	Camp ...	Turshiz ...	Halt ...	Camp ...	Zurmir ...	Turbat-Haidari.
Jam column ...	Duraz Kol	K.-i-Mushak	Badasia ...	Camp ...	Farogh Olm	Camp ...	Gardan Diwar.
Marghilan column	...	...	...	...	...	...	...

Troops.	96th.	97th.	98th.	99th.	100th.	101st.	102nd.
Atak column ...	...	...	...	...	...	...	...
1st division of re-inforcement.	Turukh ...	Sangbast...	Farimun ...	Halt ...	Camp ...	Burdu ...	Mahmud-abad.
2nd division of re-inforcement.	Camp ...	Camp ...	Himatabad	Shahr-i-Nao	Mushadi Reza	Karez ...	Halt.
Jam column ...	Halt ...	Yunt ...	Unai Pass	Sar-i-Chashma	Jalrez ...	Rustum Khel.	Argandeh.
Marghilan column	...	...	...	...	...	...	...

Troops.	103rd.	104th.	105th.	106th.	107th.	108th.	109th.
Atak column ...	...	...	...	...	...	...	...
1st division of re-inforcement.	Shaikh Jam	Halt ...	Camp ...	Karez ...	Kohsan ...	Halt ...	Camp.
2nd division of re-inforcement.	Kohsan ...	Camp ...	Ghorian .	Zindehjan ...	Ab-i-Jalil ...	Herat ...	...
Jam column ...	Kabul ...	...	...	...	...	...	...
Marghilan column	...	...	...	...	...	...	...

Troops.	110th.	111th.	112th.	113th.			
Atak column ...	...	...	...	...			
1st division of re-inforcement.	Ghorian ...	Zindehjan	Ab-i-Jalil	Herat ...			
2nd division of re-inforcement.	...	...	...	...			
Jam column ...	...	...	...	...			
Marghilan column	...	...	...	...			

If the Turkistan columns had not received their orders before the Caucasus troops, the situations on the respective days would be as follows :—

Troops.	61st.	62nd.	63rd.	64th.	65th.	66th.	67th.
Atak column ...	Sarakhs ...	Dinkala ...	Naurozabad	Camp ...	Adam Yolan	Agrachash-ma.	Halt.
1st division of re-inforcement.	Baku ...	Crossing	Caspian	Kurd Mohala	Astrabad ...	Camp ...	Finderisk.
	Petrovski						
2nd division of re-inforcement.	Darband			"	" ...	" ...	Gulugah.
Jam column ...	Halt ...	Lailakan ...	Shirabad ...	Guzkishlak...	Kepir Bolak	Kempir Degan.	Kalif.
Marghilan column	Camp ...	Gharum ...	Kamchurik	Chehl Dara...	Halt ...	Talidarah	Saghr-i-Dasht.

Troops.	68th.	69th.	70th.	71st.	72nd.	73rd.	74th.
Atak column ...	Camp ...	Kizil Bulak	Kombun ...	Halt ...	Camp ...	Kusam ...	Ghorian.
1st division of re-inforcement.	Pisarak ...	Camp ...	Halt ...	Camp ...	Obah Chakir	Camp ...	Nowsherwan.
2nd division of re-inforcement.	Badkan ...	Halt ...	Asp-o-Neza	Shahkoh ...	Tash Rabat...	Shahrud ...	Halt.
Jam column ...	Passage of	Oxus ...	Sardoba ...	Khan-i-Naobat	Charbagh ...	Palmast ...	Balkh.
Marghilan column	Talbur ...	Sar-i-Pul ...	Khawaling	Mominabad	Kolab ...	Halt ...	Halt.

Troops.	75th.	76th.	77th.	78th.	79th.	80th.	81st.
Atak column ...	Zindehjan	Ab-i-Talil	Herat ...	...	...	...	...
1st division of re-inforcement.	Camp ...	Karoguez	Halt ...	Rabat-i-Ask	Camp ...	Showgan ...	Camp.
2nd division of re-inforcement.	Khairabad	Camp ...	Maiomai ...	Miandasht ...	Abbasabad ...	Mazinan ...	Halt.
Jam column ...	Halt ...	Halt ...	Mazar-i-Sharif.	Bakaolang ...	Kishindeh Pain.	Kishindeh Bala.	Dara-i-Yusuf.
Marghilan column	Sarchshma	Samti Bala	Halt (cross Oxus).	Chalab ...	Rustak ...	Ilkashan ...	Sarai Dara.

Troops.	82nd.	83rd.	84th.	85th.	86th.	87th.	88th.
Atak column ...	...	...	...	...	...	...	...
1st division of re-inforcement.	Hajugan ...	Dowlatabad	Halt ...	Camp ...	Camp ...	Rabat-i-Gaz.	Pahnay.
2nd division of re-inforcement.	Mehr ...	Camp ...	Subzawar	Halt ...	Bigwat ...	Badraskand	Naobullia-kim.
Jam column ...	Garmub ...	Walishan...	Halt ...	Chashma-i-Duzdun.	Zardgia ...	Band-i-Char-Asman.	Camp.
Marghilan column	Faizabad ...	Halt ...	Ditto ...	Camp ...	Chapchi ...	Camp ...	Ditto.

Troops.	89th.	90th.	91st.	92nd.	93rd.	94th.	95th.
Atak column ...	...	...	...	...	...	...	...
1st division of re-inforcement.	Halt ...	Madan ...	Hissar ...	Nishapur ...	Kadamgah...	Camp ...	Sharifabad.
2nd division of re-inforcement.	Saadadi ...	Camp ...	Turshiz ...	Halt ...	Camp ...	Zurmir ...	Turbat Hai-dari.
Jam column ...	Chehl Burj	Yak Aolang	Camp ...	Tagao-i-Bark	Halt ...	Siah Dara	Duraz Kol.
Marghilan column	Tirgaran...	Halt ...	" ...	Camp ...	Zebak ...	Halt ...	Camp.

Troops.	96th.	97th.	98th.	99th.	100th.	101st.	102nd.
Atak column ...	...	...	...	...	...	...	...
1st division of re-inforcement.	Turukh ...	Sangbast...	Farimon...	Halt ...	Camp ...	Burdu ...	Mahmud-abad.
2nd division of re-inforcement.	Camp ...	Camp ...	Himatabad	Shahr-i-Nao	Mashadi Reza	Karez ...	Halt.
Jam column ...	Kotal-i-Mushik.	Badasia ...	Camp ...	Farogh Olm	Camp ...	Gardan Di-war.	,,
Marghilan column	Camp ...	Camp ...	,, ...	Camp ...	,, ...	Camp ...	Chitral.

Troops.	103rd.	104th.	105th.	106th.	107th.	108th.	109th.
Atak column ...	...	...	...	...	...	...	...
1st division of re-inforcement.	Shaikh Jam	Halt ...	Camp ...	Karez ...	Kohsan ...	Halt ...	Camp.
2nd division of re-inforcement.	Kohsan ...	Camp ...	Ghorian ...	Zindehjan ...	Ab-i-Jalil ...	Herat ...	...
Jam column ...	Yurt ...	Unai Pass	Sar-i-Cha-shma.	Jalrez ...	Ruskam Khel	Argandeh	Kabul.
Marghilan column	...	...	...	...	...	...	...

Troops.	110th.	111th.	112th.	113th.	114th.	115th.	116th.
Atak column ...	...	...	...	...			
1st division of re-inforcement.	Gohrian ...	Zindehjan	Ab-i-Jalil...	Herat.			
2nd division of re-inforcement.	...	...	...	...			
Jam column ...	...	...	...	...			
Marghilan column	...	...	...	...			

We are now able from the foregoing remarks to realize what Russia can do towards threatening India. That is to say, within two months of any given day (to-day or to-morrow, or a month ago) she can place in round numbers—

(1) 23,000 within 190 miles of Herat.
(2) 10,000 ,, 370 ,, Kabul.
(3) 6,000 ,, 270 ,, Chitral.
(4) 3,000 on the Kashmir frontier.

Without necessarily breaking off relations with the English, and if matters were cleverly managed, news of her throwing off the mask at Sarakhs, Kilif, Samti Bala, Terek Diwan could not reach the English Government for the number of days shown below, *viz.*,—

Movement No. 1	for	2	days.
„ „ 2	„	7	„
„ „ 3	„	9	„
„ „ 4	„	12	„

These forces would then be in the following positions :—

No. 1	within	170	miles of	Herat
„ 2	„	310	„	Kabul
„ 3	„	160	„	Chitral
„ 4	on the Kashmir frontier			

before their approach was known.

If the English Government was forewarned of and prepared for such moves on the part of Russia, no doubt she might do much to prevent these enterprises; but as the whole military history of England goes to show that she never is prepared, and it would be the particular aim of the Russian Government to take her at a moment when she is elsewhere engaged, or is otherwise off her guard,* it will perhaps be allowed that Russia would have a very fair chance of arriving at her objectives—Herat, Kabul, and Chitral—before the English could take any steps to prevent her; and looking to the very great distances which would still intervene between the English forces and the Russian objectives, and the seriousness of undertaking any operation with a view to driving brave and civilized forces from positions they would have had some time to prepare, it may perhaps also be granted that there would be some hesitation in the English Councils before decisive measures were even determined on and commenced.

In this interval of time, the Russian Commanders would have time to improve their defences and mature their future plans. Their plan would be, I submit, to hold on to Herat at all hazards, reinforcing it to any extent necessary from the Caspian; to hold on to Kabul, thence threatening India, long enough to draw the English into entangling themselves in a campaign in North Afghanistan in the winter; to play the same game with the Chitral column by threatening to advance on Peshawar through Dir, and to use the Pamir column to keep up a constant irritation on the Kashmir frontier; to embroil the English in every way with the Afghans, and so exhaust her that she would be glad to seek a *modus vivendi*; then to offer to evacuate Chitral and Kabul and withdraw the Pamir column, for acquiescence in a new Russian frontier drawn from the crest of the Terek Diwan Pass south by the watershed of the Pamir to the Hindu Kush, then by the crest of that range to the Koh-i-Baba, and then to include the whole of the country of the Hazaras and the province of Herat to the Farah Rud, and, if possible, to the Khash Rud.

This new frontier would be all that Russia need aim at in the first campaign, as it would give her all the necessary points from which she can advance with a great probability of success in the final attack on India.

There are no doubt many Englishmen who would raise their voices against any acquiescence in such demands, and propose rather a continuance

*As in Egypt, the Soudan, &c.

of the war: but among the English people there is a party whose cry, even now, is "perish India"; there would be very many who, averse to a long, expensive, and possibly unsuccessful war, would say "sufficient for the day is evil thereof," who would look on the loss of Herat as a *fait accompli*, and crying *aprés moi le déluge*, and would wish to acquiesce in the Russian demands; and if that Power remained firm, there is fair reason for supposing she would in the end be in the possession of the frontier described.

Then Russia could afford to wait; she could let the Central Asian question slumber for a number of years, and spend the interval in improving her communications. That is to say, she would continue the Atak Railway to the Farah Rud; she would finish a cart road to Gardan Diwar; and by making a railway from the Caspian to the Oxus and by improving the navigation of that river, put Balkh in easy communication with Russia. She would then bring the whole of Afghan Turkistan, Northern Khorasan, and the Hazarajat under her rule, taking care that it be a light and popular one, so that she could raise, when necessary, large forces from the Turkomans, Char Aimaks, and Hazaras, the Ozbaks of cis-Oxus, the Duranis of Kabul and Herat, and the Kohistanis of North Afghanistan. She would then also direct her attention to extending her influence over the whole of Afghanistan, and the ramifications of her intrigues into every city of India.

By following these plans she might rest assured that when the time came for further action, there would not be a "ghazi" from the Oxus to the Indus, not an Indian Prince from Lahore to Travancore, who would not be eagerly looking for the day when the real invasion of India would commence. And on that day she might be certain that, in addition to having the big battalions on her side, she would have the power of taking the initiative and all the prestige, "the ikbal."

A plan such as the above might be drawn out by anyone sufficiently interested and sufficiently acquainted with the facts of this great question. I have given my readers all data on which to work out the whole problem for themselves, and prove whether it is feasible or not.* I challenge anyone to disprove either my premises or conclusions. I hold that Russian troops can arrive at certain places in certain stated times, and I challenge anyone to prove they cannot. But remember, I ask for proof. I do not want vague statements about impassable rivers, impracticable deserts, stupendous mountains, want of food, bad water, enormous distances, heat, invincible sepoys, and enthusiastically loyal Indians. If anyone does not agree with me, let him show why and wherefore. If he can show me that no army ever has, or ever can, for some reason I know not of, accomplish one or more or the whole of the marches I have given, I will be glad to consider whether it is impracticable or whether that point cannot be turned in some way. If he can prove to me that no army can go to Herat from the Caspian in 77 days, I will, on being convinced, show how it can be done in 80 or 90 or 100; or if he can give good evidence to show it cannot be done at all, under any circumstances, by any army, then I will rejoice with him and draw a black mark across that line in my map and mark it impracticable. But if he only tells me the usual imbecilities that Russia is too good to covet anything English, and least of all India; that she is bankrupt and cannot feed her army; that she will soon break up into a dozen States; that an invasion of India is beyond the imagination of a 19th century commander, or the power of a 19th century

* It may indeed have already been drawn up by the Russians themselves.

army; or that it is too remote for us to begin to think about it even,—I shall still continue to raise my voice to point out what I believe to be a danger, a very formidable and near approaching danger.

I do not propose at this stage to go further in the consideration of the question of the invasion of India. In showing how Russia can place herself in a position to make that invasion possible, I think I have done enough at present. It is time I should take a look at home and see how far we are ready to meet moves I believe to be imminent, and how far we may prevent them altogether.*

* I would here acknowledge gratefully the able assistance I have received from Major the Hon'ble G. Napier and Lieutenant J. M. Grierson, R.A., especially the latter, in the preparation of this chapter.

CHAPTER II.

INTERNAL DEFENCE OF INDIA.

In the first Chapter of this paper I have shewn, I hope clearly and correctly, what the Russians can do. I leave the question of whether they will attempt to do it to those who are fonder of political speculations than I am. I have shewn that the Russians are now, or very soon can be, in a position to take and hold Herat, and to take up such commanding positions in the directions of Kabul and Chitral as will enable them at some future date, convenient to themselves, to still further threaten India, inasmuch as an invasion of India will—if they choose to sufficiently improve their communications meanwhile—then become a perfectly feasible operation of war.

I now turn to the question of what we should do. But before this can be answered satisfactorily, we must first see clearly what we *can* do, because undoubtedly the maintenance of a secure hold on India is our first duty, as well as the most difficult part of the whole problem I have set myself. If India was entirely peopled by a race thoroughly loyal to us, we could meet Russian advances with a very light heart. I know there are some who profess to believe this is the case; but there are others who think, on the contrary, that India is a "seething mass of disaffection." I do not go with either of these opinions. I believe there is much loyalty in India. I believe the majority are indifferent and passively loyal. But I believe there is an influential minority* who are thoroughly disloyal; who would take advantage of our hands being full in a Russian war to raise up rebellion to the utmost of their power. At all events, I don't suppose the most enthusiastic Indophilist would soberly recommend, in the event of a war with Russia, that India should be left to the care of the police and the babus; and therefore it is incumbent on us to review our position in India dispassionately and thoroughly before attempting to consider what our power for offence beyond our present frontier is. I will try in the following pages to lay this before my readers clearly and plainly, not taking credit for what we have not, and not viewing our situation from too gloomy a standpoint.

It is no use in a case of this sort to talk vaguely about our having a numerous, a highly disciplined, and well-equipped army, or to say we spared 60,000 men on the last Afghan war, and we could do so again. The subject must be approached in a calm and judicial spirit. It has but little analogy to an Afghan war; it is not the Power of Afghanistan we shall have to meet, but that of Russia; not the efforts of a few thousand incoherent and undisciplined men, but those of a scientific, well-disciplined army, backed by an incalculable number of irregular troops drawn from the whole of Asia.

The question which must be now answered before we can even consider how many men we can spare for military operations out of India is—"In the

---

* Probably nearly all the Mahomedans would be more or less disaffected.

event of a war with Russia beyond the North-West Frontier, how many men must we retain, and what dispositions must we make for the proper defence of India?"

In order to present a satisfactory answer to this question, I must put before my readers the requirements of each province in India; and I hope to do so in a manner which will enable him to see for himself whether I am right in the conclusion I shall draw. I shall show in this part of my paper (as I showed before in considering what Russia can do) the data on which I found my assumptions, and every reader will then be able to judge for himself.

Before, however, considering the requirements of each province, it is necessary that I should state shortly the general principles on which I base the following scheme for the defence of India. These are:—

(1) It is absolutely necessary to maintain a firm hold on all places of strategical importance, *i.e.*, on all places containing arsenals, depôts and factories of warlike stores, and on all places of first commercial and political importance.

(2) Our communications throughout India must be securely held, and all important junctions, bridges, and workshops must be adequately garrisoned.

(3) Places of refuge must be provided at stations which, though not of first importance, are still of a certain political value.

(4) Moveable columns must be provided at all the principal strategic centres throughout India, and arrangements must be well thought out and prepared beforehand for making the utmost, most prompt, and decided use of them.

(5) All this must be done at a minimum of expense, lest the cure should become worse than the disease.

(6) The garrisons of all the above places must be mainly, and often entirely, British.

BENGAL.

Taking the province of Bengal first, it is evident from the opinions of Sir Ashley Eden and Sir Steuart Bayley that there is very little cause to fear any serious rebellion in that province. "Notwithstanding certain frothy utter- " ances of the local press and local orators, there is said not to be any general " feeling of hostility of disloyalty to our Government amongst the bulk of the " population. The only sources of possible political disquiet in the province are " to be found among the Ferazis in Eastern Bengal and the Wahabis of Patna; " but these are said not to be in any way formidable, and there is no reason to " suppose that, if agrarian riots occurred, they would be beyond the power of " the provincial police to deal with."

But if there is not much fear of internal disturbances, it must not be forgotten that the Calcutta defences are far from being in a satisfactory condition; and, as long as this continues, it must be allowed that it is open to attack from the sea, especially in the event of a Russo-French alliance being formed against us. The defence of Calcutta and all our Indian ports is certainly more of a naval than a military question; but still it will not do for us to rely on naval assistance from England alone, and therefore all that we can do on land should be done.

In Bengal, therefore, the chief points we have to look to is the security of Calcutta and the repression of possible minor rebellions.

To attain the first object, the Hughli defences must at once be completed and armed, and a sufficient garrison provided for them and for Fort William. Lately something has been done towards the first object; but it has never yet been taken up in a proper spirit; and though years succeed each other, the Hughli defences still retain much of their appearance of ancient Roman fortifications. This must be rectified. I think we should be ashamed to play with this and other similar questions in the *dilettante* spirit we have hitherto displayed.

If the defences of the Hughli are put into proper repair, I think that with a garrison of one garrison battery of artillery and half a battalion of British infantry the port of Calcutta may be considered quite safe, and there will be less reason for maintaining a large garrison in Fort William; and this I would therefore entrust to 2 companies British infantry, 1½ batteries garrison artillery, and the Calcutta Volunteers. The volunteers would also be available to turn out in sufficient strength in aid of the police to put down disturbances in Calcutta or its vicinity, as, in addition to them, there is a large European population which could be, and should be, made available to man the defences of the fort at a pinch. The vacated barracks and buildings in Fort William would accommodate a large number of women and children, and many more could find refuge in case of necessity in the shipping. But in order that there might be no confusion when the time arrived, the volunteers of Calcutta should now be practised in taking up their position in the fort, so that all might become familiarised with the work.*

In Bengal there are no other places of first strategical or political importance; but the following places should be held as long as possible with the garrisons named:—

Soane bridge,—100 infantry (50 at each end), 2 machine guns.

Patna,—200 infantry, half battery garrison artillery. A small fort should be erected at this place to command the city.

Lakisarai,—100 infantry, 2 machine guns.

Jamalpur,—200 infantry, 2 machine guns.

Bardwan,—100 infantry, 2 machine guns.

Dacca,—200 infantry, 2 machine guns. A small fort should be erected at this place to overawe the city.

Places of refuge to be held by the available Europeans and trustworthy Natives should be provided at the following places: Motihari, Muzaffarpur, Darbhanga, Darjeeling, Rangpur, Mymensing, Faridpur, Chittagong, Jessore, Midnapur, Cuttack, Doranda, Bhagalpur, Monghyr, Arrah, and Gya. In order to maintain the railway communications in Bengal, I think that armoured trains should be provided, each consisting of one engine and tender, two 3rd class carriages (bullet proof), a truck with a light field-piece or machine gun on a circular platform, and a truck with spare rails and sleepers. As, however, these trains have not yet been introduced into India, it will be advisable at once to assemble a committee of one infantry and one artillery officer and a railway official to design one, and then to have a sufficient number made up for all India in the different workshops. These armoured trains should carry 50 infantry with water and rations for three days (and among these a proportion should be accustomed to platelaying), besides a truck or trucks for labourers. In Bengal armoured trains should be at Patna, Jamalpur, Bardwan, Howrah, Sealdah, Saraghat, and Muzaffarpur. Their duties would consist of running up and down the line, to keep it open, and to relay it at once where destroyed.

---

* It has been suggested to me that this would look bad; but I believe as a fact the natives never notice what the volunteers are doing.

I think it will be sufficient if one moveable column is provided in Bengal. It should consist of 2 companies British infantry, 1 battery field artillery, and 2 regiments Native infantry. Ordinarily it would be posted at Calcutta; but of course it would be moved to wherever its services were most required. The whole of Bengal should be made into one military command under a Brigadier-General with staff, and the province should be divided into the following military districts, each under a selected officer. This officer need not necessarily be a military man. There are many volunteers and civilians who would do admirably for the work; but all military questions in each district must be referable to one officer. He should have the rank of Lieutenant-Colonel conferred on him for the occasion.

The military districts I would propose are as follows:—

Calcutta to include the defences of Fort William and the Hughli and the districts of Bardwan, Bankoora, Beerbhoom, Midnapur, Hughli, 24-Pergunnahs, Calcutta, Nuddea, Jessore, and Murshedabad. The officer in this case must be a military officer.

Darjeeling to include all the districts of the Rajshahye Division and Cooch Behar. No particular necessity for a military officer.

Dacca to include all the districts of Dacca Division. Military officer not necessary.

Chittagong to include all the districts of the Chittagong Division and all the west littoral of British Burma and also Hill Tipperah and the Lushai frontier. A military officer should be appointed to this command.

Patna to include all the districts of Patna and Bhagalpur Divisions. A military officer would be required here.

Cuttack to include all the districts of the Orissa Division. Military officer not necessary.

Hazaribagh to include all the districts of the Chota Nagpur Division. Military officer not necessary.

The strength and distribution of the Bengal Command would therefore stand as follows:—

District	Station		Force
Head-Quarters (Calcutta) District.	Fort William	...	¾ British infantry; 1½ garrison artillery; 1 battalion volunteers; 1 company sappers; 4,500 able-bodied Europeans.
	Hughli defences	...	¼ British infantry; 1 garrison artillery.
	Bardwan	...	2 machine guns; 100 volunteers, or 144 able-bodied Europeans; 1 armoured train.
	Midnapur	...	54 able-bodied Europeans.
	Jessore	...	35 able-bodied Europeans.
	Howrah	...	1 armoured train.
	Sealdah	...	1 armoured train.
	Moveable column	...	¼ British infantry; 1 field artillery; 2 Native infantry.
Rajshahye District.	Darjeeling	...	105 able-bodied Europeans.
	Rangpur	...	10 able-bodied Europeans.
	Saraghat	...	1 armoured train.
	Chittagong	...	260 able-bodied Europeans.
Patna District.	Patna	...	¼ British Infantry; ½ garrison artillery; 2 machine guns; 339 able-bodied Europeans.
	Motihari	...	50 able-bodied Europeans.
	Muzuffarpur	...	50 able-bodied Europeans; 1 armoured train.
	Darbhanga	...	60 able-bodied Europeans.
	Bhagalpur	...	42 able-bodied Europeans.
	Monghyr	...	237 able-bodied Europeans.
	Lakisarai	...	100 volunteers.
	Jamalpur	...	200 volunteers.
	Soane Bridge	...	½ British infantry; 2 machine guns.
	Gya	...	All able-bodied Europeans available.
Orissa District.	Cuttack	...	All able-bodied Europeans available.

Chota Nagpur District. } Doranda ... 350 able-bodied Europeans.

Total 1½ British infantry; 3 garrison artillery; 1 field artillery; 10 machine guns; 2 Native infantry; 1,200 volunteers; 6 armoured trains, 300 men; 6 field guns; and all the able-bodied Europeans available, probably about 3,000 in all.

The present strength of troops and volunteers now in the Bengal province is as follows:—

Stations.		Artillery. Batteries. Horse.	Field.	Garrison.	Total.	Guns.	Cavalry. Regiments of British cavalry.	Regiments of Native cavalry.	Infantry. Regiments of British infantry.	Regiments of Native infantry.	Sappers and Miners. Companies.	Military authority.	Remarks.
Alipur	...	...	...	...	...	...	...	...	...	1 071 / 1¼*	...	General Officer Commanding Presidency District.	
Barrackpore	...	...	167 / 1	...	1	6	...	...	90 / ½	812 / 1	...		
Buxa	...	...	...	...	...	...	...	...	...	482 / ¾	...		
Doranda	...	...	...	...	...	...	...	...	...	593 / ¾	...		
Dum-Dum	...	...	...	...	...	...	...	...	839 / ½	...	...		
Fort William	...	...	...	77 / 1	1	...	...	136 / ¾	698 / 1	828 / 1	30 D.A.		
Hazaribagh	...	...	...	...	...	...	...	...	...	149 / ¾	...		
Dinapore	...	...	158 / 1	...	1	6	...	...	797 / ½	823 / 1	...	General Officer Commanding Allahabad Division	
Segowlie	...	...	...	77 / 1	...	...	...	406 / ¼	...	...	...		
Total	...	...	325 / 2	77 / 1	3	12	...	542 / 1	2,396 / 2½	4,758 / 6	30		

Besides the above, the following volunteers are posted in Bengal:—

Behar Mounted Rifles	...	283	Head-Quarters Muzaffarpur.
Calcutta Volunteers	...	340	" Calcutta.
" Cadets	...	310	" "
" Naval Artillery	...	120	" "
Cossipore Volunteer Artillery	...	53	" "
Eastern Bengal Railway Volunteers	...	180	" "
East Indian Railway Volunteers	...	1,220	" Jamalpur.
Tirhut Railway Volunteers	...	47	" Somastipur.
Sibpur College Volunteers	...	36	" Sibpur.
Northern Bengal Railway Volunteers		295	" Darjeeling.
" " " Cadets	...	69	" "
Akyab Volunteers	...	66	" Akyab.
" Cadets	...	89	" "
Total	...	3,408	

* *N.B.*—The lower figure given in the above and similar returns that follow shews the number of units of the different arms.

The total strength of European and Eurasian population of Bengal is 41·453, and these are distributed as follows :—

Bardwan	...	533* / 144
Bancora	...	33 / 8
Beerbhoom	...	91 / 26
Midnapur	...	217 / 54
Hughli	...	1,399 / 350
24-Pergunnahs	...	4,466 / 1,116
Calcutta	...	19.661 / 4,9[illegible]5
Nadea	...	213 / 54
Seoni	...	141 / 35
Murshedabad	...	311 / 78
Dinajpur	...	21 / 5
Chittagong	...	1,042 / 200
Noakholly	...	227 / 57
Chittagong Hill Tracts	...	30 / 7
Patna	...	1,3[illegible]6 / 339
Gya	...	120 / 30
Shahabad	...	403 / 101
Muzaffarpur	...	217 / 52
Sarun	...	124
Champaran	...	[illegible] / 23
Monghyr	...	948 / 237
Bhagalpur	...	169 / 42
Purneah	...	311 / 7[illegible]
Rajshahye	...	101 / 25
Rangpur	...	41 / 10
Bogra	...	19 / 5
Pabna	...	35 / 8
Darjeeling	...	420 / 105
Jalpaiguri	...	33 / 8
Dacca	...	9,961 / 1
Faridpur	...	84 / 210
Backerganj	...	154 / 38
Mymansing	...	96 / 25
Tipperah	...	51 / 33
Sonthal Pergunnahs	...	218 / 33
Maldah	...	37 / 9
Cuttack	...	404 / 101
Pooree	...	24 / 6
Balasore	...	1 / 20
Tributary Mehals	...	1
Hazaribagh	...	1,403 / 351
Lohardaga	...	95 / 235
Singhbhoom	...	22 / 5
Manbhoom	...	53 / 13
Cooch Behar	...	
Hill Tipperah	...	

A study of these figures will, I think, certainly shew that the following districts are well able to take care of themselves: Bardwan, Midnapur, Hughli, 24-Pergunnahs, Calcutta, Nadea, Darjeeling, Dacca, Chittagong, Noakholly, Patna, Shahabad, Muzaffarpur, Saran, Champaran, Monghyr, Purneah, Cuttack, and Hazaribagh.

Now, we have in Bengal—

British infantry.	Field artillery.	Garrison artillery.	Native cavalry.	Native infantry.	Sappers.	Volunteers.	Able-bodied Europeans.
$2\frac{1}{8}$	2	1	1	1	1	3,048	7,364

and we only require—

British infantry.	Garrison artillery.	Field artillery.	Machine guns.	Field guns.	Native infantry.	Sappers.	Volunteers.	Able-bodied Europeans.
$1\frac{1}{8}$	3	1	10	6	3	1	1,203	6,000

N.B.—The upper number gives the total population; the lower probable number of able-bodied men

Therefore we have in excess—

British infantry.	Field artillery.	Native cavalry.	Native infantry.	Volunteers.	Able-bodied Europeans.
1½	1	1	4	2,300	4,500

but we require 2 more garrison artillery, 10 machine guns, 6 field guns.

The Army Organization Commission (page 24) states the following to be the necessary obligatory garrison for the undermentioned stations :—

		Field artillery.	Garrison artillery.	Native cavalry.	British infantry.	Native infantry.	Company sappers.
Calcutta	...	0	1	⅛	½	2	1
Subsidiary stations—							
Darjeeling	...	0	0	0	0	0	0
Doranda	...	0	0	0	0	½	0
Dinapore	...	½	0	0	½	½	0
Total	...	½	1	⅛	1	3	1

But in this statement no allowance is made for the Hughli defences or the Soane Bridge, and I therefore prefer to stick to my figures as being more adapted to the probable necessities of our position. It would be suicidal in a war with Russia to leave the Hughli without any defences; and the same may be said as to neglecting the protection of the Soane Bridge, over which a very large proportion of our munitions of war for the North-Western Frontier would pass.

Therefore I prefer to adhere in this case to my own calculations, which make 1½ British infanty, 1 field artillery, 1 Native cavalry, 4 Native infantry available for operations beyond the command. The 2,200 volunteers and 4,500 able-bodied Europeans might, I am of opinion, be so far trained and organised that in three months I should consider it quite safe to withdraw the whole of the military garrison from Bengal, and leave it entirely to the Europeans residing in it. I should have no fear whatever of the result. The fact that we are in this command two batteries garrison artillery short points to the advisability of a larger proportion of the Calcutta Volunteers being trained to artillery practice; and if one company was trained to lay down torpedoes, it might also be practicable to withdraw the Sapper Company; but this is not important.

ASSAM.

We next come to Assam. Here there is "little danger of any organized "aggression of a foreign enemy, and none at all from internal rebellion; but, on "the other hand, there is an immense extent of external frontier to be protected "from the barbarous tribes who live beyond it. Speaking generally, none of "these tribes have any cohesion; none of them act together; but it might very "easily happen, not by design, but accidentally, that we might be called on to "meet Lushai incursions in the south and Abor incursions in the north, while "a Naga expedition was going on in the middle of the province; and it is "therefore necessary to make arrangements to meet these incursions by punitive "measures."

The strength of the military force in Assam is as follows :—

	1 regiment Native infantry at Shillong	... ...	883
	1 regiment Native infantry at Cachar	... ...	773
	1 regiment Native infantry at Dibrugarh	... ...	850
	1 regiment Native infantry at Kohima	... ...	869
Total	4		3,375

Besides, there are 1,899 frontier police, who approach near enough to soldiers for the purposes of this frontier, and there are the following volunteers :—

Sylhet Volunteers	... ...	128
Shillong Volunteers	... ...	32
Lakhimpur Volunteers	... ...	110
	Total ...	270

The measures which would seem, therefore, to be necessary in this province are to raise the frontier police to 4,000; to raise one of the Assam regiments to 1,200 bayonets by recruiting and calling in pensioners; to provide a half battery Native mountain artillery; to enrol the whole European population of Assam; to call on the Manipur Raja, who has a force of 5,800 regular infantry and 505 artillery and 700 Kuki horse, to provide, as he is bound by treaty to do, a contingent of 1,200 men to be fully armed by us; to provide river steamers on the Brahmaputra and on the Surma for 600 infantry; and to keep up always ready at Sadiya, Golaghat, and Cachar land transport for 600 men. Kohima should be entrusted to 400 frontier police, and all the frontier guards should be increased by about 50 per cent., while two moveable columns of 600 were kept up—one on the Brahmaputra and one on the Surma—to move on any threatened point in support of the police. The civil stations of Assam should be entirely entrusted to the care of the European and Eurasian population, the civil police, and such local levies as the civil officers on the spot should consider it safe and expedient to arm. At the stations of Shillong, Gauhati, Golaghat, Goalpara, Dubri, Sibsagar, Dibrugarh, Sylhet, and Cachar places of refuge should at once be selected and put in order.

The command of all military, volunteers, frontier police, and contingent should be placed under the command of the Brigadier General Commanding on the Eastern Frontier, who should have a fast steamer placed at his disposal to enable him to move quickly from any part of this enormous command to any other.

This force would consist of Military, 1,200; Frontier Police, 4,000; Volunteers, 270; Manipur Contingent, 1,200; and other European and Eurasian adults, 300 (about)—total 6,970: and these should be sufficient with a proper state of command to secure the whole province and to admit of two of the Assam regiments and the Cachar regiment being withdrawn for other duties. This estimate also agrees with the proposal of the Army Commission and, I believe, with the views of the Chief Commissioner.*

NORTH-WESTERN PROVINCES.

In the North-Western Provinces, Sir George Couper states the feeling to be one of general loyalty. "The landholders have everything to gain by the "continuance of our power. The same may be said as to the trading classes.

* It is not really of vital importance to us to hold Assam.

"As regards the great mass of the rural population, the general feeling is "one of contented indifference. The lower stratum of Muhammadans, and such "of the higher middle class of the same as are too proud to beg and too lazy "to work, constitute the really dangerous classes. But they are not united; "they have no leaders to look up to, and no principle of action to guide them "in a definite line of policy beyond religious antagonism and the desire for "plunder. The chief places where danger may be apprehended are—Meerut, "Moradabad, Bareilly, Allahabad, Agra, Benares, Jhansi, Cawnpore, Lucknow, "and Faizabad."

The chief strategical points in the North-Western Provinces appear to be Rajghat, Allahabad, Jumna Bridge (East Indian Railway), Cawnpore, Lucknow, Faizabad, Bareilly, Ganges Bridge (Oudh and Rohilkhand Railway), Moradabad, Agra, Meerut, Jumna Bridge (Sind, Punjab and Delhi Railway); and these should undoubtedly be held in strength. The garrisons which would appear to be necessary to secure the safety of these places would be—

	British infantry.	Volunteers.	Able-bodied Europeans.	Artillery.	Total.
Rajghat and bridge ...	1/8	100	90	20	= 210
Allahabad ...	[illegible]	400	400	80	= 880
Jumna Bridge ...	[illegible]	100	90	20	= 210
Cawnpore ...	[illegible]	200	100	40	= 340
Lucknow ...	[illegible]	200	900	80	= 1,180
Faizabad ...	[illegible]	200	0	20	= 220
Bareilly ...	[illegible]	400	50	40	= 490
Ganges Bridge (Oudh and Rohilkhand Railway) ...	[illegible]	200	0	20	= 220
Moradabad ...	[illegible]	200	0	40	= 240
Agra ...	[illegible]	200	360	80	= 640
Meerut ...	[illegible]	100	250	20	= 470
Jumna Bridge (Sind, Punjab and Delhi Railway) ...	1/8	200	100	20	= 320
Total ...	3 regiments	2,400	2,350	460	= 5,210

This would come to three regiments British infantry, 2,500 Europeans, and 4 batteries of garrison artillery.

The places which would have to be held for political reasons may be divided into those for which some garrison of Europeans could be provided from volunteers and other adults, and those for which practically no garrison could be provided, and which therefore could only be held as long as no rebellion broke out.

Under the first category I may place Naini Tal 199 volunteers, Rurki 200, Mussoorie 200, *Fatehgarh* 100, *Chunar* 100, Saharanpur 200, *Aligarh* 60, and Ghazipur 100; and these places would, I should imagine, be able to hold out without troops for a considerable space of time. At all these places of refuge should be provided, except those italicised, which are already provided.

In the second list I would place Azamgarh, Jounpur, Gorakhpur, Gonda, Rae Bareli, Sultanpur, Sitapur, Shahjahanpur, Bijnor, Muzaffarnagar, Bulandshahr, Muttra, Mainpuri, Etawah, Jhansi, and Banda. At all, except Jhansi, places of refuge would have to be provided; and although it might be necessary, sooner or later, to abandon them, it may be hoped that the facts of our holding the main strategical points as given above, and that no place would be very far from a moveable column, would enable us to retain our hold on them for very long.

I will now consider at what points moveable columns should be provided. These I take should be at Bareilly, Lucknow, Allahabad, Meerut, and Aligarh; and they should consist of the following strength:—

		British infantry.	Horse artillery.	Field artillery.	British cavalry.	Native infantry.	Native cavalry.
Bareilly	...	1 regiment	½	1	½	2	1
Lucknow	...	1 ,,	1	1	½	3	1½
Allahabad	...	1 ,,	0	1	½	2	1
Meerut	...	1 ,,	1	1	½	3	1½
Aligarh	...	1 ,,	0	1	0	1	½
Total	...	5 ,,	2½	5	2	11	5½

This would come in round numbers to 5,800 British, with 45 guns and 10,500 Native troops.

We therefore require for all purposes in the North-Western Provinces:—

		British infantry.	Garrison artillery.	Horse. artillery.	Field artillery.	Able-bodied Europeans.	British cavalry.	Native infantry.	Native cavalry.
For garrison	...	3	6	0	0	2,500	0	0	0
Moveable column	...	5	0	2½	5	0	2	11	5½
Total	...	8	6	2½	5	2,500	2	11	5½

The Army Commission recommend the following obligatory garrisons in the North-Western Provinces:—

		Field artillery.	Garrison artillery.	Native cavalry.	British infantry.	Native infantry.
Allahabad	...	½	1	½	½	1
Cawnpore	...	½	0	0	½	½
Fatehgarh	...	0	0	0	0	½
Lucknow	...	1	0	½	1	1
Bareilly	...	1	0	0	½	½
Meerut	...	1	0	0	½	1
Delhi	...	0	1	½	½	½
Agra	...	1	0	1	1	½
Total	...	5	2	2½	4½	5

But these are meant evidently for garrisons only, for which my allowance is three British infantry regiments and six garrison batteries. No allowance is made by the Commission for moveable columns, which are evidently meant to be drawn from the troops available for field service.

The troops now maintained in the territory under the Government of the North-Western Provinces and Oudh are as follows:—

Stations.		Artillery. Batteries. Horse.	Field.	Garrison.	Total.	Guns.	Cavalry. Regiments of British cavalry.	Regiments of Native cavalry.	Infantry. Regiments of British infantry.	Regiments of Native infantry.	Sappers and Miners. Companies.	Military Authority.	Remarks.
Allahabad and Fort	...	...	158/1	83/1	2	6	...	550/1	690/1	820/1	......	General Officer Commanding Allahabad Division.	
Benares	...	...	151/1	...	1	6	...	...	271/[illegible]	713/[illegible]	......		
Cawnpore	...	...	154/1	...	1	6	...	370/[illegible]	652/1	823/1	......		
Chunar	...	...	...	...	...	...	...	...	66/[illegible]	76/[illegible]	......		
Faizabad	...	...	155/1	...	1	6	...	...	795/1	829/1	......	General Officer Commanding Oudh Division.	
Gorakhpur	...	...	...	...	...	...	...	...	...	807/1	......		
Lucknow	...	157/1	157/1	23/D.A.	2	12	392/1	542/1	1,419/2	1,638/2	......		
Sitapur	...	...	...	...	...	...	...	178/[illegible]	528/[illegible]	...	......		
Banda	...	...	..	...	...	...	...	...	...	340/[illegible]	......	General Officer Commanding Saugor District.	
Jhansi and Lalitpur	...	...	...	...	...	...	...	325/[illegible]	411/[illegible]	832/1	......	General Officer Commanding Gwalior District.	
Almora	...	...	...	...	...	...	...	...	...	695/[illegible]	......	General Officer Commanding Rohilkhand District.	
Bareilly	...	...	151/1	...	1	6	...	550/1	747/[illegible]	820/1	......		

Stations.	Artillery. Batteries. Horse.	Artillery. Batteries. Field.	Artillery. Batteries. Garrison.	Artillery. Batteries. Total.	Guns.	Cavalry. Regiments of British cavalry.	Cavalry. Regiments of Native cavalry.	Infantry. Regiments of British infantry.	Infantry. Regiments of Native infantry.	Sappers and Miners. Companies.	Military Authority.	Remarks.
Moradabad ...	...	...	...	...	...	...	...	168/½	469/½	......	General Officer Commanding Rohilkhand District.	
Naini Tal ...	...	...	...	...	...	...	...	...	90/½	......		
Pithoragarh ...	...	...	...	...	...	...	...	...	87/½	......		
Ranikhet ...	...	...	...	...	...	...	...	1,011/1½	30/D. A.	......		
Shahjahanpur ...	...	...	...	...	...	...	...	257/½	359/½	......		
Agra and Fort ...	...	163/1	115/1	2	6	...	...	876/1	1,444/1½	......	General Officer Commanding Meerut Division.	
Chakrata ...	...	...	...	...	...	...	...	753/1	...	......		
Dehra Dun ...	...	...	...	...	...	...	...	...	888/1	......		
Fatehgarh ...	...	...	...	...	...	...	...	155/½	150/½	......		
Meerut ...	317/2	314/2	...	4	24	408/1	502/½	501/½	822/1	......		
Muttra ...	...	...	...	...	...	405/1	...	...	...	......		
Rurki ...	...	...	...	...	...	...	...	490/1*	...	793/7		* 1 company Royal Engineers not included (78 men).
Total ...	474/3	1,402/9	221/2	14	72	1,205/3	3,017/5½	9,700/13	12,795/15½	793/7		

Total { British ... 13,002
Native ... 16,605

The strength of volunteers in the North-Western Provinces is as follows :—

Allahabad Volunteers	... 250	Head-quarters,	Allahabad.
Lucknow „	... 326	„	Lucknow.
Cawnpore „	... 69	„	Cawnpore.
„ Cadets	... 24	„	„
Naini Tal Volunteers	... 186	„	Naini Tal.
Rohilkhand	... 121	„	Bareilly.
Agra Volunteers„	... 208	„	Agra.
Thomason College Volunteers	... 26	„	Rurki.
Mussoorie Volunteers	... 255	„	Mussoorie.
Farakhabad „	... 40	„	Fatehgarh.
Ghazipur „	... 225	„	Allahabad.
Total	... 1,728		

Besides a portion of the East Indian Railway Volunteers would be available. Besides these, there are the following adult Europeans not included in the above :—

Meerut and Ghaziabad	250
Saharunpur and Rurki	440
Aligarh	60
Bareilly	50
Agra	100
Cawnpore	100
Allahabad	400
Benares	90
Chunar	100
Lucknow	900
Total ...	2,590

I cannot ascertain the number of Eurasians; but as it is probably small, neither it nor the number of Native Christians need be considered here.

This gives a total in the whole province of about 18,000 Europeans capable of bearing arms.

The total available strength in the province in European fighting men is—

Horse artillery.	Field artillery.	Garrison artillery.	British cavalry.	British infantry.	Native cavalry.	Native infantry.	Sappers.	Volunteers.	Able-bodied Europeans.
3	9	2	3	13	5½	15½	7	1,728	2,590

and we require for internal defence—

Horse artillery.	Field artillery	Garrison artillery.	British cavalry.	British infantry.	Native cavalry.	Native infantry.	Volunteers
2½	5	6	2	8	5¾	11	2,500

We have therefore available for exterior operations—

Horse artillery.	Field artillery	British cavalry.	British infantry.	Native infantry.	Volunteers
½	4	1	5	4½	1,800

but we are short of four garrison batteries of artillery. These should, I think, be provided for by extending the volunteers and training 400 of them in the duties of garrison artillery. It is evident that if the Europeans were trained, one or two British Infantry regiments could be spared.

In addition to the above, it would be necessary to provide armoured trains at the following places :—Allahabad, Rajghat, Lucknow, Bareilly, Cawnpore, Agra, and Aligarh.

PUNJAB.

When asked in 1879 his opinion as to the state of feeling and elements of danger in the Punjab, Sir Robert Egerton stated "he is able to record his "deliberate opinion, founded upon long experience of the people of the Punjab "and the testimony of many experienced and able officers, that the state of feel- "ing in this province is excellent; and he does not believe in any province in "India there will be found an equal amount of sympathy between the rulers and "the ruled, so much identification of the interests of the people with those of "the Government, so much real, hearty, and active loyalty as in the Punjab. "The Muhammadans are far less fanatical and less swayed by religious bigotry "than elsewhere in India. The Sikhs look upon the English with an entirely "friendly spirit, and undoubtedly feel some common natural pride in the vic- "tories of the British arms which they have been permitted to share; and the "Hindus are a source of no apprehension. The excellent spirit of loyalty of "the people of British territory is worthily supplemented by the active loyalty "of the Native Independent States in political connection with the Punjab "Government."

On the other hand, and however true this may be, it must not be forgotten that the Punjab is edged on the west by a frontier beyond which lie numerous independent, warlike, and very troublesome tribes, all of whom are Muhammadans and fanatical, and who are said, perhaps with some exaggeration, to be able to turn out 170,000 fighting men. And moreover, although I do not doubt the loyalty of the Sikh States, it should be remembered that popular belief has more than once pointed to the propensity of the Maharaja of Kashmir for outside intrigue; and it is necessary also to consider that the whole of the people of the Punjab are more or less warlike, and have only quite lately been conquered; and from the situation of the province they live in, with reference to the subject of this paper, they must necessarily be more interested in, and excited by, the occurrences of any campaign undertaken beyond the Indus border for the defence of India.

I therefore hold that Sir R. Egerton's high opinion of the loyalty of the Punjab would not justify our neglecting to hold it in sufficient strength to meet all the above possibilities.

The most important places in the Punjab in a military view are Multan, Ferozepore, Lahore, Rawalpindi, Peshawar, Delhi, Amritsar, and the bridges over the Jumna between Ambala and Saharanpur, over the Sutlej at Ludhiana, and over the Beas, the Ravi, the Chenab, the Jhelum, and the Indus; and I think it cannot be gainsaid that all of these must be held in strength. The garrisons, therefore, which I consider sufficient are as follows :—

	British infantry.	Volunteers.	Garrison artillery.
Delhi Fort	4/8	200	1
Jumna Bridge	2/8	0	½
Sutlej Bridge / Ludhiana	2/8	0	½
Beas Bridge	2/8	0	½
Ferozepore	4/8	100	1
Lahore	4/8	400	1
Ravi Bridge	2/8	0	½
Chenab Bridge	2/8	0	½
Jhelum Bridge	2/8	0	½
Rawalpindi	4/8	100	1½
Attock Bridge	2/8	0	½
Peshawar	4/8	100	1
Multan	2/8	100	½
Amritsar	2/8	100	½
Total	4 6/8	1,100	10

In addition the following places, which are of secondary importance, but still absolutely necessary to hold, should be garrisoned as follows :—

	Native infantry.	Native garrison artillery.
Dera Ismail Khan	1	$\frac{1}{3}$
Bannu	1	$\frac{1}{3}$
Kohat	1	$\frac{1}{3}$
Total ...	3	1

The following places, the head-quarters of civil districts, should be held as long as possible; but as no garrisons can be provided for them from the army, these should be arranged for as far as possible by civil officers from the police and local levies: Gurgaon, Rohtak, Hissar, Karnal, Sirsa, Simla, Ludhiana, Jalandhar, Hoshiarpur, Kangra, Gurdaspur, Gujranwala, Sialkot, Gujrat, Jhelum, Abbottabad, Shahpur, Jhang, Montgomery, Muzaffarnagar, Dera Ghazi Khan, and Rajanpur; and places of refuge should therefore be provided at these places to enable the small number available to hold out as long as possible.

Then moveable columns as under should be formed at the following places :—

	Field artillery.	Horse artillery.	British infantry.	Native cavalry.	Native infantry.	British cavalry.
Delhi	1	0	1	1	2	0
Ambala	2	0	1	1	2	$\frac{1}{2}$
Lahore	2	1	2	1	3	1
Multan	1	0	1	1	2	0
Peshawar	2	1	2	1	4	$\frac{1}{2}$
Pindi	2	0	1	1	2	$\frac{1}{2}$
Thal for Kohat	1 N.M.A.	0	0	1	2	0
Dera Ismail Khan	1 Do.	0	0	1	2	0
Total ...	10 2 N.M.A.	2	8	8	19	$2\frac{1}{2}$

All these troops should be kept equipped with transport, so as to enable them to move at a moment's notice.

The total number of troops therefore which will be required for the internal defence of the Punjab will be—

	British cavalry.	British infantry.	Horse artillery.	Field artillery.	Native mountain artillery.	Garrison artillery.	Native cavalry.	Native infantry.	Volunteers.
Garrisons ...	0	$4\frac{5}{8}$	0	0	0	10	0	3	1,100
Moveable columns ...	$2\frac{1}{2}$	8	2	10	2	0	8	19	0
Total ...	$2\frac{1}{2}$	$12\frac{5}{8}$	2	10	2	10	8	22	1,100

The Army Commission recommend obligatory garrisons in the Punjab as follows:—

	Field artillery.	Garrison artillery.	Mountain artillery.	British infantry.	Native infantry.	Native cavalry.	Sappers and miners.
Lahore and Amritsar ...	1	1	0	1⅜	1	0	0
Ferozepore ...	0	1	0	6/8	½	0	0
Rawalpindi ...	0	½	0	⅛	1	0	0
Abbottabad	0	0	0	0	1	0	0
Attock ...	0	½	0	⅛	0	0	0
Nowshera ...	0	0	0	⅞	1	0	0
Murdan	0	0	⅓	0	1	1	0
Peshawar ...	1	0	0	1	2	⅞	0
Outposts ...	0		1	0	3	⅛	1
Kohat ...	0	1	0	0	1	½	0
Bannu ...	0	0	0	0	1	1	0
Kuram ...	1	0	1⅓	2	2	2	1
Multan ...	0	0	0	⅞	½	0	0
Dera Ismail Khan ...	0	0	0	⅛	1	½	0
Tonk ...	0	0	⅓	0	1	½	0
Dera Ghazi Khan ...	0	0	0	0	1	½	0
Rajanpur ...	0	0	0	0	0	1	0
Total ...	3	4	3	7½	20	8	2

It is not clear in this statement how many of these troops are meant for purely garrison duties, and how many would be available for moveable columns. It seems probable, however, that the wants of both are meant to be supplied by the above force.

Compared with my statement of the requirements of the province, it shows as follows:—

	Horse artillery.	Field artillery.	Mountain artillery.	Garrison artillery.	British infantry.	Native infantry.	Native cavalry.	Sappers and miners.	British cavalry.
Army Commission ...	0	3	3	4	7½	20	8	2	0
Mine ...	2	10	2	5	11¼	21	8	0	2⅓

Therefore my estimate is—

Horse artillery.	Field artillery.	Garrison artillery.	British infantry.	Native infantry.	British cavalry.
2	7	1	3¾	1	2⅓

in excess, while that of the Army Organization provides 1 mountain artillery and 2 companies sappers more than I do.

The figures cannot be reconciled, as it is not clear at all whether the terms of the Army Organization Commission "available for field service elsewhere" includes service in India or beyond the frontier.

The troops now maintained in the territory under the Punjab Government are as follows :—

Stations.	Artillery. Batteries. Horse.	Field.	Garrison.	Total.	Guns.	Cavalry. Regiments of British cavalry.	Regiments of Native cavalry.	Infantry. Regiments of British infantry.	Regiments of Native infantry.	Sappers and Miners. Companies.	Military Authority.	Remarks.
Delhi and Fort ...	...	...	113/1	1	...	...	[illegible]	800/½	830/1	......	General Officer Commanding Meerut Division.	
Ambala ...	307/3	...	...	2	12	488/1	551/1	783/1 (a)	319/1	......	General Officer Commanding Sirhind Division.	(a) 4 companies are located at Solon during summer months.
Dagshai ...	...	...	...	...	...	...	...	876/1	...	......		
Jutogh ...	...	99/1 (b)	...	1	6	...	...	[illegible]	...	......		(b) Mountain Battery.
Sabathu ...	...	...	...	...	...	...	...	[illegible]	...	......		
Fort Ludhiana ...	...	...	...	...	...	...	...	...	[illegible]	......		
Fort Phillour ...	...	...	...	...	...	...	...	...	[illegible]	......		
Jalandhar ...	...	167/1	...	1	6	...	...	860/1	624/2	......		
Mian Mir ...	...	334/2	...	2	12	...	550/1	736/1	1,468/1½	......	General Officer Commanding Lahore Division.	
Fort Lahore ...	...	...	[illegible]	1	...	...	...	53/Det.	70/½	......		
Multan and Fort ...	...	155/1	...	1	6	...	* 547/1	883/1	839/1	......		* See note opposite Quetta District,—Statement No. 10.
Ferozepore and Fort ...	...	167/1	110/1	2	6	...	...	849/1	838/1	......		
Fort Govindgarh ...	...	...	21/Det.	...	...	...	...	...	...	......		
Amritsar ...	...	...	...	...	...	...	...	336/½	118/½	......		
Dharmsala and Fort Kangra ...	...	...	...	...	...	...	...	...	878/1	......		
Bakloh ...	...	...	...	...	...	...	...	...	909/1	......		

Stations.	Artillery. Batteries. Horse.	Field.	Garrison.	Total.	Guns.	Cavalry. Regiments of British cavalry.	Regiments of Native cavalry.	Infantry. Regiments of British infantry.	Regiments of Native infantry.	Sappers and Miners. Companies.	Military Authority.	Remarks.
Rawalpindi (a) ...	156/1	147/1	...	2	12	398	546/1	452/½	1,533/1½	108/1	General Officer Commanding Rawalpindi Division.	(a) See remarks opposite Kuldunna, &c.
Jhelum ...	...	...	...	...	...	...	548/1	...	831/1	...		
Campbellpur ...	...	95/1 (b)	88/1 22/Det.	2	6	...	...	...	...	...		(b) Heavy Field Battery.
Fort Attock ...	...	...		...	...	...	...	78/⅛	113/⅛	...		
Sialkot ...	150/1	...	...	1	6	490/1	542/1	443/⅜	832/1	...		
Kuldunna (c) ...	...	...	...	...	...	...	...	336/⅜	...	...		(c) These troops are concentrated at Rawalpindi during winter months.
Baragully (c) ...	...	90/1 (d)	...	1	6	...	...	...	...	...		
Kalabagh (c) ...	...	103/1 (d)	...	1	6	...	...	...	...	...		(d) Mountain Battery.
Changlagully (c) ...	...	...	...	...	...	...	...	137/⅜	...	...		
Khyragully (c) ...	...	120/1 (d)	...	1	6	...	...	...	...	...		
Gharial (c) ...	...	...	...	...	...	...	...	384/¾	...	...		
Peshawar ...	...	111/1	...	1	6	...	400/⅝	1776/2 (e)	2227/2⅜	327/2	General Officer Commanding Peshawar District.	(e) 9 companies are sent to Cherat during summer months.
Shabkadar ...	...	...	...	...	...	...	39/Det.	...	84/⅛	...		
Michni ...	...	...	...	...	...	...	7/Det.	...	92/⅛	...		
Abazai ...	...	...	...	...	...	...	48/Det.	...	84/Det.	...		
Nowshera ...	...	...	...	...	...	...	470/1	756/⅞ (f)	685/⅞ (f)	...		(f) 2 companies ditto.
Fort Jumrud ...	...	...	...	...	...	...	83/⅛	...	92/⅛	...		
Total Royal Artillery ...	810/6	1,068	434	20	96							

Abbottabad ...	Natives.	165 / 1 (g)	...	1	6	...	...	...	...	...	General Officer Commanding Punjab* Frontier Force.	
Hoti Mardan ...		...	...	...	...	...	851 / 1	...	1717 / 3	...		
Kohat ...		179 / 1 (g)	74 / 1 (h)	2	6	...	801 / 1	...	891 / 1	...		
Edwardesabad ...		169 / 1 (g)	...	1	6	...	904 / 3 / 6	...	2400 / 3	...		
Dera Ismail Khan ...		162 / 1 (g)	...	1	6	...	602 / 1	...	1044 / 3	...		
Dera Ghazi Khan ...		...	...	...	...	...	649 / 1	...	1633 / 2	...		
Rajanpur ...		...	...	...	...	...	550 / 1	...	830 / 1	...		
Total Native Artillery ...	...	675	74	5	24							
GRAND TOTAL ...	620	2,283	508	25	120	1,235	6,094	10,712	23,187	320		

Total ... British ... 14,609

Total ... Native ... 24,744

(g) Native Mountain Artillery.

(h) Native Artillery.

N.B.—The troops of the Punjab Frontier Force furnish detachments for outpost duty on the North-Western Frontier.

* See note opposite Quetta District,—Statement No. 10.

The volunteer force consists of—

1st Punjab Volunteers	526
2nd Punjab Volunteers	343
3rd Punjab Volunteers	705
Total ...	1,574

Besides, it has been calculated that there are about 1,500 more adult Europeans and Eurasians scattered about the province.

The total force now maintained in the Punjab consists of—

Horse artillery, 4; Field artillery, 12; British mountain artillery, 4; Native mountain artillery, 4; Garrison artillery, 3; Native garrison artillery, 1; British cavalry, 3; British infantry, 13⅞; Native cavalry, 14; Native infantry, 28; Sappers, 3; Volunteers, 1,574; and able-bodied Europeans, 1,500.

And of this we quire for internal defence—

Horse artillery.	Field artillery.	British mountain artillery.	Native mountain artillery.	Garrison artillery.	Native garrison artillery.	British cavalry.	British infantry.	Native cavalry.	Native infantry.	Volunteers.	Able-bodied Europeans.
2	10	1	1	9	1	2½	12⅝	8	22	1,100	1,500

So that there will be available for exterior operations—

Horse artillery.	Field artillery.	British mountain artillery.	Native mountain artillery.	British cavalry.	British infantry.	Native cavalry.	Native infantry.	Sappers.	Volunteers.
2	2	3	3	½	⅞	6	6	3	474

All the principal places being strongly held as above, provisioned and provided with ammunition, each moveable column would have entrusted to it the duty of putting down rebellion in a particular area of country,—*i.e.*, the Delhi column would move in the Hissar, Ulwar, Meerut or Agra direction; the Ambala column would look after all the country between the Jumna and the Sutlej; the Lahore column would operate between the Sutlej and Chenab; the Multan column would support the Dera Ghazi frontier and keep the Bari, Rechna, and Sind Sagar Doabs quiet; the Peshawar column would maintain order in that district and support the Kohat or Abbottabad frontier; the Pindi column would operate between the Chenab and the Indus and support Abbottabad and Kohat; the Kohat column would move along the western frontier, and be always ready to meet any ingression of the tribes from the Kohat Pass to the Bain Pass; and the Dera Ismail column would take up the rest of the frontier, especially the Waziri portion.

Arrangements should be well thought out by which two or more of these columns could, at the shortest notice, be concentrated in any one district; as, for instance, Lahore might be reinforced by railway in a few hours by the Multan and Ambala columns, thus raising the strength of the force in the capital of the Punjab to—

British artillery.	British infantry.	Native cavalry.	Native infantry.	British cavalry.
5	4	3	7	1½

—a force which well handled should be able to put down any rising with a high hand and in a very short time.

It would be necessary to provide armoured trains at Delhi, Meerut, Ambala, Beas Bridge, Lahore, Chenab Bridge left bank, Jhelum Bridge left bank, Rawalpindi, Attock, Peshawar, Multan, Sutlej Bridge, and Adamwahan.

BOMBAY.

In the Bombay Presidency the sources of danger are well described by Sir R. Temple in his minute dated 31st July 1879 :—

"There is a considerable Mahratta nobility called Sirdars of the Deccan, "once powerful, and, though no longer powerful, still influential. Although "there was, as I understand, anxiety about them in 1857, they are now esteemed "to be personally well disposed. But much as we may confide in each chief "individually as we see him now-a-days, it is to be remembered that these "people are the descendants within two generations of those who formed the "court and camp of the Peishwas; that their immediate ancestors enjoyed "wealth, power, honor—all which inevitably pass away in consequence of a "foreign rule like ours; that despite all the arrangements which we can "reasonably be expected to make for the partial continuance of their emolu-"ments for limited periods, despite also such concession in perpetuity as may "be allowed consistently with the interests of the country, these people must "be much worse off under our rule than under the preceding rule; that they, "whose families were in by-gone times above all law, now feel the restrictions "of a civilized administration; and that all these circumstances affect, not only "the heads of houses, but their numerous dependants and retainers. All this "should be weighed in estimating the chances of trouble. During the earlier "days of our rule, it would have had more potential import than at present, "and it may decrease gradually year by year. But it still exists in some "degree, and so far it should be borne in mind.

"There are certain classes among the humbler orders in some of the cities, "such as Poona, Satara, and Nasik, who appear to be hostilely disposed and "who might, under certain circumstances, become a turbulent mob.

"The educated classes, fast growing in numbers and intelligence, are as a "rule loyal; indeed, I should say they must necessarily be loyal and well-"disposed to Government. But among them there are unfortunate excep-"tions to this good rule,—men who are many in the abstract, though not "numerous relatively to the whole of the upper and middle classes; men whose "minds seem discontented and unsettled, and who are, it is to be feared, ac-"tually ill-disposed towards Government. There are also scattered among the "community individuals who are of a restless, intriguing, plotting disposition, "seemingly irreconcilable to British rule, and of an ambitious nature, who "might under some circumstances readily conceivable become influential for "mischief. Indeed, they are mischievous already, both directly by their own "conduct, and indirectly by their influence upon others; and of this there are "many indications abroad.

"Of the Native States above mentioned, some had at times during British "rule, even up to recent years, been centres of political mischief, with a "tendency to work in combination. But these evil characteristics have of late "decreased,—perhaps almost disappeared.

"Throughout the whole of the Deccan the mind of the people is, I believe, "affected by the past associations of Mahratta rule, which, so far from being "forgotten, are better remembered than would ordinarily be expected, and by "the long-retained memory of the Mahratta uprising against the Muham-"madans.

"There is a general tendency also to criticise to an extreme degree, not "only the proceedings of Government and its officers, but also the national "conduct and policy of the British in respect to India. Though much of this "criticism is legitimate, and is not at all to be confounded with disaffection, "still some of it often verges towards that degree which is hardly distinguishable from disloyalty.

"The Canarese people are peaceable and loyal. In the Concan proper, "the principal class are the khotes or superior landlords, who are, as a rule, all "that could be expected in respect to loyalty.

"The Native States of Sawantwari and Janjira are well disposed. Experience even up to recent times, however, indicates that, if any political "trouble arose in the Deccan, the excitement would spread to the Concan.

"In Gujrat are included the rich country from Surat to Ahmedabad, the "Native States of Rewakanta, Mahikanta, Palanpur, and Radhanpur, and the "large State of Baroda.

"The peasantry are prosperous and loyal, and generally free from excitability; but there are some tribes among them—Kolis and others—of a "turbulent disposition.

"Of the landed gentry, some are of excellent and undoubted loyalty. "Others are broken in fortune and doubtful in character; and respecting some "of these, the caution I have expressed regarding the Mahratta aristocracy of "the Deccan is applicable.

"Of the large urban population in this province, the inhabitants of Surat "and Broach have alone evinced a turbulent disposition.

"Of the present management of the Baroda State, of the loyal disposition "of its chiefs and people, I formed a very favourable estimate. But experience "and information convince us that, in the event of any sort of trouble in the "Deccan, there will be sympathy with it among some individuals—perhaps "some classes at Baroda; or, *vice versâ,* if the trouble be at Baroda, there will "be a sentiment aroused in the Deccan. This circumstance must, I think, be "regarded as a political factor.

"Kattyawar was once much infested by lawless people, but of late years "all these elements of trouble are fast disappearing. The disposition of this "large cluster of chiefs is quite loyal. The temper of the peasantry is peaceful "and industrious. The improvement in Kattyawar within this generation "reflects honour on British rule in Western India. Still the smouldering or "hardly extinguished elements of trouble might break out again in the event "of a general disturbance. Similar remarks may be applied to Cutch.

"In Sind the temper of the cultivating peasantry is quite loyal to the "Government. So also, I think, is the disposition for the most part of the "landlords, large and small.

"Along the whole sea border of the presidency from Karachi, past Cutch "and Kattyawar, past Gujrat and the Concan and Canara, down to the confines of Madras, there are hardy maritime classes once dangerously piratical, "but now addicted to lawful ocean-borne trade, and very well affected.

"In the great city of Bombay the population is in the main thoroughly "loyal. There is not one disloyal class; while some classes, such as Parsis, "are conspicuously loyal.

"There is no Muhammadan fanaticism anywhere in the presidency; and, "if there ever was any Hindu fanaticism, it has long ago been subdued by "education.

"But if religious Brahmanism be decaying (as many believe it is), still "political Brahmanism is not extinct in those parts of the presidency which "were subject to Mahratta rule. The Brahman caste has not forgotton—will "probably never forget—that it was at the head of the great Mahratta confederation.

"There is generally some fermentation in the public mind among the "natives of Western India whenever the British Government is engaged in "wars or in grave political affairs. In any event which might cause British "power to shake, even in the slightest degree, such fermentation would "speedily become aggravated. Then the several elements of mischief I have "mentioned would become active, while (as is usual with Oriental nations) "most of the numerous elements of good would remain comparatively passive; "and so Government would be left to deal with its difficulties, unaided even "by its loyal subjects. Under such circumstances, the conduct even of the "agricultural classes would not be satisfactory in respect of co-operation with "the Government.

"The elements of danger will be gathered from my foregoing remarks "regarding the state of feeling among the people. They may be summarized "thus:

"Political ambition among certain classes, which can hardly be satisfied "under British rule.

"A certain degree of disaffection, which, though very partial, is not "likely to be removed, or even mitigated, by any remedies which a foreign "Government can adopt.

"A Native aristocracy which has unavoidably suffered in wealth and position by the introduction of foreign rule."

The most important strategical positions in the Bombay presidency would appear to be Bombay, Poona, Dhond, Manmad, Bhosawal, Asirgarh, Khandwa Mhow, Neemuch, Nasirabad, Ahmedabad, Deesa, Baroda, Surat, and Karachi; and the principal bridges over the Nurbada by the Indore State Railway and the Bombay, Baroda and Central India Railway, and over the Tapti on the Great Indian Peninsula and on the Bombay, Baroda and Central India Railway, and over the Indus at Sukkur; and it must be allowed that all these should be held in sufficient strength as shewn below:—

	British infantry.		Volunteers.	Garrison artillery.
Bombay	1		2,000	2
Kirki	4/8		400	1
Dhond	1/8		100	1/4
Manmad	1/8		100	1/4
Bhosawal	1/8		100	1/4
Asirgarh	2/8		0	1/2
Khandwa	2/8		100	1/2
Mhow	4/8		0	1
Neemuch	2/8		0	1/2
Nasirabad	2/8		0	1/2
Ahmedabad	4/8		0	1
Deesa	3/8		0	1/2
Baroda	2/8		0	3/4
Surat	2/8		0	1/2
Karachi	4/8		200	1
Nurbada bridges, I. S. R. ...	1/8		100	1/4
Nurbada bridges, B. B. & C. I. R.	1/8		100	1/4
Tapti bridge, G. I. P. R. ...	1/8		100	1/4
Tapti bridge, B. B. & C. I. R. ...	1/8		100	1/4
Sukkur bridge ...	2/8		100	1/4
Total ...	6	regiments,	500	11¾

In addition to the above, it would seem to be advisable to keep up moveable columns as given below :—

		Horse artillery.	Field artillery.	British cavalry.	British infantry.	Native cavalry.	Native infantry.
(1)	Poona ...	1	2	½	2	1	4
(2)	Ahmedabad ...	0	2	½	1½	1	4
(3)	Mhow ...	1	1	½	2	1	3
(4)	Nasirabad ...	0	1	0	1	1	2
(5)	Sind ...	0	1	0	½	½	2
	Total ...	2	7	1½	7	4½	15

The first would keep all the country quiet in the triangle Bombay, Asirgarh, and Poona; it would be available to form junction either with the Mhow and Ahmedabad columns and a column at Bellary, or to reinforce Bombay.

The second would act towards Bombay, Kattyawar, or Nasirabad. The third would be employed principally in keeping Holkar in order; but it might also be useful in the direction of Rajputana, the Central Provinces, or Gwalior.

The fourth column could co-operate either with that at Ahmedabad, Delhi, or Mhow.

The Sind force would be posted wherever seemed most suitable for internal defence of the province.

The total force therefore required for the internal defence of the Bombay presidency, Rajputana, and Holkar's territory would be—

	Horse artillery.	Field artillery.	Mountain artillery.	Garrison artillery.	British cavalry.	British infantry.	Native cavalry.	Native infantry.	Sappers.	Volunteers.
Garrisons	0	0	0	11¾	0	6	0	0	0	3,500
Moveable columns	2	7	0	0	1½	7	4½	15	0	0
Total	2	7	0	11¾	1½	7	4½	15	0	3,500

The following statement shows the distribution of troops now maintained in the territory under the Bombay Government :—

Stations.	Artillery. Batteries. Horse.	Artillery. Batteries. Field.	Artillery. Batteries. Garrison.	Artillery. Batteries. Total.	Guns.	Cavalry. Regiments of British cavalry.	Cavalry. Regiments of Native cavalry.	Infantry. Regiments of British infantry.	Infantry. Regiments of Native infantry.	Sappers and Miners. Companies.	Military Authority.	Remarks.
Bombay ...	...	...	2½¹	2	...	...	...	471 / ½	1,376 / 1½	......	General Officer Commanding Presidency District.	
Tanna ...	...	...	...	...	...	...	...	...	98 / ½	......		
Janjira ...	...	...	...	...	...	...	...	...	16 / Det.	......		
Bushire ...	...	...	...	...	...	...	...	...	33 / Det.	......		
Bagdad ...	...	...	...	...	...	...	...	...	25 / Det.	......		
Jask ...	...	...	...	...	...	...	...	...	87 / Det.	......		
Muscat ...	...	...	...	...	...	...	...	...	16 / Det.	......		
Ahmedabad* ...	...	† 98 / ½	...	½	4	...	...	64 / ½	834‡ / ½	......	General Officer Commanding Northern Division.	* 14 men of the 21st Bombay Infantry attached to the Indian Marine not included. † 4 guns. ‡ Includes the depôt of a regiment.
Deesa ...	...	1/10 †	...	1	6	...	384 / ½	89 / ½	•1/10	......		
Baroda ...	...	§ 47 / ½	...	½	2	...	13 / Det.	117 / ½	701 / ½	......		§ 2 guns.
Rajkot ...	...	...	...	...	...	...	137 / ½	...	715 / ½	......		
Bhuj ...	...	...	...	...	...	...	...	...	•1/7	......		• The depôts of the Native Infantry regiments are located at the station.
Surat ...	...	...	...	...	...	...	...	...	338‖ / ½	......		‖ Includes the depôts of three regiments.
Dwarka ...	...	...	...	...	...	...	...	...	96 / ½	......		
Palunpur ...	...	...	...	...	...	...	15 / Det.	...	...	......		
Sadra ...	...	...	...	...	...	...	...	...	64 / ½	......		

Stations.	Artillery. Batteries. Horses.	Garrison.	Field.	Total.	Guns.	Cavalry. Regiments of British cavalry.	Regiments of Native cavalry.	Infantry. Regiments of British infantry.	Regiments of Native infantry.	Sappers and Miners. Companies.	Military Authority.	Remarks.
Poona …	…	*100/1	…	†1	4	…	551/1	942/1¼	2,371/2⅞	…	General Officer Commanding Poona Division.	* Native mountain battery. † Artillery is shewn as it will be after next relief. ‡Includes 1 company Royal Engineers.
Kirkee …	184/1	‡295/2	…	3	18	…	…	122/‡⅜	184/⅜	293/2		
Ahmednagar …	…	149/1	…	1	6	…	…	480/⅜	491/1	…		
Satara …	…	…	…	…	…	…	…	140/⅜	497/⅜	…		
Malegaon …	…	…	…	…	…	…	…	…	831/1	…		
Sirur …	…	…	…	…	…	…	559/1	…	…	…		
Yerrowda …	…	…	…	…	…	…	…	…	37/Det.	…		
Ganesh Khind …	…	…	…	…	…	…	…	…	14/Det.	…		
Karachi …	…	149/1	…	1	6	…	…	478/⅛	825/1	…	General Officer Commanding Sind District.	
Hyderabad …	…	159/1	…	1	6	…	…	225/⅜	838/1	…		§ See Note.
Jacobabad …	…	…	…	…	…	…	§130/⅜	…	791/1	…		
Poolaji …	…	…	…	…	…	…	30/Det.	…	…	…		
Shahpur …	…	…	…	…	…	…	30/Det.	…	…	…		
Lehri …	…	…	…	…	…	…	35/Det.	…	…	…		
Sui …	…	…	…	…	…	…	47/Det.	…	…	…		
Ghoranari …	…	…	…	…	…	…	34/Det.	…	…	…		

Toj ...	...	...	...	...	...	...	25 / *Det.*	...	...	...		
Kushmore ...	...	...	...	...	...	...	...	...	14 / *Det.*	...		
Thull ...	...	...	...	...	...	...	...	...	14 / *Det.*	...		
Belgaum ...	...	186 / 1	...	1	6	...	...	552 / ½	1,618 / 1½	...	General Officer Commanding Belgaum District.	
Kolhapur ...	...	...	...	...	...	...	...	97 / ½	...	...		
Dharwar ...	...	...	...	...	...	...	...	...	345 / ½	...		
Kaladgi ...	...	...	...	...	...	...	...	...	82 / ½	...		
Aden ...	...	...	920 / 3	2	...	...	‖ 100 / ½	595 / 4½	674 / 1	94 / 1	General Officer Commanding Aden Force.	‖ Aden Troop.
Perim ...	...	...	...	...	...	...	...	...	50 / *Det.*	...		
Quetta ...	...	¶ 90 / 1	111 / 1	2	6	... (c)	364 / ½	9½ / 1	1004 / 2	96 / 1	General Officer Commanding Quetta District. (b)	¶ Mountain mule.
New Bazaar ...	...	...	...	...	...	...	91 / ½		416 / ½	...		
Sharigh ...	...	...	...	...	...	...	91 / ½		416 / ½	...		
Thal-Chotiali ...	...	910 / 1	...	1	6	...	273 / ¾	(c)	624 / ½	...		
Sibi ...	...	...	...	...	...	...	182 / 36		...	...		
Thulli and Quat Mandi ...	...	...	...	...	...	...	91 / ½		208 / 36	...		
	186 / 1	1,698 (d)	570 / 4	17	70	...	3178 / 7	5,205 / 7	10358 / 36	482 / 5		(d) Includes 385 natives.

(a) Native mountain battery.
(b) *Note.*—The garrison fixed by Military Department No. 118 S.D., dated 22nd June 1883, is shewn.
(c) Approximate.

Total ... { British ... 7,332
Natives ... 23,401 }

The Volunteer force in the Bombay Presidency consists of—

Great Indian Peninsula Railway Volunteers	...	1,006	Head-quarters,	Bombay.
Bombay Volunteers	...	652	„	„
„ Cadets	...	124	„	„
Bombay, Baroda and Central India Railway Cadets	...	249	„	„
Sind Cadets	...	310	„	Karachi.
Rajputana Cadets	...	542	„	Ajmir.
Total	...	1,983		

I have not been able to get very reliable information about the number of Europeans in the Bombay presidency; but it may be taken for granted that there are at least 3,000 able-bodied adult Europeans, besides the volunteers.

It would also be necessary to provide armoured trains at the following places: Khandwa, Manmad, Bombay, Poona, Dhond, Surat, Ahmedabad, and Ajmir.

From a consideration of the above, I find that the total force in the Bombay presidency is as follows:—

Horse artillery.	Field artillery.	Mountain artillery.	Garrison artillery.	British cavalry.	British infantry.	Native cavalry.	Native infantry.	Sappers.	Volunteers.
1	8	3	5	1	7	7	26	5	1,983

And of this we require for internal defence—

Horse artillery.	Field artillery	Mountain artillery.	Garrison artillery.	British cavalry.	British infantry.	Native cavalry.	Native infantry.	Volunteers.
2	7	0	11¾	1½	7	4½	15	3,500

Therefore we are short of one horse artillery battery (but for this a field battery can be substituted), 6¾ batteries garrison artillery, ½ regiment British cavalry, and some 1,600 volunteers, which, however, could be made up from the 3,000 able-bodied Europeans noted above; and these could undoubtedly also supply men for the garrison artillery short. The result of these figures therefore is that no British troops whatever could be spared from this presidency, and only 3½ regiments of Native cavalry, 11 regiments of Native infantry, 5 companies sappers, and 3 batteries mountain artillery.

I understand that there are no places of refuge, properly so called, in Bombay at all. Therefore there is no doubt that early arrangements should be made to collect all the women and children, and either send them on boardship, or distribute them in a few safe places; and I consider it of the utmost importance that places of refuge should at once be arranged for at Sukkur (for Shikarpur), Larkhana, Dhulia, Manmar, Nasik, Dharwar, Kolhapur, and Bijapur. There are forts in existence at Ahmednagar, Belgaum, Satara, Neemuch, Surat, Sholapur, and the sooner these are made suitable for small garrisons the better.

CENTRAL INDIA.

Sir Henry Daly, writing on 11th August 1879, No. 1227, says there are 71 Native States in Central India, big and little, with a population of about 1½ millions, and an area of about 89,000 square miles.

" Four of the States, composed chiefly of Rajputs, are held by Mahrattas—
" Scindia, Holkar, Dhar, Dewas,—who almost within the memory of living
" man ruled by plunder and bloodshed. Peace and order, established by the

"British Government and maintained by British garrisons, bringing with them "security, have now brought the people to habits of industry and almost con- "tentment. But the feeling displayed in 1857-58 by Rajput Thakurs towards "Scindia, round Gwalior and Holkar in Malwa, showed that the old spirit is "not dead. A word would have put them in arms.

"The Muhammadan rulers, especially Bhopal and Jowra, foreigners "though they are, have been more fortunate in winning their hold on the "people. Their rule is popular.

"In Bundelkhand, amongst Bundels, Ahirs, Gujars, the feeling towards "the Chiefs is feudatory and strong. The same amongst Baghels. Despite "oppression and hard poverty, the spirit is loyal to the hereditary Chief.

"With regard to the state of feeling in Native States towards the British "Government, my experience confirms the observations and conclusions of "Colonel Sutherland, than whom no sounder Englishman has lived amongst the "Chiefs and people of India, that in Native States and Native Courts the pre- "sence of an English officer is hailed as a safeguard against oppression. The "visit of the Governor General's Agent to a Native Court, his passage through "a State, is the event of the year. Chiefs and people invest the Agent with "mysterious influence, and all receive his camp with acclamation. The Chief "thinks his position and dignity strengthened. Thakurs and subjects hold that "they owe peace and prosperity to the great Government which the Agent "represents. The Agent comes into no collision. He has nothing to assess: no "tax to levy. He is the mediator between the people and the Chief, between "the Chief and the Government of India.

"This feeling plainly spoke in results during the troubled time of 1857-58. "While in British territory an Englishman hardly found a resting place for "his feet, in Native States he was welcomed and sheltered.

"*Elements of danger*.—Under this head general opinion, handed down from "the days when the armies of Scindia and Holkar struggled with the British "for mastery, holds that the armies of the present day are still formidable, and "that Scindia's is specially so as he passes thousands of his subjects through "the ranks, thus making reserves of his people.

"The Political Agent, in reviewing the state of the Gwalior regular army "in March last, having seen all available paraded at a camp of exercise, com- "manded by the Maharaja, reported that recruiting had not kept pace with the "dismissals, resignations, and casualties. The force was 2,100 combatants "below the treaty number of all arms of disciplined troops (*viz.*, 7,200).

"The men who form this force are mainly drawn from the British prov- "inces. The cavalry (about 1,200) are chiefly Muhammadans from the North- "Western Provinces, with pay of Rs. 22 per mensem; infantry (3,600), Rs. 7 "(Chandoree). In this body there may be 800 or 900 Gwalior subjects, mostly "wandering Muhammadans—a poor class. There is not a Mahratta in the "ranks. The few Mahrattas who remain are silladars in the irregular service.

"The artillery are efficient and well cared for—two batteries of 6-pounders, "horsed; five field batteries, 9-pounders (bullocks); two 18-pounders (elephants). "The treaty number (480) is not maintained, the present strength being about "100 short. The men are chiefly our own Poorbeahs, with some 50 or 60 men "from the Deccan. The high price of food which has prevailed in Gwalior "during two years of famine has led to a reduction in the Gwalior force through "resignations and dismissals. The element of danger here would be, supposing "mutiny in the Indian Army, the effect on British-born sepoys in the Gwalior "service; but there is little in that poorly-armed body to cause anxiety.

"*Indore.*—Holkar has no army worthy the name. Three regiments of "Poorbeahs, fairly drilled; cavalry, also from British India, badly drilled and "mounted. The artillery (bullocks) in use is good and well appointed, manned "by Poorbeahs.

"Bhopal has a small body of troops in fair order for the work they "have to do.

"In Bundelkhand the people are a warlike race, and capable of being first "class soldiers; but they shrink from regular service. Every man bears sword "and matchlock.

"*Baghelkhand, Rewah.*—The Thakurs and Baghels are a splendid body "of men, living in a state of semi-independence. The disciplined soldiers in "the service of Rewah were chiefly refugees—British sepoys of the mutiny "period,—now dying out.

"One conspicuous element of danger in 1857-58 was the want of roads "through Native States in which rebel sepoys sought shelter and plunder. "That difficulty has been removed. Metalled roads now intersect Bundelkhand, "Malwa, and Central India. Mhow, which was unapproachable in the rains "of 1857, is now linked to Gwalior by a metalled road. The rail courses past "it, and will soon be at Neemuch and in communication with Nasirabad and "Agra by the Rajputana State Railway.

"Whenever our next struggle comes, guns will play a prominent part "against us. The superiority of our small arms will be even more conspicuous "than heretofore; but the number and weight of guns must always tell in "a country in which the people may be hostile. Scindia's army, which we see "composed of old Poorbeahs and discharged sepoys, indifferently armed, is to "my mind a small matter; but the serviceable guns which he and Holkar "could put into the field—probably not less than 300,—few of which we see, "is far from being a small matter. In Bundelkhand there is hardly a big city "in which the art of gun-making is unknown. Natives in this respect have "not lost their cunning nor their taste. My views are that our garrison, espe-"cially Native States, should be few and so strong as to be beyond question, "and that we should leave the rest to the people themselves, with here and "there local corps with selected officers living amongst them."

The following statement shews the distribution of troops now maintained in the territory under the Government of the Central India Agency :—

Stations.	Artillery. Batteries. Horse.	Field.	Garrison.	Total.	Guns.	Cavalry. Regiments of British cavalry.	Regiments of Native cavalry.	Infantry. Regiments of British infantry.	Regiments of Native infantry.	Sappers and Miners. Companies.	Military Authority.	Remarks.
Gwalior	...	...	104/1	1	...	...	...	316/½	32/Det.	...	General Officer Commanding Gwalior District.	
Morar	...	*248/2	...	2	12	...	512/1, 40/Det.	808/1	1026/2	...		* Includes 1 heavy field battery.
Sipri	...	...	...	...	...	...		...	...	...		
Nowgong	...	156/1	...	1	6	...	324/½	141/½	686/½	...	General Officer Commanding Saugor District.	
Sutna	...	...	...	...	...	...	80/½	...	...	...		
Mhow	...	†248/2	...	2	12	298/1	...	647/½	333/1	...	General Officer Commanding Mhow Division.	† 1 heavy field battery.
Indore	...	...	...	...	...	...	...	112/½	271/½	...		
Mehidpur	...	...	...	...	...	...	...	...	30/½	...		
Asirgarh	...	...	...	...	...	...	...	198/½	...	...		
Augur	...	...	...	...	...	...	493/1	...	...	...		Under the orders of the Agent to the Governor General for Central India.
Goona	...	...	...	...	...	...	493/1	...	...	...		
Sirdarpur	...	...	...	...	...	...	...	...	616/1	...		
Sehore	...	...	...	...	...	...	...	...	648/1	...		
Total ...	...	667/4	104/2	6	30	298/1	1612/3½	2148/2½	4891/6	...		

Total { British ... 3,298
Native ... 6,633

There are no volunteers and too few Europeans in the Central India Agency to enable me to count on any aid from these sources; but in considering the requirements of the Bombay presidency, which furnishes most of the troops employed in these districts, I have provided a garrison for Mhow of one garrison battery and four companies British infantry. Round this all the Europeans in the Indore State would concentrate; and I have also provided a moveable column of—

Horse artillery.	Field artillery.	British cavalry.	British infantry.	Native cavalry.	Native infantry.
1	1	$\frac{1}{2}$	2	1	3

To Neemuch half battery garrison artillery and two companies British infantry; and this would afford protection to Europeans from the Northern States of the Central India Agency, as well as to many from Rajputana, while the moveable columns from Mhow and Nasirabad would still further protect this place in case of necessity.

In addition I think the Gwalior Fort should be strongly held by one garrison battery, four companies British infantry and all Europeans and Eurasians from the neighbouring States, and a moveable column of—

Horse artillery.	Field artillery.	British infantry.	British cavalry.	Native cavalry.	Native infantry.
1	1	1	$\frac{1}{2}$	1	3

should be maintained to keep Scindia in check, as well as any other chiefs who might be disposed to be turbulent. I will note the necessary arrangements for the protection of Bandelkhand, and of the portions of the Central Agency east of the strip of British territory which runs down from Jhansi to Saugor, when I come to speak of the Central Provinces.

The total force at present maintained in the Central India Agency is—

Field artillery.	Heavy artillery.	Garrison artillery.	British cavalry.	British infantry.	Native cavalry.	Native infantry.
3	2	1	1	$2\frac{5}{8}$	$3\frac{4}{8}$	6

I have provided for Mhow and Gwalior from the Bombay and Bengal Armies—

Horse artillery.	Field artillery.	Garrison artillery.	British cavalry.	British infantry.	Native cavalry.	Native infantry.
2	2	2	1	3	2	6

so that it is evident that only $1\frac{1}{2}$ regiments Native cavalry can be spared, and one more battery field or horse artillery, one garrison artillery, and $\frac{3}{8}$ths of British infantry will have to be added to the garrison.

Armoured trains should be provided at Mhow, Neemuch, Gwalior, and Bhopal.

RAJPUTANA.

The Agent to the Governor General in Rajputana, Colonel Bradford, gives his opinion in regard to the state of feeling and elements of danger in the provinces under his supervision as follows:—

"I may confidently assert that throughout the British district of Ajmir "and the State of Rajputana, whether Rajput, Jat, or Muhammadan, a spirit "of loyalty towards the British Government pervades all classes. Our connec-"tion with Rajputana has now lasted for more than sixty years; and during the "whole of this period, though in the exercise of the varied responsibilities of "our position we have been repeatedly compelled to interfere by force of arms "either to prevent the anarchy caused by mal-administration on the one hand, "or unprovoked rebellion on the other, or to put an end to the forays of predatory "tribes, in no one instance has there been any sign of disaffection towards our- "selves, or any disposition to combine in resistance to our authority, on the part "of the population of Rajputana. It would be too much to assume that the "interference we have so often been forced to exercise has been welcome to those "on whose behalf it has been required; but, at any rate, it has never been "actively resented by any class. And this I believe to be due to the moderation "we have invariably displayed in our dealings with these States, and to the "prompt withdrawal of our forces on the attainment of the objects with which "they were despatched

"The confidence which the chiefs and people of Rajputana have learnt to "repose in the justice and magnanimity of the British Government, and the "certainty they feel that we shall never place too strict and too literal an inter- "pretation on the compacts which bind them to us, reconcile them to their "subordinate position and to acquiescence without demur in the restrictions we "find it necessary from time to time to impose both on the authority of the "chiefs and on the pretensions of the nobles. So long, then, as we adhere to "the principles that have hitherto guided us in our dealings with the Rajput- "ana State, we may, I feel sure, count on the continued loyalty of the inhabit- "ants.

"The motives which keep the different classes faithful to us may possibly "vary; but it may be said of the people generally that they are wedded to old "traditions, and free from the restlessness and love of change so characteristic "of some other Indian races.

"*Elements of danger.*—The first consideration naturally occurring to those "not brought personally into contact with these Rajput States is, that there "must be a danger of an effective combination of the chiefs against us. The "possibility of this has been repeatedly urged as a reason for maintaining a larger "body of troops than would be necessary if this element of danger could be elimi- "nated from our calculations. So far as Rajputana is concerned, I believe that "it may be left out of consideration. I have alluded to the only circumstances "which, in my opinion, could unite the conflicting interests of the different "parties so invariably found in every State in Rajputana; but I can conceive "no possible train of circumstances by which a treasonable movement, if set "on foot in one State, would affect simultaneously any of the others. The "jealousies which have for centuries existed, and still exist, between the various "Durbars are so inveterate, that not even the proposed annexation of one State "would rouse the others to arms in its defence; and so strong is my conviction "that these causes would infallibly prevent any combined action against us, "that, in considering the military requirements of the province, such an even- "tuality need not be taken seriously into account. Granting, however, for the "sake of argument that such a combination is possible, it follows that for it to "be successful it must be supported by force of arms; and in that case it might "fairly be asked whether the armies maintained by the State of Rajputana are "not, or could not, become a source of danger to us. To this I would reply "that there is no State in the whole province that has a body of men who "would dare to take the field against a very much weaker detachment of dis- "ciplined troops.

"The terms in which I have spoken of the efficiency of these armies gener- "ally require some qualification if applied to Bhurtpur. There are in all "1,460 regular cavalry and 3,000 regular infantry in Bhurtpur of the tribe "of which the chief is the head; and their fidelity to him is consequently more "assured than is the case with the bodies of men employed by the other chiefs; "their organization and discipline is also slightly better. The conclusion to "be drawn from these observations is that, as far as regards imperial interests, "no real elements of danger exist in Rajputana; but that in a country where the "whole population is armed, and the criminal tribes are still unreclaimed, we "must always be prepared for sudden outbreaks on a small scale. Against such "insignificant occurrences there is no necessity to make special provision."

The distribution of the troops now maintained in the territory under the Government of the Rajputana Agency is as follows:—

Stations.		Artillery.					Cavalry.		Infantry.		Sappers and Miners.	Military Authority.	Remarks.
		Batteries.											
		Horse.	Field.	Garrison.	Total.	Guns.	Regiments of British cavalry.	Regiments of Native cavalry.	Regiments of British infantry.	Regiments of Native infantry.	Companies.		
Nasirabad	...	...	156 / 1	...	1	6	...	156 / ½	601 / ½	818 / 1	...	General Officer Commanding Mhow Division.	
Neemuch	...	...	138 / 1	...	1	6	...	395 / ½	267 / ½	527 / ½	...		
Deoli	...	...	...	...	...	...	...	167 / ½	...	712 / 1	...		Under the Agent to the Governor General for the States of Rajputana.
Erinpura	...	...	...	...	...	...	...	164 / ½	...	634 / 1	...		
Khairwara	...	...	...	...	...	...	...	...	...	691 / 1	...		
Ajmir	...	...	...	...	...	...	...	...	...	712 / 1	...		
Total	...	...	294 / 2	...	2	12	...	882 / 1½	868 / 1	4094 / 5½			

Total { British ... 1,162
Native ... 4,976

In Rajputana there are between 800 and 1,000 adult males who might be considered effective as combatants in case of necessity.

A garrison has been provided for Nasirabad in considering the wants of the Bombay presidency of ½ battery garrison artillery and 200 British infantry; and it is probable that to these may be added some 300 adult European and Eurasian males. This, with the provision of a fortified place of refuge at Abu and another in Taragarh at Ajmir, for each of which ½ garrison battery and 1 company British infantry should be provided, will be sufficient for the protection of all the Europeans in the province, the precaution having, if possible, been here taken, as in all other provinces, of getting rid of as many non-combatants as possible beforehand.

I have also provided a moveable column for Nasirabad of—

Field artillery.	British infantry.	Native cavalry.	Native infantry.
1	1	1	2

and I consider that, with the aid it might receive from Ahmedabad, Mhow, or Delhi, this will be quite sufficient to maintain order.

The total force now maintained in Rajputana consists of—

Field artillery.	British infantry.	Native cavalry.	Native infantry.
2	1	$1\frac{1}{8}$	$5\frac{1}{2}$

We require for internal defence—

	British infantry.	Garrison artillery.	Field artillery.	Native infantry.
Garrisons	$\frac{3}{8}$	$\frac{3}{4}$	0	0
Moveable columns ...	1	1	1	2

so that the present garrison of Rajputana would have to be increased by $\frac{3}{8}$ British infantry and $\frac{3}{4}$ garrison artillery, while $\frac{1}{8}$ Native cavalry and $3\frac{1}{2}$ Native infantry could be spared for exterior operations.

It would be advisable to maintain an armoured train at Nasirabad.

CENTRAL PROVINCES.

"In the Central Provinces there do not appear to be many signs of "danger; the population is mostly agricultural with no ambitious tradi- "tions, and not tied together by a hereditary and territorial bond. On the "other hand, there is a large aboriginal population in a low state of civiliza- "tion, who may easily be led astray by men of superior position; so that "in times of excitement there might be small rebellions at various points, "yet none of sufficient magnitude to cause anxiety need be apprehended.

"The chief places in the Central Provinces are—Nagpur, the head- "quarters of Government, with a large native population (84,444, Kampti "48,831). It was the residence of two former dynasties, Gond and Mahratta, "and there is a fort and arsenal at Sitabuldi. Jabalpur has a population of "55,188; it is the head-quarters of a Commissionership; it has a consider- "able European and Eurasian population (477); it is the junction of the "Great Indian Peninsula and East Indian Railways, and commands the "passage of the Nurbada. Saugor (population 46,655) has an importance "owing to its being the head-quarters of one of our districts, and because it "forms a good position for the control of the Bundelas. Nowgong is also "a place of importance; and when the railway from Bhopal to Jhansi and "Manikpur is finished, there may be other points."

These places should be garrisoned as follows:—

	British infantry.	Garrison artillery.	Native infantry.
Sitabuldi } Nagpur }	$\frac{4}{8}$	1	0
Saugor	$\frac{3}{8}$	$\frac{1}{8}$	0
Jabalpur	$\frac{3}{8}$	$\frac{4}{8}$	0
Nowgong	$\frac{1}{8}$	$\frac{4}{8}$	0
Raipur	0	0	$\frac{4}{8}$
Sambalpur	0	0	$\frac{4}{8}$
Total ...	$1\frac{3}{8}$	$2\frac{1}{8}$	1

and I think there should be moveable columns as under :—

		British infantry.	Field artillery.	Native cavalry.	Native infantry.
Nagpur	...	4/8	1	1/2	1
Saugor	...	2/8	1/2	1/2	1
Jabalpur	...	3/8	1/2	1/2	1
Nowgong	...	3/8	1/2	1/2	1
Total	...	1 4/8	2 1/2	2	4

There are no volunteers in the Central Provinces; but there are about 1,050 British-born males, exclusive of soldiers, and this should produce at least 250 men capable of bearing arms in an emergency.

The following is the distribution of the troops now maintained in the territory under the Government of the Central Provinces :—

Stations.		Artillery. Batteries. Horse.	Field.	Garrison.	Total.	Guns.	Cavalry. Regiments of British cavalry.	Regiments of Native cavalry.	Infantry. Regiments of British infantry.	Regiments of Native infantry.	Sappers & Miners. Companies.	Military Authority.	Remarks.
Jabalpur	...	...	...	...	...	...	...	66 1/8	631 3/8	775 1	...	General Officer Commanding Saugor District.	
Saugor	...	...	156 1	...	1	6	...	434 4/8	201 3/8	773 1	...		
Kampti	...	...	164 1	...	1	6	...	373 1	506 1	1,668 2	...	General Officer Commanding Nagpur Force.	
Sitabuldi	...	...	...	...	...	...	...	...	46 *Det.*	446 4/8	115 1		
Raipur	...	...	...	...	...	...	...	...	...	763 1	...		
Hoshangabad	...	...	...	...	...	...	...	...	...	358 4/8	...		
Sambalpur	...	...	...	...	...	...	...	...	...	325 4/8	...		
Total	...	...	2	...	...	...	...	1 5/8	2	6 4/8	...		

The total force maintained in the Central Provinces now is—

Field artillery.	British infantry.	Native cavalry.	Native infantry.
2	2	1 5/8	6 4/8

We require for internal defence—

Field artillery.	Garrison artillery.	British infantry.	Native cavalry.	Native infantry.
2½	2½	2⅘	2	4

Therefore while ½ field artillery, 2 garrison artillery, and ⅘ British infantry are required to make up the necessary garrison, 2½ Native infantry can be spared for exterior operations.

I have already noted that there should be armoured trains at Khandwa and Bhopal, and these, with trains at Jabalpur, Nagpur, and Amraoti, should for the present be sufficient. No doubt with the extension of railways more will be required hereafter.

MADRAS.

All authorities are agreed that there would be very little danger of rebellion in the Madras presidency. My task in this case is therefore very much simplified; but still we must not forget that there are the large Native States of Mysore and Travancore in its limits, and the descendants of Tippoo have not yet died out, while there have been serious riots in some parts of it lately.

The places which it is absolutely necessary to hold in strength are as follows :—

	British infantry.	Garrison artillery.	Volunteers.	Native infantry.
Madras	⅖	1	700	0
Bangalore	⅖	½	400	0
Cannanore	⅕	0	0	0
Maliapuram	⅕	0	0	0
Calicut	⅕	0	0	0
Mangalore	0	0	0	½
Quilon, Trichore, Trivandrum	0	0	0	½
Bellary	⅕	½	0	0
Vellore	0	0	0	1
Vizianagram	0	0	0	½
Berhampore	0	0	0	½
Cuttack	0	0	0	½
Trichinopoly	0	0	0	1
Total ...	1⅗	2	1,100	4½

Besides the above, there should be moveable columns at the following places :—

	British infantry.	Field artillery.	Native cavalry.	Native infantry.
Bellary	⅘	1	½	2
Arcot	0	1	½*	1
Salem	-	½	1	1
Bangalore	⅘	½	1	1
Total ...	1⅗	3	3	5

* Body-Guard.

The distribution of the troops now maintained in the territory under the Government of Madras is as follows:—

Stations.	Artillery. Batteries. Horse.	Artillery. Batteries. Field.	Artillery. Batteries. Garrison.	Artillery. Batteries. Total.	Guns.	Cavalry. Regiments of British cavalry.	Cavalry. Regiments of Native cavalry.	Infantry. Regiments of British infantry.	Infantry. Regiments of Native infantry.	Sappers and Miners. Companies.	Military Authority.	Remarks.
Fort St. George ...	...	...	46/⅛	⅛	...	...	...	614/¾	1,621/2	...	General Officer Commanding Eastern District.	
Pallavaram* ...	...	...	...	...	...	...	...	...	502/½	...		* 53 artillery veterans not included.
St. Thomas' Mount ...	...	317/2	65/⅛	2⅛	12	...	...	...	299	...		
Vellore ...	...	...	...	...	...	...	...	...	822/1	...		
Vizagapatam† (Waltair) ...	...	...	...	...	...	...	...	...	734/¾	...		† 12 infantry veterans not included.
Samalkot ...	...	...	...	...	...	...	...	...	100/⅛	...		
Vizianagram ...	...	...	...	...	...	...	...	...	809/1	...		
Berhampore ...	...	...	...	...	...	...	...	...	402/½	...		
Cuttack ...	...	...	...	...	...	...	...	...	701/1	...		

Station												Command	Remarks
Bangalore	...	160/1	311/3	...	3	18	446/1	380/1	69/1½ ‡	1,523/1½	771/5	General Officer Commanding Bangalore District.	‡ Includes 1 company Royal Engineers.
Ootacamund	...	...	...	...	...	...	...	...	...	110/½	119/1		
Trichinopoly	...	...	...	...	...	...	...	...	...	1,600/2	...		
Cannanore	...	...	...	...	...	...	...	...	797/½	799/1	...	General Officer Commanding Western District.	
Maliapuram	...	...	...	...	...	...	...	...	98/½	...	...		
Calicut	...	...	...	...	...	...	...	...	93/½	...	...		
Mangalore	...	...	...	...	...	...	...	...	...	777/1	...		
Quilon	...	...	...	...	...	...	...	...	...	619/½	...		
Trichore	...	...	...	...	...	...	...	...	...	138/½	...		
Trivandrum	...	...	...	...	...	...	...	...	...	83/½	...		
Bellary	...	...	161/1	...	1	6	...	385/1	919/1	1,652/2	...	General Officer Commanding Ceded Districts.	
Total	...	160/1	789/5	111/1	7	36	446/1	765/2	3,487/4½	13,372/16½	890/6		

Total { British ... 4,993
Native ... 15,027 }

M

Nair Brigade.

Stations.	Artillery field batteries.	Guns.	Native cavalry regiments.	Native infantry regiments.	Body-Guards.	Remarks.
Trivandrum and outposts ...	30	4	...	$\frac{1420}{2}$	159	

Total Natives 1,609.

Mysore Troops.

Stations.	Artillery.	Guns.	Native cavalry regiments.	Native infantry regiments.	Remarks.
Bangalore	...	...	$\frac{408}{1}$	$\frac{651}{1}$	
Mysore	...	...	$\frac{408}{1}$	$\frac{651}{1}$	
Shimoga	...	...	$\frac{408}{1}$	$\frac{651}{1}$	
Total ...	...	...	$\frac{1,224}{3}$	$\frac{1,953}{3}$	

Total Natives 3,177.

The volunteers in the Madras Presidency consist of—

Madras Volunteer Artillery Guards ...	93	Head-quarters,	Madras.
Madras Volunteer Guards	612	"	"
Bangalore Volunteers	298	"	Bangalore.
Bangalore Cadets	100	"	"
Nilgiri Volunteers	240	"	Ootacamund.
Total ...	1,343		

No further aid could be looked for from the European population.

The total requirements therefore for the internal defence of the presidency would appear to be—

	British infantry.	Garrison artillery.	Field artillery.	Native cavalry.	Native infantry.	Volunteers.
Garrisons	$1\frac{3}{4}$	2	0	0	$4\frac{1}{2}$	1,100
Moveable columns.	1	0	$2\frac{3}{4}$	2	4	0
Total ...	$2\frac{3}{4}$	2	$2\frac{3}{4}$	2	$8\frac{1}{2}$	1,100

The total force at present maintained in the Madras Presidency is—

Horse artillery.	Field artillery.	Garrison artillery.	British cavalry.	British infantry.	Native cavalry.	Native infantry.	Sappers.	Volunteers.
2	8	7	2	9½	4	32	10	1,343.

and there would therefore remain as disposable for exterior operations—

Horse artillery.	Field artillery.	British cavalry.	British infantry.	Native cavalry.	Native infantry.	Sappers.	Volunteers.
2	6	2	7½	2	24	10	243.

HYDERABAD.

The state of feeling and elements of danger in the Berars and Hyderabad is thus described by Sir Richard Meade writing in 1872 :—

(c) State of feeling.

"The state of feeling of the people in His Highness the Nizam's domi-"nions may be considered under two heads, *viz.*, "in regard to its bearing (1) towards the Nizam's "Government, and (2) towards the British Government, the relations between "which are so close and intimate, in consequence of the long-standing and still "existing treaty engagements between the two Governments.

"On this subject I would premise by stating that so lately as 25 years "ago Hyderabad was a most turbulent country, rendered so by, among other "evils, the system that then, and for many years previously, existed of farm-"ing out to contractors, saukars, Arabs, &c., the collection of the revenue, "partly in payment of their own dues, and partly on behalf of the State. "These collectors frequently sublet their contracts or entrusted their working "to naibs, who, for the maintenance of their own position, and for the purpose "of enforcing their demands, employed armed foreigners. Zemindars, and other "wealthy owners of property, again, for their own protection, also employed "mercenaries. Disputes often arose between the people and the troops, or "between zemindars themselves, or sometimes these latter became refractory; "and it was hence found necessary on the part of the State to coerce them, or "otherwise to quell disturbances that arose from these causes. The Nizam's "Government frequently was unable to do this, and called on the Resident to "assist with the Contingent troops, which were employed on the duty after the "Resident had first satisfied himself that such was warranted by the facts of "the case. In this manner, the people of the country became familiar with the "use of arms; and being at liberty to move about armed at all times, they "gained for themselves the reputation of being a class who were always ready "to fight. They continue still to carry arms as they did at the period here "referred to; and there is thus at the capital and throughout the Nizamat "a large class of men used to arms, and in case of disturbance the element for "feeding the same will not be found wanting.

"The agricultural classes, as distinguished from the armed class de-"scribed above, are a peace-loving people, who have been much oppressed by "the unprincipled and grasping officials who have been put in authority over "them. They appear to chafe much under the present system, which has given "employment to a large number of strangers from other parts of India, who are "generally personally unpopular, and against whose proceedings many com-"plaints are made. Most of the districts are managed by persons of this class, "who are said to fill all subordinate offices with their own relations and friends, "and there is much discontent in consequence.

"The Nizam, while still a vassal of the Mogul empire, and before he "assumed independence, had created a class of nobles and sirdars in Hyderabad, "upon whom he conferred grants of land or the State revenues for their own "support and the maintenance of their retainers, on conditions which generally "conveyed to them hereditary rights in such grants. Any interference with "these rights in after-years was invariably resisted by the grantees; and where "such interference was persisted in, disturbance and bloodshed were the "result.

"The zemindars and hereditary landholders are described as being in "some cases much dissatisfied with the course His Highness's Government "has for some time past taken towards certain persons of their own class. "These classes are much connected by intermarriages; and individual griev-"ances are commented on by many, far and near. The contrast between "Berar and Hyderabad in the treatment of the rights of hereditary landhold-"ers is much discussed amongst them. The British Government does not "interfere with the internal administration of Hyderabad, and the grievances "of these classes have not as yet been put forward in a way to demand its "notice; but they are the cause of much complaint and dissatisfaction.

"The trading classes are generally well-disposed towards the British "Government, but not equally so towards the Nizam's—especially the bankers "at Hyderabad, who have large unsettled claims against His Highness's Gov-"ernment. Every description of article comprising the home trade finds its "way into the Hyderabad country. The exports are limited. No oppression "is exercised towards traders; but they find some difficulty in recovering their "dues from the nobles and others at the capital, as they receive very little "assistance from the courts.

"In regard to the more wealthy class mentioned above as dissatisfied—"*viz.*, the bankers,—the Nizam's Government has from time to time borrowed "large sums from numerous firms at Hyderabad which have remained unpaid "for years, to the ruin of the bankers, who have thereby in many instances "been reduced from wealth to bankruptcy. The nobles and others have "followed the example of Government; and while decrees are often given in "favour of complainants against such persons by the courts, no adequate assist-"ance is rendered in obtaining execution of the same, and the decrees are thus "in many cases of no use whatever.

"These remarks will explain the ground for the opinion I entertain that "the state of feeling of the people throughout the Hyderabad territory cannot "be described as one of contentment and good-will towards His Highness's "Government; and where the feeling is not one of discontent, it may perhaps "be best described as one of indifference.

"This feeling has to some extent extended itself towards British officers, "to whom in the interior ill-will is occasionally shown, the slightest provoca-"tion on the part of a European being apt to be immediately, and sometimes "violently, resented. It is, at the same time, a fact that persons of all classes, "who are discontented with the existing system and state of things, appear "to look for relief from the action sooner or later of the British Government.

"While expressing myself thus freely on this point, I do not question "the existence, amongst certain classes and persons, of good feeling towards the "Executive. Those who are exceptionally well treated, or who compose or are "connected with those in power, and may be termed the ministerial party, are "well content. These, however, are, as a rule, cordially disliked by the more "influential of the court or Hyderabad party. Their ranks are filled from

"Hindustan; and the Nizam's own subjects are naturally indignant at seeing "the State favours in a large degree allotted to, and almost appropriated by, "persons whom they consider to have no claims thereto.

"Surrounded as Hyderabad is by British territory, no immediate external "elements of danger exist. The internal elements of danger, I regret to say, "are more serious. Apart from the sources of evil mentioned above, wherein "exists the nucleus of future possible trouble, the condition and character of "the armed forces of the State are, and must always continue to be, a subject "of anxiety so long as they are maintained as at present.

"Besides, the two British forces, called the Hyderabad Subsidiary Force "and Hyderabad Contingent, which are maintained under treaty for all mili-"tary purposes in the Hyderabad country, large State forces and levies are "kept up, the greater part of which are located in the city of Hyderabad and "its suburbs. One of these is the force termed the "reformed troops," the "cost of which must be greatly in excess of the services it renders, at present "at all events. This force has a political significance, to which I shall refer "by and bye.

"Another element of insecurity is to be found in the system permitted at "Hyderabad by which almost every nobleman maintains a set of armed re-"tainers at the expense of the State, who are so attached to the person of "their master as to forget the allegiance and obedience they owe to the head "of the Government, against whom they would probably not hesitate to act, "if prompted to do so by their immediate superior.

"Possible trouble might also be found to spring from the free admission "into Hyderabad of foreigners from Hindustan, who, in the event of any *émeute* "occurring from religious or other causes, would probably sympathise with and "join in the same. As long as the Hyderabad Subsidiary Force is located at "Secunderabad, and the Hyderabad Contingent garrisons Bolarum and other "stations in the Nizam's country, no serious danger from this cause need, how-"ever, it is thought, be apprehended. The British troops of these forces at the "capital are quite sufficient to cope with the armed rabble of the city, even if "it were joined by the Nizam's reformed troops, who are mostly recruited from "Hindustanis. Should, however, a *general rising* take place in the city against "His Highness's Government, in which the Arabs and other levies took part, "the case would no doubt be one of much gravity. In such event the rebels "would at once secure the persons of the Nizam and his chief nobles, whose "residences surround the palace, and hold them and His Highness's family as "hostages; and the operations of the British force against the city under such "circumstances would be attended with much difficulty and risk, as there would "be fully 25,000 armed men to oppose it in any attempt to suppress the out-"break and rescue the chief.*"

The troops within the territory of the Nizam's Government are—

	Horse artillery.	Field artillery.	Heavy artillery.	British cavalry.	British infantry.	Native cavalry.	Native infantry.	Sappers.	Volunteers.
Hyderabad Subsidiary Force	1	1	1	1	2	1	4	2	382
" Contingent ...	0	4 N.	0	0	0	4	6	0	0
Total ...	1	5	1	1	2	5	10	2	382

* A late and very well informed authority remarked here: "Hyderabad is thoroughly danger-"ous, and is almost certain to be in confusion if any serious trouble occurs. The city is hostile, "and the country full of armed ruffians."

These consist of troops under command of British officers. Besides, there are troops and police of the Nizam's Government as follows :—

Details of Troops.	Men of all Grades.			Cattle.	
	Combatants.	Non-combatants.	Total.	Horses.	Bullocks.
I.—Dewani Troops.					
(1) *Reformed Regular Troops*—					
(*a*) Cavalry (4 regiments)	1.263	444	1,707	1,227	...
(*b*) Artillery (3 batteries)	351	170	521	140	53
(*c*) Infantry (3 regiments)	2,297	218	2,515	...	...
Total (1) ...	3,911	832	4,743	1.367	53
(2) *Reformed City Troops*—					
(*d*) Infantry (2 regiments)	1.458	128	1,586	...	...
(*e*) His Highness the Nizam's own regiment of Arabs and Rohillas, or "Jamait Nizam-i-Myboob."	935	179	1,114	...	...
Total (2) ...	2,393	307	2,700	...	...
Totals (1) and (2) ...	6,304	1,139	7,443	1,367	53
(3) *Irregular Troops*—					
(*f*) Cavalry	3,604	292	3,896	3,616	...
(*g*) Dismounted Cavalry (*Barghcers*) ...	136	330	466	3	...
(*h*) Arabs	5,835	727	6,562	82	...
(*i*) Rohillas, Sindis, Turks, and Beluchis ...	1,444	47	1,491	...	...
(*j*) Sikh	906	46	952	5	...
(*k*) Rathore, Burkundauz, and Barjowan ...	8,924	540	9,464	12	...
(*l*) Loda, Aligole, and Carnatic ...	161	10	171	...	...
Total ...	21,010	1,992	23,002	3,718	...
I.—Grand Total Dewani Troops (1), (2), and (3).	27,314	3,131	30,445	5,085	53
II.—Surfi Khas Troops	5,307	1,753	7,060	338	76
III.—Pagah Troops	7,315	...	7,315	1,378	73
IV.—Minister's Troops	601	159	760	51	...
Grand Total ...	40,537	5,043	45,580	6,852	202

The strength and distribution of His Highness the Nizam's police is as follows:—

In the city and suburbs	4,606
Aurangabad	867
Beerd	526
Purbunny	571
Beder	631
Nandair	796
Nuldrug	526
Kummum	901
Nulgoondah	676
Nagur Kurnool	931
Goolburga	661
Shorapur	436
Raichore	451
Lingsugur	436
Indore	1,246
Elgimdul	751
Maiduck	603
Total ...	15.615

The force is mostly armed with swords and firearms.

Besides these, Sir R. Meade records that "almost every nobleman maintains a set of armed retainers."

It is therefore pretty evident that our forces in Hyderabad are not too numerous if we are to keep the whole of the Nizam's dominions in quiet; but if, on the other hand, the loyalty, or at least the neutrality, of the Nizam can by any means be rendered certain, it is evident that the sooner some of these native troops are got out of this country the better.

The measures which are necessary in Hyderabad may be confined to—*1st*, providing for the safety of all the Europeans; *2nd*, to keep the Nizam and the city of Hyderabad in order. For the first a proper fort should at once be provided and should be put in a state to hold all our supplies, ammunition, and non-combatants and a garrison of 1 garrison battery and 4 companies British infantry; and the second should be secured by the maintenance at a suitable position of a moveable column of—

Horse artillery.	Field artillery.	Heavy artillery.	British cavalry.	British infantry.	Native cavalry.	Native infantry.
1	1	1	½	1	2	5

The rest of the province not being ours should be left to take care of itself, and it is not easy to suppose that much serious resistance could be attempted in Hyderabad against us when the above force is considered, and it is remembered that the moveable columns from Poona and Bellary could be thrown into Hyderabad in a few days. Besides reinforcements could probably be spared from Bangalore.

There would therefore be required for internal defence—

Horse artillery.	Field artillery.	Heavy artillery.	Garrison artillery.	British cavalry.	British infantry.	Native cavalry.	Native infantry.	Native field artillery.
1	1	1	1	1	2½	4	7	2

and only 2 Native batteries, 1 Native cavalry, and 3 Native infantry regiments could be withdrawn, while another half battalion British infantry would have to be added to the garrison.

MYSORE.

With regard to Mysore, the Chief Commissioner, Sir J. Gordon, records that he is of opinion that the province "is particularly free from danger "from within, and that any disturbance in Coorg is unlikely; and as now the "government is in the hands of its own Raja, it is evident there is no necessity "to retain any imperial troops in Mysore, except for the protection of British "property and lives in Bangalore itself."

In Bangalore there are 973 adult European and Eurasian males, and the ordinary garrison consists of—

3 batteries Royal artillery	...	...	...	388 men.
1 regiment British cavalry	...	...	...	3,874 "
1 regiment British infantry	...	...	...	904 "
5 companies sappers	...	...	...	771 "
1 regiment Native cavalry	...	...	...	326 "
2 regiments Native infantry	...	...	...	1,523 "

It is therefore very evident that if one battery of garrison artillery and four companies of British infantry, as already allowed for in considering the defensive measures in Madras, were left to give the European adults cohesion and discipline, it would be enough, and the rest of the garrison could be withdrawn. There would therefore be available for outside purposes—

Field artillery.	British cavalry.	British infantry.	Native cavalry.	Native infantry.
1	1	½	1	2

BURMA.

In Burma there are considerable chances of excitement, and this arises from the unsteady, excitable nature of the people. Their history has accustomed them to sudden and extreme changes of political fortune; and these elements would assuredly be worked on in times of excitement, both by evil disposed persons in our own territories and by the authorities at Mandalay. These remarks apply to the pure Burmese, of whom we have in this province about 2,600,000 souls. On the other hand, the Arakanese, Talaens, and Karens are universally well affected to our Government; and, though much assistance could not be expected from them, they would certainly not join the Burmese against us.

Further, British Burma is exposed to attack in all three divisions of the province from Upper Burma; and though the Burmese army is contemptible and quite incapable of effecting anything in regular operations in the field, it would be capable of causing an immense amount of mischief if we were to show any disposition to be in action. Portions of it could penetrate far into our territory on every side, sacking the villages and slaughtering the people, or compelling them to join them. To stand on the defensive in such a case would be suicidal, and therefore the only step to take would be to invade Upper Burma.

To make British Burma fairly safe, the following measures would have to be adopted :—

Rangoon should be left to the protection of the navy and the volunteers and a battery of garrison artillery. This would produce 118 artillery, 393 volunteers, about 400 Europeans and Eurasians, and 2,000 alien races enrolled. In this, as in all places in Burma, all the women and children should be put on boardship, and either sent to Europe or to Madras.

Moulmein should be left to the protection of 105 volunteers, 150 Europeans and Eurasians, and 1,000 alien races.

Akyab would have 53 volunteers, 92 Europeans and Eurasians, and 1,000 alien races.

Bassein would have about 100 Europeans and Eurasians and 500 aliens. Prome about the same. Thayetmyo and Tonghoo would be protected by the moveable columns. All other places, Henzada, Mergui, Tavoy, Shwegeen, Amherst, Thonkwa, Sandoway, Kyouk Phyoo, and Salween, should be abandoned on the approach of serious danger as soon as the chief civil officer considered that the place could not be held on any longer. In this case the European and Eurasian inhabitants would retreat into boats and ships, which should be kept ready for them.

At Thayetmyo it would be necessary to have a garrison of ½ garrison battery and 200 Native infantry; and a moveable column consisting of 7 companies British infantry, 770 men, 1 mountain battery, 89 men, 1 company sappers, 116 men, and 16 companies Native infantry, 160 men—total about 2,700—should be equipped with both land and river transport.

At Tonghoo a garrison should be left of ½ garrison and 2 companies Native infantry, and a moveable column formed of 7 companies British infantry, 770, 1 mountain battery, 126 men, 10 companies Native infantry, 1,100 men—total about 2,000 men. At both Thayetmyo and Tonghoo an auxiliary force of as near 2,000 men each should be raised from such of the natives as seemed likely to be faithful. These should be armed and equipped and used as scouts, and for all petty guards, so as to leave the moveable columns intact. It is evident that Port Blair with 14,000 convicts could not spare a single man of its present garrison, *viz.*, 2 companies British infantry, 4 companies Native infantry.

From the foregoing it is evident Burma could not spare a single man; indeed, it would require a first rate man to keep things going with so few troops.

The railways to Alanmyo and Tonghoo should be completed, and one of the most urgent measures is the completion of a good road between Thayetmyo and Tonghoo. The river above our frontier should be torpedoed; and, in addition to the land transport for the moveable column, it will be absolutely necessary to keep up river transport for the whole of them. If a good General is left in command, and good arrangements are made for reinforcing Burma from Madras, I think we might safely hope to keep it pretty quiet.*

In another paper will be found a statement of the measures necessary to protect Rangoon from a sea attack. Owing to the paucity of troops, it is of course absolutely necessary this should be entrusted to the Royal Navy.

---

* Burma can be temporarily lost without serious harm; I mean without vital harm like Assam: except that it is very rich; its loss would not really hurt us, and we could retake it without an effort if we held our own in the north of India. I would therefore without hesitation strip it of troops at a pinch.

The strength of the Burma Division is as follows :—

Stations.		Artillery. Batteries.					Cavalry.		Infantry.		Sappers and Miners.	Military Authority.	Remarks.
		Horse.	Field.	Garrison.	Total.	Guns.	Regiments of British cavalry.	Regiments of Native cavalry.	Regiments of British infantry.	Regiments of Native infantry.	Companies.		
Rangoon	...	...	...	118/1	1	...	...	...	650/½	966/1	116/1	General Officer Commanding British Burma Division.	
Thayetmyo	...	...	89/1*	118/1	2	6	...	...	506/½	996/1	......		* Mountain battery (mules).
Tonghoo	...	...	126/1†	...	1	4	...	...	386/½	796/1	......		† „ „ (elephants).
Moulmein	...	...	...	...	...	...	...	...	...	496/½	......		
Port Blair	...	...	...	...	...	...	...	...	143/½	302/½	......		
Camorta	...	...	...	...	...	...	...	...	...	51/Det.	......		
Total	...	...	215/2	236/2	4	10	...	...	1,685/2	3,607/4	116/1		

Total { British ... 2,136
Native ... 3,723

Besides, there are the following volunteers :—

Akyab	...	...	...	...	53
Rangoon Artillery	...	...	...	...	54
Rangoon Rifles	...	...	...	...	198
Rangoon Railway	...	...	...	...	141
Moulmeim	...	...	...	...	105
			Total	...	551

And there are adult European and Eurasian males in the province—

Arakan	...	...	...	92	after deducting volunteers as above.
Pegu	...	...	...	2,911	
Tenasserim	...	...	...	912	
				3,915	

At the following places the number of Europeans and Eurasians would form a very efficient aid for their defence :—

Rangoon, Moulmein, Akyab, and Bassein.

There are besides the following races alien to the Burmese, who, if organized, could certainly assist, *viz.*, Karens, Shans, Toungthoos, Chinese, and Siamese, 100,632 adult males. Of these, 10,000 might perhaps be organized as I have proposed.

And finally there are 7,318 police in the province.

Therefore to recapitulate, the total available strength in the province consists of—

			British and Eurasian.	Native.
Artillery and infantry	...	...	2,140	...
Volunteers	...	...	551	...
Other adult Europeans	...	...	3,915	...
Native infantry	...	...	...	3,723
Alien races	...	...	...	10,000
Police	...	...	...	7,318
			6,606	21,031

I may now shew in one glance what force it is absolutely necessary we should retain for the internal defence of India, *viz.*,—

Province.	Batteries horse artillery.	Batteries field artillery.	Batteries mountain artillery.	Batteries garrison artillery.	Regiments British cavalry.	Battalions British Infantry.	Regiments Native cavalry.	Battalions Native infantry.	Companies sappers.	Remarks.
Bengal ...	...	1	...	3	...	1½	...	3	1	Can be dispensed within three months.
Assam ...	...	...	1	...	...	...	...	1	...	
North-Western Provinces ...	2½	5	...	6	2	8	5½	11	...	

Province.	Batteries horse artillery.	Batteries field artillery.	Batteries mountain artillery.	Batteries garrison artillery.	Regiments British cavalry.	Battalions British infantry.	Regiments Native cavalry.	Battalions Native infantry.	Companies sappers.	Remarks.
Punjab ...	2	10	2	10	2 3/8	12 6/8	8	22	...	
Bombay ...	2	7	...	11 3/4	1 3/8	7	4 3/8	15	1	
Central India	2	2	...	2	1	3	2	6	...	
Rajputana ...	...	...	...	1	...	1 4/8	1	2	...	
Central Provinces ...	...	2 1/2	...	2 1/2	...	2 4/8	2	4	...	
Madras ...	1	2 1/2	...	2	...	2 3/8	2	8 1/8	...	
Hyderabad...	1	1	...	2*	1	2 1/8	4	7	...	* 1 heavy.
Burma ...	...	...	2	2	...	2	...	4	1	
Total ...	10 1/2	31	4	42	8	43 3/8	29	82 1/8	2	

The strength of the army of India as it now stands is as follows :—

Presidency.	Batteries Royal horse artillery.	Batteries field artillery.	Batteries mountain artillery.	Batteries heavy artillery.	Batteries gun artillery.	Regiments British cavalry.	Regiments Native cavalry.	Battalions British infantry.	Battalions Native infantry.	Companies sappers.	Remarks.
Bengal Presidency[1] ...	7	21	4	2	8	6	17	32	44	10	[1] Exclusive of Bombay and Madras troops in Quetta and Presidency Districts.
Troops not under His Excellency the Commander-in-Chief (Body-Guard, Punjab Frontier Force, Hyderabad, Rajputana, and Central India troops).	...	4[2]	4[3]	...	1[3]	...	10 1/8[4]	...	23	...	[2] Hyderabad Native. [3] Punjab Native.
Madras Presidency[5] ...	2	8	2[6]	1	3	2	4	9	32	10	[4] Guides 1/8, Body-Guard 3/8, Rajputana 1/8, Punjab 4, Central India 2, Hyderabad 4.
Bombay Presidency[7] ...	1	11	3	1	3	1	6	8	25	4	
Total ...	10	44	13	4	15	9	37 1/8	49	124	24	[5] Exclusive of Mysore and Nair troops. [6] 1 with elephants.
Deduct for defence ...	10 1/2	31	4	1	42	8	29	43 3/8	82 1/8	3	[7] Exclusive of troops at Aden.
Balance available ...	0 1/2*	13	9	3	0†	1	8 1/8	5 5/8	41 4/8	21	* 1/2 battery short. †27 " "

But in thus providing for the defence of India, I must state that my proposals are based on the opposition that the Russian advance will be met by us at once, and that the Russian forces are nowhere allowed to come beyond the present frontier of Afghanistan as marked in the last map of the Surveyor General.

Of course if the Russians are allowed to seize Herat, and gradually absorb up to the Hindu Kush, as the danger from them will then become so much more pronounced, the chance of rebellion in India will become much more probable, and in that case I distinctly say that the British garrison for the defence of India must be increased. According to the above figures, it would, under the circumstances of our meeting the Russian advance at once, consist of about 55,000 British troops and 520 guns; but, under the different circumstance I have described in Chapter V, it must be increased. That is, if the Russians are in possession of Herat and the Hindu Kush frontier, to at least 70,000; if they are in possession of Kabul and Kandahar, to at least 100,000 men; and if we had to fight them on our present frontier, I feel pretty sure that we could not maintain our grasp of India under 125,000 British troops.

I will now make a few general remarks on the principles which should govern the defence of India.

In meeting rebellion, one of the first necessities is to have good information, and therefore it is absolutely necessary that on the first signs of danger, that is to say *now*, all district officers should be enjoined to take immediate steps to keep themselves thoroughly well acquainted with the state of feeling and the probable elements of danger within their districts, and to keep the Government and the neighbouring districts and the chief military officer always well informed of all that goes on.

The next step which should be taken—and it is evident to be of any use it must be taken before the actual outbreak of any rebellion—is to ascertain who are the men most likely to prove leaders, and then to make arrangements effectually, but as quietly as possible, to have them seized and deported. As, however, if this was done by districts, it would inevitably fail in most districts, it should be done by an order from the Government of India to all Governments; the actual day and hour should be fixed, and at the appointed hour all dangerous characters should be seized and sent to certain selected residences. Of course it is evident that unless measures are taken at once to ascertain who are the really dangerous characters, such a measure might result in many harmless characters being seized, while many of the most dangerous escaped. Therefore all district officers should be enjoined, if they do not already do so, to keep a list of all such characters and make monthly reports on the state of feeling in their district.

There is nothing more likely to hamper our action in defence than having large numbers of women and children scattered about the face of India;* and I therefore am of opinion that immediately on the approach of danger all Europeans should be ordered to send home all their women and children, transport in India and by sea being provided by Government. I am aware that it may be said that this would show such distrustfulness of the natives as would most likely precipitate a rebellion. To this my answer is, if we are prepared for a rebellion, it cannot be precipitated; if we are not the sooner we become so the better. If the movement of all women and

* I calculate there are not less than 32,500 European and 28,000 Eurasian women, and something like 15,000 children of the above classes in India.

children is carried out under good arrangements and in time, we ought not to lose one of them; and the fact of our having disencumbered ourselves of all impedimenta, instead of having a bad effect on the natives, cannot fail to have a good one. To hold the contrary is like saying that a would-be murderer would be more likely to carry out his intentions if he knew his victim was ready for him than if he was not.

I have before shown the places at which it will be necessary to provide places of refuge, and there is no more to be said on this subject than to implore the Government ere it is too late to take steps to have all these at once put into order; for no man knows when the storm will burst. If it bursts and finds us unprepared in this respect, I hold that the deaths of all who are killed for the want of a place to fly to will be at the door of those members of the Government of India and England who, having had the danger pointed out to them hundreds of times, have wilfully neglected to take steps to guard against it. It seems a most extraordinary thing—yet it is true—that a Government which puts by 1½ millions per annum to provide against famine should neglect to take any steps to, and grudge the money which would, secure the lives of their own countrymen and women scattered all over India doing their service. It is not possible now to calculate what would be the expense of doing this, for the projects for places of refuge have never received sufficient encouragement from Government to get to the stage of estimate; but the cost would certainly not be great, and, if it was, it is as clearly the duty of Government to provide for the defence of those in their service as it is to pay them their wages regularly.

The places of refuge once established on a proper footing and our women and children arrived at places of safety, the sting of a rebellion would be already gone, and there would remain only a few Englishmen to face fearful odds; but their mind would be at ease with regard to those dearest to them and their right arms would be free; and facing odds is no new thing for Englishmen, as our whole military history sufficiently proves.

But it is not only necessary to provide places of refuge, but there should be clear instructions in the possession of each European what he is to do on the outbreak of a rebellion in the district he resides in. He should know clearly the place of refuge or rendezvous, and the best way of getting there; and to secure this latter end the knowledge of the district officer would be most useful. In every district of India there would, I believe, be found some influential native willing to throw in his lot with us; and if these were known, it might generally be easy for stray Euopeans to place themselves under his protection until he could arrange to forward them to the nearest military station or defensible post held by his countrymen; and therefore it is no less necessary for the district officers to have lists of men on whose loyalty they can rely than of those who are to be distrusted.

Plans for each place of refuge should aim at selecting as good a point as can be got with special reference to the following points :—

(1) It should be easily accessible to most of the Europeans round, with no native city or bazaar between.

(2) It should be compact and suited to the number of men likely to be available.

(3) Its water-supply should be well under command and unfailing.

(4) The building should be such as can readily be prepared for defence.

And the following steps should not be neglected. Supplies for six months should be laid in, 20 per cent. spare rifles for all the European adult males should be kept in store, and all male Europeans over 15 years of age should be provided with rifles and 100 rounds of ammunition. A store of powder should be kept. Tools for the necessary preparations should be stored.

It is impossible to say at what time places of refuge should be occupied; this must be left to the discretion of district officers, who, however, should be warned that it is better to occupy them too soon than too late. Neither is it possible to say whether at the time an outbreak took place it would be advisable to hold all the places I have named above. Of course it would be advisable to keep our hold on as many districts as possible; but this must be entirely guided by the circumstances of the time, and no attempt should be made to hold a place where there does not seem reasonable hope for believing that, considering the garrison available, and the position to be held, the garrison can hold out without aid for three months at least.

Finally, I would impress on Government the necessity of directing all Local Governments and Administrations to show without delay the steps which, in their opinion, should be taken for the protection of all the Europeans in their Governments. With regard to the defence of fortified places in India, there should only be one watchword—"Never say die." No place once taken up should ever be surrendered, whatever the odds against it. On no other principal can success be attained or even hoped for. In the words of Sir H. Lawrence, I would say to the defenders—"Entrench, entrench, entrench;" fight, fight, fight to the bitter end; never give in; remember Lucknow, Jellalabad, the house at Arrah, and Rorke's drift, and do not forget Cawnpore and the surrender of Kabul.

With regard to moveable columns, I have already shewn what I consider necessary. Each one should be fully equipped with transport for three days' supplies and 300 rounds ammunition. Plans of moving at a moment's notice on every point likely to require assistance, on or every town likely to require punishment, should be carefully thought and arranged beforehand. Arrangements should be made for utilising railways for concentrating and uniting with other columns, and everything down to the preparation of time tables be ready. *Au reste*, the motto of every commander of a moveable column should be "frappez fort et frappez vite." Small *émeutes* as well as big rebellions must be crushed at once; there must be no hesitation, no counting the odds. Wherever rebellion shows itself, on that spot should come a blow suddenly and inexorably.

There is one other point in connection with the defence of India which should also be arranged for, that is, the protection of our main communications. All the principal bridges must be guarded, and everything possible done to prevent the railways being destroyed. This is a very difficult matter, for the distances to be protected are so enormous. Still I would not despair, and would suggest that for every hundred miles of rail there should be provided an armoured train to carry two machine guns and 50 riflemen, the engine and carriages to be bullet proof, with tenders to carry coal and water for a 50-mile run. By these arrangements, and by giving clear warning that any village within a certain distance of any point where destruction of railway was attempted would be most severely dealt with, I should hope to maintain our railway communication pretty intact.

In the first part of this paper I have shewn that Russia can in 77 days after issuing the orders* put about 23,000 men into Herat, with a reserve of a like strength, which could arrive in from 40 to 50 days afterwards; with 12,000 more possibly available within 20 days of Herat. She can in from 70 to 100 days also after the order has been given put about 13,000 men into Kabul, with a similar strength in reserve, and her communications all strongly held. She can in 90 days put 7,000 men into Chitral and 4,000 men on to the Kashmir frontier. *In short, Russia can in from 80 to 100 days after the orders issue from her War Office put 95,000 regular troops into positions, from which we can hardly drive her, and from which she can undertake the invasion of India at her own convenience, and with a very fair expectation of success !!*

And what can we do? The answer will be found in succeeding parts of this paper. To meet 95,000 Russian troops (all of whom are equal in fighting power to the best of our own, and decidedly superior to most of our Native Army) (without counting any Uzbaks from the Khanates, Turkomans from the Atak and Merv, besides an unknown number of Afghans, Hazaras, and Char Aimaks, *we in the present state of our military affairs can bring*—

Field artillery.	Mountain artillery.	British cavalry.	Native cavalry.	British infantry.	Native infantry.	Sappers.
13	9	1	$8\frac{1}{8}$	$5\frac{6}{8}$	$41\frac{3}{8}$	21

or, taking these units at their present war strength, about 10,000 British, 37,000 Natives—a *total of 47,000 men, without reserves. !!!*

And this is not all or the worst. The Russians have been preparing for this for years—*we have not been preparing.* They are therefore in all probability thoroughly ready to carry out their schemes—*we are certainly not ready* even to put this 47,000 men into the field. By prodigious efforts, such as I believe only Englishmen driven into a corner are capable, this 47,000 men might, it is true, be put on to our frontier in something under one month. But where is Herat, where Kabul, where Chitral? Still 520, 190 and 191 miles respectively distant. Of these 47,000, not less than one-half would be used up on the communications, and of the remaining half *perhaps* ¾ might arrive fit to fight. We shall have 46,000 Russians at Herat, 13,000 at Kabul, and 7,000 in Chitral. How are we to divide the 20,000 or 30,000 men we have? The thing is a farce. One weak division might go to Herat and die there;—that is all! This is the pass we have come to!

Notwithstanding the unmanly, the unsoldierlike taunt that K.C.B. mania is the cause of Russophobia, I have, I am proud to say, been one who has consistently raised his voice to warn; but till I had worked out these two chapters, I did not know how true had been the instinct which had induced me, whenever occasion offered, to sound the alarm. But I know now. If the incontrovertible evidence of these two chapters does not induce our authorities now, at last, to sound the 'assembly,' our case is indeed hopeless. Yet I will not despair; through evil report and through good I will still raise my voice. Whatever may have been our follies, we are still Englishmen; the game is not lost quite yet; and if we are true to ourselves, it shall not be lost. If I have conjured up a spectre, I will show how he can be laid, and in the next chapters offer my humble opinion as to what can still be done to win the grandest game Englishmen have ever been engaged in.

* My firm belief is that, while this paper has been written, these orders were given. Rumours from a variety of independent sources have been rife during the last 6 months of large concentrations of Russian troops. I have in vain tried to ascertain their truth. The fact is we have *no* system of getting information; and while we have been playing, the very operation I have sketched as probable had begun. Whether it has now been temporarily abandoned I know not, nor does any Englishman know; but if Providence has so beneficently given us yet a little breathing time, let me entreat our Government at last to take up this vital question and face it like—alas! that it can be said Englishmen were wont.

CHAPTER III.

DIPLOMATIC MEASURES NECESSARY.

In the foregoing pages I have shewn that Russia can, in from eighty to one hundred days after the order is given, seize the points Herat, Kabul, Chitral, besides holding the necessary lines of communication strongly and reinforcing her advance force, and that we could not put a larger army in the field than about 47,000 men, without any reserves!

This is but a poor look-out. Some seeing how bad it is, may even accuse me of taking too gloomy a view of the situation; but if they think so, I ask their reasons. It is not, I think, that I take too gloomy a view, but that the outlook is indeed sombre. I cannot make the distances from the Russian base to the Russian objectives less. I cannot make the deserts and mountains more impracticable than they are, nor can I multiply our forces by any given number to suit the views of others. I say again, as I said before, if any one can prove to me that my figures are wrong, I shall be glad. I don't want to pile up the agony; but I will not consent to say less than a careful study of the question induces me to believe is the truth. I will have nothing to do with the *suppressio veri* or the *suggestio falsi*; it is clearly my duty to say what I think, whether any one may dislike what I have to say or not.

But if the outlook is gloomy, what then? Let us meet it in a right spirit. I believe that events have placed us in a very difficult position—a position which it will require all our energy, determination, and skill to meet adequately; but I no less believe we *can* meet it. I have purposely avoided saying anything to shew how I think we have got into the present fix: one might write reams to prove who was to blame for getting us into it, and then we should be no nearer getting out of it. What we have to do is, not to waste words in talking about how we got into it, but to get out of it. What I have to do now is to shew how I think we may do so. But it is no use any one reading what follows unless I have in the foregoing portion of this paper satisfied him that the time for half measures has gone by. I will recommend none such. If any one thinks that the situation can now be met by an exchange of diplomatic notes with the Russian Government, in God's name let him think so. I don't think so. I am sure the situation can only be met by ridding ourselves of all illusions and humbug, and looking the difficulty fairly in the face, by treating it as one of the highest national importance. If I can get the English nation to see this, I shall have no fear.

In considering the diplomatic measures which should be taken in aid of our defence of India, I may rightly divide them into measures which can be taken in Europe, in Asia, and in India.

But first let me say that, as in war all things are fair, no single stone should be left unturned that will aid us in the smallest degree. The spirit which must run through all our operations, warlike as well as diplomatic, must be that Russia *shall not* invade or threaten India with impunity. Let us not be mad enough to follow the councils which would have us wait for her attack, and meet it passively behind the Indus ;* but let us force her beforehand to dread meddling any further with us. Let us resolve that this war, if forced on to us, shall be one to the knife, and that any attempt shall not only be beaten off, but must be rendered frightfully disastrous to Russia. Let her feel that the war once begun shall not cease till she recoils on her snows, crippled and ruined at every point.

Were such a resolve really made known and believed by her, I believe we should have little more trouble with the Russian advance. But, as Marvin truly remarks, " violent outbursts of English public opinion against Russia " have never yet succeeded in exercising a restraining effect upon her advances " in the East, and the political history of the last twenty years is rich in " instances of the impotence of mere diplomatic expostulations and protests " ; and inasmuch as we have hitherto played with this all-important question, we must now bear the fruits of our folly. Russia would not now believe us, even though the words of warning were said by a Pitt. She would look on any such declaration as a flash in the pan, and, laughing in her sleeve, would at most draw in her horns till the fit passed away. Therefore we must without delay take certain preliminary steps which will make her at last believe that she has reached the limit of unquestioned aggression towards India; for that she has now reached what we should consider that limit is, I think, proved beyond dispute by the remarks I have made in the first portion of this paper.

But the danger of Russia becoming possessed of vantage points with regard to India is so imminent, and we are really so unprepared to meet her by force, that I am convinced that it is everything for us to gain time. If we can put off any further movements on the part of Russia for two years, we can then be in a position to take the high hand with her. I regret to have to say we are not in such a position now.

But how are we to stay her ? She is so nearly master of the situation, that it would be folly for her to stop now ; and the question is, can we offer her sufficient inducement to do what we wish ?

The answer can, I think, be found in a consideration of the fact, that one of the principal reasons Russia has for wishing to take up a threatening position with regard to India is to enable her to cripple England's action in regard to her schemes on the Bosphorus.

If she thought she could gain that end by conciliating England, would she be so anxious to annoy her ?—I think not. Therefore let us strive to induce her to believe that she is more likely to gain her ends by conciliating England than by forcing on her an unwelcome war. Everything is fair in war ; and we must be regarded as to all intents and purposes at present at war with Russia on the Russo-Indian question. Russia has hitherto had a monopoly of diplomatic success in this question, because she has, wisely in her own interests, played with us and deceived us with promises, meant only to serve their time. We have believed everything she has said, and we have acted fair ; but this is folly. As well might a General promise to desist from surprises, stratagems, and night attacks, if his enemy would do the same. He would be

---

* Skobeleff says very truly that if we did this, our army would consider itself half-beaten before any collision occurred.

an ass to promise anything of the kind, and the enemy's General would be an imbecile if he believed him. Why then should we continue to do this thing diplomatically? It is no use disguising the fact: the buttons are off the foils in this struggle between us and Russia, and what we are fencing for is our existence as a first-class Power.

Anyhow, if we are so righteous as not even to attempt a subterfuge of this sort, it is right we should quite realize what our high-flown moral rectitude may bring on us.

The fact is, *we are not ready to meet Russia*, and we *must* have time to get ready. Leading Russia to believe that her ends *may* be gained by conciliating us may give us that time; and therefore I hold we shall be simply mad if we refuse to avail ourselves of this chance for fear of what Mrs. Grundy will say. But, of course, two can play at this game; and we have ample reason for believing that Russia will have no such scruples. She will listen to us and promise as usual. She may remove a Governor-General* of anti-English proclivities, and she may order a few regiments back to Russia; but she will all the time do what she can to resume her former *rôle* whenever it suits her convenience.

The present is a good time for the experiment; and it is certainly worth the candle. We have a Liberal Government in power, and rightly or wrongly Russia believes Liberal statesmen to be more friendly to her than their opponents. Therefore, if the move is made *now*, there will be more chance of its being successful; and if the chances and changes of parties should decree that our Liberal Government is to be replaced by a Conservative Ministry, and that Ministry takes up the game in the same spirit, I think we have good reasen for hoping that an era of apparent mutual trustfulness will set in.

Russian statesmen may, it is true, be too clever for us and not change their tactics one iota. Still I should doubt their not doing something to gain such a prize as we would dangle before them. Of course, I don't suppose this would give us relief from Russian machinations for ever. Even if she got Constantinople with our blessing added, she would afterwards go on with her schemes against India; but if we can get breathing time, and *if we utilize that time* to the utmost, we can then defy her. And I think there would be some chance of her finding that grapes guarded by a thoroughly prepared army of Englishmen were somewhat sour and not worth the picking.

The first thing we have to do, I repeat, is to get time to get ready. *We must have* it, for *we are not ready now*. I have heard all that has been said about our having a highly-trained and well-disciplined army; but I have no hesitation in asserting that this is a simple *suggestio falsi*. We have an army it is true; it is well-trained, it is well-disciplined, and I believe a good deal of it is trustworthy,—but it can't do miracles. 10,000 British troops (superior if you like to the Russians) and 37,000 Native troops, with no reserves, cannot meet 95,000 Russian troops with some 400,000 to 500,000 more to draw on. This is the problem, and there is no use shirking it. We must do nothing, or we must do all we can. If we do nothing, India will pass from our grasp; but if we rise up and do what we can, it shall not. The first course will meet the views of those gentlemen who hold that *apres moi le deluge* contains the acme of human wisdom; but I am not writing to bolster up such councils.

---

* Since this was written Tchernaieff has been removed.

I want to save India for all time. The great men who went before us won it; it is our duty to hand their legacy down to our successors. To do this, we must have time. To gain time, we must by hook or by crook induce Russia to stay her hand for say two years;—then let her come.

The next step I propose should be taken is to inform the Russian Government that any further step now taken towards the concentration of troops in the direction of the frontiers of Afghanistan will be regarded by Her Majesty's Government as a hostile act, which must lead to the rupture of friendly relations, and authorising our taking such steps as seem to us best in our own interests, even to the immediate declaration of war, and the resumption by England as against Russia of *the 'right of search.'*

This (which we weakly gave up by the declaration of Paris,—an act of our ambassador, Lord Clarendon, which was never ratified by Parliament) has always been one of the clearest rights of belligerents. The law upon this subject is thus summed up by Lord Stowell: "The right of visiting and "searching merchant ships on the high seas, whatever be the ships, whatever "be the cargoes, whatever be the destinations, is an incontestable right of the "lawfully commissioned cruisers of a belligerent nation. I say the ships, the "cargoes, the destinations, what they may, because till they are visited and "searched, it does not appear what the ships or the cargoes or the destinations "are; and it is for the purpose of ascertaining these points that the necessity "of this right of visitation and search exists. This right is so clear in "principle, that no men can deny it who admits the legality of maritime "capture. All writers on the law of nations unanimously acknowledge it. "In short, no man in the least degree conversant with subjects of this "kind has ever that I know of breathed a doubt upon it. The penalty for "the violent contravention of this right is the confiscation of the property so "withheld from visitation and search; and a neutral vessel refusing to suffer "to be searched would be condemned on that single ground alone as being "good prize."

In addition to this, all Russian ports should be blockaded; and the ease with which this can be done is one of the chief reasons for the Russians being so anxious to get a port in the open sea. If England is alone at war with Russia, she can easily blockade all the Russian ports; but if she is in alliance with Germany and Turkey, it becomes far easier, as the former is strong enough to close the Baltic, and the latter can of course close the Dardanelles, to all Russian ships or all other ships going to Russian ports. The Russian Government would, of course, realize that these measures simply mean that Russian sea-borne commerce would cease to exist.

In order, however, to shew how this can be, I here give a few notes on the trade of the Russian Empire.

It is very difficult to arrive at an exact statement of the trade of the Russian Empire on account of the want of general statistics of late date. The date of the latest general return (as published in the *Almanach de Gotha* for 1883) is 1880, which, on account of the war excitement, was quite an exceptional year. The statistics of the three previous years may also, on account of the war and its consequences, be considered exceptional. Again, the statistics make no mention of the amount of traffic by sea and by land. Under those circumstances, it is best to consider first the latest general returns of Russian trade, then, under separate headings, sea-borne trade, trade with Europe by land, and Asiatic trade.

I.—General Returns of Trade.

The following table shows the amount of imports from and exports to the various countries in 1879 and 1880 :—

Country.	1879.		1880.	
	Import.	Export.	Import.	Export.
	£	£	£	£
Germany ...	24,949,800	18,413,900	27,426,800	13,812,200
Great Britain ...	14,656,000	18,436,200	15,048,500	14,864,000
France ...	2,278,500	8,604,400	2,241,000	5,760,000
Austria ...	1,993,600	3,286,500	2,306,200	3,254,700
Turkey ...	1,541,900	1,386,900	2,037,000	1,534,000
Belgium ...	721,300	2,680,100	742,300	1,889,900
Holland ...	857,300	3,874,400	751,800	2,820,500
Italy ...	1,193,900	1,221,800	631,000	581,300
Sweden and Norway ...	352,000	1,219,800	292,500	1,212,500
Denmark ...	...	520,600	71,600	576,600
Greece ...	316,100	215,000	221,900	221,100
Roumania ...	188,200	905,000	178,600	995,600
United States ...	642,300	...	1,020,400	523,400
South America ...	3,201,200	...	1,597,200	1,000
China ...	1,900,300	198,200	2,278,000	252,000
Persia ...	719,100	342,200	686,000	394,000
Other countries ..	2,591,600	387,000	1,738,000	250,000

This trade may be divided into—

(*a*) Articles of consumption,—cereals, drinks, tobacco, fruit, animals.
(*b*) Raw materials,—minerals, metals, cotton, and other stuffs, wood.
(*c*) Manufactured articles,—pottery and glassware, cloth, machinery.
(*d*) Various.

The following table shows the amount of commerce in each with Europe, Finland, and Asia :—

	Class of merchandise.	1879.		1880.	
		Import.	Export.	Import.	Export.
		£	£	£	£
Europe.	Articles of consumption ...	10,003,800	44,716,800	13,354,300	30,269,600
	Raw materials ...	16,794,600	14,519,300	15,930,200	15,317,700
	Manufactured articles ...	18,709,400	540,200	17,753,600	483,300
	Various ...	9,313,500	865,100	10,795,300	1,565,900
	Total ...	54,821,300	60,641,400	57,833,400	47,636,500
	Precious metals ...	1,387,400	711,600	1,239,000	2,877,800
	Grand Total ...	56,208,700	61,353,000	59,072,400	50,514,300

Class of merchandise.		1879.		1880.	
		Import.	Export.	Import.	Export.
		£	£	£	£
Finland.	Articles of consumption ...	179,300	681,500	258,400	506,100
	Raw materials ...	370,800	229,100	302,500	237,800
	Manufactured articles ...	369,400	174,200	583,300	216,300
	Total ...	919,500	1,084,800	1,144,200	960,200
Asia.	Tea ...	1,864,800	8,900	2,235,500	11,900
	Cloth ...	275,500	306,400	176,700	344,000
	Raw silk, cotton, &c. ...	128,300	325,500	145,100	419,300
	Leather and skins ...	50,700	84,500	90,600	143,000
	Fruit and vegetables ...	209,700	2,400	154,800	...
	Cereals ...	89,000	87,800	106,500	30,100
	Others ...	412,600	235,100	394,400	322,200
	Total ...	3,030,600	1,050,600	3,303,600	1,270,500
	Precious metals ...	89,600	307,200	...	291,600
	Grand Total ...	3,120,200	1,357,800	3,303,600	1,562,100
Grand Total.					
Merchandise ...		58,771,300	62,776,800	62,281,200	49,867,200
Precious metals ...		1,477,000	1,018,800	1,239,000	3,169,400

II.—Sea-borne Trade.

The following table shews the movement of ships in 1880:—

Ports.	Ships entered.			Ships cleared.		
	With cargo.	In ballast.	Total.	With cargo.	In ballast.	Total.
Baltic ...	5,969	2,544	8,240	7,335	814	8,149
Black Sea ...	2,493	2,772	5,265	3,662	1,461	5,123
White Sea ...	337	545	832	871	...	871
Caspian ...	919	52	971	579	185	764
Total ...	9,445	5,913	15,358	12,447	2,460	14,908
Including steamers ...	3,868	2,080	5,948	5,068	831	5,899

(*a*) Articles of consumption,—cereals, drinks, tobacco, fruit, animals.
(*b*) Raw materials,—minerals, metals, cotton, and other stuffs, wood.
(*c*) Manufactured articles,—pottery and glassware, cloth, machinery.
(*d*) Various.

Of the trade with Europe in 1879 and 1880 (not including precious metals), there was carried by sea :—

From and to ports.	1879.		1880.	
	Import.	Export.	Import.	Export.
	£	£	£	£
Baltic	21,447,700	23,212,500	21,743,300	20,057,100
Black Sea	5,543,000	20,168,900	6,232,700	13,504,100
White Sea	94,800	1,044,200	78,000	1,021,600
Total ...	27,085,500	44.450,600	28,054,000	34,582,800
Out of a total trade of	54,821,300	60,641,400	57,833,400	47,636,500

The following are the principal articles of export and import from the ports on the different frontiers :—

NORTHERN PORTS
- *Exports.*—Cereals, flax, hemp, and wood (1,373 out of 2,932 ships leaving Riga were laden with wood in 1881).
- *Imports.*—Coal, iron, cotton, machinery of all sorts, tobacco, and ironware.

SOUTHERN PORTS
- *Exports.*—Cereals and wool; naphtha from Poti.
- *Imports.*—Cotton and cotton goods, ironware, coal, coffee, fruits, petroleum, wine, machinery, tea, tobacco.

Principal depôts.—In the south the principal ports are—on the Black Sea, Odessa, Nicolaief, Sevastopol, and Poti ; on the sea of Azov, Taganrog and Genichensk ; in the north, Riga, Wiborg, Cronstadt, Helsingfors and Liban. To all of these railways run from the interior. The minor ports (without railway communication) are in the south, Batoum on the Black Sea, Mariapol, Yeisk, Temriouk, Berdiansk, and Kertch on the Sea of Azov ; and in the north, Pernau on the Baltic, and Archangel on the White Sea. The table (Appendix I) shows, as far as statistics are available, the amount of exports from each in 1881 and 1882 (1880 and 1881 for the Baltic ports). The returns from the Black Sea ports are tolerably complete, and show a steady increase of exports (£14 millions in 1881, £18 millions in 1882) over those of 1880. Those from the Baltic are unfortunately farfrom complete. There are apparently no British consuls at Cronstadt and Helsingfors, two of the principal ports, and therefore no returns from those ports. In those returns it must be noted that the crops of 1880 were a failure, and therefore trade was bad in 1881. In 1881 the crops near the BlackSea coast were a failure, but those in the interior were abundant. The imports at the various ports (so far as statistics are available) are shown in Appendix 2.

Trade routes.—Except for the ports of Wiborg, Riga, Odessa, and Taganrog (and even those are incomplete),no returns are available as to the countries whence the ships arrived and to which they sailed. In Appendix III, however, is shown the *flag* under which the various ships arrived and sailed in 1881 and 1882 from the different ports, which may give some slight idea. In this table it will be noted how small the number of Russian ships is, and how much Russian commerce is carried on on foreign bottoms. In Appendix IV is shown for Riga and Wiborg in 1881 the number of ships arriving from and sailing to the ports of foreign countries, and also the number of *British* vessels arriving at and sailing from Odessa and Taganrog from and to foreign ports.

Russian mercantile marine.—In 1878 (according to the *Almanach de Gotha*, 1883) this consisted of—

3,643 sailing ships	=	...	...	308,230 tons
259 steamers	=	...	...	74,324 „

at the end of 1879 (according to the *Stateman's Year Book*, 1883) of—

2,568 seagoing vessels	=	...	...	522,462 tons

comprising 629 ships trading to foreign countries and 1,780 coasting vessels. The number of Russian ships entering various foreign ports in 1881 and 1882 is shown in Appendix 5. No return of Russian vessels entering British ports is available. Of the vessels shown as entering Russian ports in 1880—

2,746	were	Russian.
2,660	„	English.
2,573	„	German.
2,047	„	Swedish and Norwegian.
1,380	„	Turkish.
1,088	„	Greek.
892	„	Danish.
668	„	Austrian.
576	„	Dutch.
	&c., &c.	

The Baku petroleum trade.—As an article of fuel, Baku petroleum has not yet driven that of America out of the markets of Europe. In Russia it is superseding it, but beyond that country to the west it has made little progress. It is a rising trade, however, and bids fair with improved means of communication to rival the American article. In 1881 the export from Baku was 58 million gallons of kerosine.

III.—Trade by Land with Europe.

No statistics are available as to commerce by land with Germany, Roumania, and Turkey. The total amount was—

	1879.		1880.	
	Import.	Export.	Import.	Export.
	£27,735,800	£16,190,800	£29,779,400	£13,053,700
of which with Austria—	£3,300,000	£2,760,000	£3,680,000	£3,590,000

Principal depôts.—Wilna, Lomja, Warsaw, Lublin, Kiev, and Kishinev. The *principal routes* are of course indicated by the railways leading over the frontier to Königsberg, Danzig, Posen, Breslau, Cracow, Lemberg, Jassy, and Galatz.

IV.—Asiatic Trade.

The table given on page 110 shows a total Asiatic trade of—

						£
1879	Imports	...	...	...	...	3,120,200
	Exports	...	...	...	...	1,357,800
1880	Imports	...	...	...	...	3,303,600
	Exports	...	...	...	...	1,562,100

but no details are available, nor is it stated whether Persia is included in this statement or not. With the exception of Persia and China, our details are not of recent date; and with improved communications the amount of commerce may reasonably be expected to have increased considerably. To compete with English trade in Central (and more especially Western) Asia, proposals have recently been made to stop, or at least prevent by high duties, the transit of English (and other foreign) goods through the Caucasus. In 1881 £700,000 and in 1882 £900,000 worth of foreign goods passed through the Caucasus destined for Persia and Afghanistan. These measures have been partially carried out already, and English goods will be compelled probably to take the more roundabout road by Trebizond, Van, and Bayazid.

(*a*) *Trade with Persia.*

The figures given on page 109 show—

		£
1879	Imports	719,100
	Exports	342,200
1880	Imports	686,000
	Exports	394,000

The entire export trade of the Astrabad and Shahrud districts converges at Gez, where all goods are put on board Russian ships, the Persians not being allowed to have a single vessel on the Caspian. Thence goods for Constantinople and Western Europe go to Baku, Tiflis, and Poti. A large portion of the import trade from Persia must go by land, as the figures for the port of Gez for 1880-81 are as follows:—

Exports.—£86,280, of which silk, £40,000; furs, £21,200; fruit, £8,000; cotton, £4,000; wool, £4,000.

Imports.—£287,000, of which piece-goods, £256,000; tea, £12,000; crockery, £7,520.

(*b*) *Trade with Afghanistan.*

This is as yet in its infancy. Lessar, Alikhanoff, and O'Donovan make hardly any mention of trade between the new trans-Caspian province and Herat.

(*c*) *Trade with Khiva.*

The latest date of statistics is 1868-69; and in that year the following were the figures:—

	£
Exports	11,204
Imports	29,488

The principal depôt of trade in Khiva is New Urgunj, whence caravans march *viâ* Kazala to Orenburg. A new trade route has lately been opened out from Kungrad to Yan Airakti on the Caspian, which will probably supersede that by Kazala, and make Astrakhan the depôt for Khivan goods instead of Orenburg. From Kungrad to the Caspian is 298 miles; from Urgunj *viâ* Kazala to Orenburg is about seventy day's march (short stages).

(*d*) *Trade with Bokhara.*

The statistics for *1867* were—

	£
Exports	621,468
Imports	431,021

Bokharan trade takes two directions,—one to the west, the other to Tashkand. Tashkand, as a trading centre, will be considered later. To the west there are two routes *viâ* Kazala to Orenburg* and *viâ* the Amu to Khiva, and thence by the same routes as Khivan goods. Goods reach Moscow *viâ* Orenburg from Bokhara in 77 days in summer and in 92 in winter, and Orenburg may still be considered as the depôt of Bokharan goods.

(*e*) *Trade with Kashgar.*

Trade with Kashgar *viâ* the Naryn post was in *1871*—

	£
Imports	47,333
Exports	14,037

From the Naryn post the merchandise is mostly directed on Tokmak and Viernie, thence on Orenburg.

(*f*) *Tashkand as a trading centre and its communications with Russia.*

Tashkand may now be considered as the Russian advanced trade depôt in Central Asia, and to it the merchandise of part of Bokhara and the surrounding Russian provinces of Ferghana (lake Khokand) and Zarafshan converges. In *1873* the amount of trade at Tashkand was—

	£
Imports	1,093,816
Exports	629,918
Transit trade	95,429

This was before the annexation of Khokand. A fair is annually held in Tashkand, and the following figures shew the amount of imports from and exports to various provinces and countries from this fair in the last six months of 1873 :—

	Imports. £	Exports. £
Orenburg	194,191	...
European Russia (*viâ* Orenburg)	87,196	...
Syr Darya district	110,192	101,045
Zarafshan	13,123	25,045
Bokhara	9,479	1,279
Khokand	76,436	119,907
Khiva	...	1,498

Little of the Bokharan trade goes farther than Tashkand; the greater part only as far as Samarkand. From Tashkand to Orenburg the old post road leads by Chimkend, Perovski, Kazala, Uralsk, and Orsk, and there is a second route to Orsk *viâ* Turgai. By either of these routes goods from Tashkand reach Moscow—

in summer	70 to 90 days
in winter	85 to 105 days

at a cost of not more than two roubles per pud (36 lbs). With this route, however, a new route is competing. A railway from Nijni Novgorod *viâ* Kazan to Tiumen is now under construction; and thence water carriage will be available to Semipalatinsk, which is 1,195 miles from Tashkand by road as against 1,280 from Tashkand to Orenburg, the latter being across barren steppe. Attempts are also being made to turn the Syr and Amu into the Caspian; and if those efforts succeed, a new highway for commerce will be opened up into the heart of Central Asia.

* *Viâ* Orsk, 1,160 miles from Bokhara to Orenburg (47 days for carvans).

(g) *Trade with China.*

According to the table on page 109, the total trade in 1879 and 1880 was—

		£
1879	Import	1,900,300
	Export	198,300
1880	Import	2,278,000
	Export	252,000

The above figures are from the *Almanach de Gotha*, 1883; but the *Chinese Directory*, 1882, gives the following:—

Total value of Imports and Exports.

	Taels.*		£
Russia *viâ* Odessa	28,818	=	8,234
Siberia *viâ* Kiakhta	4,055,310	=	1,158,660
Russian Manchuria	413,098	=	118,028
Total ...		=	1,284,922

which is about £800,000 less than the figures of the *Almanach de Gotha.*

The amount of tea exported in 1880 was to—

	Piculs.†		lbs.
The Continent of Russia	41,218	=	5,495,733
Siberia *viâ* Kiakhta	296,869	=	39,581,433
Mongolia *viâ* Fanchêng	107,636	=	14,351,466
Russian Manchuria	19,238	=	2,564,067

For 1881 we have only the figures of the Consular Reports from Shanghai and Hankow. These give—

Shanghai.

		Taels.		£
From and to Russian Manchuria	Imports	25,530	=	7,294
	Exports and re-exports ...	398,540	=	113,869

—all by sea.

Hankow.

Value of tea shipped to—

	Taels.		£
Odessa	1,022,570	=	292,163
Siberia	1,050,840	=	300,240

Kiakhta appears to be the chief point through which the Chinese overland trade with Siberia passes. Roads lead thence from Pekin and to Irkutsk, Omsk, and Semipalatinsk, whence goods go by water to Tiumen. Trade by this route, however, does not appear to be increasing, as in 1875 the imports at Kiakhta were £1,075,000, the exports £250,000—total £1,325,000 against £1,158,000 in 1880.

From the foregoing we find that Russian commerce divides itself into three natural channels,—*1st*, sea-borne trade with Europe or Asia; *2nd*, land-borne trade with Europe; *3rd*, land-borne trade with Asia.

The first goes in Russian or foreign ships from the south from Odessa, Nicolaieff, Sevastopol, Batoum, and Taganrog; and from the north from Riga, Wiborg, Cronstadt, and Helsingfors, &c., and there is no doubt we could blockade all these ports, and thus effectually stop all Russia's sea-borne trade.

* 3½ taels = £1. | † picul = 133⅓ lbs.

Of course we know that Russia intends, in the event of war with England, to equip as many cruisers as she can to prey on English commerce. This, no doubt, would be very inconvenient for us; but Russia's efforts in this direction would be altogether puny compared with what we could do. For every cruiser Russia could put on the sea we could put twenty; and I am pretty sure this plan would do her far more damage than she could do us.

But the effect of stopping her trade by sea would be to give a stimulus to her trade by land; and in order to still more effectually cripple her, we must arrange to stop this also, that is to say, we must arrange with the European Powers—Germany, Austria, and Turkey—through whose territories it would then pass; and this brings me to a consideration of another step we should take, *viz.*, what alliances in Europe should we enter into.

Before answering this, I will take a short survey of the present relations of the great Powers with each other. Russia has no vital interests in Africa; France has none in the area of Asia coveted by Russia. On the other hand, Russia finds herself opposed everywhere in Asia by English interests; and France cannot realise any of her Eastern schemes without placing herself in direct antagonism to England. In this manner there is a solidarity of interests between Russia and France. Both would gain, and gain immensely, by our downfall; and on this account the possibility of Russo-French alliance against England must never be lost sight of by our statesmen. Such an alliance may even now have been concluded, and the restlessness of France in those countries which bring her into collision with the English may, for all we know, only be the premonitory signs of an approaching storm. It would be everything for Russia to know that England was irrevocably embroiled with France, and it behoves our statesmen to be very careful this shall not take place, else, in trying to protect our petty interests in West Africa, at Madagascar, and in the Gulf of Tonquin, we may find we have endangered the far greater interests of India. I consider, therefore, that it is out of the question that we can make any satisfactory alliance against Russia with France: on the contrary, it seems likely that in the complications which will assuredly arise before this question is settled, France will be found ranged with Russia.

In regard to Germany, Austria, and Turkey the case is diffrenet. None of their interests clash with ours, and all have good reason to be suspicious of, if not hostile to, Russia; and the strongest of them—Germany—must for a long time to come be antagonistic to Russia's most probable ally—France.

In fact, the time has more than come for entering into an offensive-defensive alliance with Austria, Germany, and Turkey, such as I believe was formerly in contemplation. Notwithstanding the obvious objections which may be made to such an alliance, the fact that national interests must always come before national susceptibilities gives us good grounds for hoping such an alliance could be concluded, and that it would be for the peace of the world that it should be. The state of the case seems to me to be as follows: Germany and France know that another war is likely to break out between them, and of course both wish for allies. The most powerful ally that France can get is Russia; but Russia has her own schemes, which do not include an attack on Germany. Therefore the most that either can expect from the other is a benevolent neutrality; that is, France will make no objections to Russia's schemes against Turkey or India, and Russia will, in the event of a war between Germany and France, threaten the former, so as to force her to keep a considerable portion of her force on her eastern border. Austria and Turkey have every reason to fear Russia,—the first because of her Slavonic population; the last because Russia clearly wishes to deprive her of more territory in order to gain a Mediterranean port. It is therefore probable that till matters change Austria, Germany, and Turkey will hold together, and that it would be our best policy to join them. For what else can we do? We cannot join Russia; all her schemes are directly antagonistic to us. We should not join France, because she can do nothing for us, and, moreover, her interests are also against ours everywhere.

The advantages of such an alliance to England are obvious; for it is quite certain that if Russia was threatened by these Powers, she would not, and could not, attempt anything serious in the direction of India. The only disadvantage really is that we shall at last be forced to select our friends and our enemies, and we may be drawn into a war with France; but surely we must have degenerated lamentably if such a fear can influence us, especially when Russia acts in a manner so regardless of our interests and susceptibilities as she has been doing lately.

An alliance should therefore be at once entered into between these four Powers to maintain the *status quo*, and it would be of no use whatever unless it was, and was known to be, offensive and defensive. All four Powers should bind themselves to attack with their forces either Russia or France, should either threaten or attack the territories of any of the contracting parties.

It may be said that England could not give any army to speak of; for, in the contingency of a war with France, her forces would barely suffice for the defence of her own island; but I am inclined to doubt this, for it is certain the military power of England is very much greater than we get credit for. However this may be, she could give her navy, and that navy, with such assistance as Germany, Austria, and Turkey could give, could without doubt clear the seas of any French or Russian ships; and if the "right of search" was resumed by England, the sea-borne commerce of those Powers would cease.

If such an alliance was formed, the land-borne trade of Russia must also cease. I have shown that the land trade of Russia goes from Warsaw, Lomja, Warsa, Lublin, Kiev, and Kishinev; and it is evident that if this alliance was concluded, no trade could be carried on from any of the above but the last. No doubt from Kishinev some trade could go into Roumania, Servia, Montenegro, and Bulgaria; but it would be purely local traffic, as beyond these petty States are surrounded by Austria and Turkey.

I look on an alliance with Austria, Germany, and Turkey as absolutely indispensable to the safety of India, as Russia can place in the field such enormous forces that she can simply overwhelm us, and by no other means can we make such an impression on her. I believe the mere fact of its being known that such an alliance had been concluded would do more to stay Russian progress towards India than anything we can now do; as even in the case of these Powers only agreeing to maintain a friendly neutrality towards us, Russia would have to keep over a million of men ready to defend her western and southern frontiers.

I do not expect Germany or Austria or Turkey to attack Russia in our interests any more than I would expect France to attack Germany in those of Russian. But I think if we could get them to agree (first) to threaten the Russian frontier, (second) to stop all commerce with her, we should gain several very important moves in the game. First, a very large portion of the Russian army would be retained in Russia; second, the expenses of Russia would be enormously increased; third, her resources in transport and supplies would be greatly diminished; fourth, her commerce would almost cease to exist, thus crippling her already ruined finances to a very dangerous extent; and in consequence of the above the probability is that Russia would not, as long as we could maintain such an alliance, come to open war with us, and even if she did she could not possibly keep it up long.

And for all this, what should we have to give? Only the money necessary to keep the allied forces in a threatening position on the Russian frontier; and in the event of a war between Russia and Germany, Russia and Austria or Turkey, or between Germany and France, we should give our fleet and certain further sums of money.

As to the destruction of Russian commerce in Asia, of course it will not be possible to do this altogether; but the mere fact of there being a state of war existing in Central Asia will necessarily result in great damage to her commerce.

After all Russian commerce with Asia only takes the following lines:—

To Turkey.—Were Turkey in alliance with England, this would die of itself.

To Persia.—This would be much crippled by the absolute necessity the Russians would be under in using a vast amount of Persian transport for the purposes of the war. The consequence would be that the cost of transit would run up till any trade became impossible; and this would especially be the result if England seized the opportunity to push her trade into Persia through Turkey and Afghanistan and the Persian Gulf.

To the Khanates.—There can be little doubt that, on the occurrence of the events considered in this paper, the demands of the Russians for transport and the excitement and unrest of the people would be so great, that there would be little opportunity or inclination for trade.

There remains the overland trade with China. But this also would be stopped, because if our diplomatists did their work well, there should exist at least considerable tension between Russia and China. It is, therefore, on the whole, evident we could, in the event of war, *kill Russian trade.*

What Russia is aiming at is not necessarily the immediate invasion of India, or an immediate open rupture with England; but she is taking as many steps in that direction as she safely can without coming to open war with us. We must therefore as far as possible make the ground on which she proposes to put her feet to take those steps unsafe for her.

Better if we had done this ten years ago, when her expedition to Khiva gave us the opportunity. If we had then firmly vetoed her making any use of any base south of the great Turkoman desert, we might not now be deploring the fact that the whole of this tract has become Russian territory. The Russians would have had no excuse for interfering with the Turkomans or for advancing along the Atak. However, it is no sort of use crying over spilt milk. What has passed has passed. We have to look to the future and see how we can make any further advance dangerous, or at least dangerous-looking, to her.

Russia's object is, of course, to creep up as near to India as she can without notice; but Afghanistan intervenes, and therefore she is now trying to contract the boundaries of that country by making out that the boundaries she agreed to are not correct, and that the really Afghan power does not extend so far towards the Oxus. The points which particularly call for our earnest and immediate attention are on the north-west from Karki to Sarakhs, and on the north-east on the north bank of the Punjah river. Mr. Marvin remarks: "Rightly or wrongly, the region between Sarakhs and Herat on the Afghan "side of the Hari Rud is regarded by the Turkomans as their territory,* and "it is obvious that Russia, in conquering them or establishing a protectorate "over them, will acquire those pretensions and skilfully employ them to her "advantage. This condition of things invites the most careful attention of "English statesmen, for it is folly to expect the Russian advance to be "arrested by boundary lines which exist only on paper."

The direction which this consideration should take undoubtedly lies in the immediate appointment of a commission of English officers to demarcate the whole of the north and west boundary of Afghanistan. What I recommend in this respect may be seen by the following extract from a memorandum which I have furnished the Indian Foreign Office on the north and west boundary of Afghanistan.

The frontier which, in a military point of view, would be advisable is, as between Persia and Afghanistan, it should commence on the south from the Godar-i-Lard-i-Zard on the Lash-Birjand road where the Seistan Boundary Commission left off, and should thence run north, on the desert of Dasht-i-Naumed side, of the Tabas range to a point between Burj Gulwarda and Shorab, the latter becoming Afghan. Thence it should run in a straight line to Kafir Kala, which is undoubtedly Afghan. This would include a place called Yezdun, which is a fertile little oasis in the desert. There is good water here, and it might be made a very strong little outpost of the Afghans, as it is admirably situated for checking any raiding from the west into Afghan territory. This is not taking much of the territory marked on our maps as Persian, and there is no doubt that formerly all the territory east of the Koh-Mominabad, including the district of Suni Khana, were Afghan.

From Kafir Kala it is of the very greatest importance to maintain the line of the Hari Rud, and I think that the left bank of that river up to Pul-i-Khatun should be the boundary. From this it might cross to the right bank, which it should keep till a point due west of the present Persian fort of Sarakhs was reached. From this the boundary should run straight through the desert to Karki on the Oxus, excluding the Kara Turkomans, but including the Alieli and Sariks. This line is very important, as it will be noticed that, whereas north of this line all roads go to Merv and Persia, south of it all roads go to Afghanistan; and it is only just the Afghans should have the control of all the roads from the Oxus to their own country. Karki should be Afghan most undoubtedly. From this the boundary should keep on the left of the Oxus right up to the fort of Bar Panjah.

From this commences another important bit. From this the main stream would not be a good boundary: it is a mere rivulet at this point; and I am strongly of opinion that the boundary line should leave the river above Bar Panjah and take to the watershed of the ridge which bounds the Aksu Valley on the south. It should then run along this ridge to the Irim Yas Pass, and then right across the Pamer east to the peak marked 10,250′ on the map, where it would meet the Chinese boundary, which should most certainly be brought right up to the crest of the main watershed of the Pamer, *i.e.*, that from which water drains east to Chinese Turkistan and west to the Oxus. If this frontier is obtained for the Afghans, we should have done for them all that is possible.†

* Lessar says Badkheis belongs to no one.

† It should, however, be noted here that as there is little doubt that Roshan and Shignan have, for the last 300 years, been tributary to Badakhshan, these districts should be included in Afghanistan.

It should, I think, be quite understood that there should be no argument with Russia about the frontier. It is taken for granted that the boundary of Russia does not yet touch the Afghan frontier, and therefore what we lay down cannot affect her. We should say what the frontier is to be and show it all to any Russian officer appointed to accompany our Mission, and give him a map for the information of his Government. If questions should arise with Persia, they should be settled with that Government, and the same thing applies to Chinese Turkistan.

A Commission for the settlement of so important a question should be very strongly constituted, both as to numbers and the character and ability of its members. As to its constitution, I think we have a good precedent in the Mission of Sir John Malcolm to Persia in 1810. This Mission was meant to create an effect by the numbers of its members and escort, which are given in the margin. The senior officer should, I am inclined to think, be a military officer of high rank, and of firm, decided character.

Ambassador—
Genl. Sir John Malcolm.
Capt. Pasley, Secy.
Lieut. Stewart, 1st Asst.
Mr. H. Ellis, 2nd ,,
,, A. Jukes, 3rd ,,
Lieut. Briggs, Asst. Supdt.
,, MacDonald, ,,
,, Little ,,
Surg. Colhoun.
,, Cormick.
Capt. Grant, Comdg. Escort.
Lieut. Frederick. }
,, Martin. }
,, Lindsay. } Attached.
,, Johnson. }
,, Fotheringham. }
Mr. Monteith. }

The escort consisted of 1 sergeant, 2 corporals, 1 trumpeter, 16 privates, 17 lancers, 1 subadar, 1 jemadar, 2 havildars, 2 naiks, 20 gunners, Madras H.A., 1 subadar, 1 jemadar, 2 havildars, 2 naiks, 40 sepoys, Bombay Native Infantry.

Attached to the Mission as Joint Commissioner, there should be a Civilian thoroughly acquainted with the political views of the Government.

There should be, I think, four Secretaries, who might be either military or civil. They should have a knowledge of Persian and French, and all the better if they know some Pushtoo and Russian in addition.

There should be two Persian Secretaries, who should be intelligent and thoroughly trustworthy. I think it would be advisable to have in addition four attached officers under the name of Aides-de-Camp, and it would be as well if they were chosen from each branch of the service. There should be a strong survey party, under an officer of acknowledged reputation in the scientific world.

The escort should consist of 50 cavalry, as per margin. All should be Kazlbashes, or thoroughly trustworthy Afghans, from good regiments.

1 English officer.
1 resaldar.
1 jamadar.
1 kote-dafadar.
6 drummers.
2 trumpeters.
2 farriers.
50 sowars.

The infantry escort should consist of 100 bayonets as per margin, with two British officers. It should consist of Sikhs, Dogras, and Gurkhas in equal proportions, and some of them might be taken from the Sappers.

2 British officers.
2 subadars.
2 jamadars.
2 color-havildars.
8 havildars.
4 buglers.
100 sepoys.

None but men very carefully selected, both physically and professionally, should go.

There should also be an officer to take charge of the Commissariat and Transport Departments.

The Commission should go in considerable comfort and state. Every officer and man should have his full uniform, in addition to a special equipment of service clothing. Every one might be allowed as regards baggage, tentage, and transport, &c., about double the Kabul scale, and everything should be carried on mules or yaboos.

A good supply of stores should be taken for officers and of native condiments not procurable in Afghanistan.

No large sums of money should ever travel with the Mission, but the Commander should have power to draw through Hindoostan and Persia.

The time which a Boundary Commissioner would probably take in going over this frontier cannot, of course, be calculated with any certainty; but the following route* shows the country which would have to be passed over.

The route by Nushki is chosen, as it altogether avoids Afghanistan; and though it is difficult, I think it would not be insurmountable if proper precautions and arrangements were made beforehand. Supplies would have to be arranged for by timely notice being given to the various Afghan authorities.

Communications with the Mission should be kept up by telegraph through Meshed by means of a cypher and by a special dâk service through Kandahar, Herat and Kabul, Balkh and Kabul, and Gilgit and Kashmir, according to the positions of the Mission at the time of despatch of letters.

I calculate that from the Bolan to Jamu round the whole W. and N. Afghan border would be about 200 marches, so that it would not be expected that the Mission would complete its work under one year.

The best time to start would be in September, as the Baloche desert could hardly be crossed before then. The cold in part of the journey would doubtless be great, but not too great, and it is impossible to arrange so that it can be avoided altogether. The coldest part, *viz.*, up towards the Pamer and Gilgit, would be passed over in the summer.

Measures should be taken at once to secure the willing acquiescence of the Amir Abdur Rahman.† This should have undoubtedly been kept quite secret; but I regret to notice that the intentions of our Government in this respect have already got into the papers. The result of this will be that when the Commission arrives, the Russians will be ready with all sorts of claims on account of Persia, the Sarek and Salor, and Ersari and Alieli Turkomans, and Bokhara, and in the extreme north of the petty States of Roshan, Shighnan, and Darwaz, and the consequence will be that our Commissioners will find all who could have given evidence on the other side will be driven away. This happened in Seistan; and as the Russians must have read Sir F. Goldsmid's acknowledgment of the difficulties he met with, they will be much too clever not to profit by them. To meet this certainty, I would at once despatch a thoroughly trustworthy native to collect information on the west and north-west frontier of Afghanistan, so as to have as much evidence as possible ready on the Anglo-Afghan side of the question.

With regard to the north-east portion of the frontier, there would be but little difficulty or danger in its being visited by an Englishman; and I would therefore depute an officer at once to that part of the frontier to collect evidence of the same kind as the above.‡

The two most important points to look to in the delineation of the Afghan frontier are to see that Russia gets no footing on the Afghan side of the Oxus. Of course we cannot prevent her now from claiming all the country containing the direct road from Bokhara to Merv; but we should endeavour by

* Appendix R.

† The sooner the Amir is brought down to India the better. It is high time that a clear understanding should be come to with him as to our relative positions.

‡ As it would take too long for one commission to traverse the whole frontier, I think on reconsideration it would be better to have two commissions,—one to settle the N.-W. frontier, and the other the N.E.

all means to secure for the Afghans the part of the district of Karki which lies above the village of Astana Baba, as from Karki town is a direct road to Andkhui, and this should undoubtedly be under command of the Afghans. The place itself is said to be strong, and could be readily utilized for offensive purposes by a Russian column from Karshi, and might be a very valuable outpost in the hands of the Afghans.

It is also very important so to delineate the Afghan frontier in the north-east as to cut off Russia from any direct contact with the dominions of Kashmir. If it is true, as I hear, that the Chinese Government have a post at Sarikol, the Afghan boundary should be taken right across the Pamer to the north of Wood's Lake to the Chinese frontier.

If the above frontier is secured, we shall have done all for the Afghans we can. Of course, no one supposes that a boundary-mark on a map will prevent the Russians going for Herat when they are ready; but it will prevent them creeping any nearer to that place till *they are ready* to break openly with England.

Having thus cut Russia off from any secure stepping place within Afghanistan, either towards Herat or Kashmir, the next, or rather I should say another equally, important step to take is to make Herat quite safe from a *coup de main*. Of course, if we thus prevent Russia from gaining a footing in Afghanistan, we shall not quite do this, because she will undoubtedly then, even if she has not already done so, make another treaty with Persia by which the district of Kalat-i-Nadir will be ceded to her; and on this the boundaries of that district will become sufficiently elastic to include country down as far as Zorabad. But the approach to Herat on the left bank of Hari Rud is very much more difficult than that through Badkheis by Lessar's route, and so it will not be quite so easy to reach that place suddenly.

Therefore what we must do is to place Herat beyond the possibility of a *coup de main*. At present its fortifications are in very bad order, and we have no party whatever in the place. If the contrary were the case, it follows that Russia would not undertake an attack on that place until she was ready to break with England, and until she had assembled a sufficient force to enable her to be pretty sure of taking it within a month. All this means more delay on their part and more time for us.

But how are we to do this? We must send officers there at once, and hold a light division in readiness to move from the Khojak at a moment's notice, equipped entirely with mule carriage. With regard to this division, I refer my readers to a succeeding portion of this paper.

I may be told that public opinion is not ripe for such a bold step. All I have got to answer is, then public opinion had better become ripe as soon as may be, for it is absolutely necessary.

I think that as soon as the Boundary Commission reached Kohsan or Sarakhs, some of the officers should be detached to Herat with something like ten lakhs of rupees to put the defences into thorough repair, and to arrange for some trustworthy garrison to hold them.

At this point I will extract largely from a very valuable paper by Mr. H. Barnes, Political Agent in Pishin, which embodies as succinctly as may be views which I have long held on the subject. To gain complete possession of Herat is of the utmost importance, and I can see no other way than to have that province assigned to us, as Mr. Barnes recommends:—

"This paper starts with the assumption that, in view of the complications "likely to arise from the onward march of the Russians, it is desirable in the "interests of the British Empire in India to obtain sufficient control over "Herat to prevent the possibility of that place falling into Russia's hands.

"I do not wish to argue at length on the justice of this assumption. "The question is discussed in a variety of published books and papers, and this "memorandum is written mainly for those who believe the assumption made "to be correct. But it may be worth while to mention briefly one or two of the "principal arguments on which the assumption is based, because they are "generally admitted to be sound by most people who have taken the trouble to "study the question. In short, these arguments are not so much arguments "as facts, of the truth of which there is very little question, as everybody who "examines them can judge for himself. The first fact is, that in a very short "time, four or five years perhaps at the most, Russia, if unopposed, will be in "possession of Merv.* This fact admits, I think, of no doubt. Russia is al- "ready at Askabad, and it is unreasonable to suppose she intends to stop "there if she can help it. She will naturally do all she can to connect that "outpost with her Turkestan possessions; and only the other day Nur Verdi "Khan, the Tekke Chief, is said to have suggested the establishment of a "Russian cantonment at Kyuik Tapa in Merv territory. According to later "news, Russian troops are already established on the banks of the Tejend. "The second fact is that, in the event of a quarrel between England and "Russia, Russia, if at Merv, could at any moment occupy Herat by a *coup "de main* before we could possibly do anything to save the place either from "India or elsewhere. This is also beyond doubt. It is only necessary to "examine the map, and to compare distances and the configuration of the in- "tervening countries to be convinced of its truth. Merv, it will be seen, is "within easy reach of the Herat Valley, along a road everywhere well supplied "with water from the Murghab.

"The third fact is that, if the Russians were to take Herat, it would be "extremely difficult, if not impossible for us, to turn them out of it by force "of arms. In the event of general war, we might beat Russia in Europe, or "we might put such pressure on her from the sea that, at the restoration of "peace, we might be able to insist on the abandonment of Herat. This is "quite possible. But failing this, it would be risky, if not impossible, to "enforce the abandonment by means of an army marching from India "through Afghanistan. All the reasons urged against the possibility of an "invasion of India from Merv would in this case apply to us.

"So far, I think, there is no flaw in the argument, and no part of it "which admits of any difference of opinion. There is one proposition left "which completes the chain of argument, and which, if admitted, establishes "soundness of the assumption with which this paper begins. This is the "proposition that the occupation of Herat by Russia will be extremely dan- "gerous to the British power for India. There was a time when probably no "Englishman would have hesitated to accept this proposition as true; but "latterly there has been so much indecision and confusion of thought on the "subject of the danger to be feared from Russia, that there may be some "people inclined to question its validity. To such people I can only recom- "mend a careful consideration of the following arguments. First, no one is "afraid of an invasion of India by Russia from Askabad. Secondly, the "flood of argument which has been let loose to prove that any such invasion "would be ruinous to the invaders is altogether beside the mark. Thirdly, "the real danger to be feared is not an invasion commenced from her present

---

* Ere this paper reached me, Russia had already taken possession of Merv.—C. M. M.

"frontier, but a gradual advance of Russia to some place within easy striking "distance. If Merv is occupied, and we make no sign, Herat will also follow. "If Herat is taken, and still we insist in remaining quiescent behind our "own frontier, there is really no valid reason why Kandahar should not next "be occupied, and no one will question the possibility of an invasion of India "then. However, without advancing further than Herat, Russia would "speedily make us feel the inconvenience of having her so near our border. "She would be *within* Afghanistan. We should be outside. And every one "acquainted with Afghan character knows this means that the Afghans will "necessarily be on the side of Russia, and that our influence in the country "will be gone. There is no greater fallacy than to suppose that the occupa- "tion of any part of Afghanistan by Russia would make the mass of the "Afghans her foes. Afghans respect power above all things, and Russia has "a knack of making her power felt. There is a great deal of truth in Skobe- "leff's dictum, that the true way to deal with Asiatics is to stirike hard and "to inspire terror once for all. Russia will strike hard, and she will never "have any further trouble. Moreover, if the hostility of the Afghans to us is "alleged in answer to this argument, it should be recollected that it was the "want of permanency about our own occupation of the country which reduced "the number and weakened the resolution of our friends. On the other "hand, where Russia comes, she will remain; and the prestige of her arrival, "coupled with the knowledge of her intention to stay, will at once create a "party in her favour at least as strong as any we could raise against her. "This would be true of any part of Afghanistan, and it is especially true of "Herat, and its comparatively peaceful and unbigoted inhabitants. Russia's "presence in Herat would mean therefore the total eclipse of English in- "fluence in Western Afghanistan; and this influence could only be partially "regained by the occupation on our part of Kandahar. Most military "authorities, I believe, consider that the occupation of Kandahar would be "inevitable if Russia reached Herat. But whether we went to Kandahar or "not, in either case we should have to increase our Indian Army, to "strengthen our frontier, and adopt an attitude of constant readiness, which "would lay a very heavy burden on our Indian finances. These arguments "may be amplified and illustrated to almost any extent. But it is sufficient "merely to state them here, and I imagine that by the majority of those who "have seriously studied this question they will be thought to establish the "truth of the proposition that the occupation of Herat by Russia will be "dangerous to India; and once this is admitted, the assumption made at "the beginning of this memorandum will not be found very much at vari- "ance with the facts.

"This being so, it remains to consider in what way we can best "establish the necessary control over Herat. One simple and obvious way "would be to annex Afghanistan, and to make Herat our frontier province. "But though this would be a very complete solution of the problem, it "is equally obvious, I think, that it is impracticable. In the first place, we "should have to begin with a war of conquest, which, though it would be "easier and less costly than is generally supposed, would at any rate involve "considerable expenditure. Next, the plan would accomplish too much; for, "besides gaining, what after all is the only object aimed at, the control "of Herat, it would also necessitate the occupation and administration of "large areas of barren and unprofitable country, which are of no value "to us in any sense, and which would never pay the cost of administration. Thirdly, though the mass of the people would soon be sufficiently content "with our rule, we should permanently alienate all the ruling and all the idle "classes of the community, and these might hereafter be a source of danger "in the event of an attack from without. On the principle that it is not "advisable to make more enemies than we can help, this risk should not be "incurred, if it is possible to obtain the result aimed at in some other way.

"Finally, the magnitude of the undertaking is such, and it would more-"over be so much exaggerated, that there is not the slightest chance of any "English Government agreeing to undertake it. This solution of the problem "may therefore be rejected as out of the question.

"A second plan would be to arrange with the Amir for a purely military "occupation of Herat, the administration remaining Afghan as at present. "This plan has been recommended on very high authority, and it means, I "understand, the occupatiop by British and Indian troops of the outposts of "Ghorian Kuhsan and Bala Murghab, and the occupation and fortification "of the Herat city. If it were likely to succeed in practice, this plan would "possibly, from a purely military point of view, suffice to meet all the neces-"sities of the case. But there is one objection to it so formidable, that I think "it also may be left out of consideration. This is, that all our experience "shows us that native rule, supported by English bayonets, is about the very "worst and most unsatisfactory form of government with which it is possible "to afflict a people; and in a country like Afghanistan, where the rulers are sure "to be impatient of advice, and the people are always impatient of tyranny, its "adoption would soon lead to our being thoroughly disliked and detested. Re-"cent instances in point are the government of the Wali in Kandahar, and the "government of the Khan's Naibs in Quetta before we took over the manage-"ment ourselves. In Kandahar it was a common remark that the people would "be glad to be governed by us; but they hated a rule of their own on whom, "owing to the presence of English troops, they could not enforce the salutary "checks supplied by discontent and rebellion. The mere fact that the gov-"ernors are free from these natural checks to the exercise of arbitrary power "tends to make their rule far more severe and tyrannical than it would be if "we were not there to enforce order. The people in Herat would continually "appeal from us to their Afghan rulers, and still more often from their "Afghan rulers to us. If we did not interfere, we should be held responsible "for, and share the unpopularity of, all tyrannical acts of the Amir. If we "did interfere, we should have trouble with the Amir's officers. Indeed, I "consider the political difficulties that would gradually arise would soon be so "intolerable, that we should have no alternative but to withdraw or to take "over the administration ourselves. I do not admit that the position of the "Native States in India at all weakens the force of this argument. It is "quite true that in most of these States native rule is quite tolerable, although "anything like serious disorder is prevented by the proximity of British "troops; but it should be recollected that this was not always the case, and "it is only the case now after a century of interference and example. To get "a correct idea of what is likely to occur in Herat, we must go back to the early "days of our relations with Native States in India. To give only one instance "out of many. We had to assume the administration of the Berars because "the mismanagement of the Nizam's government was so great, that it failed "to perform its treaty obligations; and at one time, for a period of eight or "ten years, the remainder of the Hyderabad districts had to be placed for "similar reasons under the control of British officers. If this was the case "with India, it is much more likely to prove the case in Afghanistan, where "the ruling race is entirely Mussalman, notoriously suspicious of foreigners, "and excessively vain and arrogant in the exercise of authority. We cannot "afford in Herat to wait till a better state of things arises, nor can we afford "to incur the unpopularity with both people and rulers, which in the meantime "is certain to be our lot. Nor, on the other hand, could we venture to "interfere in the administration without the risk of political difficulties with "the Amir. I look upon it therefore as an axiom that, if we occupy Herat, "the administration of the valley must be also in our hands; and not only do "I think this, but I consider that in carrying on the administration, we "should employ as few Duranis as possible, and should endeavour by every "reasonable safeguard to exclude the possibility of interference or meddling "on the part of the Afghan authorities. If I am correct in the opinion, it "is obvious that the scheme of a military occupation only would not succeed "in practice. Minor objections to the proposal are—first, that under native "rule the great capabilities of the Herat province and the Herat trade would "remain undeveloped. Second, that our military force would have to consist "entirely of British or Indian troops. Not having the administration in our "own hands, we could do very little to raise local troops, and we should have "no revenues from which to pay them. Thirdly, as we should be debarred "from sharing in any prospective increase of the Herat revenues, the plan "would be far more expensive than it need be if different arrangements were "made. The full force and meaning of these objections will be better under-"stood when I come to describe the third alternative I have to suggest. But "the main objection to the scheme is that first given; and I am most strongly "of opinion that, if political difficulties are to be avoided, it is essential that "the places we think it necessary to occupy with troops should be under our "political administration also.

"This brings me to my third alternative, which is briefly this, that the "Amir, or whoever may be the ruler of Herat, should be induced to assign to "us the administration of the Herat Valley up to and including the frontier "towards Persia and Merv in consideration of an annual quit-rent equivalent "to the gross revenue now derived from the province. This proposal is inten-"tionally worded in its present form for reasons which I will now give, and "which it is as well to allude to at once before I proceed to discuss the "merits and advantages of the proposal. First, I say 'the Amir or the "ruler of Herat, whoever he may be.' I believe myself that if the above "proposition were placed before the Amir in proper light, he would without "much difficulty be induced to accept it. The reasons we can urge are such "as he can readily appreciate, because they appeal direct to his self-interest. "It is obvious, as already shown, that Russia will be soon at Merv, and that "in the event of a war or even a misunderstanding with England, she will "certainly occupy Herat. This province will thus be irretrievably lost to the "Amir; and as in that case we should probably find it necessary to occupy "Kandahar, the whole of South Afghanistan would consequently pass out of "his hands. This result may be looked on as inevitable, and it may be so "represented to the Amir. We, however, do not require Kandahar, but only "Herat. Our occupation of Herat would therefore save Kandahar for the "Amir. He would also get a full equivalent for the revenues of the Herat "Valley; and the country being only assigned, and still nominally his, he "would be spared the odium of ceding to another power the full sovereignty "of any part of his dominions. All these considerations are of real import-"ance in dealing with the Amir, and I believe if they were properly placed "before him, he would raise no objection to the scheme.

"I have already given my reasons for thinking that where we occupy "with troops, we must necessarily have the administration too, and I recommend that the administration be assigned, and not ceded in full sovereignty, "because, while the result to us is the same, the difference to the Amir is of "the greatest importance. Vanity alone would induce any Afghan ruler to "refuse absolutely any proposal to cede an inch of territory of his own free "will. On the other hand, an assignment in consideration of receiving the "equivalent of the revenues saves his honour, and would probably be agreed "to. We have learnt the full value of this distinction to the Oriental mind "owing to our negotiations with the Khan of Kelat regarding Quetta. The "Khan would never have agreed to cede Quetta, but he was glad to assign it, "and the district is now held on terms exactly identical with those proposed "for Herat. Next, I have suggested that the equivalent to be given to the "Amir for the assignment should be the amount of the present gross revenues "of the valley. I have rejected the ordinary phrase, *viz.*, "the surplus revenues "after payment of the cost of administration," because this still leaves room "for the Amir's interference with our management; and if the arrangement "is to work smoothly, I assert again that all possibility of interference by "any of the Amir's officials in the administration must be absolutely and "rigidly excluded. Here, again, our Quetta experience is useful. As in "Quetta, so in Herat, the revenues would increase enormously under our "administration. This would not escape the Amir's notice, and any stipulations about surplus revenue would result in calls for accounts and discontent "with the sums given; and this would certainly lead to misunderstandings, "which, I need hardly repeat, it should be our object to avoid as much as "possible. It is better therefore to fix the sum payable at once and for ever "as we have now done in Quetta. The revenues of Herat are about 15 lakhs "of rupees, of which about 4 or 5 are paid away in pensions and allowances "(most of which we should have to maintain), only 10 or 11 lakhs reaching "the Amir. I would be generous and fix the sum payable at the total gross "revenues, *viz.*, 15 lakhs, first, because the Amir would marvel at our generosity, and probably agree all the more readily, because he would imagine "he had got the better of us; and secondly, because we may safely assume "that under our administration the revenues of the province would speedily "produce us double that sum. To give an instance. Sibi yielded 10,000 a "year to the Amir. It now gives 1¼ lakhs. Similarly the revenue of "Quetta was Rs. 20,000, of which only about Rs. 10,000 reached the Khan. "This now amounts to a total from all sources, including the town, of nearly "Rs. 1,50,000 a year. We cannot of course expect the Herat revenues to "increase in similar proportion; but the trade of the city is naturally very "large; and both the trade and the area of cultivation would expand to such "an extent under our rule, that I should think we could safely look forward "to a revenue of 30 lakhs at least within a year or two of our occupation.

"So much in explanation of the terms of my proposition. I now proceed to point out its advantage and to discuss its details. First, in the list "of advantages is the important consideration that we should hold the Herat "Valley with the full consent of the Afghans, and under conditions which "would render any misunderstandings or any political difficulties with the Amir "most unlikely. This freedom from all anxiety as to our relations with the "Afghans is of the first importance. Secondly, the administration of the "Valley being in our hands, we could set ourselves to develop its resources, and "we should pocket the whole of any increase in its revenues. Thirdly, this "increase in the revenues can be set apart for the purpose of raising and "maintaining a body of local troops, who would supplement the forces sent "from India; and on these local troops we should mainly rely for the "external defence of the province. Fourthly, these local troops, being paid "from Herat revenues, would be no burden to India, while they would double "and treble our means of resisting, if necessary, any further advance of "Russia, and would probably prevent any further advance being thought of.

"Next as to details, I would suggest that the whole of the proposed "quit-rent of 15 lakhs should be paid to the Amir by the Government of India "direct. This is a fair charge on the Government. and it should be noticed "that the sum named is only 3 lakhs in excess of the sum we are already paying "the Amir for nothing at all. The extra burden on the Indian revenues would "therefore be nominal. Similarly the cost of the contingent of Indian troops "at first sent to Herat would continue to be paid by Government, and the extra "cost would only be the difference between the expense of maintaining the "troops in India and the expense in Herat. This would set free the whole "revenues of Herat for the purpose of paying—first, the cost of civil adminis-"tration, which would be small; and secondly, the cost of raising and main-"taining a large body of local troops. The troops sent from India* would only "be a nucleus, intended to protect the officers entrusted with the administra-"tion, and their duty would probably be simply to garrison the city. The "native element of this force should be composed chiefly of Sikhs and "Punjabi Hindus—first, because the climate requires the men to be hardy; "and secondly, to avoid any possibility of combination with local Mussal-"man troops, and so to reduce to a minimum the danger of a possible mutiny. "These men should be paid from Herat revenues; and though possibly a "grant-in-aid would be required at first from India, it is not at all unlikely, "for the reasons already given, that the Herat revenues would in a short "time prove ample for the support of a body of 15,000 or 20,000 men. All "this would be impossible if we adopted the scheme of a military occupation "only, and the force of the minor objections to such a scheme referred to "above will now be appreciated.

"Finally, it remains to be considered whether the scheme would meet the "object in view, *viz.*, of checking the Russian advance. That it would have "this effect, there can be very little doubt. If that result can be attained by a "military occupation of the Herat frontier, it would be much more certainly "attained by the scheme now proposed. Instead of having to rely on Indian "troops alone in the midst of a population who, having experienced none of the "benefits of our rule, would, from the very circumstances of the position, regard "us as intruders, we should be amongst our own subjects, supported by a large "and efficient local army, with some regular European and Indian troops in sup-"port. I see no reason why with a good system these native Herat and Persian "troops should not be thoroughly attached to us. They would have no more "reason to play us false than the sepoys who won us India; and it is certain "that the Russians would think twice of advancing across the desert from "Askabad or Sarakhs in the face of a large force of trained soldiers, command-"ed by English officers.

"There are of course a number of petty objections to the scheme which "are sure to be brought forward, such as the difficulty of relieving the nucleus "of Indian troops, the difficulty of officers getting to Herat, the difficulty of "communicating with India, and the danger of being so far from supports.

* I think Mr. Barnes puts the force required from India too low. I do not think we should have less than a division of about 12,000 men in Herat, and another division of the same strength on the communications.

"All these admit, I think, of a ready answer. With the Amir on our side, "troops in relief can always march through Kandahar, and reliefs would not be "required oftener than once in two years. Officers travelling alone can always "go, *viâ* Meshed, till the force of European contact on both sides has resulted "in a strong government and safe roads in Afghanistan. Telegraphic communication with Meshed can also be speedily opened; and as regards supports, "the Herat force from its nature would be self-contained and self-supporting. "The province would, in fact, be a little dominion in itself, with its own revenue "and its own army. In the event of an overwhelming attack from Russia, "assistance can always be sent in time from England and India.

"What we are afraid of is the quiet, absorbing advance which our presence in Herat, in the manner proposed, would most effectually check.

"This completes my description of what seems to me the best course to "pursue regarding Herat. Although the scheme may appear visionary and "absurd to those who do not know Afghanistan, and who are still dominated "by that dread of the country which is our legacy from the events of 1842, "I think very few of the officers who are daily engaged in the task of managing and governing Pathan and Biluch tribes will see any great difficulty in "the administration of Herat. For myself I am convinced that the scheme "proposed is perfectly practicable, and contains all the elements of success. It "is based on experience of similar circumstances on a small scale in Biluchistan, "and I see no reason for anticipating either failure or risk in carrying it out.

"If the scheme were adopted, it would probably be necessary to send "our troops to Herat with some secrecy, to prevent a simultaneous Russian "advance. This could be very easily arranged. The troops could go nominally to Kandahar, and they would be in Herat before their real movements "could be ascertained. With Ayub's or the Amir's assistance, there would be "no difficulty in safely marching the force to Herat; and officers could be "sent simultaneously to Meshed to arrange for the completion of telegraphic "communication with Herat immediately on our arrival, and to make some "preliminary arrangements for raising the new troops, the necessary arms "for which could be carried with the force from India. Once at Herat, there "would be no fear of a sudden rush by Russia on Merv. Diplomacy and our "presence on the spot would prevent that. In the course of time routes "connecting Herat with Lash Jorven, Seistan, and with the sea-coast could no "doubt be opened for general traffic, and a direct road to the sea would give "us an alternative line of communication. Great care would of course have to "be displayed in the selection of the officers to command the expedition. The "whole of the military arrangements, as well as the government of the Herat "province, should be entrusted to the General Commanding. It would not "do to have two responsible authorities. The officer appointed should merely "be supplied with a small and experienced civil staff to conduct the revenue "administration under his orders. Provided similar care were displayed in "all the arrangements, and in the selection of the officers told off to raise "the new local troops, I see no reason why the whole scheme should not be a "complete and thorough success.

"I should like to take this opportunity to add a few remarks on the "importance of the question discussed in this paper. The reality of the "Russian advance, and the certainty of Russia's arrival before long on the "borders of Afghanistan, may not perhaps be fully appreciated in England, or "even in Calcutta, at a distance from the scene of operations. But to those "who, like myself, are stationed on the frontier, not a day passes with-

"out some reminder of the near approach of our rivals. It is only necessary "to read the Kandahar and Herat news-letters in order to see how large a "space of Afghan thought is occupied by this question. Rumours as to "Russian movements, and speculation as to Russian plans, form the com- "monest topic of conversation throughout Afghanistan. To take a recent "illustration of the groove in which people's thoughts are running, there is "a pretty general impression (not perhaps altogether ill-founded) that Ayub, "hopeless of any recognition from England, will endeavour to make some "sort of bargain with the Russian officers at Askabad or in Turkistan; and we "can scarcely expect that the ambitious and pushing officers on the Russian "frontier will not try to make some capital out of such a circumstance. It "cannot be too often repeated, and indeed it must be clear to every one, that "in view of possible complications with England in Europe or Asia Minor, "it would be a great advantage to Russia to be able to threaten Afghanistan "at her will. Skobeleff himself in his St. Petersburg speech congratulated "the Emperor on his wisdom in foreseeing the advantage of what he called a "*place d'armés* on the Afghan border; and it is surely most unreasonable "to suppose that the Russians will forbear to grasp this advantage merely "out of consideration for us. They will, of course, act as they deem best for "their own interests, and it would be foolish to assume that they will ever "act otherwise. As a means of neutralising our opposition to any plans she "may entertain in Europe, Russia has everything to gain by advancing; and "advance she, of course, will so long as we allow her to do so. At present "we are not without a remedy."

I am afraid that there will be few who will be inclined to recommend Government to face our difficulties in the resolute manner which Mr. Barnes proposes. The distance to Herat is so great, and lies through such inhospitable regions, and through the country of such wild and unfriendly tribes; the distaste of the sepoy to prolonged service away from India is believed to be so great; the difficulties of supply would be so enormous, and the reinforcing our force would be so Herculean a task—that most of us would simply shy from considering the subject at all.

But is all this true? Are we quite sure that it is not the dark shadows of the view that we are afraid of? The distance from our base Pir Chowki is exactly 576 miles. Now, is 576 miles* anything so very awful? The history of India teems with instances of our forces having marched quite as long distances. To mention only a few that I can remember at once. Lord Lake marched 325 miles in 18 days in pursuit of Holkar, and General Smith did 628 miles in 44 days; while we all remember General Roberts' march from Kabul to Kandahar, 320 miles, in 24 days. And if we are 576 miles from Herat, the Russians are 533 miles from it at Kizil Arvat. They are not afraid to stretch out their hands so far for offence. Are we afraid to go 576 miles for defence? Clearly it is not the distance that is a *real difficulty*.

I grant that the road lies through a bad country, and among wild tribes. But is the country from Quetta to Herat worse than that from Krasnovodsk to Herat; and are the tribes on the former road in any way more wild than the Turkomans of Merv? The answer to this must also be in the negative. The difference lies in the fact that the Russians have resolutely grasped their nettle, while we are even afraid to put out our hands.

I heard a good deal in Kabul of the distaste of the sepoy to prolonged service away from his home; but I made a good many enquiries about it, and

* And this should be reduced before very long to 365 miles, or 25 days' march.

I am convinced that the distaste was no more in degree and no different in kind to that which was displayed by all the troops, officers as well as men. No people in the world like kicking their heels in an out-of-the-way place doing nothing—and, for all they can see, for nothing. The feeling did not altogether arise from 'nostalgia,' but also from the tedium of idleness and the indefiniteness of their future. When the order came to go to Kandahar,—most of us were certainly eager to do so.

Besides, it is a fact that if sufficient inducements are held out to them, natives of India are not so very unwilling to go beyond the seas for definite periods; and this is proved by the fact that the Police in Hongkong and Singapore and Perak are largely composed of Sikhs. If you take a Britisher and a Sikh to Singapore or Herat for an apparently definite object, and you keep him there an indefinite time without any definite object apparent to him, both will grumble and long to get back. But if you tell Sikhs or other natives of India you want them to serve for a specified number of years in any place on enhanced pay, and if you make arrangements for the care of their families that satisfy them, I don't think they will be unwilling to go.

Again, just ponder this question. Granting that a certain "*mal du pays*" will come over your native troops, and that it has a certain infinitesimal effect on recruiting in India, will the effect of its being known in India that we have let the Russians go to Herat, and are afraid to turn them out, be less or more injurious to us in India than a certain home sickness amongst our native troops? That is the point. We are shirking a small inconvenience to court a great danger.

Then, with regard to the difficulty of supplying and reinforcing our division at Herat. Granting they may be great, the real question is, are they greater than those which would have to be met by the Russians if they take the place we are so afraid of approaching? They will not certainly be greater, nor so great. For after all to overcome such difficulties is a simple matter of organization. They might appal a man to whom the supply of two days' rations to Brighton Volunteers is a feat; but I am sure if my friends Colonel Badcock or Major Rind were to be told to arrange it, they very soon would do so.

In regard to the route which a force would take to get to Herat, I will speak in another place. I have already prepared a scheme by which I would undertake to put 12,000 British troops in Herat under 60 days.* I have, in fact looked the bogie in the face, and I do not find it so very awful. I think the first division should be equipped entirely with mules and march light by way of Kandahar, and I should not have the very smallest fear of its getting to Herat in the time I have named.

Mr. Barnes says that in the course of time a route could be opened connecting Herat with Lash Jorven, Seistan, and the sea. I have no doubt of this also; and in speaking of the part of my paper which comes under the heading of communications, I will show that it will be necessary and possible to open up regular caravan routes from Herat to the sea at Gwadar and to Jacobabad; the last quite independent of the Kandahar Road. The connection of Herat with points accessible to us, but not accessible to the Russians by roads which lead away from India, is a necessary part of the strategical part of this problem, and my readers will find it all duly discussed in another part of this paper.†

---

* Such a force could be put down at Pir Chowki and Nari in 10 days after the order was given. It could reach Kandahar by the 30th day, and Herat in under 60 days.

† *Vide* Appendix S.

I hope these remarks will drive away that bogie which seems to so many to sit on the Herat road barring our way, for it is only a bogie after all. But if they do not, I ask another question, and I want an answer to it, as I cannot concoct one for myself. What measure, short of taking over Herat as above proposed, will *effectually* keep the Russians out of it?

Till this is answered, I shall remain satisfied that Mr. Barnes's plan is not only the sole manly English way out of our difficulties, but *it is the only feasible one.*

If this is done, we shall have secured so valuable a strategic position, that I think I would guarantee the English Government from any trouble in the direction of Herat for a good many years to come. If Herat is held by us, it will require a very large Russian force to take it from us; and if they did do so, and we held on to Lash Jorven, and had a well organized line of communications with India, but running *away* from it, nothing but an overwhelming Russian force would dare to advance beyond Farah. But remember there is no time to be lost. This must be done *now.*

The next step I shall take up is the vital importance of our at once taking steps to gain over the Char Aimak and the Hazaras heart and soul to our side. They are ripe for it now, and I would spare no money or trouble to accomplish this object. Soon, very soon; this too may be too late. The Char Aimak number 20,000 and the Hazaras about 90,000 fighting men* hostile to the Afghans. I need not dilate on what a power these would be, if properly armed and organized. The situation and impracticability of their country places them in a position of the last strategical importance in this problem; and it must be evident from a glance at the map that no advance could take place from Herat towards Kandahar, or from Balkh towards Kabul, as long as this formidable force, commanded by English officers, was on the flank of any army attempting these roads. In the Afghan campaign, whatever bad blood was caused between us and the Afghans, there is no ill-feeling between us and the Hazaras. The soil is ready; we have only to sow the seed. Let half a dozen English officers therefore be sent there at once to sow rupees and rifles, with the certain prospect of a crop of invaluable warriors devoted to our cause.†

The Amir of Ghain and the Khan of Khaf also hold very important positions strategically. Through their territories come the only roads by which the direct Mashad-Herat road can be turned to the south. From what I saw of the former, I should say that he had his price; and no doubt Colonel Stewart has made friends with the latter.

I attach the greatest importance, as will be seen further on, to our being able to concentrate quickly and operate by the line of the Gomal or near Ghazni. The whole of this country is in the hands of the Ghilzais; and as the sections of them called Povindahs are entirely in our hands, owing to the fact that if we stopped their trade with India they would be ruined, I think we should take advantage of this to make satisfactory political arrangements with the Southern Ghilzais at least. I don't think this will be very difficult; and if money is judiciously used amongst their Chiefs and *their Mulas,* I should

* The Char Aimak consist of Hazaras 3,000 foot, Jamshidis 2,000 foot, Feroz Kohis 4,000 foot, Taimanis 8,000, besides 3,000 horse for all—total, 20,000.

The Hazaras consist of the following clans:—Dehzangi, 10,000 families; Behsud, 11,000; Jaghatu, 7,000; Karabagh, 7,000; Jaghuri, 8,000; Dehkundi, 10,000; Mazaristan, 8,000; others 9,000—total, 70,000 families, or about 350,000 souls, or 90,000 fighting men.

† I have been asked how I would open communications with the Hazaras. In the first instance, I should do so by letters addressed to their leading men, whom I understand to be Mir Nasir Beg, Buniyad Khan, &c. In these letters I would ask them to send down confidential agents to confer with us; and once they came, I think we should very soon worry out some *modus operandi.*

expect to see them fall in with our views, especially as we do not want very much from them. What we want is simply the right of unmolested way through their country from our frontier to the Hazara country. We want transport and supplies from them, and safe conduct for our supply caravans; and we want them to trust in us rather than in the Amir. All this we could and should pay for handsomely.

But these steps will only close the road to Kandahar. It is certainly the most dangerous line to us; but it is not the only one, and I have shewn in the first part of this paper how the Russians can also advance on Kabul and Chitral. I will show in Chapter V of this paper how to meet the first of these; but as it belongs purely to the military part of the problem, I need not do more than allude to it here.

With reference to Chitral, however, it is different. Here we must adopt the same plan as I have recommended for securing Herat and the Kandahar road. We must take up a position to protect the north-eastern corner of Afghanistan by taking over from the Chief of Chitral, the Amir, and the Kashmir Government on the same terms as at Herat all the country which lies between the north-eastern strip of Afghanistan about the Pamer and Kashmir territory, *i.e.*, the districts of Vakhan, Chitral, and Yasin.

To these places the distances are no doubt great, and the country is no doubt difficult; but the communications, with the rear are quite safe, lying as they do through the territories of an ally who dare not openly oppose us. I therefore propose to send officers at once to Chitral to organize those districts, and to gain over and arm and organize the Siahposh. I imagine neither of the above-named chiefs gets much from these districts; but it would be well worth our while to pay them 50,000 rupees or so in return for the assignment of these districts to us. In them we should have a position of incalculable strategical importance in the problem of the defence of India.

"The Kafirs," according to Mr. MacNair, "inhabit a country which at "present embraces an area of 6,500 square miles. It is bounded on the north "by the Hindu Kush, on the south by the Kabul and Kunar Rivers; for its "western limit it has the Alishang, with its tributary the Alingar, and its "eastern boundary may be roughly taken as the Kunar river from its junc- "tion with the Kabul River to where the former receives the water of the "Kalashgan at the village of Ain, thence following up this tributary to its "source, and a line drawn from that point to the head of the Dura Pass. "The population is estimated at over 100,000 souls. The men are of fine "appearance, keen, penetrating eyes, and daring to a fault. It is purely due "to combination and the absence of blood feuds that these people have "succeeded in holding their own against the Mahomedans, by whom they are "hemmed in on all sides. The Kafirs have nothing in common with their "neighbours, and are in fact incessantly waging petty wars against them. "They are exceedingly well disposed towards the British Government, and I "do not hesitate to assert they would willingly place their services at our "disposal, and the sooner steps are taken to secure their friendship the better. "Their arms at present consist merely of bows, arrows, and daggers; but "they have the materials of real good fighting stuff in them."

It is against human nature to suppose that if we are the *first* to hold out the hands of friendship to this brave people (who have for centuries been harried by the Mahomedans), they will not accept it; and their proverbial bravery shows how formidable they might become if armed and organized by us. I do not think it is too much to say that if the Russian Government knew we had such Highlanders at our disposal, they would not for long entertain any idea of threatening us from Chitral; and a look at the map will convince that not only is the position we should thus gain of incalculable importance to us in the strategical problem of defending India, but it would give us a very potent hold over the tribes of Dir and Swat, if they knew that, in addition to being attacked from the south, they might have such implacable enemies down on them from the north.

If we secure Herat, the Hazaras and Char Aimaks, the north-eastern districts of Afghanistan and the Siahposh, and we gain over the Ghilzais, we have the Duranis under our thumbs. For what is Afghanistan?—A country inhabited by Duranis, Ghilzais, Hazaras, and Yaghistanis! If we gain over the second and third at once, we can get the fourth whenever we please, as easily as the Duranis can. Then where would they be?—They would be our slaves!

I am afraid there can be little hope of our at this late period getting Persia to act hostilely to Russia; but the aid of Persia to us is a matter of such importance, that I think every effort should be made to secure, if not her hostility to Russia, at least a benevolent neutrality to us. It is not too much to say that if Persia could be induced to withhold any aid to Russia in the matter of supplies and transport, any sudden enterprise on the part of Russia against Herat on her part must end in failure, because it is only by having these supplied to her at the necessary points that she could as matters now stand put a force into Herat before we could. And even if it is found that the ruling family at Teheran is heart and soul against us, and that nothing we can do will prevent them from aiding Russia, I would not despair of gaining the necessary end by other means. The Central Government in Persia is notoriously weak; and there can be little doubt that various governors of districts in Khorassan are open to golden arguments*; and I therefore propose that Colonel Stewart be given orders at once to perambulate along the districts, and ascertain what steps should be taken to gain any or all of them over to our side, to the extent at least of inducing them to withhold supplies and transport.

These orders may be sent to him now by telegraph, and other officers should start at once for Persia. One should be directed to travel about between Tiflis, Baku, Petrovski, and Astrakhan. Another should reside in the province of Astrabad, and move about towards Shahrud and the Gurgan. A third should roam between Burjnurd, Kuchan, Daragaz, and Kalat-i-Nadir. These officers should beforehand make arrangements to have in their pay numerous native spies whom they could send to places in the hands of the Russians where they would not be allowed to enter. Colonel Stewart might continue his *rôle* of prowling about the east districts of Khorassan.

By these means we should at least be sure that nothing was being done or prepared for in these countries of which we had not very certain information. But an even more important duty of these officers would be to ascertain the resources of their beats in transport and supplies; and they should be ordered that if signs shewed themselves of any intention to transport large bodies of troops on the Caspian, it was to be at once reported, and orders should be sent to them to buy up all the supplies, and to hire or buy as many transport animals, especially mules, as they could lay hands on, and have them driven south to Yezd or east into Afghanistan, in order to denude as many districts as possible of these vital necessaries. I am convinced that in this manner a very great deal might to done to paralyse a Russian advance; and as a good many of the

* Lessar, as the result of his experience in Khorassan, says: "In general the rulers of the feudatory provinces of Khorasan when bold enough are hostile to Russia. They, and they only in Persiar, are dissatisfied with the subjugation of the Akhal Tekke."

animals might be driven towards Kandahar to meet a force coming from that direction, the money spent in their purchase would not be all lost.

It is because they foresee that some such plan may be attempted by us that the Russians are so anxious to push on their Atak Railway, as by means of it they can collect in sufficient force to push a detachment on to Herat and take it by a *coup de main ;* and it requires no further argument to show what an excellent move denuding the country of Khorassan of transport and supplies would be. Of course, when the Russians have, as I believe they intend to, absorbed the whole of Kalat-i-Nadir, they will at once extend their railway up to the extreme confines of that district, and then the above arrangement will become of less value, as they will be able to collect troops and stores and transport behind their new frontier, and then make a rush on Herat, supposing we are not in it.

Up to Kizil Arvat this railway was opened for traffic in 1881. Immediately afterwards Gospodin Lessar was employed in preparing plans for the extension of the line to Ashkabad. His surveys having demonstrated the feasibility of the railway to this point, General Annenkoff instructed him to proceed beyond, and report whether the nature of this ground was favourable for its extension to Sarakhs. Lessar successfully accomplished his task and reported that the ground was level nearly all the way from Ashkabad to Sarakhs. He was then instructed to obtain the same information regarding its extension to Herat; and he has lately finished this work, and has demonstrated the perfect ease with which Russia can extend her railway system to that point.

The present state of the railway I believe to be as follows.

From Michaelovsk to Kizil Arvat 144 miles is now working. It is said to have cost £648,000.

With regard to extensions, it will first be necessary to take up part of the line from Michaelovsk and relay it from Krasnovodsk to some point on the line to Kizil Arvat such as Mula Kari. The distance is 95 miles, and it may be estimated to cost £427,500.*

Beyond Kizil Arvat the line was not laid, but a narrow 20″ gauge line worked with 2½ tons petroleum locomotives on Decauville's system was laid to Bami, 65 miles. This, however, has since been picked up and laid to the Naphtha hill.

It will therefore be necessary to lay down the whole line to Ashkabad, 146 miles. This will cost £504,000.

On to Sarakhs, 185 miles, will cost £742,000; and to Herat, 202 miles, £910,000 more, making a total extension still required of 523 miles. Mr. Marvin says they can be done at a cost of a little under 2¼ millions; but this I doubt, and should be inclined to estimate it at nearer £9,000 a mile than £4,500.

This brings me to a consideration of the very insufficient state of our means of getting information of the movements of Russia in Asia. In making this accusation, I do not in any way wish it to be understood that I make any reproach against the Intelligence Branch of the Quarter Master General's Department. The work of that office consists in collecting information about the various countries which may be the field of operations of our Indian army, and I am proud to believe that nowhere can such complete information regarding the topographical features and resources of such countries be found as in it. But the Intelligence Branch has not the funds to

---

* Calculated at the same rate as the Sarakhs-Herat section.

enable it to get information regarding Russian movements; and if it had, I am pretty sure that our making any such attempt would be entirely discouraged, if not actually forbidden.

The channel through which, by our system, such information should reach us is through the Foreign Offices in India and London; but I don't think I am stating anything inconsistent with facts if I say those offices have no sufficient system of gaining *early*, *accurate*, and *regular* information. At all events with regard to the Indian Foreign Office, I am sure this is the case; and judging from the admission by Sir C. Dilke in the House of Commons lately, I would not mind laying odds that it is equally true of the English Office.

The means of information of the Indian Foreign Office consist in the stationing news-writers in Kandahar, Kabul, Herat, and Mashad, &c. These men are quite well known to the local authorities; and even if their letters are not actually read by them, it is certain they cannot be looked on as of any value whatever. One may read pages of these news-letters without coming on any information; they are the merest bazaar rumours, and I have no hesitation in saying are almost worthless.

With regard to gaining *early*, *accurate*, and *regular* information of the actual movements of Russian troops from the Caucasus and Russia towards Turkistan and trans-Caspia, which is really what we most want, we have absolutely no system beyond having a few Russian papers translated by Mr. Mitchell. As if the Russian authorities ever allowed anything they wished kept secret to appear in the papers!

If the case was reversed, there might be some sense in the Russian Foreign Office refusing to go to much expense to get information of our doings, as in our case: not only is every movement of troops published, but if any of them are towards the frontier, care is always taken by our editors to explain exactly what the true cause of the movement is.

But lest it should be said I am talking without the book, I will give a very recent instance of our hopeless ignorance on a subject which may even yet be of the last importance to us. On the 4th May 1883 Colonel Swaine, our Military Attaché at Berlin, wrote giving some information regarding the concentration of Russian forces in Central Asia from an "unquestionable source." This information is as follows: "Since the victory of Geok Tepe, "and the conclusion of the Treaty of Kuldja with China, the Russians have "worked for a better concentration of troops in Central Asia. This concen-"tration has taken place at points within a much more convenient distance "of the Afghan frontier, and consists of 45,000 infantry, 7 batteries of artillery "of 8 guns each, an enormous body of cavalry, all Cossacks, and of 11,000 "local troops, quite excellent of their kind."

This very important report filtered through Lord Ampthill, Earl Granville, the India Office, the Indian Foreign Office, and on the 28th June 1883—fifty-five days after Colonel Swaine had written it—it reached His Excellency the Commander-in-Chief in India!

Colonel Swaine wrote that since the victory of Geok Tepe, *i.e.*, since March 1881, this concentration had been going on; yet the first sound we hear of it comes twenty-seven months afterwards!

On receipt of this information (which was only forwarded to us in the ordinary course of business from the Indian Foreign Office) nothing whatever was done. Something was attempted; but it fell quite flat. It was clear the Government attached no importance to a rumour (said by one of our officers to come from an "unquestionable source") that Russia was concentrating a force of not less than 60,000 men towards the Afghan frontier, and this view has been upheld by after-events; for from that day to this the Government of India in the Military Department have made no allusion whatever to the subject.

But it seems to have engaged the attention of the Indian Foreign Office sufficiently to induce them to prepare (seven months afterwards—on the 17th January 1884) "A note on the concentration of Russian troops in Central Asia." From this note, which reached us on the 16th February 1884 (the serene leisureliness of this procedure is to be admired), I get the following extra information:—

"In September 1883 the Amir sent us a news-letter from Samarkand, "containing the following statements:—25,000 troops had arrived at the "town of Turkistan; 15,000 men had been sent to Khokand; 4 battalions sent "from Tashkand to Charjui had been stopped on the road; 2 battalions were "said to have been ordered to Kilif, where the Russians intended to build a "cantonment.

"In November 1883 the Amir sent us a second news-letter from Samar-"kand, in which the writer repeats his former statement that 25 battalions had "recently arrived from Russia; and he further states that 4 of these batta-"lions had gone to Urganj and 4 to Ush. Four battalions were destined "for Charjui and 2 for Kilif.

"The same news-writer reported in a letter received in December 1883 that "12 battalions with 18 guns had arrived at a place called Joban Atta. Their "destination was variously reported to be Khiva and Afghanistan.

"As to the troops of Bokhara, which may be considered as subsidiary forces, "we heard in November last from Miyan Rahat Shah that 3,000 irregu-"lar cavalry, one battery of artillery, one battalion of infantry, and one regi-"ment of regular cavalry had been stationed at Kulab, while 6,000 men were "said to be encamped on the Darwaz and Shighnan border.

"In 1882 the Russian forces in the Akhal consisted of 5,500 infantry, "800 cavalry, and 500 artillery, with 77 guns.

"In July 1883 the Amir's news-writer at Askabad reported the arrival of "four fresh battalions. He further stated that the number of guns had been "brought up to 90. Some of these were heavy guns drawn by 18 horses. "Four were machine guns. We also know that the Russians now dispose of "500 Turkoman cavalry.

"In October 1883 the Meshed Agent reported that the Russians had 10,000 "men in the Akhal. Of these, 2,000 were cavalry.

"In the same month 1,200 cavalry went to the Tejan, but returned again "within a fortnight.

"Colonel Stewart reports in his letter, dated 8th November, that the "garrison at Askabad has been largely reinforced, and that Gawars, where there "used to be a small post of Turkoman cavalry, is now garrisoned by 700 "infantry, with four guns. He also writes that the Russians apparently in-"tend to establish a post at Kara Band on the Tejan. Kara Band is about 90 "miles from Merv, and could, with very little work and expense, be made a "place of considerable importance. It was in former times well cultivated, "and had a considerable Turkoman population. The extent of desert to be "traversed between Kara Band and Merv is less than 60 miles.

"Mr. Thomson telegraphs on the 28th December 1883 that 1,000 Russian "infantry, 500 cavalry, and 10 guns have left for Tejan, probably in order to "occupy Kara Band.

"Reducing the numbers given by native correspondents to a minimum, it "may be said that Russia has now about 70,000 men in Turkistan and 10,000 "in the Akhal, or a total of not less than 80,000 men. In 1877, when an "expedition to Afghanistan was contemplated, there were no troops in the "Akhal, and the total number in Turkistan did not exceed 40,000. Of these, "15,000 were on the Chinese frontier, where Kuldja and Kashgar required "special attention, 10,000 were considered sufficient for the garrisons, and "15,000 were available for the expedition. At present the Chinese border is "quiet, and it may well be supposed that 20,000 men would suffice for all "purposes. There is consequently an excess force of about 60,000 men available for any emergency, and concentrated principally in the direction of "Bokhara and Merv, or rather Sarakhs. The increase in strength is of recent "date, and appears to continue, which is the more remarkable when it is "remembered that the area of the Turkistan district last year was reduced by "nearly one-third through the formation of the 'Steppe' Government with "separate administration and separate army."

Can anything speak more forcibly of the state of our information? Here are at least 60,000 disposable Russians reported (from different independent sources) to be concentrated towards Afghanistan, and we do not know to this day whether it is true or false!

If my readers will turn to the first chapter of this paper, they will see that in considering the possibilities of a Russian advance against Afghanistan, I have shown that the concentration of Russian troops in the Atak and Turkistan necessary for that purpose would take a long time and be done secretly; and here we have a statement averring that, though it has taken a long time, it has been done secretly, and we knew nothing of it.

Then, as the first intimation we had of it was on 4th May, we must assume that the concentration was completed before that time. But even supposing it had only been completed on the 4th May, for 55 days afterwards the Indian Government knew nothing of it! And if something of the same plan as I have supposed they would adopt had been carried out on the 28th June, the day the Commander-in-Chief in India was informed of it, the various columns might have been in the following positions:—*1st*, the Atak column at Herat; *2nd*, the Jam column at Kabul; *3rd*, the Margilan column at Chitral; and *4th*, the Pamer column on the Kashmir Frontier. It would have taken us, in the present state of our preparedness, nearly one month (say 20 days) to put columns on our frontier at the Khojak, and 20 days at Lundi Kotal, and seven days more to put the south column into Kandahar, and thirty days more to place the northern at Kabul; and by that time the Russians would have been in possession of all the vantage points *necessary to make an invasion of India quite a feasible operation.*

These reports, coupled with that which says that Tchernayeff had a plan ready for the invasion of India, make me think that the reports of the concentration were true, and that the actual attempt was only stopped at the last moment by orders from the Russian Government. If, then, we have by an accident escaped this danger, can any sane man any longer doubt the necessity for our establishing at once a system of gaining *early, accurate,* and *regular* information of *every* movement of Russian troops*?

Now, what should this system be? I confess it is not easy to answer; but if the necessity for it is allowed, I am sure the rest will come all right.

---

* I have since heard from Colonel Trench, Military Attaché at St. Petersburg, that no such concentration has taken place.

The information that we really want is—first, we must have an *accurate* distribution return of the whole Russian army; second, we must every week receive a statement, by telegraph when necessary, of every single change made in that distribution.

Of course, it will not do to trust to one source for this or any other such important information; but it must come from as many independent sources as possible. I think our Military Attachés at St. Petersburg, Berlin, and Vienna should have distinct and stringent orders to regard it as one of their most important duties to get such returns, and transmit them and any kindred information, whenever necessary by telegraph, direct to the Indian Government, as well as to the Foreign Office in London. I am pretty sure the War Offices in Vienna and Berlin must have such information, and I really don't see why they should not give it to us.

In addition to the above, I would like to see really secret English agents at once established in Tiflis, Baku, Astrakhan, Orenburg, Tashkand, Samarkand, Ush, Petro-Alexandrovsk, Ashkabad, and Krasnovodsk. Some of these men might be Europeans, some might be natives; but none should be known to each other, or to any one but the Foreign Secretary, and all should have some distinct and ostensible calling to justify their presence at the places named, and the only possible system of gaining good information should be applied to them: they should be paid only by results. No rule can be laid down as to the amounts; it must depend entirely on the value and accuracy of the information, and the celerity and secrecy with which it is despatched. For instance, if the report about the concentration of Russian troops above noted had been true, and had been reported directly it had begun or was contemplated, and each phase of it had been accurately reported as it happened, it might have been cheap at £100,000, as it might have put Her Majesty's Government in a position to protest in time to save a war.

In addition, our Consuls at Batoum, Astrakhan, Resht, Astrabad, &c., &c., as well as Her Majesty's Legation at Teheran, should have very stringent orders to pay most particular attention to the acquisition of early information about movements of Russian troops; and I would continue the beautifully frank, but somewhat childish, system of having news-writers at all the principal places in Turkistan, the Caucasus, Eastern Persia, and Afghanistan. They at all events give the bazaar rumours, and these are useful sometimes as corroborative evidence, and in a measure would withdraw attention from our *real* secret informers.

Of course, the system of getting translations from Russian papers should be kept up, as these articles at all events show the direction of Russian thought: only care should be taken that they are sent out to India much more speedily than has been the case hitherto, and that important items are telegraphed.

A speech made by General Korupatkin also suggests another way of bringing the screw on to Russia. That officer recently said "he greatly feared "an attack from China, as it was impossible to say where it would end. The "Chinese were arming slowly, but continuously. No one knew the strength "of an army the Chinese might be able to throw across the frontier; and it "might prove so stupendous in numbers that no force Russia had available to "place in time to meet them would have the power to stem so destructive a "wave of Celestials."

I am much obliged to the General for the suggestion, or rather, as I had thought of it before reading his speech, for this confirmation of my opinion.

Therefore no time should be lost in instructing our Ambassador at Pekin to take steps to induce the Government of that country to attempt, in the event of a war with England, to regain the provinces south of Siberia which have been from time to time taken from them by Russia.

The complications which have arisen between France and China offer a peculiarly favourable opportunity for in certain contingencies making an alliance with China; for even if they are for the present settled without open war, any settlement the French will agree to is not likely to be agreeable to the Chinese, and there will therefore remain for a long time a soreness against France which may be made the greatest use of. An alliance between Russia and France seems likely; and I cannot help thinking that in that event we should at once make an alliance with China against both France and Russia, giving her officers and arms to direct against the French settlements in Cochin-China and Annam, and against the Russians on the Amur and Kuldja.

I also think that this *rapprochement* between England and China should be open and ostentatious, and our Ambassador should be instructed to make the most of it in his communications with the Russian Foreign Office. It is undoubtedly a screw the Russians fear our handling.

Another step which I would propose would be to send native emissaries to Khiva, Bokhara, Khokand, Kashgar, among the petty trans-Oxus States of Hissar, Kabul, Karatagin, and among the Merv Turkomans, to ascertain and report what chances there would be of organizing rebellion against the Russians. This is a mere preliminary step, and I should say there must be many Natives available in India who would be admirably suited for the work. At first they would only make themselves thoroughly acquainted with the real state of feeling with regard to Russia among the Chiefs and people of those countries, and, if it proved to be unfriendly, to form an opinion as to how rebellion could be best incited and organized, and what assistance would be necessary when the time came. A swarm of such emissaries, with bags of rupees, could not fail very materially to affect the Russian plans; and if this was kept secret till the last, it might even have the effect of making the Russians pause in their accomplishment. In Kashgar I should say that Mr. Dalgleish might be a very fit agent to employ.

The value of such a measure is made abundantly evident by the following extracts from a letter written by the late General Skobeleff to a Russian diplomatist abroad in 1879:—

"The near future will show us, I believe, that England is about to make in "this direction a series of attempts and efforts, bearing at first a purely commer- "cial character, but which will eventually result in our borders being threatened "by a mighty offensive force of Mussulman elements, armed and organized "in European fashion, but none the less inspired by that spirit of religious "fanaticism so characteristic of the people of Asia, and so dangerous in fight- "ing them.

"When once these results, attained by the fulfilment of this first part of "the programme, are sufficiently established, I am convinced that even with "the most peaceable—if such an expression is permissible,—with the most "Gladstonian Ministry, England will be drawn into the paths of invasive "action, at first, perhaps, indirectly against our possessions in the Caucasus "and in Central Asia, and also against the preponderating influence which "guaranteed the observance of the Treaty of Turkmentchai for us both at the "Court of Teheran and throughout Persia.

"At the same time, our position in Central Asia can only be considered "comparatively secure so long as our influence meets no rival. Our uninter-"rupted successes during ten years in this country have been attained not "only by numbers and the strength of our battalions, but mainly by the "unquestioned nature of our influence.

"At the present moment, after General Kaufmann's abortive attempt of "last year, when the natives have found out that there are fire-breathing giants "on the other side, too, of the Hindoo Khoosh, who might even compel us "to turn tail, our influence must inevitably be shaken, and may even be trans-"ferred to the English. From the moment that this occurs, security within "our own boundaries is at an end. The Mussulman population of those dis-"tricts, mastered by us, but still quivering feverishly, will remain submissive "to us only in proportion as it believes that might is still on our side.

"If we have hitherto been able to encounter and suppress the outburst of "Mussulman fanaticism amongst the population of the conquered provinces "with our extremely limited fighting means, we are indebted for this success, "in the first place, to the state of dependence on us in which we have placed "the Khans of Khiva, leaders of the Turkoman tribes (except the Akkal Tek-"kes), the Emir of Bokhara, the Begs of Shakhrisiab, Karatiagan, and of the "Kara Kirghiz of Alai, and the consequent impossibility of making these "districts the centres of political and religious opposition. How clearly the "danger of such a turn of affairs was evident to all persons standing at the "head of our Central Asian administration, is shown by the fact that when "Kashgar, under Yakoob Beg, tried to raise the standard of the Prophet, it was "understood in Tashkent it was absolutely necessary either to conquer "Kashgar by force of Russian arms, or give it over to the Chinese hordes. As "is well known, the last alternative was chosen. In the second place, we "were much assisted by the dissensions existing between all these petty Mus-"sulman Princes, who out of selfishness, envy and fear of our arms quietly "looked on when we attacked their neighbours.

"One man alone in Central Asia understood then that unity was the "pledge of power—and that was Yakoob Khan.

"But even now, when Yakoob Khan is dead, the danger continues to "exist. The eldest son of the Emir of Bokhara, Katta-Tiouria, exiled from "Bokhara and shut out by our influence from successive dreams of revenge, "finds for his restless energy a field not only in Afghanistan, but even beyond "the Indian frontier. Personal bravery and a life full of adventure have made "him in some sort the unquestioned leader of the Mussulman party and repre-"sentative of Mussulman fanaticism. In the hands of the English such a man "may become a powerful and dangerous weapon. The idea of an alliance of "the Mussulman rulers and peoples in Central Asia destroyed, apparently, by "our military successes, may spring up once again, and with greater vitality, "under English influence, which will certainly make itself felt after the con-"quest of Afghanistan, thanks to the financial and military power of England. "The treaty of 4th June 1878, giving the Sultan into the hands of England, "by that also gave the latter influence over all the orthodox Mussulmans of "Central Asia.

"What must not we Russians fear in Central Asia, seeing that England "has succeeded in entangling with a thousand snares him whom the orthodox "of Central Asia consider to this day their leader in war, and the represent-"ative of the Prophet?

"To the advance of the English, who will very soon endeavour to turn "our present vassals into open enemies, and will threaten the security of our "own frontiers, we ought to oppose at any cost a point whence we could (a) "sever the independent Khanates on our frontiers from Afghanistan (under "British influence), by the exertion of material force and moral influence; "and (b) secure Herat from sudden seizure—the 'Key of India,' as the "English call it, and the possession of which would bring with it inevitably "a complete predominance of English influence at Teheran, and—more important still—a military organization of the Turkoman hordes. This point "should be Merv."

The aims of Russia as regards England are altogether so aggressive and unprovoked, that I hold we are justified in using every means in our power, in the event of war, towards breaking up the Russian Empire into fractions that cannot for a long time become dangerous to us; and I therefore now come to consider what steps might be taken towards this very desirable disintegration of the Russian Empire, though I only throw out a few hints with the greatest diffidence.

Russia, owing to her aggressive spirit and eager land-hunger, has, fortunately for our purpose, not one single friend among the many States by whom she is surrounded. There seems to be a natural antipathy between the Germans and Russians; the interests of the Austrians must always be bitterly opposed to those of Russia; Turkey has the best reason to hate and dread her; Persia and the Khanates have also nothing to gain from her, and everything to lose; while England has the best of reasons for unrelenting animosity to her, till she is reduced to more peaceable councils.

The step which I think we should take would be to form, as soon as possible, a grand coalition against her consisting of England, Germany, Austria, Turkey, Persia, Turkistan, Afghanistan and China, and offer to each, as the price of her assistance, certain parts of the present Russian Empire, most of which have been taken from them at one time or another.

The history of Russia is one long tale of aggression and spoliation for the last 150 years. She has effaced the Khanates of Turkistan and the Turkoman country from existence, and she has every intention of still further subjecting them. From Persia she has taken all right of navigating the Caspian, Ashurada, the provinces of Karabagh, Erivan and Talish, the whole of the territory now known as trans-Caspia, and she will endeavour at some future period, if not to take all Persia, at least the provinces of Ghilan, Mazanderan, Astrabad, and Shahrud. From Afghanistan she has as yet taken nothing; but it is quite incontrovertible that she wishes to take at least the whole of Afghan Turkistan and the province of Herat. From Turkey she has taken in Asia the whole of the country south of a line from Poti to the sources of the Arpachai, and thence down to Mount Ararat; and she will not hesitate, when the time comes, to take any more of Asiatic Turkey that will give her a port in the Mediterranean. In Europe she has deprived Turkey of Bessarabia, Moldavia, Walachia, Bulgaria, Servia, and Roumelia, and she has every intention of seizing Constantinople and the Dardanelles. In Europe she has effaced Poland, and holds the German provinces of Esthonia, Curland, Livonia; and has deprived Sweden of Finland. And finally, she aims at depriving England of India.

Surely here are good grounds for the formation of a coalition. Surely the above Powers would like to get back what they have lost, and to retain what they still have; and I feel convinced it is in the power of all to do so, if they will only hold together for a time.

It is a matter for serious consideration whether it would not be best for the interests of Austria and Germany to reconstitute the old Polish Kingdom under proper guarantees, or at least to construct a kingdom consisting of Russian Poland, Lithuania, and Volhynia; and to give to Germany Curland and Riga, and to Austria Podolia and Roumania, or such equivalents as might be desired by them.

I am no advocate for continuing Turkish rule over Christians, and I should therefore be quite averse to recovering for her anything beyond a nominal sovereignty over Servia and Bulgaria, and drawing her real frontier at the Balkhans, leaving to her the whole of Roumelia and Albania. But in Asia the case is different, and here her frontier should include all the Mussalman districts Russia has taken from her.

The provinces of Karabagh and Talish and the region now known as trans-Caspia, and the right to navigate the Caspian, should be returned to Persia, if she joined the coalition heart and soul. But of this I am doubtful, as she is so completely under the thumb of Russia, that she can hardly be called a free agent.

I should not much regret Persia's not joining, as it would give us the opportunity of further rewarding Turkey by giving her the provinces of Azarbaijan and Persian Kurdistan; of restoring to Baluchistan the whole of Persian Mekran; and of giving to Afghanistan Seistan, Ghain, Khaf, and Turbut Shekhjam. Further, Persia might be broken into two States,—the northern to consist of Ghilan, Mazanderan, Astrabad, Khorasan, including trans-Caspia, Khemseh, Teheran, Hamadan, Kum, and Kashan; and the southern, under a ruler completely under our influence, of Yezd, Kirman, Laristan, Fars, Khuzistan, Ispahan, Nain, Kermanshah, and Luristan. I conceive there would be little difficulty in arranging this.

As to the Caucasus, if the whole of this was taken from Russia right up to its northern foot, and formed into two States—one Christian, consisting of Georgia, Russian Armenia, and the Christian tribes of the Caucasus; and the other Mahomedan, consisting of Daghistan, Lesgistan, the Tchetchens, &c.,—it would have the effect of throwing Russian aggression in the East back by some 100 years.

There is another part in which Russia can still be mulcted of territory, and that is to the north of China and north of Kashgar; and the Chinese frontier in these directions should certainly be rectified.

In conclusion, the Khanates of Khiva, Bokhara, and Khokand could be re-established and restored to their old boundaries, Roshan and Shighnan going to Afghanistan. Under this arrangement, the boundaries of Khiva would be as follows,—west Caspian; south, the Balkhan hills, and a line drawn from them across the desert to Kabakli on the Oxus; east, a line thence north to the north of the Kazil Kum desert, about lat. 45° 30′, then on the north across the Aral to the Caspian.

The boundaries of Bokhara would be—west, the Khivan boundary; north, by the Airekti Mountains and Turkistan chain to the head of the Zer-Afshan, then by the Alai Range to the head of the Alai Valley; east, across the Pamer to the spur forming the south watershed of the Wanjab Valley to the Oxus; and south, the right bank of the Oxus to the village of Astana Baba, then including all the cultivation on the left bank to the Khivan frontier as above.

The State of Khokand should comprise the whole of the country draining to the Syr Daria, and its boundaries would be,—east from the head of the Alai Valley by the main watershed to the Suek peak, then north by the northern watershed of the Syr Daria to the west end of the Kara Tagh Range, then a line drawn north of the Aral to the mouth of the Emba.

These are, briefly stated, the measures which I would propose, and I may recapitulate them here :—

(1) Diplomatic trifling with Russia.
(2) The resumption of the 'right of search' and destruction of Russian commerce.
(3) Coalition with Germany, Austria, and Turkey, &c.
(4) Despatch of a Commission for delimitation of the North and North-Western Afghan border.
(5) Assignment to us of the province of Herat.
(6) Alliance, offensive and defensive, with Hazaras and Char Aimaks.
(7) Assignment of districts of Vakhan, Chitral, and Yasin, and organization of the Siahposh.
(8) Endeavours to gain over Persia, or at least to neutralize her giving assistance to Russia.
(9) Proposals for improving our means of gaining intelligence of Russian movements.
(10) An immediate *rapprochement* with China.
(11) Despatch of emissaries to raise rebellion in the Khanates and among the Turkomans.
(12) Disintegration of the Russian Empire by means of a coalition.

It is impossible to state exactly which of these measures are the most important, and which should therefore be taken in hand first. The fact is all are of very great importance, and should all be undertaken without delay. If any one is frightened at such an extensive programme, I can only say it is not my fault that many of them were not taken in hand long ago. I have got to show what diplomatic measures I consider necessary, and I have done so above. If some of them had been undertaken years ago, we should not now be reduced to the pass we are. For instance, the Germano-Austro-Turkish alliance might have been arranged, and rumours might have been allowed to escape about it. The Afghan boundary might have been settled, and Herat assigned to us after the war of 1880, when Russia was simply powerless to make a protest even. All our arrangements for gaining intelligence might long ere this have been perfected. Attempts might have been in progress to gain Persia over; to come to an agreement with China. And our emissaries might long ere this have got us the information we want about raising rebellion in the Khanates. In fact, there is not one of the steps I propose which should not, and could not, have been carried out by this time.

But I have no wish to cry over spilt milk, even now though nearly four years have been lost. I hope we are not too late; but this remains to be proved. And if we are too late for some, we are not for all; and therefore there is all the more reason for at last facing our difficulties in a right spirit.

These measures have the advantage that they can all, whether carried on secretly or openly, be put into force without any declaration of war. They are preliminary and precautionary on our part, and will not fail to prove premonitory to Russia, and they may cause her to desist for a time at least. This is all we want; the rest is in our hands. If we look the thing in the face and organize to meet it, I think Russia will yet regret the day she at last succeeded in rousing England in earnest.

CHAPTER IV.

HOW ARE WE TO PROVIDE A SUFFICIENT FORCE TO MEET RUSSIAN OPERATIONS.

It is, I think, necessary and convenient that I should once more recapitulate the main points in this problem.

In the first chapter I have shown that Russia can in 77 days put about 23,000 men into Herat, with a reserve of a like strength, which would arrive in 40 to 50 days afterwards, besides having 12,000 on her communications, available, on great emergency, within 20 days of Herat. She can in from 70 to 100 days put about 13,000 men into Kabul, with a similar strength in reserve, and all her communications strongly held. Further she can put 7,000 men into Chitral and 4,000 on to the Kashmir frontier in 90 days.

The total of these forces amounts to about 95,000 troops, and it must be remembered that all are regular Russian troops. I have made no mention of the irregular hordes she may call to her aid, because these are, and must always be, an unknown and a very unreliable quantity.

In the second chapter of this paper I have shown that after providing for the keeping a proper grip on India we have over—

13 batteries of field artillery,	$8\frac{4}{8}$ regiments Native cavalry,
9 batteries of mountain artillery,	$5\frac{6}{8}$ regiments British infantry,
3 batteries of heavy artillery,	$41\frac{4}{8}$ regiments Native infantry,
1 regiment British cavalry,	21 companies sappers,

and that we are $\frac{1}{2}$ battery of horse artillery and some 27 batteries of garrison artillery short.

The question, therefore, which must now be considered is this. To what extent must our military forces in India be increased to enable us to meet the advance of 95,000 Russians, excluding all irregular levies, into Afghanistan.

Surely, when we consider the superior fighting quality of such a Russian Army to our own, no one would recommend Government to attempt to meet them with under 120,000 of the best men we can get in India, with a due proportion of British troops.

Before proceeding further, I must therefore take for granted that the number I have stated is considered absolutely necessary. I cannot conceive any one imagining that fewer will do, though doubtless many may think I have underestimated our needs. Where, then, are these men to come from? This question I cannot answer until I have considered how these 120,000 men should be composed. This done, I can then show how many units of each branch are required for this army, and then we can see how many units we are short.

I would propose to form this army of 120,000 men into ten divisions. My reasons for making some difference on the constitution of divisions will be shown in the next chapter of this paper; and I give the strength of the various units as follows :—

Battery of horse artillery—established strength,	162 men;	war strength,	150 men,	6 guns.
Battery of field artillery	„	162 „	„	150 „	6 „
Battery of heavy artillery	„	100 „	„	100 „	6 „
Battery of mountain artillery	„	100 „	„	100 „	6 „
Battery of garrison artillery	„	120 „	„	100 „	6 „
Regiment British cavalry	„	476 „	„	400 „	
Regiment British infantry	„	912 „	„	800 „	
Regiment Native cavalry	„	550 „	„	500 „	
Regiment Native infantry	„	832 „	„	750 „	
Company Native sappers	„	116 „	„	100 „	
Battery Native artillery	„	177 „	„	160 „	

The divisions would be formed as follows :—

1st division.

One brigade cavalry.	1 British cavalry	400	men	1,900 „
	3 Native cavalry at 500	1,500		
	Total ...	1,900 „		
Three brigades infantry, each	1 British infantry	800	„	9,450 „
	3 Native infantry at 750 ...	2,250		
	1 company sappers	100		
	Total	3,150 „		

Artillery	1 horse artillery, British ...	150 men,	6 guns	880 „	36 guns.
	1 field artillery British ...	150 „	6 „		
	1 mountain artillery, British ...	100 „	6 „		
	3 mountain artillery, Native ...	480 „	18 „		
	Total ...	880 „	36 „		
	Grand Total 1st division ...			12,230 „	36 guns.

2nd division.

One cavalry brigade as above	...	...	...	1,900 „	
3 infantry brigades as above	...	...	...	9,450 „	
Artillery ...	1 horse artillery ...	150 men,	6 guns.		
	3 field artillery ...	450 „	18 „		
	2 heavy artillery ...	200 „	12 „		
	Total ...	800 „	36 „	800 „	36 guns.
	Grand Total 2nd division ...			12,150 „	36 guns.

3rd division.

Cavalry and infantry, as in 1st	...	11,350 „	
Artillery.	1 horse artillery 150 men, 6 guns; 4 field artillery 600 men, 24 guns	750 „	30 guns.
	1 heavy battery 100 „ 6 „	100 „	6 „
	Grand total 3rd division...	12,200 „	36 „

4th division.

Infantry, as in 1st	...	...	...	...	9,450 men,	
Artillery { 3 British mountain artillery		200 men,	12 guns	... }		
Artillery { 4 Native mountain artillery		640 „	24 „	... }	840 „	36 guns.
Total	...	840 „	36 „			
Cavalry, 2 Native cavalry	...	...	...	...	1,000 „	
Grand Total 4th division				...	11,290 „	36 guns.

5th division.

Same as 1st division	...	...	...	...	12,230 „	36 guns.

6th division.

Same as 3rd division	...	...	...	...	12,200 „	36 guns.

7th division.

Cavalry and infantry, as in 1st		...	...	...	11,350 „	
Artillery { 1 horse artillery	...	150 men,	6 guns	... }		
Artillery { 3 field artillery	...	450 „	18 „	... }	920 „	36 guns.
Artillery { 2 mountain artillery	...	320 „	12 „	... }		
Total	...	920 „	36 „			
Grand Total 7th division				...	12,270 „	36 guns.

8th division.

Same as 3rd division	...	...	...	...	12,200 „	36 guns.

9th division.

Infantry, as in 1st division		...	...	...	9,450 „	
Cavalry, 2 Native regiments		...	...	...	1,000 „	
Artillery { 2 British mountain artillery		200 men,	12 guns	... }		
Artillery { 3 Native mountain artillery		480 „	18 „	... }	680 „	30 guns.
Total				...	11,130 „	30 guns.

10th division.

Same as 3rd division	...	...	...	...	12,200 „	36 guns.
* Grand Total of Army				...	120,100 „	354 guns.

That is to say, we require for the field army—

				And we have only—†	Therefore we are deficient—
8 batteries horse artillery	...	...	...	1/3	8 1/3
23 batteries field artillery	...	...	...	13	10
8 batteries heavy artillery	...	...	...	3	5
6 batteries mountain artillery, British	...	...	...	6	0
14 batteries mountain artillery, Native	...	...	...	6	8
8 regiments British cavalry	...	...	...	1	7
30 regiments British infantry	...	...	...	5 5/8	24 3/8
28 regiments Native cavalry	...	...	...	8 1/6	19 5/6
90 regiments Native infantry	...	...	...	41 1/8	48 7/8
30 companies Native sappers	...	...	...	21	9

* It will be noted the total of cavalry comes to about 1/6 and of artillery to a little less than 3 per thousand, the sappers to about $\frac{1}{40}$; but the latter will be practically increased by the presence of some Pioneer regiments, and probably some more heavy batteries may be required.

† After providing for defence of India.

How is this large deficiency to be met? I will take each branch of the service in turn—the British first—and attempt to show how it can be provided with the least possible cost and in the shortest possible time.

British cavalry.—We require 8 regiments for the field army and 8 for the home army—total 16 regiments of 3 squadrons, or 48 squadrons in all. We have got 9 regiments of 3 squadrons. If these 9 are raised to 4 squadrons each, we should have 36 squadrons, and, therefore, if 3 regiments of 4 squadrons were sent from England we should have all we require. This would undoubtedly be cheaper than getting out 7 more regiments of 3 squadrons, and I think it would certainly also be better for efficiency. We should then have 12 regiments of 4 squadrons each. Of these, I think we should require 8 for the field army and 4 for the home army.

British infantry.—We require 43⅝ battalions for internal defence and 30 for the Field Army—total 73⅝. The strength of these battalions has been taken at 800 men, making a total of about 59,000 men. Now in India we have already 49 battalions; and if their strength was raised to 1,000 each; this would give us 49,000 men and leave only 10,000 to be provided from England in 10 battalions of 1,000 men each. But of the 59 battalions thus provided, I think we should require 30 for the field army; and this would only leave 29 battalions, or 29,000 British infantry, for the defence of India; whereas we require 43⅝ battalions at 800 each, *i.e.*, 34,600, or, say, 35,000 men: therefore the total number of fresh battalions really required from England would be 16.

British artillery: horse.—We require 10 batteries for the home army and 8 for the field army. We have only 10 in India, and are therefore 8 short. The simplest plan would be to reduce one of the batteries and transfer their men to 3 others, then to raise the other 9 to 8-gun batteries in peace. In war these could be made into 18 batteries of 4 guns, and if 2 guns for 18 batteries, *i.e.*, 36 guns, with their complement were sent out from England, we should have 18 batteries of 6 guns each. To this the answer will probably be, that this would upset the artillery organization at home, which is for 6-gun batteries. It would do this certainly, but it must be remembered that the only alternative is to send out 8 complete batteries from England, and my plan is much cheaper and quite equally efficient.

Field artillery.—We have 40 field batteries. We require 31 for the home army and 24 for the field army—total 55. We are therefore 15 batteries short. Undoubtedly the simplest and most economical plan is to raise the whole 40 at present on the establishment to 8-gun batteries, and then, on the outbreak of war, transform them into 55 batteries of 6 guns each, and bring out one fresh battery of 6 guns from England. If this is not approved, we should require 15 fresh batteries from England.

Heavy batteries.—The number in India is 4, and we require 2 for defence and 6 for the field army. We are therefore 4 batteries deficient. If the 4 batteries existing were raised to 8 guns each, they could be turned into 8 batteries of 4 guns and be made up to 6 guns from England hereafter.

British mountain artillery.—The number required are available..

Garrison Artillery.—The provision of the deficiency in this branch is a more difficult question than the others, because we are not less than 27 batteries short of our requirements, that is to say, while there are only 15 garrison batteries in India, 42 are required for the garrison of the various posts it would be necessary to hold. Moreover, the batteries intended for the defences of Calcutta, 3; Bombay, 2; Karachi, 1; Aden, 2; Madras, 1—total 9, must not be touched in any way. This, therefore, leaves us with only 6 batteries to provide for the work of 27. Luckily, the rest of the work required from the garrison artillery would not, probably, be of a very difficult nature, or require very highly trained gunners. It would consist in furnishing the artillery for our various posts in India, and the only enemy likely to come against them would certainly have worse trained artillerymen.

I therefore propose to make use of the 6 batteries to give a lead, as it were, to the new gunners, who I would provide from the infantry and volunteers.

The establishment of a garrison battery consists of 1 major, 1 captain, 3 lieutenants, 1 sergeant-major, 5 sergeants, 5 corporals, 5 bombardiers, 97 gunners, 2 trumpeters. The total strength therefore of the garrison artillery in India therefore is 15 majors, 15 captains, 45 lieutenants, 15 sergeant-majors, 75 sergeants, 75 corporals, 75 bombardiers, 1,455 gunners. I propose to leave 9 batteries almost intact, only taking 15 men per battery to promote in the other new batteries and to fill their places from the infantry. These 9 batteries would therefore consist of a total of—

9 majors, 9 captains, 27 lieutenants, 9 sergeant-majors, 45 sergeants, 45 corporals, 45 bombardiers, and 900 gunners taken from the Royal artillery and 135 gunners from the infantry—and this leaves;

6 majors, 6 captains, 18 lieutenants, 6 sergeant-majors, 30 sergeants, 30 corporals, 30 bombardiers, and 555 gunners—total 651, from which to form 33 batteries required to make up the total number of 42 batteries.

But for these 33 batteries we require—

33 majors, 33 captains, 99 lieutenants, 33 sergeant-majors, 165 sergeants, 165 corporals, 165 bombardiers, and 3,201 gunners. We are therefore short—

27 majors, 27 captains, 81 lieutenants, 27 sergeant-majors, 135 sergeants, 135 corporals, 135 bombardiers, and 2,646 gunners. The majors and captains, and 27 of the lieutenants, should, I think, be supplied by the Royal artillery, 27 lieutenants from the infantry, and 27 from the volunteers from those who have shewn most aptitude and liking for artillery work.

The non-commissioned officers short—27 sergeant-majors, 135 sergeants, 135 corporals, and 135 bombardiers—total 432 should be supplied by promotions from the whole 15 batteries in existence, and their places taken from the gunners still available.

This would leave us with only 123 gunners out of a total of 3,200 required. There are two sources from which these can be supplied,—1st, from the infantry, 2nd, from the volunteers. The infantry are directed by Bengal Army Regulations to have 60 men in each battalion instructed in heavy gun drill, and supposing this order to have been carried out, there ought to be in the 49 battalions of British infantry in India 2,940 infantry soldiers able to work heavy guns.

In the volunteers, of the 8,443 efficients, 280 are said to be artillery volunteers, so that there ought to be 3,220 trained gunners in the infantry and the volunteers, while we require only 3,077.

I would propose, however, to provide half, or, say, 1,500 from the infantry and 1,577 from the volunteers; then in each of the 33 batteries we should have all the non-commissioned officers and 4 gunners artillerymen, and the rest of the gunners would be about half each from the infantry and the volunteers.

This proposal may seem to have rather an amateur ring about it, and we all know that to the amateur, when dealing with army matters, nothing is sacred.

But, on the other hand, I think we military men are too conservative and too much wedded to regulations. Perhaps anyone having to defend a post would rather have regular gunners to man his guns; but that is not the point. It is, would not a scratch team of gunners, as laid down above, be quite good enough to enable a commander to make a good defence against natives of India? I think they would, and have therefore recommended this way out of our difficulty in the matter of garrison artillery. Of course, if these scratch batteries were not brought together till all India was in a blaze, they might not be very serviceable; but I propose nothing of this kind. I show that we require so many batteries (42) for the defence of India, of which 33 will have to be improvised; but I do not say put off your preparation till the last moment. On the contrary, I say practice now what you will have to do in the event of a Russian war, and train your infantry and volunteers now to act as garrison artillery. But if this also is not approved, then there is nothing for it but to warn the English Government that we shall want 27 garrison batteries from them.

The established strength of the British forces in India is (including those at Aden):—

	Batteries.	Officers.	Men.	Horses.	Officers.	Men.
Royal horse artillery ...	10	at 5	167	178 =	50	1,570
Royal Artillery field batteries ...	40	at 5	157	110 =	200	6,280
Royal Artillery heavy ...	4	at 5	95	5 =	20	380
Royal Artillery mountain ...	6	at 5	94	5 =	30	564
Royal Artillery garrison ...	18	at 5	115	... =	90	2,070
		Total artillery		...	390	10,864
9 cavalry regiments ...		at 22	454	396 =	198	4,086
50 infantry battalions ...		at 28	884	... =	1,400	44,200
		Grand Total		...	1,988	59,150

The effective strength on the 1st March (figures for Madras troops for February) was—

	Officers.	Men.
Artillery	392	11,354
Cavalry	162	4,117
Infantry	1,163	40,689
Total ...	1,660	53,537

showing a surplus* of 2 officers and 490 men† in the Royal artillery, 31 men in cavalry, and a deficiency of—

	Officers.	Men.
Cavalry	36	...
Infantry	237	3,511
Total ...	273	3,511

The number that are now short of the establishment, namely, 36 cavalry officers and 237 officers and 3,511 non-commissioned officers and men of infantry‡ should, of course, be sent out from England at once; indeed, that the

* District staff are included in returns, and not in above calculation. Many batteries are short of 1 lieutenant.

† This excess is only temporary, and is caused by drafts from England having arrived and men for England not having embarked on the above date.

‡ In addition if my recommendation about garrison artillery was adopted we should require 1,500 more infantry soldiers to fill the place of those withdrawn for garrison artillery.

strength of British troops in India should never be allowed to get below the establishment, on any pretence whatsoever, should be an axiom with our military authorities. If this is done, it would make our strength up to 1,988 officers and 59,150 men. But to make our strength up to what is required for internal defence and the field army we want 2,960 officers and 91,268 men, as I shall now show.

The total number of British troops to make up the required strength and keep it at war strength would be as follows :—

	Officers.	Non-commissioned officers. and men.
To make up 9 regiments of British cavalry to 4 squadrons ...	54	1,302
3 fresh regiments of British cavalry of 4 squadrons ...	84	1,806
To make up 49 battalions of British infantry to 10 companies each	294	10,731
16 fresh battalions of British infantry of 10 companies each ...	544	17,648
To make up 9 batteries of horse artillery to 8 guns ...	9	450
Complement for 36 guns to make 18 horse artillery batteries of 4 guns each to 18 batteries of 6 guns each	18	900
To make up 40 batteries of field artillery to 8 guns each ...	40	2,000
1 fresh battery of field artillery	5	157
To make 4 heavy batteries into 8 gun batteries	4	76
To make 8 heavy batteries of 4 guns into 8 batteries of 6 guns ...	8	152
Total ...	1,060	35,222

If all these were supplied, we should then have in India :—

						Officers.	Non-commissioned officers. and men.
18 batteries horse artillery	at	5 officers,	157	men each	...	90	2,826
54 batteries field artillery	„	5 „	157	„	...	270	8,578
12 regiments British cavalry	„	28 „	602	„	...	336	7,224
65 battalions British infantry	„	34 „	1,103	„	...	2,210	71,695
6 batteries heavy artillery	„	5 „	95	„	...	30	475
6 batteries mountain artillery	„	5 „	94	„	...	30	470
				Total	...	2,966	91,268

And to *keep* these up to war strength will require that about 30 per cent. of this number, or about 988 officers and 30,422 non-commissioned officers and men should be kept ready to be sent out as wanted. That is to say, that for our purposes we require an increase to the strength of the British army in India of 1,966 officers, 62,530 men, or a total of 3,954 officers and 121,690 British soldiers to be maintained in India.

This may seem a very large demand to make on England; but the following return, taken from the Report of the Commissioners appointed to enquire into the organization of the Indian army, 1858 (Appendix No. 16, page 23), will show it was nearly equalled in the rebellion of 1857-58:—

Strength of troops of Her Majesty's Regular Army on the Indian Establishment.

15th October 1858.

	EFFECTIVE—ALL RANKS.								
	Cavalry.	Foot Guards.	Infantry.	Royal Artillery.		Royal Engineers.	Military Train.	Medical Staff Corps.	Total.
				Horse.	Foot.				
East Indies	...	...	...	...	...	...	...	...	...
Bengal	3,269	...	49,310	429	2,670	259	239	73	56,249
Bombay	3,384	...	15,616	247	1,211	226	...	...	20,684
Madras	1,345	...	10,484	238	713	...	...	...	12,780
Total in India and on passage out ...	7,998	...	75,410	914	4,594	485	239	73	89,713

Return showing the strength of the European local force in India.

Bengal infantry (1st Sept. 1858.)	... ...		2,743
	Artillery and sappers, including recruit battalion ...		3,187
	Light cavalry		1,522
	Camel corps		152
	Invalid battalion		146
	Yeomanry cavalry and other irregular horse ...		599
	Eurasian battalion		75
			8,424
Madras infantry (1st July 1858.)	... ...	2,745	
	Artillery and sappers	2,110	
	Veterans	318	
			5,173
Bombay infantry (1st Jan. 1858.)	... ...	2,656	
	Artillery and sappers	1,832	
			4,488
	Total ...		18,085

SUMMARY.

East Indies.

Her Majesty's regular army	89,713
European local force	18,085
Grand Total ...	107,798

If the English Army as it stands at present could not spare such a large extra call on it, there is only one other way to arrange it, and that is, to add to the reserve of the English Army enough men to supply the wants of

India as stated above, and for the Government of India to pay for the cost of these extra reserve men, which would be kept for its purposes alone.

Supposing that the number of British troops now short of the establishment, *viz.*, 237 officers and 3,511 men, has been provided, the first reserve of the British army in India would consist of the officers and men necessary to make all units now in India to the increased strength proposed above, that is to say, of—

—	officers,	1,500	infantry soldiers for garrison batteries.
54	"	1,302	men for 9 regiments of British cavalry.
294	"	10,731	" 49 battalions of British infantry.
9	"	450	" 9 batteries of horse artillery.
40	"	2,000	" 40 batteries of field artillery.
4	"	76	" 4 batteries of heavy artillery.
401		16,059	"

and I must say I think the sooner these are provided the better.

The second reserve would consist of the extra troops required to put the whole army in India on a war footing, *viz.*,—

3 regiments British cavalry	84	1,806
16 battalions British infantry	544	17,648
Extra complement for 18 horse artillery batteries ...	18	900
One battery field artillery	5	157
Extra complmeent for 8 heavy batteries	8	152
Total ...	659	20,663

The third reserve would consist of the 988 officers and 30,422 non-commissioned officers and men necessary to feed the above units during war.

Besides the above, to make matters quite safe, a complete *English* army corps should be mobilised, and when wanted in the East should come fully equipped in every way.

I now turn to the Native army.

With regard to the Native mountain artillery, I propose that the existing 6 batteries of 4 guns should be turned into batteries of 8 guns, and these, on the approach of war, would be transferred into 12 batteries of 4 guns, and augmented in the same way as those of the Punjab Force are now, into 6 guns each. This would leave us still 2 batteries to provide, and these, I think, should be arranged for by raising one more battery of 8 guns as soon as possible.

All who saw the hastily formed British mountain batteries in Afghanistan will admit that a mountain battery cannot be made up on the spur of the moment. This would certainly increase the strength of our Native artillery by 36 guns in peace, and so may be said to be against the axiom that as few guns should be entrusted to Natives as possible; but it is absurd to say there would be any real danger in such an increase, and no more efficient batteries exist in the world than the Punjab batteries, nor are there more loyal troops in the whole Indian army than their gunners.

Native cavalry.—We have available in India 37⅝ regiments of Native cavalry. We require 29 for the defence and 28 for the field army—total 57, or 171 squadrons. If we take 38 regiments as the number available, we require 19 regiments or 57 squadrons to make up necessary strength of this arm.

I would propose, therefore, to raise each regiment existing, *viz.*, 37 to 4 squadrons. This will give us 144 squadrons and to add 2 squadrons to the 38th regiment*—total 152 squadrons. This will still leave us 5 regiments of 4 squadrons short; and though we might, of course, re-raise the regiments lately reduced, *viz.*, the 16th and 17th Bengal Cavalry, 4th Punjab Cavalry, 3rd Sind Horse, and form one other regiment to be named 20th Bengal Cavalry, I think that if all regiments of Native cavalry were raised to 4 squadrons, we might do with the number of cadres we have by a little redistribution of the regiments. In the field army, if all the regiments are 4 squadrons, each cavalry brigade should consist of 1 British and 2 Native cavalry instead of 3 Native cavalry. Thus 19 regiments would do for the home army and 19 for the field army.

Native infantry.—We have available in India 124 regiments of Native infantry of 8 companies. We require for defence 82 regiments of 8 companies and for the field army 90 regiments of 8 companies—total 172 regiments of 8 companies—total 1,376 companies. If the 124 are raised to 10 companies each, we should have 1,240 companies, and still have to provide 136 companies, or 14 regiments of 10 companies each. This might be done by raising again the 34th, 35th, 36th, 37th, and 41st Bengal Native Infantry; the 18th, 34th, 35th, 36th, and 37th Madras Native Infantry; and the 6th, 11th, 15th, 18th Bombay Native Infantry; but, as in the Native cavalry, I do not think it would be necessary. If all the regiments are raised to 10 companies each, we should only require 60 regiments for the field army, and in the same ratio about 55 for the defence; but as the regiments for defence would be more distributed, it would be as well to reckon on 64 for this purpose.

Sappers and miners.—We have in India 25 companies. We require for defence 3 companies and 30 companies for the field army—total 33 companies of 100 privates. We are therefore 8 companies short. In considering how this deficiency had best be made up, I must note that the strength of the unit of sappers varies in the three Presidencies; in Bengal it consists of 100, in Madras of 105, and in Bombay of 80 privates per company. Therefore the total number of privates we have got is 2,450, and we want 3,300. If all the companies are raised to 120, we should then have 3,000 privates, and there would only remain 3 companies more to be raised. These need only be of a strength of 100 privates as they would be used for defence. These three companies might be raised by adding 3 to the Bombay Sappers.

The total number of Native troops which would therefore be required to make us up to war strength would be as follows:—

	Officers.	Non-commissioned officers and men.
1. To make up 6 batteries of Native mountain artillery into batteries of 8 guns	12	984
2. To make 6 batteries of 8 guns into 12 batteries of 6 guns	18	1,302
3. To raise one new battery of 8 guns	5	328
4. To make 2 batteries of 6 guns of the above	3	232
5. To add to 37 regiments Native cavalry 1 squadron ...	74	9,030
6. To add to one regiment Native cavalry 2 squadrons ...	4	380
7. To add to 124 regiments Native infantry 2 companies each	372	25,792
8. To add 20 privates to 10 companies of Bengal sappers ...	...	200
9. To add 15 privates to 10 companies of Madras sappers ...	...	150
10. To add 40 privates to 5 companies of Bombay sappers ...	...	200
11. To raise 3 new companies of sappers " " ...	3	300
	491	37,254

* Guide Cavalry.

If this is done, we should then have in India—

		Officers.	Non-commissioned officers and men.
14	batteries of Native mountain artillery of 6 guns ...	56	3,850
38	regiments of Native cavalry of 4 squadrons	380	27,892
124	regiments of infantry of 10 companies	1,488	128,960
28	companies of sappers	56	3,898
		1,980	164,600

To keep these up to war strength, we should require about 30 per cent. of reserves, that is to say, about 650 officers and 55,000 men.

The total number of trained Native troops in India would then be about 220,000 men* (with 2,630 English officers).

I think that items as under should be raised with as little delay as possible, *i.e.*,—

	Officers.	Non-commissioned officers and men.
Item	...	156
„ 1	12	984
„ 3	5	328
„ 11	3	300
Total	20	2,768

Then, the men necessary to complete items 2, 4, 5, 6, 7, 8, 9 and 10, *viz.*, 471 officers and 35,886 men, required to make up units to war strength, would constitute the first reserve of the Native army.

The second reserve would consist of the men necessary to keep these units at war strength, and would be about 30 per cent. of the total war strength, (*viz.*, 1,980 officers, 164,600 men) namely, 650 officers and 55,000 men.

In addition, I am of opinion that a third reserve of 20 per cent. should be enlisted as soon as the second reserve had been mobilized. These men should be attached for instruction to the depôts of the regiments for which they had been enlisted, and they would in all probability be sufficiently trained before their services were required.

This third reserve would give us 770 Native mountain artillery men, 5,578 Native cavalry soldiers, 25,792 infantry soldiers, and 779 sappers, or a total of 33,000 men.

The grand total of the reserves of the Native Indian army would therefore be—

	Officers.	Non-commissioned officers and men.
1st reserve	471	35,886
2nd reserve	650	55,000
3rd reserve	396	33,000
Grand Total ...	1,517	123,886†

* Immediately before the mutiny of 1857 there were in India a total of 232,224 Native troops, of which 15,750 were artillery !!

† I do not go into details as to how this reserve should be organized. My object is to show that this number is necessary if the Indian army is to be put into a state to meet the Russian advance. I think if this is allowed, there will be no difficulty, and need be no delay in determining the details of the organization of the reserves most suitable to the Indian army.

The Army Organization Commission of 1879 proposed to keep up a reserve as follows:—

1st reserve	... ...	19,000 infantry.	
2nd reserve	... ...	33,000 ,,	6,000 cavalry.
Total	...	52,000	6,000
		58,000	

But this was only meant to feed a field army of about 58,000 men and 180 guns, whereas my numbers are calculated to feed an army of 120,000 men and 354 guns.

The Army Organization Commission pointed out in their report that about 8,000 Native soldiers are absorbed into the population every year, therefore it is evident that my proposals do not increase to a very appreciable degree the danger which must always arise from maintaining a reserve of mercenary troops.

I propose that in the Native army all men who have been non-commissioned officers and 20 per cent. of the best privates (who are likely to be fit for promotion to non-commissioned rank) should be allowed to serve with the colors till they completed 32 years' service for pension, and that all others should be required to go into the 1st reserve after 10 years' service, and that they should pass into the 2nd reserve after 21 years' service. The 3rd reserve would be specially formed on outbreak of a Russian war only.

Those in the 1st infantry reserve should receive Rs. 2 annas 5 per mensem, and those in the 2nd reserve Rs. 4 annas 10, while, on completing 32 years' service, all should receive Rs. 7 per mensem pension.

The Army Commission, while strongly recommending that reserve men should be employed, as much as possible, by local Governments, were only able to get promises of employment for about 7,200. This number seems to me ridiculously small when compared with the strength of the Police Force in India, which has a total of 158,000 men.

I think that local Governments should be required to keep at least 20 per cent. of these places for reservists. This would provide for 32,000. Then when the army of chaprassies, peons, railway porters, &c., &c., are considered, it seems very evident to me that a very much larger number of reservists would be able to find employment if Government interfered.

If these measures are accepted, it will be necessary to make certain changes in the constitution of the field divisions and in the distribution of the home army.

In the first, all the British units would remain the same in number as is given above, the only differences being that there would be 148 sabres more in each cavalry brigade, to which British cavalry has been attached, and 303 more bayonets in each British infantry regiment—a change which must be allowed to be for the better.

In the Native portion of the divisions the change necessary would be to substitute 2 regiments of Native cavalry of 1,334 sabres for 3 regiments of 1,431 sabres in each cavalry brigade, and 2 regiments of Native infantry of 2,080 bayonets for 3 regiments of 2,250 bayonets.

The field divisions would then be constituted as follows:—

	Batteries horse artillery.	Regiments British cavalry.	Regiments Native cavalry.	Batteries field artillery.	Batteries British mountain artillery.	Batteries Native mountain artillery.	Heavy batteries.	Regiments British infantry.	Regiments Native infantry.	Companies sappers.	Total British.	Total Native.	Guns.	Grand Total.
1st Division ...	$\frac{150}{1}$ 6 guns	$\frac{624}{1}$	$\frac{1334}{2}$	$\frac{150}{1}$ 6 guns	$\frac{100}{1}$ 6 guns	$\frac{320}{3}$ 18 guns	...	$\frac{3309}{3}$	$\frac{6240}{6}$	$\frac{408}{3}$	4,333	8,302	36	12,635
2nd " ...	$\frac{150}{1}$ 6 guns	$\frac{624}{1}$	$\frac{1334}{2}$	$\frac{450}{3}$ 18 guns	...	...	$\frac{200}{2}$ 12 guns	$\frac{3309}{3}$	$\frac{6240}{6}$	$\frac{408}{3}$	4,733	7,982	36	12,715
3rd " ...	$\frac{150}{1}$ 6 guns	$\frac{624}{1}$	$\frac{1334}{2}$	$\frac{600}{4}$ 24 guns	...	...	$\frac{100}{1}$ 6 guns	$\frac{3309}{3}$	$\frac{6240}{6}$	$\frac{408}{3}$	4,683	7,982	36	12,665
4th " ...	...	...	$\frac{1334}{2}$	...	$\frac{200}{3}$ 12 guns	$\frac{480}{4}$ 24 guns	...	$\frac{3309}{3}$	$\frac{6240}{6}$	$\frac{408}{3}$	3,509	7,982	36	11,491
5th " ...	$\frac{150}{1}$ 6 guns	$\frac{624}{1}$	$\frac{1334}{2}$	$\frac{150}{1}$ 6 guns	$\frac{100}{1}$ 6 guns	$\frac{320}{3}$ 18 guns	...	$\frac{3309}{3}$	$\frac{6240}{6}$	$\frac{408}{3}$	4,333	8,302	36	12,635
6th " ...	$\frac{150}{1}$ 6 guns	$\frac{624}{1}$	$\frac{1334}{2}$	$\frac{600}{4}$ 24 guns	...	...	$\frac{100}{1}$ 6 guns	$\frac{3309}{3}$	$\frac{6240}{6}$	$\frac{408}{3}$	4,683	7,983	36	12,665
7th " ...	$\frac{150}{1}$ 6 guns	$\frac{624}{1}$	$\frac{1334}{2}$	$\frac{300}{3}$ 18 guns	...	$\frac{320}{2}$ 12 guns	...	$\frac{3309}{3}$	$\frac{6240}{6}$	$\frac{408}{3}$	4,383	8,302	36	12,665
8th " ...	$\frac{150}{1}$ 6 guns	$\frac{624}{1}$	$\frac{1334}{2}$	$\frac{600}{4}$ 24 guns	...	...	$\frac{100}{1}$ 6 guns	$\frac{3309}{3}$	$\frac{6240}{6}$	$\frac{408}{3}$	4,683	7,982	36	12,665
9th " ...	...	...	$\frac{1334}{2}$	...	$\frac{200}{2}$ 12 guns	$\frac{320}{3}$ 18 guns	...	$\frac{3309}{3}$	$\frac{6240}{6}$	$\frac{408}{3}$	3,509	8,302	30	11,911
10th " ...	$\frac{150}{1}$ 6 guns	$\frac{624}{1}$	$\frac{1334}{2}$	$\frac{600}{4}$ 24 guns	...	...	$\frac{100}{1}$ 6 guns	$\frac{3309}{3}$	$\frac{6240}{6}$	$\frac{408}{3}$	4,683	7,982	36	12,665
Total ...	Bats. 8 Guns. 48	8	20	Bats. 23 Guns. 138	Bats. 6 Guns. 36	Bats. 11 Guns. 66	Bats. 2 Guns. 12	30	60	30	43,550	81,100	254	124,650

With regard to the redistribution of the home army, I give it in the following table :—

		Horse artillery.	Field artillery.	British artillery.	British mountain artillery.	Native mountain artillery.	Garrison artillery.	British cavalry.	Native cavalry.	British infantry.	Native infantry.	Sappers.
BENGAL ...	Former...	0	1	3	0	0	0	0	0	1⅜	3	2
	Altered...	0	1	3	0	0	0	0	0	1	2	2
ASSAM ...	Former...	0	0	0	0	1	0	0	0	0	1	0
	Altered...	0	0	0	0	1	0	0	0	0	1	0
N. W. P. ...	Former...	2⅓	5	6	0	0	0	2	5½	8	11	0
	Altered..	2⅓	5	6	0	0	0	1	3½	6 4/10	9	0
PUNJAB ...	Former...	2	10	10	0	2	0	2½	8	12⅜	12	0
	Altered...	2	10	10	0	2	0	1½	5	10	19	0
BOMBAY ...	Former...	2	7	11¾	0	0	0	1½	4½	7	15	2
	Altered...	2	7	11¾	0	0	0	1	3	5 4/10	12	2
RAJPUTANA	Former...	0	1	2	0	0	0	0	1	1⅜	2	0
	Altered...	0	1	1¾	0	0	0	0	0	1	1 6/10	...
CENTRAL INDIA ...	Former...	2	2	2	0	0	0	1	2	3	6	0
	Altered...	2	2	2	0	0	0	½	1	2 4/10	5	0
CENTRAL PROVINCES	Former...	0	2½	2¼	0	0	0	0	2	2⅝	4	0
	Altered...	0	2½	2¼	0	0	0	0	1	2	3	0
MADRAS ...	Former...	1	2½	2	0	0	0	0	2	2⅝	8½	1
	Altered...	1	2⅔	2	0	0	0	0	1	2 2/10	7	1
HYDERABAD	Former...	1	1	1	0	1	1	1	4	2⅝	7	0
	Altered...	1	1	1	0	2	1	1	3	2	5 6/10	0
BURMA ...	Former...	0	0	2	2	0	0	0	0	2	4	1
	Altered...	0	0	2	2	0	0	0	0	1 4/10	3	1
TOTAL ...	Former...	10⅓	31	42	2	6	1	8	29	43	82½	6
	Altered...	10⅓	31	42	2	6	1	5	17½	35 6/10	77 6/10	6

Above I have shown what force we require for the internal defence of India, and to provide a sufficient field army to provide Russian operations. I have supposed that all the reinforcements required must come from England. This will, no doubt, be the best solution of our difficulties if it is practicable ; but we must remember, 1st, that the English army is weak ; 2nd, it may be called on to provide for the defence of Great Britain, or to put an army in the field in Europe (at the same time as complications in India arise), or both. The army in England may not, therefore, be in a position to afford us all the aid we require, and therefore it behoves to survey our resources in India, and see to what extent we can reduce our demands on England.*

* I do not, however, wish it to be understood that I recommend that our demands on England should be appreciably reduced. I think that England should always be able to meet a demand for an increase of the British troops in India by at least 63,000 men. If the organization of the British army will not permit of this, the British troops in India and their reserves must be organized locally and independently of the home army.

In the first place, let us turn to our strength in volunteers. The following gives the distribution and strength of the volunteers in India on the 1st October 1883 :—

		Corps.	Strength.	Head-quarters.
1.		1st Punjab Volunteer Rifle Corps ...	534	Lahore.
2.		2nd Punjab or Simla Rifle Corps ...	335	Simla.
3.		3rd, or Sind, Punjab and Indus Valley Railway Volunteer Rifle Corps	716	Lahore.
4.		Behar Mounted Rifle Corps ...	272	Mozufferpore.
5.		Calcutta Volunteer Rifle Corps ...	608	Calcutta.
6.		Calcutta Cadet Companies ...	(318)	Ditto.
7.		Eastern Bengal Railway Volunteer Rifle Corps	159	Ditto.
8.		East Indian Railway Volunteer Rifle Corps	1,133	Jamalpore.
9.		Tirhoot State Railway Volunteer Rifle Corps	33	Somastipore.
10.		Seebpore College Volunteer Rifle Corps ...	42	Seebpore.
11.		Nagpore Volunteer Rifle Corps ...	75	...
12.	N.W.P. Voltr. 1st Ad. Bn.	1st Allahabad Volunteer Rifle Corps	184	Allahabad.
13.		2nd Lucknow Volunteer Rifle Corps ...	299	Lucknow.
14.		3rd Cawnpore Volunteer Rifle Corps ...	60	Cawnpore.
15.		3rd Cawnpore Volunteer Cadet Company	(24)	Ditto
16.		4th Naini Tal Volunteer Rifle Corps ...	187	Naini Tal.
17.		5th Rohilkhund Volunteer Rifle Corps	127	Bareilly.
18.	N.W.P. Voltr. 2nd Ad. Bn.	1st Agra Volunteer Rifle Corps ...	268	Agra.
19.		2nd Thomason College Volunteer Rifle Corps.	26	Roorkee.
20.		3rd Mussoorie Volunteer Rifle Corps	200	Mussoorie.
21.		4th Farakhabad Volunteer Rifle Corps	37	Fatehgarh.
22.		Ghazipur Volunteer Rifle Corps	241	Allahabad.
23.		Northern Bengal Railway Volunteer Rifle Corps	284	Darjeeling.
24.		Northern Bengal Railway Cadet Company	(69)	Ditto.
25.		Moulmein Volunteer Rifle Corps ...	117	Moulmein.
26.		Rangoon Volunteer Artillery ...	77	Rangoon.
27.		Rangoon Volunteer Rifle Corps ...	180	Ditto.
28.		Rangoon Cadet Companies ...	(162)	Ditto.
29.		Rangoon and Irrawaddy State Railway Volunteer Rifle Corps.	176	Ditto.
30.		Akyab Volunteer Rifle Corps ...	75	Akyab.
31.		Akyab Cadet Company ...	(89)	Ditto.
32.		Berar Volunteer Rifle Corps ...	137	Akola.
33.		Sylhet Volunteer Rifle Corps ...	128	Lungla.
34.		Hyderabad Volunteer Rifle Corps ...	355	Secunderabad.
35.		Shillong Volunteer Rifle Corps ...	33	Shillong.
36.		Rajputana-Malwa Volunteer Rifle Corps ...	499	Ajmere.
37.		Lakhimpur Volunteer Rifle Corps ...	110	Dibrugarh.
38.		Toungoo Volunteer Rifle Corps ...	35	Toungoo.
39.		Madras Volunteer Artillery ...	59	Fort St George.
40.		Madras Volunteer Guards ...	619	Ditto.
41.		Bangalore Volunteer Rifle Corps ...	321	Bangalore.
42.		Bangalore Cadet Company ...	(97)	Ditto.

	Corps.		Strength.	Head-quarters.
43.	Nilgiri Volunteer Rifle Corps	...	245	Ootacamund.
44.	Great Indian Peninsula Railway Volunteer Rifle Corps.		942	Bombay.
45.	Bombay Volunteer Rifle Corps	...	670	Ditto.
46.	Bombay Cadet Company	...	(122)	Ditto.
47.	Bombay, Baroda, and Central India Railway Volunteer Rifle Corps.		240	Ditto.
48.	Sind Volunteer Rifle Corps	...	292	Karachi.
49.	Calcutta Naval Artillery	...	110	Calcutta.
	Total	...	12,421	

According to form 111A, vol. II, of the Census Report of 1881, there are in India a total of 106,412 British-born and other European* and of 31,283 Eurasian males, that is to say, 137,698 European and Eurasian males in India. Of these, 55,931 were in the army and 2,966 in the Civil Service, and of the remainder, $\frac{1}{10}$th (7,880) are below 20 and above 60, so that we have, as nearly as possible, 71,000 adult European and Eurasian males in India. Of these, 12,421 are already enrolled in the volunteers, so that there must be 58,500 adult male Europeans, who, if properly enrolled, could assist in the defence of our principal places and the maintenance of order generally throughout India.

But it is quite impossible from the Census Report to make out where these 58,500 men are, and therefore I cannot make any suggestions as to their utilization in the defence of India; but I commend this fact to the notice of the Government of India. There are in India 58,500 European and Eurasian adult males, nearly all of whom are capable of being made use of, to aid in the defence of India, if you will only take the trouble to find out where they are and to consider how they can be utilized. In order to do this, Government should take a fresh census of all the Europeans and Eurasians, and the following information should be asked from each male :—Age; usual residence; employment, whether in Army, Civil Service, or Volunteers, whether able-bodied or not.

When this information has been collected, it will probably be found that the bulk of the Europeans and Eurasians are settled in the principal towns of India, such as Calcutta, Bombay, Madras, Karachi, Lahore, Simla, Delhi, Lucknow, Allahabad, Hyderabad, Poona, Bangalore, &c., &c., and it will be quite easy to organize some system by which the service of these men can be made use of for the defence of these places and thus probably free a large number of soldiers for the field army. I hold that every able-bodied European and Eurasian in India should be enrolled into a militia, armed, trained, and bound to serve as a soldier in the defence of his usual city of residence, whenever called on by Government to do so.

In the next place, there are 31,152 Goanese in India. Deduct $\frac{1}{3}$rd of these as being under 20 and over 60, and we have 20,768 adult males of this class. Say, moreover, that $\frac{1}{10}$th of these are incapacitated from military work, still there will remain over 18,000 adult male Goanese. I am quite aware that a Bombay boy armed with a spit is not a very formidable creature; but inasmuch

* I would note that the terms "British-born," "Europeans," "Indo-Britons," "and Eurasians" are very vague.

as he *must* be faithful to us, I do not see why he should not be drilled and organized, so that when armed with a Henri-Martini he should not be equal to most of the natives he would be likely to meet.

Another race which is bound to be faithful to us, because, if they showed the smallest signs of disaffection, we could in a week turn the whole race out of India, are the Parsis. There are 43,598 male Parsis in India. This would give about 30,000 adults, and if we deduct 10 per cent. as above, we should have 27,000 adult male Parsis capable of being organized into a fairly serviceable militia.

That is to say, leaving out the Army, the Volunteers, and the members of the Civil Service, who would be so fully occupied as not to be available, we have the following unused reserve for the defence of India :—

Europeans and Eurasians	58,500
Indo-Portuguese	18,000
Parsis	27,000
Total ...	103,500

I have said that till we can get proper information about the European population in India, it will be impossible to show how these can be organized; but this much I can say, that if the reserve (103,500 men) shown above were organized efficiently, it is not too much to say that many of our arsenals, internal forts, bridgeheads and places of refuge could be fully and efficiently garrisoned by them; and if this were done, it would set free for field purposes a large body of regular troops.

The proposals in Captain Collen's memorandum on the establishment of a European and Eurasian militia for India should, without a day's further delay, be adopted. These are all sensible and necessary, and may be said, shortly, to be as follows :—

"Obligatory universal militia service for all non-military Europeans and "Eurasians capable of bearing arms to be carried out at once. The first object "would be the formation, into organized bodies, of those capable of bearing "arms, whose interests and feelings are identical with the safety and "supremacy of the British Government in India.

"The employment of those bodies should be in the following manner:— "Garrison of fortresses at the capital; garrison of fortified posts at the various "stations; keeping open lines of communication.

"An Act should at once be passed making it compulsory on all male "British subjects to serve for the defence of the Empire, and this Act should be "applied to all Europeans who, after the date of the Act, came to live in India.

"The terms of the Act should provide for all males between the ages of 18 "and 60 being called out, and these should be divided into four classes, *viz.*, "1st class, 18 to 30, unmarried; 2nd, from 30 to 45, unmarried; 3rd, 18 to 45, "married; 4th, 45 to 60.

"And it should provide for an active and a reserve. The active should "consist of those who in time of war volunteered to serve away from their "homes; and in case of necessity the number of these should be filled by ballot "of all under 45. The reserve would consist of the remainder."

There is such consideration for the feelings of the ladies shown in these proposed terms, that I should be very sorry to disturb it, were it not, that I am convinced it could not possibly work. The fact is that the 1st class given above would absorb ⅘ths of the whole number; and, besides, I see no object in having any classes. If any men volunteered to serve out of their place of residence, they could be formed into active companies; and with reference to the rest, it would be best to leave it entirely to the Officer Commanding at the time to say what uses should be made of the men.

Now if we deduct from the 968,888 Christian males in India the following:—

Europeans and Eurasians	...	137,698	168,850,
Indo-Portuguese	...	31,152	

we arrive at 800,038 as the total number of Native Christian males in India.

Let us say 270,000 are under 20 years of age, while as many as 50 per cent. of the remainder are physically incapacitated for any military service, we still should have about 260,000 Native Christians, who, at all events, are physically able for service; and though it is, under present circumstances, improbable that many of these would be able to do much in the fighting line, I should say that they could be brought into quite sufficient order to enable us, with the aid of the Europeans and Eurasians, &c., to hold the whole of South India and Bengal, and to aid in the defence of posts and places of refuge. Of course, the first step—and it should be an immediate one—is to commence forming Volunteer Corps of the races above mentioned, because every day that passes and shows these hitherto despised Eurasians, Indo-Portuguese, and Native Christians that they are trusted, tends to make them more valuable to us: there is nothing truer than the saying "call a dog a bad name and hang him." This, to my mind, is one of the directions which our steps towards creating a reserve for the army in India should take. The Native army is, and must always remain, a danger to us; and seeing that we have not enough for our wants, one of the most perplexing problems which can be presented to military organizers is how to provide this reserve without unduly increasing the danger of another military rebellion. There are, as I have said above, 260,000 Native Christians physically able for service; these are nearly all stationed in the south, where the danger of the rebellion is least, and where the population is generally despicable as enemies. Surely 100,000 of these Christians could be got, who, when trained and armed, could, with the addition of the Europeans and Eurasians and with English officers, keep the whole of Southern India quiet.

Another means of assisting ourselves in India in the event of a Russian war lies in the crews of the large number of ships frequenting Eastern waters.

According to the "Annual Statement of the Trade and Navigation of British India for the year ending 31st March 1882," the following number of vessels entered the various ports in India:—

		Steamers.	Tons.	Sailing.	Tons.
Bengal ports	...	1,047	949,777	481	547,685
Bombay "	...	1,291	1,257,025	209	221,547
Madras "	...	2,133	2,556,908	326	234,258
Total	...	4,471	4,763,710	1,016	1,003,490

From another return I have procured from the Shipping Master, Calcutta,* I find the average number of European seamen visiting Calcutta during each month of 1880, 1881, and 1882 was 1,500, and this represents an average of 1 seaman to about 50 tons. If, therefore, we apply these figures to the total tonnage visiting British ports for the year ending 31st March 1882, I find that about 20,000 seamen visit British ports in the year. Of course, it is not possible to make out without further data how many of these are Europeans, but I have shown that an average of 1,500 European seamen are to be found in Calcutta in any month in the year, and it is probable that, comparing the tonnage which enters Bombay and Madras ports with that which comes to Calcutta, there would be about the same number in Bombay and over 2,500 in the Madras ports; and it is evident, if the question is gone into, that a considerable number of these could be calculated on to aid in the defence of these ports on an emergency and for a limited period.

Another step which might be taken is to ascertain from Australia, Canada, the Cape, and New Zealand what number of volunteers India might reckon on receiving from these colonies in the event of a Russian war; and lest this should be objected to, I would call to memory that Canada in the Indian mutiny offered to send a contingent of 10,000 men, and, besides that, in a war with Russia such as I am contemplating, our colonies would be practically in no danger, and could therefore spare their surplus population.

The population of Canada in 1861 was 3,000,000; it is now about 4½ millions, so that she could now offer us a larger contingent; but taking the

* *Note.*

Month.	Seamen visiting Calcutta			Total.	Average.	Remarks.
	During 1880.	During 1881.	During 1882.			
January	1,160	1,580	1,836	4,576	1,525	12 steamers, aggregating
February	1,454	1,337	1,850	4,641	1,547	21,033 tons and carrying
March	1,062	1,231	1,365	3,678	1,226	498 men = 23,677 men
April	1,094	882	1,201	3,177	1,059	per 1,000 tons.
May	948	984	1,429	3,361	1,120	
June	1,087	1,104	1,812	4,003	1,334	12 sailing vessels, aggre-
July	1,208	1,024	1,698	3,930	1,310	gating 12,131 tons and
August	1,359	1,562	1,747	4,668	1,556	carrying 250 men =
September	1,785	2,307	1,993	6,058	2,019	20,603 men per 1,000 tons.
October	1,754	1,614	2,196	5,566	1,855	
November	1,436	1,518	2,074	5,028	1,676	
December	1,896	1,943	2,074	5,913	1,971	
Total ...	16,236	17,066	21,277	54,599	18,199	

By these figures it will be seen that there is an average number of over 1,500 sailors in the port of Calcutta every day. These men, armed and assisted by artillery and volunteers, should be ample to hold Calcutta and the Hughli defences.

contribution which Canada once offered us, *viz.*, 10,000, or 1 for every 300 head, I find we might perhaps get from the above colonies the following force :—

	Population.	Contingent.
* Canada	4,500,000	15,000
† Cape Colony Proper	720,000	2,400
New South Wales	780,000	2,600
New Zealand	530,000	1,700
Queensland	220,000	700
South Australia	280,000	900
Tasmania	120,000	400
Victoria	880,000	3,000
West Australia	32,000	...
	Total ...	24,300

or, let us say, in round numbers, 24,000 men.

It is, therefore, evident that there is a possibility of our adding to the fighting strength simply by a little timely forethought and organization the following numbers over and above the army :—

	Europeans.	Natives.
European and Eurasian adult males ...	58,500	...
Indo-Portuguese	18,000	...
Parsis	...	27,000
Native Christians	...	100,000
Europeans from Marine	6,000	...
British Colony Contingents	24,000	...
Total ...	106,500	127,000

Even allowing that all these would not be available, I think it is as well to give these figures to show what unthought of mines of wealth of fighting resources we have in India without asking the mother-country for a man.

But this strength would only provide a field army of sufficient strength to give us a fair chance of defeating the efforts that Russia would, looking to the comparatively barren theatre of war, now make. I have said nothing hitherto about the troops necessary to be maintained on the lines of communications. To show this, I must forestall in a measure what I have got to say in Chapter V of this paper, in order to see how many men we shall require for our lines of communication.

The first of these will be from Pir Choki, Sibi, to Herat. The total distance is about 600 miles, divided into 45 stages; and this distance, when the railway to the other side of the Gwaja is finished, should be reduced to 445 miles of 35 stages. The points on this line which would have to be held in strength are Peshin, Kandahar, Girishk, Bakwa, Farah, and Sabzawar, and, besides, there would have to be posts at each stage consisting of 1 company

* In Canada the militia consisted in 1879 of 45,000 active militia and of 655,000 reserve. The Australian Colonies could turn out 40,000 trained men.

† It is doubtful whether this colony could spare any men.

of infantry and ½ troop of cavalry. The garrisons, therefore, required to keep up communications on this line would be—

	British infantry.	Field artillery.	Native infantry.	Native cavalry.	Sappers company.
Peshin	½	1	2	1	...
Kandahar	1	1	2	1	1
Girishk	½	1	2	1	1
Bakwa	...	...	1	½	...
Farah	½	1	2	1	...
Sabzawar	...	...	1	½	...
35 posts of 1 company Native infantry, ½ troop Native cavalry ...	...	...	3½	2	...
Total ...	2½	4	13½	7	2

The second would be from Gomul to Gardan Diwar, a distance of about 350 miles in about 30 stages. The points on this line which would have to be held in strength would be Gomul, Zurmelan, Utman, Kala-i-Langar, Karabagh, and a couple of posts in the Hazara hills. The garrisons required for these would be—

	British infantry.	Field artillery.	Native infantry.	Native cavalry.	Sappers company.
Gomul	...	...	½	¼	...
Zurmelan	¼	½	1	1	...
Utman	¼	½	1	1	...
Kala-i-Langar	1	1	2	1	1
Karabagh	½	1	2	1	...
1st Hazara post	½	1	2	1	...
2nd Hazara post	½	1	2	1	...
25 posts of 1 company Native infantry, ½ troop Native cavalry ...	...	...	2½	1½	...
Total ...	3	5	13	7	1

The third would be from Jamrud to Kabul, a distance of 179 miles, in 18 stages. The points on this line which would have to be held in strength would be Landi Kotal, Bhasawal, Jellalabad, Gandamak, Jagdalak, Seh Baba, and Lataband :—

The garrisons required for these would be—

	British infantry.	British mountain artillery.	Field artillery.	Native infantry.	Native cavalry.
Landi Kotal	½	½	...	1	½
Bhasawal	½	...	½	1	½
Jellalabad	½	½	...	1	1
Gandamak	1	...	1	1	1
Jagdalak	½	½	...	1	¼
Seh Baba	¼	½	...	1	¼
Lataband	¼	½	...	1	¼
11 posts of 1 company Native infantry, ½ troop Native cavalry ...	...	...	...	1½	¾
Total ...	3½	2½	1½	8½	4½

The fourth would be from Jamu to the Baroghil Pass, about 450 miles, and 40 stages. The points on this line which would have to be held in strength are Gilgit, Yasin and Mastoj, and about ten other small posts. The garrisons which would be necessary would be—

	British infantry.	Mountain artillery.	Native infantry.	Native cavalry.
Gilgit	¼	½	1	¼
Yassin	¼	½	1	¼
Mastoj	½	1	1	½
10 posts of ⅓ company Native infantry and 12 Native cavalry ...	...	...	⅓	¼
Total ...	1	2	3⅓	1¼

The total force therefore required for the lines of communication is as follows:—

	British infantry.	Field artillery.	Mountain artillery.	Native infantry.	Native cavalry.
1st, Herat	2⅓	4	...	13⅓	7
2nd, Gardan Diwar	3	5	...	13	7
3rd, Kabul	3⅔	1½	2½	8⅓	4½
4th, Baroghil	1	...	2	4	1½
Total ...	10	10½	4½	39	20

But, as *all* these could not be supplied from the regular army even if increased to the extent I have proposed, it will be necessary to see what other arrangements could possibly be made.

It seems that this is a duty we might safely entrust to the troops of the various rajahs of India and to local levies, both being commanded by English officers. I do not, of course, propose to entrust the whole of the communications to these, but only to an extent which will be shown hereafter.

Now, as to local levies, I gather the following information from the Gazetteer of the North-Western Frontier of India.

Commencing with the Dera Ghazi Khan district, I find in the Baloches residing in and beyond our border a perfect mine of hitherto unworked warlike material. These tribes, commencing from the north, are—

Within the border.	Adult males.	Beyond the order.	Adult males.
Kasranis	800	Kasranis (part)	500
Nutkanis	800	Bozdars	2,500
Lunds of Sori	2,000	Hedianis } These are Gorchanis and Lagaris, *q.v.*	
Kosahs	4,500	Durkanis }	
Lagaris	3,500	Pitafis }	
Gorchanis	1,100	Bugtis	1,200
Lunds of Tibi	450	Khetrans	2,500
Mazaris	1,800	Maris	4,000
Drishaks	1,200		
Kosahs of Sind ... ... }	500		
Burdis ... ... }			
Dumkis ... ... }			
Samalis ... ... }			
Jatnis ... ... }			
Rinds ... ... }			
Sakranis ... ... }			
	16,700		11,200

About 28,000 adult males.

I do not suppose that we should get all these; but I do not see why, with proper arrangements, we should not get about a quarter of them. Then the contingents furnished by each would be in round numbers as follows:—

Kasranis, hill and plain, 400; Nutkanis, 200; Lunds of Sori, 500; Kosahs, 1,000; Lagaris, 900; Gorchanis, 300; Lunds of Tibi, 100; Mazaris, 500; Drishaks, 300; Bozdars, 400; Bugtis, 400; Khetrans, 600; and Maris, 1,000—total, 6,600 men.

The value of such auxiliaries may, I think, be gathered from some remarks I made in the article "Baloches" in my Gazetteer of the North-Western Frontier:—

"The Baloches are a hardy, warlike race; their style of fighting is "peculiar, and much more deadly than that of their neighbours, the Pathans. "The Baloch dismounts and pickets his mare, and then enters the *melée*, "sword and shield in hand, while the Pathan engages with his matchlock "from a distance, if possible under cover, and seldom closes with his adversary.

"Their prevailing faults are pride, over-sensitiveness, and indolence. "They look down with contempt on the Jat and other inhabitants of the "country; they think it beneath their dignity to labour, although they are "getting out of this by degrees.

"There are many good points in their character, which render them very "valuable subjects or feudatories. They are not bigoted, and have no fana-"ticism, nor any hatred against us on religious grounds (and these remarks "refer to the hill tribes as well as those in the plains); and should ever "another crisis occur like that of 1857, or should there be a combination of "Pathan tribes against us, they would prove a most valuable aid.

"The courage of the Baloch is certainly of a sterner kind than that of "the Pathan, and this is shown not so much in their encounters with us—"though, all things considered, they have fought better against us than the "Afghans ever did—as in their tribal feuds, and in the infinitely bolder "manner in which they carry out their raids on our territory. An Afghan at "feud with his neighbour gets into a tower or behind a rock, and waits till he "can murder him in cold blood; a Baloch collects all the wild spirits of his "clan and attacks his enemy in force and sword in hand, generally losing very "heavily. The determined gallantry of the 700 Bugtis who refused to sur-"render to Merewether's horsemen, though escape was hopeless, but allowed "themselves to be shot down till more than two-thirds had fallen, is worthy "of a page in history.

"There are some other characteristics in their character which give them "a decided superiority over their neighbours, the Pathans; these are—faith-"fulness, truthfulness, and their custom regarding their women. The "Afghans swore not to molest our troops when retiring from Kabul, and the "result is known; the Baloches (Maris) swore to keep faith with Captain "Brown and his garrison in Kahan, and escorted them safely to the plains of "Kach, although quite at their mercy, and dependent on them even for water.

"It is a remarkable fact that although, as a race, they are very poor, "living from hand to mouth, they will not be induced to take regular "service, as they will not wear uniform or undergo discipline, and are impatient "of control. They are glad to take irregular service in the frontier militia, "in which they are most useful.

"This disinclination, however, of the Baloch to service is fast being got "over. I do not mean that many of them do enlist, but that a fair number of "them would, if lightly treated as to their prejudices. I took some trouble "in going along the Baloch border to get at the opinions of the Chiefs as to "military service under Government, and I believe I am fairly stating the "objections of Baloches to our services when I declare them to be as follows:— "1st, they are afraid of their hair being cut; 2nd, they object to any but "white or rather dirty white clothes; 3rd, they do not wish to leave their "homes. These objections will, I think, be allowed to be very much those "which any wild race would advance to put in their neck under the yoke for "the first time. I can fancy the wild Bunerwal saying, much as the unclaim- "able Vaziri says now, that he would serve, but he must not go beyond "Peshawar or wear aught but blue, or be obliged to wash; yet how "many Bunerwals had we before the Ambela campaign who had served "at Delhi, Lucknow, or China, who had not only been washed, but liked "it, and were clad in all colors, from khaki to scarlet. It is, in fact, "with the Baloches as with all wild races at first—they require careful hand- "ling, and they will wear anything, go anywhere, and do anything they are "asked. Unless, indeed, it be advanced that it is necessary for a soldier to "have short hair or wear red, I can see no reason why Baloch recruits should "not be as numerous in our ranks as they would be valuable; for I really "think they would be valuable, and I am of opinion they are just one of the "races of India who should look for encouragement from us, being compara- "tively weak in numbers and cut off from all other Muhammadans as much by "their total want of bigotry as their liking for us. The experiment to my "thinking is worth trying; and were an officer who was really fond of Baloches "entrusted with the task, I think we might raise several Baloch regiments that "would more than justify their entertainment in the hour of trial."

In the Dera Ismail Khan district also valuable fighting material is to be found, namely, in the following tribes:—*

	Adult males.
Gandehpurs	1,800
Daolat	200
Mean Khel	600
Babars	500
Ustaranas	200
Total ...	3,300

From this number perhaps we might raise a body of some 1,000 men.

In the Banu district the tribes from whom we might raise fighting men are—

	Adult males.
Khataks	3,500
Vaziris	3,500
Lohanis	16,000
Total ...	23,000

As, however, most of these are settled down to an agricultural life, it would not probably be so easy to get them as fighting material. Still I think that 5,000 of them might be raised under favourable circumstances.

In the Kohat district there are the following tribes who may be relied on—

	Adult males.
Khataks	19,000
Bangash	10,000
Total ...	29,000

* I would refer those of my readers who wish for more information regarding these tribes to my Gazetteer of the North-West Frontier.

I should be inclined to say that 6,000 of these could be enlisted for the special service required of them.

In the Peshawar district the fighting tribes are—

	Adult males.
Yusafzais	27,000
Khataks	1,500
Mohmands	9,000
Khalils	6,000
Daudzais	5,000
Total ...	48,500

From these perhaps 10,000 men could be raised.

There are not many men in the Hazara district of much use as fighting material; but still from the Bombas, Dhunds, Karals, and Gakars, the Tanawalis, Swatis, and tribes of Afghan origin, I should say there would not be much difficulty in raising 3,000 men of more or less valour.

From the six districts of the frontier we might then be able to raise as follows:—

	Adult males.
Dera Ghazi Khan	7,000
Dera Ismail Khan	3,500
Banu	5,000
Kohat	6,000
Peshawar	10,000
Hazara	3,000
Total ...	34,500

All tribal levies that may be used by us should be organized into tribal companies or battalions according to their numbers under their own Chiefs. They should be armed and supplied with ammunition by us, and they should be paid regularly. Uniform is not wanted: each tribe should be encouraged to have a tribal badge and banner by which they might be known. I do not say they would turn out first-class soldiers, but as they are just as plucky as the Afghans, and just as cohesive and well disciplined, I really do not see why they should not do to aid us in the work before us. And there is no doubt their absence from the frontier would be an aid to us in another way, inasmuch as it would reduce the elements of danger we should leave behind.

Besides the above, there are many other fighting races in India whose warlike strength has not been called on to anything like the extent it would bear.

For instance, of Sikh adult males we have only 15,105 in our army; only 8,756 Dogras; only 1,360 Mazbis; only 3,000 Jats; only 6,378 Gurkhas; only 14,600 Brahmans and Rajputs of Hindustan; only 569 Kumaonis; only 20,553 Hindustani Muhammadans; only 8,772 Punjabi Muhammadans; and only 1,580 trans-border Pathans, out of over 100,000 men.*

There could be little danger in enlisting these races up to treble the number now in our ranks, and there cannot be much doubt that levies of them armed by us would be quite equal to aiding in the internal defence of India, thus freeing some of our regiments for the communications of our field army.

I now proceed to consider what troops at present in the service of the Rajahs of India would be available for this purpose. In such a war as I am considering, I am of opinion that it should be taken for granted that every Rajah in India is anxious to help the British Government to the

* I make out from the Census Report that there are about 600,000 adult male Sikhs, but I have been unable to find out the numbers of the other races.

utmost of his power, and I think that some help should, as a matter of policy, be accepted from each one. Those who have sufficiently good troops should be called on to provide contingents either for the maintenance of order in India or for the communications of the field army, and those who have no troops suitable should be called on to provide transport and supplies, all according to their several positions and resources.

The following remarks from a report of Sir C. Aitchison,* when Foreign Secretary, are useful in considering this subject:—

"Many Native States of India, especially the smaller ones, such as the "Punjab Hill States, the States on the South-Western Frontier of Bengal, "and the like, are in so complete subordination, that there is practically little "difference between them and some parts of British territory. Some, indeed, "like the Chiefs of the Delhi territory, the jaghirdars of Sattara and the "Southern Mahratta Country, hold their estates on a military tenure, being "required to furnish men for our service or to pay money instead. They are, "however, all bound to co-operate with the British Government in time of "war.

"The Chiefs of the Jyntia and Cossyah Hills, for instance, acknowledge "the right of the British Government to establish cantonments and forts in "any part of their States, and are bound to obey all orders issued to them.

"The Rajah of Munipore is bound to assist with carriage in the event of "war with Burma and troops being sent either to protect Munipore or ad-"vance beyond his frontier; and in the event of anything happening on the "Eastern Frontier of British territory, he must, when required, assist with a "portion of his troops.

"The Sikkim Rajah is bound to join with the whole of his military force, "and afford every aid and facility to British troops when employed in the hills.

"The Chiefs of the South-Western Frontier of Bengal must cordially "yield obedience and report to Government all that occurs.

"In the Cuttack tributary mehals the Chiefs are required to afford sup-"plies at fair prices to Government troops, and to depute a contingent force "of their own to co-operate with the British troops, if any neighbouring rajah "or any other person whatsoever offers opposition to Government.

"The Rajah of Gurhwal holds his estates on condition of good behaviour "and of service, military and political, in time of danger and disturbance.

"In the Punjab the whole of the hill Chiefs also, including Puttiala, so "far as his hill estates are concerned, must, in the event of war in the hills, "join the British army.

"On the Bombay side, the Sattara and the Southern Mahratta jaghirdars "generally pay small tribute in lieu of horsemen.

"In Bundelcund, for instance, we have formally engaged to protect the "Rajahs of Tehree, Duttia, and Sumpthur from the aggressions of any foreign "power, and guaranteed to them their possessions. The Rajah of Tehree is "bound to defend the roads and passes through his territories, and whenever "Government sent troops or wish to station them in his State, he must con-"sent and furnish supplies. In addition to similar obligations, the Rajahs of "Duttia and Sumpthur are required to employ their troops at their own ex-"pense, whenever called upon, and to place them in subordination to the "Officer Commanding the British forces. These three Chiefs have treaties "with the British Government; the other Chiefs hold their territories under "sanads or grants from us. Although their engagements differ somewhat, it

* Written about 1868.

" may be said, as a general rule, that they are bound to defend their passes, " to supply guides and provisions to British troops, to entertain no greater " force than is required for the collection of the revenue and the dignity of " the Chief, and generally to be submissive to the will and commands of the " Government.

" The States of Puttiala, Jhind, and Nabha are bound to assist and " furnish the British troops with grain when marching through their States, " and should an enemy approach, the Chiefs are bound to join the British " army with their forces and co-operate with the British Government in " expelling the enemy.

" The position of Cashmere on our extreme frontier, lying between our " own territories and those of the independent nations of Central Asia, is " exceedingly peculiar. The boundaries of Cashmere on the north have never " been defined. The Maharajah once boasted that the boundary in that direc- " tion which he recognized was the limit to which his arms could carry it. " We have, however, recently impressed on him the necessity of abstaining " from aggressions. In the treaty with him indeed it is stipulated that the " boundaries of the State shall not at any time be changed without our con- " sent. The Maharajah is bound to refer to us all disputes with his neigh- " bours. He has therefore no pretext for aggressions. We on our part, " moreover, are bound to aid the Maharajah in protecting his territories from " external enemies, and would naturally object to any course of action on his " part calculated to provoke an invasion of Cashmere. The Maharajah, more- " over, acknowledges our supremacy and engages to join, with the whole of " his military force, the British troops when employed within the hills or in " the territories adjoining his possessions.

" The other Native States may be divided into two classes; those in " which we maintain subsidiary forces and those which are bound to subor- " dinate co-operation. Those in which we have to maintain subsidiary forces " are Gwalior, Indore, Hyderabad, Travancore, Cochin, Baroda, and Cutch.

" Scindia further agreed to maintain a body of auxiliary horse to co- " operate with the British troops and to assign funds for their support. It is " further agreed that the military force of all arms to be hereafter maintained " by His Highness shall at no time exceed—artillery, 48 guns with 480 " gunners; infantry, 5,000 drilled soldiers; cavalry, 6,000 sowars. Sindia " besides pays a contribution of Rs. 19,656 a year to the Malwa Bheel Corps.

" Our agreements with Holkar in regard to military matters are contained " in the treaty of Mundesore concluded in 1818. The Maharajah agrees to " retain in service an auxiliary force of not less than 3,000 horse.

" In Hyderabad we are bound to maintain a subsidiary force of eight " battalions of sepoys and two regiments of cavalry with the requisite guns. " Of this number, unless with the Nizam's consent, there must be stationed " within the Hyderabad territories never less than five regiments of infantry " and one of cavalry, with a due proportion of artillery, and the rest must be " brought in on demand. The expenses of this force is met from the revenue " of the ceded districts of Madras. Its duties are the protection of the " Nizam's person, the overawing of rebels, the protection of Hyderabad " against foreign invasion, and the like. Besides the subsidiary force, " Government maintain an auxiliary force or contingent of 5,000 infantry, " 2,000 cavalry, and four field batteries to be employed at all times, whenever " required, throughout the Nizam's dominions, and to quell rebellion or

" resistance to the Nizam's just claims or authority. This force is paid for from " the Hyderabad Assigned Districts. In time of war the subsidiary force, " with the exception of two battalions, and also the contingent, are available " for service, the Nizam being required to furnish no other troops to co- " operate with ours.

" By the treaty of 1799, the Maharajah of Mysore is required to pay " seven lakhs of pagodas a year for a subsidiary force. He was also required " to contribute in time of war such portion of his revenues as Government " might consider just and reasonable. This latter obligation, however, was " commuted in 1804 into an obligation to maintain an auxiliary force of 4,000 " horse, Government agreeing to pay for any more troops that might be re- " quired.

" In the Madras Presidency there are two States, Travancore and Cochin, " with which we have arrangements for a subsidiary force. In Travancore " we are bound to defend and protect the territories of the Rajah against " all enemies whatsoever, and the Rajah pays 8 lakhs a year for a subsi- " diary force. If a larger force is required, the cost is to be borne jointly " by Government and the Rajah; and if Government have reason to apprehend " failure in the payment of the funds, they have power to introduce regula- " tions for the management of the Travancore revenues, or to bring a portion " of the State under their direct management. With Cochin the stipulations " are almost precisely similar, the subsidiary payment, however, being only " two lakhs.

" In the Bombay Presidency also there are two States, Baroda and " Cutch, with which we have similar arrangements. The Baroda subsidiary " force is 4,000 Native infantry, two regiments of cavalry, and one company " of European artillery, paid for from territories ceded by the Guickwar. Its " duties are the same as those of the Hyderabad subsidiary force. The Guick- " war is also required to keep up an auxiliary force of 3,000 cavalry, and in " time of war to bring forward the whole of his military resources. We on " our part are bound to protect and defend him. In Cutch the Rao pays two " lakhs for a subsidiary force, and is bound to aid Government upon its requisi- " tion with such military force as he possesses. He cannot allow Arabs, " Seedees, or foreign mercenaries to remain in Cutch without our consent; " the importation of military stores is forbidden, Government agreeing to sup- " ply the requirements of the State at a valuation.

" In those States which are allied to us by engagements of subordinate " co-operation, the conditions generally are that we protect and guarantee " the integrity of the State, while the Chief is bound to furnish troops on " our requisition according to his means. These conditions are common to " Bhawulpore, Rewah, Oodeypore, Jodhpore, and the Rajputana States gen- " erally, Bhopal, Dhar, and Dewas. But besides these common obligations, " Oodeypore contributes Rs. 50,000 to the Meywar Bheel Corps. Jodhpore " contributes Rs. 1,15,000 in lieu of a contingent of 1,500 horse, which he " was required to keep up by the treaty of 1818. Kotah pays two lakhs a " year for an auxiliary force. Tonk is forbidden to keep up a larger army " than is required for the internal management of his possessions; and in " Serohi we have the power of raising a local force to be disciplined by Euro- " peans. By the treaty of 1818 Bhopal was to furnish a contingent of 600 " horse and 400 foot for British service, but in 1849 this was commuted to an "annual payment of two lakhs a year, from which is maintained the Bhopal "Battalion. The Dhar State pays Rs. 19,656 a year for the Malwa Bheel "Corps, Dewas Rs. 33,022, and Jowra Rs. 1,58,614 for the same corps. "Besides the above, the Rajputana States pay the following tribute :—

	Rupees.
Udeypore	2,00,000
Jeypore	4,00,000
Jodhpore	98,000
Kotah	1,84,720
Boondee	1,20,000
Jhallawar	80,000
Pertabgarh	72,700
Banswarrah	27,387
Doongurpore	27,387
Serohi	7,500

"The following States pay no tribute :—Tonk, Kerowlee, Kishengarh, "Dholepore, Bhurtpore, Ulwar, Bikaneer, and Jussulmere.

"In his able sketches on our political relations published in 1837, Colonel "Sutherland strongly advocates an extension of the system of Native contin- "gents, by which means he considers that the armies of Native States may best "be brought to support our interests in the dominions of their princes, and to "aid in the general military defence of the Empire. I give the following "extracts from his work as showing more particularly what were his "views :—

"The only question of really vital importance to the British Government, "beyond that of maintaining universal tranquillity, is the degree of authority "which it is entitled to exercise over the armies of the several States for the "general defence of the Empire. Those armies are of sufficient magnitude to "render it in the highest degree important that we should look to the nature "of their temper and the degree of their organization. The very existence "of this military force is at present almost unknown to us; it rests quietly "in its several positions, and apparently subject to our will. But should "anything occur to call our forces to an advanced scene of action, or which "may be calculated to disturb the stability of our power, we shall find "this enormous mass of men rise into active existence, if not in combination, "or directly immediately against us, at least for the purpose of exerting the "authority, and aggrandizing the power of their several Sovereigns.

* * * * * *

"Next in importance to the efficiency of our own army for the general "defence of our position in India is the extent of the armies of the several "States, the nature of their organization, and the manner in which they "stand affected towards us. An estimate has already been made of their "numbers. The nature of their organization, except in the few instances "where they are under the control or command of British officers, is of the "very worst description—ill-paid, undisciplined, and dissatisfied to a degree "which renders their allegiance to their own Sovereign a matter of very "doubtful contingency, and prepares them to enter on any enterprise promis- "ing better pay or prospect of plunder, yet all disposed to look upon us and "our power as the principal cause of their degradation.

"It has at all times been found impossible for the Native States of "India to maintain, without the assistance of European officers, a regularly "disciplined army. The absence of system and energy in the native character "seems unsuited to this; but above all the absence of any regular system of "payment where the prince has a private as well as a public treasury, "and draws into the former every farthing that he can appropriate without "any reference to the wants of the latter.

* * * * * *

"To be efficient for our purpose, those troops must be under the "immediate command of our own officers, dependent on them for the regu- "larity with which they are paid, for their promotion, and relying on our "Government for the permanency of their service. Holding these essentials "in our hands, the contingents may be composed of the old soldiers of the "Native States, for there is nothing national in the character of their armies "which need lead us to fear that in the day of our adversity they will turn "against us, as the German contingents did against Napoleon after the "battle of Leipsic. We have in the conduct of the Mysore, the Hyderabad, "the Poona, and the Nagporé contingents during the last war proof that "under this form of organization their gallantry and fidelity to our cause "will not be inferior to those qualities in the troops of our service.

"Most of the Native States are bound by treaty to aid the British "Government in time of war with the whole or a specified portion of their "armies. But those stipulations would be little binding on them, nor "could we under any circumstances of adversity calculate on their fidelity "or usefulness, unless like the contingent of the Nizam, they were placed "under the command of our own officers. No one will doubt the importance "to our cause of the services of such auxiliaries thus organized, either for "the purpose of fighting our battles in advanced positions or for the "maintenance of our interests and of general tranquillity in internal India, "when it may be necessary to call our own army to other scenes of action.

"We have not generally the right of drawing portions of the Native "armies from their Sovereigns in a degree that would render them useful "to us. And it is at present doubtful how, or whether ever, this most "important of our political objects can be attained. We may be sure that "the Native Powers will not readily or voluntarily render up their armies "to our control, for their confidence is not, and probably never will be, so "great in our good faith and in the permanency of our power as to lead them "implicitly to trust to us for their defence. The real condition to which "they have resigned themselves by treaty or to which they have fallen in the "progress of time and in the course of events is very different from that "which they would arrogate to themselves. Cut off from foreign relations "and protected as they substantially are and have been for the last fifteen "years almost without an exception to the contrary, each against the "aggression of his neighbour and of all other powers, their armies have "virtually become useless, except for the purpose of internal government.

"It is a question whether without an army a Government can exist even "for the purposes of internal administration, and the instances which we "have of late seen of the necessity which Government are under in more "civilized countries than India of calling for the aid of troops in support "of civil institutions, may serve to convince us that even for this purpose an "army is necessary.

"We must calculate upon such portions of these contingents as are "placed under British officers being as entirely withdrawn as our own "troops from the support of the Native Government in its internal "administration, and applicable only to the general defence of the Empire.

"Some of the States already pay a subsidiary force for this purpose, "others pay tribute, and in addition nearly all promise to supply a specific "contingent, or to hold their whole army at our disposal. It is on this "latter account that we may consider ourselves justified in endeavouring "to gain a control over such portion of the Native armies as is extra to "what they require for internal Government. From the nature of their "organization and their temper, those armies are at all times dangerous to us; "and on these accounts, when we were assailed from without, might become "destructive to our power. Self-preservation therefore requires that when we "have the right these portions of the Native armies should be brought under "our authority for the purpose of fighting their battles and our own.

* * * * * *

"Great difficulty will necessarily be experienced in gaining such control "over the contingents of our allies as would render them efficient and faithful "to us. When we proposed lately to render up one of three thousand horse "maintained for general service by the Guickwar, provided he would place "the remaining two thousand on a footing considered more desirable by us, "he would not yield to the arrangement. Yet until this control over those "armies has been obtained, our situation in India, under particular circum- "stances, must become highly critical, for it is obvious that we cannot afford "to pay an army in India sufficiently to fight our frontier battles, and to support "our position against hostile combinations within. It will become a house "divided against itself.

"No opportunity should therefore be lost of taking advantage of every "opening promising a result so favourable to us. It is the point on which the "greatest importance to ourselves now hinges in our relations with the States of "internal India. Every man gained is a double gain by strengthening our- "selves, and taking away from them their strength and their power to do us "harm.

"In their present condition the Native armies are not at all formidable "to us. In time of danger indeed they proved most valuable auxiliaries. "The Cashmere troops did excellent service at Delhi, so did the troops of the "cis-Sutlej States. In the majority of Native States, so long as we treat "the Chiefs with consideration and in a spirit of truthfulness rather than sus- "picion, and so long as the Chiefs govern fairly well and do not alienate the "affections of their people, we may rely on the fidelity and co-operation "of their troops. For field operations, indeed, their troops are not of much "value. But for escorts and keeping open communications so as to relieve our "trained toops for actual fighting, they would be very valuable and become "a tower of strength to us.

"In one point I think we have been too negligent. We have not suffi- "ciently made use of our power to employ the troops of Native States and "to station our own troops in Native territories. In every military affair in "the neighbourhood of a Native State I would require the State to join, "even if it should be only for a parade or to take a baggage guard. In any "expedition on the Punjab Frontier, for instance, the troops of Cashmere "and Bhawulpore should be required to take a part, as we have suggested "to the Military Department that Munipore and Tipperah should do in the "Looshai Expedition."

I propose now to show as correctly as the limited information at my disposal enables me, and as succinctly as possible, the armed strength of the various Native States, adding a few remarks as to their efficiency.

Travancore.—Artillery, 6 guns, no cattle; cavalry, 60 men, no use; Infantry, the Nair Brigade, 1,211 men, officered by British officers, armed with smooth-bore Enfields—might be of some use near their homes.

Baroda.—Artillery, 12 iron 6-prs., 4 brass 6-prs., 4 brass howitzers, 4 brass 6-prs., horsed, rest drawn by bullocks.

Cavalry, 3,000 at the disposal of British Government—badly mounted, might be useful on communications.

Infantry, 3,000 regulars, commanded by Europeans; divided into 3 battalions, *viz.*, Okmandal, Dhar—pretty fair, might be useful. 2,000 infantry for forts and 4,000 irregulars, undrilled and without uniforms.

Kattywar States.—Artillery, 68 guns, of which only 4 are thoroughly serviceable.

Cavalry, 432 regulars, 1,292 jagirdar horse, 2,309 irregulars.

Infantry, 1,055 regulars, 2,575 fort garrisons, 5,306 irregulars, 6,370 tehsil sepoys.

Kutch.—12 serviceable field guns, 200 regular cavalry, and about 1,400 irregular, inefficient, 3,000 jagirdar horse, 400 regular infantry.

Kolhapur States.—63 guns, only 16 guns said to be serviceable, but only 10 are in use; 150 cavalry, tolerably well mounted; 530 infantry under English officers, 972 police.

Sawant Wari.—Only 3 serviceable guns and a local corps, 462 strong, with 2 European officers and two 3-pr. brass guns.

Mahi Kanta.—14 guns, 400 cavalry, and 500 infantry.

Rewa Kanta.—No guns, about 300 cavalry, Arabs, Pathans, Mekranis, &c., and about 1,500 infantry.

Pahlanpur—18 guns, only 4 moveable, 300 cavalry, 700 infantry, under the Political Superintendent—said to be efficient.

Cambay.—5 guns, 200 cavalry, 900 infantry—mostly a rabble.

Cuch Behar.—2 9-prs., serviceable, and 100 guards. In the Bhotan war this State provided 100 cavalry and an infantry regiment, which were very serviceable.

Hill Tipperah.—412 infantry, 80 or 90 Gurkhas, and 198 drilled.

Rampur.—26 serviceable guns, 500 cavalry, 900 regular infantry, 1,000 irregular infantry, 3 troops cavalry, drilled and commanded by an Army Native officer. Infantry poorly drilled, little better than rabble—more likely to go against us.

Mysore.—4 5-prs., 1,200 Siladar Horse—very efficient, about 2,500 irregular infantry.

Cis-Sutlej States—

Patiala—85 guns, serviceable, 20 horsed, the rest drawn by bullocks, 2,000 regular cavalry, 3,000 regular infantry; cavalry rough and badly mounted; infantry good.

Jhind.—12 guns serviceable, 360 cavalry, 1,200 regular infantry, both very efficient. Cavalry armed with breech-loaders. Infantry with smooth bores.

Nabha.—6 serviceable guns, 2 camel guns, 450 regular cavalry, 277 irregulars, 1,000 regular infantry, not so good.

Maler Kotla.—120 cavalry, 400 infantry, 2 guns, } some of these are
Kalsia.—60 cavalry, 200 infantry, 2 guns, } drilled.

Hill States.—

Sirmur.—10 serviceable guns, 100 cavalry, 400 infantry, efficient.

Kahlur.—4 serviceable guns, 40 cavalry, 600 infantry, efficient.

Kapurthala.—8 serviceable guns, 200 cavalry, 800 infantry, very efficient.

Mandi.—1,700 infantry, inefficient, 6 guns.

Suket.—350 infantry, inefficient, 3 guns.

Bahawulpur.—6 guns, serviceable, 360 cavalry, 900 infantry, of which 100 cavalry, 400 infantry, efficient.

Faridkot.—4 serviceable guns, 50 cavalry, 150 infantry, efficient.

Kashmir.—96 serviceable guns, *viz.*, 4 10-pr. batteries of 6 guns, 4 4-pr. batteries of 6 guns, drawn by horses, 4 mountain batteries of 4 guns on mules, 1,200 gunners, cavalry about 1,300, infantry 24,000 in 28 regiments, of which 13,000 are serviceable, mostly Dogras,—good material, very active, good marchers, and faithful. Besides there are 1,600 sappers.

Hyderabad.—Artillery, 8 guns, horsed, 12 drawn by bullocks and 2 by elephants.

Cavalry, 3,000 regulars, 5,000 irregular cavalry.

Infantry, 24,000 Arabs, Rohillas, Africans, &c. About 6,000 of these are well disciplined and well equipped ; the rest are a rabble.

Nipal.—600 serviceable guns, 10 field batteries fit for immediate service, about ⅔rds mounted and carried on coolies, of whom there are 5,000 enlisted ; cavalry 100, useless ; infantry, 24,000 divided into 27 regiments, could be doubled in 3 months and quadrupled in 4 months. All indifferently drilled, but much superior to most Native States armies, and would be very serviceable.

Indore.—Six 6-prs., horse artillery, horsed, ten 9-prs.

Cavalry, 4,500 regulars, 1,500 irregulars, indifferently mounted, but efficient.

Infantry, 4,500, regulars, 4,500 irregulars, well armed, chiefly Oudh men, said to be efficient.

Jowra.—6 serviceable guns, no horses or bullocks kept up, 100 cavalry, 900 infantry, inefficient.

Rutlam.—3 serviceable guns, 80 cavalry, 600 infantry, inefficient.

Bhopal.—12 serviceable guns, horse artillery, good, 400 regular cavalry, 500 irregular, 400 regular infantry, 900 irregular infantry. Regulars of cavalry and infantry efficient.

Bundelcund States.—30 in number, 141 serviceable guns, drawn by bullocks.

2,600 cavalry, 21,000 infantry, badly armed, not drilled, but with much good material among them.

Dhar.—Two 3-pr. guns, 270 cavalry, 790 infantry, all indifferent; 50 cavalry and 150 infantry, fairly drilled.

Rewah.—6 serviceable guns, 800 cavalry, 600 regular infantry, 1,000 irregular cavalry, indifferently mounted, badly armed, but serviceable for rough work. Baghel Rajputs in the infantry. One regiment efficient and well drilled, armed with smooth-bores.

Gwalior.—Artillery, one battery horse artillery, 6 field artillery, one heavy artillery, with 44 serviceable guns, *viz.*,—12 6-prs., 30 9-prs., 2 18-prs.

Cavalry 4 regiments, 550 of all ranks, efficient, indifferently mounted; infantry, 6 regiments, 750 of all ranks.	All well drilled, armed with smooth-bores, equipped with some transport, nearly all Purbiahs and Hindustanis; efficient and hardy, and well disciplined.

Besides there are irregulars, cavalry about 5,000 and 10,000 infantry, who are without discipline or organization.

Udaipur.—14 serviceable field guns, one battery horse artillery, fairly efficient; in others carriages bad, but bullocks plentiful. Cavalry, 300 regulars, fairly efficient, 4,000 Fudal Horse, and 1,600 irregulars, inefficient; infantry, 1,200 regulars, fairly trained, 13,000 irregulars, inefficient.

Jaipur.—30 guns, of which 24 are fit to take the field, *viz.*, four 18-prs., four 24-pr. howitzers; six 9-prs.; six 6-prs.; and four 3-prs., 2,300 artillerymen.

Cavalry, 700 regulars, 3,000 irregulars, very indifferent.

Infantry, 2,000 regulars, 4,500 irregulars; the first imperfectly drilled, the rest a rabble, armed with sword and matchlock.

Jodhpur.—40 serviceable guns, 1,500 regular and 1,800 irregular cavalry, 2,000 regular and 3,000 irregular infantry, badly armed and inefficient.

Jaisalmir.—2 serviceable guns, 500 irregular cavalry, 400 irregular infantry, armed with swords and matchlocks. A large force of Rajput horse could be raised.

Bundi.—Artillery, four 3-prs., eight 6 and 9-prs. drawn by bullocks, and 25 camel guns; 100 regular cavalry, 2,000 Jaghir horse; 2,000 infantry, of which 150 are regulars.

Tonk.—A battery of 4-prs., horsed, 22 heavy guns and howitzers, 3 mortars and 26 field guns; 400 regular cavalry, 2,000 Jaghir horse, fairly equipped and efficient.

Infantry, 800 regulars, drilled and disciplined, and superior to most Native States, mostly Mahomedans, 2,000 irregular infantry.

Kotah.—Artillery, four 6-prs., horsed, sixteen field guns drawn by bullocks, and 80 camel guns.

Cavalry.—2 troops 240 men, Sikhs and Mahomedans, partially drilled; 700 irregulars, very indifferent, and 2,000 Jaghirdar horse might be raised besides.

Infantry, 1 regiment of regulars, 800 men, mostly Rajputs, fairly drilled, one regiment of Purbiahs, and about 4,500 irregular infantry, mostly Rajputs, and all "riff-raff."

Jhallawar.—Artillery, four 4-prs., horsed, twelve 6 and 9-prs. drawn by bullocks, and 50 camel guns.

Cavalry, by 400 poorly equipped and armed Sikhs, Pathans, Rajputs; infantry, 2,000 regulars, one regiment fairly good, chiefly Oudh men and s me Pathans.

Ulwar.—Artillery, four 3-prs. horse artillery, horsed, two 6-prs. drawn by bullocks, and some camel guns.

Cavalry, 300 regulars, 600 Jaghir horse, Rajputs, 1,600 irregulars, both indifferent; about 1,200 of the cavalry are well mounted.

Infantry, 1,000 regulars, imperfectly drilled, 4,000 irregulars, useless.

Bhartpur.—25 serviceable guns drawn by bullocks, 2,000 regular cavalry, well drilled, 2,700 regular infantry, drilled, 1,600 irregulars. These troops are the best in Rajputana.

Kerouli.—400 cavalry, fair, 3,000 infantry, a rabble, 250 of them are Pathans.

Dholpur.—13 serviceable guns, 500 cavalry, 500 regular infantry, slightly drilled, and 1,000 irregulars, said to be fine material, but not trained.

Bikanir.—16 serviceable guns, including 4 howitzers, 400 cavalry of sorts, and 1,600 infantry, of which some 400 are rather better than the rest.

Manipur.—About 10 brass 3-pr. guns, 400 Cavalry mounted on ponies, fairly good, 5,000 infantry, fairly serviceable, armed with percussion and flint muskets, besides 4,000 coolies and 400 ponies and 30 elephants could be turned out.

I find therefore that, in round numbers, there are available 1,050 guns of sorts, 15,000 regular cavalry, 53,000 irregular cavalry, 93,000 regular infantry, and 182,000 irregular infantry, or a total of 1,050 guns and 348,000 fighting men, exclusive of all artillerymen.*

Now the question is, what use can we make of these men. It is evident that the more of them we can draw away from India and from their own States, the less danger will there be of disaffection either in India or in particular States. But although there are great advantages in withdrawing these "elements of danger" from India, there is undoubtedly great difficulty in utilizing their services. In the first place, I do not think it would do to utilize them in the defence of India, as they might fraternise with the natives in a rebellion; and in the second, there are probably not many of them who would be good enough to be utilized on the communications in a war in Afghanistan. Still I think that some of them would be good enough, and that it is very advisable to make as much use of them as possible.

I will, therefore, turn again to my estimate of the number of men we should require for the communications of an army in Afghanistan.

For the Herat line we require 2½ British infantry, 4 field artillery, 13½ Native infantry, 7 Native cavalry, and 2 companies sappers. The British infantry and field artillery and sappers must, of course, be provided from the Field Army. I think we might substitute levies and Rajahs' troops for half a regiment Native infantry at Peshin, Kandahar, Girishk, Bakwa, Farah, and Sabzawar, and also at all the road posts; only I would put double the number of levies at these places: this will enable us to do with 7 regiments Native infantry on this line instead of 13½. In the same way levies and Rajahs' troops may be substituted for regiments Native cavalry, enabling us to do with 2½ Native cavalry instead of 7.

The troops on the Herat line of communications would then be as follows:—

	British infantry.	Field artillery.	Native infantry.	Native cavalry.	Regiment Native infantry levies.	Regiment Native cavalry levies.
Peshin	½	1	1½	½	1	...
Kandahar ...	1	1	1½	½	1	1
Girishk	½	1	½	½	1	1
Bakwa	...	...	½	¼	1	½
Farah	½	1	1½	½	1	1
Sabzawar			½	¼	1	½
35 posts of 2 companies levies, Native infantry troop, cavalry levies ...	...	...	...	...	7	9
	2½	4	7	2½	13 800 men each	14 480 men each.

* In giving the above armed strength of the Native States, all petty States have been omitted; also all guns said to be unserviceable and all troops that are clearly not worth counting.

The levies required would be 10,400 infantry and 6,750 cavalry—total 17,150. These I should propose to furnish as under:—

Levies from the Dera Ghazi Khan District ...	...	6,600
„ Bahawalpur, 300 cavalry, 1,000 infantry	...	1,300
„ Multan District	...	1,000
„ Khan of Kalat	...	2,000
„ Baroda, 500 cavalry, 2,000 infantry	...	2,500
„ Bhopal 500 „ 1,500 „	...	2,000
„ Gwalior, 500 „ 1,500 „	...	2,000
Total	...	17,400

These levies should always come with their own Chiefs, and should be armed, as far as was necessary to put them on equal terms with Afghans, from our arsenals. An English officer should be allowed to every 1,000 of them. They should be kept together as far as the exigencies of the service would allow, and of course be paid by us with extreme regularity.

For the second line, namely, from Dera Ismail Khan to Gardan Diwar, we require 3 British infantry, 5 field artillery, 13 Native infantry, 7 Native cavalry. The British infantry and field artillery should, as above, be furnished by the Field Army, and instead of 5 Native infantry and 4 Native Cavalry at the larger posts, I would substitute levies, while all the smaller posts should be held by levies.

The troops on the Gomal line would then be as follows:—

	British infantry.	Field artillery.	Native infantry.	Native cavalry.	Infantry levies.	Cavalry levies.
Gomal			¼	⅛	⅓	¼
Utman ...	¼	½	½	¼	1	½
Zurmelan ...	¼	½	½	¼	1	½
Kala-i-Langar ...	1	1	1	½	2	1
Karabagh ...	½	1	1	½	2	1
1st Hazara Post ...	½	1	1	½	2	1
2nd ditto ...	½	1	1	½	2	1
25 posts of 2 companies infantry levies, 1 troop cavalry levies	...	...	...	...	5	3
Total	3	5	5¼	2⅝	15⅓	8¼

The levies required would come to 12,400 infantry and 4,000 cavalry—total 16,400 men. These I should propose to furnish as under:—

Levies from Dera Ismail Khan District		...	...	1,000
„ Banu District	...	...	...	5,000
„ Holkar	500 cavalry,	2,000 infantry	...	2,500
„ Nipal		3,000 „	...	3,000
„ Karpurthala	100 „	400 „	...	500
„ Mandi		500 „	...	500
„ Sirmur and Kahlur	100 „	400 „	...	500
„ Bundelcund	500 „	3,000 „	...	3,500
		Total	...	16,500

On the third line, namely, from Peshawar to Kabul, we require 3½ British infantry, 2½ mountain artillery, 1½ field artillery, 8½ Native infantry, 4½ Native cavalry. The British infantry and artillery should, as above, be furnished from the Field Army, and instead of 4 Native infantry and 2 Native cavalry at the large posts, I would substitute levies, while all the smaller posts should be held by them,

The troops on this line would then be as follows :—

	British infantry.	British mountain artillery.	Field artillery.	Native infantry.	Native cavalry.	Infantry levies.	Cavalry levies.
Landi Kotal ...	½	½	...	½	¼	1	½
Bhosawal ...	½	...	½	½	¼	1	½
Jellalabad ...	½	½	...	½	¼	1	½
Gandamak ...	1	...	1	½	¼	1	1
Jagdalak ...	½	½	...	½	⅛	1	¼
Seh Baba ...	¼	½	...	½	⅛	1	¼
Latabund ...	¼	½	...	½	¼	1	¼
11 posts of 2 companies infantry levies, 1 troop cavalry levies.	...	...	...	...	...	3	3¼
Total	3½	2½	1½	3½	1½	10	6½

The levies required would come to 8,000 infantry, 3,200 cavalry—total 11,200 men. These I would propose to furnish as under :—

Levies from the Kohat district	1,500
" Peshawar district	2,000
" Hazara district	1,000
" cis-Sutlej States, 800 cavalry, 2,400 infantry	3,200
" Rajputana States, 1,000 cavalry, 3,000 infantry	4,000.
Total ...	11,700

On the fourth line, from Jamu to the Baroghil Pass, we require 1 British infantry, 2 mountain artillery, 4 Native infantry, 1¼ Native cavalry. The British infantry and artillery should, as above, be furnished from the Field Army, and instead of 3 Native infantry and 1 Native cavalry, I would substitute levies. All these could easily be furnished by the Rajah of Kashmir, who should, therefore, be called on to supply about 4,000 infantry and 500 cavalry.

The total of levies and Rajahs' troops required for our communications will therefore be :—

For the Herat line	17,400
" Gomal line	17,000
" Kabul line	11,400
" Kashmir line	4,500
Total ...	50,600

In the above pages I have shown that we must be able to put in the field an army of 120,000 men and 354 guns; and in addition to this we must have the aid of about 50,000 levies and Rajahs' troops.

With regard to the British troops, I have said that, in the event of a war coming on us suddenly, there is nothing for it but to get what we want from England; but I have pointed out that if we use the resources in men which we have in India and organize them, we may eventually be able to do with less men from England. I have not entered into the question of the best way of organizing these men, as it would take up too much time; but that they can be so organized as to give us material assistance, I am convinced. In the same way I have shown what assistance we may be likely to get from the half-caste population and those natives who must be faithful to us, come what will.

No doubt the measures I have proposed will be very expensive ; but that is not the question. Whether expensive or not, they, or something very like them, will have to be undertaken sooner or later. The evil day should not be put off one hour longer. It may be put off nominally : it can never be so in reality.

Procrastination and temporising may defer the storm for a brief season ; but every hour that is spent in mere procrastination, without taking advantage of the lull to face our difficulties, will only cause it to acquire accumulative force, and the steps which would have been sufficient to cause it to break harmlessly round us in 1884 will require to be doubled in 1885 or 1886. I repeat, with all possible emphasis, the only thing now left for us to do is to grasp our nettle and to take up such a strong position in defence of our Indian frontier as will make Russia see the hopelessness of attacking us. Nothing short of this will do.

CHAPTER V.

OFFENSIVE-DEFENSIVE MILITARY OPERATIONS FROM INDIA.

I HAVE now to consider what offensive-defensive military measure should be taken up by us to defeat Russian attempts to seize certain commanding positions in Afghanistan, namely, at Herat, Kabul, and Chitral.

If the diplomatic measures (which can all be put into effect, whether war is openly declared or not, and which should, I have said, be undertaken at once) have been carried out, the ground for the military operations which I now propose to sketch will have been a good deal prepared; but it may be as well to indicate again what these measures are. First, after some diplomatic trifling to gain time for us, Russia will have been informed that if she makes any move to cross the Afghan frontier in any direction, war will be declared, and the right of search will be put into operation against her, and a fleet of fast cruisers will have been arranged. Second, an offensive-defensive alliance will have been concluded with Germany, Austria, and Turkey, &c. Third, officers will have reached Herat, put that place in such a state of defence as to place it beyond the probability of falling to a *coup de main*. These officers will have gained over the Char Aimak and Hazaras, who will be ranged on our side. Fourth, officers sent to Persia will be in a position to give us the earliest information of Russian offensive movements, and they will have arranged to buy up supplies and transport, and denude Khorasan of these necessaries as far as possible. These officers will also have done all that is possible to deter the Chiefs of Khorasan from aiding the Russians. Fifth, our emissaries in the Khanates and among the Turkomans will, it is to be hoped, have so far succeeded in stirring up the people as to make it very unsafe for the Russians to withdraw any forces from these parts towards Afghanistan. Sixth, an alliance will have been concluded between England and China, and the latter power will be ready to threaten the Russian possessions on the Amur and towards Kulja. Seventh, our emissaries will, it is hoped, have gained the alliance of the Ghilzais. Eighth, arrangements for the assignment to us of the province of Herat and of the districts of Vakhan Chitral, and Yasin will be in hand.

Before going further, however, it may be as well if I anticipate here any remarks tending to the adoption of a purely passive defence of India with the means we have got.

At present our whole disposable force consists of—

13 batteries field artillery.	$8\frac{4}{6}$ regiments Native cavalry.
9 batteries mountain artillery.	$5\frac{6}{8}$ regiments British infantry.
3 batteries heavy mountain artillery.	41 regiments Native infantry.
1 regiment British cavalry.	21 companies sappers.

That is to say, 78 field guns, 54 mountain guns, and 27 heavy guns, about 400 British cavalry, about 4,300 Native cavalry, 4,800 British infantry, and about 30,000 Native infantry—total 40,000 men and 159 guns.

With such a force we might advance at once and seize Kandahar. One division, consisting of 3 brigades of infantry, each of 1 British infantry, 3 Native infantry, 3 batteries of heavy artillery, and 3 batteries of field artillery, with 6 companies sappers, would be sufficient for the defence of the place. This would leave us with enough to form a field division, consisting of 1 brigade of cavalry, of 1 British cavalry regiment, 3 Native cavalry, 1 field battery, and 3 brigades of infantry, consisting each of 1 British infantry, 3 Native infantry, and 1 mountain and 1 field artillery, and 1 company sappers; and we should then only have over 6 batteries field artillery, 6 batteries mountain artillery, 6 regiments Native cavalry, 23 regiments Native infantry, 12 companies sappers. Of these, not less than 2 regiments Native cavalry, 6 regiments Native infantry, 1 field battery, and 2 mountain batteries would be required for communications.

By utilizing volunteers and British adult males in India, we might free enough British troops to make up the balance of the troops still at our disposal into two more divisions; but I hold it would be very risky to reduce the garrison of British troops in India under such circumstances.

These two divisions would each be composed as follows:—

1 brigade of cavalry of 1 British and 3 Native cavalry regiments.
3 brigades of infantry of 1 British and 3 Native infantry regiments.
6 batteries of artillery.
3 companies sappers—numbering about 12,000 men.

It is very difficult to say what should be done with these. At present I am inclined to think that if the Russians get into Herat they will rest quiet for some years; but when they do advance, it will be in very great strength on the Kandahar and Kabul lines, and in lesser strength on the Chitral line. To meet them, if we go on the principle of cutting our coats according to the cloth actually in store, we shall have four divisions of about 12,000 men each. One of these will be required for the defence of Kandahar, and the other three, if well handled, would, no doubt, suffice to keep in check on the Kandahar line any number of Russians up to 50,000. But, in the first place, the Russians, when they advance against Kandahar, will probably have not less than 80,000 men, and I do not think I can be accused of taking too gloomy a view of the circumstances if I say that it will be very doubtful if 48,000 men with no reserves can make head against 80,000 with any number of reserves, besides the assistance of hordes of irregulars.

And even if our 48,000 men could make head against the 80,000 Russians advancing on this line, we should *not have one single man* to meet the 30,000 men I suppose they would, as I am pretty sure they could, send by the Kabul route, and the 10,000 by the Chitral route. Under such circumstances, the Russians would advance unopposed to Kabul and on to Peshawur, where they would be joined by the Chitral column through Dir. We should have to try to meet them somehow. But how? We should have no men. Our army at Kandahar, already heavily over-weighted, could not spare a man, and from India no aid could come, because to produce the Kandahar army we should have had to reduce our Indian garrisons to a dangerous extent.

It will be seen from the above I am no advocate for such measures. I feel sure that, as they will be begun in fear and trembling, they will but end in defeat and disaster. Under such circumstances, I see no reason why the Russians should not drive us over the Indus in one campaign. I hope no Englishman will be able to contemplate such an event with equanimity. The policy of cutting your coat according to your cloth is a very good one. We have, it is true, at present only about enough cloth to turn out 40,000 men; but is that any proof there is no more cloth in existence?

To drop metaphor. Because we, out of a pure peace establishment, can only spare 40,000 men, is that any reason why we should not get more men? Will any one care to tell me that we, who, before the mutiny, could maintain 230,000 Native troops, who, during it, had a force of 108,000 British troops in India, cannot now put our hands on more than 40,000? To say such a thing is to insult the majesty of the English nation, and to laugh to scorn the whole military intelligence of soldiers in India and England.

Therefore, before going farther with this part of my paper, I must assume that we have a disposable field army of 120,000 men, with all arrangements as regards reserves, transport, supplies, care of communications, &c., ready to enable it to take the field at a day's notice. For, of course, if the number is not forthcoming, we shall lose the power of the initiative, and be reduced to conform to Russian movements, making all the resistance we can.

It is not possible to consider the operations which it may be necessary for us to undertake under one heading only. War is made up of "ifs and ands," and the whole difficulty of it lies in the fact that we generally know very little of our enemy's plans. If I knew exactly what the Russians would try to do, and when they would try to do it, my task would, indeed, be beautifully simple; but this is not the case, and, therefore, in the following remarks I must perforce study the probabilities.

I have said I do not think any one supposes that the Russians are going to start straight from the Caspian and invade India to-morrow or the day after; but that they will endeavour to gain certain vantage points which will so much facilitate their doing so that they will really try to invade India hereafter.

Now the points from which India can be seriously threatened are Herat and Kabul. They can make demonstrations in the Chitral direction, but nothing very serious can, I take it, come on us from this side.

And, as what we ought to do depends entirely on the position of affairs at the commencement of the campaign, it becomes necessary that the question of what offensive-defensive measures can be undertaken by an army from India should be examined under the following heads:—

1st.—Provided Russia remains in her present positions till we are ready to undertake operations to cover Afghanistan.

2nd.—Supposing she takes up positions at Herat, at or near Kabul, and at or near Chitral, before we are ready.

3rd.—If, having gained these positions, she advances towards India.

4th.—Admitting that we have been so supine as to take no adequate steps to meet her, and we are driven out of the Kandahar-Kabul line, and have to fight on a line from Jellalabad to Quetta.

5th.—Allowing that we have been defeated on this line and driven back to our present frontier.

As things stand at present, I have shown that we have many grounds for fearing that we are already too late, and that Russia is now within striking distance of the vantage points which she will seize before making any serious attack on India. It is very lamentable to have to confess that our Government is entirely ignorant on such a vital point; and, though perhaps we may hope for a little more intelligence and activity in our intelligence arrangements in future, it is also evident that the Russians will make the greatest endeavours to keep their future movements secret, and that they will maintain the advantages of position which I hold they now possess.

In the first case, *viz.*, Provided Russia remains in her present position till we are ready? Now the first point that strikes one here is, Russia is already so near Herat that she can get there before us, and if we make an attempt now to get there she might forestall us, and we should thus lose for ever this important point and bring on a war before we were in the least prepared for it.

This is a very serious state of affairs, and I think my readers will now agree as to the importance of our endeavouring by every means in our power to induce her to stay her hand and withdraw her forces from the dangerous position they are now in. Perhaps this will be impossible, but it is well worth attempting; and meanwhile not a minute is to be lost in endeavouring to improve our position.

It is very difficult, I allow, to do this without attracting notice. The movement of every company in India is at once reported to the English papers, and they immediately commence to speculate on its destination. But I have great faith in the patriotism of Indian Editors, and I believe that if a very confidential '*communique*' was addressed to them, they would be careful to exclude any mention of the true reason of the movement of troops towards the frontier. With regard to the Native Press, the contrary is unfortunately the case; and as the liberty of allowing every man to say what he pleases (however seditious and distinctly damaging to the Government it may be) is, I believe, considered the inalienable right of every British subject, it is difficult to see how news can be stopped from getting about. Still, the fact is it must be stopped, and I think the only way to do this is to hoodwink the whole Native Press, and to stop all telegrams on the subject of any movements of troops to the north-west from leaving India.

I have said that I think the only way to make Herat secure is to occupy it ourselves, and for this purpose I would tell off a division as detailed in Chapter IV of this paper. But, before any orders are given to it to move, we must have a plan ready for hoodwinking the Press, and this I propose should be done as follows:—Let it be reported by Sir R. Sandeman* that the Zhob-wals are endeavouring to form a combination against us to drive us out of the Thal and Bori Valleys, and that he thinks reinforcements should be sent. Let this report be repeated, and at last let it come out that Government proposes to strengthen the Thal frontier by sending a brigade (the 1st Brigade, 1st Division) up as a reinforcement. Then let it be reported that Sir R. Sandeman fears a greater combination, and that a division will be required to undertake operations against the Zhob-wals to protect the flanks of the force advancing into Zhob and to hold the frontier of Peshin. This will provide a reason for the despatch of a division, and enable one to be sent up as far as Peshin without suspicion; and once there, if specially stringent orders are issued as to the transmittance of information of its movements by telegraph, and, as far as possible, by letter, I do not see why the division should not be well on its way beyond the Khojak towards Kandahar before the Indian Press heard anything about it; and then if the Telegraph Department had orders not to let any telegram alluding to this division leave India, except special and secret telegrams from the Viceroy, it would be fully three weeks before any news got to the ears of the public in England; and if the Government at home took the Press in

* This was written before the late scare on the Zhob frontier. The ease with which the papers swallowed all that was told them shows, I think, that my instinct has here not failed me.

England into its confidence in the same way, I see every reason to hope that our division would have arrived within the distance of a few forced marches of Herat before the Russian Government knew anything of the real object of the move at all.

Supposing, for instance, the division received its new orders on such and such a day, which I will call the first; in seven days after, on the 7th, it would be at Kandahar, and in 30 days after that at Herat. Supposing some one with the force wrote (he could not telegraph) on the first day that the Division had gone on to Kandahar, it might reach the nearest paper, the *Civil and Military*, on the fifth day, but the Editor of that paper, having been warned, would say nothing about it. However, it would certainly leak out somehow, and though no Editor might allude to it, it would be a strong rumour by the seventh day. Government would now declare that the division had been sent to Kandahar to prepare a strong position there for a force of 10,000 men. Then some one with benevolent or malevolent intentions would try to telegraph this to England or Russia. His telegram would be received, but not sent. But as he would in all probability write at the same time, a mistake might delay the mail trains sufficient to cause the steamer to go without them, and it would take from 18 to 25 days before any such letter got to England, *i.e.*, it would be from 25 to 31 days before the news got abroad that a force had gone to Herat. Then, of course, it would be telegraphed to Russia; but on the 31st day I calculate the division would be beyond the Farah Rud and within 100 miles, or four forced marches, of Herat! I hardly think the Russians would be quite ready enough to forestall us under these circumstances. I think they would be inclined to acquiesce in the *fait accompli*, especially if at the same time they received from our Foreign Secretary a firm and dignified explanation of the fact, accompanied by a solemn warning that any attempt to disturb our division would immediately be followed by war, and a solemn guarantee that no operations beyond the Afghan frontier would be attempted by us.

This, it must be acknowledged, is a deep and very bold game to play; but then we have an exceedingly crafty and most vigorous and dangerous enemy to deal with. But the question is, is it foolhardy? Would we be daring too much? Some may say, in the first place, you are presuming too much on your power to keep the movements of the Division secret. You could not do so for so long, and the result would be that you would find a Russian force in Herat to meet you, or at all events the gates shut in your face in Russian interests; and as the Russians would come up within ten days after your arrival before Herat, you would be in this predicament, that with tired troops you would have to meet a superior force, with several hundred miles between you and your supports.

This, I take it, is about the worst that can be made of the move, and I will therefore examine these objections *seriatim*. With regard to not being able to keep the secret for so long, we have certainly found that news of Russian movements do not fly with such celerity; and if it has been possible for the Russians to *reach* Merv before we heard of their intention to go there, I really do not see why, with good management, it should not be possible for us to reach more than half way to Herat before they heard of it. I feel pretty convinced that, as regards India, intelligence could be stopped from getting out of India, and the only other way that intelligence could reach the Russian General would be by the route our force was itself travelling. But, as not even our General would know he was going beyond Kandahar till he got there, our division would be on its march from Kandahar before any one in the force or out of it could know that it was going to Herat. Then, no doubt, a special messenger could be sent, and, by hard riding, he could reach Mashad, the nearest telegraph station, and 552 miles distant, in five days, and by the sixth the news could be telegraphed to Ashkabad. This, it must be confessed, would be awkward, as our division would then not be much beyond the Helmund, and still nearly 300 miles from Herat. But Ashkabad* is 370 miles from Herat, and even supposing the Russians were ready to start the next morning, they could not reach Herat till the 26th day after we leave Kandahar, and by that time we should be at Herat or very near it.

Still I allow this is running it rather close. Therefore, all I have got to say is, that *no messenger must reach Mashad or Herat with news of our advance.* A man on such an errand would certainly ride by the shortest road, and would in all probability go alone, or at all events with a very small escort indeed. We must, therefore, arrange beforehand to *have him intercepted* at several different points of the road by which he must go. Nothing must be left to chance. Arrangements for stopping any messengers must be made before we moved from Kandahar.

But, even allowing that messengers did manage to out-manœuvre us and slip past, the question then is, would the Russian General not have to wait for orders from St. Petersburg before he precipitated his troops on a course that would certainly lead to war with England. Because, remember, I am supposing that a step so totally unlike the usual action of England has taken the General and the Russian Government completely by surprise, and therefore would not the Russian Government first ask for explanations? These would (not too hastily) be given in the sense I have noted on page 187, *viz.*, "Her Majesty's "Government is determined to hold Herat, and to hold it even at the risk of "war with Russia. If this decision is opposed by the Imperial Government, "Her Majesty's Government, once for all, warns them that war, if forced on them, "shall be carried out to the bitter end. At the same time Her Majesty's Gov- "ernment has absolutely no feelings or intentions hostile to the Russian Gov- "ernment, and solemnly pledges itself to confine the operations which it may "find necessary for the safety of the Afghan border to within that frontier."

Under these circumstances, I hold the Imperial Government would hesitate; and even if it considered it advisable to take the extreme measure of declaring war, Russia would surely realize that a war with England was a much more serious measure than a campaign against the Tekkes, and would require more time for preparation. Every minute of this time would be gold to us, for we could then have time to put the defences of Herat in order and prepare ourselves; and if we had only one month to do this, I very much doubt any force Russia could send turning us out.

I acknowledge that I fear this audacity will find favour with few. That may be; but the question is, are we warranted in being so bold. I think we are. I think that Russia must be kept out of Herat at all hazards, and I see no other way of doing this but by taking the initiative and getting there before her. And, after all, what are these great risks that render us so timid? We shall have to send 12,000 men 576 miles from their base through Afghanistan to Herat. Is it the distance or the Afghans that make the picture so appalling? If so, the spirit of Clive, of Wellington, of Lake, of Nott, and of Pollock, must be strangely gone from us. 576 miles is less than the distance from Calcutta to Cawnpore; and as for the Afghans, will they be different in

* I am of course supposing the Russians have no large force nearer than Ashkabad.

any way to the men whom Nott and Pollock, Stewart and Roberts overcame?* The very idea of any man putting forward such coward counsels makes me redden with shame. I say there are a dozen officers in India who would lead that division to Herat despite distance, Afghans, Russians, or anything else; and I add that, if nine-tenths of them left their bones to whiten on the desert plains of Afghanistan and only one-tenth arrived, it would be well worth the sacrifice. I am sure not a soldier would murmur at his fate if he felt that in giving his life he was saving his country from a terrible and disastrous future. The spirit of our men would, I am sure, not be less than that grand soldier, Skobeleff, expected of his Russian soldiers in considering an advance against India;† and therefore I will paraphrase his noble words: "From the "troops that would be fortunate enough to participate in such an expedition, "more should be exacted than self-sacrifice, even in the highest sense of the term "among military men. The Helmund once crossed, I believe the conviction would be kindled on the breast of each combatant that he had gone to "Herat to conquer or die. This his Queen demands of him, and there would "be no reproaches made if our banners remained in the hands of the foe after "every English soldier had fallen."

It is difficult to advise as to what should be the exact date of the despatch of this division, as so much depends on what Russia will do, and what measure of preparedness in the sense of my remarks in Chapter IV we shall accomplish in the next few months.

I think every nerve should be strained to induce Russia to withdraw as many troops as possible from trans-Caspia and Turkistan, so that in September, when our Mission should start for the Afghan frontier, *her* state of preparedness shall have been reduced to the lowest ebb. As soon as the Mission gets to Herat, an able officer, with suitable staff, should be detached to put its defences into thorough repair and to *arrange for some sort of trustworthy garrison to hold it in our interests for a time.*

I calculate the Mission should get to Herat near by the 1st November, and therefore I think that the division should start about the 1st October, its real purpose, as I have said above, being cloaked to the latest possible hour.

In the days between this and 1st November, we should strain every nerve to get at least four divisions, such as I have detailed, ready in every way. Low as our military establishments have been allowed to fall, I think we could do this; and if we went on with our preparations, we might still further checkmate the Russians. But if we got to Herat before them, I hold that it is almost

* The following shows the forces with which our Generals have in former times performed marches quite as dangerous as that with which I propose:—

Pollock, to Kabul, 1843—7 battalions, 9 squadrons, 2 or 3 companies of sappers, 15 guns, with a Sikh contingent of 500 horse and foot, and 5 guns.

The force that moved on Kabul from Jalalabad amounted to—
8,000 men and 17 guns.

Nott, to Kabul, 1842—7 battalions, 6 squadrons, 22 guns, say—
6,000 combatants.

Stewart, to Kabul, 1880—7 battalions, 9 squadrons, 2 companies sappers, 22 guns—
7,200 combatants, with 7,230 followers.

Roberts, to Kandahar, 1880—12 battalions, 12 squadrons, 18 mountain guns—
10,000 combatants, with 8,000 followers.

† *Vide* Skobeleff's scheme for the invasion of India.

certain Russia will not declare war. She is not ready for war under such circumstances, though, if we do not take immediate steps to get hold of Herat, she may consider herself ready enough to run the risk of war for the sake of Herat. There is no doubt that the belief is very strong amongst the Russians that even their taking Herat, if they do it cleverly, will not drive us to declare war. I do not know whether they are right in this belief or not; but it is evident that, if they think that the chances are in favor of our putting up with even this loss, there is very great danger in their risking it. *The only way, therefore, is to forestall them.* I would prepare to do so at once. Happily the scare about the Zhob-wals has given a pretext for massing troops in the autumn about Peshin; and I am convinced that, if the matter is cleverly managed, no one, not even our own people, need know anything of our real intentions until the division was well over the Khojak.

Supposing, then, that a first division, constituted, as I have said, moves from India on the 15th September or so, by the 1st October it would be on the Khojak frontier, by the 8th October at Kandahar, and by the 8th November at Herat. As soon as it was no longer possible to cloak our real intentions, a second division would move up at once to Kandahar, a third would move to Quetta, and a fourth would be held in readiness to move in support.

Under this arrangement the second division should leave India about the 1st November, and would arrive at Kandahar about the 15th November, the 3rd division would arrive at Quetta on the 8th November, having left India on the 1st.

Thus, by the time the first division reached Herat, the position of each would be—

One division at Herat.	A third division at Khojak and Quetta.
A second division at Kandahar.	A fourth division ready in India.

The first division would either get to Herat before the Russians, or they would not. If they did, the Russians would either acquiesce, or they would declare war. If they acquiesced, the possession of Herat would be a *fait accompli;* its defences would be immediately so strengthened that it could hold out for a very long time, even if the Russians should then care to attack it. Any way, we should have won that trick.

I hold that the Russians would openly acquiesce, though they would really seek to discover some other means to get a grip of us. If we were in Herat, the question whether it would be worth while then going there would assume an absolutely different aspect. It is one thing to *risk* a war with England with *the certainty of having Herat in their possession,* it is another thing to deliberately *declare war* with England with only a remote chance of their being able to get hold of that place. Therefore, I feel sure the Russians will not go to war with us if we forestall them; they will acquiesce and turn the direction of their schemes into another channel.

But if we do not *at once* take steps to get to Herat first, *we may now be only days off a war with Russia.* Because *we dare not acquiesce in a Russian occupation of Herat,** for I believe that no English Ministry would live for

* Mr. Grant Duff says in an article :—"As to one point there is no difference of opinion be- "tween any of the persons who have considered this question. We all agree about what it would "be necessary to do if Russia *really* threatened Herat. That would mean war with England all "over the world. We have no choice in the matter. In the first place our engagements to "Afghanistan are such that we could not tolerate anything of the kind. In the second place the "safety of Herat has been so often and so loudly proclaimed by successive British Governments as "a matter of paramount importance that we could not now recede from our position without "appearing to confess weakness, which is wholly out of the question."

24 hours after they had made any declaration to that effect. But if Russia did declare war on our going to Herat, we should then be in the best position for fighting her. We should have our army in a very strong position with supplies for a year; she would have to bring up her supplies and siege guns over an interminable line of communications, and would find absolutely nothing in the Herat Valley that she could lay hands on.

And having chosen to risk all the consequences of a war with us under such circumstances, I am quite sure that, looking to the much greater seriousness of her venture to what I have sketched in Chapter I, she could not put into the field a sufficient force to attack Herat held by Englishmen under three to four months after the declaration of war; that is, if war was declared early in November, it would probably be the middle of February before the siege of Herat could begin, even if we did nothing all the time.

But then we should indeed be roused, and I have no fear of our doing nothing; and I will now show what I think we should do. In the first place, we must remember what would be the peculiarity of such a campaign. It would be that neither we nor the Russians could keep very large forces in the field at the front, because a large force could not be fed.

I do not think that the Russians could, under the circumstances we should create for them, keep at the front more than 50,000 men; and I think that if we had 10,000 English and Indian soldiers and 10,000 Hazaras and Char Aimaks in Herat, it would take a good many months for the Russians to get in. Because, besides the stubborn resistance of the garrison themselves, we should have two other divisions outside Herat, constantly threatening and attacking their communications.

That is to say, I would propose that the second division, instead of moving directly up to Herat, should throw itself into the Hazarajat, and (raising all the Char Aimak and Turkomans they could) advance towards Panjdeh, which would also be garrisoned in our interests, and endeavour to completely sever the Russian communications with the Atak. Now may be seen the advantage of gaining the Hazarajat.

But it may be that the Russian main line of communication would be through Khorasan. I should very much doubt this, though I dare say this line would be used. In order, therefore, to threaten and attack this line, I would advance a third division from Kandahar to Lash; and basing it on that place and Birjand would advance through Anardara and Yezdun towards Khaf and Turbat Haidari.* Here may be seen the advantage of gaining the Ameer of Ghain to our side and of opening a line of communications from India with the Helmund and Seistan.

The fourth division would be at Kandahar, maintaining the communication with the aid of levies.

The importance of seizing Herat is so great that I propose to attempt it without any further delay. I know, in the present state of our preparation, it would be dangerous for us to bring on operations that might lead to a war with Russia prematurely. Still I think we must risk it. Though we are not ready now, we shall scarcely be really so for another year, and in that time I take it as certain that the Russians will be in Herat; and although the risk may be great, I do not see how it can be helped, as it is the only way of making Herat secure. Myself I am very much inclined to doubt if Russia would

* I am quite aware that these operations are risky; but boldness in the right direction is success in war. The difficulty would be in supplying our troops; but I know the country, and I believe it could be done: not easily, but by Indian Commissariat and Transport officers it could be done.

go to war on our going to Herat. She is as yet by no means bound to do so, and history shows us that whenever Russia has been boldly faced, it has, as long as her honor is not at stake, had the effect of making her pause and draw in her horns. If we succeeded, as I believe we may, in getting into Herat before Russia could prevent us, I believe the Russian Government would thoroughly realize the seriousness of the effort required to turn us out, and that they would, therefore, while protesting, not actually take such a step as declaring war with us. Of course Russia, if she withdrew, would only do so with the intention of striking us a heavier blow elsewhere hereafter; but this would take time, and having time, it would distinctly be our own fault if we were not then ready to meet any attack she might make.

The gain in the step I propose is the absolute safety of Herat and an immense accession to our prestige throughout Asia. The risk is a possible premature declaration of war by Russia, and the loss might be that we might not succeed in getting hold of Herat, and would have to retire. But even if we did fail, I do not think the effect in India would be so bad as if we tamely acquiesced in a Russian possession of Herat.

Supposing that our division did not succeed in getting to Herat before the Russians threw a light force into it, I would still see no cause for despair. Any force that the Russians could throw into Herat before us must necessarily be a small one; and if our division was strong enough, it should at once attack the Russian division. If it was not, every nerve should be strained to bring up a second and third division to its aid, and immediately on their arrival a decisive battle for Herat should be fought. In the meanwhile, before these divisions arrived, the cavalry of our first division would, in combination with the Hazaras and Char Aimak, make persistent and determined attacks on the Russian communications, endeavouring to destroy all supplies and watering places, so as to retard the arrival of Russian reinforcements as much as possible.

Of course, if matters came to such a pass, we should be committed to a war with Russia, and then would be the time to strain every nerve to form a coalition against Russia, so as to enable us to threaten her rear and her base of operations on the Caspian. The operations which should be undertaken in this case will be found fully considered in another part of this paper. In this part, which exclusively deals with the operations undertaken by us from India, I will confine myself to endeavouring to sketch out the probable fortunes of the divisions which we would have launched against Herat; but of course it is impossible to do more than indicate probabilities and possibilities in a vague manner.

If the army composed of our three divisions, and such auxiliaries as we might be able to raise from the Hazaras and Char Aimak, proved unable to dislodge the Russians from Herat, it would then depend on the circumstances of the moment what would be the best course for the General in command to adopt. If we were not threatened in other directions, and it was possible for us to still further reinforce our divisions in the front, we should do so, and again try the fortune of war in another battle. But if at the same time, as they held possession of Herat, the Russians threatened us in the direction of Kabul and Chitral, it would be absolutely necessary for us to meet these demonstrations in an adequate manner, as they might very easily, if the roads were open, be turned into very serious attacks. In such a case, I hold we should not be able to spare more men to reinforce the Herat divisions; and I should, therefore, direct them to fall back to Sabzawar and Obeh to pull themselves together again. As soon as possible after this had been accomplished, the Sabzawar division should advance towards Khaf, leaving a force at Sabzawar to hold it. It would advance by Yezdun and Charakhs on Khaf, and thence towards Mashad-i-Reza to cut the Russian communications through Khorasan.

The Obeh division in the same way would advance to Kala Nao, and thence into Badghis to cut the Russian communications with the Atak.

This is supposing that the Russians had adopted two lines of advance, one through Khorasan and the other by the Atak; but if they were relying on only one line, these divisions, while taking care to avoid battle with a superior force, would endeavour to concentrate in rear of Herat, without losing their own communications.

If the Russians were too strong for them, and they could neither regain Herat nor block the Russian communications, there would be nothing for it but to retreat. But even in retreating the General should always bear in mind that he should never go further back than was absolutely necessary, and he should retreat by lines that would enable him to paralyse any attempt of the Russians to advance further than Herat and to retake the offensive again immediately on the opportunity offering, and he should always try to keep on interior lines. That is to say, he should retreat by two lines to Khaf and Obeh, and if the Russians advanced from Herat, the Khaf division would march by Charakhs, Yezdun, and Anardara to Farah, while the Obeh division would move west down the valley and endeavour to seize the Shah Bed Pass on the direct road to Sabzawar.

It is not probable that the Russians would show much wish to follow our retreating divisions from Herat. They could not do so unless they had an overwhelming force. They could not have an overwhelming force unless the war had gone on for some months; and if they had it, they would have to reorganize their transport and supply departments before making any further advance. Meanwhile our divisions would be hovering round them, making their hold very insecure, to say the least.

If they advanced beyond Herat, they would have to fight at the Kotul-Shah Bed or thereabouts, at Sabzawar, at Jeja, and at Farah, and all the while the Obeh division, based on the Hazara country, would be constantly attacking or threatening their left, while the Khaf division would make their right insecure. But if they triumphed over all these obstacles, they could not advance beyond Farah, as our defeated divisions would then retire on Lash Jorwen (which by that time would have been made very strong) and Taiwara, and a fresh division would be advancing from India in their front. I therefore hold that Farah would be the furthest limit of Russian advance in the first campaign.

I must now turn to the other side of Afghanistan. In the first part of this paper I have shown how a Russian division could be thrown into Kabul. But I think the Russians will only attempt this under one or other of the following circumstances. First, if we permit them to occupy Herat before we do, a Russian division will certainly advance from the Oxus by the route I have given. Second, if we occupy Herat and the Russian Government make it a *casus belli*, this advance will also certainly take place. On the other hand, if the Russians acquiesce in our retaining Herat, any advance on this line which may take place will only be for the sake of trying our nerves.

The question, therefore, now before us is, if the Russians advance on Kabul what should we do? In the first place, let me remark that an advance on

Kabul by the Russians would be a long and difficult operation, and nothing but a scandalous inefficiency in our intelligence should enable them to get very far before we heard of it. But before we heard of it, we should have a fifth division encamped at the Gomal ready to advance to Karabagh, and a sixth should be ready mobilized to move in support.

If the Russians advanced, our fifth division would march with all possible speed up the Gomal route and make for Karabagh, at or near which place an entrenched camp should be constructed. From Karabagh it should enter the Hazara country, draw to it all the Hazaras possible, and, sending them on under English officers to contest the passes of the Hindu Kush, it would make for the Behsud district.* If the division arrived there before the Russians had got to Kabul, as it undoubtedly should be able to do, I think we should be able to cry 'check' to them; for there can be no doubt that 15,000 to 20,000 Russians could not dare to advance on Kabul with 12,000 British troops and an unknown number of Hazaras directly on their communications. And if thus checked, they could as certainly not stay where they were; they must either advance in the hope of disastrously beating our division, or they must be forced back by the impossibility of supporting a force in such a country. But the *rôle* of our General would be to avoid being beaten either disastrously or otherwise. If not strong enough to be sure of victory, he would not let himself be enticed into a fight, but would retreat, leaving his Hazara allies to harass the Russian flanks. It is certain the Russians could not afford to follow our troops for many days, for every step they went after us would take them away from their objective; and so, as in the case of Herat, they would require very large reinforcements before they could hold us in check and take Kabul also.

If the Russians advanced on Chitral and the Kashmir frontier, as I have supposed in Chapter I of this paper, I think the way to meet them would be to place a seventh division with as little delay as possible on the Gilgit frontier, and there, raising the tribes of Siahposh, make it impossible for such a small force as they could bring to advance beyond Chitral, even if they got so far. The *rôle* of the General Commanding this division should be to entice the Russians by every means in his power to cross Hindu Kush, and even letting them get possession of Chitral. This might be difficult to accomplish; but if care was taken to make the Russians believe we had only a weak brigade in Gilgit, and did not mean to do more than block that road, and if the Siahposh, while really bound to us, could be induced to apparently help them, perhaps a Russian General with wind in his head might try it.

Then our division would go by the Ishkaman Valley and the Darkot and Baroghil Passes into Vakhan, and cut the Russian communications completely. The Siahposh would then be instructed to rise and cut off all supplies; and when the Russians began to retreat, as they most certainly would, they would be attacked in front and rear and all sides, and I should be much surprised if many of them saw the Oxus again.

Of course, in the event of the Russians being defeated in the Herat Valley or in the Hindu Kush, our General would be instructed to press their retreat as much as possible and to raise all the tribes that could possibly be induced to turn against them. A crushing defeat, followed by a killing pursuit, and perhaps a surrender of the remnant of the Russian army, would be worth a great deal to us; and I really do not see, in such a campaign, why we should not have as good a chance as they.

---

* *Vide* Route, Appendix.

Before concluding this part of my subject, I wish to call attention once more to the main points in my suggestions. First, I propose, by a timely exhibition of boldness and energy, to seize Herat with as little delay as possible by a *coup de main*. This, if it succeeded, would be invaluable to us, even if it precipitated a war with Russia. But the chances are it will not do this. Second, even if we did not get to Herat before the Russians, as we *must* fight on this question, we should, by taking the above step, have four divisions pretty near it, and we might be able to turn them out before their reinforcements arrived. If we did turn them out, I am sure they could not regain it except by a prodigious effort, which would require a great deal of time to prepare for, and of course all delay tells equally in our favor.

If Russia declares war and advances on the Chitral and Kabul lines, I think we should be able to destroy both these forces.

If Russia does not declare war on the Herat question, we shall have won the first trick and given her a very decided check. This will strengthen our hands in every way, both in giving us time to prepare further efforts and in raising our prestige throughout Asia, and especially in India.

Now to turn to the second head of this survey. Supposing that Russia has been allowed to gain a possession of Herat and to take up positions at or near Kabul and at or near Chitral.

In this I take it for granted that the Russian frontier will then include the whole of the Herat Province up to the Khush Rud; the whole of the Hazarajat,* that is to say, the whole country between the Herat-Sabzawar road and the Gulkoh range, which divides the drainage of the Argandab from that of the Turnak. From west of Ghazni they would probably take their frontier up the main ridge to the Koh-i-Baba, and thence continue it along the Hindu Kush to the Dorah Pass. Then it would include the whole of Chitral and Vakhan right up to the Kashgar frontier. I do not say that the Russians would at once proclaim this; but they would certainly gradually extend to these limits in the manner of which we have had such bitter experience in north and east Persia. If they seize the important point of Herat, the rest will follow. Now I ask any man to take his map, draw this line on it, and then sit down and ponder deeply over it, and ask himself what it will mean.

It will mean a firm base within striking distance of Kandahar, Kabul, and Peshawar. When they get this frontier, the Russians can afford to let the Russo-Indian question slumber; *for they will have gained the outworks of India*. It may take them five years, or ten, or twenty, to make a railway from the Caspian to Farah; to make a railway from Yaman Airakti to Kungrad; to make the Oxus practicable for steamers and barges to Kilif; to make a cart-road from Kilif to the Behsud Valley through Balkh; to make a cart-road from Ush to Faizabad; to store Herat, Behsud, and Faizabad with supplies and munitions of war; to thoroughly subdue and incorporate the Turkomans, the Uzbaks, the Hazara, the Char Aimak, and Siahposh; to so tamper with the Duranis, the Ghilzais, and the wild tribes of the Peshawar frontier that they will be straining like greyhounds in the leash to be let free for the "blood and rapine" Skobeleff talks of; but make and do all these things they as certainly will as I am writing these words. What will be the position then when all these things have come to pass?

On the one hand, the Russians, with overwhelming power, will be standing ready within striking distance of Kandahar, Kabul, and Peshawar; on the other,

* Although, of course, we should not give up one foot more than is absolutely necessary.

we shall be waiting expectant. From the day that we allowed the Russians to get into Harat, the knell of British rule in India will have struck, or at least it will seem so to the countless millions of our dusky subjects, and if a few brave hearts refuse to despair even then, their look-out will be black indeed. From the day that Herat passes beyond our power, such a blow will have been struck at our prestige, such a wedge will have been driven into the heart of India, that the whole country will become "one mass of seething disaffection," every ambitious man, every discontented man, every scoundrel in India, be he Hindu or Musalman, Mahratta or Sikh, will be welded into one expectant and inimical crowd, strai ning their .eyes to catch the first gleam of Russian steel. Our British army will, whatever economists may say, have had to be permanently increased to double, perhaps even treble, its present number; our native army will also have had to be increased to a thoroughly dangerous extent; our frontier will perforce have attained that happy millennium of the men who have so long blinded England's eyes, and will run along its whole length with that of a civilized power—Russia. Kandahar must be ours, Kabul too, and Ghazni, for at least then the neutral zone theory must have collapsed. We shall have (in the years intervening between the fatal day when the gods so maddened us as to let Herat pass from our hands and the fateful hour when Russia is ready to strike once more) had innumerable petty wars, with the Kabulis, the Kohistanis, the Ghilzais, the Afridis, and other Yaghistanis; and these wars will have fused them into a "united Afghanistan" but united only in their undying hatred of us. India meanwhile will have been seething; petty, if not serious outbreaks, induced by Russian intrigue, will have occurred and have had to be suppressed. Trade cannot flourish under such circumstances, and, therefore, with all this will come reduced finances, lessened means of increasing them, and enormously increased expenditure. This will be caused by the necessity for making Kabul, Kandahar, Ghazni, Jellalabad, and other places in Afghanistan into strong fortified positions, by having to maintain large forces so far from their bases in a state of war, by having to erect first class fortresses at Peshawar, Thal, Banu, Gomal, on the Kojak, at Multan, Ferozepore, and Lahore. And then we shall have to meet the final advance with all the "ikbal gone from us." Yet, bad as this may be, we should not even then despair.

Under such circumstances what should we do? I must first premise my remarks by saying what I think we should have been doing in the interval that is left to us. We should have first class fortresses at Kandahar, at Kabul, and at some place near Karabagh or Mushaki, held by strong garrisons. We should have to increase the garrisons of every place in India, so as to maintain a still firmer grip over it. We should have a field army of at least 150,000 men, and the proportion of British troops would have to be increased to one half. The armies of all Native States should be swept away. If a coalition with Germany, Austria, Turkey, &c., is advisable now, it will be ten times more so then. If efforts to detach Persia and stir up the Turkomans and the Khanates are expedient now, they will be far more applicable then. In addition to the railways I have noted as necessary now, lines will have to be constructed placing all our bases of military strength in direct communication with the north-west frontier. All the frontier stations will have to be connected with each other and with their reserves at Pindi, Lahore, and Multan; the roads from Kabul to Kandahar, Kabul to Peshawar, Gomal to Karabagh, Dera Ghazi to Kandahar, Gomal to Kandahar, will all have to be made practicable for carts.

The utmost activity should prevail everywhere in our military preparations and in our diplomatic measures. The utmost firmness and decision should permeate our Councils; for then the cloud which ten years ago was no bigger than a man's hand will have grown blacker and larger, and it is certain that Englishmen will have to enter into a struggle likened to which any which have gone before, or even that they may yet face, will be but as child's play. But of course we should not despair; no man is beaten till he throws up the sponge, and we would not do that. Englishmen may be foolish in many ways in not acting with foresight in military matters, but they are hard to beat if once roused.

I do not suppose that the Russians would really make any attempt to invade India until all their communications to the rear were in perfect order; at least they would be very foolish if they did so. It would only be by having railway communication from the Caspian to Farah that they could hope to collect sufficient supplies and munitions of war to enable them to make any advance, and it would be necessary for them to keep the minimum number of troops in their front till the last moment.

In the first part of this paper I have supposed that the Russians would attack Herat with about 46,000 men, Kabul with 13,000, and Chitral with 7,000 men in the front line. But of course if they contemplated an invasion of India, they would not attempt it with such forces. These would be largely increased, and as they have a practically unlimited supply of men, and as their communications would have been perfected, it is clear that they could produce any number that might be required.

Now what number would be required? The work which the Russian Commander-in-Chief will have before him will be to drive us out of Kandahar, and to seriously threaten us from the direction of Kabul and Badakhshan, so as, if possible, to prevent our concentrating at Kandahar a sufficiently large force to drive them back.

Kandahar will have been very strongly fortified and held by a garrison of 10,000 British and Native troops, and we may be able to concentrate an army of 50,000 men to prevent its being besieged. To meet a possible number of 60,000 British troops, I do not think the Russians will venture to advance from the Herat-Farah line with less than 80,000 men; and, moreover, I think this is about the limit she could reasonably expect to feed and maintain in the field on one line. Her advance posts will be on the Farah Rud. To this point a railway will have been laid, by which all supplies, transport, and munitions of war will have arrived; and I calculate that it will have taken them at least six months to make the necessary preparations. I do not go into the calculation of this here* but ask that this time may be accepted as at all events approximately correct.

From Farah to Kandahar the road lies for the most part over a very barren country, though there are no difficulties as far as the road is concerned; and the great difficulty of the Russians in such an advance would be to supply their army. This they would arrange for from their own province of Herat, from Seistan and Birjand, and from the Duranis of Darawut, Zamindawar, Terin, Nish, and Khakrez, and the Hazaras on their left flank; and it is evident that, unless their arrangements were very carefully thought out and executed, there would be very great risk of failure. Still, though I admit the Russians would find it very difficult to feed such an army, I do not think we have sufficient reason for assuming that adequate arrangements cannot be made by them.

---

* Though it would be easy to do so.

At the commencement of the campaign, before the actual declaration of war, I suppose that the Russian forces, divided into three *corps d'armée*, are assembled at Sabzawar, Farah, and Lash Jorwen, and that they will advance thence in three parallel columns.

The first corps would advance from Sabzawar by Chah-i-jahan, Girani, and Washir on Haidarabad, 225 miles in 14 stages. The second corps from Farah by Khormalik, Bakwa, Hasan Gilan, Shorab to Girishk, 161 miles in 14 stages; and the third from Lash Jorwen by Khash to Kala Bist, about 214 miles in 16 stages. These columns would be in communication laterally, and would move as follows:—

Day.	1st Corps.	2nd Corps.	3rd Corps.
1st	Aisabad.	Farah.	Lash Jorwen.
2nd	Camp.	Ditto.	Ditto.
3rd	Chah-i-jahan.	Ditto.	Camp.
4th	Camp.	Ditto.	Ditto.
5th	Ab-i-Kurmeh.	Ditto.	Minar-i-Khoja Siah.
6th	Right bank, Farah Rud.	Haozi Khalsa.	Chaodri.
7th	Shaiwan.	Khormalik.	Chakansur.
8th	Shahrak.	Karez.	Pir Kaisri.
9th	Lajward Karez.	Chiagaz.	Ab Khawas.
10th	Tut-i-Rasarman.	Kala Ibrahim.	Guzar-i-Khash.
11th	Nalakh.	Ditto.	Ab Khor, Rustam.
12th	Ibrahim Jui.	Ibrahim Jui.	Khash.
13th	Khash Rud.	Ditto.	Wisht.
14th	Washir.	Dilaram.	Talkhab.
15th	Khushk-i-Sufed.	Hasan Gilan.	Kurki Tagrish.
16th	Doshakh.	Dalhak.	Camp.
17th	Zirak.	Shorab.	Ditto.
18th	Sadat Kala.	Haoz.	Duvalah.
19th	Kareza.	Ditto.	Camp.
20th	Haidarabad.	Girishk.	Kala Bist.

From these three several points, I must leave the Russian divisions, as they would then be in collision with our own troops, and the future of the campaign would pass from the strategical to tactical, and it can therefore have no place here.

Now, in such a case, what we should have to face would be simply this—80,000 Russians on the Helmund. We could not delay them long there, for every position that can be taken up on the Helmund is liable to be outflanked and turned, and indeed it is doubtful whether there is any position between the Helmund and Argandab that is not liable to this disadvantage. I hold, therefore, that unless we could do something to strike at the Russian communications, we would simply have to take up the best position we could in the immediate vicinity of Kandahar and fight it out there.

What then would be possible in this way? First, I hold we could threaten their right flank, and, secondly, we could threaten their left; and if we did so, their centre advance would be paralysed.

In order to threaten their right, we must have a railway direct from Nushki or Shorawak to the Helmund, and an entrenched camp at about Landi or above it.* Then 15,000 men despatched to this point could operate on the Russian right flank. From Landi to Kala Bist the road goes along the

* To secure for ourselves the means of striking at the flank of a Russian advance from Herat on Kandahar is of the most vital importance, and this seems to me the best way of doing so.

Helmund with plenty of water, forage, and fuel. The distance is 186 miles. If this was done, the Russians would have to leave 20,000 men at Kala Bist, even if they dared to advance so far. I do not think they would, as a British force at Landi would be as near Chakansur as they would be at Kala Bist.

In order to threaten their left, it would be necessary to detach a force of 20,000 men from Karabagh to Kilat-i-Ghilzai. From this it would advance to the Argandab Valley, and thence down it to a position which, while it would very seriously threaten the Russian left, would at the same time not lose command of a shorter line of retreat to Kilat-i-Ghilzai. Not less than 25,000 Russians would be required to render their left safe, and they would then be left with only 35,000 men to advance on Kandahar, which would be held by 10,000 British troops, with a field army of 15,000 to 20,000 in support. Under such circumstances, I hold the Russians would not dare to advance; but if they did, I think that the result of a battle in which 30,000 British troops would be in a prepared position against 35,000 Russians should not be doubtful. And if we succeeded, the forces in the Argandab Valley and on the Helmund being in communication with Kandahar by telegraph could concentrate to cut off their retreat. Of course, the Russian right of 20,000 men and their left of 25,000 men would concentrate also to succour their centre; but as the Russians would necessarily be demoralized by their defeat, we with 20,000 men from the Argandab Valley and 20,000 from Kandahar should be able to surround them before succour arrived.

Then if our forces concentrated on Girishk, we should be able to advance from that place with 50,000 men on Farah, and *we should be on interior lines;* therefore the Russian retreat would necessarily be extremely hurried. Their left might succeed in escaping, but if we used the fickle Afghan and Hazara properly, it is very probable it might become something very near a *sauve qui peut.* As to their right, we ought to be able to cut them off from Farah altogether, and detaching 25,000 men from our army, should be able to drive them into Seistan and bring them to a decisive battle, in which defeat to them would simply mean surrender or death, and to us would only mean retiring on interior lines to our old positions.

Of course, it may be said that the Russians would send more than 80,000 men; but even supposing they could do so and could feed them, the only reply possible is, then we must send a number equal to enabling us to maintain the strategical advantages of our position.

But it would not in all probability be enough to stop one, the Kandahar, door to India. We must remember there is another by Kabul, and it is almost certain that at the same time that they advanced by Kandahar they would also advance by Kabul.

Before going further in the consideration of what we should do to stop them on this line, I must lay great stress on the necessity for our having done all possible to retain a hold upon the Hazaras and Ghilzais. If the Russians get to Herat, it may be taken for granted that the Char Aimak will go over to them in a body; but it may still be possible for us to maintain our hold over the Hazaras. It is of the utmost importance we should do so; and, therefore, in what I have to say now I will accept that this has been done.

If the Russians advanced on Kabul, they would probably form their advanced base at Mazar-i-Sharif. Their troops would gather at this place principally from Russia by way of the Yaman Airakti Bay, Kungrad, and the Oxus, and their advance posts would be pushed probably as far forward as Bajgah and Walishan, on the Bamian and Chehlburj roads respectively, and up to these points good cart-roads would have been made.

Here they would collect about, say, 30,000 men, which, with the troops necessary for their communications, would necessitate an increase to their army in Turkistan of not less than 50,000 men.

From Mazar-i-Sharif they would advance in two columns, the first by Walishan and Chehlburj, the second by Bajgah and Bamian, their objective being Kabul.

Long before they reached Walishan and Bajgah, we should require to have 30,000 men in position at Karabagh and 20,000 men at Jellalabad, and we should have the Ghilzais and Hazaras so well in hand that we could fairly expect them to be faithful to us, except in case of our defeat, when, of course, all would turn against us.

The position of the contending forces would then be—

At Walishan, 1st Russian Division	...	...	15,000 strong.
At Bajgah, 2nd "	...	...	15,000 "
In advance of Karabagh a British Force	...	...	30,000 "
At Jellalabad "	...	...	20,000 "

The Russian advance would then have to take the following lines :—

			1st Division.		*2nd Division.*
1st day	...	...	Walishan	...	Bajgah.
2nd "	...	...	Chashmai Duzdan	...	Camp.
3rd "	...	...	Zardja	...	Kamard.
4th "	...	...	Band-i-Char Asman	...	Camp.
5th "	...	...	Chehlburj	...	Saighan.
6th "	...	...	Yakalang	...	Sokhta Chinar.
7th "	...	...	Tagao-i-Bark	...	Akrabat.
8th "	...	...	Siah Dara	...	Surkh Dar.
9th "	...	...	Darazkol	...	Bamian.
10th "	...	...	Kotal-i-Mushak	...	Tokchi.
11th "	...	...	Badasia	...	Kalu.
12th "	...	...	Farogh Alm	...	Kharzar.
13th "	...	...	Gardan Diwar	...	Gardan Diwar.
14th "	...	...	Yurt	...	Yurt.
15th "	...	...	Unai Pass	...	Unai Pass.
16th "	...	...	Sar-i-Chashma	...	Sar-i-Chashma.
17th "	...	...	Jalrez	...	Jalrez.
18th "	...	...	Rustam Khel	...	Rustam Khel.
19th "	...	...	Argandeh	...	Argandeh.
20th "	...	...	Kabul	...	Kabul.

The English advance would be as follows :—

The Karabagh force at Badasia, twelve days after leaving Karabagh, and this should be at least a week before the Russians left their advanced posts. The Jellalabad force could be at any spot this side of Kabul that was necessary, or it might very properly stay at Jellalabad till events developed themselves a little.

Now if 20,000 British troops, or even 15,000, gained Badasia, it must be evident that no Russian force of nearly equal strength could advance on Kabul by Gardan Diwar until either the British force was defeated disastrously or annulled by an equal force left at Daraz Kol or thereabouts.

Supposing, however, that the Russians determined to hold our force at Badasia in check with the Walishan division, and instead of advancing further than Bamian with the other, preferred to attempt to get into Kabul by the Shekh Ali route, which goes off the Bamian road by Irak into the Ghorband Valley, and thence by that valley and the Koh Daman to Kabul.

News of such an attempt should certainly reach us by means of our agents at Bamian, and it would take the Russians not less than 15 days to reach Kabul by this route. By that time we could have concentrated 10,000 men from Badasia by the Unai Pass and Maidan to the Koh Daman, 5,000 from Karabagh by Ghazni, 15,000 from Jellalabad. Under these circumstances it would certainly be advisable to draw the Russian force on, as it is quite clear that nothing but the most hideous blundering on the part of our General could possibly save it from being destroyed or surrendering, and its right division could not advance to its aid as long as we had even 10,000 remaining at Badasia. Because, if they did so, they would, before going as far as the Unai Pass, find themselves between our division from Badasia and that which had gone, as above proposed, by the Unai Pass and Maidan towards the Koh Daman, and even then we should still have 20,000 men to meet 15,000 Russians coming from Ghorband.

Again, the Russians might mass their two divisions after crossing the Koh-i-Baba; but even if they did so, they could not hope to advance with 20,000 British troops on their flank, at all events until they disastrously defeated us. And as our General would have orders not to be entangled in a decisive action in the Badasia Valley, it would be impossible for them to get rid of the Karabagh force without following them so far that their own communications with the north would be in danger to our force, which by that time would have advanced from Jellalabad.

Therefore, whichever way they attempted to gain Kabul, I do not think it is too much to say that such a disposition of our troops would completely checkmate them.

There is only one other way in which the Russians could annoy us, and that would be by the route from Ush by Kolab and Badakhshan. I feel pretty convinced that no serious attack could be made on India by this route. Still there is no doubt that a Russian force cantoned in Chitral could occasion us very serious annoyance by stirring up the fanatical Yaghistanis of Dir, Panjkoras, and Swat, &c., to make descents into the plains of Peshawar. I doubt not that about 10,000 men would be the limit they could send in this direction, so that we should probably require 15,000 men to meet them. As by the time these events could come off we should have a railway right into the heart of Kashmir, it would of course be easier to put that number of men into Gilgit than it would be to place a smaller division there now. And as I have already shown what dispositions I would make to meet such a demonstration, I need not repeat them here.

The next point I have to consider is, supposing that Russia is in possession of the Kandahar-Kabul line, and thence advances to the invasion of India. In this case her frontier would probably be the Khojeh Amran range, thence to the Sufed Koh, by the main range separating the water of the Helmund from that of the Indus, then east of Kabul at least as far as Gandamak, and over the Kabul river to the Kunar Valley.

Russian railways would have been made from Farah to the west foot of the Khojak, as far as possible from the Oxus towards Kabul, and from Kabul to Gandamak, from Kabul to Kandahar, and from this line to the head of the Gomal. A good cart-road would have been made from Herat to Kabul direct, from Ush to Chitral, and on down the Kunar Valley. The Russians would of course have completely dominated and subdued the whole of Afghanistan, and vast stores of supplies would be forthcoming from Kandahar and Kabul. The concentration of troops for the effort would, of course, have to be gradual; but it could be carried out without any effectual remonstrance from us, or any power in our hands of taking the offensive, at least from India, before Russia was ready. We should only be able to look on and wait.

Our first line of positions would be at Gaokuch, Jellalabad, Kuram, Matun, Urganj, Zurmelan, Zhob, Bori, Quetta, and Kelat, and our second line at Peshawar, Thal, Banu, Gomal, Vihowa, Mangrota, Vidor, and Harand. These would have to be all fortifiedand held. They could not it is true do much to stay the advance of overwhelming forces, but they might just give us a little more time by delaying the Russian advance.

The Russians, I think, if they were wise, would prefer to rest awhile between their second and third campaigns. Delay could only improve matters for them, while it would be very fatal to us. They would require time to reorganize their forces and relay the several lines leading to our frontier. They would then gather in strength and sweep down on us. From Peshawar to Sakar all roads would be open to them; from Kabul to Quetta, every man would be ready to help them. They could form an army of 200,000 men; but this would only be the head to the spear with which they would strike at the heart of India; the shaft would be composed of every ruffian from the Caspian to the Indus whose shoeleather would hold out long enough to enable him to join them. They might, as before, attempt to force back our left, break our centre, or attack our right. It is impossible to be sure what they would do; but I think the best thing they could do would be to base themselves on Kabul, Logar, Ghazni, and Karabagh, from all of which they could draw abundant supplies, and protecting their right by a force advanced from Kandahar to advance quietly and cautiously, maintaining lateral communications as far as possible by the Kabul, Kuram, Khost, and Dawar and Gomal routes to the plain of the Indus. Their greatest strength would be on the Peshawar line and on the Gomal. They would, however, use all the other routes in order to make us disperse our forces as much as possible, and would concentrate the forces on intermediate lines to their right and left, directing all their efforts to gaining possession of the Attock and Dera Ismail Khan crossings. Having got hold of these, their left, still further reinforced, would advance, while they refused their right awhile, till Pindi was in their hands. Then their right would advance and threaten our communications with Lahore, and both of their armies would advance on that place.

On our side it will have been absolutely necessary for us to make our communications, both lateral and rear, absolutely perfect. All the above posts will certainly have to be connected to the rear with their supports by railway. As far as possible, the outer line will have to be connected by railway also, *viz.*, a line from Quetta by Zhob to Zarmelan, Matun, and Kuram, and the inner line from Peshawar to Harand will have to be connected by railway. Lines will have to connect Banu and Thal with the salt railway, and a line from Dera Ismail to Gomal and Zarmelan, a line to Peshin by Thal and Sanghar, and a line from Larkhana by the Mula to Kalat will have had to be made. Every post will have to be connected by telegraph.

The Russians will be able to put very large forces in the field, and I do not think they would employ less than 120,000 from Kandahar, 70,000 from Kabul, and 20,000 from Chitral.

Our garrisons will eat up at least 60,000 men, and we should require not less than 240,000 men in addition to any increase required in India, and of the field army certainly not less than five-eighths will have to be British troops.

A study of the map will, I think, show first that an advance from Kandahar offers the advantage of several routes, that is to say, forces can advance by the following lines :—1st, Kandahar-Quetta-Bolan ; 2nd, Kandahar-Peshin-Harnaī ; 3rd, Kandahar-Peshin-Thal ; 4th, Kandahar-Peshin-Bori-Sanghar ; 5th, Kandahar by the Rahi Maruf to Dera Ismail Khan ; 6th, Kandahar-Kilat-i-Gilzai-Gomal to Dera Ismail Khan, but these routes have the disadvantage that they are very liable to flank attacks.

On the other hand, the roads from Kabul are the shortest (it being only some 115 miles from Gandamak to Peshawar), and while three parallel routes can be used, none of them are exposed to a flank attack. The three routes I allude to are :—1st, Kabul, Khurd Kabul, Haft Kotal, Tezin, Hisarak-Pesh-Bolak-Bazaar-Peshawar ; 2nd, Kabul-Butkhak-Lataband-Jagdalak-Gandamak-Jellalabad-Dhaka-Khaebar-Peshawar ; 3rd, Kabul-Butkhak-Lataband-Lughman-Jellalabad-Alibaghan-Chardeh-Dakha-Shalman-Tartara-Peshawar.

The central group of routes start from Ghazni, and they consist of—1st, the Kuram road ; 2nd, the Khost road ; 3rd, the Banu and Dawar ; 4th, the Rah-i-Vaziri ; 5th, the Gomal road. All these roads are more or less practicable : from the north they are not liable to flank attack, but they are from the south.

It is not possible for me or any one else to conjecture which roads would be used, or whether the Russians would prefer to threaten some of these roads and mass on one of them, or would advance in three or four parallel columns of about 50,000 or 40,000 men each respectively, and the great difficulty we should have to contend against would be the uncertainty as to the point of real attack.

It is, therefore, evident that we must have the most perfect lateral and rear communications for all our forces. All our posts must be connected with the rear and both flanks by telegraph, and we must have a most elaborate and reliable system of intelligence; and while all our forces must be kept in a state of absolute readiness to move, the bulk of them must be placed in a central position from which any point can be easily and quickly reinforced.

It seems to me that this point is clearly Dera Ismail Khan. This place would be connected by railway ; to the rear, with Multan, Lahore, and Jhelam to the flank, with Peshawar and Sakar ; to the iron. with Peshin on the left flank, and with Multan on the right.

The positions we should have to hold in the front line would be somewhere about Jellalabad, Kuram, Matun, Urganj, Zarmelan, Zhob, Bori, Quetta, and Kalat. At each of these places there would have to be a strong citadel armed with heavy guns capable of holding an average of 3,000 men and forming the centre of an entrenched camp for 50,000 men. Again, in rear of these would be our second line of positions, *viz.*, Peshawar, Thal, Kohat, Banu, Gomal, Vihowa, Mangrota, Vidor, Harand, and Sakar.

Our third line would be Torbela, Attock, Khushalgurh, Isakhel, Dera Ishmail Khan, Dera Fateh Khan, Dera Din Panah, Dera Ghazi Khan, Chachur, Kasmore, and Rohri.

Our fourth line would be Rawal Pindi, Sahival, Multan.

I have supposed that we should require an army of at least 300,000 men, of which 180,000 should be British troops. Of this number 60,000 would be used up in garrisons and 240,000 would be disposable as a field army ; and this, I think, should be distributed as follows :—Jellalabad, 30,000 ; Gomal, 30,000 ; Peshin, 30,000 ; Rawal Pindi, 50,000 ; Lahore, 50,000 ; Multan, 50,000.

It will be a necessity of our position that we should be most accurately informed of the exact distribution of the Russian troops and of the after-movement of every battalion. I have supposed that the Russians would have 120,000 men at Kandahar and 70,000 at Kabul; but of course this total of 190,000 might be distributed more or less along the Kabul-Kandahar road. We should have to watch this distribution narrowly, as according as the Russians are disposed we should be able to a certain extent to foresee their intentions. We may take it for granted that no serious attack would be made on any line with under 50,000 men. Therefore if the Kabul army was reduced much below that strength, it would indicate an intention to use the southern lines. If Ghazni was reinforced either from Kabul or Kandahar, it would indicate that an attempt was about to be made by some of the central lines. If neither Kabul nor Kandahar was reduced, it would indicate that the attacks would be made from the Russian right and left. It therefore comes to this: the Russians must either attack with their right and left and feint in their centre, attack with their centre and right, and feint with their left, or attack with their centre and left and feint with their right. If they adopted the first plan, we should require 90,000 men to meet the left attack and 120,000 men to meet the right attack, and we should have 40,000 men to keep off feints from being serious. To meet the first attack, 50,000 men would be sent up from Pindi to Jellalabad by railway. These, joined with the 30,000 at Jellalabad, would have to stay the Russian advance. There would be little room for strategical movements on this line, as the theatre of operations is so circumscribed, and the struggle would therefore resolve itself into a campaign of positions. We should take up successive positions, holding them as long as we could, and then retire to a second position. These positions would be placed centrally between the Kabul river and the north foot of the Sufed Koh, and should be arranged in echelon from the centre; that is to say, 40,000 men would hold the centre position, and, advanced on either flank within striking distance, would be two wings of 20,000 men. If the enemy tried to overwhelm the centre, that body would, after holding on as long as possible, retire to its next position in rear, and its flank supports would wheel round forward to support its flanks and prevent their being turned. If the enemy tried to force either flank, it would have our centre on its flanks, supported by our other flank. Of course all the details of this plan would have to be carefully thought out, and positions prepared beforehand, and every opportunity would be seized of taking the offensive; while every care would be taken to prevent our losing command of our communications with the rear, and every effort would be made to bribe the Khugianis, Shinwaris, and Afridis to aid in the defence, especially by attacks in the rear and on the convoys of the enemy. If it was safe to do so, with reference to operations on the southern lines, the Peshawur force would be reinforced so as to enable it to defeat the enemy decisively.

If at the same time that the enemy made a serious attack from the left they also undertook one on their right, the following measures would be necessary to meet them. We should have 30,000 men at Zarmelan and 30,000 in Quetta. It would be necessary to reinforce the first force by sending 30,000 men from Lahore to Dera Ismail Khan direct, while 20,000 went round by

Jhelum for Banu and 30,000 would go from Multan to Derajat by way of Dera Ghazi Khan, and we should still have 20,000 men at Multan. The main body of the enemy would advance either towards Dera Ismail Khan, Mangrota, or Sakar, while the other routes were threatened. Within a very few days after his leaving Kandahar it would become evident which line he had selected for his main attack.

If he determined to push through by the Peshin-Sakar direction, he would be met, first, at the Khojak; second, in Peshin by the 30,000 men there stationed, and 60,000 men from Zarmelan would advance to attack his flank. This would place him between the horns of a dilemma. If he advanced from Peshin to Sakar, he would necessarily have to detach at least 60,000 men to keep the Zarmelan army in check and continue his advance with the balance of his force which would certainly have been much reduced by losses in forcing the Khojak and detachments which he would have sent to make feints in other directions.

If he purposed to advance from Peshin by Rori to Mangrota, he would be met by 30,000, who would have advanced from that place and have 60,000 from Zarmelan on one flank and 30,000 from Peshin on the other.

If, again, he advanced by Zhob, he would have 60,000 in his front and 60,000 on his right flank, and either of these could in a few days be increased to 80,000 from Multan.

If the enemy from the first committed himself to an advance by the Rah-i-Maruf and the Gomal, the Zarmelan force would detach 10,000 men to cover the approaches from the Zhob to the Derajat by the Draband Pass, and would, after holding Zarmelan as long as possible, fall back to Kotkai. The Peshin corps would advance to Zhob and be joined there by the Mangrota corps, and both would advance to cut the enemy's communications. If he turned on this force, the Zarmelan corps would then threaten his communications. If he tried to hold one force in check and force back the other, he could not safely do so without leaving at least 60,000 men for the purpose, and we should reinforce whichever of our corps was attacked, by 20,000 more men from Multan. In such circumstances, I hold the enemy could not make good his advance.

The only other possible mode of advance would be for the enemy to endeavour to breach our centre by advancing by the roads from Ghazni. For this purpose he certainly could not spare more than 140,000 men. Because he would have to leave a large force in Kabul and detach smaller forces to threaten other routes. He could not further advance from Ghazni without making the necessary preliminary concentrations, and once having done so, he could not seriously resume attacks from his right or left without great delay.

In the meanwhile, we should have made the following dispositions:—The Jellalabad corps would be increased to 50,000 from Rawal Pindi; a division of the Peshin corps would advance to cut the enemy's communications at Kalat-i-Ghilzai; a corps of 60,000 men would be thrown into Banu, and the Zarmelan corps would be increased to 60,000; while 40,000 would be held in readiness to reinforce either. The enemy's advance must take place either by one of the four routes—by Kuram, Khost, Dawar, through the Vaziris, or by the Gomal. The upper parts of the two first are very difficult, but they have the advantage of being less open to flank attack. There would be serious objections to using the Vaziri road, which is also difficult, and the Gomal road, though easy, is very open to flank attacks. It seems probable, therefore, that the Dawar road (which is the shortest as well as easiest) would be mainly used. The enemy would, therefore, be met in front by from 60,000 to 100,000 men, and in flank from Zarmelan by 60,000, and his communications be completely cut.

The last stage of these considerations is that which supposes that we have been driven back from Afghanistan to within our present frontier. Our position under such circumstances may be likened to that of a man sick to death, with serious internal disorder, having to make a stand against another in perfect health. We should have arrived at the millennium of those men who have recommended our waiting to meet Russia on our frontier. She would then be on our frontier, not weakened and fatigued by long operations through desert mountains, as such would have us believe, but thoroughly rested and invigorated, full of elation, with the near approaching completion of her long-cherished dream of making herself mistress of India.

We should not be exactly in a state of elation. India, having simmered ever since we lost Herat, would now be boiling over; our finances would be almost bankrupt; our native army but a broken reed; our feudatories excited, and, with very few exceptions, all eager for change; and we should have a disheartened army to meet one flushed with success, and perhaps, worst of all, those who now cry 'Perish India,' might have become a strong party, and we could not be sure even of hearty support from home.

Our first line of posts would be Peshawar, Kohat, Thal, Banu, Gomal, Darband, Vihowa, Vidor, Harand, and Jacobabad; our second on the line of the Indus; our third, Pindi, Sahiwal, Multan, and Bahawalpur. At Lahore we should require to have a very strong position. Further, Fazilka, Ferozepore, Ludhiana, and Ruper must be held; and, finally, our last stand would have to be made on the line of the Jumna.

Meanwhile a Russian division of 15,000 men would have advanced from Chitral through Dir, and, reinforced by the whole Yusafzai clan, would work through Buneyr to the Indus, and, effecting a crossing, would move down on Hasan Abdal, and endeavour to cut the communications of our Peshawar force. Another division of 15,000 men, joined by the whole of the Raja of Kashmere's troops, would, by moving through Kashmere to Sialkot or Gujarat, threaten our communications with Lahore.

What we should have to meet then would be—1st, an advance of 100,000 men from Kabul; 2nd, an advance of 100,000 men from Logar, Ghazni, and Karabagh; 3rd, an advance of 15,000 men from Chitral through Dir on Peshawar; 4th, an advance of 15,000 men from Chitral through Kashmere on Sialkot or Gujarat. All these forces would be joined by incalculable numbers of Afghans and other rag-tag.

To enable us to meet them with any prospect of success, we should require at least 350,000 men, of which, owing to the uncertain temper of our native troops, we should require to have two-thirds at least British soldiers. We should have a somewhat difficult game to play; but there would be no cause for despair. The Russians, it is true, would have two great advantages; the prestige would be on their side and also the initiative. They could threaten us along the whole line so as to induce us to disseminate our forces, and then burst through in overwhelming strength at one or two points

But, on the other hand, we should have a certain superiority in being stronger than them, in having perfect lateral communications by rail, and in having all our resources close up. Yet all these would be of little use, unless we had absolutely perfect information of their movements. The Russians could certainly threaten us at many points; but with good information we should not be deceived as to the real points of attack. There are a hundred passes into India, and they might all be threatened at first; but many could not be used without exposing the Russian columns to the danger of being attacked and defeated in detail; and once a large column was committed to any one line, it could not be transferred in such a mountainous country as Afghanistan to another without our having ample warning.

Therefore, it seems to me that our dispositions should be as follows:—100,000 at Multan, 100,000 at Dera Ismail Khan, and 100,000 at Rawul Pindi and Peshawar. The most perfect arrangements should be ready for transferring any part of these forces to any other part of the line. Our cavalry and spies should be employed well to the front. Our telegraphing and signalling should be perfect. The garrisons of the frontier posts should be prepared to die; there could be no surrender.

A corps of 20,000 men should be detached to smash up the Dir-Russian column, and a division of 10,000 should from Baramula threaten the Kashmir-Russian column. 120,000 English troops collected at Peshawar should make any entrance of the Russian-Kabul column into the Peshawar Valley impossible; and the remainder of our force should be so disposed as to bar the exits of Kuram, Dawar, and Gomal, and at the same time, from the centre, take the enemy in detail and in flank, and utterly destroy them. Then, collecting in Miranzai, our troops would force their way through Tirah, and fall on the rear of the Russian army endeavouring to break through into Peshawar. At the same moment our Peshawar army would take the initiative, and both would endeavour to destroy the enemy once for all.

If the Russians made good their advance into the valley of the Indus, we should have to be very careful to prevent their getting in our rear and seizing the crossings of that river, and thus cutting our line of retreat. Our posts on the river would be very strong by this time, and not a skiff would be procurable by the Russians in the whole stretch of the Indus. Stubborn battles would have to be fought to cover our retreat at the various passages of the river, and then all the bridges would be blown up, while our troops took up positions to prevent the enemy from following, and they would be still further stayed by heavy-armoured trains on the left bank and small armed launches with one heavy gun each.

If the enemy still further succeeded and made good their crossing, the following dispositions would become necessary:—1st.—Our Dir division would retire on Torbela and cross there, and, joined by 20,000 more men, would threaten the flank of any Russian advance on Pindi. The rest of the army would retire in good order on Pindi, Sahiwal, and Multan, breaking up the railway and taking off all rolling stock, devastating the country and drawing off all transport. The largest body would be at Sahiwal, Chinot, and Pindi Bhatian able to reinforce the right or left, and to hold the passage of the Jhelum and Chenab. Battles would have to be fought at Pindi, Multan, and Sahiwal. If Pindi fell, the Dir and Kashmir divisions would effect a junction and take up a position at Jhelum. The Pindi army would retire fighting on Jhelum. The enemy would now probably concentrate on his left and swing that flank round to Jhelum, refusing his right. We should hold on to the line of the Jhelum like grim death, and swing our left round from Multan to break the enemy's communications with Peshawar through the Salt Range. If the enemy forced the Jhelum, our right would retire on the Chenab, and our left, which would then be too far forward, would retire on Multan, and then concentrate on Lahore.

If we were no more successful on the Chenab than the Jhelum, our right would retire towards Gurdaspur and threaten the enemy's left in his advance on Lahore, while the Multan army contested the passage of the Ravi.

If the enemy forced the Ravi, Multan fort would have to be blown up; and the railways Multan-Lahore, Multan-Bahawulpur, and the Adamwahan bridge would have to be destroyed, and our right would retire by Gurdaspur to the line of the Beaseour centre by Amritsar, and our left to Ferozepore.

Our line of defence would now be the line of the Sutlej from Rupar to Bahawalpur, and it would be necessary to contest this important line to the last. But if we did not do so successfully, our lines of retreat would be to Bahawalpur, Fazilka, and Ferozepore to Delhi, Ludhiana to the Jumna. On this river our last great stand, before giving up the Punjab, would take place.

Though I thus conduct my reader through an unsuccessful defence, I only do so to show what lines of defence are open to us, and should be successively adopted. I by no means wish to imply that I think we should be so disastrously beaten as to force us to give up all this ground. On the contrary, provided our forces are in any way equal to those of our enemy, I am convinced we should have the best of the game, and believe our enemy would find our resistance so stubborn and well planned that he would exhaust himself long before he got to the Sutlej.

We should, even if forced back, always have all our arrangements ready for retaking the offensive; and these measures should take the deadly shape of striking at the enemy's communications. With all the best arrangements in the world, his line of supply through such countries and at such a distance from his base must be to the last degree precarious, while ours were absolutely perfect; and once he was checked, he would be lost. With the whole of Afghanistan, Persia, and the Punjab denuded of supplies, his only chance would be to force us to make a peace on the basis of each side holding what they had got. But of course we never could consent to any terms, and as the aim of the enemy would be driving us out of India, peace should only be made with him on his being driven over the Caspian and back to his boundaries of 1854.

Before concluding this part of my subject, I will summarise my proposals. It will be noticed that, in considering the questions of meeting—1st, a Russian advance on Herat, Kabul, and Chitral from their present frontier; 2nd, a similar advance from their frontier as it will be after we have allowed Herat to slip from our hands. I propose substantially the same measures. These are, while holding them in check on the main lines of advance by strong fortified positions, to operate as much as possible on their flanks. The only difference is that, whereas in the first case I think a field army of 120,000 men will be sufficient, in the second I hold that we shall require not less than 170,000 men for the field army, and an army at least one-third stronger for the defence of India. It may be taken as an incontrovertible axiom that the nearer Russia gets to India the more must we increase our army, and consequently our expenditure; and, further, as we cannot dare increase our native army beyond a certain limit, the nearer Russia comes the greater must be the increase in the British element. It is a very simple sum. If 180,000 men was large enough army for India before the Russians crossed the Caspian, how many will be sufficient? 1st, now they are at Merv; 2nd, when their frontier is the Hindu Kush; 3rd, when the Kandahar-Ghazni-Kabul line is in their hands; 4th, when they have the line of the Indus. The result will not be pleasing to financiers; but it is something to prove that the best course, in a military, national, and manly point of view, is also the cheapest in the long run.

It may not be altogether thrown away if I here make a very rough calculation to show what number of men we shall require to meet Russian operations under the different circumstances I have sketched above.

1st.—If we take up the game at once, a field army of 120,000 men and a Home army of about 150,000 men, total 270,000 men, would suffice.

2nd.—If we lose Herat, we shall require a field army of 170,000 men, and the Home army will have to be increased by at least one-fourth. The total force we should require would, therefore, be 355,000 men.

3rd.—If we lose Kandahar and Kabul, our field army would have to be increased to 300,000 and the Home army by at least another fourth, thus making a total of about 430,000 men.

4th.—If we have to fight on the Indus, we should require a field army of 350,000 men; and to hold India quiet, we should want probably not less than 250,000 men, that is to say, in the last stage, 600,000 men would be necessary.

I leave it to financiers to calculate the difference in cost of the stitch-in-time which I recommend and that of the last stage to which masterly inactivity cannot fail to bring us.

Of course the above are mere estimates; but it would be easy to go into the same details as I have done in considering the men I hold to be necessary now, given in Chapter IV. It is possible that such a consideration might result in a reduction of some of these apparently high figures; but I feel sure that no very appreciable reduction would be attained.

Such figures will doubtless frighten some. We in the English Army are so accustomed to deal with such small numbers, that anything above 50,000 or 60,000 alarms us. But after all what are the figures I have given to those which continental military administrations are accustomed to deal with.

Besides, it must be remembered that the matter will not be in our hands. It is an inexorable fact that if your enemy brings 'big battalions' against you, you must simply meet him by 'big battalions'; and if the Russians can bring against us 95,000 men, 120,000 men, 210,000 men, and 230,000 men according to the operation they have in hand, I must say I think that he who recommended our meeting them with less than 120,000, 170,000, 300,000, and 350,000 men respectively should be the one who should rightly be called to task. Not I who propose by meeting all Russian movements adequately, would make success as near a certainty as anything on war can be.

The conduct of a war is not as so many English administrations seem to think, an occasion for gambling, and to meet your enemy with inadequate forces, when by putting your hand in your pocket and exercising necessary forethought you *can* provide sufficient, is gambling of the very worst and most reprehensible nature.

It may be said, and this is the only other argument worth considering, that we could not raise such a number of men, and if we could, the game would not be worth the candle. Such a statement I most entirely refuse to admit. I fearlessly assert that England can raise enough men and can pay them, and for the rest, I am one of those who think that no sacrifice is too great to face when national honor is in danger.

CHAPTER VI.

COMMUNICATIONS.

SOME time ago an essay was written on the causes which led to the pre-eminence of nations in war, in which the writer gave his views very ably and clearly; but I remember when I read it, the thought that struck me was, there is only one cause which leads to pre-eminence in war, and that is, the determination to win—a determination to win in all wars before they take place; the determination to win in any war during its continuance; and a settled determination after any war to win in the next. In the possible war I have been considering this is no less the case, and I hope that the spirit I have breathed through it all will sufficiently show this. With this spirit always in view, I have gone into details to show how many men we should have to enable us to win, and how we should get them. But there is another detail which must not be lost sight of, especially in this war, and that is, the very important part which the state of our communications must play in any operations for the defence of India. Other things being equal, that side will win whose communications are in the most perfect order.

Therefore, in the same spirit as I have endeavoured to display above, let me consider what is the present state of our communications and those of our possible enemy. First, Russian communications at present are not in a satisfactory state from their point of view, though we could put up with them in an even less perfect condition. The base of Russian aggression in Asia is the heart of Russia; and to make that aggression serve its proposed ends, it is absolutely necessary that Russia should connect her base with her advanced posts, both now and after each successive advance. Formerly the base of Turkistan and Russian aggression from that quarter was Orenburg; it is so no longer—it can never be so again. Her base is now the west coast of the Caspian, at Astrakhan, Petrofski, and Baku. From Astrakhan to Kabul is now a long weary track, and the same may be said to a less degree of the south road from Krasnovodsk to Herat. But there is no sort of reason why this should continue: in fact, it is as certain as anything can be that, ere many years are past, Krasnovodsk and Yaman Airakti will be connected with the west coast of the Caspian by fleets of transports powerful enough to fulfil all that is required of them. A railway will be made from Yaman Airakti to Kungrad, and thence a powerful service of steamers will stem the Oxus to Kilif. From Kilif, at least to the latitude of Walishan, a railway will be made; or, if the Oxus proves unsuitable to river traffic, the railway will run from Yaman Airakti to Kungrad, and thence to Kilif, Balkh, and Walishan. From Walishan to Kabul there can be no insuperable difficulty to making a good cart-road, and this will therefore assuredly be made. From Krasnovodsk to Herat, and as much further towards Kandahar as the Russians succeed in gaining a footing, a railway can, and undoubtedly will, be made; and good cart roads will run from Tashkand to the northern foot of the Hindu Kush. All these improvements will be made, and made for the one single purpose of threatening, and possibly of invading, India and breaking the power of England; and there can be no doubt that the only way to meet these strategic extensions and improvements of Russian communications is to extend and improve our own in such a manner as will enable us to keep the strategic advantages which the rugged features of Afghanistan now gives us, in our own hands.

I will now consider how this can be done. For the sake of clearness, I will divide this subject into the following heads: *1st*, communications within India necessary for internal purposes; *2nd*, communications to the North-West Frontier necessary for offensive-defensive purposes; *3rd*, communications beyond the frontier which require to be at once improved; *4th*, improvements in communications which will become imperative in the event of our losing command of Afghanistan, partially or wholly; and with reference to the latter, I may remark that they will certainly increase at a tremendous ratio according to the manner in which we meet the dangers which now beset us.

With reference to the two first of these considerations, I cannot do better than offer to my readers an able memorandum on the development of the Indian Railway system with reference to strategical exigencies, which has been prepared by Major R. M. Stewart, Assistant Quarter Master General.

With reference to India, it seems to me the principal centres of internal danger should be connected with as many places where our garrisons are placed as possible. These centres are as follows:—

Lahore.—To this centre troops could be poured in from Bombay by way of Karachi and Sukkur; from Peshawar and Pindi; from the North-Western Provinces by Delhi and Meerut; another line will soon connect Moradabad with Umballa by Saharanpur, and also one from Delhi to Ferozepore. On the whole, therefore, the Punjab will soon be adequately supported.

Rohilkhund.—To this centre troops can now be poured in from Bombay by the Rajputana line, Agra, and Aligarh; from Central India by Indore, Agra, Aligarh; from the Central Provinces by Jubbulpore, Allahabad, and Lucknow; from Calcutta by Benares, Fyzabad, Lucknow; and by Allahabad, Cawnpore, and Lucknow; and when the Saharanpur-Moradabad line is finished, an additional line from the Punjab will be provided, thus giving all that seems necessary, both for this province and Oudh, which is served by the same lines.

Rajputana.—At Ajmere, lines from Bombay, Khandwa, Agra, and Delhi meet, and it does not seem probable that any more are required.

To *Central India* there are now the following lines:—From Bombay, by Khandwa; from the Punjab, by Delhi and Ajmere; from Agra, by Gwalior; and from the Central Provinces, North-Western, and Bengal, by Allahabad, Jubbulpore, and Khandwa. In addition to the above, lines are projected from the Great Indian Peninsula through Bhopal to Jhansi, from Gwalior through Jhansi to Jubbulpore, Jhansi to Rutlam and Cawnpore, and Allahabad by Manikpur to Jhansi. When these are finished, I think we may rest satisfied with our hold on these parts.

Hyderabad—Another centre of danger is now only entered by the line from the Great Indian Peninsula at Wadi; but a line is projected from Hyderabad, which will place it in communication with Nagpur, and eventually Calcutta. The projected line from the Godavery to Hyderabad will also give an alternative route for troops from Madras, which will be useful; and if there was a line from Sholapur to Bhosawal, Hyderabad would be placed in a ring fence, from any part of which troops could be despatched to its interior.

The *Northern Mahratta country* about Baroda is very well served at present and will be more so when the Jhansi, Rutlam, and Baroda Railway is finished. *The Central Mahratta country* about Poona is also sufficiently well supported from the direction of Bombay, Madras, and the North-West. *The Southern Mahratta country* is at present badly served, the Great Indian Peninsula only skirting its northern confines; but when the Sholapur and Bellary line and the Poona-Dharwar lines are finished, there will be no cause for anxiety on the score of communications in this district.

With reference to the centres of danger external to India other than the North-West Frontier, they can only come from Nipal, the North-East Frontier, and Burma. With regard to Nipal, the only line that would aid us at present is the Tirhut State Railway to Bettia, and there are apparently no other lines proposed. I think a line from Fyzabad to Bettia by Gorakhpur would be very useful from a military point of view, as in the event of war with Nipal all our troops would have to come from the North-West. For the North-East Frontier and Burma, the lines now proposed seem to answer all purposes.

The following is the Memorandum on the development of the Indian Railway system with reference to strategical exigencies to which I referred above:—

" Points for discussion.

"1. The points which seem to demand "special attention are—

"(i) The extension of railways to those points of the Indian frontier "which are of chief importance for offence or defence.

"(ii) The adaptation of the railway system to secure the rapid and easy "concentration of reinforcements from all parts of the empire "on places of strategic importance.

"(iii) Facility of inter-communication between strategic points, especially "those which are depôts of supply; and the direction of the lines "of inter-communication, so that they are as safe as possible from "interruption or destruction by an enemy.

"It may be assumed that the North-West Frontier of India from Kash-"mir to Karachi is the portion which chiefly demands consideration as most "likely to be the scene of extensive and important military operations. In "addition, the frontiers of Nipal and Assam require attention, though to a "lesser extent."

"The North-West Frontier how sup-"ported from the rear by the present "railway system.

"2. Looking, then, first of all to the North-West Frontier from Pesha-"war to Karachi, we find this line well sup-"ported on the north-east flank by the main "arterial system of Upper India Railways, "which afford direct connection with Calcutta "and the principal depôts and garrisons of the Bengal Presidency, and by a detour "*viâ* Allahabad join the eastern part of the frontier with the seaport of Bom-"bay and the garrisons of the Bombay and Madras presidencies.

"The south-western flank is connected with the port of Karachi by "railway, but has no direct and unbroken communication with the western or "southern portions of the Empire, which are reached either by the long detour "*viâ* Mooltan, Lahore, Allahabad, or by the use of the sea route from Bombay "to Karachi. Moreover, the only railway which directly supports the south-"west extremity of the frontier is situated on the right bank of the Indus, in "a position which a reverse on the frontier would render insecure.

"The central portions of the frontier line are not as yet connected by railway with any of the stations by which they are directly supported These stations, *viz.*, Rawalpindi, Lahore, Mooltan, and Karachi, are themselves in uninterrupted communication by rail, excepting only the break at Sukkur, where a bridge will shortly supply the necessary link. They are also well supported from the south, though their communications with the west of India are indirect. The principal arsenals, Rawalpindi and Ferozepore, are suitably placed for the supply of the frontier stations, but direct communication with Ferozepore is severed by the unbridged Sutlej river.

"Importance of Mooltan and the plain country west of the Indus from the Derajat to Sind. Necessity for direct railway communication with Bombay.

"3. The geographical conformation of the North-West Frontier gives a peculiar strategic importance to Mooltan. The country between Peshawar and Lahore affords special facilities for opposing a direct attack from the northward, owing chiefly to the direction and volume of the rivers by which it is traversed; but a position in the Punjab north of Lahore would be turned and rendered insecure by the capture of Mooltan and an advance along the valley of the Sutlej. Covered by Pishin or Kandahar, Mooltan is secure so long as the frontier in that direction remains unbroken; but its security and that of the Derajat, probably the most vital portion of the whole of the frontier, would be greatly enhanced if the line Mooltan-Karachi could be supported and reinforced directly from the rear, and if the railway communication on the south bank of the Sutlej were as complete as that now existing along the south of the Ravi and Chenab rivers.

"In view, therefore, to the improvement of the position of our Western Frontier on the Biluch side and Derajat, the construction of a railway connecting Bombay direct with the Lahore-Karachi line of railway seems most expedient. It is of the utmost importance that troops could be moved with rapidity and facility into this portion of our territory, both to secure it from attack, or to enable an advance to be made from Pishin or Kandahar.

"To supplement existing communications, a direct line from Bombay and Madras is most desirable.

"As a very important line of inter-communication may be placed that which could be run along the south of the Sutlej river *viá* Ludhiana, Ferozepore, Adamwahan, connecting Ferozepore directly with the main routes to Peshawar and the Kandahar-Karachi Railway, and conferring on Ferozepore that security and importance which its peculiar position demands, whether for defence or offence. Besides the above points, the connection of the posts of Kohat, Bannu, Dera Ismail Khan, and Dera Ghazi Khan with the railway system has to be considered, so that these guardians of the passes leading into India from Afghanistan may be reinforced with the utmost rapidity from the base.

"Thus the questions for discussion are—

"(*a*) A line of railway from the Bombay system to the Indus.

"(*b*) A line of railway from Ludhiana to Adamwahan *viá* Ferozepore.

"(*c*) Lines connecting frontier posts with the Punjab system.

"How connection between the Sind and Bombay systems can be effected.

"4. The proposals hitherto made for a line of railway to connect the Sind and Bombay systems have, after careful surveys, resulted in the advocacy of two alternative routes—

"The northern, from Palanpur on the Rajputana-Malwa Railway *viá* Deesa, Nagar Parker, skirting the Runn of Cutch, to Hyderabad.

"The southern, from Wadhwan through Cutch, *vid* Bhooj and Lakhpat, "to Hyderabad.

"Neither of these lines, nor any line constructed in this part of the country, "can be a commercial success. The country is poor and in many parts desert. The "cost of the lines will be great consequent on the absence along the greater part "of their length of lime, building and ballast materials, and fresh water. The "northern line is estimated to cost 316½ lakhs and the southern 397½ lakhs, both "estimates including a bridge over the Indus at Kotri (50 lakhs). No doubt "any line of railway constructed in these parts must be made chiefly on political "and military grounds. For military purposes either line seems equally suit-"able; but the southern is shorter and therefore better, and it would pass "through Deesa. It would, however, suffer from the unfortunate break of "gauge on the Rajputana Railway, which cripples so much the power of that "line for military transport; and if the northern route be adopted, the line "Palanpur to Ahmedabad should be relaid on the broad gauge. It is impera-"tive, to preserve uninterrupted communication, that the connecting line be-"tween the Bombay and Sind systems should be throughout on the broad "gauge.

"The crossing at Hyderabad-Kotri, which would cost 50 lakhs, might be "avoided by continuing the line of railway to Sukkur, there using the bridge "over the Indus. This railway would be of great importance, not only as a "means of communication between the Sind and Bombay systems, but as an "alternative line on the left bank of the Indus, strengthening greatly the posi-"tion in rear of that river and securing independence of the trans-Indus branch "of the Punjab Railway system. Hyderabad is distant from Sukkur about 200 "miles, so that this extension would not cost less than 120 to 130 lakhs, from "which might be deducted the saving of 50 lakhs by neglecting the construction "of a bridge at Kotri. As this line would be so costly, and cannot be urged on "commercial grounds, it might be cheaper, and would certainly be as useful, to "connect Sukkur directly with the Bombay railways either at Deesa or Jodhpur, "and relay the portion of the Rajputana Railway on the broad gauge. For "military purposes such a line would undoubtedly meet all requirements, as well "as the lines whose construction has been considered and cost estimated.

"Whatever course be adopted, the completion of this railway would cer-"tainly confer additional strength on the frontier at a point of great importance. "It would connect Sind and the Derajat directly with Bombay and Madras, "and enable these presidencies to reinforce the south-western extremity of our "frontier line with the utmost rapidity. At present the only alternative line *vid* "Allahabad, Lahore, and Mooltan is exceedingly long. There is also, no doubt, "the sea route Bombay to Karachi. To adopt this entails a break from railroad "to shipboard, and again transfer from shipboard to railroad. Such breaks like "those of gauges by railway seem rare, and are trifling when movements are "trivial; but accumulate delays in a proportion which increases continually with "the magnitude of the movements, and finally impede continuity of transport to "a dangerous extent when unusual demands are made on carrying capabilities. "Further, the monsoon presents an obstacle during a considerable portion of the "year, especially to the carriage by sea of horses and transport animals; and, "on the whole, it is probable that the one existing circuitous route by railway "would be employed to reinforce the Western Frontier in preference to the "shorter route by sea. Irrespective of the length of the journey, it would be "impolitic to tax the powers of a single line of railroad to provide for the "needs of a force guarding so large an extent of frontier; and for the efficient support of that frontier a supplementary line of railway is most necessary, especially when it is considered that the portion now without direct support is that which perhaps possesses the greatest strategical importance, in that it lies on the main road to India from Central Asia, and if ever reached or occupied, would confer an admirable base for further action both to the north-east and south-west. The acquisition of the Derajat and Sind would probably entail the conquest of India north-west of the Indus and Ravi, and leave India shorn of the larger portion of the Punjab, Sind, and Biluchistan.

"It is unfortunate that, in order to connect a district which is of such strategical importance with the principal base of operation by a direct railway, military needs do not coincide with commercial gains; but perhaps further investigation may prove that the creation of a railway for the purpose of securing the defence of the frontier may not be unattended with the promotion of that trade and profit which ultimately follows the development of railroad communication. Moreover, while Government are prepared to expend money on unproductive lines to prevent famines, occasional expenditure for military reasons may be fairly urged.

"Construction of a line of railway from Ludhiana *viâ* Ferozepore to Adamwahan.

"5. The Ferozepore arsenal, which may be considered the main ordnance depôt for the frontier, has no direct communication with any part of that line. It is separated from Lahore and from the railway terminus at Gunda Singh Wala by the Sutlej, which, though bridged during the winter months, can only be crossed by a ferry throughout a large portion of the year. The nearest point on the railway south of the Sutlej is Ludhiana, and between this and Ferozepore bullock train transport alone exists.

"Ferozepore is not only important strategically on account of the existence there of a large arsenal, but as the salient point on an inner line of defence behind the most southern of the Punjab rivers—on a line behind which concentration could be effected with good prospect of success, whether defensive or offensive operation were in contemplation. The territory included in the triangle formed by the Sutlej, Ferozepore, and Ludhiana has a special strategic value, and the connection of the points of the triangle by rail would add importance to an already important area, and confer the strength which it now wants. The necessity for connecting Ludhiana with Ferozepore is further strengthened by the fact that interruption of railroad communication over the Beas and Sutlej rivers on the main line has already occurred. Owing to defects in the original designs of the bridges over these rivers, the bridges themselves have been the cause of much anxiety and considerable expense; and although from the measures now adopted they may be less liable to danger than formerly, their immunity cannot be secured. It is therefore advisable to supplement these means of communication.

"Ferozepore will before long be connected *viâ* Hissar and Rewari with the Rajputana Railway by a metre gauge railway, which is already constructed from Rewari to Sirsa. This line will, no doubt, be a great support to Ferozepore, but cannot be held to suffice for the efficient connection of Ferozepore with stations dependent on the arsenal, or to maintain sufficiently the strength of a strategic position conferred by geographical situation and configuration. Moreover, this railway has been taken so much to the eastward that it will be necessary to run a branch line to Fazilka—an important place on the Sutlej, which would perhaps be better and more economically included in the Adamwahan-Ferozepore line of railway.

"To bridge the Sutlej at Ferozepore and complete its connection with Raiwind would cost about 56½ lakhs; and, owing to the uncertainty of the "channel of the Sutlej, it is doubtful whether a bridge at Ferozepore would ever "be quite reliable. A flood which would wreck the Beas bridge at Phillour "might cause similar damage at Ferozepore, less than 100 miles distant; hence "a bridge at Ferozepore would not only be very costly, but would not satisfac-"torily supplement the defective communication over the Sutlej already noted. "The cost of the line from Ludhiana to Ferozepore is estimated at 43¼ lakhs. "To continue this line along the Sutlej to Adamwahan would neither be difficult "nor costly. The distance is about 250 miles, and a railway would perhaps cost "150 lakhs at most. Now Ferozepore is said to be 'a mine of wealth to any "Railway Company that will seek its traffic,' and to open a direct route for "the grain trade of the district to Karachi would, no doubt, ensure a consider-"able revenue. Be this as it may, the value of a railway of this sort behind the "Sutlej seems from a military point of view very great, both as enabling "Ferozepore to communicate directly and uninterruptedly with the frontier and "other garrisons at all seasons of the year, and as strengthening an important "defensive position in rear of the Sutlej, which would bar the road to Delhi "and the North-Western Provinces, or enable a force to concentrate for active "operations in the Punjab or Sind.

"The line proposed seems to possess very great military importance. "The extension to Adamwahan has not, it is believed, been yet proposed, nor "does it find place in any of the projects discussed in the latest reports on "Railway Administration in India.

"Connection of frontier posts with "railway system.

"6. There are two methods by which the frontier posts can be connected "with the main railway system—one by running railways from the base to the posts; "the other by running a line down the Indus "to connect the posts. The last plan is the one preferred by the Punjab "Government, which thinks that, 'if rapid communication with Dera Ismail "Khan was required from military and political points of view, the route should "be *viâ* Mooltan, and not *viâ* the Punjab Northern Railway.' Such a line "would, no doubt, run from Mooltan across the Chenab, along the left bank of "the Indus, and join the Punjab Railway at Khushalgarh or Attock. Valuable "though this railway would undoubtedly be, there are several points in this "scheme which present themselves for consideration before deciding whether "it would effect the connection of the frontier posts with the railway system in "the way best adapted to suit military exigencies. There is, in the first place, "the difficulty of bridging the Chenab near Mooltan; and secondly, the question "whether points near a frontier line are best protected by securing their inter-"communication or by direct support from their base. The connection of "strategic points which lie in security behind a defensible frontier line is a "matter of the utmost importance. Facile inter-communication enables assist-"ance being sent at once to any threatened portion of the frontier without "risk of exposing the communications to be severed or occupied by the enemy. "Inter-communications between outposts are liable to be severed or to fall into "the hands of the enemy, in which case they enable him to complete his "offensive concentrations with rapidity. On the other hand, direct communi-"cations, even if occupied, can be disputed foot by foot, and give no aid to "that lateral movement which is so valuable when combination of forces is "necessary. Unless, therefore, the frontier of India were extended beyond "the Suliman range, so that the present frontier posts were well inside the "frontier line, it would seem premature to adopt the mode of connection of "these posts by a railway along the frontier rather than by connecting them "directly with the nearest railway system. No doubt the possession of Pishin "and posts in Biluchistan has advanced the frontier line, and has thus rendered "more secure the line of posts east of the Suliman range; but it is question-"able whether this extension is yet sufficiently consolidated to justify the "Indus being considered secure enough to allow the construction of lateral "communications along the river rather than direct lines to the posts near its "banks; or whether lateral communications, if they existed, could efficiently "supersede the shorter lines connecting the posts with the nearest railway. "Possibly a combination of both systems will be found most efficient, prefer-"ence being given in the first instance to that direct communication which our "present position seems to enforce, and admitting that hereafter our situation "on the frontier may so far secure our Indus line as to make it a base of "support rather than a line of defence.

"7. Two attempts to reach the frontier from the Punjab Railway system "have been commenced. The most northerly, *viz.*, the Khushalgarh extension, "was completed to the left bank of the Indus in April 1881. About the same "time a line to Pind Dadan Khan, on the left bank of the Jhelum river, was "constructed; but Pind Dadan Khan station was closed in June of the same "year, as a considerable portion of the line between Miani and the river bank "was swept away by floods in the Jhelum. The line from Miani was extended "to Bhera along the district road in 1882. During the winter of that year a "temporary bridge, partly on piles and partly on boats, was made over the "Jhelum river, and for three months the passenger and goods traffic were "conveyed across that river. After March 1883, floods necessitated the "removal of the bridge.

"The Khushalgarh Branch was used during the return of the troops em-"ployed in the late Waziri expedition. Since that date the military movements "along this line have been trifling. The line runs through a poor and sparsely "cultivated country, follows none of the main traffic routes, and is useless as a "railway feeder. There is, therefore, no present prospect of a successful "financial result from its construction.

"The traffic over the Lala Musa-Pind Dadan Khan line is, on the contrary, "very considerable, chiefly owing to its connection with the salt mines. Pro-"posals for the extension of this line to the Indus opposite Dera Ismail Khan "have been discussed; but as this question involves a bridge over the Jhelum, "the best site for which work has not yet been determined, the consideration "of the question has for the present been postponed.

"Commercially, then, the Khushalgarh extension has proved a failure. "From a military point of view, it cannot, in its present form, be pronounced "a success, though, no doubt, the positions at Bannu and Kohat are somewhat "strengthened by the development of railway traffic so far as the left bank "of the Indus. To complete the line would necessitate a bridge over the "Indus—a costly undertaking, which might be avoided by the construction "of a line from the point where the Punjab Railway reaches the right bank "of the Indus towards Kohat and Bannu. Such a line would support "directly both these stations, and the materials employed for the Khushalgarh "extension would assist in the construction of a railway, which would be more "satisfactory from a military point of view, and might prove a greater com-"mercial success than the Khushalgarh extension.

"The prolongation of the Salt Range Railway to Dera Ismail Khan would "materially strengthen that important post, and the traffic on this line, "already great, would be considerably increased by the trade from Afghanistan "and Central Asia, which yearly pours through the Gomal Pass into India, "and needs only ready transport into Indian markets to develop its capabi- "lities.

"To bridge the Indus would be a formidable operation; but even were the "extension made to the south bank only, a great impetus would be given "to trade, and an important addition made to the defensive power of the "North-West Frontier. While promoting and encouraging trade, influence "with traders would be strengthened, friendship with the tribes that control the "passes would be cemented, and the important routes which lead from Afghan- "istan to India would be gradually prepared for use when wanted. It might "be feasible hereafter to connect Dera Ismail Khan with the Khyrabad- "Bannu extension already alluded to; and if this were accomplished, we should "have an additional line of communication north of the Indus available at all "seasons of the year. But the position of such a line would be questionable so "long as the present frontier is maintained, and could never take the place "of the direct route from Pind Dadan Khan. Viewing the position of "Dera Ismail Khan with reference to the Gomal and adjoining passes "through the mountain range that now forms our frontier, and the possibility of "future extension of roads, and perhaps railways beyond that frontier, through "the Afghan Valleys which lead directly to Kandahar, Khelat-i-Ghilzai, and "Ghazni, and the probabilities of trade which ready transport would develop, "the connection of Dera Ismail Khan with the nearest railway system "seems a question which can be urged as important to the defence of the "frontier now and adapted to suit the probable expansions of communications "in the future.

"The position of Dera Ghazi Khan with reference to Mooltan, its immediate "point of support, offers considerable difficulties. To bridge the Chenab and "Indus rivers would be a costly and unprofitable undertaking. There seems "no reason why existing communications should not be improved; and this "could be done by leading light rail or tramways to the river banks, and by "the employment of efficient steam ferries or boat bridges over the rivers. These "arrangements would at least improve the existing communications, and in "process of time they might be replaced by a permanent railroad carried over "bridges. Looking to the situation of Dera Ghazi Khan, not only as guarding "outlets through the Suliman range, but as blocking any advance from the Shikar- "pur plain to the north-east along the Indus, the importance of a direct com- "munication with Mooltan from Dera Ghazi Khan becomes evident. At the "same time it is questionable whether the advance of the frontier into "Biluchistan and Pishin has not materially superseded the military importance "of the Dera Ghazi Khan post, and conferred on it the value that attaches to a "secondary point, which would be valuable only in the event of the loss of the "advanced posts. Nevertheless, to maintain its position on an inner line of "defence, the connection by rail with Mooltan is a matter of considerable import- "ance; and to complete the defensive system on the Indus, the connection of "Mooltan by rail with both Dera Ghazi and Dera Ismail Khan seems a necessary "measure, though less pressing than the direct connection of Dera Ismail Khan "with the Punjab Railway system. The lines of rail proposed will be valuable, "whether it be desired to support and reinforce a frontier advanced to the west- "ward of the present boundary or to secure and defend the existing frontier.

"8. Before proceeding to discuss railway extensions which do not directly "contribute to support frontier positions, it "seems desirable to allude to the Kandahar "Railway, which more than any other line contributes directly to the defence "of the frontier from Karachi to Dera Ismail Khan. Present projects propose "the extension of this line to the Khwaja Amran range, the terminus being "probably at or near Gulistan Karez. Looking to the main object with which "this line is constructed, and the fact that between the proposed terminus and "Kandahar the Khwaja Amran range alone offers any considerable obstacle, "the preparation of that range for the reception of the railway seems impera-"tive, in order that, when the time arrives, the railway may be pushed on "rapidly to its fitting strategic terminus. The task of taking the railway to "Gulistan will be incomplete without the preparation of a road to the west side "of the hill range which bars the way of the railway to Kandahar.

"Kandahar Railway.

"9. Of the railway extensions which are important as indirectly affecting "the strength of the North-West Frontier by "promoting easy and rapid concentration of "troops at important positions, and by con-"necting those positions directly with posts or depôts in their rear, the Central "India systems occupy a prominent place. There is ever a keen competition "between the two guaranteed railways which focus in Bombay to obtain the "traffic in the Ganges Valley, and to connect Bombay as directly as possible "with Cawnpore. From these endeavours various schemes have been evolved. "The routes proposed are numerous. Some centre at Ujjain on the Rajputana "Railway, and thence run *viâ* Jhansi to Cawnpore; others centre at Rutlam, a "little north of Ujjain, and connect Rutlam with the Bombay and Baroda "Railway at Godhra near Pali, proceeding from Rutlam to Cawnpore *viâ* "Gwalior. Another extends the Bhopal Railway from Itarsi on the Great "Indian Peninsula Railway to Cawnpore *viâ* Jhansi, and a modification of this "proposal is to take the Bhopal Railway to Cawnpore direct *viâ* Tehri and "Mau-Ranipur.

"Railway systems which indirectly "support the North-West Frontier.

"Of all these schemes, the one that seems best and most suitable is the "extension from Bhopal *viâ* Jhansi to Cawnpore; but the blank between "Jhansi and Gwalior must be bridged. There would then be unbroken com-"munication by rail between Agra, Cawnpore, and Bombay by a comparatively "direct route. The use of the broad gauge throughout is imperative. Toondla "and Cawnpore are both suitable junctions for the halt or despatch of troops. "The connection of this line with Gwalior would probably be urged as much "on grounds of commercial expediency as of military necessity. The traffic on "the Sindia State Railway is as yet small, and needs the development which "the proposed expansion would, no doubt, effect.

"The Jhansi-Banda-Manikpur line of railway, though useful as a feeder "and connecting line, cannot be classed among those of strategic importance. "This railway has been sanctioned as a protective work, but the gauge to be "adopted has not yet been finally decided. Most probably the metre gauge "will be employed; and though, doubtless, the broad gauge would, for mili-"tary purposes, be more efficient, the actual strategic value of the line seems "insufficient to demand a pecuniary sacrifice merely to suit military ends.

"The other extensions which have been proposed in the Bundelkhand "system of railways are as follows:—

"*Etawah-Katni-Bilaspur*, starting from a point near Etawah on the pro-"jected Bhopal-Jhansi extension, passes through Saugor, joins the East Indian

" Railway at Katni, and then trends south-east through the Central Provinces " to Bilaspur, where it would meet the projected Bengal-Nagpur line.

" *Jhansi-Nowgong-Sutna*, connecting the sanctioned Jhansi-Manikpur line " with Nowgong and the Great Indian Peninsula Railway system.

" Both these lines will be exceedingly useful as connecting links between " the military stations of Jhansi, Nowgong, and Saugor, and may be urged as " valuable adjuncts to the communications existing and proposed. Provided all " military stations and posts are reached by the railway, these lines do not " usually demand any sacrifice to military requirements, and may be constructed " in the way that best suits the special necessities for which they are designed; " but to this general principle one exception may be made. Whatever line " may be designed to connect Jubbulpore with the Bhopal-Jhansi extension " should be on the broad gauge. Most likely the line Etawah-Saugor-Katni " will have a branch at Dumoh leading to Jubbulpore, and in this case it is " urged that the Etawah-Jubbulpore extension should be on the broad gauge, " for reasons which will be more fully stated hereafter.

" The connection of Bhopal with the Ujjain, though useful, cannot be con- " sidered a work of special military importance. No doubt it will be effected by " and by.

" Extensions in Bengal and Central " Provinces.

" 10. The railways which are projected to feed the proposed Bengal- " Nagpur line and to traverse Orissa and the " Central Provinces, though primarily intended " for protection against famine, will open up " for the passage of troops a country at present wild and liable to disturbances, " and must therefore be regarded as useful military factors.

" The Bengal-Nagpur Railway is itself of great importance as shortening " the through route from Bombay to Calcutta, connecting Nagpur with these " ports, and opening up districts which could hitherto be traversed with consi- " derable difficulty. The route adopted for this line runs from Sitarampur, on " the East Indian Railway, through Manbhoom, *viâ* Bilaspur and Raipur, to " Nagpur. It will be on the broad gauge throughout, so that it will be neces- " sary to convert the present Nagpur-Chhattisgarh State Railway from the " metre to the broad gauge.

" The connecting railways which join this line are an extension of the " Patna-Gya Railway southwards to Cuttack, the Vizagapatam-Raipur Rail- " way, Katni-Bilaspur Railway, and Benares-Cuttack.

" It seems desirable that the Patna-Gya extension should pass through or " close to Dorunda. These railways will presumably be constructed on the metre " gauge, to which exception cannot be taken, as they are feeders only.

" Western System of railways and " connection between Northern and Cen- " tral India and the Deccan.

" 11. Of the Western System of railways, the Southern Mahratta deserves " special mention, and an exceedingly import- " ant series of connections are in progress be- " tween Jubbulpore and Hyderabad (Deccan). " These, when united, will form a direct line of communication through Central " India from Madras to Jubbulpore.

" The Southern Mahratta Railway system is designed on the metre gauge, " and comprises the Western Deccan Railway—Poona to Belgaum, and the " Marmagao-Bellary Railway—from the Portuguese Frontier to Bellary *viâ* " Hubli. The Southern Mahratta Railway is already under construction. It

" is possibly a defect that this line is on the metre gauge, as Bellary and Poona " are both on broad gauge railways; but there are not sufficient grounds to " urge any change. One point is noticeable. While the Portuguese port of " Marmagao is connected with the Western Deccan Railway, the British port of " Karwar, though nearer to Hubli, is still isolated. There is no engineering " difficulty on the Hubli-Karwar line, and the connection of that port with the " railway seems expedient.

" The extensions of railway which will ultimately connect Jubbulpore with " Hyderabad are being carried out piece-meal, and the value of the line which " will be formed by the ultimate connection of the fragments suffers from a " want of unity in the general scheme. First of all, there is the Jubbulpore-" Baraila-Seoni-Nagpur project. This will probably be on the metre gauge.

" Nagpur is joined to Warora by the Great Indian Peninsula Railway on " the broad gauge, which will shortly be extended to Chanda.

" From Chanda an extension on the metre gauge is projected to Hyderabad " where junction will be effected with the Nizam's Railway, which is broad " gauge. It has already (paragraph 9) been urged that whatever line may " ultimately connect Jubbulpore with the Bhopal-Jhansi extension should be " constructed on the broad gauge. It is further urged as a matter of moment " that the Jubbulpore-Nagpur and Chanda Hyderabad lines should be on the " broad gauge. There would then be uninterrupted communication from Pesha-" war to Madras by the most direct route, *viz.*, Lahore, Agra, Jubbulpore, " Nagpur, Hyderabad. It would seem a grave error to allow this most import-" ant line of railway to be ruined for military transport by a jointed patchwork " railway such as now projected. There is still time to embrace the opportunity " presented of securing an uninterrupted line of communication through the " centre of India, from north to south, from the extreme frontier at Peshawar " to the garrisons of the Madras presidency. There may be some difficulty in " the matter, as a considerable length of the new line will run through the " Nizam's territory. This portion will probably be commenced before long, as " an influential private company has, it is believed, taken the matter in hand. " If, therefore, action be held necessary, it should be taken at an early date.

" Assam and Nipal Frontiers.

" Behind the Assam and Nipal frontiers the systems of railway proposed " will connect the valley of the Brahmaputra " with the Tirhoot, Oudh, and Bengal Railways, " while advanced posts, like Dibrugarh, Darjeeling, Bettiah and Segowlie, " Baraitch and Ranikhet, lying within the range of the Himalayas, which con-" stitutes our frontier line, will all be connected with the main lines of railway " in their rear.

" The chief projects under consideration are as follows. The connection of " Dibrugarh with Dhubri by a line along the Brahmaputra, and extension from " the opposite banks of that river through Tirhoot to Muzaffarpur, whence a line " to Sonepur on the Ganges connects Assam with the East Indian Railway at " Patna, and ultimately with the Oudh system of railways *viâ* the project-" ed Patna-Baraitch Railway.

" In Assam it is further proposed to connect Gauhati with Dacca *viâ* " Mymensing and Dibrugarh with the sea at Chittagong *viâ* Cachar. The " connection of Dacca and Chittagong by rail is also under consideration. " In Oudh, Fyzabad and Baraitch have been lately connected, and an exten-" sion from Bareilly to Philibit is under construction.

"In Tirhoot the extension to Segowlie and Bettia is in progress; and "in Rohilkhand a line is being pushed forward from Bareilly to the foot of "the Kumaon hills. Other minor projects for continuing the railway system "along the North-East Frontier, and for connecting it with the main Indian "Railways, are under consideration. The majority of these lines will be on "the metre gauge, and, when completed, will amply suffice to meet the probable "requirements of the military service.

"Further north, the Umballa-Kalka and Amritsar-Pathankot extensions "will bring the hill stations north of Kalka and those of the Kangra Valley "and Dalhousie nearer to the plains, and will thus produce increased facility "of concentration on the North-West Frontier or elsewhere. The Rawalpindi-"Murree connection is still in abeyance, but will, it is hoped, be found feasible, "and may hereafter be pushed on into Kashmir territory. Sialkot is already "joined to the Punjab Northern State Railway, and an extension to Jummoo, "which seems desirable, is under consideration.

"The military requirements of our frontier on the north-east will be well "met by the railways constructed or projected; and there seems but little to be "said regarding the systems on this side of India, save to urge their completion "as rapidly as circumstances will admit, especially where they reach garrisons "at hill stations, where transport cannot easily be obtained.

"At present the delay consequent on bringing these garrisons to the "nearest point in the railway system is obstructive to rapidity of mobiliza-"tion.

"Consideration of military needs ne-"cessary to give security to commerce.

"It is not feasible in a memorandum of this nature to enter minutely into "the details of each project, or discuss each "proposal in its bearings on the development "of railway transport to suit military needs.

"That an investigation of this nature is desirable, past experience proves. "It is needless to argue that railways in India should be constructed and adapt-"ed to secure India from external attack or internal tumult. The safety of the "empire is as important as improvement of its trade or protection of its inhabit-"ants from famine. It seems, therefore, necessary that, before the execution of "any railway project is commenced, the views of the Commander-in-Chief "thereon should be expressed. Such a procedure would promote security with-"out interference with commercial progress.

"(Sd.) R. M. S."

On this valuable Memorandun Colonel Sanford, Deputy Quarter Master General, gave the following opinion:—

"Assuming that the Kandahar Railway is already decided upon, its primary "value need not be further discussed.

"I would give the second place to direct communication between Bombay "and Madras and Sukkur. Whichever way it is taken, it should be broad "gauge throughout, as it seems likely that military use of it would be on a "very large scale. For direct connection with the Kandahar line without "another Indus bridge, Rohri should be one end of it. And to enable it to be "used by troops from Bengal proper, as well as Madras and Bombay, Ajmere "would be a suitable starting point. To make it fully useful, the Rajputana

"Railway should be converted to broad gauge, which would much facilitate its "use for trooping purposes. If the line between Ajmere and Khandwa were "broad gauge, the system would be complete for the use of Madras troops, "either by the Dhond-Manmad or by the future connection between Jubbulpore "and Hyderabad. The movement of troops from Bombay or from Madras "*viâ* Ahmedabad, and any new lines thence towards Hyderabad (Sind), has the "disadvantages of the descent of the ghats into and delay in Bombay, and also "that after reaching Hyderabad the Indus must be crossed to make use of the "railway in Lower Sind, which is exposed on the wrong bank of the Indus. "Direct connection with Rohri would render this exposed part of the line less "vital than it now is.

"I concur with Major Stewart in deprecating any railway connection of the "posts beyond the Indus. It is best to run branches from the existing system "directly towards the more important of these posts, and to stop them on the "left bank. The line to Peshawar is very valuable with its Indus bridge. The "Sukkur bridge is more valuable still. These two are sufficient. The Khushal-"garh Branch is good, as it points to Kohat and the Kuram. The extension of "the Salt Range line to the Indus opposite Dera Ismail Khan is the line now "wanted to facilitate movement on the Gomal and other passes north of the "Takht. In this the line must be broad gauge, and the Chenab must be bridged, "but not the Indus.

"I attach little importance to railway communication from Mooltan "towards Dera Ghazi Khan and the Thull-Chotiali District. To bridge the "Chenab alone here would be an enormous outlay on so short a line. A first "class military road and steam ferries are all that are required. Tramways "could rapidly be laid on the road if wanted.

"Better railway communication through Bundelkhand and Malwa is very "desirable, and the line Bhopal-Cawnpore with a branch to Gwalior, all broad "gauge, seems likely to meet military requirements.

"The Calcutta and Nagpur Railway, with its branches and transverse line "from Jubbulpore to Hyderabad, are all valuable. They give access to large "districts seldom traversed by troops, and facilitate military inter-communica-"tion generally between the three presidencies. These lines will probably all "be completed as commercial enterprises, but the broad gauge on the main lines "of this system should be enforced, as the confusion of gauges up to the pre-"sent is prohibitive as regards the movement of large bodies of troops.

"(Sd.) G. E. L. S."

My own remarks on the Memorandum are as follows:—

"The most important railway in a military point of view is the Kandahar "line. Every effort should be made to push this, with as little delay as possi-"ble, as far as we can possibly get it, at all events through the Gwaja.

"The next is a line from the Salt line at Miani to opposite Dera Ismail "Khan, and then on to as far up the Gomal Pass as we can get it; at all events "it should be made up to the mouth, and I do not see any difficulty in making "it. This line would pay to a certain extent. It is of the utmost strategical "importance, especially in the event of our losing Herat, as it leads directly to "the key of the remaining portion of Afghanistan.

"I think Bombay should be in direct railway communication with Sukkur. " Either of the proposed lines would do, and perhaps it might be worth while " surveying the country between Jodhpur and Sukkur.

" A very important line would be one leading from Madras to Hyderabad, " Nagpur, Jubbulpore, Gwalior, and Agra. Such a line has been proposed, " but it should undoubtedly be all on the broad gauge.

"I think the Baraitch-Fyzabad line should be connected with Bettia. " In case of complications with Nipal, all our troops would have to come from " the North-Western Provinces and the Punjab; all stores would come from " Calcutta, and it would be as well to have two distinct lines. This, however, " is not *very* pressing.

"The Kandahar Railway has been sanctioned, but stress should be laid " on its being carried on to the extreme limit of our frontier. The next in " importance is the extension of the Salt Railway to Dera, and then the " extension of the Rajputana line to Sukkur. I think the most valuable " line strategically would be across the desert by Jodhpur and Jessulmere to " Sukkur."

In regard to lines of railway that are of strategical importance with reference to the Russo-Indian question, my views are fully explained in the memorandum above referred to. What we require is to be able to send troops and stores with celerity to the North-West Frontier from every part of India; and as Indian lines are all single, it is of great importance that we should have as many lines as possible.

In addition to those already existing, namely, the Northern State Railway to Peshawar and the Indus Valley Railway to Sukkur from Lahore and Karachi, it is of urgent importance that we should have the Sukkur-Kandahar line finished as far as possible. If we cannot have it done to Kandahar at once, it should certainly be taken to the other side of the Khwaja Amran range. I think it is much to be regretted that the time which has elapsed since the stoppage of the Kandahar Railway should not only have been utterly thrown away, but no attempt been made to be sure that in adopting the Harnai route we are taking the line which is best for all our purposes. When the Harnai line was chosen, there was no time to go into the question of the best line thoroughly; but since the end of 1880 there has been ample time, and it would have been well if we had utilized it to go into the whole question thoroughly. The reason for which we require a railway to Southern Afghanistan is not alone to provide easy transport from our frontier to Kandahar, though that is one of them. There is another reason, and, if this Russo-Indian question had ever been thoroughly considered in its strategic bearings, it could not have failed to become apparent. The fact is that the great danger to us of the Herat road being used by Russia lies in the fact that, owing to the mountains on the north of it and the desert to the south, it would be extremely difficult to strike at the Russian communications; and till this is remedied, it is evident that a contest for Kandahar must be a simple hammer and tongs one, into which strategical considerations can hardly enter.

But because at present it would be impossible to strike at Russian communications, it does not in the least follow that it need always be so. A glance at the map discloses, as I have said, that the Herat-Kandahar line is protected on the north by the mountains of the Hazaras and on the south by the desert of Biluchistan, and the question occurs whether there is no possibility of annulling this protection. Of course, any line of railway that only goes direct to Kandahar will not help us; but it is evident that if we could get a line of communications that would lead direct to the Helmand, we should acquire a position of quite incalculable strategical importance in the defence of the Kandahar gate of India. This has been fully shown in Chapter V of this paper. Therefore it seems to me a pity that the line for Kandahar has not been designed to aid in this purpose. However, as we seem to be committed to the Harnai Railway now, any further chopping and changing would be distinctly detrimental; and I do not of course propose to interfere with its being pushed on as rapidly as possible. Still, looking to the very great importance of our having in our hands an alternative route to Herat, clear of Kandahar, and a means of seriously checkmating any Russian advance to the Helmand, I have no hesitation in saying that we should lose no time in making a line from the Indus Valley Railway from some convenient spot, such as Larkhana to Gandava, thence by the Moolla pass to Sohrab, and thence by the easiest line to Nushki, and then across the desert of Biluchistan to a convenient spot on the Helmand, such as Landi or Bandar Juma Khan whence the line should eventually be continued to Herat.

Another line of railway, which should be made at once, is from the Salt line to opposite Dera Ismail Khan, and from that town to the entrance to the Gomal.

Of the lines in India, the most important seem to me to be, *first*, a line from Palee, on the Rajputana Railway, by Jodhpur and Jessulmere to Rohri. This would repair the terrible military blunder of having our main communication between Bombay and Quetta on the right bank of the Indus. This line is in every way preferable to the two more southern lines which have been proposed from Palanpur by Deesa and Nagar Parker to Hyderabad, and from Ahmedabad by Bhooj and Lakhpat to the same place. Of course the blunder of laying the Rajputana line on the narrow gauge should be repaired at the same time.

Second, a line from Ludhiana through Ferozepore to the Adamwahan bridge, on the left bank of the Sutlej, is very important, and is in all ways preferable to attempting to connect Ferozepore with Lahore, thus making another bridge over the Sutlej.

Third, we require greater facilities of communication between Madras and the north-west, and it seems to me this would best be secured by lines running (*a*) Hyderabad to Nagpur (this is projected, but it should certainly be on the broad gauge), thence to Jubbulpore by Seoni, then to Gwalior by Damoh or Saugor and Jhansi; (*b*) a line from Bangalore to Bellary, thence to Sholapur (this is in hand I believe), and then from Sholapur to Bhosawal.

Besides the above railways, which are, I consider, absolutely necessary at once, I think there are several lines of road which should be undertaken :—

1st.—A line of communications by the nearest possible line from the Indus Valley Railway to the Helmand should be organized. This is the line I have proposed for the railway above, but till that can be done, this road should be put in order. There will be no money thrown away on it, as it will in any case be necessary to have a road to enable the railway to be made. In addition to making the road passable for carts, attention must be paid to arrangements for storing forage, grass, fuel, water, and supplies at convenient stages. There can be no good reason why this should not be undertaken at once.

2nd.—An alternative line of communication should be made practicable from Dera Ghazi Khan by the best line to Pishin.

3rd.—All possible improvements should be made in the road from the Gomal to Karabagh. I think the worst part of this road, which is nearest our frontier. should be commenced at once.

4th.—Advantage should be taken of an expedition to Zhob in the autumn to make a good road from the Gomal to Pishin.

5th.—First class ferry arrangements should be kept up at Dera Ismail Khan, Khushalgarh, Dera Ghazi Khan, Shere Shah, and Shahpur. That is to say, Government should maintain proper ferry steamers. In the cold weather of course boat bridges should be maintained at these places. And it may be of the last importance if we are ever worsted on our present frontier that very perfect arrangements should be made for the passage of the Indus and all Punjab rivers at all points nearest to the debouchures of the passes.

6th.—All railway bridges over the large Indian rivers should at once be made practicable for the march of troops. It may seem incredible that they were not made so at the beginning; but it is true.

I have hitherto confined myself to a consideration of the improvements in our communications which should be undertaken at once. I cling to the hope that the Government will at once grapple with the difficulty which now besets them. I have shown in Chpater V that as surely as they do not do so, so will our military difficulties increase, and that while a possible, but by no means certain, increase to our army, now of 80,000 men, will bring us triumphant through the troubles which surround us, if action is put off, it may come to this, that we shall require something like 400,000 men to save ourselves hereafter.

And I regret I have no more comfort to offer to Government in this section of my subject. I have shown above what improvements to our communications should be undertaken at once; but I distinctly add that these, expensive though they may seem and be, will be as nothing to the cost and extent of the necessary improvements in our communications, which will become absolutely necessary to save us from sheer disaster and defeat, if the Russians are allowed to advance any further.

As in regard to the number of men, where one man will be enough now, five will barely suffice later on. So where one mile of railway will be enough now, ten miles will scarcely see us through it later.

For instance, in the event of the Russians having got possession of the Herat province and Afghan-Turkistan, we shall require railways from Rawalpindi to Sonamarg in Kashmir, from Peshawar to Jellalabad, from Dera Ismail Khan to Karabagh, from Zarmelan to Pishin, from Pishin to Dera Ghazi Khan; these all beyond our present frontier. Within our frontier trans-Indus, we shall require a railway from Khushalgarh to Thal, from Isa Khel to Thal, from Mooltan to Dera Ghazi, and from Peshawar along the frontier to Jacobabad; and cis-Indus, Dera Ismail Khan will have to be connected with Mooltan and Lahore.

If things go further against us, we shall require, in addition to all the above, a line along the left bank of the Indus from Torbela to at least Dera Ghazi Khan. A line along the left bank of the Chenab from Jummoo to at least as far as Jhang, and a line from Amritsar to Gurdaspur, with railway bridges over all the large rivers. And as none of these lines will be of the slightest use, except for military purposes, none of course will pay.

CHAPTER VII.

OFFENSIVE-DEFENSIVE MEASURES FROM OTHER POINTS THAN INDIA.

In addition to the offensive-defensive measures which can be undertaken from India, there are many other operations which can, and certainly should, be attempted from other directions.

I have said in Chapter III that I think it of very great importance for us to form a coalition against Russia with Germany, Austria, and Turkey, and that every effort should be made to gain over Persia, the Khanates, and China.

I think there is every reason for us to fear a coalition between Russia and France; and if this took place, it would intensify our difficulties to an alarming extent. While Russia advanced towards India by land, France would at the least hold England in check and attack our sea communications with India. Without going the length of saying we could not alone face such a coalition with fair prospect of success, it must be evident that it would increase our difficulties enormously; and I hold that our best chance would be to conclude a coalition with Germany and Austria and Turkey.

I confess I cling to this quadruple alliance. It seems to me the best and most reliable issue from our difficulties. If it can be concluded, it is impossible that Russia can threaten, far less invade, India. But can it now be concluded? There was a time when, I understand, we were in fair way of concluding such an alliance; but since the efforts in that direction have ceased, we unfortunately seem to have been drifting further and further away from it.

The reason seems to me to be because of the policy of isolation which has been so unfortunately followed of late years by English Ministers. England has tried to live alone, caring for no one and loved by none. Swathed in purely selfish instincts and pursuits, she has gone on accumulating wealth at a fabulous rate, and has hoped that she will be allowed to enjoy her riches in peace, though surrounded by needy and covetous neighbours.

But poor human nature itself forbids that this could ever be the cases even if she had made all her riches and had them stored within her own land. But the fact is that in extending her commerce, she has had to extend her possessions and responsibilities, and her riches are no more the result of local efforts within Great Britain than they are all stored in those boundaries. England is, therefore, not in the position of a rich miser, with all his wealth stored in one iron box, on which he can sit to guard it. Her riches are scattered over the face of the earth, divided from her by other peoples strong as herself, whom greed or envy may any day make enemies. The prudence and foresight which has shown her how to store her riches seems in these latter days to have altogether failed her when called upon to take care of them. She must see her enemies all round her, yet she will not conciliate or buy any of them; and without the power to defy them, her attitude is really a defiance to the whole world.

But luckily other nations are not so blind as ourselves to their own interests, and so Germany, Austria, and Turkey were once ready to buy our aid. Now apparently they are not so; they have seen that nothing will induce us to risk anything; and so they have withdrawn to seek other alliances. I regret that it seems possibly too late to make the coalition I recommend. I am afraid that the bargain between Germany and Russia has been made, and that bargain probably is that Russia will be neutral in a war between Germany and France, on condition that Germany makes no objection to Russia's schemes in the East.

Still it may not be too late; and I think no effort should be spared to secure the alliance with Germany. If we can do so, the Russo-Indian question will surely die, or at least go to sleep. It is impossible that Russia could undertake anything serious against India if Germany, Austria, and Turkey even hinted that such schemes were distasteful to them and might lead to war.

But of course none of these Powers will ever agree to such an alliance without a distinct equivalent being offered to them. What this should be must be left to the ingenuity of our diplomats to devise. I will only say that I cannot believe that these countries are above a price or that we cannot pay that price. Certain it is, that what will be demanded from us, will be that we shall throw off the mantle of selfish isolation, choose our friends, and be prepared to stand by them through thick and thin.

It seems to me that were such a coalition formed, it would undoubtedly cause Russia to rush into the arms of France; but I deny that it would be likely to cause a war. Both sides of the coalition would be too strong to permit of either wantonly incurring such a risk. The foreign politics of the above countries may be summed up as follows. England, everyone must allow, is thoroughly non-aggressive. She wants no more territory, and will take no more, except with a purely defensive view. She will not attack either Russia or France, if these Powers will let her and her foreign possessions alone. But if threatened in India, she will certainly make the possession of Egypt permanent, and she will take up such positions in the countries between India and Russia as may seem advisable for purely defensive purposes.

Besides the direct defence of her Indian Empire, England finds it necessary to make certain alliances to aid her in the indirect defence of India, that is to say, she will endeavour to conclude an offensive and defensive alliance with Germany, Austria, and Turkey against Russia and France, and in consequence of this she will undertake to support either of her allies whose territories are attacked by either Russia or France with her whole power.

The whole key to French foreign policy lies in the insane and criminal wish of her people to be revenged on Germany, and there can be no more doubt that she will do so if she finds an opportunity than that the sun is now shining. In addition, France seems to have an idea that it is necessary to maintain their prestige in other directions when not able to do so at the expense of Germany. In pursuance of this idea, she has lately been taking up positions in Madagascar, Tunis, and Tonquin; and though she abandoned overt opposition to England in Egypt, there can be no doubt that she will take up an offensive attitude on this question whenever it suits her purpose to do so. To enable her to gratify her first wish, she must have an ally. The only ally strong enough to help her is Russia, and to gain her aid against Germany she would probably connive at that Power's designs against England.

It is, therefore, evident that there may be two causes of quarrel between England and France. First, French schemes of aggrandisement in the East may bring them into collision with the English. Secondly, an alliance with Russia for the purpose of threatening India would certainly do so. Consequently, there seems every reason to believe that French and English interests will be for some time antagonistic.

Germany is also purely non-aggressive. The great danger she is exposed to is having to fight France and Russia single-handed for the maintenance of her present frontier. If France loses the power of attacking her, Germany will certainly not wantonly attack France.

Austria is composed of such discordant elements, that she cannot be aggressive. Her only probable cause of disquietude lies in the chance of Russia possessing herself of a port in the Mediterranean and attempting a Slav propaganda in her territory. It is, therefore, directly to her interest to prevent Russia getting stronger.

Turkey's only object in life is clearly self-preservation. She has long passed the stage at which she could be regarded as an aggressive Power. She certainly will never attack Russia.

Russia, like France, is a purely aggressive Power. Her great wish is to get into the open sea. Those who stand in her way are Austria, England, and Turkey. Austria, because she fears her getting more powerful; Turkey, because she knows that the realization of the Russian wish will mean extinction for her; and England, because the preservation of her Indian possessions make it necessary for her to seek an ally in Turkey. These three Powers must, or certainly should, always hold together on this question; and though it would undoubtedly deprive Germany of any interest in the Eastern question, her very natural distrust of Russia must always impel her to seek the alliance of the above three Powers. In order to carry out her designs, Russia must attack Turkey and take more of her territory; in order to paralyse England, she must also threaten India; and to annul Austrian action she must threaten her with a Slav rebellion.

But if Russia could thus make arrangements so much to our detriment, is there no other hope for us but in the quadruple alliance I have advocated? If Germany and Austria refused to join us, could we not by any means detach France from Russia? I am afraid it would be very difficult, if not impossible, to do so. Sentiment has very little to do with such alliances; it is self-interest which in the end rules: and unfortunately both the sentiment and self-interest of the French are against us. It is true that France once joined us against Russia; but everyone by this time has realized that it was not France which was on our side, but the Emperor Napoleon III, and that he concluded the *entente cordiale* purely in the interests of his own dynasty. On the other hand, England and France have been enemies since the beginning of history; and even if this was not the case, it may be doubted whether the temptation of reducing England to the position of Holland and succeeding to her territory in India, Egypt, China, and the Straits, and taking to herself the best part of her Eastern commerce, would not be too great for the latter Power to withstand.

We can offer nothing that would appeal either to French cupidity or vanity without at the same time ruining ourselves. Gibraltar, Malta, Egypt, Aden, India, the Straits, and Hong-Kong are all necessary to our existence as a first class Power. Madagascar, Tonquin, Siam, and perhaps part of China,

France will take without our leave. America would not let France touch Canada or the West India Isles. The Australian Colonies would protect themselves; and the Cape is not worth having: and there is nothing else left.

It is then evident that in the event of a coalition of Germany, Austria, Turkey, and England against Russia and France, neither of the latter Powers can go to war with any chance of success; and as neither of the former wants war, the peace of the world would, as far as human prescience can foresee, be secured by such an alliance.

This may be seen at a glance by the following figures, which give the available forces of the powers named in the above considerations:—

	Men.	Guns.
Austria	1,064,307	1,580
Germany	1,492,104	2,808
Turkey	850,000	1,548
England	780,766	754
Total ...	4,187,177	6,690
Russia	2,087,169	3,986
France	1,567,150	2,952
Total ...	3,654,319	6,938

But while all other Powers are probably unable to produce more men or guns than they now maintain, England could certainly increase her forces in England and India by at least 400,000 men, and her guns by any number that might be requisite. So that the above quadruple alliance would be so strong that neither Russia nor France would be likely to attack any of its members.

If, however, war did break out, it is quite clear that the Austrian and Turkish fleet could dispose of the Russian, and the English and German of the French. And if Germany was aided by 300,000 Austrians, she would clearly overmatch the French.

Then there would remain—Austria, 764,307; Turkey, 850,000; England, 780,766: total, 2,395,073 against Russia's 2,087,169.

One cannot study these figures and believe that any war would arise under such circumstances; and I do not, therefore, see the use of entering further into any consideration of what offensive measures against Russia such an alliance would enable us to undertake.

The quadruple alliance is probably also the only real safe course for Germany; for if she does not join it, the Power of Russia and France combined will be so nearly equal to that of England, Austria, and Turkey that war is much more likely to ensue; and if the result of it should be unfavourable to the latter Powers, the former could, and probably would, turn their united forces on Germany, who would then be left without any possible ally.

Still Germany may not enter into such coalition. All she cares about is not to be attacked by France and Russia together; and if she can make arrangements with the latter (as indeed she appears lately to have done) to remain neutral in a war between her and France, she would naturally not be particularly anxious to risk getting mixed up in the Eastern question, which really does not concern her directly. The great reason why Germany should join a quadruple alliance with Austria, Turkey, and England is because she cannot trust Russia's sincerity and adherence to her engagements.

It thus seems to me to be demonstrated that the safest course for Austria and Germany is to join England and Turkey; and I hold that it will be very unwise if our Government does not do all in its power to conclude this quadruple alliance.

Supposing that the above alliance had been concluded, it may be taken for granted that Germany and France would provide sufficient amusement for each other. This would leave England, Austria, and Turkey with over two millions of men against Russia with about the same number; but while of the allied Powers, England and Austria would not have to fear an attack from other directions, and could denude their territories of troops, Russia's dominions are so widely extended and so heterogeneous, that she would have to keep large numbers in hand simply to preserve her sway in her own dominions intact.

Under such circumstances, I think an attack on Russia should proceed from three directions,—1st, on Poland; 2nd, on the Caucasus; 3rd, on Turkistan.

For the 1st, the Austrians would put 600,000 men in the field and the Turks would aid them with 200,000 men; for the 2nd, the English would give 60,000 men and be aided by 200,000 Turks; and for the 3rd, India would provide 120,000 men.

The numbers that Russia would have to maintain to preserve internal order and protect her other frontiers may be taken as follows:—

	Men.
On the German frontier	200,000
Eastern Turkish frontier	150,000
Turkistan and Siberia	60,000
Internal defence	600,000
Total ...	1,030,000

This would leave her rather under 1,000,000 men to meet the attack of about 1,200,000.

In regard to the first, I will not say much. The operations would rest entirely in the hands of the Austrian Government, and they would undertake and carry out whatever operations they were capable of. I think, however, it would be a good plan to send some English officers to the Turks to induce them to work in accord with the Austrians. If the Austrians and Turks were to bring 800,000 men against Russia in her Polish frontier, it is quite evident that Power could make no counter-stroke against Turkey in European Turkey, and besides Turkey could, after providing two armies of 200,000 men each, still have something like 400,000 men available, and she could thus certainly protect her own frontier.

The 2nd operation would be an attack on the Caucasus by a combined English and Turkish army with 260,000 men, and the object would be to drive the Russians back over the Caucasus and re-establish the Circassians in their own country and constitute a Christian State of Georgia, and, above all, keep the country south of the Caucasus in the hands of a friendly Power, so as to give us at any further date the power of reaching the Caspian. Before peace was made, it would be a *sine quâ non* that Russia should lose the exclusive right to navigate the Caspian, thus depriving her for ever of the possibility of putting pressure on Persia and of using the Caspian as a base against India. These objects are of most undoubted importance, and, therefore, every effort should be made to place our success beyond question. On the one hand, the outside number Russia could place in the field in the Caucasus would be 200,000 men. The English should be able to give two corps d'armée of 60,000 each, and the Turks, say, six corps d'armée of like strength. In addition to these, every able-bodied Circassian in Turkey should be enlisted. There are, I believe, over 100,000 of these men who have been driven from their homes by the Russians, and there could not be much doubt of their becoming very zealous allies. But supposing after weeding they could only produce 60,000 men. Under such circumstances, I think we could rely on the aid of the Persians; they are doubtless now completely under the influence of Russia; but if such a combination was formed, I do not imagine Persia would be able to stand the temptation of endeavouring to recover her lost provinces, and this would especially be the case if Persia was solemnly warned that if she did not join she would be ruthlessly dismembered. However it may be that we should not be able to overcome her fear of Russia, and we should have to do without Persia, yet even in this case, though Northern Persia would be against us, there can be little doubt that Southern Persia would go with us, and we should be able to raise considerable forces from the Bukhtiaris, Levis, Arabs, Kurds, and the southern provinces.

The force to operate against the Caucasus would then stand as follows:—

English troops	60,000
Turkish troops	180,000
Circassians	60,000
Persians	40,000
Total ...	340,000

Now as to the use to which we should put these forces. There are two ways of attacking the Russians in the Caucasus,—1st, to base ourselves on the Black Sea and advance direct on Tiflis; 2nd, to base ourselves on the Tigris or Persian Gulf, and advance from the south on Erivan.

In the first case the force should, I think, consist of English 60,000, Turks 120,000, Circassians 60,000: total 240,000. We should be stronger on this line than the Russians; for I do not think they could face us with more than 150,000 men.

Having the complete command of the sea, we can of course select our own base of operations. We might land at Trebizond and march by Erzeroom and Kars and Gumri on Tiflis; but the disadvantage of this would be that the distance would be great, and we should have to take the two strong fortresses of Kars and Gumri, and, moreover, our line of operations would be very much exposed. I am therefore inclined to think that we should land either at Sukam Kale, Poti, or Batum, and I think the manner of carrying out this should be as follows. The English and Turkish forces would be collected at Constantinople with the declared intention of making a descent on the Russian coast at Odessa and advancing to aid the Austro-Turkish operations against Russian Poland. Having embarked and sailed out of the Bosphorus, the fleet would change direction as soon as it was dark and steer for Poti. At the same time the Circassians would advance through Lazistan on Batum, and would attack it aided by our fleet and a detachment landed for the purpose. Having seized Batum, the whole force would be collected on the railway line in advance of Poti. The railway would, of course, have been destroyed; but as the whole line was made by English engineers, we should be prepared to relay the line to bring up stores for the army. The advance on Tiflis would go on, and would be timed so as to fit in with the advance of the army of the South. From Poti to Tiflis by the road is 213 miles, or about 8 stages; so that, allowing for a progress of only 10 miles a day, we should reckon on appearing before Tiflis in 21 days (*vide* Appendix U). The Russians would doubtless make every effort possible to defeat us and retain hold of the capital; but as they would be numerically weaker, their communications with Vladikafkaz and Baku would be threatened, and they would be fighting in the midst of a hostile population. I do not think they could hope for success.

The 2nd operation I propose would be undertaken either from the Tigris or the Persian Gulf, and it may be well if I here say a few words as to the various lines of operations that are open to us in this direction. They consist of the following roads: 1st, from the Tigris at Jezireh, by Bitlis on Erzeroom—Appendix (*c*); 2nd, from the Tigris at Mosul by Rowandiz, Urumiah, and Khoi on Erivan—Appendix (*d*); 3rd, from Sulimania to Erivan by Sehna or Suj Bolak—Appendix (*e*); 4th, from Bagdad by Kirmanshah, Sehna, Maragha, Tabriz, on Erivan—Appendix (*f*); 5th, from Dizful by Khoramabad, Kirmanshah, and then as above—Appendices (*g*) and (*h*); 6th, from Dizful by Khoramabad, Bururujid, Kum, Tehran, Shahrud—Appendix (*k*)—to cut the Russian communications at Astrabad. Which of these would serve our purpose best?

If the Russians were actually holding Herat at the time, or engaged in operations for its capture, I think the last would be the route we should choose, as our sending a force to seize the Russian base on the Caspian could not fail to paralyze them completely. But I hold that if the combinations I have proposed were carried out, Russia could have no men to spare for offensive operations against India; and as she would be engaged in a struggle for dear life, she would have to concentrate every available man she could spare from Europe and Turkistan on the Caucasus. There would, therefore, be no object in using this line.

Our object should be to paralyze her in the Caucasus, and the best *rôle* that could be assigned to our army of the south would be to advance in the first instance and seize the line of the Aras. Our force would consist of Anglo-Indian troops, 40,000; Persians, 40,000; Turks, 60,000: total 140,000, or about five corps d'armée. These I would distribute as follows: 1st, Turkish Corps at Mosul; 2nd, at Sulimania; Persians I would collect at Kirmanshah and the Anglo-Indian force at Dizful, and the advance would then go on according to the following programme. Details of the routes will be found in appendices.

From Mosul to Rowandiz would take about 15 days, from Rowandiz to Khoi 20 days, and from Khoi to Erivan 15 days, or, say, 60 in all.

From Sulimania there are two roads over into Persia,—the first to Suj Bolak would take, say, 15 days; the second to Sehna 20 days; from Sehna to Tabriz would take 30 days; and from Tabriz to Erivan about 20 days, or, say, 90 days for this column.

From Kirmanshah to Erivan by Tabriz would take about 60 days. From Dizful to Kirmanshah would take 45 days; and 60 days on to Erivan.

The most favorable time to begin all these operations would be about February, so that the various columns should take the spring up with them and arrive at Erivan in the summer. I do not go into calculations of the details of this scheme, but of course these could easily be worked out in a very short time.

The result of these combined operations would be to place nearly 500,000 men into the Caucasus; and as Russia would be very fully occupied in Europe, I do not think the result could be doubtful.

---

* See Appendix V, Route from Batum to Tiflis; Appendix W, Route from Sukum Kaleh to Tiflis; Appendix X, Route from Erzeroom to Tiflis; Appendix Y, Account of the Poti-Tiflis Railway, Appendix Z, Description of Poti—(*a*) Description of Batum; (*b*) Description of Sukum Kaleh.

There are other routes by which the Caucasus could be approached from the Mediterranean and the Persian Gulf, namely, from Iskandarun to Tiflis *viâ* Marash, Kharput, Mush, Erzeroom, and Kars, 874 miles—Appendix (*m*); from Iskandarun to Tiflis *viâ* Diarbeker, Mush, Erzeroom, and Kars, 971 miles—Appendix (*n*); and from Baghdad to Tiflis *viâ* Mosul, Bitlis, Erzeroom, and Kars, 910 miles—Appendix (*o*); but these are in no way preferable to the roads I propose should be adopted.

The third operation would be an attack on the Russians in Turkistan. This would simply be reversing the operation I have sketched in the first chapter, in considering a possible Russian advance from Samarkand on Kabul.

The Russian force in Turkistan could not number more than 60,000 men under the above circumstances; and therefore, I think, that if 50,000 British Troops were sent, it would be quite sufficient, as they would be aided by the Afghans and by the Uzbaks, who would, it may be supposed, rise in a body. The force destined for such an operation would advance in four divisions,—one by the Kuram route, Logar, Maidan, and Bamian; another by the Khost route, Logar, Maidan and Bamian; a third by the Dawar route, Ghazni, Behsud, and Chehlburj; and a fourth by the Gomal route as above.

Every effort would be made to raise corps of Afghans, Hazaras, and Uzbaks, and arrangements would be made to light up insurrection among the Turkomans and in Khiva, Bokhara, and Khokand simultaneously, and the Chinese would be instigated to advance at the same time from Kashgar and Kuldja.

The result of these measures, if skilfully carried out, could hardly fail to cause the Russians to retire along their whole line; and if they were carefully combined with the operations in Europe and the Caucasus, there can be little doubt that Russia would be crippled to a frightful extent.

I must say I think that the best course we could pursue would be to take the initiative and attack Russia in this manner, and the sooner it is done the sooner will the Central Asian question be set at rest, for there can be no real end to it till this is done.

If Germany will not join such a coalition, we should be left with only Austria and Turkey as allies against France and Russia.

In this case France with her 1,567,000 men, being free from fear of attack from Germany, might be tempted to invade England, who would have only some 500,000 or less available. This would be very serious for us, especially as France could probably spare enough men to seize Egypt; but even though her army is so much more numerous than ours, I should very much doubt its being in the power of France to invade England successfully, especially if she was threatened by Austria on the east.

If Austria attacked France, it would make it easier for England to repel the attack of the latter; but it would make it more difficult for the Turks to withstand the attack of Russia.

The forces on either side, in the event of such alliances being formed, would be—

		Men.	
Austria	...	1,065,000	Total 2,115,000 men.
Turkey	...	850,000	
England	...	500,000	
India	...	300,000	
Russia	...	2,087,000	Total 3,654,000 men.
France	...	1,567,000	

I think that if France attacked England, endeavoured to seize Egypt, and generally threatened the British possessions in the Mediterranean, it would be about as much as she could manage. She could never be quite sure of Germany, and would have to keep so many men ready to meet that Power that it is improbable she could spare any force for offensive operations against Austria.

It would therefore come to this, that the three other Powers—Austria, India, and Turkey—would have to face Russia. Their united forces would amount to 2,115,000 men, while those of Russia are only 2,087,000 men.

To attack Turkey aided by Austria, Russia would have to put into the field very much larger forces than she did in the last war. In this she had 313,000 men in the field in European Turkey and 123,000 in Asiatic Turkey. But to meet Austria and Turkey and India she would require—

		Men.	
On her German frontier	... ...	300,000	
Internal defence	... ...	500,000	
Austrian frontier	... ...	400,000	
European Turkish frontier	... ..	300,000	
Caucasus and Asiatic Turkish frontier	...	200,000	
Turkistan and Siberia	... ...	100,000	if threatened from India.
Total	...	1,800,000	

The allies could bring against her something as follows :—

Austria, after deducting an army to threaten France and for her own internal defence, not more than 300,000 men ; Turkey, 700,000 men ; India, 150,000 men ; total, 1,150,000 men. In this case the allies would be so nearly equal to ther enemy that it would not do to disseminate their forces too much ; and I think the plan of operation most likely to cripple Russia would be for Austria and Turkey so to dispose their forces in Europe that Russia could not advance to the attack of either without exposing her flank to the other and to act generally on the defensive on the left of the theatre of war.

In the centre I would suggest an attack on the Caucasus with—

100,000 Austrians,
200,000 Turks,

landed on the east coast of the Black Sea, and 50,000 Anglo-Indian troops aided by 60,000 Persians or Circassians advancing from Erzeroom and the Persian Gulf.

Russia could hardly reinforce her army in the Caucasus, as, if she did, she would denude her European frontier, and Austria and Turkey would at once take the offensive in this direction. With 100,000 Russians in Turkistan, we could not at first spare more than 50,000 men from India ; but if the operations of the allies were successful in the Caucasus, the Russian Army in Turkistan would almost certainly be reduced , then an attempt might be made from India to raise the whole of Turkistan against them by advancing an army of 50,000 from Kabul.

This campaign would certainly not be so sure of a successful issue as that which I have outlined before. Very much would depend on the harmony and generalship of the allies ; but I think that if they persisted in it long enough, even this alliance should be sufficient to secure to us what should be the great aim of England to dive Russia out of the Caucasus and Turkistan.

But in addition to squaring Germany as above, Russia might, by some means I cannot think of, also arrange for the neutrality of Austria, while she also gained the alliance of France against England. In this case, to which I call paticular attention, as it is one which is very likely to be attempted by Russia, England would be prevented aiding India or Turkey by having to provide for her own defence and that of Egypt and her communications with India against France, and Russia would only have to fight Turkey single-handed and attack India.

In such a case I apprehend that the following would be approximately the distribution of the Russian forces :—

			Men.	Guns.
On the German frontier	...	...	200,000	1,600
„ Austrian „	...	...	150,000	450
Turkistan and Siberia	...	...	60,000	180
Internal police	...	...	500,000	1,500
Caucasus and Asiatic frontier	...	...	200,000	600
Invasion of Turkey	...	...	700,000	1,500
„ India	...	...	200,000	600
	Total	...	2,010,000	5,430

If Russia could attack Turkey with 700,000 men and threaten India with 200,000, there would be considerable fear of her being successful. The Turks could not withstand the attack of such a force, and certainly India could not send a man to their aid.

Having conquered Turkey, gained ports in the Mediterranean and Persian Gulf, annexed as much of Turkish territory, and absorbed as many of her people as may be necessary, Russia would then be free to turn her whole attention to India and invade it at her leisure.

If England was paralyzed by France, Turkey conquered, India would have a very hard struggle to maintain herself. Then would come to pass one of the operations I have outlined in Chapter V ; and it is certain that if the Russians attacked India with 200,000 men, we must meet her, as I have said, there with at least 250,000 men and keep at least 200,000 men for the internal defence of India.

I will now sum up this part of my subject by saying, if we conclude a quadruple alliance with Germany, Austria, and Turkey, Russia and France will never attack either of the Allied Powers, and they will have the power, if they will only act offensively, and take the initiative, of completely crippling Russia and France and thus permanently securing the peace of the world for a long time, or at least till fresh interests and ideas cause fresh combinations to become necessary.

If we are only able to secure Austria and Turkey as allies against France, we may still cripple Russia most seriously ; but nothing like to the same extent as stated in the other combination I propose ; and France, even though she may be foiled in her attack on England, will still remain the disturbing element in European affairs she is now. On the other hand, it is quite possible that Russia and France may win in this contest, and this will leave us and our allies less fitted to meet another war.

If only England and Turkey have to meet Russia and France, the chances are we shall be beaten all along the line. We may make a good fight ; but the odds will be very much against us, and the war may end by Turkey being finally conquered, England very much subdued, and India losing her Afghan frontier for ever.

In conclusion, I will say this, that everyone I have asked seems to say we cannot conclude the quadruple alliance now, whatever may have been the case ,formerly though all admit its value to us. I suppose, therefore, I must sorrowfully admit this ; but this does not in the least shake me in my opinion as to the vital necessity of our straining every nerve to secure it. I believe in it alone lies the least chance of the peace of the world and the safety of India.

EPILOGUE.

In the foregoing pages I have tried to point out, as shortly as the vastness of the subject will allow, what I, and probably at this time the majority of Englishmen who have any knowledge of the subject, believe to be a great danger hanging over our Indian Empire, and consequently—for the two are inseparable—the honour of England. My aim has been to state what I believe to be "the truth, the whole truth, and nothing but the truth."

If there should be any at this stage of Russian aggression who still refuse to believe, and who would still resort to the favorite device of the "masterly inactionists," of calling every one who raised a note of warning Russophobists, I can expect no better fate at their hands. I suppose they will say I have exaggerated the danger, and have proposed measures so grandiose that no Ministry would ever contemplate putting them in hand.

As to my having exaggerated the danger, it is very easy to make such an accusation; but I protest against its being made, unless it is backed up by some arguments which will really cut away the ground from under my feet. The whole question really lies in a nutshell. Has Russia the wish and the means to attack us in India, and is such an undertaking a feasible operation of war? As to the wish, I think the whole history of her advance eastwards for the last hundred years sufficiently proves this, at least to those who are open to conviction. I have not troubled my readers with any sketch of this advance, as there is no necessity to repeat what can be found in a hundred different books, articles, and letters.

As to the means, I have shown in the first chapter what these are, and in the same chapter I have sketched without bias what would be the course of any further unopposed advance by Russian troops; while in the appendix will be found the grounds on which I base the belief that an advance on India is a feasible operation of war. By these proofs (or others more trustworthy) alone can my statement be refuted. Mere assertion and hiding one's head in the sand is not proof; and I sincerely hope the English people will demand from those who, even at this eleventh hour, pooh-pooh all action, nothing less than a clear and detailed refutation of my arguments.

From those, who even now, do not believe, I only ask further honest and searching investigation of the subject. To them I say, "not only I, but the great "majority of those who have made the subject their study, believe there *is* great "danger. You perhaps do not; but unless you think us all absolute fools and "knaves, let the fact that we do, induce you to make a more thorough and more "earnest study of it than you have yet done. If the result of your labor is "to confirm your belief, let us, in the name of patriotism, hear your views backed "up by unanswerable arguments. If you can prove that I am wrong, I shall "be the first to acknowledge my error, and to welcome your reassuring con- "clusions; but in Heaven's name let us have nothing but real proofs."

As to the measures I propose being on too grand a scale for the acquiescence of an English Ministry, I can only say that if I am right as to the danger, it will not be in the power of any English Ministry to refuse to carry out, if not the exact measures I propose, other measures at least as great and expensive. If Russia does advance further, she will have to be met with adequate measures and in adequate force. An English Ministry may try to put off the evil day by timid procrastination and by tinkering; but, fortified by the experience of the past, and the prescience which a study of war in general, and this question in particular, gives, I prophesy they will fail: and just in so much as they neglect to face the danger adequately, so far, need they bring further danger and disaster on their country.

I allow that I have proposed a very extensive programme. I have done so because the peril is very great, and I am convinced that nothing short of it will meet the case; at the same time I am not so foolish as to be wedded to each detail of my plan of action. All I ask is, that enough should be done, and done in time.

With these few words by way of epilogue, I close; but in doing so I make one last appeal to all Englishmen who have followed me so far, and to do all that in them lies, to rouse the English nation to a just appreciation of the crisis which is coming on us. If this can be done, there need be no further fear or doubt.

There is, I think, only one point to which I have not alluded, namely, the possibility of our coming to some agreement with Russia. Is such a thing possible? If so, I am sure most Englishmen would hail its conclusion with gladness. Of course if Her Majesty's Government opened communications with the Imperial Government to the effect that, desirous of continuing friendly relations, they wished to see if there was no *modus vivendi* between the two Powers, the Russian Government would reply that to remain on good terms with the British was and always had been the main aim of their existence, and they would be ready to *promise* anything to secure that friendship.

But Russian promises are, I am afraid, at this moment not a marketable commodity. What we want is to be let alone. A mere promise from Russia to sin no more is incontestably not worth the breath expended in uttering it: we must have some guarantee, that we shall be let alone.

The only guarantee that would be of the smallest use to us would be the absolute withdrawal of the Russians from the east coast of the Caspian below the Yaman Airakti Bay. If the Russians would dot his, we might consider how far we could meet their wishes.

Russia's most absorbing wish I understand to be a port in the Mediterranean; but it is impossible to think how she can get this without the concurrence of Turkey; and as that Power cannot agree without losing territory, I don't see how it can be accomplished.

Myself I don't see what advantage to the commerce of Russia the possession of a port in the Mediterranean would be. I don't see even how *Russian trade* would be benefited by her possession of Constantinople, unless she got all the country intervening between Odessa and that place in addition.

The fact really is, that Russia does not want a port for purely commercial purposes, but for aggressive purposes. During peace her vessels have the freest access to the Mediterranean; but during war, Russia can be confined to the

Black Sea. If she had Constantinople and the Dardanelles, or some other port on the Mediterranean, she could gradually assemble a fleet there that might be very useful to her, because it could act on the sea communications between India and England and threaten the Suez Canal.

So that if she got a port on the Mediterranean, we should gain nothing thereby. If she is in a position to put pressure on us now, she would be in a better position to do so then, and most assuredly she would use it. She may give up the line of the Atak to gain a port in the Mediterranean; but depend upon it, that the idea that she would be so grateful to us for helping her to it that she would never again worry us on the Indian frontier, is altogether a delusion.

I therefore regret to say I can see no way of coming to a satisfactory understanding with Russia by diplomatic means. It is certain that we do not want war and will not provoke it; but it is also certain that we must fight her if she takes one step more towards India; and I solemnly assert my belief that there can never be a real settlement of the Russo-Indian question *till Russia is driven out of the Caucasus and Turkistan.*

C. M. MACGREGOR, *Major-General,*

Quarter Master General in India.

APPENDICES.

Appendix A.

Krasnovodsk.

Krasnovodsk possesses by far the finest natural harbour on the east coast of the Caspian, as it is perfectly safe at all times and with a depth of water of from 22 to 26 feet.—(*Colonel Baker.*)

The harbour is easily accessible, and possesses a natural breakwater in a tongue of land lying to the west of the anchorage. Recent soundings near the northern shore of the bay show a depth varying from 7 to 18 feet.—(*Condie Stephen.*)

The harbour is well sheltered on all sides by rising ground, and has a depth which allows of heavily laden ships of deep draught to anchor close in shore.—(*O'Donovan.*)

The presence of a long spit of land several miles in length, lying west of the anchorage and running in a south-easterly direction, renders it a perfectly safe harbour at all times.—(*Lovett.*) It is protected by a narrow sandy spit of some 20 miles in length. There is 9 to 10 feet of water alongside the pier, and a general depth over the anchorage of 14 to 22 feet.—(*I. B., H. G.*)

To provide accommodation for the numerous ships that now frequent the port, two wooden piers have been provided standing about 3½ feet above the water-level, as in the Caspian there is no tide. These run out into the bay about 500 feet each or thereabouts. The west pier is broad and has two lines of 15-inch gauge tramway laid down. These trams extend to the commissariat blocks.—(*Lovett.*) Mr. Condie Stephen says that these two piers are about 300 × 25 feet and 200 × 20 feet respectively. A correspondent of the *Civil and Military Gazette* says that one pier is 600 feet long, being built partly of masonry and partly on piles, and the other to the west of it is even broader and longer.

Krasnovodsk as a base and point for the concentration of troops has a serious drawback, *viz.*, the entire want of water for drinking purposes. This want has been more than partially rectified by the establishment of condensing machines, one on board an old steamer and two in sheds on shore. The water thus furnished is quite adequate for the ordinary requirements of the present garrison and population ; but the deficiency would probably make itself felt in the event of Krasnovodsk becoming the base of considerable military operations.—(*Condie Stephen.*)

C. M. M.

Appendix B.

Mikhailovsk.

Mikhailovsk is situated on a Gulf of the Krasnovodsk Bay, lying nearly due east of the island of Cheleken. It is the base of the railway (at present) running as far as Kizil Arvat. It is asserted that there is good anchorage for ships near the shore; but the navigation of the channel between Cheleken and the main land is so intricate and shallow, that in practice ships must anchor three miles from the shore. The port is therefore but little used as a direct line of communication from the west coast of the Caspian, and both men and goods destined for the Akhal *oasis* are first landed at Krasnovodsk and then transhipped across the bay in vessels specially designed for this purpose.—(*Trotter.*) There are at present only two tugs, each dragging three barges, in use between Krasnovodsk and Mikhailovsk. Each of these, including embarking and disembarking, could transport in 24 hours half a battalion of infantry and two *sotnias* of cavalry. The number of these barges might be increased, and a few steamers of light draught might be procured from the mouth of the Volga; but the intricacies of the channel are such that pilots of experience could not be obtained in sufficient numbers to allow of any considerable addition being made to the number of barges.—(*Condie Stephen.*)

The work of landing troops and stores is facilitated by the construction of two piers about 160 yards long with a 15-inch gauge tramway laid down to connect them with the Commissariat store-houses. These piers are about 3 feet above the level of the water.—(*I. B., H. G.*)

C. M. M.

Appendix C.

CHIKISHLAR.

Chikishlar is a roadstead extremely shallow and open to every wind. At a distance of two miles from the shore the water is only two feet deep, and it is unaffected by tide. Vessels of from two to three hundred tons cannot approach within three miles of the shore. The work of landing troops and stores is consequently both tedious and difficult. Everything has to be transhipped into Turkoman lighters, which are poled or pushed by men in the water through the sand to the head of the pier. This jetty was intended to lessen the difficulty of landing stores; but it is too short to be of any service really. It is simply a sandbank projecting about 200 yards into the sea; it was formerly a landing place of the Turkomans, and the Russians raised the bank and added a wooden jetty to it about 150 yards in length.—(*I. B., H. G.*)

To give an idea of the extreme difficulty of landing at the pier and the very gentle slope of the shore, bathers looked at from the shore when in water only up to their arm-pits appear to be quite out on the horizon. The depth of water, however, varies according to the direction the wind is blowing from, because with wind in a particular quarter the water is forced inland. The difficulties of landing are, moreover, increased by dense fogs which constantly occur: these sometimes last for days together. Violent storms, too, called 'Tenkis,' come up with great suddenness from the westward almost without warning. The force of the storms is excessive, and all vessels caught in one on a lee shore are certain to go to pieces. These tempests usually last from one to five hours. The season that both fogs and storms are most frequent is the months of February and March.—(*O'Donovan.*)

There is only one pier 500 feet long with a tramway leading to the commissariat store sheds on the beach. The shipping is obliged to lie out from the shore about three miles. In windy weather the roadstead is useless.

With steam launches, rafts, and boats it would be possible to land about 800 men and 300 horses in the day without having recourse to any extraordinary means beyond that which at the present time can be furnished by the resources of the Caspian.

An advanced force of 1,200 cavalry, 4,000 infantry, and 18 mountain guns could be conveyed to, and landed at, Chikishlar in three to four days. The ships required to convey this force would amount to 14, taking the usual sized steamer on the Caspian. That is to say, the cavalry would require four ships, the infantry eight, and the artillery two. In making this estimate it may be stated that the ship *Alexander Gendie*, belonging to the 'Mercury Caucasus Company,' has on one occasion carried 700 horses from Petrovski to Krasnovodsk and 1,200 men on another. The voyage from Petrovski to Chikishlar can be made in about 48 hours. It is not probable that a force would now be concentrated at Chikishlar owing principally to the scarcity and bad quality of the water and unhealthy climate, but would, as landed, be pushed up in detachments to some given and selected point on the Atreck.—(*Lovett.*)

On the 19th of June 1879, a storm from the west blew the sea over the lower part of the Russian camp then formed, and damaged the pier and destroyed a quantity of forage. Four days later another tempest inundated the camp and compelled a number of transports with horses on board to put to sea.

The horses on shore were thus left without water or forage for two days and suffered considerably. Great difficulty was experienced in supplying the troops with water. Owing to the infiltration of saline matter, the wells hardly remained sweet for 24 hours, and the troops were constantly employed in digging fresh ones. It was, however, found that water obtained from pipes sunk deep in the sand remained fresh, and pipes for this purpose were eventually obtained.

In 1879 about eight battalions of infantry, two batteries of artillery, and three regiments of cavalry were landed at Chikishlar to complete the numbers already there for the expedition against the Tekkes in addition to all the stores, forage, &c.—(*I. B., H. G.*)

Chikishlar appears to have some slight advantages as a port over most of the other localities which might have been selected on this part of the coasts, from the fact that the Attrek current has so far swept away the sand from its neighbourhood that the water is rather deeper here than elsewhere. The advantages thus gained are, however, small, and the landing place is a bad one, even for a port on the east coast of the Caspian. Stores and troops have to be punted or dragged ashore from a distance of three miles in Turkoman lighters. The pier is too narrow and short to be of much service. It is constructed of sand ill-supported by wooden posts at a cost of 19,000 *roubles* (about £1,900).—(*Trotter.*)

C. M. M.

Appendix D.

Route from Chikishlar to Bami.

Territory.	Authority.	Halting places.	Miles. Stage.	Miles. Total.	Description of the route.
Trans-Caspia.	Marvin (from Russian sources).	Bevun Bashi ...	20	20	First four miles shell sand, then salines, then clay soil; hard in summer; soft in winter. There are 80 wells here, many with unpleasant water. There is a Russian fort here, five miles from the Attrek.
		Delili ...	$14\frac{1}{8}$	$34\frac{1}{8}$	Road good, with occasional nullahs to be crossed; but these are easily passed. A lake here, two miles in circumference; water brackish and purges. A marsh separates it from the Attrek.
		Gudri Olum ...	$10\frac{1}{3}$	$44\frac{1}{3}$	Road good with many bends to avoid chasm. Here it touches Attrek river; here 18 feet wide; banks six feet high. Land irrigated and cultivated. A little forage. Wood and grass on Persian bank.
		Bayat Hadji Olum	$19\frac{1}{3}$	$63\frac{5}{8}$	Road good. Forage along it, but none at halting place itself. Attrek bed here half a mile wide; banks 100 feet high; many side nullahs. Water bad. Desert on both sides of river. Redoubt here usually held by two companies.
		Yagli Olum ...	$13\frac{1}{3}$	$77\frac{1}{8}$	Road good in summer, with nullahs across it, which do not impede troops. No forage the whole way. Water from river.
		Takendji Olum ...	$13\frac{3}{8}$	91	Road in three places crossed by nullahs, but marching is not difficult. No forage. River banks steep.
		Tchat ...	16	107	Road good. No forage in summer. Abundant grass, but heavy rains, and roads almost impassable in winter. Fort here, armed with eight guns, garrisoned by a battalion, and 135 feet above the Caspian. Sumbar and Attrek here unite; banks of both very high. Bed of latter 200 to 300 yards wide, but river itself only 20 feet wide and 10 feet deep in April. Ground all round Tchat is clay, and full of cracks and holes.
		Khur Olum ...	$14\frac{1}{3}$	$121\frac{1}{3}$	Road good. Columns can advance on broad front for first 11 miles, after that hillocks and chasms force it to narrow its front. No forage. Water (good) from Sumbar.
		Duz Olum ...	$17\frac{1}{3}$	$138\frac{2}{3}$	For first eight miles troops can advance on a broad front, though chasms abound; but they can be avoided by turning to the left at the foot of Khur Olum hill After that the front must be narrowed. No forage along the road. Duz Olum is at the fork of the Sumbar and Chandir rivers, and is protected on both sides by their deeply cut beds. It is 850 feet above the sea, and the climate is good. Water tolerable. Russian fort and garrison here to protect the bridge over the Sumbar.
		Beg Tepe ...	$12\frac{2}{3}$	$151\frac{1}{3}$	Six hours. Road across river and through hilly region. Water at Beg Tepe clear and pleasant.

Route from Chikishlar to Bami—contd.

Territory.	Authority.	Halting places.	Miles.		Description of the route.
			Stage.	Total.	
Trans-Caspia.	Marvin (from Russian sources).	Tarsakan ...	7⅝	159⅛	Heavy road for infantry. Six and a half hours. Tarsakan is an important place, as it commands the source of the Sumbar.
		Margiz ...	17	176⅛	Waterless road and very dusty in summer. Margiz is a small plateau surrounded with trees with a few wells with saline water.
		Khwaja Kala ...	12⅞	139	Five hours. Road broken, but could easily be made excellent. Country billy. There is an alternative road from Tarsakan to Khwaja Kala by Kara Kala, 30⅝ miles long. Kara Kala has numerous wells. Water bad. Khwaja Kala is 2,100 feet above the sea in a beautiful valley. Water good and place healthy.
		Bendesen ...	13⅛	202⅛	Road between two parallel ranges of Kopet Dagh. Clay soil and plenty of water.
		Bami ...	13½	215⅝	At eight miles road crosses Kozlinski or Bendesen pass of Kopet Dagh (5,000 feet). Very difficult and steep. Requires improving (1879) for passage of vehicles. Seventeen hours' ride for cavalry. Bami is two miles from the mouth of the pass and contained (1879) 500 kibitkas. Water abundant.

C. M. M.

Appendix E.

Route from Kizil Arvat to Sarakhs.

Territory.	Authority.	Halting places.	Miles.		Description of the route.
			Stage.	Total.	
Trans-Caspia.	Grodekoff (campaign of 1880-81).	Kodjh ...	21⅝	21⅝	Road level. Water from a stream. Some cultivation.
		Bami ...	13⅞	35½	Pass Zan at 5⅞ miles, Djengi at 8, Kizin Charhm at 10⅞: all watered by rivulets and with cultivation. A good deal of cultivation round Bami.
		Beurma ...	7⅝	43⅛	A large rivulet runs through Beurma. Road to it level, with one nullah to be crossed just before Beurma; but it is not difficult.
		Archman ...	16⅞	60	No water on the road.
		Durum ...	17	77	Pass Suncha at 8⅞, Begerden at 14 miles Field and cultivation begin at Suncha and extend to Askabad. Road level.
		Kalata ...	13⅜	90⅜	Pass Kariz-Verdi-Khan at 10 miles.
		Samurskoe ...	14	104⅜	Also called Yezan-Batir-Kala. Two forts, Kafir Kala and Isha Bashi, are passed on the way. These were all destroyed by the Russians in 1880-81.
		Yangi Kala ...	8⅛	112½	A village close to Geok Tepe.

Route from Kizil Arvat to Sarakhs—contd.

Territory.	Authority.	Halting places.	Miles. Stage.	Miles. Total.	Description of the route.
Trans-Caspia.	Grodekoff (campaign of 1880-81).	Bazmein ...	16⅝	129⅛	Pass the villages of Sher Kala, Kala-i-Adjar, Kordojov, and Bab-Arab.
		Askabad ...	10½	139⅝	Pass villages of Salik-Kala, Khari-Kala, Gekche Mirava, and Geshi. Askabad has a large Russian garrison of all arms.
		Gavars ...	22⅛	162⅛	For the first 8 miles to Annau road is level. Annau is a village of 200 tents with a fort on a stream. Thence road over smooth slope to 11¾ miles, where sand-hills are crossed. There are three forts at Gyaurs, two only being inhabited. Water from a stream.
		Baba Durmaz ...	25	187⅛	Ground slightly undulating, with very gradual slopes. Baba Durmaz is the present Russian frontier post, but is deserted. Water from a stream and slightly brackish.
		Lutfabad ...	14½	201⅝	Road over plain covered with bushes, interspersed with, from sixth mile, mounds and ruins of forts. At six miles is the fort of Artik; thence cultivation to Lutfabad; canals unbridged. Lutfabad stands in dense gardens, and is a walled town with a bazaar. Provisions and forage plentiful.
		Kahka ...	18⅝	220¼	Through a fertile and highly cultivated country, watered by the Rudkhan and densely populated. Irrigation canals unbridged. Water from a river at Kahka, which has a fort containing 600 houses.
		Khwaja Med ...	12⅞	233⅛	Road first over a low spur, then level. A settlement of 20 families. Water ceases to flow at about 600 yards from it. It lies low. A mile off are the ruins of Sermochit, visible from afar.
	Lessar.	Dushak ...	14	247⅛	Country absolutely level and open. Dushak and Chardeh form four forts. Water from the Chardeh stream, 14′ wide 2′ or 3′ deep. Banks 14′ high, but shelving. It is easily crossed.
		Mehna ...	26	273⅛	No water on the road. Marut is 12 miles to the south. Ground level, but destitute of vegetation. Cultivation begins three miles from Mehna, and extends three miles on other side of it. Forts of Mehna and Emrali contain 250 houses. Water from Mehna stream, which is of same size as Chardeh.
		Chacha ...	16	289⅛	Chacha is a ruined fort with 30 families living near it, occupied in agriculture. Water from Chacha rivulet, same size as Chardeh.
		Sarakhs ...	33½	323⅛	Road level. At 13¾ miles a reservoir nearly filled up with sand. From 20th to 24th mile road through sand hummocks seven feet high. Sarakhs is a large fortress. Supplies and forage abundant. Water from Hari Rud and canals.

C. M. M.

Appendix F.

Route from Sarakhs to Herat.

Territory.	Authority.	Halting places.	Miles.		Description of the route.
			Stage.	Total.	
Afghanistan.	Lessar.	Din Kala ...	9⅓	9⅓	Road at first south-east, then at 1,000 yards from old Sarakhs; turns abruptly south and soon crosses the Hari Rud by a ford up to a horse's belly. River in four branches; bottom gravelly; banks low. There is a fort being built here by the Merv Turkomans. Thence road along large canals. Country level. Soil sandy clay.
		Naurozabad ...	15	24⅓	Road leaves canal to right and crosses a plain 3⅓ miles to Hassan Kala; thence crosses range of gently sloping hills to Naurozabad. Descents along road to Hari Rud are easy. Road fit for wheeled traffic.
		Adam Yolan ...	27	51⅓	For 6⅔ miles to hill of Shir Tepe road along Hari Rud; then it turns to south-east. At 19 miles pass a ruined karez with water in it still. There are two wells at Adam Yolan in an elliptical cavity between hills. Water very good. Wells 14 feet deep; water at 10 feet from surface. Forage all round.
		Agar Chashma ...	8⅓	59⅔	A spring with beautiful fresh water; 500 yards up the valley is a second now filled up. Forage abundant.
		Kungrueli Rabat ...	5⅔	65⅓	Water somewhat brackish, but fit for drinking, 17 feet below surface.
		Kizil Bulak ...	26	91⅓	A rich spring with fresh water, 500 yards to side of the road in a defile leading to the Hari Rud.
		Khombon ...	24	115⅓	At 13⅔ miles the road crosses the bitter Shar Yub rivulet, thence five miles over a plain to a rabut at the foot of the pass over the Barkhut mountains. From Naurozabad to this pass the road is perfectly easy and alternately through level and undulating country. The pass is 3,100 feet above the sea, and 900 above the surrounding country. Road even now fit for wheels, along defile cut by Shar Yub. At Khombon, half-way down the pass on the south side, is a spring of fresh water.
		Kusan ...	30	145⅓	Road descends for four miles, then over level ground. Kusan is the first Afghan post.
		Herat ...	64	209⅓	

C. M. M.

Appendix G.

Route from Sharifabad to Herat.

Territory.	Authority.	Halting places.	Miles. Stage.	Miles. Total.	Description of the Route.
Persia.	Bellew.	Turukh ...	19	19	Route north-east and north over rich pasture downs by a good military road. At 14 miles cross the stream of Darud which flows east over a wide boulder-strewn bed; then through cultivated pasture lands to Turukh, which is 5 miles from Mushad. Water good from a watercourse; supplies scanty.
		Sangbast ...	17½	36½	South-east, 6½ hours. Road level for 6 miles, then undulating. Soil alluvial with granite and quartz. Rejoin the high road in half a mile, where are the ruins of a serai and mosque. Pass remains of bridge on left over dry bed of stream. At 1½ miles is a small fort with blue domes in it off right. At 2½ miles mud ruins off left. At 5½ miles ruined well on right; here rocky range approaches the road. At 6½ miles cross low ridge, high precipitous rocks on right, a steep conical rock off left with watch-tower. At 8½ miles steep descent into valley with dry bed of stream. Presently is a cistern with indifferent water on right. Hence to 13 miles cross four valleys with dry river beds. At 14 miles another dry bed and ruined mill off left. At 16¾ miles descend, cross a brackish stream and marsh, then a steep ascent to high ground, on which is fortified village of Sangbast. A large brick serai attached. Water brackish in stream; good in Kants; supplies scarce.
	Taylor, Clerk, Hardy.	Feriman ...	19	55½	South-east, 7¾ hours. Road level at extremities, very undulating in the middle. Soil alluvial. Go round the low hills on left, with mud watch-tower, and descend into broad dry bed of river, along which the road runs for some distance, turning to the right at 3rd mile. At 7 miles, ruins of fort and village in plain on left. At 8¼ miles enter defile among low hills and cross a ridge. Hence to 12 miles several deep valleys and ravines. At 11 miles defile between rocky bluffs on left; descend into plains with several towers of refuge. Encamp south-east of the village. Water good from a stream. Supplies procurable. Large flocks of sheep.
		Burdu ...	24	79½	South-east, 10½ hours. Road undulating, soil alluvial and sometimes gravelly. Pass through ploughed fields much cut up by irrigation. At 6 miles deep, dry bed of river. At 7 miles, a small mud fort in plain off left. At 8 miles, rocky hills on right. Presently dry bed of stream and a watch-tower off right in the plain. At 9 miles, another watch-tower on right. By 9½ miles,

Route from Sharifabad to Herat—contd.

Territory.	Authority.	Halting places.	Miles. Stage.	Miles. Total.	Description of the route.
Persia.	Taylor, Clerk, Hardy.				a small stream, with extensive irrigation on left. At 10 miles, village of Kalandarabad; on emerging from garden walls cross broad, dry bed of river. At 12 miles kanats and very rough and stony dry bed of river, 60 yards broad. At 14 miles is a road to Shahr-i-Nao to the right front. At 15 miles, a small spring amid rushes on right. At 16 miles a deep ravine; a little further a deep valley with small stream. Hence to Burdu, a succession of deep ascents and descents. Water good from stream running round west and north of village. Supplies scarce, except sheep.
		Mahmudabad ...	19	98½	Eight and quarter hours. Road tolerable and undulating. Soil alluvial, but stony in beds of rivers. At 1½ miles is a ruined fort on left. At 3½ miles, steep descent and dry bed of river. At 7½ miles, dry bed of river; thence ascent high ground, on which stands the village of Abdulabad, amidst fields and gardens. At 7½ miles, fine clear stream and village. At 16 miles, pass through extensive ruins of Lingar, extending for miles. At 18 miles, high-domed cistern of brick on left. Cross stream and large brick ruin of Imamzada. At 18½ miles, modern village and fort of Lingar. Descend into green hollow, on banks of stony river. Mahmudabad is on the high bank, quarter of a mile off. Gum in any quantity. Water good and abundant. Supplies scarce.
		Turbat-i-Shekh Jam	16	114½	South-east, 4½ hours. Road good; soil alluvial. At 1 mile a ruined fort on right (probably the limit of Lingar). At 3½ miles road passes through defile, and at 5½ miles emerges into the plain, whence are visible the minarets of the tomb of Shekh Ahmed Jan. At 13 miles trees and gardens of Turbat. Water good and plentiful. Supplies procurable.
		Karez ...	30	144½	South-east, 12½ hours. Road level and good; soil alluvial. Left the garden; passing on the right the village with good walls, gate and wet ditch, a level plain with fine pasture. At 1½ miles, an Imamzada with wall off left. A little beyond cross twice a deep stream, muddy and difficult. At 10 miles, a cistern of water on left. From 14th to 15th mile are undulations and two small dry beds of streams. At 17 miles, ruined brick serai of Abbasabad on right, with ruins of fort, &c., on high ground near it. Cross the dry bed of a small stream and ascend gradually. At 22 miles cross broad, dry bed of the river of

Route from Sharifabad to Herat—contd.

Territory.	Authority.	Halting places.	Miles. Stage.	Miles. Total.	Description of the route.
Persia.	Taylor, Clerk, Hardy.				Mohsinabad (village off left). At 23 miles cross ridge of low hills. At 24 miles cross similar ridge. At 29½ miles large ruined brick serai, and ruined citadel on mound; all on right: cross small stream of brackish water, and arrive at the little walled village of Karez on right. Water brackish, not bad for cooking and cattle, but unpleasant to man. Supplies none.
		Kohsan ...	21	165½	East-by-south, 9 hours. Road level and good; soil alluvial. Pass through well-irrigated cultivation. At 4 miles is a ruined fort off right. At 5½ miles, mud ruins and remains of an arch on right. At 8 miles, ruins of fine brick serai on right. At 15 miles high mound, on which is ruined fort off "Kafar Kala"; serai opposite. At 19 miles, cross the river, which is quite dry here At 20 miles, walled enclosures, ruins and remains of gardens. Pass through the village and cross small stream. Kohsan has a ruined wall with towers and encloses a great space. Citadel is surrounded with a wet ditch. Water good and plentiful. Supplies procurable.
		Ghorian ...	25	190½	South-east, 11 hours. Road generally level, little undulating midway, good, barring the water-courses towards the end; soil alluvial. For 10 minutes along lanes between garden walls. At 2½ miles low hills of gravel on left, and a river below on right. At 5½ miles ruined brick serai on right and ruined bridge, "Sir-i-pul, over Hari Rud; small watch-tower on left. At 9 miles, another tower; descend into dry bed of torrent. At 13 miles a fine brick serai in ruins on left. At 13½ miles village of Shahbash on right. At 15 miles road turns off. (That direct to Herat *viâ* Rasanek and Shakaban south-west by east.) At 17 miles cross small stream and ½ mile further cross Hari Rud, 3 feet deep. At 18 miles, village of Janjisowar on left. Large ruined serai and other buildings on right. At 19 miles ruins on left, and Rasanek 2 miles off left. At 20 miles, small fort on left. At 21 miles, extensive ruins of ancient Ghorian walls, towers, &c., cover the plain for miles; splendid irrigation all round. A stream of good water close to the tower. Supplies plentiful.
		Zindehjan ...	13	203½	East-by-north, 5¾ hours. Road level and good. Soil alluvial, with a little gravel. Wind for some distance between garden walls. At 2½ miles, ice-house on left. At 7 miles a small grove of willows on stream off left. At 10 miles the large village of Binderabad among

Route from Sharifabad to Herat—concld.

Territory.	Authority.	Halting places.	Miles. Stage.	Miles. Total.	Description of the route.
Afghanistan.	Taylor, Clerk, Hardy.				gardens and ruins 2 miles off left, on the highest bank of the Hari Rud. Hence abundant cultivations both sides. At 11½ miles curious ruins with abrabesques among trees on right; cross a small stream and ruined fort on right at 12th mile. Here road enters lanes between ruins and walls. Water good. Supplies procurable.
		Ab-i-Jalil ...	15	218½	East-by-north, 4½ hours. Road at first level; near the river undulating; then good again. Water abundant and excellent. Supplies scarce. At 1¼ miles emerge from garden walls. At 3 miles a fine stream runs along left of road for some distance; a little further a ruined fort on the left. At 7 miles another road from Zindehjan comes in from the left rear. Hence to river, very undulating and cut up by ravines and torrents. At 8½ miles cross Hari Rud, rapid and 2 feet deep; ascent gradually to village of Sangbast (9 miles) on the left. At 10 miles small walled village and ruined fort off left. At 11 miles the large village of Yadgah, with a broad stream running through it. Here the mountains on the right terminate, turning off south. Much irrigation. At 11½ miles a small fort on the left.
		Herat ...	11	229½	East-by-north, 2¾ hours. Road level, but terribly cut up by watercourses. Soil alluvial. Water abundant and excellent; supplies plentiful. At 1 mile ford a deep canal and pass a ruined fort off left. At 2¼ miles a broad and deep canal runs parallel on the right, and can be crossed by a brick bridge; but leaving it cross the deep and rapid stream, Karju, by brick bridge. An Imamzada among trees on the right. Cross numerous canals. At 3 miles are two ruined fortified villages,—one on the left, the other off right. At 4 miles a brick cistern on the right, and the large village of Nukrah off left. At 4¼ miles a ruined village with extensive enclosures on the right. At 4½ miles a small fort with towers of ornamented brick-work on the right. At 6 miles, lanes between gardens, ruins, and graveyard. At 7¾ miles a tall solitary fir among houses on the left. A little farther cross a bridge; thence amidst mounds. At 8½ miles Imamzada on the left; remains of Persian approaches zig-zig, and a ruined battery on the right. Cross ditch by wooden bridge; wind round up the steep ascent; pass through double gateway (Irak) and enter city. Splendid encamping ground on every side.

C. M. M.

Appendix H.

Route from Bandar-Gaz to Herat viâ Sabzawar and Turshiz.

Territory.	Authority.	Halting places.	Miles. Stage.	Miles. Total.	Description of the route.
Persia.	Napier.	Kurd Muhala ...	7	7	
		Astrabad ...	16	23	
		Galugah ...	29	52	
		Radkan ...	12	64	From Galugah, a small ascent of five miles over a forest-covered spur; road steep and bad, considered impassable for laden beasts after melting of snow and in rainy weather. Total ascent not less than 5,000 feet. From crest of spur, steep descent of three miles to Bagh-i-Kullah, small hamlet of eight houses. Thence four miles to Radkan, village on hillside above Asp-o-Neza or Nikah stream.
		Asp-o-Neza ...	8	72	Steep descent to stream. Follow valley south-east over good road to Asp-o-Neza. At two miles pass Mil-i-Radkan tower. At three miles road from Chashma-i-Ali strikes in from right at gorge of Sawar glen. At eight miles open ground fit for large camp at mouth of Asp-o-Neza defile. Nearest village Hajiabad.
		Shahkoh Pain ...	13½	85½	Follow up stream and at ½ mile enter narrow Asp-o-Neza defile, overhung by high cliffs. Summits of mountains 2,000 to 3,000 feet high, flat and open. At 2¾ miles defile closes in and road winds through narrow gorge, the Tang-i-Loodian, about 80 yards wide, closed in by stupendous cliffs of limestone strata curiously contorted, mostly nearly vertical. Thence defile opens out, hills recede and are well wooded. At seven miles glen opens to left, up which lies road to Hajiabad, small village on plateau. Thence one mile following stream, road stony and rough. At eight miles cliffs close in forming narrow pass ½ mile long: at one point only 50 yards broad, overhung by high cliffs; guns might pass along shallow bed of stream. Thence defile slightly more open. Hamlet and mill of Durzunday reached at 9½ miles. Thence through narrow and tortuous defile; road fairly good and passable for wheels. At 11½ miles reach Daob-i-Burzunday; road turns to left up glen to Shahkoh Bala and another up small glen to Shahkoh Pain; former said to be shorter but difficult. At 12 miles, path from Chardeh, taken at times by Persian troops, strikes in, winding down lateral glen. At 13½ miles village Shahkoh Pain, situated in deep glen at foot of high serrated line of

Route from Bandar-Gaz to Herat—contd.

Territory.	Authority.	Halting places.	Miles.		Description of the route.
			Stage.	Total.	
Persia.	Napier.				cliffs known as Shahkoh. The two villages have 100 houses; considerable wheat crops and good water.
		Tash Rabat ...	15¾	101	Leave camping ground above village on bearing about 22°; cross low spur and descend steep slope. Cross cultivated plateau, and pass down short steep descent into defile with stream flowing east-south-east, the upper course of the Nikah stream eventually bending north-east. Following streams, at 2½ miles path up glen to right to Charbagh. At 5 miles, road turns up hillside on left of defile to Shahkoh Bala, distant 1 fursakh. At 5½ miles, mill and small stream from glen to right. Following stream up narrow glen of Elyanay, at 8 miles turn up hills on left over easy pass of Chehlchalyan, road winding over slopes wooded with cyprus. At 9¾ miles, reach crest of ascent, 8,600 feet above sea, and descend over open hill slopes to 11 miles, where road enters barren defile of Sanda-Ab. Thence by fresh stream of clear water to small mud "rabat" at junction of main road to Astrabad, 15¾ miles. Camping ground in valley, up which road and telegraph line run to Astrabad. Road on the whole good and practicable for guns. Ascent to pass and descent of 1,400 feet to Tash particularly easy, and surface of road good. First two slopes below Shahkoh Pain might present some difficulty, but soil is light and easy to work. Wood, water and forage are procurable at any point. Defile leading to and from pass commanded by hills receding with easy slopes. Village of Tash, 58 houses, lies one mile from junction of roads above mentioned.
		Shahrud ...	19¾	120¾	Follow stream down defile. At 1½ miles pass ruined "rabat," right, and ascend low spur. At 3¼ miles descend easy slope, and enter wide open valley with village 4 or 5 miles right. Follow barren valley with enclosing hills running due east, and at 9 miles touch stream of good water flowing east through it. At 12¼ miles ruined fort on hill, ½ mile to right, and another at foot in plain. Shahwar mountain with snow on left. At 14¼ miles village of Kellatch, ¼ mile to left. At 17 miles turn south into valley between two rocky spurs; cross wide shallow watercourse, and continue south to gap in spur running from north to south. Cross spur at 19 miles, and bending E., at 19½ miles enter gardens of Shahrud. Road good and passable for wheels, except last rocky pass which may be turned by a detour of 2 or 3 miles. Four

Route from Bandar-Gaz to Herat—contd.

Territory.	Authority.	Halting places.	Miles. Stage.	Miles. Total.	Description of the route.
Persia.					miles from Shahrud, town of Bostam lies off to the left. Total descent 2,200 feet.
	Napier.	Khairabad ...	8	128¼	Two hours. Road level and good. Soil mostly alluvial. Skirt east side of town and cross several watercourses. At 1 mile broad dry bed of torrent from left. At 1¼ miles pass through high garden walls and cross watercourses. At 1½ miles cross two streams from left. At 4½ miles large walled village of Budusht, fine gardens and good stream, which is crossed by a bridge ½ mile further on. Here road turns and enters large plain. At 7¾ miles cross small stream from left. Encamp between it and the ruins of Khairabad. Direction for 5 miles east-by-north, the rest by south. Water good, but small supply. Supplies none.
	Taylor.	Maiomai ...	32	160¼	Nine and a half hours. Road good; soil gravelly. Pass through ruins of Khairabad and ascend gradually. At 10 miles ruined caravanserai and fort on right. At 13 miles several low ridges and dry beds of torrents. At 13½ miles sharp descent. At 14 miles ruins of fort and reservoir on right. At 16 miles low conical hill on right and range of mounds, which at 19 miles form a gorge through which the road passes. At 20 miles steep stony ascent, reaching the top in 5 minutes. Thence long descent into plains, which reach at 22 miles. At 24½ miles three small villages, with cultivation under hills on right. At 25½ miles stream from right. At 30 miles enter suburbs of town; march round walls and encamp on bank of a beautiful stream under fine palm trees. Direction east-by-south. Water plentiful and excellent. Supplies procurable; not abundant.
		Miandasht ...	22	182¼	Six and a half hours. First 5 and last 4 miles level and good; rest rough, undulating and stony. At 4 miles large village of Ibrahimabad on left. At 4½ miles a stream with trees on left, which cross 1 mile further on. At 6½ miles another stream on which is fort of Zydar; a watch-tower on right. At 6½ miles enter defile and continue among stony hills for three hours. At 9½ miles a very stony and difficult ridge. At 11 miles a stony and difficult descent through defile. Cross dry bed of torrent at 11½ miles and another at 12 miles; thence undulating till 15th mile, where is another dry bed. At 16 miles a gradual descent into a more level plain. At 17 miles a gentle ascent. At 18 miles enter an elevated plain, whence serai is visible. Water in a cistern from kanat brackish. Supplies none. Direction to Zydar south-east-by-east, after that east-south-east.

Route from Bandar-Gaz to Herat—contd.

Territory.	Authority.	Halting places.	Miles. Stage.	Miles. Total.	Description of the route.
Persia.	Taylor, Clerk, Hardy.	Abbassabad ...	19	201⅓	Five and one-third hours. Road good, except among the hills where it is stony, and soil gravelly. A level barren plain for 3⅓ miles, when enter defile; hills low, barren, and volcanic. At 6 miles cross a rocky ridge; at 7 miles dry bed of torrent; at 7½ miles rocky ridge. At 8 miles ascend, and at 9 miles a steep, stony descent into a small valley surrounded by hills. At 10 miles a dry torrent bed from left. At 11¼ miles a serai, stream, and fortified village of Elhak on right. At 11¾ miles enter defile of Elhak till 13¼ miles; then descend gradually. Road cut up by dry beds of torrents from left. Round spur of a hill Abbassabad comes into view; low, but on an eminence. At 18 miles garden on right, and a little farther spring on left. Village in tiers like Tasgird. A few good houses. Serai in ruins. Direction east by south for 13½ miles, then north-east-by-east. Water good and plentiful. Supplies none.
		Mazinam ...	21	222⅓	Six hours. Road level and good throughout, broken near old Behmanabad. Soil gravelly and alluvial. Descend from Abbassabad and cross a small watercourse. At 3 miles a small spring of brackish water on the left. At 6½ miles a deep dry bed of a river, with fine old brick bridge, Pul-i-Abruham. At 9 miles small fortified village of Sadrabad; brackish stream on left. At 14½ miles winter road branches off to left. At 18 miles scanty cultivation in gardens to left, with large walled village of Kaha on same side. At 19 miles small watercourse and cultivation. At 19¾ miles ruins of fort and mosque of Subbi. At 20½ miles extensive ruins of an ancient town and modern fortified village of Behmanabad. Mazinan is a small fortified village of 150 houses. It has two serais. Direction east-by-south. Water from Kanat good and plentiful. Supplies tolerable.
		Mehr ...	18	240⅓	Four and a half hours. Road excellent; soil gravelly and sandy. Pass a large ruined village on left. At 3¾ miles dry bed of stream. At 4½ miles, small brick reservoir on left. Water stinking. Several dry beds for next five miles, where cultivation begins, mostly cotton. At 14 miles village of Sulkhar, with trees, gardens, abundant supplies, plenty of water. One-fourth mile beyond are mud ruins and an Imamzada. From 16 to 17 miles numerous dry beds. At 17¼ miles road diverges, one to a serai, other to a village, which has almond and palm trees. Direction east-by-south. Water good and plentiful. Supplies procurable.

Route from Bandar-Gaz to Herat—concld.

Territory.	Authority.	Halting places.	Miles. Stage.	Miles. Total.	Description of the route.
Persia.		Sabzawar ...	30	270½	Eight hours. Road good; latter part excellent; soil gravelly and sandy. At ¾ mile, cross two dry beds of streams and at one mile dry river. At 4½ miles ruined brick cistern on left, and at 6½ miles road to Rewand on left, rejoining at 15 miles. At 10 miles, a small stream from left. At 11 miles, splendid brick serai on right and cistern of bad water on left. At 15 miles another cistern on left. To 20th mile several dry beds. At 20½ miles cross by broken bridge broad, dry bed of a river. At 22 miles stream, cistern, and ruins on left. At 24 miles small mud fort on left. At 24½ miles ravines and broken ground. At 25½ miles, broad dry bed of river and ruins of large village of Khushrud, with high brick minar on left; modern village same name and same side. At 26 miles an Imamzada on left; cistern and mud huts on right. At 28 miles cistern on left. At 28½ miles a stream, and a little further fort on right. At 29 miles watercourse, cistern, and large serai. Direction east-by-south. Water good and plentiful supplied by kanats. Supplies abundant. Cultivation chiefly cotton round villages; very extensive near Sabzawar.
	MacGregor.	Bigwat ...	14	284½	The road goes over a low pass and undulating country. Village; water; supplies.
		Badraskand ...	14	298½	The road through cultivation. Village; water; supplies.
		Naobulhakim ...	28	319½	The road through waste. Village; water; supplies.
		Saadadi ...	21	340½	The road through cultivation. Village; water; supplies.
		Turshiz ...	28	368½	The road is through cultivation. Water good and plentiful. Encamp on west side near kanat.
		Zurmir ...	25	393½	At 3 miles village of Mowla. At 5 miles cross a stream. At 6 miles road from Turshiz comes in on left. At 8½ miles a reservoir on the right. At 10 miles cross broad river from left and lines of kanats. At 13 miles reservoir on left and Turbat-i-Haidari road forks to left. At 13½ miles reservoir on right. At 15½ miles reservoir of rain water on right, and fortified town of Azkund 1 mile to left. At 19½ miles cross deep and rapid river from left, with steep banks, 20 feet wide, 3 feet deep. At 23 miles cross deep rapid torrent from left. Hence gentle descent to Zurmir. Road good, but slightly undulating in parts. General direction east-south-east. Soil gravelly and alluvial.
	Taylor.	Camp near Turbat-i-Haidari ...	15	408½	Cross several streams. At 7 miles cross river with high banks, 30 feet wide, 3 feet deep. Here road to Turbat-i-Haidari branches to left. At 11 miles small village with large tree to left. At 12 miles cross streams; pass rain-water reservoir on right. Gradual descent over undulating country. Cross several streams. At 14 miles villages of Jufferabad and Husainabad to left. Road good though undulating. Soil gravelly. Direction south-east-by-east.
		Himatabad ...	60	468½	Country open and undulating for first 40 miles. General direction east. For cart 20 miles road bad and crosses a difficult pass over hills by the Godakela Minar. Water and supplies procurable at Himatabad.
	MacGregor.	Shaher-i-Nao ...	14	482½	Road good, through fields and water. Village; water; supplies.
		Mushadi Reza ...	17	499½	Road good and level through waste. Village; water; supplies.
		Karez ...	14	513½	Road good and level.
		Herat ...	85	598½	See Route.

C. M. M.

Appendix I.

Route from Samarkand to Kabul* viâ *Ghozar, Ispantoda, Kilif, Balkh, Bamian, and the Unai Pass.

Stages.	Places.	Miles.	Remarks.
1	Daor ...	9	Supplies and water plentiful.
2	Jam ...	30	
3	Kara Giha ...	10	Supplies, and water from wells near surface.
4	Kok Tash ...	9	
5	Chirakhchi ...	12	Supplies, and water from stream.
6	Kara Bagh ...	9	
7	Ghozar ...	30*	
8	Name of ground forgotten	18	Water and grain scarce. Sheep, grass, wood in plenty.
9	Ispantoda ...	20	Water for animals plentiful, but rather brackish; only one well for human use; grain scarce. Sheep, grass, wood abundant.
10	Kilif ...	21	Everything abundant.
11	Sardaba ...	21	Water scarce in summer. Supplies fair.
12	Khan-i-Naoabad ...	6	Water plentiful. Supplies abundant.
13	Haiatan ...	9	As above. The shortness of these marches is due to the number of canals which cross the road. There is, however, abundance of timber at hand for temporary bridges.
14	Charbagh ...	3	
15	Charbagh-i-Saiadan ...	3	
16	Paimast ...	5	
17	Balkh ...	10	
18	Mazar-i-Sharif ...	8	
19	Naibabad ...	15	Water scarce. Supplies from Mazar-i-Sharif and Tashkurghan.
20	Tashkurghan ...	15	Water plentiful. Supplies abundant.
21	Hazrat Sultan ...	18	
22	Aibak (*Haibak*) ...	14	
23	Sarbagh ...	18	
24	Khuram ...	15	
25	Rui ...	15	Water plentiful. Grain scarce. Sheep and grass abundant.
26	Doab ...	18	Water plentiful. Everything abundant.
27	Madar ...	21	Water plentiful. Grain scarce. Sheep and grass abundant.
28	Kamurd ...	25	Water plentiful. Everything abundant.
29	Saighan ...	24	
30	Sokhta Chinar ...	12	Water plentiful. Grain scarce. Sheep abundant.
31	Akrabad ...	12	Water plentiful. Supplies of all kinds procurable in quantity, but very dear.
32	Surkh Dar ...	9	Water plentiful. Enough of everything for 1,000 men only.
33	Bamian ...	9	Water plentiful. Everything plentiful.
34	Tokchi ...	12	Water plentiful. Supplies of all kinds scarce.
35	Kalu ...	18	
36	Kharzar ...	21	
37	Gardan Diwar ...	16	
38	Unai Pass ...	12	Water plentiful.
39	Sar-i-Chashma ...	18	
40	Jalrez ...	15	
41	Arghandeh ...	15	
42	Kabul ...	14	
	Total ...	614	

Transport.

From Samarkand to Aibak camels are to be procured in great numbers, and also one-horse carts. From Aibak to Kaul camels are scarcer, and carts not procurable.

Character of Road.

Fit for wheeled guns from Samarkand to Khuram, *i.e.*, 24 marches; unfit for wheels from Khuram to Bamian.
Much work required to make this portion passable.
Unfit for wheels from Bamian to Kabul without much work, unless the Gharband routes be taken, which is easier.

* At 18 miles from Kara Bagh is Arababad, with wells, not often used by caravans as a halting ground.
NOTE.—The marches given are those used by caravans.

C. M. M.

Alternative Route from Ghozar to Kilif by Shirabad.

Stages.	Places.	Miles.	Remarks.
1	Kosh Los ...	9	Water plentiful from stream.
2	Tanga ...	8	Water plentiful, but brackish.
3	Chashma-i-Hafizan ...	14	Water scarcer.
4	Shorab ...	25	Water plentiful but indifferent.
5	Serab ...	12	Water plentiful and good.
6	Igarchi ...	9	
7	Lak-lak-kan ...	7	
8	Shirabad ...	12	
9	Gaz Kishlak ...	15	
10	Gambir Bolak ...	20	Water scarce, from a well or two.
11	Kilif ...	16	Water plentiful, abundant and good.
	Total ...	147	

Supplies and Transport.

On the above route the first four stages to Shorab have hardly any grain at all, but sheep, grass and wood. Of the remaining stages, supplies of all kinds are abundant at each except Gambir Bolak, which has a very limited quantity of grain. Sheep and grass, as well as firewood, are procurable at *every* stage.

Numerous camels; no carts.

Character of Road.

Between Tanga and Shirabad the road passes through such a difficult, mountainous country that a great deal of labor would be necessary to make it fit for wheels. From Tanga to Serab the hills are all rocky, and much blasting would be necessary. From Serab onwards the formation is an easily worked clayey soil.

C. M. M.

Appendix J.

Route from Jam to Kabul viâ Chehl Burj.

Territory.	Authority.	Halting places.	Miles.		Description of the route.
			Intermediate.	Total.	
Bokhara.	Mayeff, Minayeff, Kostenko.	Kara Kiya (village)	13	13	The road at once enters the mountains; at ¾ mile turns to the left at a granite pillar. Although fit for arabas, it is very difficult owing to the deep ruts. It runs along a stream the whole way, whose banks are steep and broken. At half-way the village of Arab-Bendi is passed, and a mile or two further on an extensive but low with spring water. The road would require some improvement, especially where it rises on to the slopes of the hills. Kara Kiya village is situated in a small valley watered by a rivulet, and is 1½ miles from the road.
		Kak Tash Wells ...	13	26	The road issues from the mountains a short distance from Kara Kiya and crosses the Uchun canal. which flows from the Kara Kiya rivulet; then crosses a steppe. There are no inhabited places on it up to the Kashka river, only kibitkas. At 300 yards from the Uchun canal a road branches off to Kara Tube, 1½ miles from Chirakchi, on the Kashka river, and also near the same canal a road branches to Char and Kitab. At 5¼ miles from its issue from the mountains the road a high ridge and 5¼ miles further on the dried up bed of the Chuyan Duryas, after which the Chuyan Kirler mountains are traversed. Close to the river bed is the Chuyan Well, 3¼ miles from Kak Tash. There are numerous wells, but all very deep, on the steppe. The water at Kak Tash is very good.
		Chirakchi (town)...	12	38	The steppe continues to Chirakchi. At 5¼ miles pass the wells of Ikezak, and at 10¼ miles the village of Kal-Tube on two canals led in from the Kashka river. Thence to Chirakchi, rice and wheat-fields. The Kashka river is passed by a ford at the town; it has usually very little water. Camping ground on a level, and dry field west of Cirakchi. Road good throughout.
		Kara Bagh (village)	16	54	Road good throughout, running through a plain covered with fields and intersected by canals drawn from the Karima canal, whose high banks are run on the right of the road. At 4 miles road to right of village of Kairma. At 10½ miles road makes a sharp bend to avoid the Igre-Kul-Sai ravine. Camping ground on the Huzar road beyond the village (on fallow wheat-fields, says Mayeff).

Route from Jam to Kabul viâ *Chehl Burj*—contd.

Territory.	Authority.	Halting places.	Miles. Intermediate.	Miles. Total.	Description of the route.
Bokhara.	Mayeff, Minayeff, Kostenko.	Huzar (town) ...	23	77	Road still good and across a plain with wheat-fields near villages. For the first two miles a group of villages is traversed. At $2\frac{1}{4}$ miles a belt of gardens along the Kamai canals is traversed. At $7\frac{1}{4}$ miles road crosses the high-road from Karashi to Yar Tube, and between it and heights to the left are some Uzbak villages called Uch Tube, whose water is brought from cisterns in the mountains. At $15\frac{1}{4}$ miles the road crosses a range of hills with easy slopes, and thence traverses a plain covered with wheat-fields to Huzar. At the foot of these heights the road crosses the Abarde canal near the village of that name. No water between Kamai and Abarde canals. Huzar is a large town with a strong citadel, and is one of the most important towns of Bokhara. The nomads drive large flocks to it for sale at the weekly market on Thursdays, 1,000 head being the average sale. They also bring in wood, salt, and lead.
		Kush Lush (village)	11	88	At two miles road rises to the crest of a gentle ascent, and at $5\frac{1}{4}$ enters the mountains and traverses the easy Huzar defile. The road requires repairing at $7\frac{1}{2}$ miles and at 10 miles where there is a very strong bit, but even in its present condition is passable for arabas. Camping ground on a broad open space in front of the village. Kush Lush is at the junction of two streams forming the Huzar river.
		Tonga ...	13	101	At Kush Lush the road bifurcates, one branch running to Durband by Tanza Khoram and Chashma-i-Hafiz-Jan to Ak-Rabat, the other by the Anar-Bulak spring on the Kultar-Minar road to Al Rabat, where both branches re-unite. To Tanga the road runs mostly along the right bank Kichi-Uru-Darya crossing it twice near Huzar, and several times further up. Especially at the beginning the road is difficult, and at $3\frac{1}{2}$ miles crosses the deep ravine of Gum Bulak, and at $3\frac{1}{4}$ miles the still steep ones of Yar Tube. From Yar Tube the broad and easy Kara Chach valley begins. The road requires repairs at the two above-mentioned ravines, at $4\frac{1}{2}$ miles at a bend of the river, and at the head of the river where the road passes under overhanging rocks.
		Chashma-i-Hafiz Jan	15	116	The road runs over a slightly undulating gravelly, and in parts stony, plain. At $1\frac{3}{4}$ miles cross the Kon-Sai river; at 3 miles the ravine of the Tuz-Sai stream flowing out of the salt mines $10\frac{1}{2}$ miles from the road. At $6\frac{3}{4}$ miles the Kon-Sai stream enters the

Route from Jam to Kabul viâ *Chehl Burj*—contd.

Territory.	Authority.	Halting places.	Miles. Intermediate.	Miles. Total.	Description of the route.
					defile of Ak-Dagan, and through this the road is very difficult. On issuing from it the broad and easy valley of Uzan Kuduk is traversed, and a well of that name passed at 8 miles, with good fresh water. The brooks in this plain dry up in summer. From this well the valley is called Sari-Kamar. At $9\frac{1}{3}$ miles the ascent of the Tashlag-Mishab mountain commences and the road rises to Ak-Rabat, the highest point at $11\frac{2}{3}$ miles. Cultivation begins extending to Chasma-i-Hafiz-Jan. Hitherto the country is completely unwooded, except a few bushes near the streams. The village of Chashma-i-Hafiz-Jan is situated on the brook of the same name. Fuel is abundant, and is principally brought from the mountains. One araba load of savin wood costs $1\frac{1}{3}$*d.* to $3\frac{3}{4}$. The road from Tanga requires repairs at the Tug-Sai ravine and in the Ak-Dagan defile where some blasting would be necessary.
Bokhara.	Mayeff, Minayeff, Kostenko.	Tash Kalama ...	7	123	Road rises from Chashma. At $1\frac{1}{3}$ miles is a well with brackish water; at 4 miles a "serai" on a stream with good water called Ak-Rabat. At $6\frac{2}{3}$ miles the highest point of the Ak-Rabat pass is reached. Here a road branches off the north by Kara Khoval and Kalta-Minar to the valley of Shahr-i-Sabz. At the bottom of the descent is the narrow gorge of Tash Kalama. The road requires repair at $6\frac{2}{3}$ miles at the Ak-Rabat pass, where it is obstructed by huge stones at the Ak-Rabat stream, and at the Tash-Kalama Gorge which blasting would be required to widen.
		Shorab ...	10	133	The road runs along the Chackhta valley through which runs the stream of that name, a very uneven and cut up locality. At $5\frac{2}{3}$ miles it enters the Iron Gate or Bazgola Khana, a narrow, picturesque and very winding gorge $1\frac{2}{3}$ miles long, very stony, but practicable for vehicles, along which flows the Chakcha brook. Thence the road lies in a broad, even, and easy valley to the "ziarat" and serai on the Shorab brook, whose water is good. The road to the end of the Iron gate requires clearing throughout, and beyond that it requires widening in places where it is a mere sheep-track on the hillside.
		Sar-i-Ab ...	17	150	The road turns eastward by the Darb and defile, the mountains bordering the left of which are called Bali-Baili. At $\frac{2}{3}$ mile a path branches to the right to the Shorab stream, which enters, one mile further on, the narrow and difficult defile of Buzzola,

Route from Jam to Kabul viâ *Chehl Burj*—contd.

Territory.	Authority.	Halting places.	Miles. Intermediate.	Miles. Total.	Description of the route.
Bokhara.	Mayeff, Minayeff, Kostenko.				through which runs the pack-animal track to Shirabad avoiding Darband. The road rises by a winding and difficult ascent for two miles and then enters the defile, through which the dry bed of a mountain stream extends, and which is very difficult. A steep and stony ascent brings the road out of it on to the broad plain of Dakh-Kara-Kand, slightly undulating and with gravelly soil, intersected in places by mountain streams. From the defile to Sur-i-Ab is eight miles. This is a most difficult march, and the road requires re-making *ab initio* except over the Dakh-Kari-Kand plain. The defile may be avoided by turning off at ¾ miles to the Shorab stream; but the ascent to the Dakh-Kara-Kand plain would be very steep, though to make a road this way would be easier than to improve that through the defile.
		Igerchi (wintering hut) ...	10	160	For 1¾ miles the road runs over even gravelly country, and then descends by a short slope into a plain intersected by three streams of good water. At three miles road rises to the Chaga-Tai valley, which is stony and intersected by ravines with steep banks. At 6¾ miles cross a deep ravine, in which flows Gazak-Su stream, across which an almost floating wooden bridge is thrown. The other ravines do not require bridges, but are wearisome to cross. At eight miles road approaches Shirabad river, and follows its right bank. Camping ground in a large dry field. Road very heavy and requires repair at the ascent to Chaga Tai plain at all the ravines, at the place where it approaches the Shirabad river, and where it crosses tributaries of the latter.
		Lailakan (village)	8	168	At 2¾ miles pass the "wintering place" of Shadi-Bai-Tugui with closer fields and meadows. Here on the right hills approach the bank of the Shirabad river along the right bank of which the road runs. Hence the country becomes very hilly with deep stony ravines. From the Punj hollow, covered with cultivation and villages a very hilly locality again commences, the hills being covered with burnt-up grass. Lailakan is situated on the Shirabad river and has good gardens. At it the road crosses the Bash-Khard-Su stream.
		Shirabad ...	11	179	This portion of the road presents the greatest difficulties. There are two roads to Shirabad from Lailakan,—one by the left bank crosses to the other bank of the Shirabad river at the village itself by a ford, rises to the heights on the bank, and enters the Nan-Dahan defile,

Route from Jam to Kabul viâ Chehl Burj—contd.

Territory.	Authority.	Halting places.	Miles. Intermediate.	Miles. Total.	Description of the route.
					the whole breadth of which is occupied by the Shirabad river, the road being in the bed itself. The other road runs by the right bank, and is comparatively much better. It runs along the elevated hilly bank and at 4 miles crosses the Shur-Ab stream, which has its course 2¾ miles from Lailakan. At 5½ miles it runs along the edge of the precipitous bank, and at 5½ miles enters the Nan-Dahan defile following its right bank on a cornice, which is nothing but a mass of heaped-up rocks torn from the bank by spring floods. Above the path are overhanging rocks undermined by water. The road is most difficult and dangerous, and the river bed itself when the water is low is usually preferred. From this defile both roads unite and run along the right bank over elevated hilly country.
					At 9 miles the gardens of Shirabad begin, and at 10½ the citadel on a high hill comes in right. This road would require making throughout, especially in the Nan Dahan defile. Shirabad is one of the most populous towns in Southern Bokhara, surrounded by gardens. Its streets are very narrow and only passable by horsemen, pack-animals and men on foot. There is not a single araba in the town.
Bokhara.	Mayeff, Minayeff, Kostenko.	Guz Kishlak (village) ...	17	196	Road runs south-west through a hilly country, passable in all directions with hard gravelly soil. At 2 miles the village of Nanvakh in fields watered by the Nanvakh Arik is passed. Hills covered with burnt-up vegetation border the road on the right. At 4¾ miles is passed Khoja Kuya the centre of a group of villages, and at 5½ miles a ruined tank. Thence the road traverses a salt steppe to the termination of the Khoja-Kuya-Tun mountains, behind which rises the Bash-Kurd range. At 8 miles, the road enters the mountains and runs in a broad, easy defile with firm gravelly soil. The ascent terminates in a level open space, after which the defile assumes a wild character with precipitous limestone rocks, the passage being also encumbered with detached rocks. This defile is called Guz-Sui. The banks of the Guz-Bulak stream are fringed with willow and vegetation. The village of Guz is at the very crest of the ascent; so that at Guz-Kishlak the defile issues on to a level valley called Karez Atlik, 20 miles broad, extending to Kalif. The road only requires repairing in the Guz-Sui defile for a distance of 4 miles.

Route from Jam to Kabul viâ *Chehl Burj*—contd.

Territory.	Authority.	Halting places.	Miles.		Description of the route.
			Intermediate.	Total.	
Bokhara.	Mayeff, Minayeff, Kostenko.	Kempir Bolak ...	12	208	Road continues over plain of Karez Atlik, which is watered by an underground canal (karez) 11½ miles long, marked by a number of wells on the steppe, along which the road, which is good and even, runs. This valley is bordered on the right by the Kintin Tau range. Wheat-fields extend from Guz-Kishlak to Yakub Bai village (2½ miles). On the left the Uch Kora hills border the road for a short distance, and where they recede from is seen the village of Zinou, 2 miles off. Opposite this begins the Katta Kamish Sai defile, formed by the Uch Kora and Katta Kamish ranges, on the latter of which are two villages. No repairs of the road are required.
		Kempir Dagan (camp beyond).	7 or 10	215 or 218	Road is good and runs in a broad valley. At 2 miles is the village of Alri, under the hills of Kintin Tau, to which the road gradually approaches. At 3 miles the defile of Kempir Dagan, through the Kasragaspur of the Kintin Tau mountains, is entered. The defile extends for four miles, and its soil is hard and gravelly, requiring no improvement.
		Kalif ...	16 or 13	231	At 2¾ miles from the issue of the Kempir Dagan defile, the village of Oguz Bulak is passed situated on a stream from the Kintin Tau, which flows in branches, one of them flowing to Kalif, the second losing itself in the steppe, and the third running to the village of Kalluk. Hence the road runs over a smooth steppe to the Amu Darya, with ranges of low hills parallel to it on both sides. At 12¾ miles a third low range, the Kura Ura, is seen. The road follows the Oguz Bulak canal, which is grown over with tamarisk bushes. For the last 3 or 4 miles of the road a salt tract is traversed, extending almost to Kalif, crumbling sand only commencing about 600 yards from the river bank. Kalif is on the right bank of the Amu, and is a small village with no bazaar or mosque.
					The river Amu is here contracted by the Khadam Gucha range on the left bank to a breadth of 500 spans. The ferrymen live on a mound on a small promontory and have three boats. Notwithstanding the swiftness of the current, the passage is carried on at high or low water without a check, and the current even assists the passage by driving the boats to the Afghan shore. In ascending the river boats keep to the Afghan shore throughout, as the current there is weaker, and there are no sunken rocks. On the opposite bank there is no village, but only a ferry post and three wretched huts. On

Route from Jam to Kabul viâ Chehl Burj—contd.

Territory.	Authority.	Halting places.	Miles. Intermediate.	Miles. Total.	Description of the route.
Afghanistan.	Mir Izzat Ullah, Burnes.				the summit of the Khadam Gucha is seen a "ziarat," and beyond this range, 26¾ miles off, is the Afghan village of Akcha, where the Chief is Masha Khan, who has 600 Sarbazis. Information as to the events and roads in Afghanistan may always be had at Kalif from Bokharan salt-drivers. There are rapids at Kalif, extending half-way across the river from the Bokharan side, and caused by sunken rocks over which the water rushes violently, and another cataract of smaller dimensions 2¾ miles from Kalif; but those can be avoided by keeping to the Afghan bank. The depth of the Amu is said by the ferrymen to be 43½ feet at the rapids, and about 120 feet elsewhere.
		Sardoba ...	18	244	"Sardoba" means a cistern or reservoir. There are only a few ruined houses here.
		Khan-i-Naobat ...	12	261	Road through steppe. No water.
		Haiatan ...	8	269	A stream flows through this place towards Charbagh.
		Charbagh ...	3	272	Road from Haiatan to Balkh runs through a country intersected by canals and covered by fertile vegetation. Charbagh is an Uzbak village near stream with good supplies.
		Charbagh-i-Saiadan	3	275	A village east of the road.
		Paimast ...	5	280	A village with a round fort.
		Balkh ...	10	290	The once prosperous city of Balkh is now a heap of ruins; but its citadel, however, is still in a tolerable state of preservation. The surrounding country is very fertile and produces large quantities of grain, fruit, &c. The new town of Balkh is open, but has a citadel in the centre. It is peopled by 10,000 Afghans and 5,000 Uzbaks.
	Intelligence Branch.	Mazar-i-Sharif ...	12	302	
		Yakaolang ...	16	318	1,000 tents, situated in a fertile plain, and inhabited by Uzbaks.
		Kishindeh Pain ...	15	333	1,000 tents, situated in a fertile plain and in habited half by Uzbaks, half by Hazaras.
		Kishindeh Bala ...	8	341	2,000 tents of Hazaras, situated in a fertile plain.
		Dara-i-Usuf ...	12	353	A fort in a wide undulating plain, near which are 1,000 tents of Hazaras.

Route from Jam to Kabul via Chehl Burj—contd.

Territory.	Authority.	Halting places.	Miles. Intermediate.	Miles. Total.	Description of the route.
Afghanistan.	Intelligence Branch.	Garmab ...	12	365	50 tents of Hazaras, situated in a narrow valley.
		Walishan ...	8	373	1,000 black tents of Hazaras, situated in a very fertile valley surrounded by hills, in which there are no houses.
		Chashma-i-Duzdan	9	382	Inhabited by Hazaras. No houses, nor cultivation.
		Zardgia ...	11	393	Inhabited by Hazaras. No houses, nor cultivation.
		Band-i-Char-Asman	12	405	
		Chehl Burj (or Shahr-i-Kohna)...	21	426	The country on this stage is rough and hilly. Across the Koh-i-Baba the place is in ruins, among which are a few black tents of the Hazaras. Very little cultivation.
		Yak Aolang ...	11	437	A large city, Hazaras with Hindu shopkeepers, in the Koh-i-Baba.
		Tagao-i-Bark ...	24	461	
		Siah Dara ...	11	472	Five forts and 100 houses, occupied by Hazaras.
		Daras Kol ...	11	483	Fifteen forts and 1,000 houses occupied by Hazaras.
		Kotal-i-Mushak ...	12	495	Two forts and 15 houses, occupied by Hazaras.
		Badasia ...	10	505	Seven forts and 700 houses occupied by Hazaras. A considerable extent of cultivated land.
		Farogh Olm ...	18	523	Thirty forts and 1,000 houses occupied by Hazaras.
		Gardan Diwar ...	18	541	A village situated at an elevation of 10,076 feet between the Unai Pass and Koh-i-Baba range on the Helmand, a few miles from its source.
		Yurt ...	7	548	Road tolerably good, passing over four rather high spurs and crossing the Helmand (2½ or 3 feet of water in July) at the beginning of the stage. Yurt is on an elevated undulating plateau 6 miles broad, forming the watershed between Kabul and Herat and Kandahar. Water is procurable, but grass scarce.

Route from Jam to Kabul viâ *Chehl Burj*—concld.

Territory.	Authority.	Halting places.	Miles.		Description of the route.
			Intermediate.	Total.	
Afghanistan.	Wood, Burnes.	Unai Pass ...	5	553	This pass consists of a succession of very steep ascents and descents, water being procurable at the foot of each. Guns require the aid of drag-ropes. A troop of horse artillery took two days to do the 5 miles. Encamp at foot of it. Water procurable. Grass long and bad.
		Sur-i-Chashma ...	9	562	Road for three miles very stony, with two steep but short descents at the beginning of the stage; for the last 6 miles very fair. The descent throughout is considerable, and the valley is narrow. Encamp at a spring, one of the sources of the Kabul river. Grass scarce.
		Jalrez ...	10	572	Road very rough, stony, and narrow. At Jalrez supplies and water are procurable, but grass is rather scarce.
		Rustam Khel ...	10	582	Road generally rough and stony, passing through a well cultivated valley. At the village of Rustan Khel supplies and water are procurable, and grass is plentiful but scarce.
		Argandeh ...	8	590	The road crosses the Argandeh pass, which is practicable for guns, and of no great height; but the descent is bad, being very rocky. At the summit is 2¼ miles undulating tableland. The ascent from the valley of the Kabul river is steep towards the top. This ghât may be avoided by marching down the Kabul river to Maidan on the Ghazni road, and then following the latter, on which is Argandeh. Supplies are procurable in small quantities; water is plentiful, but grass is scarce.
		Kabul ...	4	694	Road tolerably good, passing through a succession of gardens and fields, intersected by canals brought from the Kabul river.

C. M. M.

Appendix K.

Route from Marghilan to Chitral.

Territory.	Authority.	Halting places.	Miles. Stage.	Miles. Total.	Description of the route.
		Kuva ...	21	21	Postal Road. Practicable for carts.
		Min Tube ...	14	35	
		Aravan ...	9	44	
		Osh ...	16	60	
		Langar ...	20	80	Road runs for 2⅔ miles through gardens, then to village of Madi (5⅓ miles) through a hilly but well-cultivated country; thence across elevated steppe, and at 12⅔ miles road enters the Taldik Gorge, through which it follows the pebbly bed of the stream to Langar.
		Gulcha ...	30	110	The road bifurcates at Langar, and one branch was converted into a cart road in 1876. The other is unmade, but could easily be adapted for wheeled traffic. The cart road continues along the Taldik, and at 12⅔ miles bends to the east and traverses the Chigirchik-Pel-Su gorge leading up to the Chigirchik-Bel Pass (7,700 feet); crossing this, it descends through a gorge, and follows the Chigirchik river to its confluence with the Gulcha at fort Gulcha. On this road from Osh forage is everywhere procurable, and fuel in the shape of dried cowdung. In the Chigirchik gorges there is scrub forest. The other road from Langar crosses the Taldik by a ford and ascends by the Karvan-Kul gorge to the pass of that name 6 miles from Langar (7,400 feet). At 7⅔ miles the Tuka Pass (6,800 feet) is crossed, and at 18⅓ miles, after passing Lake Kaplan Kul (5,600 feet), the road crosses a third pass, the Kaplan Kul (7,000 feet). Thence the road descends by the Karogan Sai gorge, and at 20⅓ miles comes out into the valley of the Kurshab, which it follows to Fort Gulcha. The passes along this routes, although steep, admit of the passage of pack-animals. From Osh to Gulcha by this route is reckoned 43⅓ miles.
Turkistan.	Kostenko.	Kizil Kurgan ...	12	122	From Gulcha the road ascends the river of that name.
		Yangi Arik ...	5⅓	127⅓	Road still up Gulcha and at Yangi Arik crosses two hanging bridges, of which the second is over the Belavli, an affluent of the Gulcha.
		Sufi Kurgan ...	8⅔	136	For the first half the road is difficult and traverses a gorge, but in the second half the gorge opens out and the road runs along the bottom, which is covered with thick grass, with clumps of poplars in the last mile.
		Kizil Jar ...	14⅔	150⅔	At Sufi Kurgan a road branches to the left and runs by the Terek Su and Terek Davan passes and Fort Irkishtem to Kashgar. The road to Kizil Jar follows the Gulcha, and at 10⅔ miles a branch leaves it to the left, leading to the short pass, the most easterly in the Alai range, and 17 miles distant from the point of bifurcation.
		Koijol Davan Pass	10⅔	161⅓	At Kizil Jar a branch road to the left leads to the Archat pass (12,000 feet), 6⅔ miles off. The main road turns to the west, and runs by forts Uch Tube and Bossaga to the Koijol Davan pass (11,400 feet). There is another pass, the Taldik Davan (11,500 feet), 1⅓ miles to the west, but it is more difficult.
		Kulin Urt Pass ...	5⅓	166⅔	Road descends. This pass is through a secondary range.

Route from Marghilan to Chitral—contd.

Territory.	Authority.	Halting places.	Miles. Stage.	Miles. Total.	Description of the route.
Turkistan—contd.	*Kostenko—contd.*	Alai Valley ...	4	170¾	The Alai valley is covered with excellent grass and is well-watered.
		Darawat Kurgan ...	55	225¾	The cart road ceases, but the road is good for pack-animals, although there are some difficult places. It leads along the right bank of the Kizil-Su, an affluent of the Oxus.
		Kata Krramuk ...	19	244¾	From the west end of the Alai and eastern route to Karatigin, but probably longer by 20 miles, runs by Tuz-Altin-Su and the Tars Agar pass.
		Zinkab ...	60	304¾	On the right bank of the Surkhab a group of 10 villages.
		Gharm ...	40	344¾	The capital of Karatigin and a town of 800 houses, situated in a defile on the right bank of the Surkhab, at an elevation of 5,000 feet. There is a fort here. Supplies plentiful. The road from Kata Karamuk to Gharm is generally easy, though in places it runs high above the precipitous banks of the river.
Karatigin.	Oshanin.	Kamchurik Pass ...	10¾	355½	The road enters the pass at the hamlet of Sur-i-Pul and ascends by an easy road over soft soil to a plateau ½ mile wide.
		Childara ...	9¾	365	The descent from the plateau is stony and steep, and was formerly dangerous, but the road was widened and improved by the Bokharan army in 1877. After leaving the spur, which it follows, the road runs along the Shakh-Ab to the Darwaz Fort of Childara. Road practicable for pack-animals and south slopes of mountains covered with forests.
Darwaz.	Oshanin.	Labidara ...	16	381	A fort with high ramparts and towers on the left bank of the river Khulias, which is here bridged.
		Saghar-i-Dasht ...	10¾	391¾	The road is blocked by snow in winter. Saghar-i-Dasht is a hamlet of 40 houses on an elevated plain covered with barley fields. Another road, 16 miles long, by the Saghar-i-Dasht stream, traverses in its latter part a narrow gorge.
		Talbur ...	17	408¾	A small hill village on the Yakh Su.
		Sar-i-Pul ...	16	424¾	A small fort and village of 20 houses on the left bank of the Yakh Su.
		Khowalim ...	7¼	432	An important town of 500 houses, with a bazar.
		Mominabad ...	16	448	The road is stony and difficult. It first crosses a range of hills on the right bank of the Yakh Su by an easy pass, 2,000 feet high. Then follows the valley of the latter river. Mominabad is a town of 300 houses and 50 shops on a high and fertile plateau bounded by stone hills.

Route from Marghilan to Chitral—contd.

Territory.	Authority.	Halting places.	Miles. Stage.	Miles. Total.	Description of the route.
Kulab.	The Havildar.	Kulab ...	13½	661½	The road descends through a narrow defile to the village of Dihana. The town contains 400 houses, but its suburbs and gardens are very extensive. Supplies abundant.
Afghanistan.		Samti Bala ...	25	486½	The Oxus at Samti Bala is 600 paces wide, and is crossed on rafts of skins towed by horses. On the Afghan bank the hills come close down to the river with a cultivated strip near the bank. On the Kubab bank are extensive wheat fields. Samti Bala is a large Afghan village on the left bank with a garrison.
	Lord.	Chaiab ...	21	507½	
		Rustak ...	17	524½	A town of 5,000 houses, with two market days a week. Supplies abundant. Locality unhealthy.
		Iskasham ...	12	536½	
		Sarai Dara ...	18	554½	
		Faizabad ...	16½	571	The capital of Badakshan on the right bank of the Kokcha stream, which flows in a rocky trench-like bed. Behind the town hills rise to a height of 20,000 feet. The population is numerous, and there is a large bazar and a large garrison.
Independent.	Ibrahim Khan, January 1874.	Chapchi ...	23	594	For two miles the road runs through a rocky valley known by the name of the Tangi-i-Faizabad. The rest of the road is good. Four miles from Chapchi, a river, which comes from Jurm (probably the Kokcha), is crossed by a bridge. A little below this bridge the river just spoken of joins the Zebak river flowing from Faizabad.
		Tirgarán ...	35	629	Country on of both sides of the road is populated and well cultivated, and rice grows well. People speak both Turki and Persian. Merchants can purchase provisions here from the villagers.
Chitral.	MacNair.	Zebak ...	30	659	From Zebak there are several roads to Chitral, *viz.*, by the Dura, Nuksan, Agram, and Kharteza passes. The distance from the south, *i.e.*, from Chitral to the head of the Dura Pass (which is the easiest and is 14,800 feet in elevation) is 42 miles, or four marches. The distance from the head of the Dura pass to Zebak is much less; but eight marches for the whole journey would be sufficient.
		Chitral ...	100	759	

C. M. M.

Appendix L.

Route from Karabagh to Kajao in the Besud Hazarajat country.

Stages.	Places.	Miles.	Remarks.
1	Turgan ..	12	Road good for camels and mules, but impassable for wheels and difficult to render passable. Turgan is a place of importance, with a large fort and several villages. Inhabitants Jaghatus of the Bakhtiari subdivision. Water plentiful from springs. Wheat and ghee in abundance. Plenty of clover and lucerne, but no common grass. Firewood very scarce.
2	Baraki ...	18	Road good for camels and mules. Baraki is a large place, with several forts and villages. Spring water plentiful. Barley and grass (common) abundant. Firewood scarce.
3	Khawat ...	21	Road very good and level. *All* supplies abundant here, and water good and plentiful.
4	Korila ...	10	Road difficult, but yet fit for camels and mules. Water abundant; supplies fair.
5	Sar-i-Bokan ..	15	Road as above. Supplies of all kinds abundant, and water good and plentiful.
6	Sar-i-Bed ...	9	Road as above. Two forts and 12 houses. Supplies scarce; no grass; spring water good and sufficient.
7	Surkh-ek-bum ...	18	Road difficult, but fit for mules and camels. Bad and confined ground for encamping. Villages. Supplies plentiful of *all* kinds. Good water from a canal.
8	Kajao ...	9	Road good and quite level. Here are supplies of *every* description. Large forts and villages, and abundance of good water from a canal. The Khan is Ali Baksh, Besud. From Kajao four great roads go off, *viz.*, I.—To Gardan Diwal and Kabal. II.—To Balkh. III.—South-west through the remainder of the Hazarajat. IV.—To Karabagh and Ghazni.

The great difficulty on this route is the length of the marches, and the latter don't seem capable of being shortened by intermediate halts. The man's *kos* may however be shorter than the measurement I have given, *e.g.*, 1 kos = 1½ miles.

C. M. M.

Appendix M.

Route from Samarkand to Faizabad.

Stages.	Places.	Miles.	Remarks.
1	Ura Tepa ...	18	A small post of Russian police.
2	Kitab ...	18	Here there is a *Hakim* from Bokhara.
3	Shahar-i-Sabz ...	6	The residence for four months in each year of Amir of Bokhara.
4	Kara Tepa ...	24	A village.
5	Kalta Minar ...	18	Do.
6	Kara Khwal ...	24	A hamlet with two sarais.
7	Shorab ...	24	Do. one sarai.
8	Yurchi ...	...	Except at Shorab, where it is brackish, the water on this road is good and plentiful.
9	Kawadian ...	...	
10	Hissar Kulab ...	...	
11	Faizabad ...	...	

There are ample supplies of sheep and grain everywhere except at Shorab, where they are scarce. Firewood and grass everywhere.

Camels procurable in great numbers.

Character of road. Gulab Khan has only been as far as Shorab on this road. According to him, from Samarkand to Ura Tepa the road is fit for guns. From Ura Tepa to Kitab it is so bad that much blasting would be necessary. Pack ponies only are used. *Laden* camels cannot go by this section. From Kitab to Kara Tepa it is a good cart road. From Kara Tepa onwards it is fit for laden camels, but would require much making for wheel traffic.

C. M. M.

Appendix N.

POSTAL ROAD FROM ORENBURGH TO TASHKENT.

From Tashkent to the town of Orenburgh, Postal Road.

Province of Sir Daria, Kurama Division.	From point to point	Total between chief places.	From point to point.		Total between chief places.	
	Versts.	*Versts.*	Miles.	Fur.	Miles.	Fur.
Tashkent. Provincial town of—	...		...	...		
Khish-Kupir (Kaplan-Bek).	18½		12	2		
Ak-Jar ...	14¾		9	6¼		
Jeri ...	17		11	2¼		
Sharan-Khani ...	12½		8	2¼		
CHIMKEND DIVISION.						
Beglar-Beg ...	21½		14	2		
Ak-Tash ...	14		9	2¼		
Chimkend. Town of—	14		9	2¼		
		112½			74	3¼
Bur-Jar ...	17¾		11	6		
Aris ...	21½		14	2		
Bugun ...	24½		16	2		
Ak-Moli ...	24¼		16	0¾		
Nagai-Kura ...	21½		14	2		
TURKISTAN DIVISION.						
Ikan ...	20¾		13	6		
Turkistan. Town of—	23½		15	4½		
		153¾			101	7¼
Kosh-Mizgil ...	20¼		13	3½		
Sauran ...	25½		16	7¼		
Tash-Swat ...	27½		18	1¾		
Ak-Kum ...	17¾		11	6		
Yani-Kurgan ...	27½		19	2		
Tumen-Arik ...	21		13	7½		
PEROVSKI DIVISION.						
Sor-Kuduk ...	14½		9	5		
Kok-Irim ...	20¼		13	3½		
Julek (fortified post)	19¾		13	0¼		
		194			128	4½
Tar-Tugai ...	21¾		14	3¼		
Sari-Chaganak ...	17½		11	4¾		
Jarti-Kum ...	19¾		13	0¾		
Bor-Kazan ...	17¾		11	6¼		
Birubai ...	12¾		8	3½		
Fort Perovski ...	18½		12	2¼		
		108			71	4¾
Demitroff ...	22½		14	7¼		
Aman-Tash ...	11		7	2¼		
Petrovsk ...	16		10	5		
Seminoff ...	22¼		14	6		
Alexandroff ...	18¼		12	0½		
Vladimir ...	25		16	4½		

Remarks.

The postal route from Orenburgh to Tashkent, 1,280 miles 7¼ furlongs, is 97 marches. There is a great scarcity of water and supplies along portions of it where it runs through desert country. For above half its length, however, it runs parallel to the right bank of the Syr Daria, which it strikes about 45 miles from Tashkent at the station of "Tash-Swat," and from this point to Kasala (Fort No. 1) follows the course of the river closely. By far the worst part of the road is that from Kassala to Orenburgh on account of the region being so barren and the scarcity of water great. Commanders of districts are, however, instructed carefully to supervise the cleaning out of the wells every spring when the movements of the troops take place, and which season it is only for troops to be moved along the route with any degree of comfort, as in winter there are great difficulties in procuring fuel enough for cooking, even which is scarce at any time. During the summer the troops suffer much from the heat and thirst occasioned by it.—("Turkistan Region," by *Colonel Kostenko.*)

Lieutenant Stumm, "In the Russian campaign against Khiva," says that the road from Orenburgh to Orsk is fairly good and leads through abundant Cossack settlements and cultivated lands of the Ural Cossacks. But that from Orsk to Kasala in reality all signs of a road cease, and merely a track leads over the steppes or desert through a country quite uncultivated and without supplies, and is continually enclosed in sandy deserts. He states that the distance is 490 miles, and that during the whole of this there are no resources or supplies of any kind. Between Kasala and Chimkend he says that, although the route runs through the well-watered tracts of the Syr Daria, the character of the country alters little, except that grass grows on the steppes that alternate with

From Tashkent to the town of Orenburgh, Postal Road—contd.

Province of Sir Daria, Kurama Division.	From point to point.	Total between chief places.	From point to point.		Total between chief places.		Remarks.
	Versts.	*Versts.*	Miles.	Fur.	Miles.	Fur.	
Fedoroff ...	24½		16	2			
Victoroff ...	18		11	7½			
Fort No. 2 (Karmakchi).	20½		13	4¾			
		178			118		
Khor-Tut ...	18¾		12	8¼			
Kara-Tugai ...	17½		11	5			
Ilchibai ...	25		16	6⅓			
Kazala Division.							
Ak-Jar ...	27¾		14	3¼			
Ak-Swat ...	21⅓		14	2			
Maili-Bash ...	23¾		15	6			
Baskari ...	22		14	4⅓			
Fort No. 1, Kazala	18⅓		12	2¼			
		174¾			115	6¾	
Unisk ...	16		10	4¾			
Bik-Bauli ...	13⅓		8	7½			
Goloff ...	17⅓		11	5			
Kamishli-Bash ...	13¼		8	6¼			
Andreyeff ...	17⅓		11	4¾			
Sappak ...	18⅓		12	2			
Ak-Julpas ...	18		11	7½			
Alti-Kuduk ...	17		11	2¼			
Nicolaeff ...	16¼		10	6			
Kul-Kuduk ...	10⅓		6	7¾			
Jungurluk-Sor ...	21⅓		14	2			
Constantinoff ...	19½		12	7⅓			
Kara-Kuduk ...	19½		12	7½			
Julus ...	20¼		13	3¼			
Terekli ...	17		11	2¼			
		255¾			169	4¼	
Province of Turgai.							
Jalovli ...	32¼		21	4½			
Ak-Sai ...	23¾		15	6			
Jalanghach ...	25½		16	7½			
Irgiz. Town of—...	17⅓		11	4¾			
		99¼			65	6¼	
Buz-Gumer ...	19		12	4¾			
Kizil-Yar ...	14		9	21			
Terenuziak ...	17⅓		11	4¾			
Serali ...	13⅓		8	7¾			
Kapani (Kara-Kuduk).	17		11	2			
Kara-Sai ...	15⅓		10	2¼			
Kum-Sai ...	23⅓		15	4⅓			
Chulak-Kairakti ...	25		16	4⅓			
Ashchi-Sai ...	15¾		10	3¾			
Kara-Butak (fortified post).	16¾		11	0¾			
		177⅓			117	5¼	
Bash-Kara-Butak ...	19⅓		12	7⅓			
Damdi ...	28⅓		18	7			

the sandy deserts, and that the marshes which have to be crossed or skirted render the journey along the route very dangerous owing to their fever-laden vapours combined with excessive heat. The country is, however, partially cultivated. After reaching Turkistan the road runs through the heart of the province where cities are numerous and are surrounded by extensive and well-watered gardens capable of providing abundantly for troops on the march, and everywhere the country is inhabited. Bearing in mind the difficulties of the route from Orsk to Kazala, it is possible to picture the condition of a division of troops or train of carts on the march and the extremely difficult situation of this province in respect to the state of its communications. A detachment of troops on the march taking with them their supplies on a train of carts travels 20 *versts* daily and halts on the 4th day; at the best such a detachment could accomplish the whole journey from Orenburgh to Tashkent marching without any delays in about 4½ months.

In 1881 the communications between Orenburgh and Tashkent were in a deplorable state and almost impassable, and attention was therefore directed to the opening of a new route, *viz.*, that *viâ* Nijni Novgorod, Perm, Tobolsk, and Semapalatinsk.—*(I. B., H. G.)*

In the Khivan expedition the column that started from Orenburgh was conveyed thence to Kazala in sledges, and the distance divided into daily marches of about 40 miles. This was in the month of January. The country between Orenburgh and Orsk is bare and stony in parts, with occasional scanty brushwood. The road is crossed by many rivulets which, when not frozen, are deep in mud.

From Orsk to Kara-Butak the country, though bare of timber, is not wanting in good pasturage. Hence this grass land is replaced by stony or dreary bare tracts. Water gets scarcer, while such herbage

From Tashkent to the town of Orenburgh, Postal Road—concld.

Province of Sir Daria, Kurama Division.	From point to point	Total between chief places.	From point to point.		Total between chief places.		Remarks.
	Versts.	*Versts.*	Miles.	Fur.	Miles.	Fur.	
Bugati-Sai ...	19		12	4¾			as grows is almost too bitter for even camels to thrive on. At Irghis in spring time the inhabitants have to store up a sufficient supply of water to last them for nine months out of the year. After Irghiz the route crosses a depressed country, which is the bed of an ancient sea, in which there are salt lakes and quagmires. Ground capable of cultivation is not to be found, and anything more barren or desolate it is not easy to conceive than the surrounding country. Wells across these Aralian deserts have been dug at every 12 or 15 miles, but the water is more or less salt. The desolation of the country grows gradually less as the road approaches the Syr Daria. Even by this river the country does not indeed present a very fertile aspect; but with the aid of irrigation cereal crops give moderate returns. Fruit trees and the vine are productive. Madder and other dye roots thrive. Only in the spring, however, can it be said that herbage is at all abundant, and that, too, only close to the river.
Sari-Kamish ...	22½		14	7½			
Tasta-Butak ...	17¾		11	6			
Aral-Tube ...	21½		14	0¾			
Istemes ...	25¾		17	0½			
Ashchi-Butak ...	14½		9	5			
Tokan ...	18		11	7½			
Orsk. Town of— ...	27½		18	2			
		214½			142	0¼	
GOVERNMENT OF ORENBURG.							
Khabarna ...	26½		17	4½			
Guberlinska ...	29		19	1¾			
Podgornaya ...	26		17	1¾			
Ilinsk ...	19		12	4¾			
Nikolsk ...	19		12	4¾			
Verkhne-Ozero ...	27½		18	2			
Giriyalsk ...	21½		13	7½			
Krasnogorsk ...	22½		14	6			
Viazovsk ...	27		17	7½			
Kamenno-Ozero ...	16		10	4¾			
Nejinsk ...	14¾		9	6¼			
Orenburgh, Government town.	17	265	11	2¼	175	5¼	
Total ...		1,932½			1,280	7¼	

C. M. M.

Appendix O.

LIST OF THE ARAL FLEET.

Name of vessel.	Description.	Date of building.	Horse power.	Remarks.
Perovski ...	Steamer ...	1853 ...	40 nominal	Draws too much water for the upper portions of the river.
Obrutsheff ...	Steam tug	,, ...	12 ,,	Almost useless as a tug.
Sir Daria ...	,, ,,	1862 ...	20 ,,	
Aral ...	,, ,,	,, ...	40 ,,	
Samarcand* ...	,, ,,	1866 ...	70 ,,	
Tashkent ...	,, ,,	1870 ...	35 ,,	

* This steamer foundered in the ice in the winter of 1882.—(*Marvin.*)

List of the Aral Fleet—*contd.*

Minor vessels.

Transfer of vessel.	Description.	Cargo capacity in tons.	Date of building.	Remarks.
No. 1	Barge ...	56	1855	
,, 2	,, ...	,,	,,	
,, 3	,, ...	60	1860	
,, 4	,, ...	30	,,	
,, 6	,, ...	121	1855	
,, 7	,, ...	,,	,,	
,, 8	,, ...	130	1871	
,, 9	,, ...	,,	,,	
,, 10	,, ...	185	,,	
	7 iron ferry boats.	From 30 to 25 each.	From 1859 to 1875.	
	10 iron long boats.	From 3 to 5	From 1854 to 1859.	

(*Marvin.*)

Route on the River Sir Daria.

Ports.	Distance along the River.						Remarks.
	Between Ports.		From Fort No. 1.		From Fort Perovski.		
	Versts.	Miles.	*Versts.*	Miles.	*Versts.*	Miles.	
Fort No. 1 ...	...	...	...	...	525	346¾	Between Forts No. 1 and No. 2 navigation is carried on between the 25th March and 20th October.
,, ,, 2 ...	265	175¾	265	...	260	171¼	Between Fort No. 2 and Fort Perovski (on the Yaman-Daria), between the 25th March and the middle of September.
,, Perovski ...	260	171¼	525	346¾	...	...	Between Fort Perovski and Chinas fortified post navigation is carried on from the middle of March to the end of October.
Julek ...	175	116	700	462¼	175	116	
Uch-Keyik ...	332	220	1,032	682¼	507	336	
River Aris ...	130	86¼	1,162	769	637	422¼	
Chinas ...	482	319½	1,644	1,088½	1,119	741¾	

The period for navigation consequently averages 7½ months.

According to the *Cronstadt Gazette* of 12th May 1883, these vessels have all been handed over to a private company by the Russian Government.

The Sir Daria, though navigable and used by steamers, is of inferior importance as a line of communication, since the fair way above Fort No. II is very bad.

Great marshes and sand banks and rapids impede the navigation for the greater part of the year. The channel near Perovski is often scarcely a foot deep in summer and in spring at most from three to four feet deep. Formerly a number of canals were led from the river for irrigation purposes: there the Russians have stopped, thereby devastating whole tracts of country adjoining the river; still even then precautions have failed to make the Sir Daria a good means of communication.—(*Lieutenant Stumm.*)

From the latest statements from Tashkent it is found that the only boats on the Sir Daria are those belonging to the Russian Aral fleet, Government property, and performing only the work of the Crown. The fleet consists of six steamers, nine transport barges, seven large iron ferry boats, and ten iron long boats. These are used to convey Government stores from Rasala to Chinas, the port for Tashkent. For navigation the river may be divided into three portions—1st, from Rasala to Fort No. II, good for navigation purposes; 2nd, from Fort No. II to Perovski through the Jaman Swamp, very bad owing to the extreme shallowness; 3rd, from Perovski to China, navigable. The river is only fit for navigation from March to October. Great difficulty is experienced as regards fuel; most of the saksoul (the fuel mostly used) has been burnt up, but coal has been found about 90 miles above Kazala, but of what quality is not known. Coal is also imported to supplement the saksoul. The great drawback to the river navigation is the excessive slowness of it; vessels always have to stop at nights. The first section requires from two to three days with the stream and three to six against it to navigate it; the second section taking about the same time; and the third section takes from 8 to 14 days down-stream and 12 to 20 going up stream.—(*Marvin's* "Russian advance towards India.") Steam navigation on the Sir Daria is excessively difficult owing to the peculiar characteristics of the river, *viz.*, its sinuosity, the swiftness of the current reaching in places seven to eight versts an hour, and the shifting of the channel. In addition to which must be remembered that men and stores before embarkation have to pass over the worst part of the road between Orenburg and Tashkent. The extreme shallowness of the portion of the river named Jaman Daria running through the Jaman Swamp is also a great drawback, as it divides the river into two separate portions. In this reach, which is 130 miles in length at the most favorable time of the year for navigation, *viz.*, June and July, the water is only 3 feet deep and at other times only 1 foot deep. For this reason it was found best to employ one set of steamers on the upper portion and another on the lower, the steamer *Tashkent* serving as a connecting link between them in the 2nd section of the river. It is a common thing for the steamers on the Sir Daria to stick on a sandbank and to remain there for some time. The steamers cannot run at night. For transporting cargo the flotilla has nine barges carrying in all 894¾ tons. The greatest amount of cargo, &c., carried in a season by the flotilla was in 1875 and reached 3,130·18 tons. The greatest number of troops was in 1874, 4,480, and in that year the cargo amounted to 2,940 tons.

Several attempts have been made to deepen the channel of the Jaman Daria, but all have proved useless, and the project has now been given up.—("Turkistan Region," Vol. II, by *Colonel Kostenko.*)

C. M. M.

Appendix P.

*From the Town of Turkistan to Orsk** viâ *the town of Turgai.*

Camping grounds.	From point to point.	Total between chief places.	From point to point.		Total between chief places.		Remarks.
	Versts.	*Versts.*	Miles.	Fur.	Miles.	Fur.	
Turkistán. Town of—	...	...	...	...	...	...	*Turkistan.* Town of—The distance from the town of Turkistan to the camping ground on the Shurnak

canal is 21¼ *versts* (14 miles ¾ furlong). The road leaving Turkistan in a north-west direction passes at first for 1½ *versts* (1 mile) between the walls of gardens as far as the Jinishki canal, and from thence to the camping ground through a level and open country, grown over here and there with salt-soil herbs, "jantak," a thorny bush, and "miya;" the former makes excellent food for camels, and the latter, in its dry state, passable fuel. At 8 *versts* (5 miles 2½ furlongs) from the town the road crosses the Karachik stream, which, except for fifteen days in the spring of the year when the water in it is very high, is always easily practicable at the ford; at 11 *versts* (7 miles 2½ furlongs) the road crosses the dry bed of the Karsakti stream: at 18 *versts* (11 miles 7½ furlongs) the Kos-Mezgil canals, in which the water does not always reach the road, as it is distributed over the fields above; at 22 *versts* (14 miles 4¾ furlongs) the Shurnak canal (camping ground) with good pure water. At the camping ground on the Shurnak there is little food for camels, but sufficient fuel, roots of "jusan" and dung.

Camping grounds.	From point to point.	Total between chief places.	From point to point.		Total between chief places.		Remarks.
Shurnák-Arik canal.	21¼	...	14	0¾	...	...	*Shurnák Canal* (Sauran-Arik)—From the Shurnák canal to the Bish-Arik stream is 35 *versts* (23 miles 1¼

furlongs). From the Shurnák canal the road separating from the postal route takes an almost northerly direction over level country, intersected with dry shallow hollows. At 21 *versts* (13 miles 7½ furlongs) the road crosses the dry bed of the Maidan-Tal stream, the water from which is drawn off into the "Arik"—irrigation cut—of the same name, flowing parallel to the course of the river and very close to it at 26 *versts* (17 miles 2 furlongs) the road crosses the tolerably deep but dry bed of the Satim-Sai stream; at 34 *versts* (22 miles 4½ furlongs) crosses the dry bed of the

* This route was measured and described by Lieutenant Startseff. The Cossack *sotnias* of the Orenburg army take this route in and out of the district.

From the town of Turkistan to Orsk viâ *the town of Turgai*—contd.

Camping grounds.	From point to point.	Total between chief places.	From point to point.		Total between chief places.		Remarks.
	Versts.	*Versts.*	Miles.	Fur.	Miles.	Fur.	
							Bish-Arik with steep, but not high banks; and about 1½ *versts* (1 mile) further on reaches the Bish-Arik canal, into which the whole water of the stream of the same name is drawn off. The road on this march passes through a level, salt-soil country, occasionally crossing, almost imperceptible, flat eminences. The whole locality between the above-named camping grounds is grown over with the "jusan" herb, furnishing good food for camels, and, in addition, its roots supply good fuel. At the camping ground on the Bish-Arik there is little "jusan;" water good and very plentiful, and sufficient fuel ("jusan"). At Bishak-Arik the caravan road into Turkistán, by which all caravans from Turgai enter Turkistán and leave it, branches off through the village of Babai-Kurgán.
Stream Bish-Arik ...	35	...	23	1½	...	...	*River Bish-Arik.*—From the Bish-Arik to the Krach spring is 23 *versts* (15 miles 2 furlongs). The road from Bish-Arik rises on to a plateau, and up to the Krach spring passes through an undulating country, intersected by dry and shallow hollows. At 9 *versts* (5 miles 7¾ furlongs) from the camping ground the road crosses the Dimbai spring; at 13 *versts* (8 miles 5 furlongs) the Toktamish-Bulák spring near the cemetery of that name, and finally, at the 23rd *verst* (15 miles 2 furlongs) reaches the Krach spring. At all the springs named the water is good and sufficiently plentiful, but the best of all both in the quantity and quality of the water is that of Krach-Bulák at the camping ground; the road between Bish-Arik and Krach is over hard, stony ground. There is no grazing or vegetable fuel at all at the Krach spring.
Springs of Krach-Buálk.	23	...	15	2	...	...	*Krach Bulák Springs.*—From the Krach-Bulák spring to the Jidéli stream is 28 *versts* (18 miles 4½ furlongs); throughout this distance the road lies in an undulating country, which, however, presents no difficulty in the way of ascents and descents. At 11 *versts* (7 miles 2¼ furlongs) road reaches the springs of Kuttu-Kuja-Bulák with good water; about the springs is the cemetery of the same name; at 20 *versts* (13 miles 2 furlongs) the road crosses the dry bed of the Shalgain-Kelti stream, in the bed of which to the right of road are springs with good water. At 28 *versts* (18 miles 4½ furlongs) the road reaches the Jidéli stream, the bed of which is also dry, but in it are many good and plentiful springs of water. From Krach to the Shalgaia stream the road is over hard, stony ground, but from the Shalgaia to the Jidéli stream over a salt-soil, and the whole of this locality is covered with light brushwood of "baialich," amongst which are found small bushes of "saksaul." At the camping ground on the Jiédli stream there is a great deal of water; fuel (the small bushes of "baialich" and "saksaul") is plentiful, and there is also sufficient food for camels—"jusan."
Stream Jidéli ...	28	...	18	4½	...	...	*Jidéli Stream.*—From the Jidéli stream to the Min-Bulák springs is 28 *versts* (18 miles 4½ furlongs). The road for this distance lies in a somewhat undulating country, occasionally intersected with wide, but not deep river channels; at 7 *versts* (4 miles 5 furlongs) are the tank and spring of Kotan-Bulák, with good water; at 11 *versts* (7 miles 2¼ furlongs) the road crosses the dry bed of the Aristandi stream, the banks of which are grown over with tamarisk bushes; at 26 *versts* (17 miles 2 furlongs) the road descends to the valley of the Min-Bulák, over which are scattered a number of springs with good fresh water. Throughout the whole march the road lies on hard, stony soil, except in a few places in the hollows in which the soil is salt. Throughout the whole distance there is plenty of "baialich." At the camping ground there is plenty of water, and also a great quantity of "baialich" for fuel; there is only plenty of herbage for forage in the spring, as after that it is eaten up by the Kirgiz nomads.
Springs of Min-Bulák.	28	...	18	4½	...	...	*Min-Bulák springs.*—From the Min-Bulák springs to those of Daut-Kazgán is 53½ *versts* (35 miles 3¾ furlongs). The road from Min-Bulák to the Daut-Kazgán springs lies on the spurs of the Kára-Tourange between the mountains of Kára Murun and Diermen-Tau; the ascents and descents of the spurs are not steep, and present no difficulty. At 16½ *versts* (10 miles 7½ furlongs) on the right of the road under the Diermen-Tau hill are two springs of the same name, in one of which the water is rather salt and bitter, and in the other good, but only in small quantities, perhaps sufficient for a small passing detachment of about 200 men without baggage animals. If both springs were cleaned out a large quantity of water could be counted on. From the 22nd *verst* (14 miles 4¾ furlongs) from the camping ground, the road in some places passes over smooth salt soil, and at 37 *versts* (24 miles 4½ furlongs), diverging from the paths leading to the Ak-Kuduk well, perceptibly changes its former northerly direction for a north-westerly one, and as far as Daut-Kazgán-Tau runs on salt-soil;

From the town of Turkistan to Orsk viâ *the town of Turgai*—contd.

Camping grounds.	From point to point.	Total between chief places.	From point to point.		Total between chief places.		Remarks.
	Versts.	*Versts.*	Miles.	Fur.	Miles.	Fur.	
							between not very large sand hillocks, grown over with "saksaul." At 47 *versts* (31 miles 1¼ furlongs) it again enters the Daut-Kazgán mountains through which it runs as far as the springs at the exit from these hills. The road on this march is on stony soil, except at the salt marshes above named. At the camping ground at the Daut-Kazgán springs there is no grass for forage; a little fuel (bushes of "baialich") and sufficient water in the springs for a detachment of 800 men with all their baggage animals. *N.B.*—As the march from Min-Bulák to the Daut-Kazgán springs is excessively long, it is necessary to carry with one as much water as the vessels permit of. The part of the water used on the first third of the march can be replenished at the Diermen-Bulák spring. In hot weather it is better to make this march at night.
Spring of Daut-Kazgán.	53½	...	35	3¾	...	...	*Daut-Kazgán springs.*—From the Daut-Kazgán springs to the Tele-Kul Lake is 44 *versts* (29 miles 1¼ furlongs). The road between these camping grounds passes over a very level, salt-soil country, grown over with occasional bushes of "saksaul" and "baialich." On approaching Tele-Kul the saksaul bushes become less frequent, and finally, when about 7 *versts* (4 miles 5 furlongs) from the lake, there are none to be found. At the camping ground there is plenty of herbage for forage, and sufficient fuel ("baialich"). The water in the lake is somewhat saltish.
Lake Tele-Kul (south side).	44	...	29	1¼	...	...	*Camping ground on the south shore of the Lake Tele-Kul.*—From the camping ground on the south shore to that on the north shore of the Lake Tele-Kul is 40 *versts* (26 miles 4 furlongs). From the camping ground on the south shore the road takes a north-west direction and runs along the edge of the lake through a level, salt-soil country, thickly overgrown with "saksaul" and tamarisk. At 30 *versts* (19 miles 7 furlongs) the road reaches a narrow arm of the Lake Tele-Kul, across which a dam* about 58½ yards long is constructed, which serves for crossing to the north shore of the lake. From the point of passage to the camping ground the road for a distance of 10 *versts* (6 miles 5 furlongs) runs along the north side of the lake in an easterly direction. At the camping ground on the north shore of the lake there is plenty of meadow grass for forage; there is no fuel; the water in the lakh is fresh.
Lake Tele-Kul (north side).	40	...	26	4	...	...	*Camping ground on the northern shore of Lake Tele-Kul.*—From the camping ground on the northern shore of Lake Tele-Kul to the springs of Kámish-Bulák is 71 *versts* (47 miles ½ furlong). After leaving the lake 12 *versts* (7 miles ¾ furlong) in a north-east direction, the regular caravan road leading to the Kámish-Bulák springs is struck; at 42 *versts* (27 miles 6¾ furlongs) the road descends from the flat level plateau to the basin of Lake Aris, a salt lake; at 54 *versts* (35 miles 6¼ furlongs) the road leads past three wells of Kára-Kuduk, which are on the very shore of Lake Aris. The water in the Kára-Kuduk wells is very salt, and, in addition, so little in quantity that it might be sufficient for 200 men without baggage animals. At 56 *versts* (34 miles 1 furlong) on the right of the road there are also on the margin of the lake the springs of Tuz-Bulák, the water of which is salt and bitter and not much in quantity. At 65 *versts* (43 miles ¾ furlong) the road passes near the brackish spring of Kil-Bulák, whence perceptibly turning to the left, it runs over friable salt-soil to the Kámish-Bulák spring (the halting place). From the very lake of Tele-Kul to the descent into the Aris basin, the road runs over level high ground of clayey soil, mixed with small pebbles; this high ground is studded with an occasional bush of "baialich." After descending into the basin, the road runs over salt-soil intersected in many places with salt marshes, which are difficult to pass in spring. From the wells of Kára-Kuduk to the Kil-Bulák spring for a distance of nearly 11 *versts* (7 miles 2¼ furlongs) the road passes through deep sand between hillocks grown over with "saksaul." At the camping ground at the Kámish-Bulák springs there is plenty of water, which is saltish to the taste; round about the springs are some green reeds, which serve for fodder for horses and baggage animals; there is no fuel. The march of 71 *versts* (46 miles ½ furlong) from Lake Tele-Kul to the Kámish-Bulák springs over an enormous waterless expanse of country is very hard

* This dam was constructed on the 15th/27th June 1874 by men proceeding on indefinite furlough from Tashkend. It was made of "saksaul" and tamarisk found on the shore of the lake; three hours were expended in making it. As the dam mentioned may perhaps be injured by the pressure of water in spring or even carried away, in consequence of which a new one would have to be erected, this circumstance should be borne in mind by commanders conducting marching detachments, in order that on leaving Tashkend they may provide themselves with the necessary quantity of spades, which are also necessary at some of the camping grounds for clearing out the springs and wells.

From the town of Turkistan to Orsk viâ *the town of Turgai*—contd.

Camping grounds.	From point to point.	Total between chief places.	From point to point.		Total between chief places.		Remarks.
	Versts.	*Versts.*	Miles.	Fur.	Miles.	Fur.	
							both on men and baggage animals, and requires to be done at night, at which time camels do not get so quickly wearied, and men also suffer less from thirst: camels have to travel uninterruptedly for twenty-one hours; it is necessary to take water supplies for the road.
Springs Kámishli-Bulák.	71	...	47	0½	...	...	*Kámish-Bulák springs.*—From the Kámish-Bulák spring to Sari-Bulák is 28½ *versts* (18 miles 7¼ furlongs). The road between the springs named runs at first for 7 *versts* (4 miles 5 furlongs) over light salt-soil, cut up with salt marsh, and beyond this to the camping ground of Sari-Bulák over sandy salt-soil, studded with bushes of baialich and saksaul. At 8 and 9 *versts* (5 miles 2¼ furlongs and 5 miles 7¾ furlongs) from the camping ground a quantity of springs are met with scattered on both sides, in some of which the water is fresh, in others brackish; the low ground in which these springs are found is covered with good meadow grass. At 24 *versts* (15 miles 7¼ furlongs) on the left of the road there is a small spring of sulphurous water. The water in the Sari-Bulák spring is clear, ferro-sulphurous, and bitter to the taste; "jusan" furnishes food for camels at the camping ground; and there is plenty of fuel ("saksaul" and "baialich").
Springs Sari-Bulák.	28½	...	18	7¼	...	...	*Sari-Bulák springs.*—From the Sari-Bulák springs to the Espe-Sai stream is 31½ *versts* (20 miles 7 furlongs). The road from Sari-Bulák to the Espe stream is over level country, intersected in three places by broad river channels. At 15 *versts* (9 miles 7½ furlongs) from the camping ground the road passes near the spring of Kutin-Bulák, with bitter water. Throughout the whole march little "saksaul" and "baialich" is met with. In the bed of the Espe stream there is no running water, but there are many springs and ditches with good fresh water; to obtain water in the bed it is sufficient to dig a few spades—full and clear fresh water at once appears; the Kirghiz dig down to the water with their hands even without the aid of any instrument. The valley of the Espe stream about ½ *verst* in width (583 yards) is covered with short green herbage furnishing very good food for horses and camels; there is plenty of fuel ("saksaul" and "baialich").
Brook Espe-Sai ...	31½	...	20	7	...	...	*Espe-Sai stream.*—From the Espe-Sai stream to the Tuz-Bulák springs is 22½ *versts* (14 miles 7¼ furlongs). The road between these camping grounds is over quite level country on salt-soil, and only at 17 *versts* (11 miles 2¼ furlongs) it begins to cross the flat spurs from the high ground of Sandik-Tau, over which rises not very steeply to the camping ground the springs of Tuz-Bulák. At the camping ground there are four springs, of which two are in the ravine by which the road rises and the others, 400 *sajens* (933 yards) to the left of the road, in another hollow; the water in the whole four springs will perhaps suffice for a detachment of about 800 men without baggage animals; the water in the springs is bitter to the taste. At the camping ground there is good food for camels and sufficient fuel ("baialich").
Spring Tuz-Bulák (Sandik).	22½	...	14	7¼	...	...	*Tuz-Bulák springs (Sandik).*—From the Tuz-Bulák springs to the camping ground on the Kalmak-Kirgán river is 31 *versts* (20 miles 4½ furlongs). Between the Tuz-Bulák springs and the Kalmak-Kirgán stream the road crosses a flat highland of hard, sandy soil; along the road are met with small patches with "baialich" bushes. At 6 *versts* (3 miles 7¾ furlongs) the road crosses the broad channel of the Ak-Sai, and at 7 *versts* (4 miles 5 furlongs) between the two wells of Kos-Kudduk water bitter; at 30 *versts* (19 miles 7 furlongs) the road descends to the camping ground in the valley of the Kalmak-Kirgán stream. The water in this river has no continuous current, but is interrupted, remaining in the deep pools of the bed like small elongated lakes and remains so the whole year through. In the pools mentioned a few fish breed (carp). The whole valley of the Kalmak-Kirgán is grown with green "jusan" furnishing very good food for horses, camels, and sheep, and consequently many Kirghiz camps of the Japas tribe are scattered along the stream; the thin bushes of the "kokpek" and "jantal" (thorny bushes) covering the valley serve as good fuel.
Stream Kalmak-Kirgán (Beleudti).	31	...	20	4½	...	...	*River Kalmak-Kirgán (Beleudti).*—From the Kalmak-Kirgán stream to the river Muldir is 34½ *versts* (22 miles 7 furlongs). From the camping ground on the Kalmak-Kirgán the road at first runs along the river valley, and at 6 *versts* (3 miles 7¾ furlongs) rises at a very decided incline; at 7 *versts* (4 miles 5 furlongs) the road crosses a not very deep hollow; at 17 *versts* (11 miles 2¼ furlongs) passes through the dry bed of the Miur; and at 35 *versts* (23 miles 1¾ furlongs) reaches the camping ground on the Muldir stream. Along the road on this march there is scarcely any vegetation, except in the valley of the dry

From the town of Turkistan to Orsk viâ *the town of Turgai*—contd.

Miur stream, in which grass grows. At the camping ground there is good water in great quantities, plenty of fodder (" jusan" and meadow grass), and a little fuel (roots of dry "jusan").

Camping grounds.	From point to point.	Total between chief places.	From point to point.		Total between chief places.		Remarks.
	Versts.	*Versts.*	Miles.	Fur.	Miles.	Fur.	
Stream Muldir (Bulánti).	34½	...	22	7	...	...	*River Muldir (Bulánti).*—From the Muldir stream to the Kugálajar stream is 46 *versts* (30 miles 6¼ furlongs). From the camping place on the Muldir the road rises, but not steeply, to an insignificant height, and at 5 *versts* (3 miles 2¼ furlongs) crosses a narrow, but deep, dry ravine; at 22 *versts* (14 miles 4¾ furlongs) it runs through a dry hollow; at 24 *versts* (15 miles 7¼ furlongs) on the right and 27 *versts* (17 miles 7¼ furlongs) on the left the road passes by two pasture fields sown with feather grass; at 31 *versts* (20 miles 4¼ furlongs) the road crosses the ravine of Taldi-Sai, in which in some places, on the left of the road, snow-water remains throughout the whole summer, and caravans often camp there. In the years in which there is much snow in winter, great deal of water remains in the Taldi-Sai ravine in the summer. Further on, the road, after crossing three slight hollows running into the dry Teresken-Sai ravine at the 34th, 37th, and 39th *versts* (22 miles 4¼ furlongs, 24 miles 4¼ furlongs, and 25 miles 6¾ furlongs), reaches the river Kugálajar at the 47th *verst* (31 miles 1¼ furlongs)—the camping ground. Throughout the whole march between the Muldir and Kugálajar streams the road runs on hard, sandy soil, studded with small "jusan," and very occasionally here and there with bushes of "baialich." At the camping ground on the Kugalajar streams there are a number of springs in its bed with a large supply of water, but there is no regular stream; there is plenty of grass for forage and a little fuel (roots of "jusan").
Stream Kugálajar (Jimike).	46½	...	30	6¼	...	...	*River Kugálajar (Jimike).*—From the river Kugálajar to the river Kargála is 41 *versts* (27 miles 1¼ furlongs). The road on the camping ground rises up the steep bank of the Kugálajar stream to a flat high land, along which it runs up to the next camping ground; on this march the road runs through several slight hollows covered with feather grass. The whole country between the Kugálajar and Kargála streams is level on hard, sandy soil and studded with small "jusan." The camping ground on the river Kargála is a very good one; the water is very good; the valley covered with many good herbs, "jusan," fine reeds, and cow-parsnip, furnishing good food for horses and baggage animals; a little fuel (roots of "jusan"). In the Kargála stream there is an excessively large quantity of fish (perch and gudgeon).
Stream Kargála ...	41	...	27	1¼	...	...	*River Kargála.*—From the Kargála stream to that of Kaïdagul is 31 *versts* (20 miles 4¼ furlongs). Having left the Kargála ½ *verst* (583 yards) the road crosses a branch of the stream and imperceptibly rises out of the valley on to a flat high land; at 14 *versts* (9 miles 2¼ furlongs) the road crosses the Kudukti-Saï ravine, which falls into the basin of the Kárakul on the left of the road, in which the spring season water sometimes remains throughout the whole summer; on the right side, near the road, in the Kudukti-Sai ravine, there is a not very deep well of fresh water; further on, at the 18th, 25th, and 29th *verests* (11 miles 7¼ furlongs, 16 miles 4¼ furlongs, and 19 miles 1¾ furlongs), the road passes some small basins, in which a great deal of the spring water sometimes remains. These holes are covered with cow-parsnip and fine green reeds. Between the Kargála and Kaïdagul stream the road runs over level country on hard, sandy soil; along the road a great deal of feather grass is met with. The Kaïdagul stream (the camping ground) only has a regular stream in spring; during the remainder of the year little lakes of good fresh water remain in the bed. There is plenty of fodder at the camping ground of a good quality; no fuel.
Stream Kaïdagul ...	31	...	20	4¼	...	...	*River Kaïdagul.*—From the river Kaïdagul to the camping ground on the south-western edge of Lake Bashche-Kul is 21 *versts* (13 miles 7½ furlongs). From the camping ground in the Kaïdagul the road runs to Lake Bashche-Kul over somewhat undulating country, full of small basins, a large number of which are covered with cow-parsnip; the road throughout the whole march is on clay soil, grown over with "jusan," and occasionally feather grass; at 14 *versts* (9 miles 2¼ furlongs) on the right of the road are ditches with fresh water. The water in Lake Bashche-Kul is fresh; on its shores there is plenty of meadow grass and reeds for fodder for horses and camels; for fuel there is in summer dung, and in autumn and winter plenty of reed cane. The Kirghis have their winter quarters at Lake Bashche-Kul.
Lake Bashche-Kul ...	21	...	13	7½	...	...	*Lake Bashche-Kul.*—From Lake Bashche-Kul to the river Jalánchik is 57½ *versts* (38 miles ½ furlong). The road from Bashche-Kul up to camping ground on the Jalánchik runs over an undulating

From the town of Turkistan to Orsk viâ *the town of Turgai*—contd.

Camping grounds.	From point to point.	Total between chief places.	From point to point.		Total between chief places.		Remarks.
	Versts.	*Versts.*	Miles.	Fur.	Miles.	Fur.	

country, full of a number of basins, the greater part of which are covered with meadow grass and fine reeds. In these basins or depressions there is spring water. Commencing at 14 *versts* (9 miles 2¼ furlongs) and up to 31 *versts* (20 miles 4½ furlongs) the road is on sands, amongst which there are some soft places. At the 31st and 34th *versts* (20 miles 4½ furlongs and 22 miles 4½ furlongs) the road runs through two deep hollows running into the low ground of the Sazánbai, with its salt marsh on the left of the road. With the exception of the 17th *verst* (11 miles 2¼ furlongs) of sandy ground, the road on this march lies the whole time on firm sand. At 58 *versts* (38 miles 3¼ furlongs) the road slopes down to the river Jalánchik, the camping ground. The water in the stream is running; the banks are grown over with meadow grass and fine green rushes; there is no fuel growing at the camping ground. There are a great many fish in the Jalánchik—pike of large size, perch, &c.

N.B.—According to the Kirghiz, caravans do not perform this march of 57½ *versts* (38 miles ¼ furlong) in one day, but camp at the wells of Sazánbai-Kuduk at 30 *versts* (19 miles 7 furlongs) from Lake Bashche-Kul. Although there are indeed wells, there is very little water in them, and that is so brackish and tainted that detachments marching should not count on these wells, but go direct from Lake Basche-Kul to the Jalánchik stream.

Camping grounds.	From point to point (Versts)	Total between chief places (Versts)	From point to point (Miles)	(Fur.)	Total between chief places (Miles)	(Fur.)	Remarks.
Stream Jalánchik ...	57½	...	38	¼	...	...	*River Jalánchik.*—From the river Jalanchik to the Batpa-Kuduk ditches is 34½ *versts* (22 miles 7 furlongs).

After crossing the river Jalánchik, on leaving the camping ground, by a deep and swampy ford, the road rises to hilly high ground from the river, and at 4 *versts* (2 miles 5¼ furlongs) descending into low ground of salt-soil, passes near an elongated basin with water in it leaving it on the right; at 7 *versts* (4 miles 5 furlongs) the road passes near the sandhill of Sarali-Tam with a tomb on it; at 11 and 12 *versts* (7 miles 2¼ furlongs) and 7 miles 7¾ furlongs) the road runs along the left side of the Kara-Tuz salt lake; at 29 *versts* (19 miles 1¾ furlongs) the road rising on to a flat high land, quickly descends again to the salt lake of Batpa-Karasu, along the north-east shore of which it runs to the hollow of Batpa- Kuduk with its cuttings where the camping ground is. The road on this march lies in a salt-soil district almost bare. At the camping ground there are many ditches, but only five with water in them. The water in the wells is good and may supply 1,000 men without baggage animals, which can be watered in the neighbouring Lake Batap-Kára-Su, the water in which is unfit for the use of men; the water in the cuts can be obtained without the use of ropes. There is sufficient fodder about the cuts; fuel there is none.

Camping grounds.	From point to point (Versts)	Total between chief places (Versts)	From point to point (Miles)	(Fur.)	Total between chief places (Miles)	(Fur.)	Remarks.
Batna Kuduk (canal)	34½	...	22	7	...	...	*Batna Kuduk wells.*—(In a small valley running into Lake Bapta-Kára-Su) From the camping

ground at the Batpa-Kuduk wells to the river Kábirga is 36½ *versts* (24 miles 1¼ furlongs). The road between these points runs in a somewhat undulating country, full of basins and lakes. At 8 *versts* from the camping ground on the left of the road is the large meadow of Chubti-Kul, in which there is much water in spring; but in summer it dries up, and this basin is covered with good meadow grass; at 17 *versts* (11 miles 2¼ furlongs) the road passes through a hollow, joining the Lakes Ala-Kul and Chukur-Kul; the latter is on the right of the road, 4 *versts* off (2 miles 5¼ furlongs) near the tomb of Hasan-Ilimes; on the shores of Chukur-Kul the Kirghiz cultivate wheat and millet; at 28 *versts* (18 miles 4½ furlongs) passes through a wide salt, marshy hollow running out from a salt lake near the road. The whole locality between the Batpa wells and the river Kábirga is on clayey salt-soil and covered with "jusan" and feather grass; basins are met with along the road for the greater part grown over with meadow herbs. The water in the river Kábirga is good; "jusan" and fine green rushes on the banks of the stream furnish good fodder for baggage animals; there is sufficient fuel (roots of "jusan").

Camping grounds.	From point to point (Versts)	Total between chief places (Versts)	From point to point (Miles)	(Fur.)	Total between chief places (Miles)	(Fur.)	Remarks.
Stream Kábirga ...	36½	...	24	1¼	...	...	*River Kábirga.*—From the camping ground on the river Kábirga the road runs at first for 1½ *versts* (1

mile) in a north-east direction along the left bank of the river, then crosses to the right bank at a point where it is dry, and turns sharply to the west, after which at 3 *versts* (2 miles) from the camping ground it descends imperceptibly to the meadow-like valley of the river Turgai; at 8 *versts* 5 miles 2½ furlongs) makes a sharp turn to the north-east, and from here to the river Turgai for a distance of 6 *versts* (3 miles 7¾ furlongs) passes through inundated meadows (water meadows) on which the spring water sometimes remains for a long time, as, for instance, up to the middle of July; but such a prolonged presence of water in the Turgai valley happens very seldom, and generally the water subsides by the 1st June. When nearly a *verst* (5¼ furlongs) from the town the road crosses the river Turgai by a well-constructed wooden bridge, which is always put together at the end of the month of May; from the time the river overflows until the bridge is put up the crossing is made by a ferry about 5 *versts* (3 miles 2¼ furlongs) above the town; the ferry is kept by Kirghiz. When the river Turgai keeps within its banks, the width

From the town of Turkistan to Orsk viâ *the town of Turgai*—contd.

is from 35 to 58 yards, and the depth inconsiderable; the water in the river is excellent. Detachments passing through camp on the right bank of the river at the bridge. In the river Turgai there are a great many fish (pike, porch, roach, and carp), catching which forms almost the chief occupation of the inhabitants of the town. From the river Kábirga to Turgai is 15¼ *versts* (10 miles 1 furlong). There are 28 gates to the town.

Camping ground.	From point to point.	Total between chief places.	From point to point.		Total between chief places.		Remarks.
	Versts.	*Versts.*	Miles.	Fur.	Miles.	Fur.	
Turgai, town of ...	15¼	775	10	1	513	7¾	*Town of Turgai.*—From the town of Turgai to the Koshelák water-cuts is 30½ *versts* (20 miles 1¾ furlongs). The road between these points runs through an almost level country on hard sand, grown over with good herbs. In the first 5 *versts* (3 miles 2½ furlongs) from the town the road runs through five not very deep hollows; at 28 *versts* (16 miles 4¼ furlongs) is the Kára-Sai hollow, in which at 2 *versts* (1 mile 2¼ furlongs) more to the right of the road are scattered many fresh wells, at which there are some Kirghiz villages; at 25 *versts* (16 miles 4¼ furlongs) on the road itself on the right there are many water cuts of Kung-Aigir with fresh water; at 31 *versts* the road reaches the Koshelák wells; the camping ground studded about in a good meadow basin at the foot of a sandhill. At the camping ground there are many wells, and the water in them is fresh, but they all require cleaning out; although the Kirghiz, who winter here, clear them out in the autumn, they again get blocked up during the winter, and remain in this condition throughout the whole summer. As the water in these wells is not more than 3½ to 5 feet below the surface of the ground, passing detachments would not require more than half an hour to clean them out; there is plenty of food for horses and camels, but no fuel growing.
Koshelák canal ...	30½	...	20	1¾	...	...	*Koshelák wells.*—From the Koshelák wells to the camping ground on the right bank of the river Ulkayak is 36 *versts* (23 miles 7 furlongs). From Koshelák to the Ulkayak stream the road runs in an almost westerly direction over undulating ground, full of basins; at 10 *versts* (6 miles 5 furlongs) it runs through the Chukur-Kára-Sai hollow, in which, on the left of the road, are many fresh wells: at 18 and 19 *versts* (12 miles 7¼ furlongs and 12 miles 4¾ furlongs) the road runs through a large basin, inundated in spring by the overflow of the river Kábirga, and furnishing the Kirghiz with rich hay crops; at 23 *versts* (15 miles 2 furlongs) the road crosses the river Ulkayak, easily fordable, and from this point perceptibly change its direction to the north-west. After crossing, the road runs along the Ulkayak on its right bank, and at 14 *versts* (9 miles 2¼ furlongs) turns to the camping ground. The soil on this march is hard sand, grown over with "jusan" tamarisk, and feather grass; the water in the Ulkayak is fresh; there is ample forage at the camping ground, but no fuel.
Stream Ulkayak ...	36	...	23	7	...	...	*Camping ground on the right bank of the river Ulkayak.*—From the camping ground on the Ulkayak the road as far as the Kára-Butak stream leads along the river, leaving about 1 to 2¼ *versts* (5¼ furlongs to 1 mile 5¼ furlongs) on the right. Only at 39 *versts* (25 miles 6¾ furlongs) does it again touch the river, which it again at once quits. The road on this march runs through many inconsiderable hollows and runs over an almost imperceptibly undulating country with hard sand soil, covered with "jusan," cow-parsnip, and feather grass; at the camping ground on the Kára-Butak the water is fresh; there is plenty of herbage (feather grass, cow-parsnip) for camels and horses; there is no fuel.
Stream Kára-Butak	42¼	28	...	...	...	...	*Camping ground on the river Kára-Butak close to its confluence with the Ulkayak.*—From the camping ground on the river Kára-Butak to the river Teris-Butak the road continues at a slight slope along the right bank of the Ulkayak; at 16 *versts* (10 miles 4¾ furlongs) from the Kára-Butak the road crosses the shallow Jantai stream by a ford; it runs through the dry hollow of Koilibai-Sai, and at 25 *versts* (16 miles 4½ furlongs) of Kiz-Sai. The soil on this march is hard sand; the whole locality is covered with good feather grass and cow-parsnip. At the camping ground on the Teris-Butak stream the water is good, and there is a great deal of grass for forage; there is no fuel.
Stream Teris-Butak	32¾	...	21	5¾	...	...	*River Teris-Butak.*—The road from Teris-Butak to Lake Ak-Chakti runs almost level on sand soil, covered with feather grass and cow-parsnip; at 8 *versts* (5 miles 2¼ furlongs) runs through one of the hollows forming the upper course of the river Ulkayak; at 26 *versts* (17 miles 2 furlongs) the road descends to low ground, and reaches the small Ak-Chakti lake, the camping ground; the water

From the town of Turkistan to Orsk viâ *the town of Turgai*—contd.

Camping grounds.	From point to point.	Total between chief places.	From point to point.		Total between chief places.		Remarks.
	Versts	*Versts.*	Miles.	Fur.	Miles.	Fur.	
							in the lake is very good; its banks are covered with grass and all the country about with excellent feather grass; there is no fuel. *N.B.*—There is a great deal of sorrel round the Lake Ak-Chakti.
Lake Ak-Chakti ...	26	...	17	1¾	...	...	*Lake Ak-Chakti.*—From the camping ground on Lake Ak-Chakti the road for the first 4 *versts* (2 miles 5¼ furlongs) passes over low ground full of little fresh-water lakes and meadow basins; at 4 *versts* (2 miles 5¼ furlongs) it traverses the broad Ak-Chakti hollow, in which the snow-water sometimes remains for a long time; at 10 *versts* (6 miles 5 furlongs) on the left of the road and close to it are fresh wells of Ak-Chakti; at 27 *versts* (17 miles 7¼ furlongs) the road descends almost imperceptibly into a vast basin containing the large lake of Aike-Kul, which lies 1½ *versts* (1 mile) to the right of the road on the shores of Lake Aike-Kul, and in its vicinity the Kirghiz mow a great deal of hay. At 33 *versts* (21 miles 7 furlongs) the road reaches the camping ground on the moderately-sized Lake Daul-Kul. The road on this march is through perfectly level country continuously covered with excellent feather grass; the water in Lake Daul-Kul is slightly salty, and according to the Kirghiz sometimes dries up: there is plenty of feather grass for forage at the camping ground, and no fuel except dung.
Lake Daul-Kul ...	32¼	...	21	3¼	...	...	*Lake Daul-Kul.*—The road from Lake Daul-Kul to the river Kazánchi-Kára-Su, taking a westerly direction, at first runs level, and at the 11 *versts* (7 miles 2¼ furlongs) rises imperceptibly on to flat high ground; at 19 *versts* (11 miles 2¼ furlongs) from the camping ground, the road passes near the inconsiderable Lake Jilán-Kul, which is almost continuously covered with reeds; at 23 *versts* (15 miles 2 furlongs) on the left of the road also lies the small Lake Chukur-Kul; at 30 *versts* (19 miles 7 furlongs) the road descends to Lake Jiti-Kul (Chelkar), which it leaves on the south, and running in a north-westerly direction reaches the camping ground at 39 *versts* (25 miles 6¾ furlongs). The road from Daul-Kul to the river Kazánchi-Kára-Su passes over hard sand soil grown over with excellent feather grass. At the camping ground on the Kazánchi stream the water is good; on the banks of the stream are many places in which meadow and feather grass grows; there is no fuel.
Stream Kazánchi-Kára-Su.	39	...	25	6¾	...	...	*River Kazánchi-Kára-Su.*—(Not far from where it falls into Lake Jiti-Kul—Chelkar.) From camping ground on the river Kazánchi-Kára-Su the road, after running for 7 *versts* (4 miles 5 furlongs) along the right bank of the river, leaves the little Lake Kára-Su, which is the source of the river Kazánchi on the right; further on, at 26 *versts*, the road imperceptibly ascends to flat high ground separating the source of the river Kokpekti from the Jiti-Kul depression and soon descends along a dry hollow to the camping ground where the hollow joins another, with water in it, and having united form the commencement of the river Kokpekti. The road on this march is level on hard sand-soil, covered with excellent feather grass; besides this there are along the road many meadows; at the camping ground on the Kokpekti stream the water is excellent; there is a great deal of meadow and feather grass, but no fuel.
Stream Kokpekti ...	34½	...	22	7	...	...	*River Kokpekti.*—From the camping ground on the river Kokpekti the road to Alin-Sai runs at first along the left bank of the Kokpekti, and at 8 *versts* (5 miles 2¼ furlongs) crossing the river at a good ford continues on over an undulating country intersected with shallow ravines; at 19 *versts* (12 miles 4¾ furlongs) the road also crosses the river Kumak at a good ford, and up to the camping ground runs over the same kind of country as on the first half of the march. Although on this march there are many ravines across the road, they in no way render movement difficult. The whole country between the rivers Kokpekti and Alin-Sai is on hard sand-soil, covered with feather grass. At the camping ground on the Alin-Sai the water is good, and there is plenty of feather grass for forage, but no fuel. *N.B.*—At 7 *versts* (4 miles 5 furlongs) from the camping ground on the Kokpekti, the old transport road, which is much more circuitous than the present one, branches off to the left.
Stream Alin-Sai ...	37¼	...	24	5½	...	...	*River Alin-Sai.*—On the march between the rivers Alin-Sai and Ak-Jár the road traverses a very undulating country, running through a great many unimportant small ravines and hollows, and in consequence has many sinuosities in order to cross them conveniently at 10 *versts* (6 miles 5 furlongs). From the camping ground the road crosses the river Issanbai, at 14 *versts* (9 miles 2¼ furlongs) the Isebai, and at 21 *versts* (13 miles 7¼ furlongs) the Kutebai. All three streams have

From the town of Turkistan to Orsk viâ *the town of Turgai*—concld.

Camping grounds.	From point to point.	Total between chief places.	From point to point.		Total between chief places.		Remarks.
	Versts.	*Versts.*	Miles.	Fur.	Miles.	Fur.	
							little water in them, and are consequently easily practicable at the fords at any season of the year; the soil on this march is clayey, and the whole country is covered with feather grass and cow-parsnip. At the camping ground on the river Ak-Jár the water is good, and there is plenty of forage for camels and horses, but no fuel.
Stream Ak-Jár ...	33¼	...	22	1¼	...	...	*River Ak-Jár.*—The road from the river Ak-Jár to the Kára-Sai estuary passes through almost level country, and only rises at half way to an inconsiderable height, from which it quickly descends into the valley of the river Or. At 11 *versts* (7 miles 2¼ furlongs) from the camping ground the road passes near the moderately-sized Lake Kyán-Kul; at 24 *versts* (15 miles 7¼ furlongs) it passes to the right of Lake Jaltir-Kul, in which the water sometimes dries up. The water at the camp on the Kára-Su estuary is very good; there is plenty of forage for camels and horses, but no fuel.
Kára-Su (tributary of the river Or).	28¼		18	7½			*Kára-Su* (an estuary of the river Or).—From the Kára-Su estuary to the town of Orsk is 27 *versts* (17 miles 7½ furlongs). The road runs in the valley of the Or, through land almost continuously planted with wheat, millet, and vegetables; at 21 *versts* (13 miles 7½ furlongs) the road imperceptibly rises to an insignificant height, from which it again at once descends into the low ground, watered by the rivers Or and Ural; in this locality the town of Orsk is situated, having about 2,000 houses. All detachments passing through are disposed of by billetting.
	27		17	7			
Orsk, town of ...		399¼			274	6¼	
Total ...		1,174¼			788	4¼	

This route avoids the worst part of the Postal route from Orenburgh to Tashkent.

For—from Orsk to Orenburgh and Turkestan to Tashkent see—Postal Route.

C. M. M.

Appendix Q.

Nijni Novgorod to Tashkend.

Kazan, 280 miles; 30 hours, steamer; river Volga; navigation easy, April to December.

Nijni Novgorod, a large town, which carries on much trade close to the banks of the river Volga, on which 300 steamers ply, and also run up the Kama to Perm. There are large dockyards.—(Siberia in Asia by Seabohen.)

Kazan, the town of, is 4 *versts* inland from the river: there is a tramway from the town to the bank.

Perm, 520 miles; 58 hours, steamer; river Kama; navigation easy, April to November.

The same steamers can run up the Kama from the Volga. Perm, a large town, about 20,000 inhabitants. There are dockyards here.

Ekaterinburg, 300 miles; 20 hours, train; railway single line.

Eketerinburg is connected with Perm by a single line railway passing across the Mul mountains. The place has about 30,000 inhabitants. There is a large foundry here. There are iron mines about 100 miles from the town, giving large outturn in the year. (Siberian Overland Route).—'Michie.'

Tienmen, 220 miles; road; road bad.

The roads are bad. The country passed through is gently undulating, well-wooded, fertile, and well populated.

Nijni Novgorod to Tashkend—contd.

Tienmen, a thriving place: everything telling of commerce and wealth; supplies plentiful and cheap; situated on the river 'Toora.' This river in winter is full of steamers frozen in, which are brought here for winter quarters. There is a dockyard here, and good steamers are turned out.

The Toora is navigable only from the spring until August for large vessels, but small vessels can ply at any time, except when the river is frozen. The Toora flows into the Tobol, which flows into the Irtish at Tobolsk. The country through which these rivers flow is flat; there are large willow beds along the low banks; Russian and Tartar hamlets and settlements numerous. Country fertile; supplies plentiful.

Tobolsk, 100 miles; 32 hours, steamer; rivers Tonga and Tobol; navigation easy between April and August.

All the country between Tienmen and Omsk and up to Tobolsk is very fertile and "living is so extravagantly cheap that there is little or no incentive to work. Beef can be purchased at 2*d*. a lb. and hay and corn are so cheap that horses can be hired for ½*d*. a mile."

From Tobolsk navigation continues up the Irtish river. The same steamer can run through. The regular ordinary steamers ply twice a week.—(Murray's Hand-book to Russia in Asia.)

Tobolsk is a large town of 10,000 inhabitants, situated at the junction of the Tobol with the Irtish; it is a thriving place.—(Siberian Overland Route.)

Omsk, 540 miles; 135 hours, steamer; river Irtish; navigation easy by day and on moon-light nights between April and the end of November.—[Central Asia (Atkinson).]

"Omsk" situated at the junction of the 'Om' with the Irtish; has 12,000 inhabitants, and is the residence of the Governor-General of Western Siberia—(Siberian Overland Route.) The country immediately round Omsk is a bare barren steppe.—(Murray's Handbook.)

Semipalatinsk; 480 miles; 120 hours, steamer; River Irtish; navigation easy by day and on moonlight nights between April and the end of November.—(Central Asia.)

Semipalatinsk, chief town of province of that name. Population 10,000; situated on a junction of Semipalatinska river with Irtish. A large trade carried on with Tashkend, Kulja, and Kashgar. Country fairly fertile. —(Murray's Handbook.)

* The communications between Orenburg and Tashkend were during the winter in a most deplorable state and almost impassable, and probably on this account attention was directed to opening a new route, which bids fair to supersede, for the greater part of the year, the old road along the right bank of the Sir Daria.

* This is the most practicable of the routes from Siberia into Central Asia. It runs parallel with Tehzhungarian border line, and it has therefore a two-fold importance in a strategical sense, for it also commands all the routes leading from the Semipalatinsk and Semiraitchen provinces to the interior of Tehzhungarian.—(Review of Russian Frontiers in Asia, by Colonel Venyukopp, translated from the Russian by Major Gowan.)

Passengers and mails for Tashkend now proceed by rail to Nijni Novgorod on the Volga, thence by steamer to Perm, where a railway runs across the Ural Mountains to Ekaterinburg. Post carts run from this town to the river Mias, where steamers ply to Tobolsk.

From Tobolsk another line of steamers run up the Irtish to the town of Semipalatinsk, about 1,000 miles distant. This closes the journey by water, and another 700 miles by post road brings the traveller to Vernoë, the depôt of the Kuldja region, and 300 miles further to Tashkend itself. This route, though longer than the old road, has been selected by the postal authorities, as it can be traversed in less time; it has also the advantage in the case of troops of being less fatiguing, as the men are spared the heat and thirst accompanying a march across the almost barren region lying between Orenburg and the Aral. Some idea may be gained of the facility this route gives for the despatch of reinforcements to Eastern Turkestan, when it is mentioned that during the spring of 1880 a steamer arrived at Semipalatinsk from Tobolsk, tugging barges and conveying in all 1,200 troops to reinforce the Kuldja Division. The objection to this route is that it is only open for a part of the year, when the rivers are not frozen.

From Tashkend to Semipaládtinsk, Postal Road.

	From point to point.	Total between chief places.	From point to point.		Total between chief places.		Remarks.
	Versts.	*Versts.*	Miles.	Fur.	Miles.	Fur.	
CHIMKEND DIVISION.							
Mánkend (Ak-Su) ...	26¼		13	4¾			The road to Varnore is a mail road, and as far as Chimkent from Tashkent is the same as the road from Tashkent to Orenburgh. From Chimkent on it is a good road, running through Russian colonies which (according to Colonel Venukoff) may be looked upon as the base of Russian operations in Turkistan.—(Routes in Asia.)
Mashat ...	15½		10	2¼			
Yas-Kichu ...	19¼		12	6½			
Tulkubásh ...	23½		15	4½			
Chak-Pak ...	23½		15	4¾			Between Chimkent and Chakpate many rivers and ravines are crossed.
AULI-ATA DIVISION.				7¼			Crosses the Talas river at Kuyak.
				0¾			Auli Ata is situated on the rapid river of Talas, and is now but an insignificant country town, but is a large market for the district round; since taken by the Russians it has increased in size and importance, but is still a straggling, shabby place on a bare steppe.—(Schuyler.)
Tersk ...	24		15				
Kuyuk ...	18¼		12				
Golovachevsk ...	17½		11	5			
Auli-Ata. Town of—	14½		9	4¾			
		196½			117½	0½	
Uch-Bulák ...	22		14	4¾			Close to the Talas river the road runs over level ground on the other side of and close to Auli-Ata; the ground is much intersected with ravines, after that as far as Merke the country is level and easy.
Ak-Chulak ...	17		11	2			
Akhir-Tube ...	21		13	7¼			
Maldabaeff ...	15½		9	7½			
Kum-Arik ...	21		14	0¼			
Tarti ...	23¾		15	5¾			
Munkinsk ...	19		12	4¾			
Merke ...	16½		10	7¾			Close round Merke the ground is cut up by ravines. Here there is a Fort, Post Office, and Telegraph Station.
		155½				0½	
Chaaldavar ...	29		19	1¾	103		

From Tashkend to Semipalátinsk, Postal Road.

	From point to point.	Total between chief places.	From point to point.		Total between chief places.		Remarks.
	Versts.	*Versts.*	Miles.	Fur.	Miles.	Fur.	
Province of Semirechia, Tokmak Division.							
Kára-Balti ...	29		19	1¾			At Aksu there is a Fort.
Ak-Su (settlement)	19		12	4¾			From Auli-Ata to Bukuluk the road runs close to the mountains of

Alexandrovski and many rivulets from this range are crossed. The chief are Shiraly, 'The Kinnuk,' 'Jilanys,' and 'Sukuluk' rivers.—(R.I.A.)

	From point to point (Versts).	Total between chief places (Versts).	Miles.	Fur.	Miles.	Fur.	Remarks.
Sukuluk ...	14¾		9	6¼			From Pishpek to Kurdai the road follows the valley of the river 'Chu' and that of its tributary 'Argaity'; at Pishpek the valley of
Ala-Archa (Pishpek)	24¼		16	4¾			
		116			76	7¼	

the 'Chu' is eleven miles wide, but gradually narrows as the road progresses.

The 'Chu' is a rapid turbid river running between great belts of reeds that protect the banks from being washed away by the current. Its current is never less than 10 feet per second. It is, however, generally fordable except in spring.

The reeds along the shore extend at Pishpek to 2 miles in width. At Pishpek there is a fort. The great dryness of the air here prevents much vegetation except a zone along the base of the Alatun mountains.

Vernei Division.	From point to point (Versts).	Total between chief places (Versts).	Miles.	Fur.	Miles.	Fur.	Remarks.
Constantinoff (Chuiska).	22¾		15	0½			At Constantinoff of the river Chu is crossed by a good wooden bridge.
Sagatinsk ...	23		15	2			From Kurdai the road leads up the valley of the Argaity across some inconsiderable mountains to the
Kurdai ...	30		19	7½			

south side of the spur of the Alatan range, and then up the glen of the Kurdai stream, and there runs close to the mountain range, and then up the Kopa valley the ground being level.

	From point to point (Versts).	Total between chief places (Versts).	Miles.	Fur.	Miles.	Fur.	Remarks.
Otar ...	32½		21	4¼			From Otar the road continues to pass up the Kopa valley and crosses several hollows and ravines and runs up to Kastek an elevation of about 3,300 feet. Here there is a Russian Fort and Post Office.
Targap ...	30		20	1¾			
Kastek ...	33¼		22	0¼			
Uzun-Agach ...	26½		17	4½			
Kiskilensk station (Lubovninsk).	27		17	7¼			

From Kiskilenski to Varnore the road runs along level ground, but crosses rivulets and gullies from the mountains which are at a distance of 4 to 5 miles.

	From point to point (Versts).	Total between chief places (Versts).	Miles.	Fur.	Miles.	Fur.	Remarks.
Vernei, chief town of province.	27		17	7¼			Fort Vanor, the centre of Russian civil and military administration, consists of a fort and military agricultural district, which has a population of between 5,000 and 6,000 in-
		252½			167	3	

habitants. The district is well irrigated and is fertile. The elevation is about 2,430 feet. It has a great range of temperature being very hot in summer and very cold in winter. Murray's Handbook.)

	From point to point (Versts).	Total between chief places (Versts).	Miles.	Fur.	Miles.	Fur.	Remarks.
Kurasui picket ...	24½		16	1¾			Plain, with ravines at foot of mountains.
Kutentai ,, ...	22½		14	7½			Pass, into the Karatal Valley.
Ili settlement ...	23½		15	4½			Plain, pass across the Karatal.
Chingildin picket ...	23½		15	4½			Plain and the undulating country.
Kopal Division.							
Kara Chekin picket	33½		22	1¾			Sharp descent to the Koksa afterwards a pass.
Kuyan-Kus ,,	27¾		18	3¼			Passage of Koksa and then over mountains.
Altin Emel ,,	27½		18	1½			Valley cut up by ravines.
		182¾			121	1	Ditto ditto.
Kugalin picket ...	22¼		14	6			Undulating country.
Tsaritsin ,, ...	25		16	4¾			Plain with a few ravines.

From Tashkend to Semipalátia Postal Road—concld.

Ports.	Distance along the River.						Remarks.
	Between ports.		From Fort No. 1.		From Fort Perovski.		
	Versts.	Miles.	*Versts.*	Miles.	*Versts.*	Miles.	
Jangar-Agách picket	20½		13	4½			Crumbling sands; passage of the Ili by boats.
Kara-Bulak (settlement).	22		14	4¾			Plain with sandy soil.
Sara-Bulak picket...	30		19	7			Ditto ditto.
Ak-Ichki ,, ...	26		17	2			Steppe with small quantity of grass.
Kopal, town of ...	27		17	7¼			Undulating country through Aiaguz and over level country.
		172¾			114	4¼	
Arasan ...	29		19	1¾			Steppe.
Abakumoff picket...	21		13	7¼			
		50			33	1	
Aksu ,, ...	25½		16	7¼			
Baskan ,, ...	28½		18	7¼			
Sergiopol Division.							
Lepsa picket ...	28½		18	7¼			Crumbling sands and hilly country.
Ashchi-Bulak picket	34		22	4¼			Slightly undulating and waterless country.
Arganatin ,,	29½		19	4¼			Steppe with sandy soil.
Jus-Agách ,,	31		20	4½			Ditto clayey loam.
Lesser Aiaguz ,,	26		17	2			Plain with scanty green grass.
Kizil-Kis ,,	26		17	1¾			Ditto fairly succulent grass.
Taldi-Kuduk ,,	23¾		15	6			Ascent to the mountains mineral springs.
Central Aiaguz ,,	29		19	1¾			Country undulating and turn flat.
Sergiopol, town of	31½		20	7			On the right bank of the Aiaguz Fort and station.
		313¼			207	5¼	
Province of Semipalátia.							
Altin-Kilat picket...	26¼		17	3¼			
Enreki ,, ...	22¾		15	0½			
Uzun-Bulák ,, ...	26¼		17	3¼			
Archan-Adir ,, ...	24½		16	2			
Arkat ,, ..	24		15	7½			At the base of Arket mountains.
Kizil-Mulin ,, ...	26½		17	4½			Undulating country.
Jertav ,, ...	26		17	2			
Ashchi-Kul ,, ...	21½		14	2			
Arkalik picket ...	27		17	7			(Review of Russian frontiers in Asia) Colonel Venyukoff.
Ulugnz ...	22		14	4¾			
Semipalátia, chief town of province.	25		16	4¼			
		271¾			180	1	
Total ...		1,803			1,195	2½	

Appendix R.

From Pir Choki to Jamu along South-West and North Afghan frontier.

1, South Kirta, 16 miles; 2, New Bibi Nani, 13 miles; 3, Mach, 13½ miles; 4, Darwaza, 16½ miles; 5, Mastang, 21 miles; 6, Babari, 13 miles; 7, Kardagaf, 17 miles; 8, Salungun, 18 miles; 9, Nushki, 18 miles; 10, Jabba, 22 miles;

11, camp west of Muhabbat, 21 miles; 12 Saitar, 22 miles; 13, Koh-i-Gao, 25 miles; 14, Chargeh, 17½ miles; 15, Tumpa Gaz, 29 miles; 16, Bahrab Chah, 23 miles; 17, Kiachah, 16 miles; 18, Rabat, 18½ miles; 19, Sukaluk, 15 miles; 20, Pulalak, 40 miles; 21, Rudbar, 36 miles; 22, Kila Jan Beg, 28 miles; 23, Charburjak, 14 miles; 24, Daki Dela, 20 miles; 25, Gabri Haji, 12 miles; 26, Nadali, 20 miles; 27, Chakansur, 20 miles; 28, Minari-Khoja, 20 miles; 29, Camp, 15 miles; 30, Lash, 20 miles; 31, Khushkrudak, 22 miles; 32, Kala Kah, 15 miles; 33, Bank of Harud, 15 miles; Chah-i-Sagak, Dorah, Abass, ; 38, Burj Gulwarda, 80 miles; Shorab, Yezdan; 43, Kafir Kalah, 80 miles; 44, Toman Agha, 25 miles; 45, Kalsan, 20 miles; 46, Karez Ilias, 20 miles; 47 Zulfikar, 20 miles; 48, Garmab, 15 miles; 49, Khuda Bux, 15 miles; 50, Pul-i-Khatun, 20 miles; 51, Daolatabad, 15 miles; 52, camp opposite Sarakhs, 10 miles; 53, Camp, 15 miles; 54, Irolan, 15 miles; 55, Camp, 15 miles; 56, Rabat Abdulla, 15 miles; 66, Kerki, through the desert, 200 miles; 70, Kilif, 70 miles; 71, Shorab Ferry, 20 miles; 73, Termez Ferry, 30 miles; 78, Aliwaj Ferry, 60 miles; 84, Hazrat Imam, 75 miles; 87, Kokcha River, 30 miles; 91, Samti Bala, 50 miles; 93, Zaghar, 30 miles; 94, Tarma Falan, 9 miles; 95, Shinazen, 6 miles; 96, Khasto, 7 miles; 97, Jagmarg, 10½ miles; 98 Udun, 9 miles; 99, Yagit, 12 miles; 100, Patkinao, Sangeo, 9 miles; 102, Kila Khum, 7 miles; 103, Razoai, 5 miles; 104, Keorun, 9 miles; 105, Wishkaro, 12 miles; 106, dak, 10½ miles; 107, Tagmai, 8 miles; 108, Gurgavat, 10 miles; 109, Pishikaro, 8½ miles; 110, Watkhud, 7 miles; 111, Gaumarg, 6 miles; 112, Amurd, 10 miles; 113, Radan, 9 miles; 114, Waznud, 9 miles; 115, Deh Roshan, 12 miles; 116, Deh Zud, 6½ miles; 117, Kila Wamar, 3 miles; 118, Akhun, 3 miles; 119, Pas Baju, 13 miles; 120, Sacharo, 10 miles; 121, Deh Shahr, 7 miles; 122, Bar Punjah, 7 miles; 123, Kuguz Parin, 20 miles; 124, Bar Shahr, 22 miles; 125, Sari Shakh, 10 miles; 126, Ishkashim, 10 miles; 127, Patur, 7 miles; 128, Kazdeh, 8 miles; 129, Ishtkaro, 12 miles; 130, Urgand, 6 miles; 131, Pigish, 10 miles; 132, Mizgar, 12 miles; 133, Kila Panjah, 8½ miles; 134, Langar Kish, 6 miles; 135, Yam Khana, 18 miles; 136, Yol Mazar, 13 miles; 137, Bilaor Bas, 12 miles; 138, Mazar Tapa, 20 miles; 139, Victoria Lake, 5 miles; 144, Aktash Valley, 65 miles; 145, Camp entrance, Neza Tash Pass, 15 miles; 146, Camp E foot, Neza Tash Pass, 17 miles; 147, Tashkurgan, 16 miles; 148, Camp E foot, Neza Tash Pass, 16 miles; 149, Camp west end, Neza Tash Pass, 17 miles; 150, Little Pamir Lake, 45 miles; 151, Langar, 25 miles; 152, Sarhad, 23 miles; 153, Chattiboi, 16 miles; 154, Camp, 16 miles; 155, Durkot, 6 miles; 156, Handur, 13 miles; 157, Hayolti, 5 miles; 158, Yassin, 4 miles; 159, Goopis, 11 miles; 160, Roshan, 4 miles; 161, Hoopar, 13 miles; 162, Gaokuch, 9 miles; 163, Sinjal, 9½ miles, 164, Gulpoor, 10¾ miles; 165, Hauzil, 10 miles; 166, Gilgit, 10 miles; 167, Minawer, 8¾ miles; 168, Chakerkot, 16 miles; 169, Boonji, 7 miles; 170, Ramghat, 9 miles; 171, Duizan, 12 miles; 172, Mushkin, 8½ miles; 173, Harcho, 8 miles; 174, Astor, 11 miles; 175, Gurikot, 7 miles: 176, Chagam, 13 miles; 177, Pukarkot, 12 miles; 178, Camp, 11 miles; 179, Mohan Das, 11 miles; 180, Gurikot, 12 miles; 181, Gurez, 11 miles; 182, Kunzalwan, 11 miles; 183, Zotkusu, 62 miles; 184, Tragbal, 9 miles; 185, Bandipur, 9 miles; 186, Sambal, 18 miles; 187, Sirinugger, 17 miles; 188, Avantipur, 17 miles; 189, Islamabad, 16 miles; 190, Vernag, 15 miles; 191, Deogol, 15 miles; 192, Ramsu, 14 miles; 193, Ramban, 19 miles; 194, Bilant, 10 miles; 195, Landar, 14 miles; 196, Mir, 11 miles; 197, Kiramchi, 13 miles; 198, Dansal, 16 miles; 99, Jummoo, 17 miles.

C. M. M.

Appendix T[1].

Table showing Exports from Russian Ports in 1881 and 1882.

A—Black Sea Ports.

Nature of Exports.	Odessa.		Taganrog.		Nicolaieff.		Berdiansk.		Mariapol.		Yeisk.		Genichensk.		Temriouk.		Batoum.	
	1881.	1882.	1881.	1882.	1881.	1882.	1881.	1882.	1881.	1882.	1881.	1882.	1881.	1882.	1881.	1882.	1881.	1882.
	£	£	£	£	£	£	£	£	£	£	£	£	£	£	£		Foreign trade.	Foreign trade.
Cereals ...	5,208,400	6,406,600	3,027,204	5,545,016	2,102,484	1,587,924	883,466	No returns.	311,043	515,203	319,706	437,858	208,279	67,354	64,154	No returns.	35,000	32,300
Wool ...	403,570	600,000	203,030	386,317	...	18,940	22,322		4,230	...	25,800	28,680	...	...	...		Coasting trade.	Coasting trade.
Other exports ...	645,030	993,400	772,814	194,699	11,685	5,851	...		...	...	72	...	...	...	6,097		66,000	72,000
Total Exports ...	6,307,000	8,000,000	3,403,048	6,126,032	2,114,160	1,612,715	905,788	1,671,158	315,273	515,706	345,578	466,538	208,279	67,354	70,251		101,000	104,300

Exports from Kertch, 1881 ... £ 133,273 } No returns available for 1882.
" " Sevastopol, 1881 ... " 606,033 }
" " Poti ... ... No returns available for 1881 and 1882.

Total Exports from Black Sea Ports.

	£
1881	14,509,692
1882	18,563,300

B.—Baltic Sea Ports.

	Total Value of Exports.		Export of Wood.	
	1880.	1881.	1880.	1881.
	£	£	£	£
Riga	5,546,890	5,501,204	1,305,387	1,131,62
Wiborg	590,130	323,177		
Pernau		822,042		
Liban		2,564,756		
Total for 1881		8,211,179		

Appendix T².

Table showing Total Value of Imports at the various Russian Ports in 1881 and 1882.

Ports.	1881.	1882.	Remarks.
	£	£	
Odessa	5,000,000	4,600,000	
Taganrog	568,510	556,708	
Nicolaieff	59,315	33,364	
Berdiansk	18,568	22,217	
Sevastopol	643,981	No returns.	
Mariapol	4,145	„	
Kertch	8,348	„	
Yeisk	5,000	„	
Genichensk	No returns.	„	
Temriouk	„	„	
Poti	„	„	
Batoum	275,302	267,000	These figures only show the coasting trade.
Riga	3,799,114	No returns.	
Wiborg	360,272	„	
Pernam	19,306	„	
Liban	996,919	„	
Total ...			

Appendix T³.

Table showing Nationalities of Ships which cleared from the various Russian Ports in 1881 and 1882.

Flag.	Odessa.		Taganrog.		Nicolaieff.		Berdiansk.		Mariapol.		Yeisk.		Genichensk.		Batoum.		Poti.		Sevastopol.		Riga.		Wiborg.		Pernan.		Liban.		Remarks.
	1881	1882	1881	1882	1881	1882	1881	1882	1881	1882	1881	1882	1881	1882	1881	1882	1881	1882	1881	1882	1881	1882	1881	1882	1881	1882	1881	1882	
British ...	126	532	193	408	156	128	7	14	14	No returns.	No returns.	No returns.	No returns.	No returns.	7	9	No returns.	No returns.	43	No returns.	603	No returns.	27	No returns.	35	No returns.	88	No returns.	At Batoum in 1881 above 1,500 very small Russian coasting vessels entered the port.
German ...	9	25	5	6	2	6	...	...	...						...	...			2		868		35		42		505		
Russian ...	183	181	40	15	1	...	5	3	4						52	52			54		480		364		13		240		
Danish ...	2	...	...	...	...	3	...	...	...						...	...			...		135		9		40		218		
Dutch ...	...	...	...	...	...	...	...	...	...						...	...			...		323		14		1		13		
French ...	47	49	4	...	2	...	3	...	4						25	26			...		20		6		2		...		
Swedish ...	...	...	1	6	...	...	...	...	...						...	...			...		136		26		5		222		
Norwegian ...	17	...	...	...	13	2	...	...	...						...	...			1		344		77		20		150		
American ...	...	...	...	...	...	...	...	...	...						...	...			...		1		1		...		...		
Belgian ...	18	18	...	2	7	3	...	...	...						...	...			...		1		...		...		...		
Austrian ...	114	134	8	...	11	10	4	6	7						52	59			9		...		4		...		...		
Turkish ...	85	75	40	...	...	...	11	20	1						12	9			4		...		...		...		...		
Italian ...	84	88	25	...	1	...	60	93							...	...			14		...		1		...		...		
Greek ...	82	104	253	20	2	1	84	112	20						...	...			34		...		...		...		...		

Appendix T⁴.

Table showing Vessels and Tonnage arriving at, and clearing from, Riga and Wiborg with cargoes (not in ballast) from and to ports of other countries in 1881.

Ports.	Riga.				Wiborg.				Remarks.
	Arrived from.		Cleared to.		Arrived from.		Cleared to.		
	Ships.	Tons.	Ships.	Tons.	Ships.	Tons.	Ships.	Tons.	
African ...	12	4,410	1	480	...	No details.	...	No returns.	1,323 ships entered Riga in ballast and 25 left in ballast. Of the returns for Wiborg in the column "Arrived," 10 ships are included which remained from 1880; also 60 ships in ballast (ports whence unknown). Of the 549 ships "Cleared" from Wiborg, 526 were with cargo.
American ...	10	5,450	1	875	6		...		
Belgian ...	44	19,900	180	64,550	1		6		
British ...	748	235,325	1,165	457,040	30		78		
Danish ...	23	2,745	42	5,900	9		19		
Dutch ...	47	9,520	510	141,980	16		37		
French ...	34	9,025	256	87,150	10		63		
German ...	261	65,270	383	81,390	45		55		
Italian ...	1	210	...	...	7		...		
Norwegian ...	49	8,140	47	7,310	..		...		
Russian ...	244	71,045	265	74,550	390		268		
Spanish and Portuguese. ...	6	1,540	13	2,790	1		3		
Swedish ...	75	16,600	48	9,445	30		22		
Total ...	1,582	457,090	2,911	933,480	564	115,012	549	....	

Table showing British vessels arriving at, and clearing from, Odessa and Taganrog in 1881, with the countries from and to which they sailed.

Countries from which arrived or to which sailed.	Odessa.				Taganrog.				Odessa.		Taganrog.		Remarks.
	Arrived from.				Arrived from.				Sailed to.		Sailed to.		
	With cargo.		In ballast.		With cargo.		In ballast.						
	Ships.	Tons.	Ships.	Tons.	Ships.	Tons.	Ships.	Tons.	Ships.	Tons.	Ships.	Tons.	
Great Britain...	210	202,720	14	13,820	8	7,537	77	60,698	132	131,280	383	310,795	
Italy ...	...	...	52	51,810	1	899	142	114,112	8	7,471	4	3,148	
Russia ...	...	...	62	61,692	5	3,879	40	33,736	59*	51,911	...	...	* In ballast.
Turkey ...	...	...	22	18,040	1	990	67	53,530	...	...	...	...	
Egypt ...	2	2,010	30	32,204	...	...	29	26,306	...	...	...	...	
France ...	...	...	21	20,346	...	...	27	21,484	61	38,740	15	11,834	
Greece ...	...	...	...	...	...	...	11	8,388	...	...	...	...	
Austria ...	...	...	...	...	...	...	3	2,354	...	...	...	...	
Belgium ...	6	5,667	...	...	1	631	...	...	} 115	119,892	{ 4	3,685	
Holland ...	...	...	...	...	...	...	...	...			4	3,655	
Portugal ...	...	...	...	...	...	...	...	...	...	...	2	1,454	
Germany ...	...	...	...	...	...	...	...	...	13	11,098	...	...	
Others ...	1	770	6	5,571	...	...	...	...	30†	26,940†	...	...	† 24 ships = 21,504 tons in ballast.
	219	211,187	207	203,483	16	13,936	306	320,608	417	407,032	412	33,454	

Appendix T[5].

Table showing the number of Ships sailing under the Russian flag and having called at the undermentioned ports in 1881 and 1882.

District.	Port.	1881. Ships.	1881. Tonnage.	1882. Ships.	1882. Tonnage.
France	Bordeaux ...	22	9,551	No re	turns.
	La Rochelle ...	1	324	,,	,,
	Nantes ...	3	636	,,	,,
	St. Nazaire ...	8	5,709	,,	,,
	Brest ...	No re	turns.	1	737
	Cherbourg ...	,,	,,	3	1.217
	Boulogne ...	5	1,241	No re	turns.
Spain	Alicante ...	7	2,010	No re	turns.
	Valencia ...	13	5,326	12	6,238
	Cadiz ...	18	7,686	No re	turns.
	Manilla ...	3	3,796	,,	,,
	Barcelona ...	25	10,393	34	16,865
	Catalonia ...	No re	turns.	9	3,357
Germany.	Bremerhaven ...	8	2,686	No re	turns.
	Konigsberg ...	6	?	,,	,,
	Danzig ...	9	5,474	,,	,,
	Memel ...	7	?	,,	,,
	Hamburg ...	7	?	,,	,,
	Wismer ...	8	1,369	,,	,,
Sweden	Gottenburg ...	14	4.235	2	695
	Stockholm ...	11	2,498	No re	turns.
	Hernosand ...	2	437	,,	,,

District.	Port.	1881. Ships.	1881. Tonnage.	1882. Ships.	1882. Tonnage.
Belgian	Ports ...	77	27,185	No re	turns.
Turkey	Aleppo ...	53	71,145	No re	turns.
	Beyrout ...	53	65,114	,,	,,
	Jaffa ...	51	42,072	51	74,516
	Salina ...	83	10,717	62	8,262
	Adana (Musqua)	48	43,059	53	67,517
	Previsa ...	No re	turns.	No	ne.
	Kustendjie ...	16	4,800	?	552
Java	Batavia ...	3	2,399	No re	turns.
	Samarang ...	4	3,034	,,	,,
	Sourabaya ...	2	1,434	,,	,,
Italy	Venice ...	2	422	No re	turns.
	Genoa ...	No re	turns.	,,	,,
	Naples ...	4	2,230	,,	,,
Austria	Fiume ...	No	ne.	No	ne.
	Trieste ...	No re	turns.	No re	turns.
North Africa	Alexandria ...	94	52,040		
	Tripoli ...	1	274		
	Mogador ...	No re	turns.	No	ne.
	Mazagan ...	,,	,,	No	ne.
	Rabat ...	No	ne.	No	ne.
	Darul Baida ...	No	ne.	No re	turns.

District.	Port.	1881. Ships.	1881. Tonnage.	1882. Ships.	1882. Tonnage.
United States of America.	Boston ...	No	ne.	2	1,147
	Mobile ...	2	1,148	2	1,262
	Pensawla ...	35	22,410	28	18,711
	S. Francisco ...	4	1,837	3	3,044
	New York ...	13	?	No re	turns.
	Baltimore ...	36	?	,,	,,
	New Orleans ...	No	ne.	No	ne.
	Galveston ...	No	ne.	No	ne.
	Savannah ...	2	1,335	2	970
	Philadelphia ...	30	20,008	No re	turns.
Japan ...	Kanaguwa ...	4	284	No re	turns.
	Nagasaki ...	9	10,752	,,	,,
	Kiogo-Osaka ...	1	498	,,	,,
	Hakodate ...	5	856	,,	,,
China, Siam, Annam.	Saigon ...	1	115	8	6,154
	Amoy ...	2	1,623	No re	turns.
	Hankow ...	2	4,315	,,	,,
	Bankok ...	2	880	,,	,,
	Shanghai ...	3	4,774	No re	turns.
India ...	All ports ...	12	12,502	17	13,512
Greece ...	Piræus ...	No	ne.	No re	turns.
Hayti ...	Iacmel ...	1	441	,,	,,
S. America ...	Panama ...	1	115	,,	,,
Cape Verde ...	St. Vincent ...	2	1,106	,,	,,

Appendix U.

From—POTI *To*—TIFLIS.

Territory.—WESTERN CAUCASUS.

Names of Stages, &c.	Distance.		Rivers.	Remarks.
	Intermediate.	Total.		
	Miles.	Miles.		
1. SAKORNAIA ...	7½			From Poti to Orpiri a post road, thence to Tiflis by cart road, officially known as the "Tmeritinian Military Road." (stages 1–7)
2. SARICH-KOPI ...	8½			
3. KODORI ...	12			
4. ORPIRI ...	12			
5. KOPETPARSKAIA ...	12			
6. KUTAIS ...	12			
7. SIMONETTI ...	12			
8. TILLIWILI ...	12½			River steamers can get up the river Rion as far as Orpiri. (stages 7–17)
9. BELOGOR ...	14½			
10. MALIT ...	11½			
11. PONKSK ...	10			
12. SURAM ...	9			
13. GARGAREP ...	14½			
14. GORI ...	17			
15. AKHAL-KALAKI ...	14½			
16. NITCH-BIS ...	12			
17. ALLOHEKTI ...	8½			
18. TIFLIS ...	13½	213½		

Appendix V.

From—BATOUM *To*—TIFLIS.

Territory.—WESTERN CAUCASUS.

Names of Stages, &c.	Distance.		Rivers.	Remarks.
	Intermediate.	Total.		
	Miles.	Miles.		
1. KOBOOLERI ...	13½			From Batoum to Ozurghetti by cart road, thence to Orpiri metalled road.
2. OZURGHETTI ...	13½			
3. BEREZHEOOLI ...	10½			
4. ORPIRI ...	14½			
Thence by Route III.				
Tmeritinian Military Road to Tiflis— a total of 18 stages ...		225½		

Appendix W.

From—SOUKOUM KALEH *To*—TIFLIS.

Territory.—WESTERN CAUCASUS.

Names of Stages, &c.,	Distance.		Rivers.	Remarks.
	Intermediate.	Total.		
	Miles.	Miles.		
1. ANASTASIEVSKOE ...	11⅓			Cart road throughout, from Soukoum Kaleh to Tiflis.
2. DZHERDSKAIE ...	15⅓			
3. MOKVSKIE ...	12			
4. BEDIESKIA ...	13⅓			
5. RECHKHA ...	16			
6. ZUGDIDI ...	16			
7. OCHKHOMOORIÉ ...	13⅓			
8. MARTVÉLÉ ...	19⅓			
9. KHONE ...	10⅔			
10. KUTAIS ...	18			
Thence by Route III.				
Tmeritinian Military Road to Tiflis—a total of 22 stages ...		295		

Appendix X.

From—Erzeroum
Territory.—Turkey in Asia and Caucasus.

To—Tiflis *viâ* Kars and Alexandropol (Gumri).

Names of Stages, &c.	Distance.		Rivers.	Remarks.
	Intermediate.	Total.		
	Miles.	Miles.		
1. Hassan Kale ...	20			[Norman.] *Erzeroum to Kars.* Not so good a road as that from Trebizond. The ascent to the Debi-Boyun is steep, but lately it had been eased off, and an excellent gun road now crosses the range. Through the Passin plain the road is excellent. Cavalry and infantry could march with a wide front on either flank as far as Khorassan. There are two other routes from Erzeroum to Kars across the Soghaly Range, but neither of them are metalled nor are the streams bridged. Guns can be freely moved by both. Supplies and transport.
2. Kuipri Kui ...	10			
3. Khorassan ...	20			
4. Mezingird ...	20			
5. Sara Kamysh ...	18			
6. Kotanli ...	20			
7. Kars ...	25	(133)		
8. Mesrako ...	15			
9. Palveran ...	10			
10. Tiknis ...	12			
11. Alexandropol ...	9			
12. Ak-Boulah ...	18			[Buchan Telfer. (The Crimea and Trans-Caucasia, 1876.)] Good post road throughout.
13. Amamly ...	14			
14. Karakilissa ...	14			
15. Gamsagheman ...	12			
16. Delijan ...	12			
17. Tarstchai ...	10			
18. Karavanserai ...	12			
19. Ouzountaly ...	12			
20. Novo Akstafa ...	11			
21. Zohr Arh ...	8			
22. Salaogly ...	9			
23. Novo Alghetka ...	14			
24. Yagloudjynsk ...	15			
25. Saganlough ...	8			
26. Tiflis ...	8			
		351		

From Erzeroum to Tiflis viâ *Kars and Alexandropol* (*Gumri*)—*Another road* —contd.

Names of Stages, &c.	Distance.		Rivers.	Remarks.
	Intermediate.	Total.		
	Miles.	Miles.		
1. Hassan-Kala ...	22⅜			Metalled road throughout.
2. Kerpikey ...	10			
3. Ardost ...	15⅛			
4. Zivin ...	14			
5. Sirbasan ...	8⅞			
6. Sarakamysh ...	16			
7. Karakhamza ...	13⅝			
8. Begli Akhmet ...	10			
9. Kars ...	14			
10. Chamchaoosh ...	11⅛			
11. Parget ...	14			
12. Argina ..	13⅛			
13. Alexandropol ...	12⅞			
14. Ak-Boulak ...	12⅞			
15. Amamli ...	13⅛			
16. Karakilissa ...	13⅛			
17. Bozikyant ...	12			
18. Delijan ...	10⅞			
19. Akh-Kayali ...	12			
20. Karavanserai ...	8			
21. Oozoontala ...	10⅞			
22. Novo Astaphinskaia.	10			
23. Shikiloo ...	18			
24. Kosali ...	10⅞			
25. Yagloojinskaia ...	13⅛			
26. Tiflis ...	13⅛	333⅛		

Appendix Y.

Note on the oti-Tiflis Railway.

General description.

The Poti-Tiflis Railway is constructed on the 5 foot gauge. It was commenced in 1867, supervised almost entirely by English Engineers, and opened for through traffic to Tiflis in 1872. The earthwork was constructed principally by soldiers, and bridges, which are almost all of iron, were manufactured and erected by English contracting firms. Landslips in the mountains are one of the great difficulties to be contended against in the construction and maintenance of this line. The railway station of Poti is on the right or north bank of the river Rion, opposite the town, with which it is connected by a bridge, and the line continues on that side of the river up to Kutais station, about 4 miles south of the town of that name and 60¾ miles from Poti. The first 40 or 50 miles of the line from Poti passes through swamps and dead forests, the railway embankment having interfered with the courses of the streams which formerly carried off the drainage of this tract of country into the Rion, and regularly drowned the trees. The mortality amongst the employés on the construction of this section of the line was very great from fever and dysentery. Crossing the Rion at Kutais the line runs through a richly cultivated plain as far as the station of Bejatubani, 108¾ miles from Poti, whence the ghât work commences, and near Suram becomes very heavy, the gradients being often 1 in 22 and in places as much as 1 in 19: the curves are also very sharp. The Engineers of the line wished to avoid a portion of the very heavy ghât work by tunnelling, but the Russian Government would not face the heavy outlay, and insisted on the line being carried over the pass. Subsequently it seemed probable that the tunnel would have to be resorted to after all, owing to the great difficulty and danger experienced in working the very steep part of the line, but the introduction of powerful "Fairlie" engines to run over this section of the line seems to have obviated this necessity, though occasionally during the heavy snow storms that occur in the winter, this portion of the line has to be closed for two or three days at a time.

The top of the pass is reached at Suran, 119¼ miles from Poti. This station is situated at the junction of the post roads from Poti to Tiflis and Tiflis to Borjon and Alchaltzik. Three miles further on is the station of Mikhailovo, situated at an elevation of about 3,000 feet above the sea on a wide, windy plain (?) miles in breadth, dotted with Georgian villages and surrounded with wooded mountain ranges; it is always cool even during the height of summer, and has been constituted the seat of management of the Poti-Tiflis Railway. Here there are extensive workshops, a locomotive depôt, and resident civil engineers. From Mikhailovo the line descends to Gori, 151¼ miles from Poti, and following the course of the river Kus across a broad desert plain, through which the river flows as in a deep cutting, reaches Tiflis, 200¾ miles from Poti, and the terminus station is at least two miles from the town. The time occupied on the journey from Poti to Tiflis is usually about 15 hours.

Station and their respective distances from Poti.	Miles.
1. Chalodidi	9¼
2. Novo Senaki	24
3. Samtrede.	41¼
4. Kutais	60¾
5. Koirilsk	80
6. Dzerula	88¾
7. Bailogozsk	95¼
8. Legvani	100

					Miles.
9.	Bejatubani	...	...	...	... $108\frac{3}{5}$
10.	Pona	...	...	...	... $115\frac{1}{5}$
11.	Suram	...	...	...	... $119\frac{1}{5}$
12.	Mikhailovo	...	...	...	... $122\frac{3}{5}$
13.	Kareli	...	...	...	... $139\frac{1}{5}$
14.	Gori	...	...	...	... $151\frac{1}{5}$
15.	Grakali	...	...	...	... $160\frac{3}{5}$
16.	Kashpi	...	...	...	... $169\frac{1}{5}$
17.	Kranka	...	...	...	... $179\frac{1}{5}$
18.	Mtskhet	...	...	...	... $186\frac{4}{5}$
19.	Avchali	...	...	...	... 194
20.	Tiflis	...	...	...	... $200\frac{3}{5}$

Branch lines.

A branch line to Batoum has been recently opened from Samtrede on the main line, $41\frac{1}{3}$ miles from Poti. The length of it is about 60 miles. Some years ago it was proposed to run a branch line from Novo Senaki on the main line, 24 miles from Poti, to Soukoum-Kaleh, the project has not been carried out as yet, but the distance would be about 80 miles.

Rolling stock.

Fairlie engines and special carriages with extraordinary brake-power are used over the ghât section of the line. The carriages are comfortable, and are built on the American car system.

Appendix Z.

Description of Poti.

Poti situated on the east coast of the Black Sea in latitude 42° 8′ north, longitude 41° 43′ east (approximate), belonged originally to Turkey, was taken by the Russians in 1812, restored under the treaty of Bucharest, and again taken by them in 1828, since which it has remained in their possession. In 1877 it was entirely deserted, as it was feared the Turks would land and burn it; they did not do so, but the Cossack and Militia garrison did so much damage to private property that in the spring of 1878 Poti had much the appearance of a town that had been bombarded and sacked.

Town and roadstead.

The town is built at the embouchure of the river Rion (ancient Phasis), which here discharges itself into the sea discolouring the water for miles. The mouth of the river is closed by a dangerous bar of shifting mud and sand, over which the water varies in depth from 3 to 8 feet according to the condition of the stream and the direction of the winds that have lately prevailed. In consequence of this bar the shipping has to lie about two miles off the shore in an exposed roadstead, dangerous during south-west winds, which occasionally blow with great violence. Loading and discharging cargo is effected by means of large lighters or "sandalls" manned by Turks, belonging to the Greek and French, and Armenian ship-brokers and agents of the port. Within the bar the river is deep, and until the opening ofthe Poti-Tiflis Railway, river steamers used to ply between Poti and Orpiri, a town about 40 miles up the river, whence the high road to Tiflis *viâ* Kutais commences. The landing place is about 200 yards above the bar. A custom-house exists, but notwithstanding this smuggling goes on briskly: the police are practically useless. Twenty years ago the site of the little town of Poti was morass, but its salubrity and adaptation to commercial purposes has been greatly improved of late years by the construction of high and well-backed wharf walls on the river's bank. The bazar itself is built mostly of brick, but many of the houses composing the streets of the town which radiate from their common centre, the quays are of the old wooden, tumble-down type, as was the bazar itself until quite recently. The *Eucalyptus globulus* has been extensively raised from seed with every prospect of success. No further efforts are being made to elevate the entire site upon which the town stands and is extending, but the effects of the noxious exhalations are partly counteracted by the houses being mostly constructed on huge logs, so that their floors are raised five or six feet above the ground, while the superstratum of the roads and footpaths is attended to numerous draining ditches have been dug, but there is room for great improvement in their maintenance. The town was originally fortified, but the old walls have now been demolished. The Molt Aqua, a deep and broad channel, supposed to be an old bed of the Phasis, runs round the north-eastern part of the town and falls into the sea some six miles to the south of it. It communicates at its northern extremity with the Paleostrom, a fine sheet of water five or six miles square. Into the Paleostrom flow several deep and sluggish rivers intersecting the marshes and dampy forests which extend for miles on every side of the lagoon but the western one (facing the sea). These rivers and the lagoon itself swarm with fish and in the winter with wild fowl of all kinds.

Climate.

Poti, as is to be expected from its situation, is a most unhealthy place, fever being particularly rife from July to October.

Population.

The population of Poti is fluctuating, averaging, it is said, 8,000 souls independently of a garrison of a thousand men. It comprises specimens of most eastern Europeans, Greeks, Turks, Dalmates, &c., in addition to Armenians, Persians, French, Russians, and the people of the country, Mingrelians. The maritime Turks, who own the native craft plying along the east coast of the Black Sea, are a fine set of men. All Anatolians from Copa, Trebizond, &c., they are excellent seamen, extremely sober and temperate, and knowing, as they do, every yard of the eastern coast from Trebizond to Novo Russisk and Anapa, would be invaluable auxiliaries in time of war to a hostile fleet.

Commercial value.

Since the Russian annexation of Batoum, Poti has been in a languishing unsettled state. After the Crimean war construction of a harbour of refuge, a railway down to it, and draining of the marshes, were talked of; but in the 30 years which have elapsed hardly anything has been done. Construction of an artificial harbour was attempted, but it was destroyed by a storm long before completion. Situated as it is in the centre of the Rion Valley, and at the mouth of a large and deep river, Poti is undoubtedly the natural commercial outlet of the Western Caucasus. The same operations as were successfully carried out at the Sulina mouth of the Danube would make it an excellent harbour of refuge for vessels of heavy tonnage.

Communications.

Poti is the terminus, on the Black Sea side, of the Poti-Tiflis Railway, an extension of which now runs to Baku, on the Caspian. The station is situated on the right or north bank of the river opposite the town with which it is now connected by a bridge. The journey to Tiflis (193 miles) takes about 15 hours to accomplish. Before this railway was opened, small river steamers used to ply between Poti and Maran (or Orpiri) about 40 miles up the river, whence an excellent road, called the Tmeritinian Military Road, leads *viâ* Kutais and the Suram Pass to Tiflis, distance 213 miles (Route III). It is kept in good condition, but the time for its commercial utility has gone by, t[illegible] railway which follows the same route being in operation, roads following [illegible] cost line lead from Poti southward to Batoum, and northward to Soukou[illegible] Kaleh, distant respectively about 40 and 80 miles.

Garrison.

From the distribution return of the Rus[illegible] Army in 1883, the garrison of Poti consists of 232 garrison artillery.

Appendix (a).

Description of Batoum.

Batoum is a small port on the east coast of the Black Sea, situated in [illegible] tude 41° 39′ north and longitute 41° 37′ east. Being the only safe port on east coast during winter, the Russians have always had a great desire to posses[illegible] During the war between Russia and Turkey, in 1828 and 1829, Batoum was taken by the Russians, and on peace being made they were very anxious to retain it, but lost it by a quibble and mistake in the spelling of a word. The river Tchor*u*k, lying some miles to the east of Batoum, having been inserted in the treaty instead of the river Tchor*e*k, which lies to the west of it, and was the boundary intended by Russia. It came into their possession, however, after the war of 1877, and is being regularly fortified, has been connected by a branch line with the Poti-Tiflis Railway, and is rising in value as a seaport and outlet for the commerce of the country.

Description of harbour and town.

The harbour, though capable of containing only a few ships, is the safest and most important on the east coast. There is deep water close up to the shore on the west side of the bay, so that vessels afloat land their cargoes over their sterns in the absence of the quay. The bay is afforded protection by the high overhanging cliffs of a spur of the Gouriel mountains. The town is built at the western entrance of the bay close to the sea. It contains several shops, coffee-houses, khans, and a mosque, all built of wood ; a few small houses are built, and gardens cleared behind the town.

Fortifications.

So long as Batoum was in possession of the Turks the fortifications were miserable. One redoubt was constructed commanding the entrance to the harbour, and another at the head of the bay, but both were completely commanded from the high ground in rear. Extensive and well planned works are required, for there are successive ranges of hills in the background, each higher than and commanding the other. The Russians are now carrying this out, an arsenal and store depôt have been constructed up a valley behind the town, heavy artillery has been landed and earthworks have been run up, which, by means of the circular railway now laid down, can be armed with 18 and 25 ton guns in a few hours.

Population.

The population is said not to have exceeded 2,000 in 1875, but it has probably increased considerably since Batoum was annexed to Russia, owing to the construction of the branch line of railway connecting it with the Poti-Tiflis line, and the increasing commercial importance of the town in consequence.

Climate.

Batoum being situated in a swamp at the mouth of the valley through which the river Choruk descends from the mountains, is unhealthy, particularly during the summer months from July to October, when it is a perfect hot-bed of fever, as is all the low ground on this coast. The higher ground on the eastern side of the bay is said to be perfectly healthy.

From its position at the furthest corner of the country to be commercially tapped, *viz.*, Mingrelia and Tmeritinia, and the country immediately behind it, instead of a wide alluvial plain enormously fertile (as the Rion valley at Poti is), being nothing but weld and precipitous mountains, only good for sheep pastures, Batoum has not really the same commercial importance as Poti. Nevertheless, it is highly probable that the Russian Government, impelled in reality more by strategic and aggressive motives than by any real desire to develop the commercial resources of the country, will insist on artificially forcing Batoum for some years to come instead of Poti, and the superiority of the harbour at Batoum gives them a plausible excuse for doing so.

Commercial value.

Batoum is now connected with the Poti-Tiflis Railway by a branch line about 60 miles long, joining the main line at Samtrede, about 40 miles from Poti.

Communications.

A cart road leads along the coast to Poti about 80 miles and another to Kutais *viâ* Ozurgheti and Orpiri about 90 miles, whence the Tmeritinian Military Road leads on to Tiflis, total distance to Tiflis about 225 miles (Route IV). Another road leads to Tiflis *viâ* Borjoin, joining the Tmeritinian Military Road at Mikhailovo. This is a much nearer way, but there is no information available to show whether this road is passable by carts throughout; numerous minor roads communicate with towns of the interior, such as Ardahan, Artivin, Akhaltrik, &c.

Garrison.

From the distribution return of the Russian Army in 1883, the garrison of Batoum consists only of 507 infantry.

Appendix (b).

Description of Soukoum-Kaleh.

Soukoum-Kaleh, the most important town of Abbasi, is situated in latitude 42° 59′ north and longitute 41° 2′ east (approximate), on the shore of a bay surrounded on three sides by wooded hills.

Roadstead.

There is plenty of water in the bay, and vessels lying in it are protected at all seasons of the year from the prevailing sea winds by the Kodorski promontory on the south and by the main Caucasian range on the east and south-east. There is a landing pier and numerous boats, manned by Greeks, ply for hire.

Fortifications.

There exist only the remains of the fortress built in 1578 by the Sultan Amirath II. This consists of four bastions in height, connected by straight, contains long, high, and thick with "bonnets" and narrow banquettes. The walls to seaward have fallen over and lie in huge masses under water.

Town.

Since 1866 Soukoum-Kaleh has been constituted the head-quarters of the Soukoum military district or division. It is quite a small place, consisting, with the exception of the Commandant's quarters, barracks, and hospitals, of about 300 small houses and huts, grouped round the custom-house and quarantine quarters, and of a bazar containing about thirty shops, poorly supplied and kept principally by Armenians.

The natives of the country, Abbasians, are an indolent people, whose only pursuit is that of rearing cattle, although their rich forests are capable of abundant supply. They are a wild race, at once distinguishable from other populations by their dark-brown clothing and by the "glitapt" or "bashklyk," which they wear universally. They are always armed, the most needy even having the cartridge cases or sockets sewn to the breasts of their coats. In lawlessness and addiction to thieving they are second only to their neighbours, the Swanny. They speak a dialect assimilating that of the Circassian tribes, and not understood by their neighbours on the south and east.

People.

The town being surrounded by marshes, which come almost up to the walls themselves, has acquired an unpleasant reputation for intermittent fevers, from which it is never free. The local authorities admit that the death-rate during the sickly season—the summer, is as high as 3 per cent.—and it is probably in reality higher, but it is said that the heights to the west of Mount Basta overlooking the bay, on which the military hospital is built, are completely free from fever.

Climate.

Soukhoum-Kaleh, not having good roads connecting it with the interior, is far behind Poti in commercial importance. Notwithstanding its good harbour, a coast trade is kept up almost exclusively with Russian and Turkish ports. The imports are mainly manufactured goods and food-grains and the exports "palmovoe" wood, honey, leather, &c.

Commerce.

Soukoum-Kaleh is connected by a postal and cart road with Poti. The road follows the coast line, and the distance is about 80 miles. Some years ago it was proposed to connect it with the Poti-Tiflis Railway by a branch line from Novo-Senaki, a station on the Poti-Tiflis Railway, 26 miles from Poti, but the scheme has not been carried out as yet. A cart road leads *viá* Tugdidi to Kutaís and thence by the Tmeritinian Military Road to Tiflis, total distance about 295 miles (Route V).

Communications.

From the distribution return of the Russian Army in 1883 the garrison of Soukoum-Kaleh appears to be only 507 infantry.

Garrison.

Appendix (c).

Memorandum on Armenia as a Theatre of War—15th December 1876.

A campaign in Armenia, under the present aspect of affairs, of course, means a campaign in which the two principals would be Russia and Turkey; and, looking to the relative power of the two countries, I think it may be taken for granted, also, that it would mean an invasion by the former and a defence by the latter.

Whether such an invasion would be a success, or as great a failure as the last attempt in this direction, depends, *1st*, on the number of troops Russia could bring into the field in this quarter; *2nd*, whether Turkey was supported in Armenia by England.

As to the first proviso, without going further into the region of ifs than is necessary, I will only say that I suppose that Russia will be forced to keep up very large forces for the protection of her Prussian frontier, in Poland, in the Galician frontier, towards the Danube, in the Caucasus, and she must largely increase her forces in Central Asia; while, if she contemplates an invasion of Bulgaria, she must employ large forces for the purpose. This allowed, it is apparent that, for the invasion of such a home of wild warriors as Asiatic Turkey, she can hardly be said to possess an overwhelming force.

I am aware that a very exaggerated idea is abroad both as to the numbers and efficiency of the Russian army; but knowing all that has been written as to the first, remembering what I have seen of the second, and taking into consideration the very many calls on her from the quarters named above, I think that she would be unable to bring into, and maintain in the field in, Armenia an army of more than 170,000 men, to which may be added, if Persia becomes, as is reported, her ally, 50,000 rabble, unofficered, unfed, and untrustworthy.

Let us now examine how many the Turks can bring to meet this array. Sameh Pasha, the Governor General of Erzeroum, in answer to my queries, produced a statement which aggregated 200,000 men; but many of these were so evidently paper-men, that I prefer to offer my own estimate, made after talking with many on the subject.

I think that, turning out every available man and calling out all the "redifs," the utmost strength of what I may call for the moment Turkish dsciplined troops in this Pashalic would be 70,000 men.

To these must be added irregular troops, who are all splendid fighting material, only requiring some organization to make them very formidable. Asiatic Turkey is indeed a very mine of warriors. Of no country in Asia, and perhaps in the world, can it be said with greater truth that all her men are strong, enduring, and brave; in none could the fire of religious enthusiasm be easier lit.

Therefore, if we add all that can be raised from these sources, we produce a force no invader can ignore, and this without following the exaggerated estimate of their numbers given by the Turks themselves. On the contrary, the following estimate of their numbers is placed at the very lowest, and the results are as follow:—Circassian tribes, 15,000, all burning with a fierce hatred of the Muscov; Koords, 30,000; Arabs, 30,000; Lazees and mountaineers, 10,000; Osmanlees, 10,000: total 95,000.

To these must be added two other sources of aid which the Turks possess ere they need turn to foreign assistance. The corps d'armée of Damascus in such a campaign would scarcely be threatened, and could therefore well spare 20,000 men, while that of Bagdad might spare 10,000. Thus the total fighting strength may be calculated at—

Regulars	100,000
Irregulars	95,000

The only fortified places of any importance the Turks possess are Kars and Erzeroum, and the garrison of these would consume not under 50,000 men; but with such garrisons these places could hope to stand a siege throughout the summer, whether attacked independently or one after the other; and whether the enemy besieged these places or blockaded them, they certainly could not accomplish either alternative with less force than 100,000 men.

If, indeed, the Russians attacked Kars with an overwhelming force, and were prepared to sacrifice 20,000 for its capture, it might perhaps fall sooner; and by going through the same process with Erzeroum, they might take it in a shorter time. But this would leave them with sadly diminished forces, and little fine weather, to crush out such further vitality of resistance as the Turks still possessed. A blockade would not improve the position very much, as it would leave them with but 70,000 men to face 50,000 regulars and 95,000 irregulars. Still there is little doubt, in either of these cases, the Russians would have the best chance of success, though it is by no means certain that they would be victorious in the long run, if the Turks remained steadfast with something of the spirit of determination expressed by a Pasha at Constantinople, who said if the Russians drove them out of Istambol they would go to heaven.

How then would it be if a corps d'armée of British troops, 30,000 strong, landed at Trebizond; if 60,000 mixed British and Indian troops advanced from Bagdad; and if the fighting powers of the Turks themselves were more than doubled by the presence of English officers at their head?

In such a case the available forces would consist of—

†	30,000	English troops.	
	60,000	Indian* ,,	
	100,000	Turkish regulars ...	Directed by English officers.
	95,000	,, irregulars ...	
	285,000		

fighting men; while, as I have estimated, the Russians would probably be unable to muster more than 222,000, of which only 170,000 are reliable.

For an invasion of Asiatic Turkey, it seems to me but two courses are open to Russia. Tiflis must be her base in any case, and she has only two lines of operation open to her—*1st*, by Delijan, Goomree, to Kars and Erzeroum as an objective; *2nd*, by Erivan, Tabreez, to Bagdad as an objective. The first has the advantage that the objectives are close at hand, *i.e.*, within 200 and 300 miles respectively of her base; and its disadvantages are that this line is barred by two fortresses, so strong that, if defended with the traditional tenacity of the Turks, their capture must be doubtful, while the line of advance is flanked by the mountains of Lazistan on the right and of Koordistan on the left; behind the first the sea being in command of Turks, and beyond the second the plains of Mesopotamia offering an excellent base and source of supply.

The second has the advantage that it lies within friendly territory to within 100 miles of its objective; but the disadvantage of a line of operations 900 miles in length through a poor country would render such an undertaking sheer madness, even if it had not the extra drawback of being dangerously open to flank attack.

The other possible lines of advance from the Russian frontier are from Erivan by Makoo and Lake Van to Bitlees; but along this line the route by the lake side is difficult, and to cross the lake by boats would require very extensive arrangements, which could only be slowly made, while the road from Bitlees to the plains or to any point of any importance passes through terribly strong mountainous country.

Again, a force might advance on Moosul by Nukhshvan, Khoee, Ooroomeea, Ooshnae, and Rowandiz; but the latter part of this route is very difficult, through wild tracts only inhabited by a few untamed Koords, and producing no supplies. To both these schemes may be applied the query—*Cui bono?* To advance and seize points of no importance, and leave the strength of his enemy intact on both her flanks, would be an amount of folly that no general could be guilty of. I therefore think a campaign against Asiatic

* One-fourth British.

† This estimate may seem to some too high; but I maintain we could produce the men if we put our shoulders to the wheel; and if we do not mean to do that, we had better not fight Russia.

Turkey must commence by the capture of Erzeroum and Kars. With these in their hands, the Russians might safely extend their conquests either south or west; but it would be madness to attempt either with them in the hands of the Turks.

Thus my survey may for the present safely be confined to a consideration of the defence of these places; and taking all the circumstances of the case into view, I am strongly of opinion that while the object was their retention in the hands of the Turks, the plan of the campaign should be offensive-defensive. That is to say, Kars should be properly garrisoned with 20,000 men, of which 5,000 should be British, while a force—the Army of Kars, consisting of 15,000 British, 50,000 Turks, 10,000 Lazees, and 15,000 Circassians—should operate to raise the siege. This force would be based on Lazistan, its line of retreat being either Batoum or Baiboort, as might be most appropriate, according to the vicissitudes of the campaign.

The Army of Erzeroum would consist of 15,000 British, 45,000 Indian* troops, 45,000 Turks, 30,000 Koords, 30,000 Arabs, there being in Erzeroum itself a garrison of 5,000 British, 10,000 Indian,* 15,000 Turks, while the rest of the available forces, amounting to 160,000, would form a separate force or forces operating to prevent its siege or to assist Kars, its line of retreat being towards the south-west.

It would be absurd to attempt to forecast any further movements in such a campaign. I have placed on the board, so to speak, the forces I believe England and Turkey could bring, and I have shown the most probable general idea of the campaign.

Troops arriving from England should sail so as to reach the coast at the end of March, and they should disembark at three points: *1, Tripolis.*—Here the majority of the infantry, cavalry, light guns, and stores suitable for pack-carriage, should debark and march to Goomishkhana, and thence by Erzinjan to Erzeroum. *2, Platana.*—This should be used as a subsidiary port only to *3, Trebizond,* where all heavy material should be debarked and marched up by the cart road (use being made of both the summer and winter roads) to Baiboort. *4, Soormeneh.*—From this a mountain road leads to Baiboort, which could be used for a light force to protect the flank of the main road.

Batoum is undoubtedly the best port and most convenient spot to land at, as, in addition to the harbour, water-carriage is available to Artveen. It would, however, probably be too much exposed to a flank attack to make its adoption advisable.

The road from Trebizond to Erzeroum is regularly made, the gradients being practicable for wheel-carriage throughout. The road is badly drained, and is consequently heavy in parts, but there are no other difficulties. Water is plentiful along the whole line, and fuel as far as the north foot of the Zuggunah pass; beyond to Erzeroum special arrangements would have to be made for its collection. Fodder is procurable everywhere except in the part mentioned as affording abundant fuel. After due notice, supplies could be collected at any part of the route. The whole distance is 170 miles. As far as Goomishkhana the ground is very confined, and difficulty would be experienced in finding room for large bodies of troops.

A force from England should bring with it a sufficient supply of Maltese carts, which is admirably adapted to the roads of Armenia. Large numbers of the Armenian carts would be available, and there are also on the road

* One-fourth of these also British.

several hundred four guns, a large, heavy, four-wheeled cart introduced from Russia. Pack-horses could be procured from Erzinjan and Sivas.

Commissariat officers should be sent on ahead to Trebizond, Baiboort, Erzinjan, and Erzeroum; and they should undertake the commissariat arrangements for the Turks also.

From Erzeroum to Kars the following routes are available:—

1. Kars to Erzeroum—

Mooshad, 4 hours—

The road is nearly level, and is quite good, over black cultivated soil, which is heavy after rain.

Chelpaklee, 4 hours—

The road goes over easy, undulating ground; heavy after rain.

Yenikevee, 6 hours—

The road is level at first, and then ascends for 1 hour by easy gradients to top of the Soghanli Dagh, whence it goes over easy, undulating ground on top of the range for 2 hours; then it descends easily for 3 hours, the last part into Yenikevee being steepish.

Zewm, 4 hours—

The road descends along a valley the whole way, and is easy.

Khorassan, 3 hours—

The road goes down the same valley to the foot of a very steep pass 400 feet above it; then over undulating ridges. This ascent is only taken to shorten the distance: the road goes on down the valley and turns this part.

Koprikevee, 4½ hours—

The road is not very good, going over frequent nasty undulations on the left bank of the Aras; but the ground is all soft, and it could easily be improved to any extent.

Hassan-Kaleh—

The road ascends an easy ridge, then descends easy over an open plain.

Koorochuk, 3 hours—

Quite level.

Erzeroum, 3 hours—

Quite level to the Nabichai; then an ascent over Deveh Boyun.

2. By Olti.
3. By Khorassan and Yenikevee.
4. By Khorassan and Meshinguerd.
5. By the valley of the Aras and Kagizman.
6. By Deli Baba and Doghanly.

The most direct route to reach Kars from the sea would, of course, be from Batoum; but, for the reason already given, this would probably not be available. The most direct route from Trebizond would therefore be to follow the Erzeroum road to Vurzuhan in the valley of the Upper Choruk, and then by Isper and Olti to Kars. This route would have to be improved.

From the south the most direct route to Kars would be to follow the Bitlees-Erzeroum route as far as Kop in the Bolanyk district, and keep the bank of the Moorad Soo to Malazgird to the Alashgird district, then cross the Koseh Dagh to Kagizman.

An army coming from India for Erzeroum is practically limited to one landline, which is the one I followed, and which I will presently describe. Some other land routes from the Persian Gulf to Erzeroum are feasible, but they are either much longer by land or else go through Persian territory. A force, for instance, might go from Shoostur to Kirmanshah or from Bagdad to Sehna, and thence through Azurbaijan, or it might go from Moosul to Khooye, and thence by Bayazeed; but these routes have no advantages, and a glance at the map will show how unsuitable they are strategically. I need say no more about them.

There is one other alternative. A force could be sent by sea by way of Suez and Constantinople to Trebizond. Though this route would be feasible, and under some circumstances it might be necessary to adopt it for part at least of a force coming from India, I think the line by the valley of the Tigris is strategically the best. An advance like this of two forces, *each able to hold its own*, from two different quarters, would be more likely to paralyse the Russians, and the plan would have the great additional advantage of more than doubling all facilities for transport and supply.*

The route from Moosul by Bitlees seeming, therefore, the only one that is practicable for a force from India to adopt, I give a detail of the route itself in Appendix A.

The whole of this route (Appendix A) is quite practicable now for infantry, cavalry, and mountain artillery, and field guns could be passed over the bad parts by hand, but with considerable labour. If timely arrangements were made for the despatch of engineer officers, and they were followed as soon as possible by sappers and pioneers, all the bad parts of the road could be rendered practicable by the stores arrived.

The road alluded to in the note to Stage 17 is very much better than the one I marched through, which, though the ordinary caravan route, is not the best. This joins the above route before reaching Bitlees, and has actually been traversed by a large body of Circassians, who carried their baggage on their own clumsy carts.

Between Erzeroum and Juzeereh water is plentiful everywhere, except at Sert, and a force should, therefore, not halt at this place, but either on the Sert river or the ravine to the north of the town. Supplies could be collected at any point on due notice being given, and at Juzeereh, Sert, Bitlees, Kop, and Erzeroum considerable depôts might be formed.

Between Erzeroum and Bitlees fuel is so scarce that it is best to say there is none. The people of the country use cow-dung and a little brushwood, but of course these would go a very little way towards supplying the wants of an army. Therefore it would be necessary to impress on all the great necessity for economy in this article, and that very special arrangements should be made for storing it.

Forage, though not abundant, is procurable on this route, and could be collected in considerable quantity.

It is of course understood that this country is not practicable for operations in the winter. Snow falls and lies from November to April; and though, if absolutely necessary, infantry and light guns could, with immense labour, make the journey in winter, it should certainly not be needlessly attempted before the end of March or after the end of November.

I will now offer a few remarks on the suitability of this route as the main line of operations of a force advancing from India either to assist the Turks or to co-operate with a force sent from Europe.

* There still remains another practicable line. To send a force by sea, through the Canal to Iskanderoon, and thence march it up to Erzeroum. Under certain circumstances this might be preferable.

The difficulties of transporting by land the enormous quantity of stores which accompany an army must always render it an object of solicitude to take off the strain as much as possible from this description of carriage. In fact, it may be taken as an axiom that water-carriage should always be used to the utmost possible extent. In this case the primary base of a force operating from India in Armenia must of course be India, and it is equally a matter of course that the whole army, with its impedimenta, must be transported by sea to the nearest point on land. This point in the present case is Busrah, which must be the port of debarkation from sea-going vessels in any event.

From Busrah to Bagdad the navigability of the noble river Tigris has been so fully tested that it is no longer matter for doubt that all the *matériel* as well as the *personnel* of an army could be transported with certainty up to that point by river. This practicability of river transport need, therefore, only be limited by the advisability of using it to its fullest extent. The Tigris will bear up all it is asked to; but, looking to the difficulty of collecting a sufficient number of boats, it would probably be better that all the animals of the force should march up to Bagdad.

From Bagdad to Juzeereh the Tigris could, it is believed, be utilized to some extent to bring up stores. At present there certainly are some obstacles to the free navigation of the river, but these are of a nature which render their removal not doubtful. These are the remains of some old stone barriers west of Khan Mizrakchi below Samurra, reefs of low rocks running across the river between Tekreet and Humam Alee, and the remains of an old stone dam called the Bund-i-Nimrood, which crosses the Tigris at Awaie, about 30 miles below Moosul, whence to Juzeereh the river is open.

While, therefore, the heavier *matériel* was transported by water, troops should march by the direct route which goes by the right bank of the river, by Tarmujeh, Soomeycha, Beled, Tekreet, Khorneyna, Abooshukat to Moosul, and thence by Telis Kof, Semiel, and Peshkhaboor. This route is practicable for carts throughout its whole length.

As the mountainous country commences above Juzeereh, it would be advisable to send the troops forward by as many parallel routes as possible; and fortunately many of these exist. Thus (1) a route goes by the Zeitoon valley, between the first and second ranges, and comes down to the Sert river, above its junction with that of Bitlees; (2) the route I travelled and which is given above: this is the most direct; (3) from Sert by Zoke and Kermetta to Bitlees; (4) from Tilo by Zoke; (5) from Juzeereh by Middo, Chelik, and Tilo; (6) from Juzeereh by Middiat, Hassan Kef, and so to Nerjik and Moosh.

Above Bitlees, a very important position is Tadvan on Lake Van, which would have to be held in some strength, as it commands a practicable route by Lake Van to Ardis, and thence by the valley of the Saook Soo to Makoo, from which routes diverge to the Russian cantonments of Erivan and Nukhshvan.

Once the high table-land of Armenia is reached, there are numberless routes leading north, and forces would have no difficulty in marching by different parallel routes and maintaining their connection with each other at the same time.

Troops should arrive from India so as to take advantage of the winter months to go through the low country. At this time the climate is splendid, so that no sickness need be feared, and the army could assemble at the northernmost points on the routes, ready to advance directly the melting of the snow made the roads practicable.

I have before remarked on the scarcity of fuel, and as this is the greatest difficulty likely to be met with, it will not be out of place if I again call attention to the necessity for timely arrangements being made for its collections at suitable spots. There are three points from which firewood is procurable: (1) from the mountains of Lazistan on the north of Erzeroum; (2) from the Soghanli Dagh range on the east; and (3) from the hills of Koordistan south of Bitlees. Arrangements would therefore be necessary to organize depôts in connection with each of these sources of supply, whence the necessary places on the various routes could be kept supplied. For the first two parts, a train of carts could be organized; and for the last, of pack-animals.

Large numbers of horses, suitable for cavalry and artillery, could be procured from the Arabs, and also from the Koords and the villages of Armenia. It would not, however, be advisable to trust too much to these sources, and therefore every arm should come fully equipped with remounts.

Baggage horses, suitable for mountain guns and commissariat, could also be procured from the country south, west, and south-west of Erzeroum. Mules are not procurable in any number, but, unless Persia was hostile, large numbers would be procurable from Kirmanshah and Looristan.

Carts of clumsy make, but very suitable to the roads, exist in every village above Lake Van, and would certainly be procurable in large quantities; and as their construction is very simple, any number more could be made in the Soghanli forests and brought down for use.

Camels and donkeys are also procurable in very large numbers from the low country of El-Jezeereh. The latter are particularly fine animals, and should by no means be despised as beasts of burden.

The people of the country would be difficult to deal with. The Armenians are said to have been so oppressed that they would perhaps not be very likely to enter very heartily into any operations which had for their object the maintenance of their oppressors. But if they could be assured of present protection and future improvement of their position, they would doubtless assist in the end.

The Koords are all robbers, and, as such, would, no doubt, give trouble by harassing the communications; and the same may be expected from the Arabs. But there would be no open, organized hostility, and their utilization to the utmost extent as carriers, labourers, guards, or light troops would gain them all to our side. There is no doubt that every man of these people are as open to the arguments of gold as their neighbours, and there is, besides, a decidedly friendly feeling to the English from Trebizond to Busrah.

As in every campaign, it would be necessary to make every possible arrangements to prepare for the arrival of the troops; I speak with deference, yet writing this on the spot with all the country and its resources fresh in my mind; and I would recommend that the following preliminary steps should be taken directly the determination to despatch an army had been arrived at.

The following officers should be sent on ahead by express steamer:—

A superior officer, who would superintend all arrangements and be responsible that everything possible was done to prepare for the troops.

Several officers of the Intelligence Department (it would scarcely be possible to send too many) should proceed at once by sea to Trebizond and thence to the frontier. So little is known of the country and the people that every moment would be valuable.

Commissariat officers should be sent at once to Erzeroum, Kars, Kop, Bitlees, Sert, Juzeereh, Moosul, Bagdad, and Busrah.

Transport officers should be sent to Erzeroum, Erzinjan, Kharpoot, Diarbekir, Aleppo, Moosul, and Bagdad.

Engineer officers will be required to improve the channel of the Tigris and the road up. They should utilize the labour of the country, but should be followed without delay by sappers and pioneers.

In conclusion, I wish to note that I am endeavouring to obtain reliable information as to the approximate numbers of boats available for river transport, and also of the average time taken in ascending the river.

With reference to the amount of land-carriage available, I have not attempted to commit myself to figures as riding through the country at the rate I did, it was not possible to procure reliable statistics.

C. M. M.

Appendix (a) and (b).

Erzeroum to Juzeereh.

1. Akjullar, 12 miles 1 furlong east.

The road leaves the city by the Eran Gate, and is pretty level for 6 furlongs (15 minutes), winding round the south foot of the Top Dagh; it then goes over undulating ground for 1 mile 1 furlong (21 minutes), when it commences the ascent of the Deveh Boyun ridge, which is 3 miles long (1 hour) and 700 feet above Erzeroum. It next descends for ¼ mile to a ravine, out of which it reascends for ½ a mile, and then descends again 1 mile (18 minutes) into the ravine of the Nubbee Chai, running from the south (650 feet below ridge). Having crossed this by a ford (this must be deep after rain), the road goes over a ridge for ½ a mile (7 minutes) to another small stream, and ascending out of this the road to Hassan Killa goes off to the left. Thence it goes over easy level ground at the foot of a terrace from the hills on the right for 1¾ miles (½ hour) to a stream from the right; then in 2 furlongs (5 minutes) it crosses another dry stream, and after 1 mile (17 minutes) a third: 1 mile from here (9 minutes) it turns up to the village of Akjullar, which is 1 mile off on a terrace of the hills.

The road over the Deveh Boyun is difficult, but is practicable for guns, and could be improved to any extent. From the Nubbee Chai ravine the road is along the south-east side of the fertile and well-cultivated plain of Paseem. The best place for a force to encamp would be on the banks of the stream 2 miles west of Akjullar, which drains to the village of Kooroo Chuck in the plain.

2. Hertev, 9 miles 4 furlongs east.

The road runs along the foot of the lowest terrace of the hills, and is quite good and nearly level the whole way. The river of Hertev coming from the south, is crossed by a ford and bridge; several villages are passed, and there is no difficulty anywhere.

3. Majeedlee, 10 miles 5 furlongs south.

The road ascends pretty steeply (400 feet) for ½ a mile (13 minutes); it then winds along the hill side, ascending and descending for 1 mile 1 furlong (32 minutes), when it descends easily to the Shaitan Dun[illegible] (600 feet below), 1 mile, in 27 minutes. It then ascends by an easy gradient, but over soil which becomes heavy and sticky after rain, for 1½ miles (40 minutes): the last part is very steep to the top of the Akgokush pass (1,100 feet above the ravine). It then descends a little, and ascends to the Sakul Dotan ridge (200 feet higher) in ¼ mile (7 minutes). There is then a descent of 6 furlongs to a stream coming from the right, which, having crossed, the road ascends ½ a mile, then descends easily for 5 furlongs (12 minutes, 400 feet); then very steeply to a ravine 2 furlongs further. There are then some small ascents and descents, winding over the Aras for ½ a mile, the road being very stony and narrow, but easy. This is followed by a steep descent of 5 furlongs (1,000 feet) to a stream coming from the right, crossing which the road continues for 2½ miles pretty level into the village of Majeedlee, on the left bank of the Aras river, the village of Eypler being left on the right above. The road on this march would have to be made practicable for guns. This would be a difficult but not an insuperable task. A better line exists from Majeedlee along the bank of the river, which turns all the above ascents and comes out into the Paseem valley, opposite Hassan Killa, and is practicable for carts.

4. Koolee, 13 miles 5 furlongs south.

The road goes along the bank of the river, over cultivated terraces and winding round bluffs, and is level and good, but narrow, for 5¼ miles. It then turns away from the river, and ascends the easy pass of Magara for 6 furlongs. From this it descends for 1 mile to a stream coming from the right, which, having crossed it, continues pretty level, though narrow and winding along the river and round spurs and bluffs. For 2½ miles it descends to the river; following it for ½ a mile, it ascends a short but very steep and impracticable pass for 200 yards, and is very narrow indeed for 100 yards further (this bit would have to be made or turned in some way); it then descends for ½ a mile, whence there is a road to a bridge over the Aras, when it continues quite good, ascending imperceptibly into Koslee in 3 miles.

5. Koslee, 17 miles 7 furlongs south-south-east.

The road goes out quite level over a grass plain for three furlongs to the river Aras, which it crosses by a ford 3 feet deep, and which would not be practicable after heavy rain. The banks of the river are easy. The road then ascends imperceptibly at first, passing *en route* the small village of Korsu on the left, but afterwards more steeply, but always very easy, over rounded earthy hills, to the top of a ridge (800 feet above Koslee), and then descends slightly, and ascends to the crest of the Tek-Dagh (200 feet higher) range in 8 miles; thence the road descends for 2½ miles, and then runs along the lower ridge of the hills all the way to Koslee by a good broad track in 7 miles (700 feet below Tek-Dagh pass).

6. Kara Kopri, 9 miles south-east.

The road is excellent all the way, descending at a gentle slope along the foot of a ridge to the left (900 feet in all), and passing much cultivated ground; about half-way, pass village of Oornas on a stream (drawing to the Khynys river), which is crossed by a ford.

7. Shekh Hamza, 10 miles south-south-east.

The road, immediately on leaving, fords the river below Kara Kopri (50 yards wide, with a good bottom and easy banks). It then enters the hills and ascends easily over round earthy hills to the top of the Zernak pass (1,400 feet above Kara Kopri) in 6 miles. This road in wet weather is exceedingly heavy and slippery; half a mile from the top, pass village of Zernak on the left, on a considerable cultivated terrace. From the pass the road first winds round the southern face of the hill, descending easily; but it is very narrow for 2 miles. It then descends along a spur for 2 miles further by an easy gradient to Shekh Hamza (1,500 feet below Zernak pass). The road on this march requires widening everywhere, but the soil is all soft.

8. Kop, 10 miles 2 furlongs south-south-east.

The road goes out quite good to the Khynys river in 1½ miles (which is crossed by a deep ford, difficult to find without a guide, and not practicable after heavy rain; bottom good; banks easy). Then it passes over a nearly level plain to the Morad Soo in 3 miles (which is crossed by a deep ford in two branches; bed ½ mile; bottom wide and good; banks easy). Thence it is again level into Onajhlee, 1¾ miles, and also on to Kop in 4 miles, all over perfectly level plain. All this march goes over fine, open, cultivated plain, everywhere suitable for cavalry.

9. Peeran, 10 miles 6 furlongs south-south-west.

The road is pretty level for 3½ miles, when it crosses and ascends a ravine easily to the village of Shekh Yakoob, whence it goes on nearly level, descending slightly 2½ miles (40 minutes), when a small lake below is seen on the right. The road continues along it for 1¾ miles, then runs more west and goes round its south shore for 3 miles to the village of Peeran, situated on higher ground above its south-west corner.

10. Pulkhoos, 9 miles 4 furlongs south.

The road ascends easily over a road covered with boulders to a ridge, and descends to the village of Khers in 4 miles. It then goes by a rocky road, along the banks of the Nazikgol Lake for 2 miles, and then turning away from it, goes over a rocky but easy ascent, followed by a descent of 3½ miles to the village of Pulkhoos.

11. Karmooj, 8 miles south-south-east.

The road is over a rocky spur of the Nimrood Dagh for 2½ hours to Karmooj. It is quite good the whole way.

12. Kizvak, 10 miles south.

The road is very good, though sandy in places, passing over undulating ground, not far from the edge of the lake. In 2 hours pass the village of Zeghak on the left of the lake, and in 1 hour further reach Kizvak by a road nearly level along the lake.

13. Alaman, 10 miles south-west.

The road is very good, over easy ground. In 2 hours pass the village of Tadwan on the lake, and in 1 hour further ascend easily to the old khan of Alaman.

14. Bitlees, 10 miles south-west.

The road descends easily and is quite good, at first over open undulating ground, then along the sides of the Bitlees, a stream. The last part is narrow and would have to be widened, and for this it would be necessary to blast in some places. The road through the town, too, is narrow, and would have to be looked to; it crosses and re-crosses the river several times by bridges, which have to be strengthened, if not entirely re-made. The town is perched over the river on ledges, and extends for about 3 miles down.

15. Dokan, 14 miles 6 furlongs south-west.

The road descends gradually along and over the bank of the Bitlees ravine, and is in fair order for 3 miles (though it is narrow and rocky in places), when it descends and passes through a hole in a rock. There is then a nasty rocky descent for 3 furlongs (10 minutes) to the junction of a ravine from the right, which it crosses and goes along its right bank for 3 furlongs. There is then for 3 furlongs a nasty narrow bit that requires blasting, and the road crosses over to the left bank, which it continues along for 1½ miles (20 minutes), when it crosses to the right. It then continues along the right bank, and is narrow and stony for 1 mile (20 minutes) to the Hormiz Soo from the right, which it crosses by a bridge. From the hole above mentioned to this the road requires a good deal of improvement as there are at least four places where considerable blasting is required to make it practicable for artillery. Thence it is a good road for 1 mile (20 minutes), where there is a steep ascent for 2 furlongs, the first part of which is very bad, requiring much blasting and clearing, though the gradient is easy. Then it is pretty level, and descends gradually to an old khan and a stream from the right in 7 furlongs. For ¾ mile on there is a very bad bit, and 200 yards farther another. It is then good for 1 mile 2 furlongs, when it crosses a stream from the right by a ford, whence it still continues good for ½ a mile. Thence it is very bad, and is nearly impracticable for 5 furlongs, needing much clearing and widening. Then it is pretty easy for 1½ furlongs, descending easily to a bridge in bad order, by which it crosses to left bank of river, whence it is very bad into Dokan (1¼ miles), an old Knan.

16. Sirs, 11 miles 1 furlong south-west.

The road ascends steadily for 4 miles 3 furlongs (2 hours). Generally speaking, the gradient is not very steep, though in some places it is remarkably so; but the road throughout is very bad indeed, being a mere track among boulders and rocks and stones. It would require a great deal of work to make this bit practicable for artillery, and if it was wished to do so for a permanence, another line had better be sought for. Still, if the object was only to get the guns over, this could be done by hand after the improvement of the present line.

The road then descends and ascends to another ridge, and continues bad and requires making for 1½ miles (35 minutes); it then descends easily for 2 miles (35 minutes), winding round hills and crossing several steamers which unite in a ravine to the left and drain to the Sert river. Then it ascends easily to another ridge for 1½ miles (½ hour), beyond which the drainage goes to the Bitlees river, then, winding round the side of the hill to the left, ascends still gradually for ¾ mile (15 minutes), when it descends by an easy gradient, though the road is narrow, for about 1 mile (20 minutes) to the village of Sirs.

17. Sert, 14 miles 2 furlongs south.

The road descends steadily and is bad in places, requiring a good deal of making, to the Tawan river, which it crosses by a ford, and then again by a bridge, in 8 miles. This is crossed by an old bridge, Kupri Agarif, which is in a rickety condition; it then ascends pretty steeply for ½ a mile (10 minutes) to the village of Taseewan. Passing this on the left, it ascends pretty easily 2 miles (35 minutes) to a fine open cultivated ridge, then it is nearly level for 7 furlongs (15 minutes); it then descends easily and passes the village of Bisheen on the left. Then it descends into a deep ravine 6 furlongs (15 minutes), out of which it again ascends, the road being stony but good for another 6 furlongs (15 minutes): it then descends easily, and afterwards very steeply into another ravine in 7 furlongs; ascending out of this, it goes over open undulating ground for 2 miles to Sert (½ hour).

N.B.—An alternative route goes from Sert to Bitlees by Zoke and Kermetta, which forms the above route close to Dokan. This has been traversed by carts on the occasion of the Circassian emigration of Mesopotamia, and could be made practicable for artillery.

18. Darghalib, 11 miles 5 furlongs south-south-west.

The road is level and good over open cultivated slopes for 1 mile 1 furlong (20 minutes). It then descends by an easy gradient, but very stony and bad, for 1¼ miles (½ hour), whence it descends by a very steep zigzag for 6 furlongs (20 minutes). This is a very bad bit, the road being almost entirely over boulders and sheet-rock, or a rough pavement of the former. It would require much work to make it practicable for artillery; but as the cliffs both up and down the river and in sheer scarps for a considerable distance, it is improbable a better line could be found. Then it is pretty level but stony for 1½ miles (½ hour) to an old Khan and ferry. Thence it is quite good, winding along over the river for 2½ miles (40 minutes). It then ascends a higher ridge up a bad, stony track, part of which is not more than 6 feet wide, under magnificent sandstone cliffs. It then goes over an earthy bluff for 2 furlongs; then there is a nasty bit, very narrow, over soft sandstone sheet-rock, and winding among huge detached rocks for 6 furlongs: one part of this is a ridge built up over the river 4 feet wide. This bit is very bad, and would require a great deal of blasting to make it practicable. Thence the road is easy, going over open, cultivated land the hills having receded off to the right for 2½ miles (40 minutes). An earthy spur now impinges on the river, and the road ascends this easy, but very narrow, to an open plateau near Darghalib in one mile. Here is a ferry. The river is about 250 yards wide, with a considerable current. The right bank is high, and shelves steeply down, leaving no span; so that good arrangements would be required here to prevent confusion and a block occurring. A broad road should be cut from the bridge, which should be made here, round to the open ground above mentioned.

19. Chelik, 13 miles 2 furlongs.

The road on crossing runs along the river, and is quite level. At 2 miles pass junction of the Bitlees river on the right, and the village of Champur, above, on the left; thence it continues level along the last terrace from the hills and over stony ground for 5½ miles (1½ hours) to the village of Mohtel. Here cross a ravine from the left, where it leaves the river and ascends on to higher ground on the left; in ½ a mile pass the village of Wahsaron, and ½ a mile further on cross a stream from the left, and ascending for ¼ mile, then descending for 2 furlongs, the road zigzags down over hard rock, requiring to be blasted, to an old Khan and ferry on the Tigris in 2 furlongs. The road then crosses a small stream from the left by a ford, but which is bridged 50 yards up. Thence it goes along the left bank of the river the whole way to Chelik in 4 miles. This is stony in places and narrow in others, but all is easily makeable.

20. Fyndyk, 14 miles 1 furlong south-east.

The road is good, but stony leading over an open cultivated terrace for 3½ miles (1 hour), when the hills on the left begin to close in and the road becomes rough and stony for 1 mile 3 furlongs, when there is a very bad bit for 8 minutes, requiring to be blasted, followed by another equally bad bit, which is very narrow and over rock, high over the river, for 2 furlongs; the road then turns and descends by a not difficult gradient to a stream coming from the left in 2½ furlongs. This is very bad, narrow, and over rock, and would require a great deal of blasting and looking to. The stream here is very swift, and is crossed by a very deep ford, which is not practicable after rain, but there is an indifferent bridge 50 yards up. Then the road ascends steeply over greasy clay soil for 1½ furlongs (7 minutes), when it resumes its former direction along the river. This bit is bad, but the hill is soft, and it could easily be improved. There is then a nasty rocky descent for 1½ furlongs; then another shocking descent over sheet-rock, ending in a regular devil's-staircase to a lower ridge over the river in 2 furlongs. This bit would require good engineering to render it practicable, but it would have to be done, as there are no signs of a better line, the cliffs being sheer scarps on either side. The road then goes over a broad ledge of sheet-rock for 1 furlong, which could easily be made better, to the river Goinan from the left. Here the hills, which have up to this closed the river in, open a little, and the road is good along an open terrace and ascending in easy bluff for 1 mile 6 furlongs. The river now turns away to the south-west, and the road goes over open ground, ascending for 1 mile 3 furlongs; then over undulations for 1 mile to the village of Yakmala, and again ascends over easy stony hills for 1 mile 1 furlong to Khowaran on a hillock on the right, and a Koord camp in 7 furlongs; it then ascends steeply up a rocky hill side, and then descends over stony ground in 1½ miles to Fyndyk.

21. Finik, 14 miles 4 furlongs south-west.

The road ascends gradually for 1½ furlongs to a ridge above Fyndyk; it then descends over the contours of a hill on the left for 2½ furlongs. It then descends over stony ground to a ravine. crossing which it is pretty level but stony along the top of a ridge for 2 miles. It then descends easy but stony for ½ a mile, and then still descends, but entirely over sheet-rock, for ½ a mile. It is then not quite so bad, the hill being more earthy, 3 furlongs in some cases. Here it crosses a ravine, and becomes more easy, going over long undulating slopes from the ridges on the left, divided by ravines, for 1½ miles, when there is a descent to a stony ravine 4 furlongs, whence there is a bad stony descent of 3 furlongs to the Abzewa ravine, which is crossed by a ford, the old bridge above being broken. From this ascend by a nasty stony path for 2 furlongs, whence the road goes over open undulating ground, and is quite good right into Finik in 5 miles.

22. Jezeereh, 12 miles 5 furlongs south-west.

The road is quite good, though narrow, over river, for 5¼ miles, to Roosul ferry to the right, and whence for 1 mile 3 furlongs it is the same to a couple of ravines. Having crossed these, the road descends in 2 furlongs to the level of the river Zaitoon, which comes through the hills from the left, flowing through a considerable alluvial plain surrounded by ridges. It then crosses this river, which is in three branches, by fords, one of which is 50 yards broad, and, going over the level alluvium, ascends in 2 miles to higher ground above the Tigris; it then turns south parallel with the river, passing the village of Mansoorieh and a stream below in 2½ miles, whence it goes on to opposite Jezeereh in 1¼ miles, and is quite good.

Total—22 marches, 260 miles 4 furlongs.

Appendix (c).

Referring to the estimates of the strength which the Russians and Turks could probably put in the field in Armenia, it may be interesting if I append the following rough statement of how they were made out. The estimates of the strength in the Caucasus are made from notes made while in that region last year; and of the Turkish, from notes made this year.

The army of the Caucasus consists of 7 divisions of Infantry, *viz.*, 1 division of grenadiers of the Caucasus and 6 of the line (namely, the 19th, 20th, 21st, 38th, 39th, and 41st), and one brigade of Chasseurs of the Caucasus. Each division has 2 brigades, each brigade 2 regiments of 4 battalions, and a war strength of 900 bayonets, or 108,000 in all.

There is one division of cavalry of 2 brigades of 2 regiments of 4 squadrons of 150, or 2,500 sabres.

The artillery consists of 42 batteries, of which 12 are 9-pounders, 14 are 4 pounders, 3 are mitrailleuse, and 4 are mountain guns; and these have a total in war of 336 guns, 252 officers, 10,298 rank and file.

The engineers consist of 2 battalions of a total of 58 officers and 2,020 men.

There are besides in the Caucasus the following:—

Local battalions	47,000
Local depots	36,000

The Cossacks of the Kooban have a war strength of 30 regiments of 6 sotnias of 100 sabres = 18,000 sabres and 5 batteries of horse artillery of 8 guns each or 40 guns and about 1,200 men.

The Cossacks of the Terek have 15 regiments and 2 batteries of the same strength each.

Thus the total strength of the troops in the Caucasus is as follows:—

Regulars.	*Men.*		*Men.*
Infantry	108,000		
Cavalry	2,500		
Artillery	10,300	336 guns	
Engineers	2,000		122,800
Local Battalions			47,000
„ Depots			36,000
Cossack Cavalry			27,000
„ Artillery		56 guns	1,700
Irregular Militia			4,000
TOTAL			238,500, 392 guns.

But in the Caucasus there are not less than 300,000 Mahomedans, who are all bitterly hostile to the Russians, and who certainly could not be kept under with a less force than, say, 100,000 men. This would leave 140,000 men of the Caucasian army only available, so that 30,000 men must be provided from elsewhere.

Appendix (d).

The Turkish army is raised by conscription among the Mahomedans, every man of whom, with certain exceptions, is bound to serve 20 years, *viz.*, 6 years in the (Nizam) active army, 3 years in the (Idatyal) 1st Reserve, 3 years in the (Rudeef) 2nd Reserve, and 8 years in the (Hiyade) Landsturn. It is divided into regulars, irregulars, and auxiliaries.

The new organization which was promulgated in 1869 was to have taken to the end of 1878 to complete, when the total force was calculated at 700,000 men.

The regulars are divided into 7 corps (ordoos), with only three of which, however, we need at present concern ourselves, *viz* :—

The IVth or Corps of	Anatolia,	with its head-quarters at	Erzeroum.
,, Vth ,,	Syria,	,, ,, ,,	Damascus.
,, VIth ,,	Irak,	,, ,, ,,	Bagdad.

Each corps consists in round numbers of about 30,000 men. To these must be added the—

1st Reserve	14,000	men.
2nd ,, ...	10,000	,,
3rd ,, ...	10,000	,,
Besides	4,000	gendarmes, who are quite equal to the regulars.
Total ...	68,000	men.

The VIth Corps has perhaps 75,000 men.

Thus the estimate I have given of the probable force that Turkey can assemble in Armenia is as near the truth as is possible—

This was—

IVth Corps	70,000	
Vth ,, ...	20,000	
VIth ,, ...	10,000	
		100,000

Again, the irregulars, which I have estimated above, are as follows :—

Lazees 10,000.—This number is probably much smaller than could be raised. They would be drawn from the mountains of Lazistan, which border on the coast of the Black Sea, and are comprised in the province vilayet of Trebizond, the population of which is given at 938,140 souls. The Lazees have already fought with great distinction against the Russians in the defence of the fortresses of Akhiska, Akhalzik, and Kars, and they are a very hardy and brave race.

Circassians, 15,000.—Over 100,000 of these people emigrated from the Caucasus after its conquest by the Russians. They are splendid material, quite equal to the Russians and superior to the Cossacks of the Kooban and Terek, and all are imbued with an undying hatred of Russia.

Koords, 30,000.—Exact information of the Koords is very difficult to obtain, but there can be very little doubt that this number represents but a small portion of the fighting strength of a race who extend in the mountains for nearly 10° longitude, and every man of whom is a warrior.

Arabs, 30,000.—The number of these people is also much a matter of conjecture, but of some pretty good information exists; and if I mention that of these the Montefik tribe alone can muster 10,000, Benilam 10,000, Delim 5,000, and the Anezeh probably 20,000, and that there are numerous other tribes, the above will not seem too large an estimate. The Arabs, no doubt, hate the Turks; but their religion forms an indissoluble link between them, and I am informed that a very strong feeling exists amongst the Arabs to be led against the would-be destroyers of their religion, as they regard the Russians.

Osmanlees 10,000.—This would include all the men who were available after the ranks of the Nizam were filled, and is undoubtedly a very low estimate.

The [vilayets] provinces from which these men would be drawn would consist of the following:—

Trebizond, population	... ...	938,140 souls.
Sivas "	... ...	571,808 "
Erzeroum "	... ...	792,104 "
Diarbekir "	... ...	708,288 "
Aleppo "	... ...	535,714 "
Syria "	... ...	518,750 "
Bagdad "	... ...	2,000,000 "
	TOTAL ...	6,064,804 souls.

Appendix (e).

The estimate for the force which Persia might place in the field has been placed at 50,000, and this without doubt is the outside force they are capable of putting into the field, though how long it could be maintained there is another matter.

These would be drawn principally, if not entirely, from the two provinces of Azarbaijan and Irak Ajumee. At least it seems to me that if the Persians could withdraw a man from Khorassan, Kirman, Fars, or Kirmanshah to aid in a war against us, it would argue something radically wrong in our manipulation of the Afghans, Beluchis, and Turks on the frontiers of those provinces. Indeed, I am of opinion that merely by judicious threatening the Persians would be unable to afford any armed assistance to the Russians at all; but I will adhere to the above estimate, and now try to show how it could be managed.

The total strength which the Azarbaijanees could turn out has been variously estimated at from 40,000 to 60,000; the former being the actual number that they were enabled to assemble in a moment of great national danger—that is, in the war of 1826; and I think, therefore, it is certainly not likely to exceed this last when the object of their mobilization was to assist the Russians, whom every Persian must regard in his heart of hearts as but a concealed foe at the best. And it is evident that the whole of this number could not be sent out of the province. Tabreez must be held, and some arrangement must be made to protect it from the Nomad tribes, who number one-fourth of the total population. Bearing this in mind, it must be considered a liberal estimate if I allow that 30,000 men might be withdrawn to co-operate with Russia.

The army of Irak Ajumee was estimated at a time when more was done to develop the military strength of the country than is now the case, at 12,000 men. To these 5,000 might be contributed by the province of Khamseh perhaps 10,000 from Mazanduran, and 5,000 from Geelan—total 32,000, This I know, that on a late occasion, when the Shah was particularly anxious to make a show at a grand review at Teheran, not more than 12,000 could be mustered.

Again, Teheran cannot be left undefended, and some arrangement must be made to protect the country, if only from marauders. To do this would really require a considerable force; and therefore I shall, I imagine, be regarded as underestimating the resources of the province if I estimate the outside force that could be collected and despatched from Irak Ajumee and the neighbouring districts would be 20,000.

By these means—that is, by crediting the Persian resources with an elasticity I very much doubt their standing— I produce 50,000 men. These could have little effect on the campaign. It must be remembered that the Turks could still mass 65,000 infinitely superior troops at Bagdad, if the Persians attempted a diversion in that direction; and if they sent their army to swell the Russian forces in Armenia, the same 65,000 making a demonstration on Kirmanshah from Bagdad, or on Ispahan from Shoostur, would, I imagine, very soon necessitate their recall.

Appendix (f).

The Tigris is eminently navigable from the sea to Bagdad at all seasons of the year by vessels drawing six feet water. In the autumn, when the river is at its lowest, there would be some difficulty; but this can always be avoided by care and with proper pilots. The period of the greatest rise varies between the end of April and the third week in May, and the average rise of the river is about 22 feet The lowest time is from the end of October till the rains, which occur about the end of November. From this date the river has always plenty of water in it till July, when it gets lower and lower to the end of October, as above stated. The Turks have eleven steamers of various sizes on the river, and there is one English steamer belonging to Messrs. Lynch & Co., another being in course of construction.

Mr. Carter, the Agent of Lynch & Co., has been kind enough to give me as the result of his inquiries that there are 1,700 native boats trading from Busrah to Bagdad, with an average tonnage of 20 tons; and on the Euphrates there are about 600 with an average tonnage of 14 tons, making the total available tonnage approximately 56,000 tons.

The best native boats are well adapted for their work. They are strongly built, and, though rough, are of excellent model. The journey from Busrah to Bagdad occupies with a single band of trackers from 40 to 60 days, with a double set about 25, the distance being about 500 miles.

The *goopa* is a wicker-work coracle covered with bitumen, and it is ordinarily used for crossing the river, but it might be used with advantage for making bridges.

C. M. MACGREGOR, *Lieut.-Colonel,*
1st Asst. Quarter Master General.

Appendix (d).—*1st Section.*

From—MOSUL *To*—ROWANDUZ.

Territory.—TURKEY AND PERSIA. *Authority.*—GERARD.

Names of Stages, &c.	Distance.		Rivers.	Remarks.
	Intermediate.	Total.		
	Miles.	Miles.		
1. Burtala ...	15	15		
2. Kellek ...	18	33		From 1 to 4 country is rich and cultivated. No difficulties of road, and supplies obtainable. In 5 road becomes rough, and 7 there is a pass most difficult for pack animals. Supplies and fodder doubtful at 5 and 6.
3. Erzil ...	22	55	Zab 150 yards wide, ferry, few boats available.	
4. Dumwach ...	12	67		
5. Herash ...	18	85		
6. Kurrak ...	12	97		
7. *Rowanduz* ...	14	111		

2nd Section.

From—ROWANDUZ *To*—KHOI.

Territory.—PERSIA. *Authority.*—AINSWORTH AND MORIER.

Names of Stages, &c.	Distance.		Rivers.	Remarks.
	Intermediate.	Total.		
	Miles.	Miles.		
1. Jeffuli ...	25	25	Stream (bridged).	Road in 1 and 2 exceedingly difficult. In 1 ascent of Sari hud impracticable, even for mule artillery. In 2 Kelishin pass (10,000′) very difficult.
2. Ghafur Khan Kila	28	53		
3. *Ushnai* ...	7	60	*Gader* (fordable).	
4. Uladi ...	25	85		Supplies at 1, 2, 4 doubtful. Abundant after 4.
5. *Urmia* ...	12	97	*Bardisur* (bridged). *Burrandaz* (fordable).	No difficulties of road after 2.
6. Gawálan ...	24	121		
7. Dilman ...	30	151		
8. Salmas ...	20	171		
9. *Khoi* ...	18	189		

3rd Section.

From—KHOI *To*—ERIVAN.

Territory.—PERSIAN AND RUSSIAN.

Names of Stages, &c.	Distance.		Rivers.	Remarks.
	Inter-mediate.	Total.		
	Miles.	Miles.		
1. Parschi ...	5	5		Forage, water, and supplies everywhere except at 2, which is in a mountainous tract, and 8, 9, 10, of which no information is given.
2. Khanava ...	20	25		
3. Nasik ...	12?	37		Good road.
4. Abásábád ...	7	44	*Arras*, bridged in dry season. Bad ferry in floods.	
5. *Nakjivan* ...	8	52		
6. Bayuk Diez ...	13½	65½		
7. Koragne ...	9½	75		
8. Bach Nurachin ...	15	90		
9. Sadarak ...	15	105		
10. Davalu ...	12	117		
11. Kamarlu ...	12	129		
12. *Erivan* ...	18	147		
1st Section ...	...	111		
2nd Section ...	...	189		
Total ...	...	447		

Appendix (e).—*1st Section.*

From—BAGHDAD *To*—SULEIMANIA.

Territory.—MESOPOTAMIA AND KURDISTAN. *Authority.*—CHAMPAIN AND RICH.

Names of Stages, &c.	Distance.		Rivers.	Remarks.
	Intermediate.	Total.		
	Miles.	Miles.		
1. Jedidah ...	20	20	Tigris (boat bridge).	No difficulties of road, first march over desert, then over level and fertile country to Tauk, after which ascends hills. Supplies procurable, also fodder, up to 7, after which no information.
2. Yenijeh ...	18	38		
3. Delli Abbas ...	27	65		
4. Kara Teppeh ...	27	92		
5. Kifri ...	21	113		
6. Taz Khurmati ...	27	140		
7. Taúk ...	21	161		
8. Leilan ...	11	172		
9. Yusuf Agas Camp	9	181		
10. Chemchemal ...	14	195		
11. Derghezin ...	15	210		
12. Kelespi ...	14	224		
13. *Suleimania* ...	8	232		

2nd Section.

From—SULEIMANIA *To*—SUJ BULAK.

Territory.—PERSIA. *Authority.*—FRASER.

Names of Stages, &c.	Distance.		Rivers.	Remarks.
	Intermediate.	Total.		
	Miles.	Miles.		
1. Akurta ...	20	20	Stream (ruined bridge)	
2. Sardasht ...	18	38	...	Humil Pass. Difficult for laden animals.
3. Nistan ...	16	54	*Aksa*, difficult ford.	
4. Jiltomar ...	12	66	...	Road steep and difficult.
5. Bairam ...	20	86	...	
6. Suj Bulak ...	12	98	...	Road wild and mountainous throughout. Water procurable. No particulars given of resources of villages.

2nd Section.—Alternative.

From—SULEIMANIA — *To*—SEHNA.

Territory.—PERSIA. — *Authority.*—GERARD.

Names of Stages, &c.	Distance.		Rivers.	Remarks.
	Inter-mediate.	Total.		
	Miles.	Miles.		
1. Naodeh ...	11	11		
2. Mama Kulan ...	10	21	*Tonkabwa-yahara*, 100 yds. wide, ford.	The road is over hilly country, but presents no great difficulties. Water is always procurable. Good grazing ground in valleys—cattle and sheep.
3. Dia ...	7	28		
4. Pengwin ...	20	48	*Mashkhal, R.*	
5. Murivan ...	18	66		No. 9 (Doissa) is at a little distance from the road.
6. Sheikh Attar ...	21	87	*Girdalan*, ruined bridge.	
7. Kilai Nadir Shah	12	99		
8. Barodar ...	15	114	*Katawal* (ford).	
9. Doissa ..	15	129		
10. Sehna ...	15	144		

For 3rd Section of this route, *vide* Route, Appendix F, 3rd Section.

Appendix (f).—*1st Section.*

From—BAGHDAD — *To*—KIRMANSHAH.

Territory.—PERSIA. — *Authority.*—GERARD AND BELLEW.

Names of Stages, &c.	Distance.		Rivers.	Remarks.
	Inter-mediate.	Total.		
	Miles.	Miles.		
1. *Bakútú* ...	33	33	Diála ...	In (1) pass Khanhein Sír at 14 miles. A few hovels and water brackish. No other halting place. Cross Diála by bridge of boats.
2. *Shahrabán* ...	26	59		
3. *Kihil Robát* ...	17	76		
4. *Khánikin* ...	18½	94½		No difficulties in 1, 2, 3, 4, 5,6, 7, 8, and 10.
5. *Kasr-i-Shírin* ...	16	110½	Ahvand ...	
6. *Sir-i-Púl* ...	18	128½	Ahvand ...	(9) Deep and muddy.
7. *Kirrind* ...	29	157½		Water procurable at all country. A good deal cultivated. So presumably there are supplies at all. Certainly at 4 and 10.
8. *Harúnábád* ...	19	176½		
9. *Máhidasht* ...	28	204½		
10. *Kirmanshah* ...	18	222½		

2nd Section.

From—KIRMANSHAH *To*—SEHNA.
Territory.—PERSIA. *Authority*.—PLOWDEN.

Names of Stages, &c.	Distance.		Rivers.	Remarks.
	Inter-mediate.	Total.		
	Miles.	Miles.		
1. *Kaklistán* ...	16	16	Kára-Sú ...	Road in 1, 2, 4 good. Supplies procurable all along the route, except at 2 which is a small, dilapidated village. Road in 3 is in some parts excellent, in others a mere bridle path. There is always plenty of water.
2. *Kamyarán* ...	21	37	Áb-i-Razáwar.	
3. *Kúrúgh* ...	21	58	Cham-i-Gahwárú	
4. *Sehna* ...	21	79		

3rd Section.

From—SEHNA *To*—TABRIZ.
Territory.—PERSIA. *Authority*.—"ITINERARIES IN PERSIA," W. O., 1880. ROUTE No. 247 (MORIER).

Names of Stages, &c.	Distance.		Rivers.	Remarks.
	Inter-mediate.	Total.		
	Miles.	Miles.		
1. Camp near Amárat.	14	14		Road all along the route is uneven, but not very difficult; narrow defile in 4; cross Kizl Ozan in 2. Abundance of good water and supplies at 11. Morier says nothing about supplies at any other place; but as the country seems well peopled and full of villages, it may be presumed that supplies of some sort will be procurable. There are a number of small rivers and streams intersecting the road; none of them large enough to present much difficulty to the passage of troops, so there would be no difficulty about water.
2. *Zágha* ...	16	30	Kizl Ozan	
3. *Diván darah* ...	12	42		
4. *Khoubatú* ...	15½	57½		
5. *Kháfilán Kúh* ...	12	69½		
6. *Súrkh River* ...	12½	82		
7. *Kizli* ...	7	89		
8. *Abás Bolák* ...	13	102		
9. *Bári* ...	6	108		
10. *Galandi* ...	18½	126½		
11. *Maragha* ...	14	140½		
12. *Akú* ...	15½	156		
13. *Cháwan* ...	12	168		
14. *Shíramín* ...	10½	178½		
15. *Deh Kargán* ...	12	190½		
16. *Khúsrú Sháh* ...	18	208½		
17. *Sardarúd* ...	11	219½		
18. *Tabríz* ...	6½	226		

4th Section.

From—TABRIZ *To*—ERIVAN.

Territory.—PERSIA AND GEORGIA. *Authority.*—CHAMPAIN AND TELFER.

Names of Stages, &c.	Distance.		Rivers.	Remarks.
	Intermediate.	Total.		
	Miles.	Miles.		
1. *Sofian* ...	24	24	...	Road is stony and bad in 4, otherwise very good. From 4 to 13 it is the post road, and fit for wheeled transport.
2. *Marand* ...	16	40		
3. *Airandibi* ...	20	60		
4. *Julfa* ...	20	80	Araxes (ferry).	
5. *Nakjivan* ...	27	107		
6. *Buikh Dhs* ...	12	119		
7. *Kyvrah* ...	10	129		The country is very fertile, except 9 and 10, and there is abundance of water.
8. *Bash Morashan* ...	15	144		
9. *Sardarak* ...	15	159		
10. *Davalu* ...	12½	171½		
11. *Kamarlu* ...	12½	184		
12. *Ahamsala* ...	10	194		
13. *Erivan* ...	9	203		
1st Section ...	...	222½		
2nd Section ...	...	79		
3rd Section ...	...	226		
Total distance Baghdad to Erivan.	...	730½		

Another route.

From—Tabriz in Persia *To*—Erivan in Persian Armenia.

Territory.—Persia. *Authority.*—Ousley, Morier, Champain.

Names of Stages, &c.	Distance.		Rivers.	Remarks.
	Intermediate.	Total.		
	Miles.	Miles.		
1. *Sofian* ...	...	24	Stream ...	Road good throughout. Chief difficulties are crossing irrigation drains and rivulets in 1, 2, 6, and 5, in which last road is stony and bad, and hilly in 2. Supplies fair throughout—poor at 1, 3, 7, 8, good at 2, 5, 9. Water at every stage; but the road dry for part of 5, 3, and 7; elsewhere plentiful.
2. *Marand* ...	20	44	Many rivulets.	
3. *Airandibi* ...	20	64		
4. *Gargar* ...	20	84		*Detail of route.*—1. Road generally good, over a flat country, crosses a river and irrigation drains frequently. Sofian a poor village; water plentiful.
5. *Julfa* ...	13	97	Arus R. Ferry.	2. Road good, but hilly, crosses numerous rivulets. At 9 miles pass ruined Caravanserai-i-Yam; then descend into the plain of Marand; rich in garden and plantations.
6. *Nakitchivan* ...	27	124	Many streams.	3. Road over grand level plains. Airandibi, an immense collection of hovels, short of which are some good villages.
7. *Dudanyah* ...	40	164		4. At 19 miles round caravanserai, otherwise no place between.
8. *Davalu* ...	28	192		5. At 8 miles cross Aras river by ferry, hence over a parched and barren country for 3 miles, and then by bad hilly road to Julfa.
9. *Erivan* ...	27	219		6. Road very good, but many streams. 7. Road for 2 miles through ruins of habitations; then lies over the magnificent plain of Chaman-i-Sharur.

8. Road over a parched and barren plain. Morier halted at Sadrall.
9. Road goes through an extensive tract of fertile land called *Gerai* (from river). Pass Virab monastery on left.

Erivan.—The capital of Russian Armenia, on the left bank of Zéuzis, a considerable tributary of the Aras, 6 miles from north foot of Ararat, some 3,000 houses, 10,000 population. Has an elliptical fort, one side of which is over a perpendicular cliff.

H. B. N.

Appendix (g).—*1st Section.*

From—DIZFUL | *To*—BÚRÚJIRD.

Territory.—PERSIA. | *Authority.*—SCHWINDLER.

Names of Stages, &c.	Distance.		Rivers.	Remarks.
	Intermediate.	Total.		
	Miles.	Miles.		
1. *Báladrúd* ...	18	18	Búladrúd ...	Road good in 1, 6, 10, 11, 12, 13.
2. *Rizze* ...	22¾	40¾		Road bad in 2, 3, 4, 5, 7, 8, 9.
3. *Púl-i-tang* ...	15	55¾	Áb-i-Zál ...	The road generally is bad in places; but it is evidently infinitely better than the one through the Bukhtujari mountains, and with a small expenditure of money Schwindler considers that most of the difficulties might easily be removed. Supplies procurable in small quantities. All along the route in larger quantities, particularly at 7, 10, 13. No difficulty about water.
4. *Cham-i-Gez* ...	14	69¾	Seihíns ...	
5. *Velmián* ...	17½	87¼	Fani ...	
6. *Badamek* ...	14	101¼		
7. *Nasrábád* ...	16½	117¾		
8. *Chínúsk* ...	15¼	133	Shíráb ...	
9. *Sháhinsháh* ...	15	148	Págin ...	
10. *Khorámábád* ...	8	156		
11. *Zághe* ...	22¼	178¼		
12. *Kelángáne* ...	17¼	195½		
13. *Búrújird* ...	19¼	214¾		

2nd Section.

From—BURUJIRD | *To*—KIRMANSHAH.

Territory.—PERSIA. | *Authority.*—CAPTAIN JONES.

Names of Stages, &c.	Distance.		Rivers.	Remarks.
	Intermediate.	Total.		
	Miles.	Miles.		
1. *Náhwand* ...	35	35		This road is the highway from Búrújird to Kirmanshah, and passes through a highly cultivated and populous country, with towns and villages every six or seven miles; a smooth broad road. Supplies and water are in abundance.
2. *Garáchea* ...	21	56		
3. *Sána* ...	21	77		
4. *Besitán* ...	14	91		
5. *Kirmanshah* ...	17½	108½		
Total miles of 1st section ...	...	214¾		
Total distance from Dizful to Kirmanshah ...	...	323¼		

There is another and more direct road from Khorámábád to Kirmanshah; but it is very winding and quite uninhabited, and is about 144 miles in length, divided into five stages.

The road presents but few difficulties and obstacles to the march of an army, except just after leaving Khorámábád, when it winds a good deal amongst the hills lying along the bed of a large stony river. No villages between these two towns, but two, one 28 miles from Kirmanshah and the other 32. So there are no supplies hardly to be had on the road.

Appendix (h).

From—DIZFUL (*viâ* the Kerkha river) *To*—KIRMANSHAH.

Territory.—PERSIA. *Authority.*—RAWLINSON.

Names of Stages, &c.	Distance.		Rivers.	Remarks
	Inter-mediate.	Total.		
Dizful to—	Miles.	Miles.		Road good generally throughout, notably 1, 2, 4, 5, 6, 9; bad places met with 3, 7, 8, 10.
1. *Balarud* ...	24	...		Not known are 11, 12, 13, 14.
2. *Huseni* ...	10	34	Balarud river.	No description available, Rawlinson having turned aside. Supplies in small quantities and water available.
3. *Kalsi Risa* ...	18	52		No information on four last stages.
4. *Pul-i-tang* ...	19	71	Karkha river.	*Detail of route:—*
5. *Ab-i-garm* ...	28	99	Ditto.	1. Road good. Sahra-i-Lort, plain, winding road; sandhills at foot of Kalai-Jangawan.
6. *Jaidar* ...	16	115	Ab-i-garm river.	2. Road good. River sometimes dangerous from sudden rises, open plain.
7. *Pul-i-gamashan* ...	16	131	Kashgar river.	3. Road good. Soft gypsum soil; two broad ravines—Dukhtawajib and Tik-tiki; difficult to cross.
8. *Seimarah* ..	14	145		4. Road good, crosses hills, leaving river at Abizat ford; 15 miles rejoins river.
9. *Sahra-i-Lort* ...	20	165		5. Road good along bank of Karkha parallel to Keileem range.
10. *Rudbar* ...	20	185		6. Road good. Past Ab-i-garm river at confluence with Karkha river, 4 miles across plains, through Chuli-Jaidar pass, difficult for guns, but no easier pass; easily made practicable. From Karkha valley along table-land all called Jaidar.
11. *Zangawar* ...	20	205		
12. *Hululan* ...	16	221		
13. *Stage* ...	22	243		
14. *Kirmanshah* ...	22	265		7. From open plain road ascends to steep and rocky pass, hardly prac-

ticable for laden mules. Very difficult road, parallel to Kashgar river.

8. No description available, Rawlinson having turned off to see ruins.

9. Road ascends all the way to Seimareh on the banks of the Karkha running north-west.

10. Road bad; but can be made practicable for wheeled carriages. Cross Lort plain, re-ascending small range, and another more thickly wooded, pass valley of Badrae, and two streams. Road descends to valley of the Sirwar river.

11, 12, 13, 14, no description available.

Appendix (k).—*Section 1.*

***From*—SHUSTAR AND DIZFUL** ***To*—BÚRÚJIRD AND KUM.**

***Territory.*—PERSIA.** ***Authority.*—SCHWINDLER.**

Names of Stages, &c.	Distance.		Rivers.	Remarks.
	Intermediate.	Total.		
	Miles.	Miles.		
Shustar to—				
1. *Ab-i-bid* (or Gavanek 16½ miles).	20¾	20¾	Karun river.	1, 2 road good; supplies moderate; country cultivated. A pass to cross in 1 near Shustar Tangi Jalibasi.
2. *Dizful* (or Gavanek 20½ miles).	17¾	38½		3 to 16, *vide* Route V, Section I. 17—23. Road fair throughout. Difficulties in crossing ridges 1, 17, 19, 20, in threading gorges, 18, 19. Country cultivated; fair supplies throughout. Good at 19, *Sultánábád.*
3—16. *Vide* Route V., Section I, to *Burujird*).	214¾	253¼		
17. *Dodjuft* ...	18¼	271½	Hissa stream.	*Detail of Route.*—1. Pass Tang-i-talikin or Reshgir at 6 miles; rich tract of Aguili: 12 villages. At 6 miles Golwand village, Kari river.
18. *Tukht-mahal* ...	19¾	291¼	Doab river.	2. Stream pass Sar-i-bishet canals. 3—16. *Vide* Route V.
19. *Sultanabad* ...	16¼	307½	Bridged stream.	17. Four ridges of 7,150′ to 6,150′. Numerous villages, a stream; most villages to Dodjuft.
20. *Mushtabad* ...	18¾	326¼	Stream.	18. Saluin village at 2 miles. Kezaz valley and two villages; a gorge between Rasthend and Shahzindbutans. At 94 miles, Ture, large village caravanserai; Doab river and 8-arched bridge.
21. *Rahgird* ...	24	350¼		19. Marun village at ½ mile. At 1 Kuzik hills; at 6 miles Nimadkah, a ridge, speak Turkish. At 8½ miles a village. At 11 miles a ridge; narrow gorge and high pass, valley of Sehdeh. At 14 miles ridge; 16½ Sultanabad, chief town of Irak.
22. *Salijun* ...	18½	368¾		
23. *Kum* ...	16½	384¼		

20. At 6 miles Sherigird village; 9 miles Mutabad village and Imamzada. At 12 miles Shave; 14 miles Karijun, 16 miles a ridge (5,970′). At 18½ miles Mushtabad, ruined village, formerly chief town of province.

21. Ibrahimabad, 3 miles. At 11 miles ridge (6,370′), followed by plateau (6,050′); at 20 miles small stream (6,099′); at 24 miles Rahgird village. Shrine, caravanserai, and cisterns.

22. At 2 miles Dizijun village, near stream; at 4 miles Imamzada; at 5 miles Zawarigers village, on other side of river; at 9 miles Salik Shimjun; at 11 miles Inadbeg (4,750′); at 15 miles edge of plateau. Sulijun at 8½ miles (4,230′).

23. At 3 miles ruined caravanserai plateau (3,770′); at 9 miles dry river bed; at 10 miles canal and village (3,530′). At 11 miles low plateau (3,450′); at 13½ miles Karr-i-Dukhtar ruins; at 14 miles single arched bridge; ditto at 14½ miles; at 15 miles a 9-arched bridge; post leave and go into Keem, a town of about 12,000 souls.

Section 2.

From—KUM *viâ* TEHERAN *To*—SHAHRUD AND ASTRABAD.

Territory.—PERSIA. *Authorities.*—TROTTER, BELLEW, GOLDSMIDT.

Names of Stages, &c.	Distance. Inter-mediate.	Distance. Total.	Rivers.
	Miles.	Miles.	
Kum to—			
1. *Pul-i-dalak* ...	15		
2. *Hauz-i-Sultan* ...	24		
3. *Kinaragird* ...	24		
2. *Tehran* ...	24		
5. *Khan-i-khatiri* ...	18		
6. *Aiwan-i-kaif* ...	27		
7. *Kishlak* ...	21		
8. *Deh-i-nimak* ...	23		
9. *Lasjird* ...	25		
10. *Samaran* ...	22		
11. *Ahwan Serai* ...	24		
12. *Ghuslúh* ...	24		
13. *Damghan* ...	23		
14. *Dehmulla* ...	26		
15. *Shahrud* ...	16		
16. *Tash* ...	18		
17. *Camp* ...	25		
18. *Astrabad* ...	14		

Remarks.

Road generally fair and practicable throughout.

Difficulties owing to barrenness of country, and bad or scant water in 1, 3, 8, 9, 12, 14, 17. Difficulty of limited supplies throughout, save at 1, Kum. 4, 5, 9, 10, 15, 18, where they are good. Road difficult by steep ascent, rockiness, &c., in 2, 3, 7 11.

Detail of Route.—1. Leave Kum masonry bridge 8 arches; along left bank of river nearly dry; through cultivated plains; past low hills, barren valleys, 9 miles village Faizabad-i-Kala. Caravanserai, well brackish water. Pul-i-dalak, caravanserai, small stream, salt water. Fair drinking water by digging holes south-east of posthouse.

2. Over part of Kavir, across low hills, volcanic rocks At 9 miles tolerable water is vaulted at Abambir, 10 miles Sadrabad serai. Then across desert plain to 23 miles. Road rugged and difficult in defile. Hauz-i-Sultan, fine serai, and tolerable water from masonry well, under highest hill of range, right of river.

3. Four miles over barren plains. Eight miles over barren hills. One rocky ascent, difficult for wheels. At caravanserai water bitter and undrinkable. Six miles more through barren hills to Davi-malik-ul-mant (18 miles). Pass fordable river, salt water, 5-arch bridge. At 19 miles an unbridged dry river bed in hilly country. Last 3 miles through a cultivated valley, few small villages. Several small swampy watercourses to Kinaragird in ruins, but with caravanserai and other small inhabited villages with cultivation. Supplies limited.

4. Much good for wheels. Cross Kinaragird plain; then a small range of steep hills; pass a high dry plateau, enter small hills to serai, and walled gardens of Husepabad, 11 miles. Cross several small watercourses and valley for 3 miles. At 10 miles the cultivated valley of Karisak; then an ascent across a barren plain to Kala-i-Khoja Ali, a small ruined fort; then across a rough plain, varied in the trees, cultivation to New Gate, Teheran. Supplies, water, &c., abundant.

5. Over undulating cultivated land, villages, corn fields, &c. At 1 mile cross stream. At 1½ miles stone bridge over dry bed of nullah. At 3½ miles stream with stone bridge. 5 miles town of Shah Abdul Azim, several villages Takiabad, Aminábád. Cross a small ridge of Mav, a stony hill skirt 6 miles to 8 miles, small streams and villages; ample water and supplies.

Section 2—contd.

From Kum viâ Teheran to Shahrud and Astrabad—contd.

Names of Stages, &c.	Distance.		Rivers.	Remarks.
	Inter-mediate.	Total.		
	Miles.	Miles.		

6. Road across Vivamin plain, skirting a hill range to left, over which towers Damavand. At 1½ miles cross dry deep nullah. Two streams from left. At 3 miles cross a stream. At 3¾ miles a village with few trees—ruined fort on mound. At 4 miles cross three streams from right; pass serai of Kabrea Gumbaz. Road, with few undulations, level. At 6 miles cross Jajrud river, 1 mile in breadth, including several watercourses. At 8 miles pass Khasran. At 11 miles Sharifábád, Aiwan-i-kaif, large village round a fort, gardens, vineyards, &c., on bank of brackish Zanrud, 50 yards wide, flows in a ravine, and drying up in August. Supplies (save fruit) scarce.

7. Good road, gravel. At 6 miles through low ridge to defile Sirda-i-kuk. Breadth from 300 to 800 yards; exit, 30 yards; cross salt stream several times. Hills mostly barren till about 20 miles, then cultivation and villages. Several watercourses. At Kishlak is the Hableh-rud, a fair large stream, brick bridge. Heights bordering the Sirda-i-kuk. Defile can be crowned with ease and turned. Water good, but muddy. Supplies plentiful.

8. Road through cultivated plain, dotted with villages. At 10 miles walled hamlet, Aradan, Telegraph. At 15 miles villages, Padish, then a gravelly desert. Water brackish. Supplies *nil.* Dehnimak, a salt village, round a fort on a mound.

9. Road skirts Khorassan desert. Soil clay, saline efflorescence; usually traversed at night; very fatiguing, waterless; several ravines, crossed by bridges; dilapidated fort and caravanserai at Tasgird and post-house; water brackish; supplies plentiful.

10. Road 20 miles cross stony, undulating desert, cut up by watercourses; 10 miles village of Surkhab. At 16 miles a dry brick cistern on left. At 18 miles lines of Kanat. Last 2 miles through fields. At 20 miles two streams of clear water. Samnan, a telegraph station; flourishing place. Good water; good encamping ground.

11. Road good for 11 miles, gravelly. 13 miles more over stony and undulating soil. Small streams and gardens up to 5 miles. Then long hill skirt. At 12¼ miles cross dry bed of torrent. At 13 miles a steep narrow winding ascent, *impracticable for guns.* A tiny spring and summit at 14 miles. Steep desert into broad ravine. 15 miles Kanat of water. Then gentle ascent up to the bed of a mountain torrent. At 15½ miles small villages. At 19 miles steeper ascent. At 21 miles reach highest summit, then undulating desert into small plain, in which at 24 miles is the wide serai and post-house of Ahwan. Pool of water beyond, and abambir. Water good and plentiful; supplies none.

12. Good, hard, gravelly road over a gently falling desert; waste-hills on either side. Cross low spur of Elburz after steep ascent. At 1¼ miles gentle descent to 5 miles, then steeper. At 6 miles road winds round spur, and descends gradually to bare plain of Damghan. At 17 miles cross dry bed of torrent. Ascend low ridge (5,600′). At 23½ miles cross dry bed torrent; deserted fort, &c. Then stream of clear water, good but limited, from pool and "abambir," though none on march. No supplies.

13. Road good and level, across stony, desert plain between hills to Aminabad, 8 miles. At 11½ miles Daulatabad with triple wall and ditch. At 13½ miles small stream, more villages. At 15 miles cross stream from left. At 21¾ miles ruins and burial ground. At 22½ miles cross stream. Water abundant and good. No supplies, save bread.

14. Road fair over barren tract. To the left sloping up to a stony skirt, and to the right dam to the salt desert. 3rd to 4th miles constant watercourses; 6 miles high round tower, "Tuppa-i-Bakr." At 12½ miles stream; numerous villages. Dehmulla, small village, with round fort on mound; large caravanserai; water good and plentiful; supplies few.

15. Route by well beaten tract over stony hill skirt, and desert on right; undulating ascent for first 3 miles. At 9 miles Kanats. 10 miles pass walled village Karvan. Road turns and ascends gradually to Shahrud in an opening of the Elburz. A walled town, 650 houses, gardens, vineyards, &c.; three good serais, post-house. Water good and plentiful; supplies abundant. Important as connecting Astrabad and Khorassan.

16. Road good and passable for wheels after first rocky pass, turnable by detour of 2 or 3 miles ascent. Leave gardens, cross shallow watercourse, passes through narrow valley, emerging from

SECTION 2—concld.

From Kum viâ *Tehran to Shahrud and Astrabad*—concld.

Names of Stages, &c.	Distance.		Rivers.	Remarks.
	Intermediate,	Total.		
	Miles.	Miles.		

rock 2½ miles 2,200′. At 5½ miles Kellateh village. Shahwar mountains 7½ miles ruined fort. Barren valley up to stream of good water. 10½ miles wide open valley; easy slopes. 16¼ miles descent from spur. At 18 miles pass "Rabat." Defile leading to and from the Chalchallyan pass commanded by hills. Tash has 50 houses.

17. At 1 mile after steep ascent reach crest of Kotal-i-Wajimaina; descend some distance to Kabr-i-Sufed. No village; ample ground for encamping; good stream. At 3 miles Haffchashna, caravanserai, road level. At 5½ miles Kotal-i-Jaling Maling. At 7 miles Rabat-i-Sufed. At 9 miles Aliabad. At 10 miles Kuzluk. Descent to plain easy; road good. At 18 miles foot of pass.

18. Ten miles to camping ground in forest-covered valley of lower range; overhead ascend road through marshy forest-covered country. Astrabad or Astar, containing from 2,000 to 3,000 houses. Supplies, water, &c., abundant.

Appendix (1).

From—TREBIZON *To*—ERZEROUM.

Territory.—TURKEY IN ASIA.

Names of Stages, &c.	Distance.		Rivers.	Remarks.
	Intermediate.	Total.		
	Miles.	Miles.		
1. Djevizlik ...	18			"An excellent hill road of an average width of 27 feet; it passes over ranges of a height of 8,000 feet, consequently the gradients in many places are steep, but are practicable everywhere for heavy guns.
2. Khamsikui ...	16			*Bridges*—All the streams are bridged over, and culverts thrown over small mountain torrents. The bridges do not admit of guns or wheeled vehicles passing each other. The stages are somewhat longer than we consider an average march, but there is good accommodation for troops at each."
3. Zigana ...	21			*Supplies* abundant
4. Gumesh Khaneh ...	27			*Transport:* arabas (country carts) and pack ponies procurable in unlimited quantities by employing local agents.
5. Khadrak ...	27			
6. Baiboort ...	15			
7. Kop ...	15			
8. Farna-kapan ...	16			
9. Kara-booyuk ...	16			
10. Erzeroum ...	27			
		198		

Appendix (m).

Route from Iskanderún to Erzeroum viâ Marash Kharpût and Músh.

1st Section.

From—Iskanderún *To*—Kharpút.

Territory.—Turkey in Asia. *Authority.*—Murray's Handbook of Asiatic Turkey.

Names of Stages, &c.	Distance.		Rivers.	Remarks.
	Intermediate.	Total.		
	Miles.	Miles.		
1. Baias ...	10	10	...	The stages and distances are all taken off the map attached to Murray's "Handbook of Asiatic Turkey."
2. Ujakly ...	10	20	Stream ...	
3. Akjar ...	15	35	" ...	There is no available information about this road at all; but as it also appears in Stielez and Keipert's maps, it is possibly quite practicable.
4. Shanakly ...	12	47	" ...	
5. Charna ...	9	56	" ...	
6. Pekmes Owázi ..	15	71	...	
7. Marash ...	24	95	Jihún Chai ...	The ranges to be crossed are the Akir Dagh and Kanlu Dagh between 7 and 8, the Baltan Dagh between 13 and 15, and the Músher Dagh between 17 and 18—close to 18.
8. Alisháhr ...	16	111	...	
9. Jellagha ...	12	123	...	
10. Albistan ...	11	134	...	
11. Til ...	13	147	...	The rivers to be crossed are the Euphrates at 16, where Murray states that there is a ferry. The Tokmansu (bridged) in 15, and numerous small streams in 2, 3, 4, and 5.
12. Dedinikoi ...	15	162	...	
13. Arga ...	32	194	...	
14. Shermiglu ...	13	207	...	7, 10, 15, 18 are biggish places on main routes. The two former on the road from Berejik to Kasariyeh, and the two latter on that from "Erzeroum to Sivas and Tokat." So probably supplies would be procurable at these places. Water would be also procurable, as there appear to be numerous streams and rivers, small and large, along the whole route.
15. Malatiyeh ...	9	216	Tokhmasu ...	
16. Eizolú ...	21	237	Euphrates ...	
17. Chaukeia ...	21	258	...	
18. Kharpút ...	12	270	...	

Route No. VII (a).—*Section II.*

Route from Iskanderún to Erzeroum *viâ* Marash, Kharpút, and Músh.

From—Kharpút *To*—Músh.

Territory.—Turkey in Asia. *Authority.*—Brandt.

Names of Stages, &c.	Distance.		Rivers.	Remarks.
	Intermediate.	Total.		
	Miles.	Miles.		No great difficulties of road, but it is rather an elevated one in many places, and likely to be closed by snow in winter. Cross over a ridge in 4, boulders in 3, long but gradual ascents and descents in 6 and 7; road rough in 7. Country well cultivated, and there would be no difficulty about supplies. Enter the Músh plain after 9, when the road is a dead flat.
1. Alishan ...	12	12		
2. Tikeh ...	12	24		
3. Palú ...	12	36	*Murad Chai* (bridged).	
4. Mezirah ...	11	47		Brandt did not actually go to Músh by his account of his march, but passed by it; so there is no record of the actual distance from Arishhan. It is probably about 10 or 12 miles.
5. Cherli ...	20	67	*Murad Chai* (fordable).	
6. Ashaguh ...	11	78		
7. Boghlan ...	18	96	*Takhta Kopri-su* (bridged).	
8. Ziyaratu ...	12	108	*Murad Chai* (fordable).	
9. Arishhan ...	12	120		
10. *Músh* ...	12?	132?		

Section III.

From—Músh *To*—Erzeroum.

For this route, *vide* Appendix (n), 3rd Section.

Appendix (n).—*1st Section.*

Iskanderún to Diarbekr.

From—Iskanderún | *To*—Erzeroum *viâ* Diarbekr and Músh.

Territory.—Turkey in Asia. | *Authority.*—Champain.

Names of Stages, &c.	Distance.		Rivers.	Remarks.
	Intermediate.	Total.		
	Miles.	Miles.		
1. Karamút ...	18	18		Road is fairly good throughout, No. 5 rather hilly and rocky.
2. Antioch ...	18	36	Orontes (bridged).	Nos. 2, 5, 8, 10, and 14 are large town with supplies. No particulars given about remaining stages, but the country is generally rich and well watered.
3. Jisr Hadíd ...	12	48		
4. Dána ...	30	78	Orontes (bridged).	
5. Aleppo ...	27	105		
6. Chúbanbeggi ...	36	141		No. 7 is an insignificant village. Scarcity of fuel at 9.
7. Sargúsh ...	42	183		
8. Birijik ...	14	197		
9. Charmelik ...	25	222	*Euphrates* (ferry).	
10. Urfa ...	27	249		
11. Karajún ...	26	275		
12. Severek ...	25	300		
13. Karabokchi ...	27	327		
14. Diarbekr ...	27	354		

N.B.—An alternative route (Pollington) from *Aleppo* (5) to *Biridjik* (8) is by *Dalsas* (6 hours), Bambuch (?), *Sadjur* (3 hours), Elifelu (? hours), Sadjus river).
Birijik (3 hours, Euphrates ferry).

2nd Section.—Diarbekr to Músh.

Territory.—ASIATIC TURKEY. *Authority.*—TAYLOR AND BRANDT.

Names of Stages, &c.	Distance.		Rivers.	Remarks.
	Inter-mediate.	Total.		
	Miles.	Miles.		
Diarbekr to—				
1. Egil ...	25	25	Arganeh Mäaden.	Road generally mountainous and difficult. In 7 over a very difficult pass. "The passage of troops could easily be arrested by a small force, and it would be quite impossible to drag artillery over it."—(*Brandt.*)
2. Jubehr Kila ...	10	35		
3. Hini ...	24	59	Debeneh-su.	
4. Ilijeh ...	20	79		
5. Darakol ...	10	89		
6. Nerjki ...	12?	101	Kok-su. Yak-su.	Water obtainable everywhere; supplies and fodder at Hini; elsewhere no particulars. Distances in 6, 7, and 8 are doubtful.
7. Shin Valley ...	20?	121		
8. Kizil Aghaj ...	12?	133		
9. Músh ...	10	143		

N.B.—This is the most direct route from Diarbekr to Músh. Another *viâ Miafarkin, Saert* and Bitlio is much longer and almost as difficult. A third, by Kezero and Kizil Aghaj, is given.

2nd Section (alternative).—Diarbekr to Músh.

Authority—VISCOUNT POLLINGTON.

Names of Stages, &c.	Distance.		Rivers.	Remarks.
	Inter-mediate.	Total.		
	Miles.	Miles.		
Diarbekr to—				
1. *Khazero* ...	36	36		
2. *Teltafi* ...	25	61	*Semes Rai*, *Semeh Surun*,	No particulars given. Distances approximately taken from time given.
3. *Kherun or Khems*	20	81	*Pokreh*, *Koh-su*	
4. Kurdish Camp ...	30	111		Road is mountainous and rough, and in 4 very bad indeed.
5. *Kizil Aghaj* ...	20	131		
6. Músh ...	14	145	Several streams	

Route No. VII (b).—*3rd Section.*

Músh to Erzeroum.

Territory.—Turkey in Asia. *Authority.*—Brandt.

Names of Stages, &c.	Distance. Intermediate.	Distance. Total.	Rivers.	Remarks.
Músh to :—	Miles.	Miles.		
1. Kirawi ...	12	12	*Murad Chai*, bridge. *Kara-su* ford	No great difficulties of road. It lies through hilly country with good grazing. Good water-supply everywhere.
2. Chak Bukúr ...	11	23		
3. Gúmgúm ...	11	34	*Char Bukár* bridge.	Nos. 5 and 7 are very small villages. No other particulars given.
4. Khinis ...	20	54		
5. Agveran ...	9	63		
6. Koli ...	10	73		
7. Eipler ...	12	85	*Bingol-su* rapid current, fordable.	
8. Hasan Kaleh ...	18	103	*Bingol-su* bridge. *Kelwen-su*, *Kurd-su* ford.	
9. *Erzeroum* ...	18	121	*Hasan Kaleh-su*	
Section I ...		354		
Section II ...		143		
Total ...		618		

Appendix (o).

Memorandum on the aid which could be rendered to Turkey from India, dated May 8, 1877.

In December last I wrote a memorandum with the object of calling attention to the practicability of the Tigris Valley route as the line of operations of a force proceeding from British India. Then war seemed doubtful; there was a hope that it might yet be staved off for another year. But now it has come. We are aware the Russians have invested Kars; we have information that a force has occupied Bayazeed; Persia is said to have concentrated forces at Khoi, and to be preparing another force at Mohumrah. Now, therefore, the whole aspect of affairs is changed; and it becomes necessary to consider the question in the new light which events have thrown on it.

If war broke out between Great Britain and Russia, and it was wished to aid Turkey by a force from India, the question cannot now be confined to the narrow limits of my former memorandum. That only treated of the practicability of the Tigris Valley line *per se;* the problem which should now be attended to is, what aid we in India can render the Turks, and how this aid can best be applied?

In my former memorandum there are two paragraphs which show that I recommend the Tigris Valley line on two conditions, the first of which was that troops shall 'go through the low country' in the winter months, and the second of which is implied, though not so clearly stated, that we should be beforehand with the Russians.

The season is, however, already far spent, and our army could not, under the most favourable circumstances, now hope to reach Erzeroum before the winter commences in November, and the probable position of the Russian forces before an army from India could reach the foot of the mountains between Mesopotamia and Armenia *might* render an advance by this line—perfectly safe if undertaken at the right time—now strategically a false one.

I will, however, consider what courses are open to us; and it seems to me the following are worthy of consideration:—

1. An advance through Persia on Tiflis.
2. An advance by the line of the Tigris to Erzeroum.
3. An advance from Iskanderoon to Erzeroum.
4. An advance from the Black Sea to Erzeroum or on Tiflis.

In regard to the first proposition, I would remark that it could certainly have the advantage of drawing the Persians off from aiding the Russians, while the prestige of a successful advance on Tiflis would be enormous throughout Asia. But it has the disadvantage that our whole line of operations would lie through a hostile country, and the conquest of Tiflis would tax our strength to such a degree that failure might at least be possible, and failure with a line of retreat through a hostile country might mean annihilation. If, however, it was determined to adopt this plan, there are two routes by which it would be feasible for a force to advance—first, from Shoostur to Kirmanshah; second, from Baghdad to Kirmanshah. If the first was adopted, troops would land at Ahwaz, three days' steam above Mohumrah, and march to Shoostur. The distance is under fifty miles, and the road is quite good, so that it might be accomplished in five days; that is to say, from the day of arrival of detachments at Mohumrah, it might be calculated that troops could be collected at Shoostur by the tenth day.

At Shoostur there would have to be a considerable halt, in order to let transport be collected. As this would be a hostile country, it is quite impossible to say how long this would take, and it is fair to conjecture that none would be procured. In this case transport would have to be collected and marched to Shoostur from Turkish territory—a by no means easy feat to accomplish, as all the country between Shoostur and the Tigris is for a considerable portion of the year a swamp; and, in fact, I know of no cross road that could be used.

However, as no attempt could be made to collect transport till the force was assembled at Shoostur in sufficient strength to detach parties to collect animals, he would be a sanguine man who would expect to get off from Shoostur under two months. Of course it would be quite feasible to bring transport from India, but the difficulty and delay that would be caused by adopting this course would be very great.

Before starting from Shoostur it would be necessary to arrange to leave a pretty strong force there to protect our line of communications, because this position is very open to a flank attack from Ispahan or from Shiraz by Behbahan.

This arranged for, the force would necessarily proceed by the route by Khorumabad described by Sir Henry Rawlinson. The distance of this road to Kirmanshah is not under 280 miles; and as the road is decidedly bad, it would probably take at least thirty days to accomplish.

Thus, if a force did not bring its own transport, it might perhaps be concentrated at Kirmanshah in something under four months from date of reaching Mohumrah.

A force might also be sent by Baghdad to Kirmanshah. In this case, which was recommended by Sir Henry Rawlinson in the war of 1854-55, it might be concentrated at Baghdad in a month after leaving Busrah; and in the time that would have intervened between the declaration of war and the arrival of the force, there seems little doubt that a very large, at all events a sufficient, amount of transport might have been collected.

From Baghdad to Kirmanshah is 210 miles, and the force could therefore be assembled at the latter place in three weeks after leaving the former; and as I think it nearly certain that a practicable road for light troops exists from Khanakeen to Sehna, that point could also be reached by an advance force in the same time that it would take the main army to arrive at Kirmanshah. In addition to being, if anything, an easier line, the Baghdad route possesses four very important advantages over the other. One, the facility of getting a sufficiency of transport together, I have already alluded to. The second is that up to Khanikeen would be in a friendly territory, and the distance to be traversed in hostile territory before reaching Kirmanshah would be 160 miles as against 439 miles. The third is that the Baghdad-Kirmanshah route is not open to a flank attack to anything like the same extent as the other, if indeed at all. The fourth is that the fine corps d'armée the Turks have at Baghdad could co-operate with us, so that our own force could move out of Kirmanshah intact. These considerations induce me to recommend this route most strongly in preference to that by Shoostur.

From Kirmanshah, where a large force would have to be left to protect the communications from a flank attack from Teheran, the onward road is perfectly practicable to Tabreez. Captain Hon'ble G. Napier, who, at my recommendation, traversed this route in 1875, reports the distance to be 342 miles, and remarks that "except in seasons of extreme scarcity, the country might be relied on to supply a very large force in all that would be necessary. Mules, camels, and horses are owned and bred in large numbers, and corn and forage are plentiful."

A force then going by this Baghdad route would occupy, speaking approximately, about ninety days to Tabreez.

If the Persians were hostile, we should, no doubt, have to fight at or near Kirmanshah, and also at Tabreez. But the latter is a straggling city, and, besides being commanded, it has no defences, so that it could not hold out long.

The hostility of the Persians seems to me so entirely out of order, that I am inclined to think it will not last long, unless our diplomacy is much at fault.

From Tabreez to the Russian frontier is only seventy miles, and the road is perfectly good, being constantly traversed by the heavy Russian 'fourgons."

But here it would be necessary to be guided in the after course of the campaign by the progress the Russians had made in Armenia and the strength of their forces between Tabreez and Erzeroum or Tabreez and Tiflis. It would, therefore, be futile to attempt to sketch any further the progress of the campaign, it being sufficient for our present purpose to know that from Tabreez to Erzeroum, 370 miles, or to Tiflis, 365 miles, are both quite practicable for troops.

The Tigris Valley route I have already considered. A force would take thirty days to concentrate at Baghdad. From that place to Jezireh is 342 miles, the road being practicable for carts, and the river could be made available for heavy stores.* This would probably take thirty-five days, and the 260 miles thence to Erzeroum would take thirty days more, so that an advance by this route would take not less than ninety-five days. For the details regarding an advance by this line, I refer to my Memorandum; but there are certain considerations connected with the question under present circumstances which must not be passed over in silence.

In the first place, the season is already far advanced, and even with the utmost expedition troops could not reach Busrah for four months after the declaration of war, to which must be added the ninety-five days it would take to reach Erzeroum from Baghdad, thus making it in all not less than eight months from the date of the order for sending a force.

Again, from May to October the plague seems to rage annually in the low country between Baghdad and Busrah, and therefore it would not be advisable to arrive at the former before the end of October, by which time it would be quite too late to hope to get to Erzeroum that season. The proper time for a force to arrive at Busrah, if the use of the Tigris Valley line is contemplated, is December 1. It would then arrive at Sert early in March, and be able to take advantage of the first opening of the passes.

Much also depends on the positions of the Russain forces in Armenia at the time we should reach that country. Clearly, under present circumstances, we could not reach Erzeroum before the beginning of April next.

If Kars and Erzeroum have fallen (as seems to me very likely to be the case) before the winter, the Russians will either winter there, or even, if they have time, they may push on either in the direction of the Mediterranean or the Tigris. In this case our further movements must depend entirely on what the position of their forces is. This much only is certain, that if we adopt this line we had better press on with the greatest practicable speed to the farthest point we can attain this side of the snowy mountains of Erzeroum. An army could winter very comfortably at Jezireh and Sert, or their vicinity; to send them beyond would only cause needless suffering without any corresponding advantage.

The third proposition is an advance from the Mediterranean to Erzeroum.

As in the other cases, I will not do more than allude to the very important part of these operations that would be embraced in the transport of the force by sea.

The point on this coast which we are always accustomed to regard as that at which a disembarkation should take place is Iskanderoon or Alexandretta; but in talking over the Euphrates Valley Railway scheme with the Governor-General of Armenia, who had been long stationed in Aleppo, he informed me

* For this statement I have the authority of Mr. Consul Brand, than whom no one was ever better acquainted with this country.

that the port in every way best suited for this purpose was at Suadia (Soiedie in a German map), or ancient Seleucia. This place is called Souediah in the Imperial Gazetteer. It is eighteen miles west of Antioch, and is said to be a remarkably healthy place, and to have considerable advantages for the formation of harbours for the accommodation of shipping. It is well sheltered, there are no sunken rocks, and the anchorage is safe.

The road to Antioch, in addition to being eighteem miles shorter from Suadia than from Iskanderoon, has no mountain pass to cross, like the other.

From Suadia to Aleppo is eighty-seven miles, and the road is quite easy. From Aleppo the road goes by Birehjik (cross Euphrates) and Urfa to Diarbekr, the total distance being from Suadia 336 miles. It would, therefore, in all probability take not less than forty days to throw a force into Diarbekr from the coast. A force could not, however, traverse the 211 miles (twenty-one days), which intervene between it and Erzeroum, unless it started from Diarbekr very early in October, as the whole country is under deep snow in the winter, and quite impracticable.

The disadvantage of this route lies in the very long sea voyage from Bombay to Suadia, which would probably take not less than thirty days to accomplish. Its advantage is that it would provide us with a double base of operations,—England and India,—and probably place the resources of nearly all the littoral of the Mediterranean at our disposal; it would provide us with a force, which might be used for Egypt, and up to the last moment the force could be sent elsewhere; and, finally, the line of operations is not the least liable to be interfered with.

The fourth and last proposal is the despatch of a force to land in the Black Sea; and first, either operate to assist the Turks in Armenia, or, second, invade Georgia. These had better be considered together. It would not be a more difficult undertaking to land on the east coast of the Black Sea than it was to land in the Crimea, if a force was sent from England; and if sent from India, it would only take perhaps ten more days than to Suadia.

The plan has the advantage that the real point of attack could not be known until the last moment, and there is no very long land journey before the objective points were reached, from Poti to Tiflis being only 195 miles. The disadvantages of the plan are that no transport could be procured at the point of debarkation, and probably but few supplies; and the low country of Mingrelia is very unhealthy, partaking of the nature of an Indian terai. From Poti to Tiflis there is a railway, which of course would be broken up. Yet, as there must be in England plans and sections of the whole line, and it was constructed by English engineers, I suppose English engineers could reconstruct it.

I believe it is not known what is the strength with which the Russians have actually invaded Armenia; but adopting the figures given in my first Memorandum, I shall say it is probable they have not under 140,000 men across their frontier. Now, whether they are able to capture Kars and Erzeroum or not, I should say that the main body of this force would be found in Armenia in the commencement of next winter, so that there would be not more than 100,000 actually in the Caucasus, of which certainly not more than 50,000 would be available to meet us, or perhaps less, if the Mahomedan tribes of the Caucasus were judiciously handled.

Directly after the intention of attacking Tiflis became evident, I think it may be taken for granted that every man that could be spared would at once be ordered to demonstrate in Georgia, and that they would even, if necessary, evacuate or raise the siege of Kars and Erzeroum in order to be strong at this point.

But, however anxious they might be to concentrate in Georgia, the question is whether they would be able to do so in time. Erzeroum is 330 miles from Tiflis, while Poti is only 195 miles from that place, and it is only 175 miles to Mtz Kheta, the really important strategical point from it being on the only Russian line of retreat over the Caucasus. To ensure the success of this attack, it would first be advisable to assemble the troops intended for it at Constantinople, giving out that the destination of the force was the Danube. This, unless the management of the affair was grossly blundered, would have the effect of inducing the Russian Government to reinforce their army on that river with every available man; and sufficient time having been allowed to elapse to permit of this concentration, the fleet would sail suddenly for Trebizond, and make a feint of landing the troops there. When this feint also had had time to work, the fleet would again sail for Batoum, Poti, Nicolaef, or other suitable point, and, debarking without delay, would advance on Tiflis in the lightest possible order.

It is a question of time. If the Russians could concentrate enough men to beat us before we got to Tiflis, our strategy would have failed; but on our part we have greater facility for throwing a force by sea to Poti than they have by land from the Danube.

Unless the Russians have large reserves ready in the south of Russia to reinforce their army in the Caucasus, it would be an extremely difficult undertaking to do so from whatever point they came. They would probably have every available man concentrated on the Danube, if we seriously threatened to land there; and from the Danube to the Caucasus troops would have to go by Odessa, Birzula, Kharkof, and Rostof to Vladi Kavkas by rail (the distance being over 1,500 miles), and thence by road over the Caucasus (133 miles).

If troops came from Moscow, the distance is almost equally great, from Moscow to Vladi Kavkas being 1,250 miles.

It is a matter for calculation how long troops would take to go from 1,250 to 1,500 miles by rail, and march 133 miles over a mighty range like the Caucasus; but we may take it for granted they ought not to do so in anything like the time troops should march 175 miles over the comparatively easy country from Poti to Tiflis. Moreover, if the time of our advance on Tiflis was arranged to take place just before the commencement of the winter, the army of the Caucasus would be cut off from all succour; for not only are the passes of the Caucasus snowed up a month before the low country between Poti and Tiflis, but navigation is very dangerous on the Caspian during the winter months.

Whichever of these alternatives was adopted, it may be questioned whether the force which would sail from India could, in our state of total unpreparedness, start under four months from the outbreak of war.

This may seem a very long time, but we are not as other nations are. A declaration of war always takes us aback. At the present moment I am not aware that we have a single bag of flour ready.

Adopting this estimate, therefore, as the time required for preparation, and supposing Bombay to be the port of embarkation, I may now calculate how long it would be before our troops could hope to come into collision with the enemy:—

1st A—

	Days.
From Bombay to Mohumrah	10
„ Mohumrah to Shoostur	15
„ Shoostur to Kirmanshah	30
„ Kirmanshah to Tabreez	40
„ Tabreez to Russians	15
	110

1st B—

	Days.
From Bombay to Busrah	10
„ Busrah to Baghdad	30
„ Baghdad to Kirmanshah	20
„ Kirmanshah to Tabreez	40
„ Tabreez to Russians	15
	115

2nd—

	Days.
From Bombay to Baghdad as above	40
„ Baghdad to Jezireh	35
„ Jezireh to Erzeroum	30
	105

3rd—

	Days.
From Bombay to Suadia	30
„ Suadia to Diarbekr	40
„ Diarbekr to Erzeroum	21
	95

4th—

	Days.
From Bombay to Poti	45

That is to say, if the declaration of war came to-morrow, by plan 1st A we might reach Kirmanshah by November 10.

By plan 1st B, we should be five days later. But both would be too late to go further, and we should therefore have to winter at Kirmanshah; and commencing operations again by April 15, we might reach Russian frontier by June 15.

By plan 2nd, we should reach Baghdad by October 25, and Jezireh by December 1. But this would be too late to advance this season; therefore we should have to winter at Jezireh, Sert, or thereabouts, and commence again about April 15, reaching Erzeroum by about May 15.

By plan 3rd, we might reach Suadia by October 15, and Diarbekr by November 25. This also would be too late, so that we would have to winter about Diarbekr, and commencing again about April 15, we might reach Erzeroum by the beginning of May.

By plan 4th, we might reach Constantinople by October 20. We might then have to wait there for some time, so we probably could not get to Poti before November 1. Then, if the winter was late, and we displayed an extraordinary amount of energy and good arrangement, we might be in possession of Mtz Kheta on the Russian line of communications over the Caucasus by December 1.

I very much doubt the possibility of our being able to anticipate these dates, and myself should be inclined to add another thirty days to them.

It is thus evident that by the first three plans we can do nothing this year, but must wait for the spring. By the last plan we might, if we had great luck right through, perhaps get to Tiflis before the winter was upon us; but it would be very risky. Still, it is the only thing we can do this year, and I think if we hardened our hearts we might do it. It would be a really brilliant operation of war, and I believe a perfectly sound one.

If, however, it is agreed that it is practically too late to send any troops this year, there would be no use despatching troops from India before—

1st A plan	January 1	2nd	January 1
1st B plan	„ 1	3rd	„ 15
4th	February 10		

But if war was declared any time before four months of the dates in the above paragraph, we need by no means sit still with our hands folded. We might not be able to send the Turks any assistance in men before the winter, but we could send them in one month assistance in officers, which I believe would prove so valuable as to enable them to hold out till the winter put an end to operations for this year; and any officers sent might collect information that would be of the greatest aid to us when we did send a force. But this is not the only measure we might undertake, if we are to be forced into a war with Russia. If we must draw the sword, let us be determined not to return it to the scabbard till we have some more substantial guarantee than Tzaric honour to guard us against a repetition of Russia's treacherous attempt to overturn the balance of power in the East.

I consider that no sane person could, and no loyal Englishman should, wish that such a war should be ended till Russia's unprovoked attack on our interests has recoiled on herself,—till her frontier is thrown back to its proper limit, or till her resources and commerce are so crippled that she will think seven times before she again provokes England.

In this view the first point that strikes me is the present attitude of Persia. The threatened intention of this State to interfere in the present war is clearly owing to the promptings of the Russian working on the natural hostility of the Sheeah for the Soonee. I cannot say that I regard this her blindness to her own true interests with any dismay. The aid she can give the Russians can hardly affect seriously the present balance; and her hostility gives us a very opportune chance of rectifying her east frontier, and at the same time binding Afghanistan and Beloochistan more closely to us.

In another paper I have recommended that a small force be despatched to Mekran directly on the outbreak of war. This could without difficulty reconquer the whole of Persian Beloochistan; and the force would be so small that it need not interfere with the aid we shall render the Turks eventually. No doubt, should war be proclaimed, the Russians will endeavour to induce the Persians to again lay siege to Herat, lending them officers to direct the operations. If she should do so, I should not regard the step with much apprehension. Directed by English officers, I think the Afghans are more than capable of holding their own. Indeed, so much is this the case, that I would recommend that, while Herat was reinforced from Kabul, a force from Kandahar might undertake the reconquest of Seistan.

I think also by taking steps I believe to be in our power to effect cohesion among the Oozbek Khanates and the Turkomans, it might be possible to drive the Russians out of Central Asia, and throw their frontier back at least as far as the Aral.

We cannot perhaps supply men for all these enterprises, but we should not forget that we can supply money and arms and officers; and let us use these sinews of war to the very utmost of our power. Officers sent promptly even now might enable the Turks to hold out till the winter.

I have not touched upon what can be done direct from England. With her small yet splendid army, with her magnificent navy, with her well-stored coffers, and the ability of her diplomatists, much, very much, may be done. Let it be our duty in India to second her efforts, by carrying out to the bitter end all the means of crippling Russia we possess, and which I have sketched above.

We have not provoked the war—then let us remember that the more we can do to the above end, the longer peace shall we bequeath to our posterity.

(Sd.) C. M. MACGREGOR.

Appendix (p).

Route from Lásh Jawain by Kásh to Kala Bíst, and thence to Kandahár.

[*Authority.*—From Chakánsúr to Dewala, Leach,—*vide* "Routes in Asia," Section II, No. 86.]

Jawain to—	Miles.	
1.		
2.	50	I can find nothing on record about this part of the route; but it appears to pass through cultivated country, irrigated from the Helmand, &c. There is a road marked on the map. By this the distance would be as nearly as possible 50 miles.
3.		
4. Chakánsúr		
5. Kadeh	16	*Chakánsúr* is a fort and village of Toki (Sanjaráni) Baluch. Thence the route, hitherto S.E., turns W.N.W., following the Kásh-rúd.
6.		
7.	46	*Kadeh* is a village. Thence to Kásh no halting places are mentioned; but as the route lies along or near the Kásh-rúd, the distance could probably be divided into 3 marches of 15 or 16 miles each.
8. Kásh		
9. Cháh-i-Kasadi	16	*Kásh* is a walled village on or near the Kásh-rúd (*Ferrier*). There is a road from Farah to Kásh given hereafter.
10. Cháh-i-Karki	20	From Kásh the route turns eastward. The next three stages (9, 10 and 11) are over a waterless tract, probably undulating gravel plain. Halting places are at wells with no habitations. Dewala (11) appears on the map nearly opposite Kala Bíst.
11. Cháh-i-Dewala	20	Distance is estimated. There is a fort across the Helmand, which is here deep and swift. Supplies, &c., procurable.
12. Kala Bíst	10	
	178	

Note I.—From Jawain to Kásh, 112 miles, *viâ* Chakánsúr, is only 60 miles in a direct line, as measured on the map. In all probability there is a tolerably straight road between the two places, avoiding the detour by Chakánsúr.

Note II.—Farah to Kásh.—This route was travelled by Ferrier, and is as follows:—

Farrah to—	Miles.	
1. Hanz-i-Kalsa	... 10½	From Macgregor's Gazetteer of Afghanistan, Route No. 40. Water, forage, and grass plentiful at Hauz. No difficulties.
2. Khosmalik	... 10½	
3. Khuspas	... 25	Ferrier is the only authority for this portion. The route leaving the Girishk road (southern route) at Khormalik turns S.W., and passes through a defile on to an immense sandy plain without water. Khuspas is a small marshy pond; water bad. Next stage (4) through same desert. Basruig is a Parsiwan village. Water from a well, bad. Still desert till the Kásh-rúd is reached, beyond which is Kásh.
4. Basruig	... 14	
5. Kásh	... 14	
	75	
Kásh to Kala Bíst	... 66	
Kala Bíst to Kandahár	... 97	
	238	

From Kala Bíst to Kandahár.

[Traversed or reconnoitred by troops under General Biddulph in January and February 1879.]

KALA BIST TO—		Miles.
1. Jui Sarkar	...	12
2. Bála Khána	...	12½
3. Gumbaz Surkh	...	12½
4. Kala Saidal	...	15
5. Shah Mir Kala	...	10½
6. Hauz-i-Madat	...	10½
7. Sinjiri	...	12½
8. Kandahár	...	11½
		97
Jawain *viâ* Chakánsúr to Kala Bíst	...	178
		275
Or if a more direct road be followed from Jawain to Kásh, about	...	230
From Farah to Kandahár, *viâ* Kásh and Kala Bíst	...	238

There are no difficulties whatever on this route Forage, &c., can be procured at every halting place, but not in large quantities, until Shah Mir Kala is reached. From thence the route turns north-east and joins the Girishk road between Ata Karez and Hanz-i-Madat. This is the best route; but if it be desired not to interfere with the movement of another column coming from Girishk, there are roads along the Argandáb to Sparwán (crossing easy), and thence to Kandahár. The country is studded with villages and highly cultivated. The only difficulty could be from irrigation channels which would to some extent impede artillery.

Appendix (q).

Notes on Kafiristan.

Kafiristan at present embraces an area of 6,500 square miles. It is bounded on the north by he Hindu Kush mountains; on the south by the Kabul and Kunar rivers; for its western limit it has the Alishang, with its tributary the Alingar.

Its eastern boundary is not nearly so well marked and defined; but taken roughly may be expressed as the Kunar river from its junction with the Kabul to where the former receives the waters of the Katashgum at the village of Ain; thence following up this tributary to its source and a line drawn from that point to the head of the Dura Pass would be well within the mark.

The population is estimated at over 1,00,000 souls. Their country is picturesque and wild in the extreme. The men of fine appearance, keen penetrating eyes, and daring to a fault. It is purely due to a combination and no blood feuds existing amongst this sect that they have succeeded in holding their own against the Mahomedans, by whom they are hemmed in on all sides. The Kafirs have nothing in common with their adjoining neighbours: in fact are incessantly waging petty wars against them.

They are exceedingly well disposed towards, and have a leaning for, the British Government: aye, I may venture further and say that they would not hesitate to place their services should an occasion require at our disposal, and the sooner some steps are taken to secure their friendship the better.

Their arms consist merely of bows, arrows and daggers. At a distance of 60 yards they seldom fail to hit an object very much smaller than that of a man.

Their wealth is reckoned by the number of heads of cattle in possession; there are 13 chiefs in all; selection is given for deeds of bravery and some consideration and allowance made for hereditary descent. Wheat is their staple food.

Routes.

Abazai to Chitral.

Abazai to Kharki, 26 miles.

Frontier outpost is on left bank of river. The last village *en route* in British territory is Bairam Deri, distant 14 miles; the first-half of this distance is over a bare plain, the remainder of journey is over fertile ground. Supplies in plenty to be had from surrounding villages; water good and on surface, but fuel scarce.

Kharki to Kotigram, 23 miles.

Distant to Malakand kotal 5 miles; the first $3\frac{1}{2}$ miles is by left bank of a running stream. No cultivation beyond Kharki. Wood and grass on the hills. The ascent to kotal is easy and will allow of laden camels. The top of the pass is very flat and well wooded; in addition, a goodly supply of water is to be had.

Traces of a made-road, executed (so it is said) by the Sikhs, is still to be seen; but being a longer one, is little, if at all, used, even by traders.

The descent of very nearly 3 miles into the Swat valley is over rough ground; but when once in the plains the going is easy. Country on both banks of river very fertile and well irrigated. The river is crossed opposite the large village of Chakdara: 7 miles beyond is Kotigram, *en route* several villages.

Kotigram to K. Rabat, 10 miles.

Four miles beyond Kotigram is the Laram Pass. The ascent is easy and practicable for all beasts of burden; water plenty; slopes of hill cultivated with hamlets scattered about: 2 large-sized tanks at top of pass that hold water for 9 months in the year.

The descent to Killa Rabat in parts very stony, getting worse on nearing fort, which is built on a low mound on left bank of river, commanding a good position.

The descent is through fir and pine forests. Water and grass plentiful; some cultivation about.

Rabat to Shahzadgai, 5 miles.

Cross over the Panj Kora,—a long, easy and level route. Arrive at the large fort of Shahzadgai, which is built at the sharp bend of river above mentioned, commanding a strong position. The valley is a narrow one, but richly cultivated. Supplies of grass and fuel sufficient for a large force.

There is an alternative route from Chakdara to Shahzadgai, which avoids the Laram Pass; but a low kotal (Katgola) is crossed, 6 miles due west from Unch, which is 4 miles from Chakdara. This alternative route is principally used by kafilas.

Shahzadgai to Barawal Bando viâ Barawal Kohat, 17 miles.

From Shahzadgai to Kotal Barawal, route is along right bank of a running stream through rich cultivation, distant 12 miles; the ascent is easy for laden beasts. The northern face of range is well clad, not so the southern.

The descent is over 4 miles through dense fir and pine forest and brushwood; soil rich. Water-supply plentiful.

The village of Bando is on right bank of stream, over which a frail bridge has been thrown. The stream admits of fording right through the year.

Barawal Bando to Dir, 16 miles nearly.

About half-way is the fort of Chutiatan at junction of stream from Barawal Bando with Panjkhora.

The path keeps to left bank of stream. After leaving the village of Sangrawal, which is 4 miles from Bando, the country falls, forming a deep gorge for the stream to rush through, in places as much as 200 feet deep. No cultivation between Bando and Chutiatan, but plenty of grass and firewood.

From Chutiatan to Dir the path is along cultivation, wheat and rice chiefly.

Dir is the name given to the fort, which is large and mud-built. It is used by the chief and his followers, whereas the village is known as Arian Koh, and is the head-quarters of Shao Baba.

The population of fort and village exceeds 10,000 souls.

Dir to Mirga, 9 miles.

Path for nearly 1 mile goes by right bank of stream, that takes its rise at Lowarai Kotal. The valley is a narrow one, but fertile. When opposite the fort of Panakot, which is half-way, an ascent of about 300 feet is made, and a similar descent thence to Mirga; the going is easy.

Mirga to Ashrath, 12 miles.

About 5 miles from Mirga the Lowarai Kotal is reached; elevation 10,450. The pass is open for laden animals for 8 months in the year, commencing from the month of May. The ascent is very easy and gradual; but the descent for 5 miles and more is difficult, the stream having to be crossed and recrossed several times. No cultivation between Mirga and Ashrath. The kotal is the north boundary of Dir territory.

During the winter months almost a hurricane blows up the valley. In May 1883 when I was going over the ground it was then well under snow, and for 2 or 3 miles the way was strewn not only with branches, but with trunks of pine and deodar that had been uprooted.

It is a stiff march from Mirga to Ashrath. Wood and grass, but no cultivation.

Ashrath to Darosh, 11 miles.

The descent continues to Mirkandi, distant 3 miles. The path here and there difficult for laden animals. From Mirkandi a sharp turn to east, and descent of a hundred feet to left bank of Kunar river; thence to Darosh easy going. Two small villages *en route* (Badalga and Galatak), with cultivation around. Brushwood and grass on hill slopes.

Opposite the fort of Darosh a bridge is thrown across the stream that can be utilized by cattle. The Darosh plain is a large one, well brought under cultivation, and fruit gardens scattered about.

The Shushai stream empties itself into the Kunar river a mile and half to north of fort. The valley is fertile, with a population of about 3,000 fighting men.

Darosh to Braz, 12 miles.

By left bank of river and at 1½ miles from fort cross Shushai stream, fordable at all times of the year; a slight ascent and similar descent is made by junction of streams. Little or no cultivation till nearing Braz. Here the soil is rich and well irrigated for an area of 6 square miles.

Five miles from Darosh fort there is a very nasty rocky spur which might easily block the route. This spur was walled some years ago, when a Punjab, ruler attempted to invade Chitral.

The going for 2½ miles and more is through an open and bare plain; next dip over a low kotal and enter the Jogor fertile plains and gardens, and traverse through it for a mile and half, ascending next a bare hill, say, 150 feet; following this contour till abreast Chitral, then descend and overshoot the fort by 300 yards, and cross over by a very fair and well constructed wooded suspension bridge and return to fort, which is merely a stone wall with bastions or raised towers, occupied by the chief, his family and menials. One face of this fort is a long river bank; the east and west face walled gardens; the south facing cornfields.

Braz to Chitral, 8 miles.

Along the four sides and corners are planted stately poplars and "chinars."

Chitral to Zebak in Badakshan viâ *Dura and Nuksan passes.*

There are two routes, which separate from fort Andarthi 15 miles from Chitral. Path leading by right bank of stream till near Shogoth, a village 1 mile south-east of Andarthi. The Uzur Valley (5,000 men) lies to north of Shogoth: 10½ miles beyond Andarthi (on Durra route) is the village of Darosh; *en route* the stream has to be crossed and recrossed several times. A large valley from south joins in ½ mile beyond Darosh, with an estimated population of 4,000 fighting men. There is another and smaller valley to north of village, containing about 100 houses.

Nine miles beyond Darosh is the isòlated fort of Gobor at an elevation of 9,150. This is the last permanent abode. The building has been run up within the last five years as a check against the Kafirs.

From Gobor to the head of pass, a distance of 7 miles, the ascent is easy and gradual; kotal reading 14,800. This pass is open for traffic for a little over 3 months in the year; laden animals can go over it. Supplies after leaving Darosh little, if any. Little or no grass or fuel.

The Nuksan pass, which strikes off from fort Andarthi; is a more difficult one. Animals laden cannot ascend; yet notwithstanding these annoyances, the pass is more in use than the Dura one, due to travellers and traders being free from any attacks by Kafirs.

The remarks bearing on supplies and period of time the pass is open are the same as those noted above.

Between the Dura and Nuksan passes there are two others—Agram and Khartiza; neither has been used of late years.

Chitral to Uchli pass on Hindu Kush, due south of Killa Panj in Wakhan District.

Route traverses left bank of stream for 13 miles; in several places path so bad as not to permit of riding; in fact with difficulty can a horse be led. Prith to Drassan *viá* Lun, 21 miles by right bank; valley open; plenty of cultivation, and going easy for all kinds of baggage animals. From Drassan to Uchli about 70 miles, with a very gradual ascent, the pass being just over 9,000 feet elevation and Drassan 6,637. Some supplies are procurable for about 20 miles from Drassan; all beyond bare and barren; scarcity of fuel as well. Pass open for 5 months in the year. From Uchli kotal to Killa Panj 22 miles over a barren and arid soil.

Drassan to Sarhad in Wakhan district viâ *Baroghil Pass.*

The route is *viâ* Mastuj on left bank of river. The valley is well populated, and supplies in plenty as far as Gazan, 44 miles from Drassan. Fuel and grass is scarce, the path does not keep to one bank of river, which is crossed and re-crossed several times.

Nine miles beyond Ghazan or Gazan and 31 miles from kotal is Topkhana Zaibek. Beyond the fort there is neither cultivation nor grass nor fuel. The stream (Yarkun) is very often frozen as far as fort Topkhana. The elevation of kotal is a little under 12,000. The pass is an easy one, and will admit of a mule battery being taken over it.

From Baroghil kotal to Sarhad a march of 15 miles; path good; country bare and sandy.

Ghazan to Gilgit viâ *Jhui Pass.*

From Ghazan to kotal 7 miles; ascent easy; height of pass above sea-level 14,812, Ghazan 8,990. No cultivation, but some grass and fuel midway. The descent to Jhui stream is a little over 4 miles; frightful going over snow when the upper crust has melted: under is ice, the accumulation of years, with here and there yawning fissures. Nine miles further east we come to the first village (Nelti); path very fair; grass and wood on hill slopes. Keeping to right bank for another 8 miles till Jhui joins with stream from Darkot pass; going easy; valley narrow; cultivation on both banks: the route to junction was going from west to east. We now turn almost due south and reach Yassan, 6½ miles beyond the meeting of the streams. There is an alternate route over hills striking off from Kaspu, a village 2½ miles east of Nelti, saving in distance quite 3 miles. The present path is very fair; with a little trouble and cost would permit of laden animals utilizing it.

Yassan is a picturesque place; the fort, a dilapidated one. There is a good deal of cultivation to south and west of fort. The population of this district exceeds 6,000 fighting men. The position of the fort is a good one, commanding as it does the entrance to three large valleys—Jhui, Darkot and Asumbar.

From Yassan to Raoshan, 16 miles. First start by right bank of stream for nearly 3 miles; here cross by frail bridge, keeping on the left side till opposite the fort of Raoshan; 3½ miles beyond the bridge above mentioned the Yassan stream is joined by the Ghizar flowing from west to east: crossing over to fort Raoshan by rope bridge; horses can ford the stream 2 miles west of fort.

Raoshan to Hopar, 12½ miles; path fair; valley narrow; brushwood and grass in plenty, but no cultivation whatever.

From Hopar to Gakuch distant 9 miles; in several places the path is quite impracticable for aught save passengers on foot; loads if any have to be carried by men. Once at Gakuch the entire appearance of country changes, and traces of civilization true in its infancy but yet marked, when contrasted with anything between the outpost of Abazai and Gakuch.

Gakuch to Gilgit is two stages,—the first of 17½ miles, the other of 19½; the road, which is a made one, was laid out under the directions of Major Biddulph, whilst he was on special duty at Gilgit.

The position of Gakuch might very easily be made strong, and at the same time a commanding one; the present fort is about ¾ mile from river bank, standing on highest ground overlooking the Ishkoman valley.

A force marching into India by Darkot valley for Gilgit could avoid Yassan and the bad pathway between Hopar and Gakuch by marching up the Asumbar valley (it is fertile and populated) and enter the Ishkoman one, 7 miles above its junction with the stream from Yassan; this latter route is frequently used by traders and others from either Chitral or Yassan.

There is a still more direct route from Gilgit to Chitral which traverses the original one *viâ* Gakuch, Raoshan and Gupis to where the Ghizar stream joins the one from Yassan; from here strike off and follow up the former valley, its entire length; ascend kotal and enter Laspur valley which empties itself opposite Mastuj. I was given to understand that this was the route taken by Major Biddulph.

Both the Ghizar and Laspur valleys are populated.

Gilgit to Sirinaggar.

The entire distance is somewhat over 160 miles by a made-road; the entire way suitable for baggage animals, and kept in very fair order. Supplies are certainly scarce between Gilgit and Astor, a distance of 56 miles. According to present arrangements the small garrison at the latter are provisioned by grain collected and sent from Astor weekly.

At Ramghat, where the Astor river joins the Indus and 37 miles from Gilgit, a strong wooden suspension bridge is thrown across; in addition to this wooden one there are two rope bridges from the bridge; an ascent (stiff) occupying 4 hours has to be made, and then a very gradual descent to Dash Kan.

The crossing of the Indus opposite Bowanji and 32 miles from Gilgit is by ferries; those at present on river cannot carry more than 20 men a trip; of these there are only two and one small craft for carrying the Maharajah's mails across.

Myself and party did the journey from Gilgit to Sirinaggar in 11 days; but it is set down as 22 regular stages.

The following were our marches:—

Gilgit to Manawar.—Eight miles; road perfect over level ground, with no fording of torrents or other inconveniences; supplies plenty.

Manawar to Chakarkot, 15¾ miles; road good; no signs of vegetation *en route* till Chakarkot is reached; three ascents, none difficult, and a similar number of descents on this march; ponies carried our loads.

Chakarkot to Ramghat, 13 miles: the first mile and half in parts nasty; a fast running torrent is crossed opposite Chakarkot village; the path follows its right bank to Bowanji by fertile but narrow valley. From Bowanji to Ramghat 7 miles; two mountain torrents have to be crossed; these occasionally during the hot weather are impassable for some hours whilst the rush lasts: the one near Ramghat is the worse of the two: after crossing the latter an ascent is made of about 200 feet by fair pathway, then a descent to Ramghat bridge. No cultivation between Bowanji and Ramghat.

Ramghat to Dashkan. The ascent occupied 4 hours, a trying undertaking owing to there being no water *en route;* an hour's further going brought us to the village of Doin; from Doin to Dashkan 7 miles through a fine forest; soil rich; several hamlets scattered about; path fairly good, but needs clearing.

Dashkan to Gurikot, 15½ miles: the first 9½ miles is somewhat unpleasant going; pass by one small village, but from Astor onwards through fertile and rich soil.

Gurikot to Darto 18 miles; going easy; route pleasant and interesting; hamlets *en route.*

Darto to foot of Kanoori Pass, 20 miles; arrangements necessary for carriage of provisions; road very fair; baggage animals keeping up with our men; wood scarce.

Foot of Pass to Gorez Fort 20 miles; our encampment was 4 miles from Kotal; the ascent is easy by fair path; trying during the rains, owing to the slaty soil; hill very wooded; the descent is also easy and through soil that would allow of being brought under cultivation. I could not help but noticing how poorly populated is the entire route from Gilgit to Sirinaggar. The soil is rich, and wood and grass plentiful.

Gorez fort to Jatkusi at foot of Kotal, distant 16 miles. We followed main stream, which is narrow but fertile, to a place known as Kazli band; thence struck off to north and halted at foot of pass.

Foot of Kotal to Bandpura about 11 miles. The ascent to Kotal is very gradual; the descent more so, and consequently longer hills, well clad; water abundant.

From Bandpura to Sirinaggar. This distance can be done either by boat or in two land marches, both easy and level.

W. W. McNAIR.

Appendix (r).

Notes on Chinese Turkestan.

The Chinese are now fairly established in Kashgaria, and perfectly able to take care of and defend themselves against internal intrigues and all border chiefs; but they are still entirely at the mercy of Russia.

True the military authorities have received orders from Pekin to repair the "forts" in every city, and at Khoten and Karashair they have begun to build new forts; but without the aid of engineers and wanting arms of precision these forts are all but useless against a European foe.

I have endeavoured to point out to Ying "Tao-Tai," that it is Sirikol, Yarkund, Kashgar, Ush Turpan, Aksu, Karashair, Turfan and Kuldja that want to be well fortified. Beyond Karashair, Russia would find campaigning no easy game, owing to an arid and unproductive country for hundreds of miles, in which her troops would be harrassed by thousands of Mongolians.

The old Amban Ying "Tao-Tai" informs me that since "Tse-Tsun-Tang," Viceroy on the North-west frontier, has been appointed President of the Board of War, China's policy in Central Asia will become more active and decided.

The "Fort of Sirikol" (Tashkurghan) now flies the Chinese flag, and the Begs of Sirikol have received new robes of honor from the Amban of Yarkund and been made to understand that the entire district of Sirikol is now under Chinese rule. This wise step I would venture to urge ought to be followed up by the Government of India directing attention to Kanjut, which would secure a shorter and easier route to Eastern Turkestan and a side gateway to India that is worth taking care of. Baltistan is only 18 stages from the fertile plains of Yarkund *viá* "Kogiar" and the "Mustagh Pass." This is the old

Baltistani route to Yarkund and is only now closed by the Kanjut people, a petty tribe of mongrels, numbering about fifteen hundred men, who live by plunder.

There is also a highroad from Sirikol to Kanjut *viâ* Kurghan-i-Yadbai; this route is comparatively easy and practicable in the summer months for laden animals.

The Chinese have now drawn their western and southern frontier in Turkestan. The western frontier extends to the Bolan mountains and follows this range in a southerly direction until it meets the northern spur of mountains that springs from the Hindu Kush. This northern spur runs in an east-south-east direction and joins the Kuen-luen range, taking in the Yengi-Dawan Pass *viâ* Kogiar, the Kilian Pass *via* Kilian, and the Sanju Pass *viâ* Sanju, and becomes the southern frontier.

The Chinese consider all to the south of the Sirikol district and the above-named three passes the territory of their friendly neighbour, the British.

The settlement of the Russian and Chinese boundary line has come to a stop for the present, the Commissioners having had a dispute about a point in the "Ala Tau" range near Kuldja. The case has been referred to Pekin and St. Petersburg.

A Russian trader passing through Yarkund on his way to Khoten informed me that the Russian Consul of Kashgar, who went back to Tashkend in December, would return in May, and would bring his family with him. He is to be accompanied also by an engineer, who is to build the new Consulate at Kashgar, and after that a large serai for Russian traders.

If the British Government desire either to check or even keep themselves accurately informed of the stealthy progress of the Russians in Central Asia; if they desire to foster the already by no means altogether insignificant trade of their subjects with Yarkund, or even to prevent the gradual suppression of this,—then I would humbly suggest that they should take an early opportunity of appointing a Consul General to Kashgar, as the only effectual countermove to that of the Russians. Of course I speak not for myself, as I am now thoroughly trusted by and known to the Chinese, and I shall gain nothing personally by the appointment of a British official. Indeed I may lose, as I shall probably become less important in their eyes when there is an official British representative on the spot; but as I am asked to give such ideas as I have on Central Asian matters, I am bound to state clearly that in my opinion this is the one measure which is all important in the interests of both India and England.

I have referred above to the Kunjut route. I do not know whether it is clearly understood that any power established in Yarkund could bring an army of any size and of all arms without difficulty to the northern base of the Mustagh, either from the direction of Yarkund or from Sirikol, to which latter there is a direct road from Khokand, without touching Kashgar territory at all.

If the Mustagh pass was seized, a practicable road for artillery could I believe be easily made, and debouching from the Mustagh pass, an army in the summer, moving by the Bundipur route, would find nothing even to delay their advance into the heart of Kashmir.

Now on the northern and north-west frontier of Kunjut there are passes, easy no doubt, but which could be defended against any advancing force. These might be seized by a sudden dash no doubt; but if Kunjut were accepted as part of our territory, these passes could not be seized without our having ample warning, and thus time afforded us to bar the Mustagh range. The passes of Kunjut in fact afford an outter line of defence, which, as time goes on, will unquestionably prove of great importance.

The Chinese will not occupy Kunjut, though they desire the route to be opened out. It was solely on my strong recommendation that they occupied Sirikol, but they would not go south of the range that forms the northern boundary of Kunjut, and I was not anxious to press it, because had they so occupied it, then when Kashgaria falls into the hands of Russia as it inevitably must, failing counteraction on our part, Kunjut would have become part of Russian territory, and the Russians would have acquired a position far more threatening to us than if they occupied Herat or even Kabul,—almost as threatening as if they held Kandahar.

Now Kunjut is no man's land. It is held by a petty tribe of robbers, whose raids are the curse of the whole country up to the Pamir. The Maharaja of Kashmir, if so directed, could take and hold the country, probably without firing a shot, and not only would the trade with Central Asia be thereby facilitated, but a strategic advantage would be gained the real magnitude of which will only be realized some years hence.

This is the second point in connection with Central Asian affairs that I consider of vital importance. I shall only add now that the Chinese have relieved British trade with Central Asia from all duties of all kinds, and all exports and imports alike go free.

If it were any use, I might point out how markedly friendly is the feeling of all the Chinese officials towards the British Government, and how thoroughly they all feel (whatever may be the feeling at Pekin) that the English are the only neighbours with whom they can safely be friends and they dwell on the apparent impolicy of doing nothing to strengthen and cultivate that friendly sentiment.

Simla, 29th July 1883. A. DALGLEISH.

Appendix (s).

Notes on a Route mentioned by Mr. Dalgleish from Ferghana to Baltistan by the Mustagh Pass.

From Osh to the Toyuksu Pass there is a well known line of route, traversed already by Russian columns and practicable for wheels; the distance is 205 miles. From the pass there is no line of route marked on any late map down the Ak-boital stream and the Ak-su; but the drainage lines of the Pamirs are easy and little depressed, and it may be assumed that some kind of road exists.

At the junction of the stream draining the "Little Pamir" the main road from Yarkund to Wakhan over the "Great Pamir" is struck in proceeding southwards, and would be followed as far as Ak-tash or some miles beyond. Thence a road to the Mustagh Pass would pass about 40 miles west of Tashkurghan, the present Chinese outpost in Sarikol, traversing the great and little Pamirs and the Taghdumtash Pamirs and which offer no difficulties.

From the south verge of the latter "Pamir" is a stretch of country about which I can find no information * It is dominated by the Mustagh range, and drains into the Yarkund river, and probably its configuration is easy. The Mustagh Pass does not appear to have been crossed by any European, and is only mentioned casually by Trotter and Biddulph. It is estimated at 18,400 feet, and the road over it lies for a great part over glaciers. It is used by the Baltis settled in Yarkund, to whose country it is the most direct route.

* Biddulph calls it the Shimsal Pamir, and mentions a difficult route over a high pass into it from the Shimsal valley. There is also a road across it to Usadboi in Sarikol.

East of Baroghil it appears, however, to be the only pass at all practicable from the Pamir country, for the Kilik Pass, though easy and open in summer and winter, leads only into the *cul-de-sac* of the Upper Hunza, from which there is no egress during summer, except for 2 months over the high and difficult Moorkon Pass. This pass is mentioned by Biddulph, who says nothing of the winter state of the defile draining the Upper Hunza. Possibly the defile is traversable there. If the Mustagh Pass is at all as easy as some of the high passes of those mountains, it may be assumed that Mr. Dalgleish is right in his assertion that a good route exists skirting the present Chinese border from Ferghana into Baltistan, and the question of sovereignty over the Kunjut country and the Mustagh range becomes of importance.

As to the population of Kunjut, Mr. Dalgleish is very much in error, unless he confines the application of the term to the Upper Hunza only. The population of Hunza is given at 6,000 (*Biddulph*) and of Nager at 10,000, and both States appear to be comprised in the term Kunjut. Politically Nager is already a dependency of Kashmir; and the Hunza Chief, judging from the mention made of his relations with Biddulph, considers himself in some sense a dependent of the British Government.

In either case there should be no difficulty in extending our nominal sovereignty to the northern base of the Mustagh range, where we should meet the Chinese border. This, assuming that Chitral and Yassin are under British protection, would complete the political frontier line of India in the direction of Ferghana, from whence Russian influence is now extending in search of that definite frontier line and established government which is alleged by the Russians to be a necessity, and the only limit to the extension of their frontiers that they can accept.

Since writing the above, I have conversed with Major Biddulph on the subject of the Mustagh Pass. His opinion is that it is quite impracticable for trade or for any military operation.

There are not less than 6 marches over glaciers and snow beds, without grass, fuel, and of course without supplies of any kind.

Mr. Dalgleish's information is certainly defective, and there can be little doubt that the only good road from the Pamir into India is by the Boroghil Pass and Yassin.

G. C. NAPIER, *Major*.

THE END